Fundamentals of Gifted Education *private copy*

The field of gifted education is characterized by a confusing array of perspectives concerning such fundamental issues as definition, philosophy, curriculum, social and emotional development, and underserved populations. The mission of this book is to provide a coherent framework that instructors and service providers can use in planning effective programs, providing appropriate counseling services, and evaluating programs for the gifted. Most sections are organized around fundamental issues confronting the field and follow a common structure: an introductory chapter that provides a historical and theoretical background and organizing questions followed by several point-of-view chapters written by experts that provide varied perspectives on the topic at hand.

Distinguishing Features:

- Comprehensive Coverage—The book's 45 manageable-length chapters cover the full range of topics that must be considered when planning programs and services for gifted students both within and outside of school.
- Coherent Structure—Section introductions provide background information and organizing questions to guide chapter authors who offer varying views of the issue at hand. The emphasis is not on the "right way" or the "wrong way" (except when clearly documented bad practice is discussed), but on how best practice stems from well-informed and logical decision making.
- Decision-Making Focus—The book's introductory chapter addresses the need for a clearly developed and consistently applied set of values to guide decision making. Likewise, each section introduction includes a decision-making framework regarding some aspect of educating, counseling, or parenting gifted students.

This book is appropriate for introductory level courses in gifted education or courses in program development and planning. It is also suitable for school personnel responsible for making program-planning decisions in the area of gifted education and for academic libraries with holdings in this area.

Carolyn M. Callahan (PhD University of Connecticut) is Commonwealth Professor of Education at the University of Virginia. She has been a principal investigator on projects of the National Research Center on the Gifted and Talented for the past 19 years. She has published more than 180 refereed articles and 50 book chapters across a broad range of topics on gifted education. She is a past president of The Association for the Gifted and the National Association for Gifted Children (NAGC). She is currently editor of *Gifted Child Quarterly*.

Holly L. Hertberg-Davis (PhD University of Virginia) is an educational consultant specializing in differentiation of instruction, advanced curriculum, and professional development. She is a former faculty member at the University of Virginia's Curry School of Education, where she taught courses in the education of the gifted, and was a principal investigator for the National Research Center on the Gifted and Talented. She has written and presented extensively on her primary research interests: differentiation of instruction, staff development, and equity in Advanced Placement and International Baccalaureate courses.

Fundamentals of Gifted Education

Considering Multiple Perspectives

Edited by
Carolyn M. Callahan
Holly L. Hertberg-Davis

Routledge
Taylor & Francis Group

NEW YORK AND LONDON

First published 2013
by Routledge
711 Third Avenue, New York, NY 10017

Simultaneously published in the UK
by Routledge
2 Park Square, Milton Park, Abingdon, Oxon OX14 4RN

Routledge is an imprint of the Taylor & Francis Group, an informa business

Library of Congress Cataloging in Publication Data

Fundamentals of gifted education : considering multiple perspectives / [edited by] Carolyn M. Callahan,
Holly L. Hertberg-Davis.
  p. cm.
  Includes bibliographical references and index.
  1. Gifted children—Education. I. Callahan, Carolyn M. II. Hertberg-Davis, Holly L.
  LC3993.F82 2011
  371.95—dc23
  2011048417

ISBN: 978–0–415–88149–4 (hbk)
ISBN: 978–0–415–88151–7 (pbk)
ISBN: 978–0–203–84817–3 (ebk)

Typeset in Minion
by Swales & Willis Ltd, Exeter, Devon

Printed and bound in the United States of America
by Edwards Brothers, Inc.

DEDICATION

We dedicate this book both professionally and personally. The professional dedication must go to Joe Renzulli. While Carolyn was lucky enough to stumble into his office as an undergraduate work–study student and find a mentor who has never failed to deliver for more years than he or Carolyn will admit to, the more important dedication is to his commitment and contribution to the field of gifted education and the people in the field. His lineage and legacy cannot be overestimated. A perusal of just this volume reveals the extraordinary influence he has had both through his insights and writing and through the students who studied with him at the University of Connecticut, and through the students of *his* students at universities all over the United States.

The personal dedication is to Carolyn's husband, Mike, Holly's husband, Kevin, and Holly's children, Cole and Finn. They all sacrificed time and attention as we worked to bring together the chapters written by others and struggled to find our own voices in the introductory chapters. Thanks to all of you for giving us the space and support we needed to accomplish our goal.

CONTENTS

PREFACE

In 1993, Sally Reis and her colleagues wrote a technical report titled *Why Not Let High Ability Students Start School in January?* (Reis et al., 1993). In that report, the authors documented what so many parents, students, teachers, and administrators have sensed for a long time—that the existing school curriculum and grade placements that characterize our schools are just inadequate for making school "fit" for learners whose ability to learn quickly amazes us, whose proclivity to absorb information from every source around them often means they know more than we do about a given topic, and who enter school each year having already mastered most of the curriculum that is going to be served up to them. Every teacher and administrator has tales to tell of these young people and the struggles faced by the teacher, the student, and the students' parents as they all seek to attain the goal of ensuring that every child has the opportunity to learn every day in school. That is why we wrote this book. We have both been those teachers and faced those students—like the student who came to algebra class on the second day and announced he was "finished" with algebra, wrongly interpreted by me to mean he was quitting the course when, in fact, he meant that he had scanned the book and could do the problems posed at the end of each chapter. We were both driven to seek understandings of who these students are, what makes them tick, and what we could do to create learning experiences that would go beyond the easy and the known for these students. Our journeys led us from those classrooms to seek deeper knowledge and understanding ourselves about these students and eventually to careers in helping to develop programs and curriculum, doing research, and teaching classes that would arm other teachers and administrators with the knowledge and skills to answer those questions for themselves and result in positive learning experiences for those children.

This text is a manifestation of our conclusion that there is no "one right way" to achieve the goal of creating exemplary services for gifted students. We do, however, believe that there are *wrong* ways to go about that process. One of these "wrong ways" is to assume that we have all the right answers. This assumption leads us to fail at examining practices that may fit some gifted students far more adequately than others. The second "wrong way" is to mix and match philosophies, definitions, programs, and curricula in such a way that the components are not aligned, and thus, the strength of services is diminished or even cancelled out by the choices we have made. Or we make the mistake of "keeping up (or down) with the Joneses"—choosing how we provide services and curriculum for a group of students based on what a neighboring school district does, even when the students in our district, the philosophy of our school district, and/or the resources available are very different. Finally, choices made based on either the charismatic speaker or attractive, easy-to-use but inappropriate curricular materials will most certainly lead us to make bad decisions.

What this text is structured to do is to guide administrators, resource teachers, classroom teachers, counselors, parents, consultants and others who are responsible for the development of gifted learners in choosing the most appropriate options based on sound interpretations of available theory *and* research, to make decisions that evidence logical and reinforcing support for high-quality services, and to evaluate whether or not those decisions are leading to the outcomes we expect for gifted learners. To that end, we have selected chapter authors who are experts in the most researched and examined approaches to the primary areas of decision making:

1. philosophies and beliefs about giftedness and definitions of giftedness and talent;
2. identification of gifted students;
3. selection of program services and program delivery models;
4. curriculum development;
5. providing services to specific populations of gifted students;
6. evaluation of and advocacy for gifted programs.

In making the choices for topics and authors, we further screened by selecting a broad spectrum of views. In the process, we have had to make many very hard choices. We were not, after all, writing a textbook on each of those topics, but providing the reader with the best overview of these topics. We hope that the developers and advocates of positions not included in detail in this book will see that we give recognition to those approaches and encourage consideration of all. For example, we could not include every curriculum model or approach, so models limited to one prospective outcome (such as models to develop creativity alone) are not included. However, the models we do include address those dimensions of curriculum and instruction for gifted students and make reference to those approaches (see, for example, the Schoolwide Enrichment Model in Chapter 21).

Our choice to give voice to others in presenting particular orientations is based on our teaching experience, in which students relate to and seem to connect to ideas when they are hearing them straight from the original authors "untranslated" by us or by other textbook authors. Of course, we recognize the need to help our readers make sense of the many points of view they will encounter in each section; to that end, we have included introductory chapters to provide readers with an overall picture of the important issues associated with each of the sections. Additionally, we include a set of guiding questions to consider in reading each chapter and when making judgments about a given approach. We provide no formula, no decrees of "best," and no testimonial to any particular model. What we have aimed for, and hope we have accomplished, is to encourage our readers to engage in the same kind of high-level thinking, creative problem solving, and independent, self-directed thinking in which we hope our gifted students will engage.

REFERENCES

Reis, S. M., Westberg, K. L., Kulikowich, J., Caillard, F., Hébert, T., Plucker, J. et al. (1993). *Why not let high ability students start school in January? The curriculum compacting study.* (Research Monograph 93106). Storrs: The National Research Center on the Gifted and Talented, University of Connecticut.

ACKNOWLEDGMENTS

Like so many other times on so many other projects we have undertaken, we owe the successful production of this text to Lisa Miller. As always, she has shepherded us up the steps of pulling together all the odds and ends that accompany producing an edited book, gently prodded authors (the steel hand in the velvet glove), done the careful organizational work, and been reassuring that we could get this done. Thanks, Lisa, for being you, and for being patient with us being *us*.

LIST OF CONTRIBUTORS

Susan G. Assouline
Professor of School Psychology, The University of Iowa.

She is also associate director for the Belin-Blank Center for Gifted Education and Talent Development, co-developer of The Iowa Acceleration Scale, and co-author of *Developing Math Talent: A Guide for Educating Gifted and Advanced Learners in Math* and *A Nation Deceived: How Schools Hold Back America's Brightest Students*. She conducts research in twice exceptionality and has received the Mensa Education & Research Foundation Award for Excellence in Research.

Amy Azano, PhD
Research Scientist, Curry School of Education, University of Virginia.

She also serves as a project manager with The National Research Center on the Gifted and Talented. Her research interests include rural gifted education, writing instruction, and the effects of place and poverty on critical literacy skills.

James H. Borland
Professor of Education, Department of Curriculum and Teaching, Teachers College, Columbia University.

He directs the graduate programs in the Education of Gifted Students at Teachers College. Author of numerous books, book chapters, and journal articles, Borland is also editor of the *Education and Psychology of the Gifted* series of Teachers College Press. He has served as editor of the Section on Teaching, Learning, and Human development of the *American Educational Research Journal* and has served on the editorial boards of *Gifted Child Quarterly, Roeper Review*, and the *Journal of Secondary Gifted Education*.

Catherine M. Brighton, PhD
Associate Professor, University of Virginia.

She is also a principal investigator on Project Parallax, aimed at developing talent in under-represented elementary students in the science, technology, engineering, and mathematics (STEM) areas, and the director of the University of Virginia Institutes on Academic Diversity. Her research interests include factors that support and inhibit teacher change and school reform initiatives; differentiating curriculum, instruction, and assessment; and qualitative methodologies. She received the National Association for Gifted Children's Early Leader Award in 2005.

Marguerite C. Brunner

Doctoral Student in Gifted Education, University of Virginia.

Her previous work in education includes teaching in both elementary and middle schools as an English teacher and a mathematics specialist. In addition to her teaching, Marguerite has 15 years' experience working with gifted students in various settings. Her research interests include differentiated instruction, fidelity of implementation, identification of gifted students, and mentoring programs for gifted children and their families.

Carolyn M. Callahan, PhD (University of Connecticut)

Commonwealth Professor of Education, University of Virginia.

She has been a principal investigator on projects of The National Research Center on the Gifted and Talented for the past 19 years. She has published more than 180 refereed articles and 50 book chapters across a broad range of topics on gifted education. She is a past president of The Association for the Gifted and the National Association for Gifted Children (NAGC). She is currently editor of *Gifted Child Quarterly*.

Jane Clarenbach

Director of Public Education, National Association for Gifted Children (NAGC).

She coordinates NAGC's legislative and advocacy initiatives and promotes the needs of high-achieving and high-potential children through her work with the media, and state and national organizations. Jane is an attorney with more than 25 years' advocacy experience in Washington, DC.

Nicholas Colangelo

Myron and Jacqueline Blank Endowed Chair of Gifted Education, The University of Iowa.

He is also director of the Belin-Blank Center for Gifted Education and Talent Development at The University of Iowa. He has produced considerable research on the counseling and affective needs of gifted students. He is co-author of *A Nation Deceived: How Schools Hold Back America's Brightest Students* as well as a co-author of *Guidelines for Developing an Academic Acceleration Policy*. With Gary Davis, he co-authored three editions of the *Handbook of Gifted Education*. He received the Distinguished Scholar Award from the National Association for Gifted Children (NAGC) in 1991 and the President's Award from NAGC in 2002.

Mary Ruth Coleman, PhD

Senior Scientist Emerita, FPG Child Development Institute, University of North Carolina at Chapel Hill.

She has taught within general, special, and gifted education programs from kindergarten to graduate levels. Her service has included the boards of the National Association for Gifted Children (NAGC), The Association for the Gifted, and the Council for

Exceptional Children, of which she was president in 2007. She has authored numerous publications including *Educating Exceptional Children* (13th edition) with James J. Gallagher.

Marcia A. B. Delcourt, PhD
Professor, Western Connecticut State University.

She coordinates the Doctor of Education in Instructional Leadership program at Western Connecticut State University. She has served as principal investigator or evaluator for over 25 state or federal grants. Her present research interests include assisting school personnel to design techniques for identifying gifted and talented children, developing inquiry skills in teachers and students, and encouraging teachers as researchers. She is presently working with educators and researchers in India to identify and mentor children with high ability in mathematics and science.

Rebecca D. Eckert, PhD
Assistant Clinical Professor, University of Connecticut.

She works in teacher preparation at the University of Connecticut. In her former role as the gifted resource specialist for the National Association for Gifted Children (NAGC), Rebecca co-edited the book *Designing Services and Programs for High-ability Learners*. Her work at The National Research Center on the Gifted and Talented included participation in the development and testing of the Schoolwide Enrichment Model-Reading (SEM-R). Her research interests include talented readers, recruitment and preparation of new teachers, arts in the schools, and public policy and gifted education.

C. Matthew Fugate
Doctoral Student, Purdue University.

Prior to attending Purdue, Matthew worked as an elementary teacher in the Houston Independent School District where he also served as a gifted coordinator and magnet coordinator. During this time, he received his Master's degree in Educational Psychology, Gifted Education from the University of Connecticut. In addition to his work with the Total School Cluster Grouping Model, Matthew's primary research interests are in the areas of twice exceptionality and the under-representation of gifted Native American students in gifted programs.

Françoys Gagné
Retired Professor, L'Université du Québec à Montréal (UQAM).

Dr. Gagné, a French Canadian from Montreal, obtained his PhD in Educational Psychology from the University of Montreal. Dr. Gagné spent most of his professional career in the department of psychology at UQAM. He is best known for his theory of talent development, the Differentiated Model of Giftedness and Talent (DMGT). Dr. Gagné has received NAGC's prestigious Distinguished Scholar Award (1996), and two awards from the Mensa Society. Although retired from his UQAM professorship since 2001, Dr. Gagné maintains international publishing and keynoting activities.

James J. Gallagher
Retired Kenan Professor of Education, University of North Carolina at Chapel Hill.

He worked in the field of gifted education for over five decades as a journal editor, and as president of NAGC, the World Council for Gifted and Talented Children, and the Council for Exceptional Children. His publications include *Teaching the Gifted Child* and over 100 articles, monographs, and research summaries. He has completed the 13th edition of *Educating Exceptional Children.*

Marcia Gentry

Professor of Educational Studies and Director, Gifted Education Resource Institute, Purdue University.

She is also director of graduate studies in gifted, creative, and talented education at Purdue University. Her research has focused on the use of cluster grouping and differentiation; the application of gifted education pedagogy to improve teaching and learning; student perceptions of school; and non-traditional services and underserved populations. Dr. Gentry developed and studied the Total School Cluster Grouping Model and is engaged in continuing research on its effects on student achievement, identification, and teacher practices. She serves on the editorial review boards of five journals in her field.

E. Jean Gubbins, PhD

Associate Director, The National Research Center on the Gifted and Talented and Associate Professor of Educational Psychology, University of Connecticut.

She is involved in research studies focusing on science, technology, engineering, and mathematics (STEM) high schools, mathematics education, and using gifted education pedagogy with all students. Her research interests stem from prior experiences as a classroom teacher, a teacher of gifted and talented students, an evaluator, educational consultant, and professional developer. She teaches graduate courses in gifted education and talent development related to identification, programming, curriculum development, and program evaluation.

Thomas P. Hébert

Professor of Educational Psychology, University of Georgia.

He teaches graduate courses in gifted education and qualitative research methods. He has served on the board of directors of the National Association for Gifted Children (NAGC). He was elected governor-at-large for The Association for the Gifted, and also served on the board of the Association for the Education of Gifted Underachieving Students (AEGUS). His research interests include the social and emotional development of gifted students, culturally diverse gifted students, underachievement, and problems faced by gifted young men. He is the author of *Understanding the Social and Emotional Lives of Gifted Students.*

Holly L. Hertberg-Davis, PhD (University of Virginia)

Educational consultant specializing in differentiation of instruction, advanced curriculum, and professional development.

She is a former faculty member at the University of Virginia's Curry School of Education, where she taught courses in the education of the gifted and was a principal investigator for The National Research Center on the Gifted and Talented. She has written and presented extensively on her primary research interests: differentiation of instruction, staff development, and equity in Advanced Placement and International Baccalaureate courses.

Lorie Hood
Doctoral Candidate in Gifted Education, University of Virginia.

She earned her BA in Psychology from the University of Hawaii and her MS in Counseling Psychology from Chaminade University of Honolulu. Her research interests include profound intelligence, parenting gifted children, and mindfulness practices as they apply to the gifted population. Her work experience includes clinical psychotherapy both in hospital and private settings as well as movement therapy with in-patient adolescent and adult populations. She is currently in private practice.

Susan K. Johnsen, PhD
Professor, Department of Educational Psychology, Baylor University.

She directs the PhD program and programs related to gifted and talented education at Baylor University. She is the author of over 200 publications including *Identifying Gifted Students: A Practical Guide*, books related to implementing the national teacher preparation standards in gifted education, and tests used in identifying gifted students. She serves on the board of examiners of the National Council for Accreditation of Teacher Education and is chair of the knowledge and skills subcommittee of the Council for Exceptional Children. She is past president of The Association for the Gifted and past president of the Texas Association for the Gifted and Talented.

M. Layne Kalbfleisch, MEd, PhD
Educational Psychologist and Cognitive Neuroscientist, and Associate Professor, College of Education and Human Development and Krasnow Institute for Advanced Study, George Mason University.

She studies twice exceptionality in gifted children with attention disorders and with autism or Asperger's syndrome (http://krasnow1.gmu.edu/kidlab). Her neuroimaging studies investigate reasoning and attention in these populations and across the lifespan, examining fundamental attributes of human ability under various contexts.

Sandra N. Kaplan
Assistant Director, National/State Leadership Training Institute on the Gifted and Talented.

Through her work with the institute, a federally funded project, she has been a consultant to state departments of education and school districts. Her work as a principal investigator for three Javits-funded federal grants has involved designing and researching curriculum in the area of social studies, "Thinking Like a Disciplinarian," and determining the effects of differentiated instruction using models of teaching. Sandra has been a state and national leader in the field of gifted education, assuming the role of president of the California Association for the Gifted and the National Association for Gifted Children (NAGC). Her honors include the Distinguished Service Award and the Ruth A. Martinson Award.

David F. Lohman
Professor of Educational Psychology, The University of Iowa.

He is a fellow of the American Psychological Association, the American Psychological Society, and the American Educational Research Association. He is the recipient of numerous awards, including a Fulbright Fellowship and the Iowa Regents Award for

Faculty Excellence. He twice received the *Gifted Child Quarterly* Research Paper of the Year Award and has received the NAGC Distinguished Scholar Award. His research interests include the effectiveness of different curricular adaptations for students who differ in ability or personality; conceptualization and measurement of reasoning abilities; and issues relating to the identification and development of talent.

D. Betsy McCoach, PhD

Associate Professor, Measurement, Evaluation, and Assessment Program, University of Connecticut.

She has extensive experience in hierarchical linear modeling, instrument design, factor analysis, and structural equation modeling. Betsy has published over 50 journal articles and book chapters, and she co-edited the volume *Multilevel Modeling of Educational Data*. Betsy has also served as the co-editor for the *Journal of Advanced Academics*. Betsy serves as a co-principal investigator and research methodologist on several federally funded research grants, including Project Early Vocabulary Intervention.

Maureen A. Marron, PhD

Associate Research Scientist, Institute for Research and Policy on Acceleration (IRPA), Belin-Blank Center for Gifted Education and Talent Development, The University of Iowa.

She also serves as an adjunct assistant professor in the department of psychological and quantitative foundations at The University of Iowa. She served on the national task force that produced *Guidelines for Developing an Academic Acceleration Policy* (http://www.accelerationinstitute.org/Resources/Policy_Guidelines/). She conducts research on and advocates for acceleration for academically talented students.

Erin Morris Miller

Assistant Professor of Psychology, Bridgewater College, Virginia.

She received her PhD in Educational Psychology from the University of Virginia. Her research interests include theories and conceptions of giftedness and intelligence, theories of problem solving and conceptual categorization, and the trajectories of development for gifted individuals across the lifespan. She may be reached at emmiller@bridgewater.edu.

Tracy C. Missett

Doctoral Candidate in Educational Psychology, Gifted Education, Curry School of Education, University of Virginia.

She is currently a graduate research assistant for the National Research Center on the Gifted and Talented. Her research interests include twice exceptional students, program evaluation, creativity, and assessment. She received her BA from the University of Virginia, her JD from the University of California Hastings College of the Law, and her Master's degree in Education at Teachers College, Columbia University.

Tonya R. Moon, PhD

Professor, University of Virginia.

She is also a principal investigator for Project Parallax and the National Research Center on the Gifted and Talented. Tonya works with school districts and schools on using better assessment techniques for improving instruction and student learning, and on the identification of gifted students. She is the chair of the Institutional Review Board for the Social and Behavioral Sciences at the University of Virginia, is a member of the board of directors of the Virginia Association for the Gifted, and a past president of the Virginia Educational Research Association. She is also an associate editor for *Gifted Child Quarterly*.

Sarah Oh
Doctoral Candidate in Gifted Education, University of Virginia.

She is a former elementary classroom teacher and earned her MEd in Curriculum and Instruction from the University of Virginia. She has been working with pre- and in-service teachers in the graduate-level courses on differentiating instruction and curriculum for the gifted. Her research interests include curriculum development, differentiating instruction, program evaluation, and identification of diverse gifted students.

Jonathan A. Plucker
Professor of Educational Psychology and Cognitive Science, Indiana University.

He is also director of the Center for Evaluation and Education Policy and the Consortium for Education and Social Science Research at Indiana University. His interests include creativity and intelligence, the psychology of giftedness, and education policy.

Sally M. Reis
Vice Provost for Academics and Board of Trustees Distinguished Professor, University of Connecticut.

She also serves as a principal investigator for the National Research Center on the Gifted and Talented. She was a public school teacher for 15 years. She has authored or co-authored over 250 articles, books, book chapters, monographs, and technical reports. Her research interests relate to children with disabilities, gifted females, and diverse groups of talented students. She is also interested in extension of the Schoolwide Enrichment Model to multiple populations of students.

Joseph S. Renzulli
Director, National Research Center on the Gifted and Talented and Distinguished Professor of Educational Psychology, University of Connecticut.

He is the 2009 winner of the Harold W. McGraw, Jr. Award for Innovation in Education.

Nancy M. Robinson, PhD (Stanford University 1958)
Professor Emerita of Psychiatry and Behavioral Sciences, University of Washington.

She is also the former director of what is now known as the Halbert and Nancy Robinson Center for Young Scholars, founded by her late husband, Hal. The center is best known for its two pioneering programs of early entrance to college, but offers summer and other opportunities as well. Engaged previously in a 30-year career in mental retardation, her research interests in giftedness have focused on academic acceleration to college, adjustment issues of gifted children, intellectual assessment, and verbal and mathematical precocity in very young children.

Stephen T. Schroth
Assistant Professor, Knox College, Illinois

Dr. Schroth holds a PhD in Educational Psychology/Gifted Education from the University of Virginia. He taught for the Los Angeles Unified School District, where he served as a classroom teacher, literacy coach, lead teacher, gifted coordinator, and arts prototype coordinator. With his colleague Jason Helfer, he has written curriculum for the Lyric Opera of Chicago and is currently chair of the Arts Network of the National Association for Gifted Children (NAGC). Drs. Schroth and Helfer have won the Mensa Education & Research Foundation Award for Excellence in Research on three occasions.

Del Siegle
Professor of Gifted Education, University of Connecticut.

He is past president of the National Association for Gifted Children (NAGC) and has served on the board of directors of The Association for the Gifted and the American Educational Research Association (AERA) Research on Giftedness, Creativity, and Talent SIG. Prior to earning his PhD, Del worked as a gifted and talented coordinator in Montana and is a past president of the Montana Association of Gifted and Talented Education. He authors a technology column for *Gifted Child Today*. Del recently joined Gary Davis and Sylvia Rimm as authors of the 6th edition of the popular textbook, *Education of the Gifted and Talented*.

Carol Ann Tomlinson
William Clay Parrish, Jr. Professor and Chair of Educational Leadership, Foundations and Policy, Curry School of Education, University of Virginia.

She is author of *How to Differentiate Instruction in Mixed Ability Classrooms* and *The Differentiated Classroom: Responding to the Needs of All Learners.* Her books have been translated into 14 languages. She works nationally and internationally with educators who seek to create classrooms that are more effective in teaching academically diverse student populations.

Joyce VanTassel-Baska
Smith Professor Emerita, The College of William & Mary, Virginia.

She developed a graduate program and a research and development center in gifted education at The College of William & Mary. She initiated and directed the Center for Talent Development at Northwestern University and also served as the state director of gifted programs for Illinois, as a regional director of a gifted service center in the Chicago area, as coordinator of gifted programs for the Toledo public schools, and as a teacher of gifted high school students. Dr. VanTassel-Baska has published 27 books and over 500 refereed journal articles, book chapters, and scholarly reports.

Kristofor Wiley
Doctoral Student in Gifted Education, University of Virginia.

After receiving his MEd in Gifted Education from Drury University, he taught for seven years in a program for profoundly gifted students in Springfield, Missouri. A former Peace Corps volunteer, he is interested in giftedness as a social construct and the application of contemplative instruction to students identified as gifted.

Frank C. Worrell, PhD
Professor, Graduate School of Education, University of California, Berkeley.

He also serves as director of the school's psychology program, faculty director of the Academic Talent Development Program, and faculty director for the California College Preparatory Academy. His research centers on academic talent development, the relationship of psychosocial variables to academic and psychological functioning, and the translation of research findings into school-based practice. Dr. Worrell is a co-editor of the *Review of Educational Research*; a fellow of Divisions 5, 16, and 52 of the American Psychological Association; a fellow of the Association for Psychological Science; and an elected member of the Society for the Study of School Psychology.

LIST OF FIGURES

LIST OF TABLES

1

INTRODUCTION

Holly L. Hertberg-Davis and Carolyn M. Callahan

The first year that I (Holly) taught the "Introduction to the Education of the Gifted" course at the University of Virginia, I imagined it as a course in which students' knowledge and understanding about gifted education would be expanded and refined. Their burning questions about "What is giftedness? How do we find it? How do we serve it?" would be answered and summarily put to rest. It was, of course, the classic case of a teacher forgetting what it was like to be a student. Because when I really think about it, I remember that during my first year of doctoral work, I walked into Carol Tomlinson's "Introduction to Teaching the Gifted" course wide-eyed, full of certainty from my own teaching experiences about what giftedness was and how to ignite and fuel it. That was September.

In December, I walked, slightly dazed, out of the final exam, thinking, "I know way more than I knew when I came in September—but I am sure of way less." Nothing was simple any more. Everything was fraught. There were so many decisions, and so much rested on every single one. By spring break, I was so overwrought, in fact, that Carol recommended that I buy the self-help book *Don't Sweat the Small Stuff*, although I think that both she and I knew that, in fact, none of this was small stuff. This was, in fact, stuff that impacted many children's lives and it *deserved* some sweat.

I recount this story to my students when they inevitably burst out, mid-semester, in frustration, "I have more questions now than I did when I started this class!" My first year, that outburst unnerved me. Now it pleases me. I know that this course can be—and ought to be—a battleground between the often simplistic conventional myths about giftedness embedded in our society and the more complex realities that research and thoughtful practice have uncovered. I know that it can be eye-opening and even unsettling to discover that the things that we were very sure of—the prized thinking skills pull-out program, our favorite robotics unit, the "no fail" identification matrix we've been using for years—may need to be rethought, retooled, or abandoned. But it is this constant thinking, rethinking, refining—and, most important, *questioning* by those in charge of designing and implementing programming for gifted students that makes for the sort of educational experiences we can call exemplary.

What Carol did for me and my classmates—and what I have since at least attempted to do for my own students—is continually force us to think not only about "what constitutes appropriate educational experiences for gifted students," but "what constitutes *defensible* educational experiences for gifted students." That is, how can we ensure that the programming, curricular, and instructional experiences we are providing to our gifted students are uniquely suited to their needs? How can we ensure that these experiences would not benefit *all* students? So much of the criticism and the skepticism about the need for gifted education come from the existence of programs in which the offered curriculum and learning experiences are not defensible, are not clearly distinguishable enough from what should be offered to *all* students. Field trips to art museums and space centers and "thinking skills" instruction presented in isolation of rich and challenging content in and of themselves do not constitute an appropriate education for gifted students. Whenever we make any decision concerning gifted students, we should ask: "Why just for the gifted?" We need to put all of our decisions to Passow's simple but brilliant "Would, Could, Should" test: *Would* all students want to be involved in such learning experiences? *Could* all students participate in such learning experiences? *Should* all students be expected to succeed in such learning experiences? (Passow, 1982).

If the answer to any of these questions is "yes," then what we are doing does not constitute an appropriate, defensible educational experience for gifted students.

There are many questions posed in this text, but it is the question: "Can we document that the educational experiences we are providing for the students we designate as gifted provide maximum benefit to those students and would not benefit students without that designation?" that to us seems the most crucial and the most worthy of returning to continually, in every decision—however small—we make. As we will continually reiterate throughout this text, there are no "right" answers in gifted education (although I think we would both argue that there are some "wrong" answers!), but we do believe that there is a right *process* involved in making decisions, a process that we outline below and redirect you to throughout your readings.

It is indeed true, and certainly not news, that there are numerous different —and sometimes conflicting—philosophies regarding what the purposes and responsibilities of the field of gifted education are and should be; and we present a broad range, but certainly not all, of those philosophies in this textbook. For some, the central purpose and responsibility of gifted education are to provide appropriate, and often separate, educational experiences for gifted students whose talents and abilities are evident and identifiable. For others, the central purpose and responsibility lie in developing the talents of a broad range of students, including those whose talents are readily identifiable and those whose potential has yet to emerge. While these two approaches may seem to be relatively similar, underlying them are divergent belief systems that lead to different methods of defining and identifying giftedness and talent, different viewpoints on the appropriate settings in which to provide services, and ultimately to the provision of different curricular and instructional experiences. The existence of multiple philosophies of gifted education does *not* mean that these multiple approaches cannot coexist. In fact, many of the most current definitions, identification methods, and programming and curriculum options in the field attempt to merge philosophies into cohesive and coherent approaches to attending to demands for both equity *and* excellence within the services we provide to gifted students.

HOW TO USE THIS TEXTBOOK

This textbook is designed to reflect a broad range of thinking in the field so that its readers can examine multiple options from which to choose those that best fit their needs and belief systems. When we first got the idea for this textbook, we imagined a book that would provide guidance—not a prescription—for educators concerned with the education of students in need of advanced instruction. There truly is no one right way to design or implement a program for gifted students; so much depends upon context— the population of students that a school serves, the resources available, the community surrounding the school. Our goal was to give the reader a sense of the range of options, knowing that we cannot, in an introductory-level text, present in-depth discussions of all options. By choosing particular points of view, we recognize that some other divergent, valuable chapters could have been included. But, in using other texts, we have often been frustrated that our students do not come away with a deep sense of any one approach or with a sense of the original "voice" of a key advocate for, or creator of, a particular approach. Hence, we chose to allow you to hear those voices and to use this text as the stepping stone for further investigation of the ideas, beliefs, and models which we perceive to be representative of the various approaches and points of view in existence— and evolving—in this field.

There is, however, a line of logic that should be followed in the program creation or revision process to ensure alignment between philosophy and definition of giftedness, identification methods, services and educational experiences offered, and evaluation of both students and the program itself (see Figure 1.1). The chapters that follow provide in-depth discussion of these components; however, a brief description here of each will provide the reader with a primer on basic elements of gifted education and an overview of the offerings of this textbook that will be helpful in providing a framework for reading.

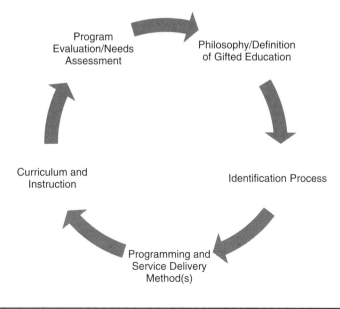

Fig. 1.1 Decision-making process in designing an aligned gifted program.

Philosophy/Definition of Giftedness

The process of creating or revising a gifted program, while essentially a cyclical process, ideally begins with consideration or reconsideration of beliefs about what it means to be gifted. The definition of giftedness that results should be reflective of the population of students that the district serves as well as the strengths and needs of the district. For example, in a district with a bi-modal population (divided between a wealthy group and a group with low socio-economic status) and general education classrooms reflecting a broad range of academic diversity, the definition of giftedness might include both high-achieving students and students with *potential* for performance at a high level. In a district with a generally high-achieving population served well in the regular classroom, the definition of giftedness might be more exclusive and include only students performing at the highest levels of achievement. Still other districts might focus their definitions on students with talents in mathematics in response to a documented need for advanced mathematics programming.

The importance of a district's definition of giftedness cannot be overstated. The definition effectively determines who will be served by the gifted program—and who will not. It answers the question: "Who are we serving?" and sets the stage for the rest of the decisions made in the process of program creation or revision. Section 1 of this textbook provides a variety of different approaches to defining giftedness, as well as the beliefs and philosophical and research bases underlying those definitions. Some criticize the field for not being in consensus on definition, but others (see Chapter 5 by Renzulli and Delcourt) view the varied approaches as a healthy and energizing aspect of gifted education. As long as underlying beliefs about what should be valued in education vary, so will definitions of educational constructs; those readers looking for definitive answers will necessarily be sorely disappointed. However, those readers who are looking for a definition that rings true to their beliefs will be heartened to see options.

Identification Processes

Once a district has determined *whom* it will serve, it then must determine the most effective and defensible process for *finding* those students. Identification processes and the assessment tools used in these processes should be closely aligned with the definition of giftedness and reflective of best practices in measurement and assessment. For example, if Sunny Valley School District determines that *giftedness* means demonstrated talent in music and the arts, and the neighboring district, Waterfield School District, determines that *giftedness* means high general academic aptitude, the identification processes used in each district should be vastly different. Detailed looks at a variety of different identification methods—from traditional approaches to those that are innovative—along with exemplary practices in identification are explored in depth in Section II of this text.

Service Delivery Options and Programming Models

Service delivery options and programming models refer to the structures through which services are provided to gifted students. Some service delivery approaches focus primarily on the settings in which gifted students are served; others encompass both the settings in which students learn and the content offered within these settings. These options should be tailored to the needs of the identified students and clearly reflect the definition of giftedness used in the district. In Sunny Valley School District (see example above), where giftedness is defined as musical and artistic ability, service delivery options might include separate advanced classes in music and art instruction, push-in services (where the gifted teacher and the general education teacher collaborate) during regular art or music classes, or a magnet school focused on music and the arts. In Waterfield, where general intellectual ability is served, service delivery options might include using cluster grouping of gifted students alone or offering a pull-out program (a separate class for the gifted) focused on extending and enriching the regular classroom curriculum. Once again, whatever approaches are utilized, these offerings must be aligned with the needs of the students identified for gifted services; Section III of this textbook provides closer and more in-depth descriptions of a variety of different service delivery methods. In this text, individual chapters focus on one service delivery approach, and often the term "the gifted program" is used to refer to that approach. However, the term "gifted program" should be used as an umbrella term in a district to cover an array of services or "continuum of services" that may be offered. A district might accelerate some students, serve some identified students in the regular classroom using a cluster group arrangement, provide a resource room for a smaller segment of that population, and offer a full-time school (e.g., in mathematics, science, and technology) for an even smaller segment of the population. Too often, districts choose only one service delivery option when an array of services would provide better matches between students and instruction.

Curriculum and Instruction

The term "curriculum and instruction" refers to the content and experiences that gifted students encounter within their gifted programs. While all components of a gifted program are important, it is the fit of the curriculum and instruction that students encounter daily that determines the degree to which a gifted student's academic—and, to a large extent, affective—needs are met. However, just as there is no single service delivery approach designed to meet the needs of all gifted students, there is no single curriculum appropriate for all gifted students. Gifted students are a diverse lot, varying from one another not only in their areas of strength and need, but also in their learning preferences, areas of interest, and backgrounds and experiences. Like every other component of gifted services mentioned thus far, the curriculum and instruction offered within a gifted program must be aligned with the specific needs of the identified students. Furthermore, even within an identified population of gifted students, student variance exists. Therefore, differentiation of curriculum and instruction within gifted programs should be considered. Section IV of this textbook explores a variety of curricular and instructional approaches to meeting the needs of the gifted.

Specific Populations

In many circles in the field of gifted education, the terms "special populations" and "underserved gifted" are used to designate student groups that bring a set of unique characteristics to the instructional setting. However, a cursory examination of the table of contents of this text will reveal that nearly every group one can parse from the overall gifted population has some set of unique traits that warrant attention across the dimensions of a gifted program: beliefs, philosophy, definition, identification, service delivery, curriculum, and even evaluation. Since the term "underserved population" does not usually include males or females, it seems more appropriate to entitle this section of the book "Specific Populations" in order to include gender differences, differences across ethnic and cultural groups, geographic locations (rural/suburban/urban), and even differing issues around students' current level of performance. But we must also remember that the issues discussed in these chapters are still generalities. Most individuals fall into several of these specific categories: the gifted African American female who lives in a rural environment may be an underachiever. Finally, the authors of these chapters present discussions of these subgroups based on the data on groups, and we caution against the creation of stereotypes or overgeneralizing from the group to particular students in the group. Section V of this textbook will guide the reader in understanding the issues and possibilities related to a broad range of gifted learners.

Program Evaluation/Needs Assessment

A critical—and often overlooked—step in the process of creating, redesigning, or refining a gifted program is assessing the degree to which a school or district currently provides for gifted students through the regular curriculum in order to determine what, if any, services need to be provided. Additionally, evaluating the effectiveness and impact of a gifted program on identified students (and those not identified for services) is necessary in creating and maintaining an exemplary, defensible gifted program. Section VI of this textbook investigates issues and processes related to effective formative and summative evaluations of gifted program outcomes.

A FINAL NOTE—AND DISCLAIMER—BEFORE READING

We noted above that we have included chapters representing a broad range of philosophies about the purposes and responsibilities of the field of gifted education, including chapters that question the need for gifted education at all. Clearly, as editors of a textbook about gifted education, we believe that as long as academic diversity exists among students, there *is* a need for gifted education just as there is a need for special education; however, we recognize the issues that complicate decision making in schools, as well as the competing philosophies underlying every decision about curriculum, about instructional grouping, and about allocations of resources. While we have tried to include those points of view that cause us—and, we hope, our readers—to pause and reflect on our assumptions, the very fact that we have made the effort to create this textbook is testimony to our belief in gifted education.

Why do we believe that gifted students exist and that there is a need for special programming for these students? That gifted persons have been recognized from the time of written history is undeniable; the terms used to describe them may have varied, but the existence of individuals with advanced abilities has not. And it is difficult to believe that the traits that resulted in the achievement of eminence for many of these individuals appeared full-blown in adulthood. It is also difficult to ignore the very real possibility that the talents of many other students were never recognized or developed. While some theorists and scholars (e.g., Tannenbaum, 1983) prefer to use the terms "potential" or "talent" to describe advanced abilities in children, the traits characterizing giftedness and gifted behavior (or whatever you choose to call it) are recognized in young children and adolescents, even if they are not fully developed. If we reflect on those traits, they suggest that the learning experiences of those children need to differ from those whose pace of learning is not as accelerated and those who do not bring the same broad and deep understanding of one or more disciplines to the classroom.

It seems to us a basic, indisputable tenet of any educational philosophy that every child has a right to learn every day in school. To that end, we must examine the degree to which that is happening for our most advanced learners in today's (2012) general education classrooms. Like all educators, our dream is that every teacher in every classroom would have both the skill and the will to adjust the curriculum and the instruction offered to the diverse students in their classrooms. And like many others, we hope that some day that will be the case. However, there is ample evidence that current classrooms fail to come close to that ideal, particularly for advanced learners.

At one time, the one-room schoolhouse was populated by a very small number of students (a very select group as most children did not access public education), giving the teacher the time to know students well and accommodate learning tasks to individual needs. Even then, it seems, not all learners' needs were addressed. As Mark Twain observed of schooling over a century ago, "I've never let school interfere with my education" (attributed to him by Holland, 1907). However, the acceptance of compulsory education and the subsequent growth in the size of schools and classrooms created very different classroom environments, characterized not only by larger class sizes, but by great diversity in readiness for schooling and learning, cultural viewpoints, exceptional learning differences, and abilities. At the same time, the solidification of curriculum by grade level began, culminating in the high-stakes testing environment surrounding the No Child Left Behind Act of 2001. These changes in classrooms and many other factors have resulted in many general education classrooms that do not or cannot address the needs of gifted learners (Brighton, Hertberg, Moon, Tomlinson, & Callahan, 2005; Hertberg-Davis, 2009). The reasons for this lack of attention are not the deliberate intentions of teachers or other educators. They stem from the circumstances described above combined with other realities of current educational environments.

While parents and many educators have long recognized the serious lack of attention to addressing gifted students' needs in America's schools, the documentation of classroom practices relative to the gifted child in the current school climate began with the report of the Marland Commission in 1972. The commission concluded:

> Gifted and Talented children are, in fact, deprived and can suffer psychological damage and permanent impairment of their abilities to function well which is equal to or greater than the similar deprivation suffered by any other population with special needs served by the Office of Education.
>
> (Marland, 1972, pp. xi–xii)

The commission reported that only a small fraction of the gifted students in the United States were receiving appropriate educational programs in any setting. This report was followed by a national survey conducted by researchers at the National Research Center on the Gifted and Talented, which documented, 20 years after the Marland Report, the continued lack of attention to modifying instruction for the gifted student.

The major finding of this study is that third and fourth grade teachers make only minor modifications in the regular curriculum to meet the needs of the gifted students. This result holds for public school teachers, for private school teachers, and for teachers in schools with high concentrations of the four types of ethnic minorities included in this research. The same general conclusion also applies to teachers and classrooms in various regions of the country (Northeast, South, West and North Central) and to teachers and classrooms in rural, urban, and suburban communities.

(Archambault et. al, 1993, p. vii)

Recent reports document that classrooms have not changed in the ensuing 20 years—20 years during which there have been many focused attempts to bring attention to the need for general education teachers to plan thoughtfully for the gifted in regular classrooms.

A follow-up study of middle school teachers found that, consistent with the Archambault et al. (1993) study findings on elementary teachers:

[L]earning contracts, tiered assignments, advanced organizers, computer programs focusing on basic skills or advanced understanding, curriculum compacting, learning centers, flexible grouping, or interest centers are rarely used in their middle school classrooms . . . a large portion of teachers also indicate never tailoring an assignment for students or varying materials based on student readiness levels. Instead, lecture, direct instruction to the whole class using the state standards and local curriculum guides, is the predominant reported modality of teaching. Students indicated, consistent with teachers' responses, that the instructional content of their classes was textbook driven and focused on student success for more formal assessments (e.g., end-of-unit tests, standardized tests). Students also indicated whole group instruction supported by note taking and all students working on the same assignment as the predominant format of their classrooms.

(Moon, Callahan, Tomlinson, & Miller, 2002, pp. v–vi)

Most recently, a national survey of teachers conducted by the Thomas B. Fordham Institute (Farkas & Duffet, 2008) and a survey of state departments of education (Council of State Directors of Programs for the Gifted [CSDPG] & National Association for Gifted Children [NAGC], 2009) reveal the lack of teacher preparation in gifted and talented instruction and lack of attention to classroom practice that challenges or supports high-ability learners. Thirty-two percent of teachers responded that advanced students are a low priority in their schools; 73 percent of teachers agree that "too often, the brightest students are bored and under-challenged in school; we're not giving them a sufficient chance to thrive"; and 77 percent of teachers agree that "getting underachieving students to reach proficiency has become so important that the needs of advanced students take a back seat." Only 10 percent of teachers in the survey report that advanced students are likely to be taught with curriculum and instruction especially designed for their abilities (compared to 51 percent who report that struggling learners receive such a curriculum), and 84 percent of teachers say that, in practice, differentiated instruction is difficult to implement (Farkas & Duffet, 2008).

But even if every teacher in every classroom could deliver a curriculum appropriately adjusted to the level and pace of all students, there remains a second, affective dimension of school and schooling that most heterogeneous classrooms will likely fail to address.

The classroom climate may be isolating for a child whose peers do not understand his or her way of thinking, who feels isolated and "different" in ways that make no sense to him or her; or who is not supported by peers in debate and in-depth discussion of new ideas.

> National efforts to increase the availability of a variety of appropriate instructional and out-of-school provisions must be a high priority since *research indicates that many of the emotional or social difficulties gifted students experience disappear when their educational climates are adapted to their level and pace of learning.*
>
> (Neihart, Reis, Robinson, & Moon, 2002, p. 286)

REASONS WHY THE GENERAL EDUCATION PROGRAM IS NOT YET READY TO MEET THE NEEDS OF GIFTED STUDENTS

Two critical aspects of the current status of teachers and general education classrooms exemplify the many forces diminishing the likelihood that gifted students will be well-served in the regular classroom. First, teachers are not trained to meet the needs of advanced students. Sixty five percent of teachers report that their education courses and teacher preparation programs focused either very little or not at all on how best to teach academically advanced students; only five states require all teachers to receive pre-service training in gifted and talented education (Farkas & Duffet, 2008; NAGC, 2009).

Second, there is tremendous pressure on classroom teachers to focus on raising the test scores of the low-performing students in their classrooms. In one of many recent studies of the impact of high-stakes testing, Moon, Brighton, Jarvis, and Hall (2007) surveyed teachers and then followed up with classroom observations and interviews to ascertain beliefs and practices. They found that both teachers and students feel a tremendous amount of pressure associated with high-stakes testing. The pressure experienced by teachers results in the use of drill and practice as the dominant mode of curriculum and instruction. Further, the high-stakes testing environment creates the greatest pressure in disadvantaged schools, resulting in more drill and practice instruction. Finally, and sadly, gifted and talented students expressed feeling great pressure to perform well to bring up the scores in their classrooms and schools, often resulting in disengagement from the learning process.

Some critics of gifted education cite elitist values and failure to be inclusive of students from all populations. Yet those critics fail to observe both the intense and vigorous efforts by the field to change identification procedures and the subsequent results of those changes. They seem unwilling to acknowledge recent changes in the demographics of gifted programs. For example, state policy changes in Georgia increased the identification of African American students in Georgia's gifted programs by 206 percent and the number of Hispanic students by 570 percent (National Research Center on the Gifted and Talented, 2012).

All of these circumstances suggest that change is not going to occur in the immediate future. Even with the best models for making all classrooms welcoming and appropriate instructional climates for gifted learners, change will take a long time and far greater commitment from educators. In the meantime, thousands of children could "just start school in January" as Reis and her colleagues demonstrated (Reis et al., 1993). Until this situation changes, we need to find alternative ways to provide appropriate services to gifted students. It is the intent of this textbook to provide the reader with the necessary breadth of understanding of current best practices within the field to do so.

REFERENCES

Archambault, F. A., Jr., Westberg, K. L., Brown, S. W., Hallmark, B. W., Emmons, C. L., & Zhang, W. (1993). *Regular classroom practices with gifted students: Results of a national survey of classroom teachers.* (Research Monograph 93102). Storrs: The National Research Center on the Gifted and Talented, University of Connecticut.

Brighton, C. M., Hertberg, H. L., Moon, T. R., Tomlinson, C. A., & Callahan, C. M. (2005). *The feasibility of high-end learning in a diverse middle school.* (Research Monograph 05210). Storrs: The National Research Center on the Gifted and Talented, University of Connecticut.

Council of State Directors of Programs for the Gifted, & National Association for Gifted Children (2009). *State of the states in gifted education 2008–2009: National policy and practice data.* Washington, DC: Authors.Farkas, S., & Duffett, A. (2008). *High-achieving students in the era of NCLB: Results from a national teacher survey.* Washington, DC: Thomas B. Fordham Institute.

Hertberg-Davis, H. (2009). Myth 7: Differentiation in the regular classroom is equivalent to gifted programs and is sufficient: Classroom teachers have the time, the skill, and the will to differentiate adequately. *Gifted Child Quarterly, 53,* 251–253.

Holland, W. B. (1907). *The Outing Magazine Advertiser, 50,* 840.

Marland, S. P., Jr. (1972). *Education of the gifted and talented: Report to the Congress of the United States by the U.S. Commissioner of Education and background papers submitted to the U.S. Office of Education,* 2 vols. (Government Documents Y4.L 11/2: G36). Washington, DC: U.S. Government Printing Office.

Moon, T. R., Brighton, C. M., Jarvis, J. M., & Hall, C. J. (2007). *State standardized testing programs: Their effects on teachers and students.* (Research Monograph 07228). Storrs: The National Research Center on the Gifted and Talented, University of Connecticut.

Moon, T. R., Callahan, C. M., Tomlinson, C. A., & Miller, E. M. (2002). *Middle school classrooms: Teachers' reported practices and student perceptions.* (Research Monograph 02164). Storrs: The National Research Center on the Gifted and Talented, University of Connecticut.

National Research Center on the Gifted and Talented. (2012). *The Georgia story: One state's approach to the under-representation issue.* Storrs: Author, University of Connecticut. Retrieved January 31, 2012 from http://www.gifted.uconn.edu/sem/The_Georgia_Story.html

Neihart, M., Reis, S. M., Robinson, N. M, & Moon, S. M. (Eds.) (2002). *The social and emotional development of gifted children: What do we know?,* Waco, TX: Prufrock Press.

Passow, A. H. (1982). Differentiated curricula for the gifted/talented. In *Curriculum for the gifted/talented: Selected proceedings of the First National Conference on Curriculum for the Gifted and Talented* (pp. 4–20). Ventura, CA: Ventura Superintendent of Schools.

Reis, S. M., Westberg, K. L., Kulikowich, J., Caillard, F., Hébert, T., Plucker, J. et al. (1993). *Why not let high ability students start school in January? The curriculum compacting study.* (Research Monograph 93106). Storrs: The National Research Center on the Gifted and Talented, University of Connecticut.

Tannenbaum, A. J. (1983). *Gifted children: Psychological and educational perspectives.* New York: Macmillan.

Section I

Beliefs, Philosophies, and Definitions of Giftedness

2

BELIEFS, PHILOSOPHIES, AND DEFINITIONS[1]

Carolyn M. Callahan and Holly L. Hertberg-Davis

Educational programming, clinical practice, and even parenting decisions are shaped and driven by beliefs and philosophies. They may not be overt or articulated, but they underlie actions from everyday behaviors to high-level policy decisions. Because the field of gifted education is characterized by not one, but many belief systems, there is a considerable variation from state to state and school to school in definitions of giftedness, identification of students for special services, programming delivery models, curriculum and instructional practices, and guidance and counseling practices. One can argue the merits of one belief system or philosophy over another, but the key to providing high-quality services to gifted children is to examine carefully the current theory and research in the field; come to a consensus on underlying principles to guide programming, based on sound reflections of what the theory and research indicate is best practice; and then create the components of a program consistent with a set of beliefs derived from careful reflection and decision making based on current knowledge.

Beliefs of parents, teachers, administrators, and the community are sometimes based on knowledge and understanding of the theory and research; but just as often beliefs are based on "one child I know" (or heard about) or the many myths that surround the field. In the past 25 years, two issues of *Gifted Child Quarterly* (1982, Volume 4, Issue Number 1; 2009, Volume 53, Issue Number 4) were devoted entirely to myths in the field. The editor for both issues found that many of the myths addressed in the first issue had not been dispelled in 2010, illustrating the enduring nature of beliefs despite evidence to the contrary.

Further, the beliefs some hold about education and educational opportunity in general may conflict with beliefs others have about what educational experiences are appropriate for gifted students. For example, the ways in which equity of educational opportunity is interpreted can lead to conflicting points of view: Some interpret equity as meaning the same for all; others interpret equity as meaning providing appropriate education for all. Therefore, it is not surprising that views about gifted education differ and sometimes collide.

BELIEFS AND PHILOSOPHIES RELATING TO THE GIFTED—DO GIFTED STUDENTS EXIST? DO GIFTED STUDENTS NEED A DIFFERENT EDUCATIONAL EXPERIENCE?

As Tannenbaum (1983) notes in his overview of the history of attention to the gifted, recognition of persons who excel in any aspect of human performance inevitably results in "some degree of public interest, suspicion, appreciation, or antipathy, depending on the temperament of their audiences" (p. 2). He posits that the "traditions of ambivalence" in our culture and over time have roots in conflicting beliefs. On the one hand, some reflect the beliefs of the ancient Greeks that great intellect is a divine gift. On the other hand, some believe that the genius is emotionally disturbed. In past times (and perhaps even in some stereotypes held now), some believed that great mental prowess was accompanied by physical weakness or social awkwardness. Today (in 2012), ironically, as noted by scholars like Tannenbaum and Gallagher, "an almost insatiable demand for newness in the arts, sciences, and humanities" (Tannenbaum, 1983, p.4) conflicts with culturally conservative views that regard creativity with suspicion and disdain. Gallagher (1997) has characterized this as America's love/hate relationship with the gifted and talented.

As a consequence of these mixed philosophies, outstanding performance in adults has long been recognized and celebrated, but educational institutions have not been uniformly (or even widely) responsive to nurturing the exceptional potentials or abilities of their most advanced students.

DEFINITIONS OF GIFTEDNESS

A fundamental belief of those in the field of gifted education is that there exists a group of children, adolescents, and adults who are different in some significant way from others of their age group in their learning profiles and behaviors. The differences these individuals exhibit are then used as a basis for creating differentiated educational programs to address those differences. If one accepts the philosophical belief that gifted children, adolescents, and adults exist, then usually there is a corresponding belief about who those individuals are and the characteristics they exhibit that warrant assignment of the label.

The belief that gifted children, adolescents, and adults exist leads to defining who those individuals are. In schools, it leads to the formal definition of what traits characterize the population of students we will identify—and serve—as gifted. An important caveat at this point is to note that a definition does not suggest that all students must start the journey at the same point or that all students will stop at all the points of interest along the way, that all will stay on the same path, or that all will reach the same destination at the same time!

The construct of giftedness has not been solidified with any agreed-upon specific definition. The range of beliefs about "who is gifted" evolves from multiple belief systems and philosophies and can be characterized as broad or narrow; from restrictive and exclusive to open and inclusive, conservative or liberal, and theoretical or atheoretical. Of course, most definitions fall somewhere on the continuum represented by each of these extremes. The field of gifted education is not unique in the field of exceptionalities in the multiplicity of definitions of giftedness offered. But in other areas of special education there are agreed-upon parameters and criteria for delineating who falls into a given category—parameters and criteria often sanctioned by federal regulations and controlled by funding associated with those parameters.

The Evolution of Definitions

The definitions that have characterized the field of gifted education in the United States have been influenced by the evolution of ideas in the field of psychology, particularly psychometrics; by historical events; and by the politics and economics of given eras. While there was some attention to biographies of individuals considered "geniuses" prior to the 20th century and some attention to programming in select places, little study of the development and education of gifted students emerged until the early 20th century. The first systematic study of the development of gifted children into adolescence and adulthood was tied to developments in psychometrics, most particularly the development of assessments to measure aptitude.

Early Influence of Psychology and Psychometrics

In the field of gifted education, most refer to the work of Terman as both the pioneering work in the study of gifted children and the basis for a narrow definition of giftedness in the United States (often referred to as the IQ definition of giftedness). The work of Terman and his colleagues at Stanford University, first published in Volume I of *Genetic Studies of Genius* (Terman, 1925), was an outgrowth of his work translating the intelligence tests created by Alfred Binet into English. The construction of the Stanford–Binet Intelligence Scale reflected a belief of intelligence as a unitary trait, and Terman defined "gifted" as those who scored in the top 1 percent on that test. The longitudinal study of the gifted individuals from childhood to maturity that followed, although it demonstrated that IQ assessed at an early age can be used successfully to predict adult achievement and dispelled the myth of gifted children as emotionally unstable, is harshly criticized for reflecting an undocumented construct of unitary intelligence, a hereditary and fixed view of ability, and for creating a field reflecting social elitism (Borland, 1997, 2005; Dai, 2010; Margolin, 1996).

The work of Terman, however, while certainly extensive and very influential, was but a small part of the emerging interest in studying and defining giftedness. Many of the alternate definitions offered during the same era were broader in conception. During the 1920s, Hollingworth (often only noted for studying students with exceptionally high IQ scores) reported on the possibility that students "may be far more excellent in some capacities than others" (1926, p. 202); Bentley (1937) called for recognition of and advanced curriculum for students who have aptitude in specific areas such as mathematics, music, or art. Witty, in 1958, developed a definition that not only recognized intellectual abilities, but also special talents in art, writing, and social leadership. While the field of gifted education was noting the call for broadened conceptions of giftedness, other psychologists were offering data that supported a concept of intelligence that included specific abilities. Perhaps the alternate definitions of intelligence as multifaceted which were offered by Thorndike and his associates (Thorndike, Bergman, Cobb, & Woodyard, 1926) or Spearman (1927) at this time did not achieve such widespread attention and acceptance in definitions of giftedness because they lacked both accompanying standardized assessment tools and corresponding study of the population defined as gifted.

Political and Social Contexts

Definitions are also greatly influenced by the social and political contexts of the times. Recognition of the possibility of outstanding performance across a wide range of performance realms has always been part of history. But the recognition of talent in children, development of educational programs to serve these children, and bestowing of honor on one domain of performance or another reflects the culture and historical events of the time. For example, Guilford (1950), in a historical address to the American Psychological Association, lamented the lack of attention to creativity in education, a lament which resulted in a rise in the study of creativity as an aspect of outstanding performance and inclusion in definitions of giftedness. Further, during the 1950s, numerous commission reports and regional and national surveys pointed to the neglect of gifted students, and several scholars called for reform to address the issue of low standards resulting in inadequate curriculum for the most able students (Tannenbaum, 1983). While these reports and articles raised issues and debate, it was not until the launch of Sputnik by the Soviet Union in 1957 that widespread attention was directed to the need to provide any special educational programming. Suddenly, serious attention (defined as changed policy and financial commitment) was paid to the need to produce an "intellectual elite" in response to worry that the United States was losing ground in scientific and military prowess. Concern that the "greatest minds of the day had outperformed ours" triggered a response from political leaders including Admiral Hyman Rickover. In 1960, he observed that "anti-intellectualism has long been our besetting sin. With us, hostility to superior intelligence masqueraded as belief in the equality of man [sic] and put forth the false claim that it is undemocratic to recognize and nurture superior intelligence" (p. 30). Not surprisingly, those students recognized as highly able or gifted and provided with services during the 1960s were those who excelled or had potential for high-level performance in the sciences and mathematics.

In the early 1970s, a federally sanctioned study of the state of gifted education led to the publication of what came to be called the Marland Report (1972). This report included the first "federal definition" of giftedness. The definition represented an inclusive approach to defining giftedness by designating the categories of general intellectual ability, specific academic aptitude, creative or productive thinking, leadership ability, visual and performing arts, and psychomotor ability as the targets for identifying gifted students. It further specified the target population as the upper 3 percent to 5 percent of school-aged children. The definition recognized the influence of Terman (general intellectual ability), Thorndike and Spearman (specific academic aptitude), Guilford's address (creative or productive thinking), and the work of early scholars like Hollingworth, Witty, and Bentley in expanding the definition to include the visual and performing arts. This definition quickly became the policy-level definition adopted by many states and school districts.

Shortly after the federal definition was put forward, dissatisfaction with the definition led Renzulli (1978) to offer an alternative definition drawn from his study of research on eminent people. Among his criticisms were the bifurcation of aptitude and creativity and lack of recognition of the importance of task commitment to the full development of giftedness. This led to a definition (The Three-Ring Conception of Giftedness; see Renzulli, 1978) and a concomitant program option (the Schoolwide Enrichment Model; see Renzulli & Reis, 1997) widely accepted as a more inclusive alternative to traditional definitions and programming.

A Return to the Influences of Psychology in a Time of Changing Demographics

The evolving work in defining and examining intelligence in the field of psychology has also influenced the conceptions and definitions of giftedness used in research and practice. As noted, early definitions and measures of intelligence led to the conflation of giftedness with high IQ. More recently, interactions between social forces and developments in the field of psychology have resulted in broadened definitions of giftedness. As theorists and researchers in the 1980s re-conceptualized intelligence and assessment of intelligence, the demographics of schools in the United States began to change radically, with increased numbers of immigrants, particularly those who were second language learners and Hispanic in origin. In addition, increasing recognition of the issues behind the widening achievement gap between students from high-poverty environments and their more economically privileged peers called for new ways to think about the nature of intelligence and talented performance. In 1983, Gardner offered a model of relatively distinct intelligences which came to be called Multiple Intelligence or MI theory. Educators in the field of gifted education translated the theory to suggest that students might be gifted in the realms of spatial, linguistic, logical–mathematical, bodily–kinesthetic, musical, interpersonal, or intra-personal domains. Despite many criticisms of lack of empirical evidence to support the theory (Sternberg, Jarvin, & Grigorenko, 2010; Waterhouse, 2006), the theory continues to receive considerable attention and has sparked a trend toward more multifaceted approaches to defining and identifying giftedness. Like Gardner, Robert Sternberg (1988) proposed a multi-faceted conception of intelligence which has had a strong influence on the field's conception of giftedness. Sternberg's Triarchic Theory of Intelligence (1988) recognizes three intelligence preferences—analytic, synthetic, and practical—to describe ways in which individuals process information and demonstrate talent. He developed assessments of these constructs and, using curriculum based on the information-processing dimensions underlying the definitions (Sternberg, Ferrari, Clinkenbeard, & Grigorenko, 1996), demonstrated the success of teaching to the strengths of students to achieve high-level performance.

Debates Surrounding Definitions of Intelligence and Giftedness

Debates Around the Concept of Intelligence and Defining Giftedness

The multitude of definitions of giftedness and the identification practices that evolve from these definitions are the subject of great debate and angst in the field. On the one hand, those most concerned with the results of using an IQ-based conception of giftedness point to the resulting racial and social inequities that result and also question the usefulness of a unitary construct. Proponents of using IQ tests note the lack of understanding of IQ assessment (Gottfredson, 2006; Kauffman, 2009; Robinson, 2005) arguing that:

1. current intelligence tests are based on both a construct of general intelligence and specific areas of ability articulated by the structure of human cognitive abilities referred to as the Cattell–Horn–Carroll theory (McGrew, 2005); and
2. the overwhelming data on intelligence tests support the validity of IQ scores in predicting school and job performance.

Others (e.g., Renzulli and Delcourt in Chapter 5 or Gagné in Chapter 7 in this book) have re-framed the debate by acknowledging the importance of conceiving of giftedness in ways that include both cognitive *and* personality factors.

Debates Around the Role of the School in Addressing the Needs of the Gifted

A school system is also fraught with political and economic realities. Hence, it is quite possible that any school division might adopt a very broad definition, but determine that it can only serve a smaller proportion or a targeted group within the broader definition. For example, a school district may adopt a definition that recognizes talent across the academic domains as well as in the arts, but its gifted program may only serve students in the academic areas. Or the definition may include students of all ages, but gifted services may be offered only beginning in third grade because of other, conflicting belief systems (e.g., assessment of young children is unreliable).

Beliefs About What Gifted Education is "For"

In considering their beliefs about the purposes of gifted education, educators must situate these beliefs in the context of their beliefs about education in general. The belief that the purpose of education is to transmit knowledge and cultural understandings leads to different educational programs than the belief that the purpose of education is to teach students to be critical thinkers, agents of social change, or problem solvers. Two common beliefs about the purposes of gifted education are:

1. We should provide educational programs to gifted students so that they may fully realize their potential and become happy and productive adults.
2. The gifted population represents our nation's greatest resource and hope for the future so we should endeavor to ensure full development of their potential for the good of the nation.

As Renzulli and Delcourt note in Chapter 5, these philosophies do not have to be mutually exclusive, but rather can work in support of one another. Whatever the belief system about education in general, and gifted education in particular, that one espouses, it is important to reflect on how these beliefs influence all decision making from the writing of a definition, to adoption of an identification procedure, to programming and curriculum development.

GUIDES TO READING THIS SECTION OF THE TEXT

As in the other sections of this text, the chapters related to definition are not inclusive of all possible definitions of giftedness, but represent instead a broad range of definitions that are the most widely accepted and applied definitions in the field. As you read the chapters, consider these questions.

1. Does the definition represent a clear philosophical position? What is that position and do you agree with it?
2. Does the definition provide guidance in making other decisions such as how to identify gifted students?
3. Does the definition seem fair and equitable in including students from all groups that include gifted individuals?
4. Is the definition theory-based? Is it research-based?
5. Would this definition be considered broad or narrow; restrictive and exclusive or open and inclusive; conservative or liberal; and theoretical or atheoretical?

6. What are the implications of adopting this definition for identification, programming, and/or curriculum?
7. Why is society appreciative of and willing to support the recognition of and devotion of resources to develop talent in athletics but not academics? Why is it acceptable for students to be singled out for special instruction on teams made up of extraordinary athletes, but not for instruction when they perform at extraordinary levels in academics?
8. The set of myths surrounding definition that were "debunked" in the *Gifted Child Quarterly* (1982, Volume 4, Issue Number 1; 2009, Volume 53, Issue Number 4) is listed below. Do the chapter authors re-enforce the myth or offer proven arguments to counter the myth?

   • The gifted and talented constitute one single homogeneous group and giftedness is a way of being that stays in the person over time and experiences.
   • The gifted constitute 3 percent to 5 percent of the population. Moreover, giftedness equals high IQ which is a stable measure of aptitude.

NOTE

1. The connections between historical events as well as the social and cultural contexts for interpreting the evolution of both definitions and events in gifted education, are borrowed from the work of Abraham Tannenbaum (1983). His work is seminal in drawing these connections, seeing the parallels between the events, and expressing them in ways that lend considerable insight into the history of gifted education.

REFERENCES

Bentley, J. E. (1937). *Superior children.* New York: Norton.

Borland, J. H. (1997). The construct of giftedness. *Peabody Journal of Education, 72*(3–4), 6–20.

Borland, J. H. (2005). Gifted education without gifted children: The case for no conception of giftedness. In R. J. Sternberg & J. E. Davidson (Eds.), *Conceptions of giftedness* (2nd ed., pp. 1–19). Cambridge, UK: Cambridge University Press.

Dai, D. Y. (2010). *The nature and nurture of giftedness.* New York: Teachers College Press.

Gallagher, J. J. (1997). Issues in the education of gifted students. In N. Colangelo & G. A. Davis (Eds.), *Handbook of gifted education* (2nd ed., pp. 10–23). Boston: Allyn & Bacon.

Gardner, H. (1983). *Frames of mind: The theory of Multiple Intelligences.* New York: Basic Books.

Gottfredson, L. S. (2006). Social consequences of group differences in cognitive ability. In C. E. Flores-Mendoza & R. Colom (Eds.), *Introduction to the psychology of individual differences* (pp. 433–456). Porto Allegre, Brazil: ArtMed.

Guilford, J. P. (1950). Creativity. *American Psychologist, 5,* 444–454.

Hollingsworth, L. (1926). *Gifted children: Their nature and nurture.* New York: Macmillan.

Kauffman, A. (2009). *IQ testing 101.* New York: Springer.

McGrew, K. S. (2005). The Cattell-Horn-Carroll theory of cognitive abilities: Past present, and future. In D. P. Flanagan, J.O. Genshaft, & P. L. Harrison (Eds.), *Contemporary intellectual assessment: Theories, tests and issues* (pp. 136–182). New York: Guilford.

Margolin, L. (1996). A pedagogy of privilege. *Journal for the Education of the Gifted, 19,*164–180.

Marland, S. P., Jr. (1972). *Education of the gifted and talented: Report to the Congress of the United States by the U.S. Commissioner of Education and background papers submitted to the U.S. Office of Education,* 2 vols. (Government Documents Y4.L 11/2: G36). Washington, DC: U.S. Government Printing Office.

Renzulli, J. S. (1978). What makes giftedness: Re-examining a definition. *Phi Delta Kappan, 63,* 180–184, 261.

Renzulli, J. S., & Reis, S. M. *The Schoolwide Enrichment Model: A how-to guide for educational excellence.* Mansfield Center, CT: Creative Learning Press.

Rickover, H. S. (1960, February 13). Don't hamstring the talented. *The Saturday Evening Post, 30,* pp. 126–130.

Robinson, N. M. (2005). In defense of a psychometric approach to the definition of academic giftedness: A conservative approach from a die-hard liberal. In R. J. Sternberg & J. E. Davidson (Eds.), *Conceptions of giftedness* (2nd ed., pp. 278–294). New York: Cambridge University Press.

Spearman, C. E. (1927). *The abilities of man: Their nature and measurement.* New York: Macmillan.

Sternberg, R. J. (1988). *The triarchic mind: A new theory of human intelligence.* New York: Penguin Books.

Sternberg, R. J., Ferrari, M., Clinkenbeard, P. R., & Grigorenko, E. L. (1996). Identification, instruction, and assessment of gifted children: A construct validation of a triarchic model. *Gifted Child Quarterly, 40,* 129–137.

Sternberg, R. J., Jarvin, L., & Grigorenko, E. L. (2010). *Explorations in giftedness.* New York: Cambridge University Press.

Tannenbaum, A. J. (1983). *Gifted children: Psychological and educational perspectives.* New York: Macmillan.

Terman, L. M. (1925). *Genetic studies of genius: Mental and physical traits of a thousand gifted children* (Vol. I). Stanford, CA: University of Stanford Press.

Thorndike, E. L., Bergman, E. O., Cobb, M. V., & Woodyard, E. (1926). *The measurement of intelligence.* New York: Teachers College Press.

Waterhouse, L. (2006). Multiple intelligences, the Mozart effect, and emotional intelligence: A critical review. *Educational Psychologist, 4,* 207–-225.

Witty, P. (1958). Who are the gifted? In N. B. Henry (Ed.), *Education of the gifted: The fifty-seventh yearbook of the National Society for the Study of Education* (pp. 41–63). Chicago: University of Chicago Press.

3

A BRIEF SYNOPSIS OF EVENTS INFLUENCING THE RECOGNITION AND EDUCATION OF GIFTED CHILDREN IN THE UNITED STATES

Kristofor Wiley and Marguerite C. Brunner

The intent of this chapter is to provide a brief, annotated timeline of major events and individuals influencing the development of the field of gifted education. Awareness of the historical underpinnings and growth over time of gifted education provides useful context for the current discussions, debates, and directions of the field outlined in this textbook.

EUROPEAN INFLUENCES

1869—Francis Galton, an English scientist and mathematician, produces *Hereditary Genius*, a study of eminent British men intended to illuminate the nature of genius. It sets a precedent of using the characteristics of creatively productive adults to identify giftedness in the general population.

1905—Alfred Binet and Théodore Simon, both French psychologists, develop the first quantitative assessment of an intelligence construct. Their purpose is to identify children likely to have difficulty in the classroom. As a result of the assessment, intelligence is increasingly transformed into a single numeric quantity, a paradigm neither scientist supports.

1916–1936: THE LABORATORY AND THE CLASSROOM

1916—Lewis Terman, an educational psychologist who spends most of his career at Stanford University, translates the Binet–Simon scales for use in America. In addition to reinforcing the concept of a unitary intelligence, the new Stanford–Binet Intelligence Scale introduces the concept of the intelligence quotient, or IQ. From this moment forward, IQ becomes the standard with which all other approaches to identifying talent in students are compared or contrasted.

1917—As World War I begins, Terman and others are invited to create two standardized assessments of intelligence to facilitate assignment of new recruits. The first, or Army A, serves to introduce the idea of intelligence as a unitary and testable quantity to millions of adult Americans. The second, or Army B, is modified so that it can be taken by recruits with limited English proficiency or language disabilities. The Army B assessment helps to anchor a thread of research on non-verbal assessments of intelligence.

1921—Lewis Terman uses the Stanford–Binet test to qualify a sample of about 1,500 children for the experimental study of the traits of "gifted children." Terman and others administer an extraordinary variety of surveys and examinations to assess physical health, social skills, favorite reading, profiles of talent, heredity, and many other variables. The results are published in *Genetic Studies of Genius*, a five-volume series, beginning in 1925.

1922—Leta S. Hollingworth begins the Special Opportunity Class for gifted students at Public School 165 in New York City. This class would yield nearly 40 research articles, a textbook, and blueprints for Hollingworth's work at Public School 500, the Speyer School. Hollingworth's use of the classroom as an "authentic" laboratory serves as a counterpoint to Terman's more controlled analytic context. In addition, Hollingworth proposes that intelligence may be responsive to environment, not purely hereditary as suggested by Terman.

1926—Hollingworth publishes *Gifted Children: Their Nature and Nurture*, considered to be the first textbook on gifted education.

1936—Hollingworth establishes Public School 500, the Speyer School, for gifted children aged between seven and nine. Upon her death in 1941, the Speyer School closes, but programs for gifted students are originated in multiple New York public schools.

1950–1971: EXCELLENCE VERSUS EQUALITY AND BROADENING CONCEPTIONS

1950—J. P. Guilford delivers a keynote address to the American Psychological Association suggesting that intelligence has multiple dimensions, including many factors which come to be thought of as "creativity." The talk represents a point of origin for creativity research.

1954—The National Association for Gifted Children (NAGC) is founded under the leadership of Ann Isaacs.

1954—*Brown v. Board of Education* ends "separate but equal education" for minorities in the United States. As the spirit of this Supreme Court decision takes root across the United States, it casts a new light on the nature of "equality" and on the idea of special classrooms for students identified as gifted.

1954—A. Harry Passow is named director of the Talented Youth Project, one of the first to study gifted children, particularly in urban schools. The article that resulted, "Are We Short-changing the Gifted?" became one of the most widely reprinted of the era.

1957—The Soviet Union launches Sputnik, calling into question the technological dominance of the United States and representing an unknown threat to national security. The country re-examines its human capital and the quality of American schooling, particularly in mathematics and science. As a result, substantial amounts of money pour into identifying the most able students for advanced mathematics, science, and technology programming.

1958—The National Defense Education Act passes in response to Sputnik. It represents the first comprehensive infusion of federal funds into education. The primary emphases at all grade levels are mathematics and science, and the legislation makes it clear that student excellence in these areas is in the national interest.

1958—The Association for the Gifted (CEC–TAG) is established as a division of the Council for Exceptional Children (CEC).

1961—President John F. Kennedy is inaugurated. He surrounds himself with advisors who represent the promise of academic excellence, and he makes a call for Americans to work hard in school in the cause of their country.

1961—Virgil Ward coins the term "differential education" which addresses the need for challenge within the curriculum for gifted students, presaging a later movement toward teaching to individual student needs.

1964—The Civil Rights Act passes. Equality of opportunity becomes a foundational principle of national legislation, and educators find themselves striving to reconcile equality of opportunity with the development of individual excellence in the classroom.

1964—The Tonkin Gulf Resolution passes, formally introducing the United States into the Vietnam War. Over the next 10 years, the academic talent once glorified by Kennedy and his advisors becomes diminished in the minds of many Americans who oppose the war. There is a widening schism between governmental action and public sentiment that can be mapped onto the debate between academic excellence and social equality.

1966—E. Paul Torrance publishes the Torrance Tests of Creative Thinking (TTCT) which become the most widely used instrument to assess creativity in schools.

1971—Raymond Cattell, a statistician and psychologist, publishes work suggesting two separate factors of intelligence: crystallized and fluid. The first represents the use of discrete elements of knowledge, while the second refers to general processes such as inductive and deductive reasoning. This dichotomy is revisited under many names by subsequent research. The distinction gives rise to a thread of research and production on "culture-neutral" assessments of intelligence and revisions in traditional intelligence tests.

1972–1983: THE MARLAND REPORT AND FEDERAL ATTENTION

1972—The Marland Report is published by Congress. The need for special services for gifted students is formalized, and the first formal definition is issued. The report encourages schools to define giftedness broadly, including academic and intellectual talent, leadership ability, visual and performing arts, creative or productive thinking, and psychomotor ability. *(Note: psychomotor ability is excluded from subsequent revisions of the federal definition.)*

1973—The National/State Leadership Training Institute on the Gifted and Talented (N/SLTI–G/T) is established with funding from the federal government to facilitate educational training programs for teachers and administrators in an effort to improve instruction and programs for gifted students.

1974—The Office of the Gifted and Talented becomes a recognized component of the U.S. Office of Education.

1975—The Education for All Handicapped Children Act is established. This federal mandate for schools to serve children with special needs does not include gifted students as part of that group.

1977—Joseph Renzulli defines the Three-Ring Conception of Giftedness, which recognizes the interplay of the components of above-average ability, creativity, and task commitment.

Late 1970s, early 1980s—Universities, including Johns Hopkins, Northwestern University, Duke, and the University of California, begin implementing national talent identification and service programs for school-age children. These programs were based on work initiated by Julian Stanley and entitled the Study of Mathematically Precocious Youth (SMPY).

1983–PRESENT: RECENT RESEARCH AND SHIFTING PARADIGMS

1983—Howard Gardner's Multiple Intelligences (MI) theory questions the idea that one measure can adequately identify a person's intelligence. His theory explores many domains of intelligence, including linguistic, logical–mathematical, musical, spatial, bodily–kinesthetic, and interpersonal. Later, naturalist intelligence is added.

1983—*A Nation at Risk* presents an unsettling report of the achievement level of U.S. secondary school students compared to international age-mates.

1985—Françoys Gagné presents the Differential Model of Giftedness and Talent (DMGT) which differentiates gifts from talents.

Mid- to late 1980s—Tracking of students into separate classes is criticized as a discriminatory practice. Due to this alteration in practice, cooperative learning strategies gain attention and mixed-ability classes become more prominent.

1988—The Jacob K. Javits Gifted and Talented Students Education Act is passed by Congress as a component of the Elementary and Secondary Education Act (ESEA). The goals of this Act were to promote research grants examining effective measures to be used in gifted education, support grants that promote gifted services for under-represented populations, and to support programs executing best practices for gifted learners. Within this Act, the federal definition is altered by removing the psychomotor component and the phrase "in order to realize their contribution to self and society." The Act includes funding for a National Research Center on the Gifted and Talented (NRC/GT) which begins as a consortium of the University of Connecticut, the University of Georgia, the University of Virginia, and Yale University. The University of Connecticut and the University of Virginia continue to carry out research under the umbrella of the NRC/GT.

1988—Sternberg's theory of successful intelligence promotes the triarchic components of analytic, synthetic, and practical giftedness.

1993—*National Excellence: A Case for Developing America's Talent*, presented by the U.S. Department of Education, reports on areas in which education of the gifted is lacking.

1994—Mary Frasier and A. Harry Passow offer a new paradigm for identifying "talent potential" in minority students and in students from impoverished environments.

1999—Carol Tomlinson's *The Differentiated Classroom* is published, offering strategies for developing curriculum and instruction to match student needs in the classroom.

2002—The U.S. Congress passes the No Child Left Behind Act (NCLB) which calls schools to focus efforts on bringing low-achieving students up to grade level. While the Jacob K. Javits Act is reauthorized as part of the legislation, the overall effect is to target resources on students achieving below desired levels.

2004—*A Nation Deceived: How Schools Hold Back America's Brightest Students* is published. This report presents the disparity between research-based practices that support the needs of gifted students and the typical educational practices in U.S. schools. A strong case is made for increased use of acceleration.

2006—The NAGC and the Council for Exceptional Children (CEC) develop research-based standards for teacher preparation programs for gifted education.

2007—The Association for the Gifted (CEC–TAG), a division of the CEC, calls attention to the need for twice exceptional learners (those identified as gifted with a specific learning disability) to have educational opportunities to meet the needs of their cognitive abilities as well as their disabilities through Response to Intervention (RtI).

BIBLIOGRAPHY

Civil Rights Act of 1964, Pub. L. No. 88–352, 78 Stat. 241 (1964).

Colangelo, N., Assouline, S., & Gross, M. U. M. (Eds.). (2004). *A nation deceived: How schools hold back America's brightest students.* Iowa City: The Connie Belin & Jacqueline N. Blank International Center for Gifted Education and Talent Development, The University of Iowa.

Council for Exceptional Children. (CEC). (2007*). Position on Response to Intervention (RTI): The unique role of special education and special educators. Retrieved January 15, 2012 from* http://www.cec.sped.org/AM/Template.cfm?Section=Home&Template=/CM/ContentDisplay.cfm&ContentID=11769

Education for All Handicapped Children Act, Pub. L. 94–142, 89 Stat. 773 (1975).

Gagné, F. (1985) Giftedness and talent: Reexamining a reexamination of the definitions. *Gifted Child Quarterly, 29,* 103–112.

Galton, F. (1869). *Hereditary genius: An inquiry into its laws and consequences.* London, UK: Macmillan & Co.

Gardner, D. P. (1983). *A nation at risk: The imperative for educational reform.* Washington, DC: U.S. Government Printing Office.

Gardner, H. (1983). *Frames of mind: The theory of multiple intelligences.* New York: Basic Books.

Hollingworth, L. S. (1927). *Gifted children: Their nature and nurture.* New York: The Macmillan Company.

Jacob K. Javits Gifted and Talented Students Education Act of 2001, Pub. L. No. 107–110, § 115, Stat. 1826 (2002). Available online at http://www.gpo.gov/fdsys/pkg/PLAW-107publ110/pdf/PLAW-107publ110.pdf

Marland, S. P., Jr. (1972). *Education of the gifted and talented: Report to the Congress of the United States by the U.S. Commissioner of Education.* (Government Documents, Y4.L 11/2: G36). Washington, DC: U.S. Government Printing Office.

National Association for Gifted Children/Council for Exceptional Children. (2006). *NAGC–CEC teacher knowledge and skill standards.* Retrieved January 15, 2012, from http://www.nagc.org/uploadedFiles/Information_and_Resources/NCATE_standards/final%20standards%20(2006).pdf

National Defense Education Act of 1958, Pub. L. No. 85–864, 72 Stat. 1580 (1958).

No Child Left Behind (NCLB) Act of 2001, Pub. L. No. 107–110, § 115,

Stat. 1425 (2002). Available online at http://www.gpo.gov/fdsys/pkg/PLAW-107publ110/pdf/PLAW-107publ110.pdf

Renzulli, J. S. (1977). *The Enrichment Triad Model: A guide for development of defensible programs for the gifted.* Mansfield Center, CT: Creative Learning Press.

Ross, P. (1993). *National excellence: A case for developing America's talent.* Washington, DC: Office of Educational Research and Improvement, U.S. Department of Education.

Sternberg, R. J. (1988). *The triarchic mind: A new theory of human intelligence.* New York: Viking-Penguin.

Terman, L. M. (Ed.). (1959). *Genetic studies of genius* (Vols. I–V). Stanford, CA: Stanford University Press.

Tomlinson, C. A. (1999). *The differentiated classroom: Responding to the needs of all learners.* Alexandria, VA: Association for Supervision and Curriculum Development.

Tonkin Gulf Resolution of 1964, Pub. L. No. 88–408, 78 Stat. 384 (1964).

4

POLICY-RELATED DEFINITIONS OF GIFTEDNESS

A Call for Change

Jane Clarenbach and Rebecca D. Eckert

Definitions of terms and concepts in any field of study provide the basis for common understanding and shared meaning while also facilitating decision making and resource allocation. They serve an important role in building credibility and consensus among theorists, researchers, practitioners, and policy makers. The field of gifted education is no exception, but as the following example demonstrates, there is still much work to be done regarding the clarity and utility of policy-related definitions of giftedness.

AN ILLUSTRATIVE CONVERSATION

Meeting on a Tuesday at the end of the school day was nobody's idea of the best way to spend a beautiful spring afternoon, but the Task Force was deeply committed to the school district's goal of getting a pilot gifted and talented program up and running by the fall. The group of two teachers, a school psychologist, and a parent had been given the task of creating a definition of giftedness for the district that could then guide the development of all other aspects of the district's program and services. Dr. Perez, the school psychologist, began the meeting by asking the Task Force members to share what they had discovered in their research.

"I think maybe we should start with me," volunteered Mr. Washington, a ninth grade teacher. "I was in charge of finding the federal definition of giftedness. I thought it would be easy, but I really had to look around for it. I made copies for everyone."

Mr. Washington then passed around papers on which the following definition was written:

GIFTED AND TALENTED—The term "gifted and talented", when used with respect to students, children, or youth, means students, children, or youth who give evidence of high achievement capability in areas such as intellectual, creative, artistic, or leadership capacity, or in specific academic fields, and who need services or activities not ordinarily provided by the school in order to fully develop those capabilities.

(No Child Left Behind Act, 2002, section 9101[22])

Ms. Swiet, a first grade teacher spoke up. "Wow! That's a lot broader than I would have expected. I bet over half of my class could be identified as gifted if we used this definition. How is this supposed to help us?"

Dr. Perez began nodding in agreement as she considered all of the testing that would result if this were the only vision of giftedness to guide educational decisions in the school district. "I agree. Although there does seem to be a threshold of need established at the end with the statement about 'services or activities not ordinarily provided by the school'."

Mrs. Miller, who had been active in her state gifted association ever since her children entered elementary school, decided to jump in. "Remember that the federal definition has to be broad enough to encompass the range of needs and beliefs in all 50 states and 14,000 school districts in this country. As I'm sure you all know, education isn't even mentioned in the Constitution—it's just one of the many governmental responsibilities delegated to the states. So, I guess what I'm saying is that I'm glad that the needs of gifted and talented students are recognized by the federal government. It's one small way to remind everyone that children are unique individuals who have the right to come to school to learn and grow."

"That's a good point," said Ms. Swiet. "The teachers and administrators in this school district do a great job of seeing students as individuals, but there are a lot of schools where students with special needs, whether it's learning disabilities or advanced math ability, wouldn't get the educational supports they need without a gentle push from some outside force, like regulations or vocal advocates. Someone could also use this definition when talking to a state legislator or a philanthropic agency about special populations of children who need funding to support their educational needs. It might help move the conversation along; however, I don't think it's going to help us identify gifted kids in my classroom."

"I found another definition from the National Association for Gifted Children," stated Dr. Perez. "The organization's definition is a little clearer, but still not really specific enough to guide all of the decisions our district has yet to make in setting up this gifted program."

> Gifted individuals are those who demonstrate outstanding levels of aptitude (defined as an exceptional ability to reason and learn) or competence (documented performance or achievement in top 10% or rarer) in one or more domains. Domains include any structured area of activity with its own symbol system (e.g., mathematics, music, language) and/or set of sensorimotor skills (e.g., painting, dance, sports).
>
> (National Association for Gifted Children [NAGC], 2010a, para. 4)

Mr. Washington spoke up. "OK. So now we're looking for outstanding, capable learners who need something more than what we already offer in the classroom. How does this align with what the state department of education says? Did anyone find another definition that would give us more direction? We've got to finish our task before the other groups can begin their work."

"I'm not sure whether this is good news or bad news, but our state definition is fairly similar to NAGC's," remarked Mrs. Miller as she passed around copies of the definition. "And I have to say, the one thing that really bothers me about this definition is that school districts in our state aren't even required by law to use it. Here, take a look."

State Definition of Giftedness[1]

"Gifted and talented" means a child identified by the planning and placement team as (1) demonstrating abilities that give evidence of very superior intellectual, creative, or specific academic capacity (in the top 10% of [the] student population), and (2) needing differentiated instruction or services beyond those being provided in the regular school program in order to realize their intellectual, creative, or specific academic potential.

"With the variety of student populations across this state, I can see why legislators might want to give school districts more freedom with this definition, but placement decisions for new students can be extremely difficult when definitions are not uniform," explained Dr. Perez. "Imagine how difficult it is to explain to a parent that his or her child may have qualified for gifted services in the neighboring school district, but doesn't qualify here because we use a different definition."

Ms. Swiet, with an eye on the clock, chimed in. "I wish that was an issue we could tackle in this Task Force, but I know that's a larger conversation with many stakeholders. I'd like to get back to the task at hand, if we could."

"You're right. We can talk with our state gifted education association to see if we can do something in the legislature to address the lack of consistency across the state, and we can certainly make sure that our final definition aligns with the one we have here. So, what aspects of the state definition match our program goals?" asked Mrs. Miller.

"I like the fact that the state definition includes a 'planning and placement' team to make these decisions," stated Mr. Washington. "It seems to me that we don't want just one person determining which students receive services and participate in programs."

Ms. Swiet nodded. "I agree, although one thing in the state definition that concerns me is the focus on demonstrated abilities. Some of my students come from homes with few resources, and a few others have limited English proficiency, so they're not demonstrating top performance *yet*. But I've talked with the kindergarten teachers and my students' families and I'm sure that with a little more support, and time, they'll be ready to soar. Is there a way to leave room for student potential in our guiding definition?"

"That's an important distinction," said Dr. Perez. "We need to be concerned about including students in the search process who may not have as many advantages at home. We could recommend adding the word 'aptitude' to the definition, which follows the NAGC and federal definitions. Then we would need to ensure that our assessments and criteria for identification are sensitive to the issues you've just described. Another strategy that we could use for identification would be to examine the local norms of our standardized tests—rather than the national or state norms—when we are looking for that top 10 percent of students. I think this is one way to give us a truer picture of who needs additional challenge right here in our own school district."

"I agree, let's try to include the word 'potential' or 'aptitude' in our final version of the definition, as I think that might be clearer for everyone," added Mrs. Miller. "And we should also make sure to explain these concerns to the steering committee when we share our final definition, so that we're sure some sort of safety valve is in place in the identification process."

Mr. Washington joined in. "Speaking of sharing our final definition, let's see what we've got so far. As I look at all of these definitions we've collected, it seems like the closer we get to working with actual students, the policy definition becomes more specific and purposeful. What I'm saying is that as great as it would be to identify in every conceivable talent area like leadership or kinesthetic learners, we don't have the resources or support to do that well. So, building from our limited state definition, we want a local policy definition of gifted that:

- recognizes advanced ability or potential;
- addresses intellectual and one or more academic areas as well as creativity;
- allows the comparison of ability or potential to others of the same age based on local norms; and
- acknowledges that gifted students often require special instruction and/or services beyond those offered in the general education curriculum."

After several more minutes of conversation and work, the Task Force adjourned with a first draft of their district definition. The members had each learned something about the complexities and importance of policy definitions in gifted education, and were confident that they had provided the guidance necessary to get the district's new pilot program started off on the right foot.

DEFINITIONS

As is evident in the Task Force discussion above, a range of definitions of giftedness exists with limited agreement about how terms and concepts related to educating high-ability students are delineated. In general, definitions of giftedness tend to be either theoretical or practical in their construction. Moon (2006) refers to the dichotomy as *conceptual* versus *operational*, and the literature on gifted education is filled with a variety of examples of both types (Sternberg, 2004). Although these conditions are not mutually exclusive, the construction of a definition is shaped by its purpose and use. These purposes can include developing a philosophical framework, defining a field of study, or guiding educational decisions. Typically, one definition does not and cannot fit all students and situations comfortably. For example, a definition describing a theory of giftedness—whether it is Sternberg's Triarchic Theory, Gagné's Differentiated Model of Giftedness and Talent (DMGT), or Renzulli's Three-Ring Conception of Giftedness—may not, without more explication, lend itself well for use as a definition that guides district and classroom practices such as identification or curriculum selection.

Policy Definitions

In the policy arena, definitions of giftedness facilitate decision making, which is inextricably tied to resource allocation (VanTassel-Baska, 2006). Ideally, policy definitions also reflect common understanding and shared meaning within a profession or community and serve as a fulcrum for research and advocacy (Gallagher, 2002). Whether it is a definition of "learning disability" under the Individuals with Disabilities Education Act (IDEA) or the definition of "safe" under the Food, Drug and Cosmetic Act, effective policy definitions must be specific enough to guide the development of processes and procedures, and yet broad enough to accommodate new understanding and withstand variations in circumstances over time.

In response to national security threats (e.g., the launch of Sputnik), federal education policy has sporadically supported advanced teaching and learning. Although there is a federal definition of giftedness, there is no corresponding federal policy for educating gifted students beyond policies that address access and equity for populations covered by civil rights laws. Even though the minimum level of federal support may benefit some gifted students, it does not provide consistent, comprehensive policy for those students described as "gifted and talented" in the federal definition. Also, unfortunately, two other areas of federal emphases have been implemented at the local level in ways that impede specialized services for this special population of children. The intensifying emphasis on both *inclusion* as a service delivery model and *proficiency* as a performance target for Pre-K–12 schools has discouraged educators and policy makers at the state and local levels from developing or expanding targeted services and programs for advanced students. Instead, most gifted students are placed in heterogeneously grouped general education classrooms (NAGC & CSDPG, 2011) where the majority of teachers are not trained to meet their needs, and where repetition and test preparation are the norm (Duffett, Farkas, & Loveless, 2008). With no mandate to provide services to gifted students or guidance from the federal government, it is up to state and local leaders to develop definitions and corresponding policies that guide decision making and allow for identification of gifted students and equitable delivery of services within the constraints of limited resources.

DEFINITIONS IN GIFTED AND TALENTED EDUCATION

Definitions of giftedness can be extremely powerful—determining not only who will qualify to receive gifted education services, but also which services are offered, when they are offered, and even why the services are offered. High stakes indeed, and from this perspective, the need for clarity cannot be overstated.

The federal definition of gifted and talented (provided above), which was first adopted in 1972 and has been revised over time, most recently in 2002, acknowledges a wide range of giftedness including intellectual giftedness; giftedness in specific academic fields; or in creative, artistic, or leadership areas; and includes a focus on capacity, or potential, for giftedness. The federal definition is silent regarding measuring giftedness based on age, but instead focuses on the regular school curriculum as a point of comparison for determining which students require specialized gifted education services. Inherent in this broad, inclusive approach to defining giftedness is the assumption that the more rigorous the regular education curriculum, the larger the number of students who will benefit in that setting. However, the question remains whether the ceiling in the classroom is high enough for the most advanced students.

Although the majority of states have modeled their definitions after the federal definition (NAGC, 2010b), there is variability among the states in the areas of giftedness recognized, whether potential for giftedness is included in the definition, and the point of comparison for determining the need for services (NAGC & CSDPG, 2011). This variability leads to large discrepancies between states regarding students identified as needing gifted education services as well as diversity in the content of the programming offered (NAGC & CSDPG, 2011). Responses to a recent survey of state departments of education indicate that "intellectually gifted" as a category of giftedness is the most common area of giftedness recognized across the United States (cited in 36 of 40 state definitions). "Academically gifted" was included in 25 state definitions and "leadership" in 18 state definitions. Four states included "highly gifted" as a category of giftedness. How states handle capacity or aptitude, as well as the factor(s) they use for determining giftedness adds ambiguity to the national picture. While 28 states use the federal reference point for giftedness—that the student requires services not ordinarily provided by the school—a full 32 states include "potential for giftedness" in their definitions. Ten states use "age, experience, or environment" as the comparison point and seven states have no point of comparison, leaving districts in those states to develop their own (NAGC, 2010b). Similarly, school districts in 16 states with definitions are left to make their own choices about the criteria and processes used to identify students as gifted (NAGC & CSDPG, 2011). Further diluting the common understanding of giftedness, four states have no state definition and an additional eight states do not require districts to follow the state definition in crafting local definitions, policies, and procedures related to this special population of students (NAGC & CSDPG, 2011).

Not coincidentally, federal and state research and data collection efforts are hobbled by a lack of consistent understanding and application of key terms such as "gifted," "talented," and "giftedness." For example, without a commonly understood definition of who the "gifted" students are, how reliable are federal surveys seeking simply the numbers of students across the United States receiving gifted and talented services? How can state legislatures accurately determine the funding needed to serve gifted students when districts define giftedness differently? How can we ensure that all students who would benefit from district gifted education services and programs are identified and served in cases where the local definition limits giftedness to demonstrated ability in mathematics? And, with all these variations in data sets, how are researchers able to make any meaningful evaluations of the effectiveness of "gifted" education programming?

DEVELOPING A LOCAL POLICY DEFINITION OF GIFTEDNESS

In the opening vignette, the Task Force members worked to create a high-quality policy definition of giftedness that could guide the development of their gifted education programming district-wide. Their discussion reflects the premise that a high-quality policy definition for the education of gifted and talented children should be sufficiently clear to avoid reliance on outside sources for guidance on the meaning of the terms used, and should include the critical components that together create a framework to guide administrators, educators, and advocates within a school district, removing the guesswork that plagues some districts and frustrates families.

- A policy definition should include the program goals as well as measurable dimensions that can be used to determine whether the goals have been met and to track how resources are allocated. For example, the definition could specify that gifted and talented students are those who perform in the top 10 percent on a combination of assessments compared to same-age peers, and that there will be services in grades P–12 through enrichment and acceleration in each academic area.

- A policy definition should reflect shared values about the types of giftedness to be developed and supported in schools and the community. For example, the definition could include reference to supporting demonstrated ability and developing latent talent, specifically stating as a goal that the resulting talent pool should reflect the entire student population and welcome students from diverse backgrounds and experiences. Decision makers need to be aware that including areas other than academics in the definition, such as fine and performing arts and leadership, serves additional students, but also requires further resources and commitment from the school and community to support them fully.

- A policy definition should provide an anchor for decision making. Specific terms affect the development of identification procedures, program offerings, teacher training requirements, and related policies and procedures that support this special population of learners. For example, the use of "shall" rather than "may" converts activities or services from optional to mandatory or required. Some definitions also reference specific service options, such as whether the students will be served in the regular classroom, in pull-out programs, magnet schools, or other specialized settings. Definitions may also reference other policy documents that detail, for example, approved assessment instruments or procedures to be used in identifying students for services.

WHAT DOES THIS MEAN FOR PRACTITIONERS AND ADVOCATES?

Although policy definitions are typically written as stand-alone statements, they are not self-executing. That is, they should be shaped by current theory and research, as well as by national standards; and should be linked to regulations, procedures, and other policy documents that specify action (e.g., guidance documents from the state education agency augmenting state laws and regulations). Essentially, it is in the implementation that definitions come to life and have an impact. The language used to craft policy definitions reflects *choices* and privileged points of view (Schiappa, 2003) and "can have serious implications for public policy and individual lives" (Skillin, 2009, p. 79). In many cases, the full implementation of a policy definition shapes which students are selected for which programs and services, as well as how critical resources are allocated.

Therefore, advocates and practitioners must be aware of the central role of a policy definition among the interdependent components of effective gifted education programming. Bear in mind that the finished policy definition should inspire and guide the creation of a cohesive set of practices, tools, and procedures that characterize an *internally consistent* program for gifted education, sensitive to the needs of the community as well as the diverse needs of individual students. In this instance, internal consistency is characterized by agreement and alignment among the stated definition and program goals, program components and procedures (including identification and instruction), and the students who are participating in the program as well as the activities that they pursue.

Imagine the confusion that would result in a school community if the policy definition, program goals, and identification procedures focused on supporting the needs of high-potential and high-ability students in mathematics and science, yet the curricular opportunities and other support services offered enrichment only to those students who were demonstrating a high degree of mastery in existing science classrooms. Despite the stated goal of seeking students with high potential (as well as ability), numerous great contributors to the field of mathematics and science would be overlooked by this program serving only straight-A students. This lack of internal consistency in the programming would not only undermine the learning and growth of the school's gifted students; it would also likely jeopardize support for, and therefore the continuation of, the gifted program. If, however, the group that was creating (or redesigning) the mathematics–science gifted program had followed the policy definition closely and been required to demonstrate how each component of the program tied back to the policy definition and program goals, it is likely that this lack of consistency could have been avoided.

As discussed in the Task Force conversation at the beginning of this chapter, the crafting of effective policy definitions is an essential precursor to program development and evaluation, and shapes subsequent decisions. Once program goals and student needs have been determined and a definition—guided by state law, best practices, and community values—is in hand, school leaders can then develop and implement gifted education programming based on the following national program standards (NAGC, 2010c) in several key areas for maximum effectiveness.

- Procedures, such as referral for identification and communication with families about the program are free from bias and should ensure that students intended to be served are not overlooked (i.e., the demographics of a gifted program should reflect the larger student population).
- Ongoing teacher training is essential, not only on the gifted education opportunities available in the district and the referral process, but also on how to effectively engage and challenge all students within a mixed-ability classroom, as this is where the majority of gifted students spend most of their time in school.
- Curriculum offerings and service options are guided by program goals and policies that are tied to the definition of giftedness, but also contain enough flexibility to meet the changing needs of students and the school community over time.
- Resource allocations and budgets should be guided by the existing policies and program goals to ensure that each component receives enough support to sustain effective programs and services.
- Related district policies should be developed and implemented that support advanced students and promote best practices as demonstrated by research and other data (e.g., early entrance to kindergarten, acceleration, dual enrollment, credit by examination), to ensure a student's smooth transition between grades.
- Evaluation plans provide school districts with opportunities to purposefully collect and examine data and to assess the effectiveness of the policy implementation. Bear in mind that the ultimate goal of the evaluation process is not punitive; it is the continued improvement of service delivery and program offerings for students.

Finally, to ensure implementation reflecting the intent of the adopted definition and to strengthen policy implementation and internal consistency over time, districts must offer regular opportunities for education and continued professional development and training of all school personnel, policy makers, students, the families of those who may be served in gifted education programs, and other interested members of the community. It is vital that all of these individuals develop a working knowledge of the needs of, and expectations for, gifted students, as well as the relevant policies and definitions. Maintaining a healthy gifted program requires thoughtful leadership, teacher preparation, and advocacy to sustain the definition's intent. No matter how well-crafted and informed, a policy definition that does nothing more than collect dust on a shelf cannot be effective.

USING POLICY DEFINITIONS TO IMPROVE GIFTED EDUCATION

Numerous theorists and philosophers have published clear, thoughtful definitions of giftedness, and yet debate about who gifted students are and how best to identify them continues to rage among scholars in the field of gifted education. This same lack of agreement among Pre-K–12 educators results in the uneven and inequitable availability of services to high-ability students across the United States. Although debate is healthy, confusion is not. The development and widespread acceptance of a common, clear, and purposeful policy-related definition of giftedness at the national and state level can significantly bolster gifted education by:

- providing a basis on which to define the type of data to be collected to track the educational progress of gifted students and allow for equitable state-by-state comparisons, rather than the current patchwork system of uncoordinated information gathering;
- supporting a research agenda for the field that encourages uniformity of terms and definitions, which would provide consistency and clarity for those translating research into recommended practices in teaching, counseling, and parenting;
- freeing the gifted education system from bias and charges of "elitism" and building recognition that students with the potential to develop as high achievers are found in all environments, social strata, and cultural groups; and
- creating obligations on the part of schools and school personnel—a published policy definition provides expectations within the community for how *all* students will be treated within a system, rather than allocating limited educational resources on an ad hoc, case-by-case basis.

CONCLUSION

For advocates and practitioners, a command of knowledge and expertise in gifted education is not enough to ensure program success or continuation. Rather, establishing a common policy definition of giftedness provides the direction needed to prod institutions and communities to develop a lasting support system that recognizes all gifted students and sustains their growth and continued educational advancement in every area of human endeavor.

NOTE

1. This "state definition of giftedness" was made up by the authors for illustrative purposes.

REFERENCES

Duffett, A., Farkas, S., & Loveless, T. (2008). *High-achieving students in the era of No Child Left Behind.* Washington, DC: Thomas B. Fordham Institute.

Gallagher, J. J. (2002). *Society's role in educating gifted students: The role of public policy.* (Research Monograph 02162). Storrs: The National Research Center on the Gifted and Talented, University of Connecticut.

Moon, S. M. (2006). Developing a definition of giftedness. In J. H. Purcell & R. D. Eckert (Eds.), *Designing services and programs for high-ability learners: A guidebook for gifted education* (pp. 23–31). Thousand Oaks, CA: Corwin Press.

National Association for Gifted Children. (2010a, March). *Redefining giftedness for a new century: Shifting the paradigm.* (Position Paper). Washington, DC: Author. Retrieved from http://www.nagc.org/index2.aspx?id=6404

National Association for Gifted Children. (2010b). *State definitions of giftedness.* Retrieved January 21, 2011, from http://www.nagc.org/uploadedFiles/Advocacy/State%20definitions%20%288-24-10%29.pdf

National Association for Gifted Children. (2010c). *Pre-K–Grade 12 gifted programming standards: A blueprint for quality gifted education programs.* Washington, DC: Author.

National Association for Gifted Children, & Council of State Directors of Programs for the Gifted. (2011). *State of the states in gifted education 2010–2011: National policy and practice data.* Washington, DC: Authors.

No Child Left Behind Act (2002). Pub. L. No. 107–110, § 115, Stat. 1425 (2002). Title IX, Part A, Section 9101(22).

Schiappa, E. (2003). *Defining reality: Definitions and the politics of meaning.* Carbondale: Southern Illinois University Press.

Skillin, K. M. (2009, July). *Beyond the classroom: Rhetorical constructions of "service learning."* (Doctoral dissertation). University of Minnesota, Bloomington.

Sternberg, R. J. (2004). Definitions and conceptions of giftedness. In S. M. Reis (Ed.), *Essential readings in gifted education Series* (Vol. 1). Thousand Oaks, CA: Corwin Press.

VanTassel-Baska, J. (2006). State policies in gifted education. In J. H. Purcell & R. D. Eckert (Eds.), *Designing services and programs for high-ability learners: A guidebook for gifted education* (pp. 249–261). Thousand Oaks, CA: Corwin Press.

5

GIFTED BEHAVIORS VERSUS GIFTED INDIVIDUALS
Joseph S. Renzulli and Marcia A. B. Delcourt

The question "What makes giftedness?" has been debated for decades, with renewed interest over the past 20 years as new theories of intelligence emerged, questions of equity were raised, and resources in schools declined. To shed light on this complex and controversial question, we will draw heavily on the theoretical and research literature associated with the study of gifted and talented persons, but our approach also reflects the point of view of educational practitioners who have devoted significant time and effort to translating research and theory into defensible identification and programming practices. In this chapter, an explanation of key features to be included in a definition of giftedness is followed by a review of the types of giftedness typically identified by school personnel and a summary of purposes for educating gifted students. Subsequent discussion of the developmental nature of giftedness and a rationale for viewing giftedness as a displayed behavior rather than a possessed trait lead to an explicit definition—the Three-Ring Conception of Giftedness (Renzulli, 1978).

CONCEPTIONS OF GIFTEDNESS

Purposes and Criteria for a Definition of Giftedness
A primary purpose of theory construction in education or psychology, which includes defining important concepts, is to add to our understanding about human condition. But in applied fields of knowledge there is also a practical purpose for defining concepts. Hence, defining giftedness effectively relies on combining theoretical and practical perspectives. Further, a definition of giftedness is a formal and explicit statement that might eventually become part of official policies or guidelines and should be used to direct identification and programming practices. Therefore, creators of definitions need to recognize the consequential nature and pivotal role that definitions play in structuring the entire field, consider ramifications of their definitions, and recognize the practical and political uses to which their work might be applied.

As long as there are differences of opinion among reasonable scholars there will never be a single definition of giftedness, and this is probably the way that it should be. However, definitions are open to both scholarly and practical scrutiny, and for these reasons it is important that a definition meet the following criteria. The definition must:

1. be based on the best available research about the characteristics of gifted individuals rather than romanticized notions or unsupported opinions;
2. provide guidance in the selection and/or development of instruments and procedures that can be used to design defensible identification systems;
3. give direction to and be logically related to programming practices such as the selection of materials and instructional methods, the selection and training of teachers, and the determination of procedures whereby programs can be evaluated;
4. be capable of generating research studies that will verify or fail to verify the validity of the definition.

Two Kinds of Giftedness

Most efforts to define giftedness stem from studies focused mainly on the concept of intelligence. Although a detailed review of these studies is beyond the scope of this chapter, a few general conclusions from earlier research are necessary to set the stage for an analysis of the concept of giftedness. First, there are many kinds of intelligence and therefore single definitions cannot be used to explain this complex construct. Criticisms of unitary theories of intelligence led Sternberg (1984), Gardner (1983) and others to develop new models for describing and explaining human capabilities. For instance, Sternberg's "triarchic" theory of human intelligence consists of three sub-theories, but having studied the three aspects of intelligence for some years, Sternberg (1996, 2001) concluded that the answer to the question of intelligence is even more than just *the amount* of a person's analytical, creative, and practical abilities.[1] A person may be gifted with respect to any one of these abilities or with respect to the way she or he *balances the abilities* to succeed (Sternberg & Grigorenko, 2002). Further, intelligence, according to Sternberg and his colleagues, is not a fixed entity, but a flexible and dynamic one (i.e., it is a form of developing expertise) (Sternberg & Grigorenko, 2002; Sternberg & Lubart, 1995; Sternberg & O'Hara, 1999). Sternberg concluded, "The notion of someone's being 'gifted' or not is a relic of an antiquated, test-based way of thinking" (1996, p. 197). Gardner (1983) posed what has come to be called "multiple intelligences," initially reflecting seven domain-specific intelligences to which an eighth one (naturalistic intelligence) was later added (Gardner, 1999).[2]

In view of this recent work and numerous earlier cautions about the dangers of describing intelligence with a single score, we conclude that this practice has been and always will be questionable. At the very least, attributes of intelligent behavior must be considered within the context of cultural and situational factors. Multiple forms of intelligence as described by Sternberg and Gardner, theories of developmental progression, and biological approaches have much to contribute to a better understanding of intelligence. "Wc should be open to the possibility that our understanding of intelligence in the future will be rather different from what it is today." (Neisser et al., 1996, p. 80).

Second, there is no ideal way to measure intelligence and therefore we must avoid the typical practice of believing that if we know a person's IQ score, we also know his or her intelligence. Even Terman warned against total reliance on tests: "We must guard against defining intelligence solely in terms of ability to pass the tests of a given intelligence scale." (1921, p. 131). Thorndike echoed Terman's concern by stating "[T]o assume that we have measured some general power which resides in [the person being tested] and determines his ability in every variety of intellectual task in its entirety is to fly directly in the face of all that is known about the organization of intellect." (Thorndike, 1921, p. 126).

Further, we should not conclude that test scores are the only factors that contribute to success in school. While IQ scores correlate moderately with school grades, they account for only 16–36 percent of the variance in later performance. Indeed, according to Jones (1982), a majority of college graduates in every scientific field of study had IQs between 110 and 120. Using a strict cut-off score on intelligence tests to exclude students from special services would be analogous to *forbidding* a youngster from trying out for a basketball team because he or she missed the "cut-off height" by a few inches! Basketball coaches know that such an arbitrary practice would result in missing the talents of youngsters who may overcome slight limitations in inches with other abilities such as drive, speed, teamwork, ball-handling skills, and perhaps even the ability and motivation to out-jump taller persons trying out for the team.

Concerns about the difficulty of defining and measuring intelligence are cited to highlight the larger problem of isolating a unitary definition of giftedness. At the very least, we will always have several conceptions (and therefore definitions) of giftedness which can first be examined by distinguishing between two broad categories found in the research literature. The first category is referred to as "high-achieving giftedness" and the second as "creative–productive giftedness." Note that:

1. both types of giftedness are important;
2. there is usually an interaction between the two types of giftedness;
3. special programs should make appropriate provisions for nurturing both types of giftedness as well as offering numerous occasions when the two types interact with each other.

High-Achieving Giftedness

High-achieving giftedness might also be called test-taking or lesson-learning giftedness. Most easily measured by IQ or other cognitive ability tests and/or achievement measures, high-achieving giftedness conceptions most often form the basis for selecting students for special programs. Students who score high on IQ tests are also likely to get high grades in school; however, the predictive nature of these scores is unclear. Dai (2010) cautions that a positive correlation between IQ and achievement "[C]an be seen as indicative of redundancy or overlap of the two types of tests rather than a causal relationship" (p. 26). Test-taking and lesson-learning abilities generally remain stable over time, leading to several conclusions about high-achieving giftedness:

a. it exists in varying degrees;
b. it can be identified through standardized assessment techniques; and
c. we should make appropriate modifications for students who have the ability to learn regular curricular content at advanced rates and levels of understanding.

Curriculum compacting (Renzulli, Smith, & Reis, 1982), a procedure used for modifying curricular content to accommodate advanced learners, and other acceleration techniques should be an essential part of school programs that strive to respect individual differences that are clearly evident from scores on cognitive ability and achievement tests.

Creative–Productive Giftedness

Creative–productive giftedness describes human activity and involvement where a premium is placed on the development of original ideas and products purposefully designed to have an impact on one or more target audiences. Learning situations designed to promote creative–productive giftedness emphasize the use and application of information (content) and thinking processes in an integrated, inductive, and real-problem-oriented manner. The role of the student is transformed from that of a learner of prescribed lessons to one in which the learner uses the modus operandi of a first-hand inquirer. In other words, creative–productive giftedness is putting one's abilities to work on problems and areas of study that have personal relevance, and which can be escalated to appropriately challenging levels of investigative activity. The roles of students and teachers in the pursuit of these problems have been described elsewhere (Renzulli, 1982, 1983).

Why is creative–productive giftedness important enough to raise questions about the "tidy," and relatively easy, test-score approach traditionally used to select students? The answer to this question is simple and yet very compelling. Research tells us that there is much more to the making of a gifted person than the abilities revealed on traditional tests of intelligence, aptitude, and achievement. Many who are moderately below the traditional 3–5 percent test-score cut-off levels for inclusion in gifted programs have shown that they can do advanced-level work (Reis & Renzulli, 1982). Furthermore, history tells us that it has been the creative and productive people of the world, the producers rather than consumers of knowledge, the reconstructionists of thought in all areas of human endeavor, who have become recognized as "truly gifted" individuals. History does not remember persons who merely scored well on IQ tests or those who learned their lessons well.

PURPOSES OF EDUCATION FOR THE GIFTED

Implicit in any effort to define and identify gifted youth is the assumption that schools will provide various types of specialized learning experiences that are responsive to and show promise of developing the characteristics implicit in the definition. In other words, the *why* question supersedes the *who* and *how* questions. There are two generally accepted purposes for providing special education for the gifted. These services:

1. provide young people with maximum opportunities for self-fulfillment through the development and expression of one or a combination of performance area(s) where superior potential may be present;
2. increase society's supply of persons who will help to solve the problems of contemporary civilization by becoming producers of knowledge and art rather than mere consumers of existing information.

Arguments are offered for and against both of these purposes, but most people agree that goals related to self-fulfillment and/or societal contributions are generally consistent with democratic philosophies of education. These two goals are highly interactive and mutually supportive of each other. In other words, the self-satisfying work of scientists, artists, and leaders in all walks of life usually produces potentially valuable contributions to society. Keeping in mind the interaction of these two goals, and the priority status of the self-fulfillment goal, it is safe to conclude that supplementary investments of public funds and systematic effort for highly able youth would produce at least some results geared toward the public good. If, as Gowan (1978) has pointed out, the purpose of gifted programs is to increase the size of society's reservoir of potentially creative and productive adults, then the argument for gifted education programs that focus on creative productivity is compelling.

THE GIFTED AND THE POTENTIALLY GIFTED

A subtle, but very important, distinction exists between the "gifted" and the "potentially gifted." Most of the research about conceptions of giftedness is based on students and adults who have been judged (by one or more criteria) to be gifted. The general approach to the study of gifted persons could easily lead the casual reader to believe that giftedness is magically bestowed on a person in much the same way as nature endows us with blue eyes, red hair, or a dark complexion. As a matter of fact, there is considerable debate regarding the origins of giftedness. While there are proponents of the notion of giftedness as fundamentally endowed by nature, others contend that giftedness is developed and enhanced by specific support in the environment. Another perspective posits that nature and nurture interact to form a person's profile. Recently, Dweck's work (1999, 2006) suggests that a construct such as giftedness *can be developed* in some people if an appropriate interaction takes place between a person, his or her environment, and a particular area of human endeavor. According to Good and Dweck (2005), individuals who view their ability as "fixed" (p. 40) are defensive about admitting to or exposing their deficiencies. Those who see their ability as "malleable" (p. 40) or changeable are better prepared to address new challenges. A growth mindset allows people to extend their levels of achievement (Dweck, 2006).

When other traits are described as components of giftedness (for example, creativity), there is no assumption that one is "born with" these traits, even if one happens to possess a high IQ. Almost all human abilities can be developed; hence, attention to the potentially gifted (those who could "make it" under the right conditions) as well as to those who have been studied because they gained some type of recognition is equally important. Implicit in this concept of the potentially gifted, then, is the idea that giftedness emerges or "appears" at different times and under different circumstances. Without such an approach, there would be no hope whatsoever of identifying bright underachievers, students from disadvantaged backgrounds, or any special population not easily identified through traditional testing procedures.

ARE PEOPLE "GIFTED" OR DO THEY DISPLAY GIFTED BEHAVIORS?

Except for certain functional purposes related mainly to professional focal points (i.e., research, training, legislation) and to ease of expression, terms such as *"the gifted"* are counterproductive to educational efforts to identify and provide services for certain students in the general school population. Rather, we propose a shift in emphasis from the concept of "being gifted" (or not being gifted) to a concern about developing *gifted behaviors* in students who have the highest potential for benefiting from special education services. This slight shift in terminology might appear to be an exercise in heuristic hair-splitting, but it has significant implications for the concept of giftedness and the ways in which the field engages in research endeavors and effective educational programming.

The implications of this shift can be placed in perspective by raising a series of questions.

1. Is giftedness an absolute or a relative concept? That is, is a person either gifted or not gifted (the absolute view); or can varying kinds and degrees of gifted behaviors be displayed in certain people, at certain times, and under certain circumstances (the relative view)? Is gifted a static concept (i.e., you have it or you do not have it) or is it a dynamic concept (i.e., it varies both within persons and within learning–performance situations)?

2. Are giftedness and high IQ one and the same? And if so, how high does a person's IQ need to be before he or she can be considered gifted? If giftedness and high IQ are not the same, what other characteristics contribute to the expression of giftedness? Is there any justification for providing selective services for certain students who may fall below a predetermined IQ cut-off score?

3. What causes only a minuscule number of Thomas Edisons or Langston Hugheses or Isadora Duncans to emerge, while millions of others with equal "equipment" and educational advantages (or disadvantages) never rise above mediocrity? Why do some people who have not enjoyed the advantages of special educational opportunities achieve high levels of accomplishment, whereas others who have experienced the best of educational programming opportunities fade into obscurity?

Research provides the most powerful argument in response to these questions for policy makers who must render important decisions about the regulations and guidelines dictating identification practices in their states or local school districts. An examination of research suggests that gifted behaviors can be developed in those who are not necessarily the ones who earn the highest scores on standardized tests. Implications of this research for identification practices are clear.

The first research-based implication will undoubtedly be a major controversy in the field for many years, but needs to be dealt with to defuse criticism directed at the gifted field. Simply stated, policy makers must re-examine identification procedures that result in a final and limited pre-selection of certain students and the concomitant implication that these young people are, and always will be, the only "gifted." This absolute approach, coupled with the almost total reliance on test scores, is not only inconsistent with the research, but almost arrogant in the assumption that assessment during a single one-hour segment of a young person's life should determine if he or she is "gifted."

The alternative to an absolutist view is to forgo the "tidy" and comfortable tradition of "knowing" on the first day of school who is gifted and who is not gifted. Rather, effort must be redirected toward developing "gifted behaviors" in certain students (not all students), at certain times (not all the time), and under certain circumstances. The trade-off for tidiness and administrative expediency is a much more flexible approach to both identification and programming, and a system that not only shows a greater respect for the research on gifted and talented people, but one that is fairer and more acceptable to educators and the general public.

Second, an effective identification system must take into consideration factors in addition to test scores. According to recent research, strict cut-off scores on IQ or achievement tests are still the primary, if not the only, criterion given *serious* consideration in final selection in spite of the multiple data points gathered in many screening procedures (Borland, 2004). When screening information reveals outstanding potential for gifted behaviors, it is almost always "thrown away" if predetermined cut-off scores are not met. Respect for other data means they must be given equal weight. That is, evaluators must come to believe in and rely on non-test criteria and shed the belief that test scores are inherently more valid and objective than other procedures. As Sternberg (1982) pointed out, *quantitative* does not necessarily mean *valid*. When it comes to identification, it is far better to have imprecise answers to the right questions than precise answers to the wrong questions. The broadened and malleable notions presented thus far led to the Three-Ring Conception of Giftedness (Renzulli, 1977) and the Revolving Door concept of gifted identification (Renzulli, Reis, & Smith, 1981).

THE THREE-RING CONCEPTION OF GIFTEDNESS

The Three-Ring Conception of Giftedness is a theory that attempts to portray the main dimensions of human potential for creative productivity. Research on creative–productive people has consistently shown that although no single criterion can be used to determine giftedness, persons who have achieved recognition because of their unique accomplishments and creative contributions possess a relatively well-defined set of three interlocking clusters of traits. These clusters consist of above-average, though not necessarily superior, ability, task commitment, and creativity (see Figure 5.1). It is important to point out that no single cluster "makes giftedness." Rather, it is the interaction

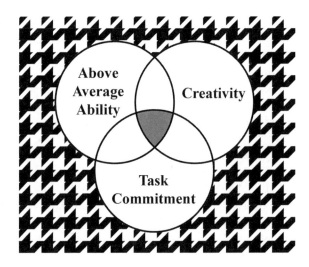

Fig. 5.1 The Three-Ring Conception of Giftedness. The houndstooth background represents personality and environment, factors that give rise to the three clusters of traits.

among the three clusters that research has shown to be the necessary ingredient for crea-tive–productive accomplishment (Renzulli, 1978). This interaction is represented by the shaded portion of Figure 5.1.

Discussion of the Three Rings

Are There Additional Clusters of Abilities That Should Be Added to the Three-Ring Conception of Giftedness?

One of the most frequent reactions to this work has been the suggestion that the three clusters of traits portrayed in the model do not adequately account for the develop-ment of gifted behaviors. Extensive examination of the research on human abilities has resulted in a modification of the original model represented figurally by the houndstooth background in which the three rings are now imbedded (see Figure 5.1).

The interaction among the original three rings is still the most important feature lead-ing to the display of gifted behaviors. There are, however, a host of other factors that must be taken into account to explain why some persons display gifted behaviors at certain times and under certain circumstances. These factors are grouped into the two traditional dimensions underlying studies about human beings commonly referred to as personality and environment. As indicated by research on the manifestation of gifted behaviors, each of the factors listed in Table 5.1 plays a role, albeit to varying degrees. What is even more important is the interaction between the two categories and among the numerous factors listed in each column. (In fact, a houndstooth pattern was selected over an earlier checkerboard design in an effort to convey this interaction.) Considering the almost limitless number of combinations between and among the factors listed in Table 5.1, it is easy to realize why so much confusion has existed about the definition of giftedness.

Each of the factors is obviously a complex entity which could be subdivided into numerous component parts. The factor of socio-economic status, for example, accounts for such things as prenatal care and nutrition, and educational opportunities. On the personality side of the ledger, MacKinnon (1965) found that the most highly effective individuals had life histories marked by severe frustrations, deprivations, and traumatic

Table 5.1 Personality and environmental factors influencing giftedness

Personality factors	Environmental factors
Perception of self	Socio-economic status
Courage	Parental personalities
Character	Education of parents
Intuition	Stimulation of childhood interests
Charm or charisma	Family position
Need for achievement	Formal education
Ego strength	Role-model availability
Energy	Physical illness and/or well-being
Sense of destiny	Chance factors (financial inheritance, death)
Personal attractiveness[a]	Zeitgeist (living near an art museum, divorce, etc.)

a Although personal attractiveness is undoubtedly a physical characteristic, the ways in which others react to one's physi-cal being are quite obviously important determinants in the development of personality.

experiences. Findings such as these highlight the complexity of the problem. The advantages of high socio-economic status, a favorable educational background, and early life experiences that do not include hardship, frustration, or disappointment may lead to a productive career for some individuals; but for others, it may eliminate the kinds of frustration that might be the "trigger" to a more positive application of one's abilities. Each of the factors above shares one or a combination of two characteristics. First, most of the personality factors are long-term developmental traits or traits that in some cases are genetically determined. Although schools may play an important role in developing traits such as courage and the need for achievement, it is highly unrealistic to believe that schools shoulder the major responsibility for overall personality formation. Second, many factors such as socio-economic status, parental personalities, and family position are chance factors in children's lives, which educators must take as givens. We cannot tell a child to be the firstborn or to have parents who stress achievement! For these reasons, the model for identification of and programming for gifted students which has evolved from the Three-Ring Conception of Giftedness is concentrated on the three sets of clusters set forth in the original model. Of course, certain aspects of the original three clusters are also chance factors, but research suggests that creativity and task commitment are modifiable and can be influenced positively by purposeful kinds of educational experiences (Reis & Renzulli, 1982). And although the jury is still out on the issue of how much of one's ability is influenced by heredity and how much by environment, psychologists and educators generally conclude that abilities (both general and specific) can be influenced to varying degrees by the quality of learning experiences.

Are the Three Rings Constant?

Most educators and psychologists agree that the above-average-ability ring represents a generally stable or constant set of characteristics. In other words, if an individual shows high ability in an area such as mathematics, it is almost undeniable that mathematical ability was present in the months and years preceding a "judgment day" (i.e., a day when identification procedures took place), and that mathematical ability will tend to remain high. In view of the types of assessment procedures most readily available and economically administered, it is easy to see why conceptions of giftedness based on ability assessments dominate decision making about placement in special programs. Educators feel more comfortable and confident with reliably and objectively measured traits, but the "comfort" engendered by the use of such tests often causes them to ignore or only give minimal attention to the other two clusters of traits.

In the Revolving Door Identification Model based on the Three-Ring Conception of Giftedness (Renzulli et al., 1981), above-average ability is the major criterion for identifying a group of students referred to as the Talent Pool, which generally consists of the top 15–20 percent of the general school population. Test scores, teacher ratings, and other forms of "status information" (i.e., information that can be gathered and analyzed at a fixed point in time) are of practical value in making certain kinds of first-level decisions about accessibility to some of the general services that should be provided by a special program. This procedure guarantees that students who earn the highest scores on cognitive ability tests have access to services that appropriately modify curriculum in areas where advanced levels of ability can be clearly documented. Indeed, advanced coverage of traditional material and accelerated courses should be the "regular curriculum" for high-ability students in areas of advanced ability.

However, task commitment and creativity are different! While "status information" regarding these constructs can be garnered from tools such as rating scales, divergent thinking tests, and personality inventories, these traits are not present or absent in the same stable fashion as mathematics ability in the example above, nor as other aptitudes might be. Equally important is recognition that they are not adequately assessed by the highly objective and quantifiable means characterizing test-score assessment of traditional cognitive abilities. A score on a test of creativity provides limited information about levels of creative capacity because the assessments examine predefined constructs such as figural divergent thinking, creative attitudes, or verbal insights, but do not indicate how an individual will use or expand upon that potential at certain times and under certain circumstances. Likewise, a measured level of achievement motivation cannot be used to predict students' indefatigable persistence in topics they have personally selected to pursue. In other words, we cannot put a percentile on the value of a creative idea, nor can we assign a standard score to the amount of effort and energy a student might be willing to devote to a highly demanding task. Creativity and task commitment "come and go" as a function of the types of situations in which certain individuals become involved; therefore, "action information" is an equally valuable, if not more relevant, assessment of an individual's readiness to pursue or engage in creative–productive activity.

Three principles guide understanding of the creativity and task commitment clusters. First, the clusters are variable rather than permanent. Although there may be a tendency for some individuals to "hatch" more creative ideas than others and to have greater reservoirs of energy that promote more frequent and intensive involvement in situations, a person is not either creative or not creative. Almost all studies of highly accomplished individuals indicate that their work is characterized by peaks and valleys of both creativity and task commitment. One simply cannot (and probably should not) operate at maximum levels of output in these two areas on a constant basis. Most productive persons have consistently reported "fallow" periods and even experiences of "burnout" following long and sustained encounters with the manifestation of their talents. Even Thomas Edison, acknowledged to be the world's record holder of original patents, did not have a creative idea for a new invention every waking moment of his life. Second, task commitment and creativity can be developed through appropriate stimulation and training. Because of variations in interest and receptivity, some people are more influenced by certain situations than others. While we cannot predetermine which individuals will respond most favorably to a particular type of experience, through general interest assessment techniques and stimulus variation, we can raise the probability of generating a greater number of creative ideas and increased manifestations of task commitment in Talent Pool students. When the Three-Ring Conception of Giftedness is applied as an identification model, the ways in which students *react* to planned and unplanned stimulation experiences has been termed "action information." Action information is used to make decisions about which students might benefit from individualized and advanced kinds of learning activities. The important distinction between status information and action information is that action information cannot be gathered before students have been selected for special programming. Giftedness, or at least the beginnings of situations in which gifted behaviors might be displayed and developed, is in the *responses* of individuals rather than in the stimulus events. This second-level identification procedure is, therefore, a critical component of the general enrichment experiences provided for Talent Pool students and is based on the concept of *situational testing* that has been described in the theoretical literature on test and measurements (Freeman, 1962).

Finally, creativity and task commitment almost always stimulate each other. A person gets a creative idea; the idea is encouraged and reinforced by self and/or others. The person decides to "do something" with the idea, and thus, commitment to the task begins to emerge. Similarly, a strong commitment to solving a particular problem will frequently trigger the process of creative problem solving. In this case, the situation undoubtedly gives rise to the adage "necessity is the mother of invention." This final point is especially important for effective programming. Students participating in a gifted program should be aware of opportunities to act on creative ideas and commitments in areas of particular interest. Similarly, persons responsible for special programming should be knowledgeable about strategies for reinforcing, nurturing, and providing appropriate resources to students at those times when creativity and/or task commitment are displayed. Further examples of the relationship between the definitions of the three clusters of traits, identification procedures, and associated programming services can be found in the Schoolwide Enrichment Model (Renzulli, Gubbins, McMillen, Eckert, & Little, 2009).

Are the Rings of Equal Size?

Originally, the clusters were presented as "equal partners" in contributing to the display of gifted behaviors. Reflection has led to the position that creative–productive giftedness requires an interaction among all three clusters for high-level performance, but all three clusters need not be of equal size; nor are the sizes of the clusters constant throughout the pursuit of creative–productive endeavors. For example, task commitment may be minimal or even absent at the inception of a very large and robust creative idea, and the energy and enthusiasm for pursuing the idea may never be as large as the idea itself. Similarly, there are undoubtedly cases in which an extremely creative idea and considerable task commitment overcome somewhat lesser amounts of traditionally measured ability. Such a combination may even result in increased ability by attainment of the technical proficiencies needed to see an idea through to fruition. Because numerical values cannot be assigned to the creativity and task commitment clusters, empirical verification of this interpretation of the three rings is impossible. But case studies based on the experience of creative–productive individuals and research on programs using this model (Reis, 1981) indicate that stronger clusters compensate for somewhat lesser strength in one or both of the other two areas. Most importantly, all three rings must be present and interacting to some degree in order for high levels of productivity to emerge.

CONCLUSION: WHAT MAKES GIFTEDNESS?

In recent years, renewed interest in the study of giftedness and related efforts to provide special educational services for this segment of our school population have occurred. A healthy aspect of this renewed interest has been the emergence of new and innovative theories to explain giftedness, and research studies with promise of greater insights and more defensible approaches to both identification and programming. Conflicting theoretical explanations abound, and various interpretations of research findings add an element of excitement and challenge that can only result in greater understanding of the concept in the years ahead. So long as the concept itself is viewed from the vantage points of different subcultures within the general population and differing societal values, there will always be a wholesome variety of answers to the question: What makes giftedness? These differences in interpretation are indeed a salient and positive characteristic of any field that attempts to further our understanding of the human condition.

The Three-Ring Conception of Giftedness reflects a belief that efforts to define this concept must be research-based and relevant to the persons most influenced by this type of work. While it represents our interpretation of the available evidence, educators must continue the search for greater understanding of this concept which is so crucial to the further advancement of civilization. The task of providing better services to our most promising young people, however, cannot wait until theorists and researchers produce an unassailable ultimate truth because such truths probably do not exist. But the need and opportunities to improve educational services for these young people exist in countless classrooms every day of the week.

NOTES

1. According to Sternberg, analytic abilities are those measured by typical IQ tests and include reasoning, critical thinking, etc.; creative abilities allow for the synthesis or generation of unique and useful solutions to novel problems; and practical abilities allow one to grasp and deal with everyday tasks in ways that maximize the outcomes of analytic or synthetic abilities.
2. The first two intelligences—linguistic and logical–mathematical—are typically valued in schools; musical, bodily–kinesthetic, and spatial are usually associated with the arts; and another two—interpersonal and intra-personal—are called "personal intelligences" by Gardner. Gardner later concluded (1999) that naturalist intelligence also qualifies as intelligence in his Multiple Intelligences (MI) theory.

REFERENCES

Borland, J. H. (2004). *Issues and practices in the identification and education of gifted students from under-represented groups*. (Research Monograph 04186). Storrs: The National Research Center on the Gifted and Talented, University of Connecticut.

Dai, D. Y. (2010). *The nature and nurture of giftedness: A new framework for understanding gifted education*. New York: Teachers College Press.

Dweck, C. S. (1999). *Self-theories: Their role in motivation, personality, and development*. Philadelphia: Psychology Press.

Dweck, C. S. (2006). *Mindset: The new psychology of success*. New York: Random House.

Freeman, F. S. (1962). *Theory and practice of psychological testing*. New York: Holt.

Gardner, H. (1983). *Frames of mind: The theory of multiple intelligences*. New York: Basic Books.

Gardner, H. (1999). *Intelligence reframed: Multiple intelligences for the 21st century*. New York: Basic Books.

Good, C., & Dweck, C. S. (2005). A motivational approach to reasoning, resilience, and responsibility. In R. J. Sternberg & R. F. Subotnik (Eds.), *Optimizing student success in school with the other three Rs: Reasoning, resilience, and responsibility* (pp. 39–56). Charlotte, NC: Information Age.

Gowan, J. C. (1978). Creativity and gifted movement. *The Journal of Creative Behavior, 12*, 1–13.

Jones, J. (1982). The gifted student at university. *Gifted International, 1*, 49–65.

MacKinnon, D. W. (1965). Personality and the realization of creative potential. *American Psychologist, 20*, 273–281.

Neisser, U., Boodoo, G., Bouchard, T. J., Jr., Boykin, A. W., Brody, N., Ceci, S. J. et al. (1996). Intelligence: Knowns and unknowns. *American Psychologist, 51*, 77–101.

Reis, S. M. (1981). *An analysis of the productivity of gifted students participating in programs using the Revolving Door Identification Model*. (Unpublished doctoral dissertation). University of Connecticut, Storrs.

Reis, S. M., & Renzulli, J. S. (1982). A research report on the Revolving Door Identification Model: A case for the broadened conception of giftedness. *Phi Delta Kappan, 63*, 619–620.

Renzulli, J. S. (1977). *The enrichment triad model: A guide for developing defensible programs for the gifted and talented*. Mansfield Center, CT: Creative Learning Press.

Renzulli, J. S. (1978). What makes giftedness? Reexamining a definition. *Phi Delta Kappan, 60*, 180–184, 261.

Renzulli, J. S. (1982). What makes a problem real: Stalking the illusive meaning of qualitative differences in gifted education. *Gifted Child Quarterly, 26*, 148–156.

Renzulli, J. S. (1983). Guiding the gifted in the pursuit of real problems: The transformed role of the teacher. *The Journal of Creative Behavior, 17*, 49–59.

Renzulli, J. S., Gubbins, E. J., McMillen, K. S., Eckert, R. D., & Little, C. A. (Eds.). (2009). *Systems & models for developing programs for the gifted & talented* (2nd ed.). Mansfield Center, CT: Creative Learning Press.

Renzulli, J. S., Reis, S. M., & Smith, L. H. (1981). *The Revolving Door Identification Model.* Mansfield Center, CT: Creative Learning Press.

Renzulli, J. S., Smith, L. H., & Reis, S. M. (1982). Curriculum compacting: An essential strategy for working with gifted students. *The Elementary School Journal, 82*, 185–194.

Sternberg, R. J. (1982). Lies we live by: Misapplication of tests in identifying the gifted. *Gifted Child Quarterly, 26*, 157–161.

Sternberg, R. J. (1984). Toward a triarchic theory of human intelligence. *Behavioral and Brain Sciences, 7*, 269–316.

Sternberg, R. J. (1996). *Successful intelligence: How practical and creative intelligence determine success in life.* New York: Simon & Schuster.

Sternberg, R. J. (2001). Why schools should teach for wisdom: The balance theory of wisdom in educational settings. *Educational Psychologist, 36*, 227–245.

Sternberg, R. J., & Grigorenko, E. L. (2002). *Dynamic measurement: The nature and measurement of learning potential.* New York: Cambridge University Press.

Sternberg, R. J., & Lubart, T. I. (1995). An investment perspective on creative insight. In R. J. Sternberg & J. E. Davidson (Eds.), *The nature of insight* (pp. 535–558). Cambridge, MA: Bradford Books.

Sternberg, R. J., & O'Hara, L. A. (1999). Creativity and intelligence. In R. J. Sternberg (Ed.), *Handbook of creativity* (pp. 251–272). New York: Cambridge University Press.

Terman, L. M. (1921). Intelligence and its measurement. *Journal of Educational Psychology, 12*, 127–133.

Thorndike, E. L. (1921). Intelligence and its measurement: A symposium. *Journal of Educational Psychology, 12*, 124–127.

6

BEING GIFTED

Erin Morris Miller

The study of the psychological constructs of cognitive ability and intelligence[1] has its roots in the work of theorists and researchers in the fields of psychometric measurement, intelligence, and developmental psychology. Giftedness as a trait of individuals is an outgrowth of the study of intelligence and cognitive abilities, and the definition of giftedness has changed over time as the study of human abilities has evolved in psychology. The study of giftedness in psychology can be traced back to Francis Galton's (1869) *Hereditary Genius*. From his observations of families of eminent persons, Galton defined giftedness as either attainment of genius or children showing the potential for genius, emphasizing the influence of heredity. Galton's beliefs about the high hereditability of intelligence and the link between measured intelligence and giftedness had a strong influence on the study of both intelligence and giftedness. This orientation continued with the work of Terman and his longitudinal study of gifted students (Terman, 1925) and the work of Hollingworth (1942) with highly gifted students. Terman defined gifted children as those scoring two standard deviations above the norm on the Stanford–Binet intelligence Scale, an assessment created by Terman. Theories of giftedness that align with the conception of giftedness as advanced cognitive ability have generally focused on performance as measured by the Stanford–Binet, the Wechsler Intelligence Scales, or other intelligence tests.

This line of study is continued today (2012) by scholars such as those taking part in the Genetics of High Cognitive Abilities (GHCA) consortium (Haworth, Wright, Martin, Martin, Boomsma, Bartels et al., 2009) and the Study of Mathematically Precocious Youth (SMPY) at Johns Hopkins University (i.e. Brody & Stanley, 2005; Lubinski & Benbow, 2006) who characterize high ability as either high general intelligence (g) or high ability on specific cognitive factors (s). The researchers and educators at SMPY define giftedness as exceptional performance in a specific area of aptitude—for example, mathematical, verbal, or spatial/mechanical. They ground their views in developmental psychology and describe these children as evidencing precocious development such that they comprehend ideas and reason in a particular academic domain like much older students or adults.

Previous theorists proposed that cognitive abilities are organized hierarchically with a general factor (g) and specific factors (s)—a position supported in empirical studies by Carroll (1993). However, there continues to be research and theorizing in this area, particularly by scholars such as Sternberg and Gardner who believe that *in addition* to the cognitive abilities represented by "g" (general ability) and "s" (specific abilities such as spatial reasoning, or mathematical problem-solving ability), there are other cognitive abilities that can be described as separate intelligences. And by extension, they suggest additional forms of giftedness.

Sternberg (1995, 2000) posits three main types of intelligence (analytic, synthetic, and practical) and multiple patterns of giftedness. Gardner defines intelligence as the ability or set of abilities that allows a person to solve problems and create products that are valued by the society in which the person lives (Gardner, 1983/2003). Gardner identifies eight dimensions that describe the different patterns of abilities that make up his Multiple Intelligences (MI) theory. These dimensions of intelligence comprise: linguistic, logical–mathematical, spatial, musical, bodily–kinesthetic, interpersonal, intrapersonal, and naturalistic. Each competency is thought to have its own developmental history and reside in a separate area of the brain (Gardner, 1983/2003).

What ties together all of these theories is that each has a clear focus on giftedness as arising from internal cognitive abilities that are a part of the individual. Research continues about how cognitive abilities are organized and whether there are additional separate types of cognitive ability or one general ability that is then supported by specific factors (e.g., mathematical, spatial, verbal); however, according to all of these theories, differences in the speed, efficiency, and power of the spectrum of cognitive abilities are at the core of giftedness. This spectrum includes such mental mechanisms as: perceptual sensitivity, identification of problems, selection of thinking tools, creation of mental representation, allocation of resources, selection of strategies, solution monitoring, encoding information, combination and comparison of information, determining what information is relevant, reaction to novelty, automatization of responses, decisions of relevancy, purposiveness, environmental adaptation, the shaping and selecting of one's environment, mental manipulation of spatial configurations, kinesthetic control, and musical pitch discrimination, to name just a few. These abilities can be applied across the range of domains of human endeavor.

Fixed or Malleable Intelligence

Carol Dweck's research on "malleable minds" investigates the perceptions people hold about the nature of intelligence and the effect of these perceptions on learning. According to Dweck, learners may believe they only have a certain amount of intelligence and that they cannot do much to change it (helpless/fixed mindset); or they may believe that no matter who you are, you can change your intelligence (growth mindset) (Dweck, 1986, 1999, 2007; Dweck & Leggett, 1988; Mueller & Dweck, 1998). When confronted with failure, individuals with a fixed mindset are likely to attribute the failure to lack of intelligence and give up or cease to attempt difficult tasks to avoid failure. Individuals with a more malleable growth mindset are likely to attribute failure to a lack of trying and continue to seek challenge (Mueller & Dweck, 1998). But there is another possible viewpoint.

Learners can believe that everyone has a certain innate set of abilities that can be used or allowed to stagnate. These abilities are fixed, but how you apply them is not. This view can apply to analytical abilities, athletic abilities, and interpersonal abilities. Very little research has been conducted examining fixed versus malleable implicit theories of intelligence among gifted individuals; however, there is tentative support for the idea that gifted students can recognize their innate ability and its importance to achievement without feeling helpless in the face of failure (Siegle, Rubenstein, Pollard, & Romey, 2010). Dweck's (2007) contention that hard work and discipline contribute more to achievement than IQ is likely to be true. But a parallel, not necessarily contradictory, view is that achievement is the result of hard work, discipline/commitment, and intellectual ability, with each of these three components having a separate and important role. In this view, cognitive abilities are important for learning and the more the better (Lubinski, 2009).

Measurement

Proponents of giftedness as a psychological construct recognize that performance on any assessment reflects the sum of innate ability and experiences. For those with a trait view of cognitive giftedness, a combination of traditional intelligence and achievement tests serves as the best measurement of the construct of giftedness. But at the same time, there is an awareness of potential for other assessments through the continued development of tests that measure aspects of contemporary intelligence theories such as those of Sternberg and Gardner.

The tests that have been in development the longest, and with the largest research base supporting their reliability and accuracy in predicting school outcomes, are those that measure general intelligence (g) and specific cognitive factors (s) and those that measure achievement in a specific domain of study. Examples include the Wechsler series of intelligence and achievement scales (i.e., Wechsler, 2000, 2009), the Stanford–Binet Intelligence Scales (Roid, 2006), the Woodcock–Johnson series (i.e. Woodcock, McGrew, & Mather, 2001a, 2001b), the Cognitive Abilities Test (CogAT) (Lohman & Hagen, 2001), and the Iowa Tests of Basic Skills (ITBS) (Hoover, Dunbar, & Frisbie, 2005). (See also Missett & Brunner in Chapter 11 in this book.) Research continues on tests that reflect the conceptions of theorists such as Sternberg (Sternberg, 1999; Sternberg, Ferrari, Clinkenbeard, & Grigorenko). Further evidence of the reliability and validity of tests measuring triarchic abilities is needed. More work on validating the theory of Multiple Intelligences is required before any tests based on these theories can be in widespread use.

Implications for Diverse Groups

One of the essential aspects of a trait view of giftedness is the belief in the universality of the giftedness and the behaviors that characterize giftedness. In other words, people from different ethnicities are not gifted in different ways; rather, all intellectually gifted individuals are gifted in the same way: through advanced cognitive abilities as described earlier in the chapter. The manifestations and applications of these abilities may be different, depending on cultural background, but the cognitive mechanisms are not (Frasier & Passow, 1994; Passow & Frasier, 1996; Scott, Deuel, Jean-Francois, & Urbano, 1996; Shaklee et al., 1994). The challenge is finding the best way to evaluate the abilities of students from various backgrounds. The commonly used standardized tests may not provide an accurate measure of a culturally diverse student's capabilities. Alternative assessments may be necessary. The key to developing these assessments is to ensure that they are valid and reliable measures of advanced cognitive abilities.

According to Robinson (2003), one must be clear that the under-representation of certain cultural and racial groups in programs for the gifted is not primarily an issue of conceptions of intelligence, giftedness, or the types of tests used. The primary reasons for under-representation are the social injustices that result in differences in prenatal care, early childhood experiences, and the quality of neighborhood services. Although innate ability *generally* explains about 50 percent of differences in performance on tests of intelligence, heredity and environment interact in different ways depending on socio-economic status (SES). The effects of shared environment are greater for children living in lower socio-economic status homes (Harden, Turkheimer, & Loehlin, 2007; Turkheimer, Haley, Waldron, D'Onofrio, & Gottesman, 2003). This means that environmental differences explain more than genetic factors about the differences in expression of ability for students from low-income environments as compared to students from more affluent backgrounds. In the United States, cultural differences and socio-economic differences are related and influence the intellectual and academic performance of certain cultural and racial groups.

EDUCATIONAL IMPLICATIONS

Theories based on a trait perspective of giftedness are often oriented in the fields of cognitive and developmental psychology. They focus on differences in trajectories of development and cognitive processes among groups and when looking at the individual gifted person. Educationally, the focus is on where a child is developmentally at a particular moment in time. As such, educational approaches are inherently child-centered and should be designed to find the optimal match between the current abilities of the individual student and the educational options available that will lead to further development of their abilities. Essentially, one seeks to match services with the students' developmental readiness for new challenges. Cognitive and developmental readiness is determined through a comprehensive identification procedure.

Identification

Exemplary identification programs work to produce strong links between identification and instruction and promote the use of identification to enhance understanding (Callahan, Tomlinson, & Pizzat, 1994; Johnsen, 1997; Maker, 1996; Sternberg et al., 1996). The ideals in measuring the psychological construct of giftedness include: measurement of universal underlying constructs (intelligence, cognitive abilities), context-appropriate measurement, valid and reliable instruments, use of multiple criteria, and flow from definition to identification to service.

The concept of universality reflects the viewpoint discussed earlier suggesting that an identification paradigm should be applicable to all students, whether they are from historically disadvantaged or advantaged groups (Passow & Frasier, 1996). All talents are present in all groups of people. They may be expressed in a different way depending on cultural context, but they are fundamentally the same constructs (Passow & Frasier, 1996; Scott et al., 1996; Shaklee et al., 1994). When identifying giftedness, one should look for constructs common to all cultural and social groups, but at the same time be sensitive to diverse expression of these ability constructs.

The importance of context and previous experience has been emphasized both in educational studies and in classical studies of cognition (Maker, 1996; Passow & Frasier, 1996; Patton, 1992; Sternberg, 2000; Tversky, 1977). The context of one's life shapes those problems viewed as relevant and how one's abilities develop. Thus, it is important to take context into account when developing assessments, particularly when developing identification procedures for a diverse student body. Changes in context can be made without changing the essential constructs being tested. However, if context cannot be brought into the test, then the test can be aligned with the context by comparing students with others who are similar in age, experience, or environmental background. This use of local norms should not be seen as a reflection of the competency of the group in question, but as a reflection of an attempt at greater validity in measurement. See also Lohman in Chapter 12 of this book.

Using multiple criteria in the identification of students who fit trait definitions of intellectual giftedness requires the use of several different types of assessment to identify potential strengths. First, identification would necessarily involve standardized testing. This psychometric approach is effective and efficient and provides reliable and educationally useful information (Robinson, 2005). It allows an evaluation of both general intelligence and specific aptitudes, both of which should be served in school. However, additional assessments should also be used, with each instrument having the potential to contribute different data to an understanding of the core set of cognitive abilities that make up giftedness. Any one criterion can get a child identified, but no one criterion can exclude a child from identification. This structure of identification procedures is highly supported in the field (Ford, 1998; Maker, 1996; Passow & Frasier, 1996; Renzulli, 1999). The philosophy is one of inclusion, not exclusion, and as such, it emphasizes both expression and potential.

CONCLUSION

The study of giftedness is the study of individual differences among human beings, and each individual is a tapestry of innate abilities and experiences. Cognitive ability is one aspect of what makes people who they are. While it is a strong thread in the weft and weave of a person's life and can be examined, measured, and studied, there are other threads that twist and turn and make up the fabric of a person's life. Cognitive ability is a strong determinant of one's capacity to learn about and interact with the world, but schools play a vital role in its development. It is both that simple and that complicated.

Dweck (2007) writes that many well-known geniuses such as Thomas Edison, Charles Darwin, and Albert Einstein were ordinary bright children who became obsessed with something, and as a result of this intense interest, ended up making world-changing contributions. Whether these geniuses were ordinary children is debatable, but they were certainly very bright. This suggests that schools should make sure that "ordinary bright children" are able to explore their passions. The work of Dweck and others in the area of motivation and learning reminds us that we need to make sure that students who are labeled as gifted understand what that label does and does not mean. The "yarn" that is giftedness is fascinating and powerful. But it must be woven with other threads to craft a life.

NOTE

1. A construct in psychology is a term used to explain an unobservable complex concept that will explain behavior. A construct may be defined in many different ways, be measured, and may have many theories surrounding what it is and how it influences behavior.

REFERENCES

Brody, L. E., & Stanley, J. C. (2005). Youths who reason exceptionally well mathematically and/or verbally. In R. J. Sternberg & J. E. Davidson (Eds.), *Conceptions of giftedness* (2nd ed., pp. 20– 37). New York: Cambridge University Press.

Callahan, C. M., Tomlinson, C. A., & Pizzat, P. M. (1994). *Contexts for promise: Noteworthy practices and innovations in the identification of gifted students.* Charlottesville: The National Research Center on the Gifted and Talented, University of Virginia.

Carroll, J. B. (1993). *Human cognitive abilities.* Cambridge, UK: Cambridge University Press.

Dweck, C. S. (1986). Motivational processes affecting learning. *American Psychologist, 41,* 1040–1048.

Dweck, C. S. (1999). *Self-theories: Their role in motivation, personality, and development.* Philadelphia: Taylor & Francis/Psychology Press.

Dweck, C. S. (2007, December/January). The secret to raising smart kids. *Scientific American MIND,* 36–43.

Dweck, C. S., & Leggett, E. L. (1988). A social-cognitive approach to motivation and personality. *Psychological Review, 95,* 256–273.

Ford, D. Y. (1998). The underrepresentation of minority students in gifted education: Problems and promises in recruitment and retention. *The Journal of Special Education, 32*(1), 4–14.

Frasier, M. M., & Passow, A. H. (1994). *Toward a new paradigm for identifying talent potential.* (Research Monograph 94112). Storrs: The National Research Center on the Gifted and Talented, University of Connecticut.

Gardner, H. (2003). *Frames of mind. The theory of multiple intelligences.* New York: Basic Books. (Original work published 1983).

Harden, K. P., *Turkheimer,* E., & *Loehlin,* J. C. (*2007*). Genotype by environment interaction in adolescents' cognitive aptitude. *Behavioral Genetics, 37,* 273–283.

Haworth, C. M. A., Wright, M. J., Martin, N. W., Martin, N. G., Broomswa, D. I., Bartels, M. et al. (2009). A twin study of the genetics of high cognitive ability selected from 11,000 twin pairs in six studies from four countries. *Behavioral Genetics, 39,* 359–370.

Hollingworth, L. S. (1942). *Children above 180 IQ Stanford-Binet: Origin and development.* New York: World Book Company.

Hoover, H., Dunbar, S., & Frisbie, D. (2005). *Iowa Tests of Basic Skills.* Chicago: Riverside.

Johnsen, S. K. (1997). Assessment beyond definitions. *Peabody Journal of Education, 72,* 136–152.

Lohman, D., & Hagen, P. (2001). *Cognitive Abilities Test.* Chicago: Riverside.

Lubinski, D. (2009). Exceptional cognitive ability: The phenotype. *Behavioral Genetics, 39,* 350–358.

Lubinski, D., & Benbow, C. P. (2006). Study of Mathematically Precocious Youth after 35 years: Uncovering antecedents for the development of math-science expertise. *Perspectives on Psychological Science, 1,* 316–345.

Maker, C. J. (1996). Identification of gifted minority students: A national problem, needed changes and a promising solution. *Gifted Child Quarterly, 40,* 41–50.

Mueller, C. M., & Dweck, C. S. (1998). Intelligence praise can undermine motivation and performance. *Journal of Personality and Social Psychology, 75,* 33–52.

Passow, A. H., & Frasier, M. M. (1996). Toward improving identification of talent potential among minority and disadvantaged students. *Roeper Review, 18,* 198–202.

Patton, J. M. (1992). Assessment and identification of African-American learners with gifts and talents. *Exceptional Children, 59,* 150–159.

Plucker, J. A., Callahan, C. M., & Tomchin, E. M. (1996). Wherefore art thou, multiple intelligences? Alternative assessments for identifying talent in ethnically diverse and low income students. *Gifted Child Quarterly, 40,* 81–92.

Renzulli, J. S. (1999). Reflections, perceptions, and future directions. *Journal for the Education of the Gifted, 23,* 125–146.

Robinson, N. M. (2003). Two wrongs do not make a right: Sacrificing the needs of gifted students does not solve society's unsolved problems. *Journal for the Education of the Gifted, 26,* 251–273.

Robinson, N. M. (2005). In defense of a psychometric approach to the definition of academic giftedness: A conservative view from a die-hard liberal. In R. J. Sternberg & J. E. Davidson (Eds.), *Conceptions of giftedness* (2nd ed., pp. 280–294). New York: Cambridge University Press.

Roid, G. S. (2006). *Stanford-Binet Intelligence Scales* (5th ed.). Rolling Meadows, IL: Riverside.

Scott, M. S., Deuel, L. S., Jean-Francois, B., & Urbano, R. C. (1996). Identifying cognitively gifted ethnic minority children. *Gifted Child Quarterly, 40,* 147–148.

Shaklee, B., Barbour, N., Ambrose, R., Rohrer, J., Whitmore, J. R., & Viechnicki, K. J. (1994). Early assessment for exceptional potential in young minority and/or economically disadvantaged students. In C. M. Callahan, C. A. Tomlinson, & P. M. Pizzat (Eds.), *Contexts for promise: Noteworthy practices and innovations in the identification of gifted students.* Charlottesville: The National Research Center on the Gifted and Talented, University of Virginia.

Siegle, D., Rubenstein, L. D., Pollard, E., & Romey, E. (2010). Exploring the relationship of college freshman honors students' effort and ability attribution, interest, and implicit theory of intelligence with perceived ability. *Gifted Child Quarterly, 54,* 92–101.

Sternberg, R. J. (1986). A triarchic theory of intellectual giftedness. In R. J. Sternberg, & J. E. Davidson (Eds.), *Conceptions of giftedness.* Cambridge, UK: Cambridge University Press.

Sternberg, R. J. (1995). *A triarchic approach to giftedness.* (Research Monograph 95126). New Haven, CT: The National Research Center on the Gifted and Talented, Yale University.

Sternberg, R. J. (1998). Teaching and assessing for successful intelligence. *School Administrator, 55*(1), 26–27, 30–31.

Sternberg, R. J. (1999). A triarchic approach to the understanding and assessment of intelligence in multicultural populations. *Journal of School Psychology, 37,* 145–159.

Sternberg, R. J. (2000) Patterns of giftedness: A triarchic analysis. *Roeper Review, 22,* 231–235.

Sternberg, R. J., Ferrari, M., Clinkenbeard, P., & Grigorenko, E. L. (1996). Identification, instructions and assessment of gifted children: A construct validation of a triarchic model. *Gifted Child Quarterly, 40,* 129–137.

Terman, L. M. (1925). *Genetic studies of genius: Vol. I.. Mental and physical traits of a thousand gifted children.* Stanford, CA: Stanford University Press.

Turkheimer, E., Haley, A., Waldron, M., D'Onofrio, B. M., & Gottesman, I. I. (2003). Socioeconomic status modifies heritability of IQ in young children. *Psychological Science, 14,* 623–628.

Tversky, A. (1977). Features of similarity. *Psychological Review, 84,* 327–352.

Wechsler, D. (2000). *Wechsler Intelligence Scale for Children (4th ed.). San Antonio, TX: Harcourt.*

Wechsler, D. (2009). *Wechsler Individual Achievement Test (3rd ed.). San Antonio, TX: Harcourt.*

Woodcock, R. W., McGrew, K. S., & Mather, N. (2001a). *Woodcock-Johnson III Tests of Achievement.* Itasca, IL: Riverside.

Woodcock, R. W., McGrew, K. S., & Mather, N. (2001b). *Woodcock-Johnson III Tests of Cognitive Abilities.* Itasca, IL: Riverside.

7

THE DMGT 2.0

From Gifted Inputs to Talented Outputs

Françoys Gagné

Since its first appearance in *Gifted Child Quarterly* (Gagné, 1985), the Differentiated Model of Giftedness and Talent (DMGT) has evolved into a full-fledged theory of talent development now referred to as the DMGT 2.0 (Gagné, 2009). No chapter-length text can encompass all the details of its contents and dynamics. Consequently, I offer the present text as a "detailed overview"—a potential oxymoron!—of the updated DMGT. This overview comprises five themes:

a. the DMGT's rationale;
b. the five components;
c. the prevalence of gifted/talented individuals;
d. the DMGT's biological underpinnings; and
e. some basic dynamic rules of talent development.

THE DMGT'S RATIONALE

The field of academic talent development uses two key concepts to label its special population: *gifted* and *talented*. Those who browse the field's scientific and professional literature soon discover that the existence of two terms does not mean the existence of two distinct concepts. Most authors use these two terms as synonyms, as in the common expression "the gifted and talented are . . ." A few scholars (e.g., Joseph S. Renzulli and Robert J. Sternberg) even hesitate to use the term talent, focusing their whole conception of outstanding abilities on the concept of giftedness. When the two terms are differentiated, the distinction may take several forms. Some apply the term "gifted" to high cognitive abilities and the term "talented" to all other forms of excellence (e.g., arts, sports, technology). Others consider giftedness to represent a higher order of excellence than talent (e.g., "she is 'just' talented, not 'really' gifted"). Still others associate giftedness with some mature expression as opposed to a vision of talent as an undeveloped ability

(U.S. Department of Education, 1993). Well over a dozen variations of definitions of these two terms can be extracted from major publications in the field. For that reason, it would not be too much of an exaggeration to associate the current status of our conceptual foundations with the biblical Tower of Babel. Yet most of the field's scholars and professionals appear quite comfortable with this lack of consensus over the definition of our basic constructs. The most significant piece of evidence to that effect is a quasi-unanimous silence on the question.

Whereas conceptions abound and often contradict one another, scholars keep mentioning one particular idea in almost every discussion of the giftedness construct. They acknowledge, implicitly or explicitly, a distinction between early emerging forms of "giftedness" with strong biological roots, and fully developed adult forms of "giftedness." Scholars will express that distinction through pairs of terms like potential/realization, aptitude/achievement, and promise/fulfillment. Here are a few examples: "Talent development is important to achieving one's full potential . . ." (Brody & Stanley, 2005, p. 28); "Being gifted means moving beyond potential to actual performance." (Cross & Coleman, 2005, p. 53); "To be born with high talent potential and later possibly be talented in some career-oriented field . . ." (Feldhusen, 2005, p. 74). The DMGT was created to take advantage of that distinction; it became the basis for the following differentiated definitions of these two terms.

> Giftedness designates the possession and use of outstanding natural abilities, called aptitudes, in at least one ability domain, to a degree that places an individual at least among the top 10% of age peers.
>
> Talent designates the outstanding mastery of systematically developed abilities, called competencies (knowledge and skills), in at least one field of human activity to a degree that places an individual at least among the top 10% of age peers who are or have been active in that field.

In these definitions, the two concepts share two characteristics: (a) both refer to human abilities; (b) both target individuals who differ from the norm or average because of outstanding behaviors. These two commonalities help us understand why so many professionals and laypersons regularly confound them. Indeed, most dictionaries, even those specializing in the social sciences, commonly define giftedness as "talent," and vice versa. Note that both definitions concretize the meaning of "outstanding" with precise estimates of prevalence: the "how many" question. Assuming that most human abilities manifest themselves as normal—or bell curve—distributions, the DMGT states that gifted and talented individuals occupy the top 10 percent of any such ability distribution (more details in "The Metric-based (MB) System," below). From these two definitions, we can extract a simple definition for the talent development process: *talent development corresponds to the progressive transformation of gifts into talents.*

As implied by the chapter's title, individuals who build upon one—or more—talent will progressively transform gifted inputs into talented outputs. These three components, giftedness (G), talent (T), and the talent development process (D), constitute the basic trio of components of the DMGT. Two additional components (see Figure 7.1)—intrapersonal catalysts (I), and environmental catalysts (E)—complete the structure of this talent development theory.[1]

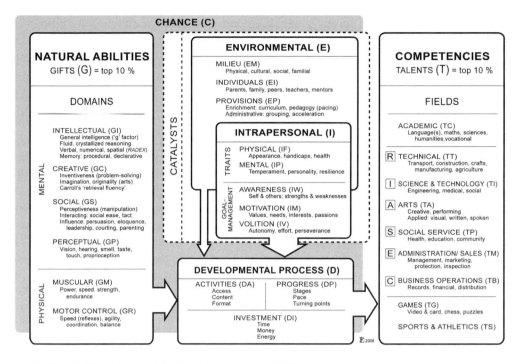

Fig. 7.1 Gagné's Differentiated Model of Giftedness and Talent (DMGT 2.0).

THE FIVE COMPONENTS OF DMGT

Gifts (G)

The G component of the DMGT clusters natural abilities into six groups or sub-components, called *domains*. Four of these domains belong to a mental group: the intellectual domain (GI), the creative domain (GC), the social domain (GS), and the perceptual domain (GP). Physical abilities are subdivided into two major groups: muscular (GM) abilities devoted to large physical movements; and (GR) abilities representing fine motor control and reflexes. Both domains of physical abilities usually contribute to complex physical activities (e.g., tennis, baseball, and gymnastics). We can observe natural abilities in most tasks that children perform in their daily activities and their schooling. Think, for instance, of the intellectual abilities needed to learn to read, speak a foreign language, or understand new mathematical concepts. Think of the creative abilities involved in writing a short story, composing a song, drawing an attractive poster, or building with toy building blocks. Notice also the social abilities that children use in their daily interactions with classmates, teachers, and parents. Finally, perceptual and physical natural abilities guide activities in the schoolyard, in neighborhood sports, or arts (dance, sculpture, crafts).

Natural abilities are not innate; they do develop over the whole course of a person's life, but probably much more during the early part of that life. Gifts manifest themselves more easily and directly in young children because only limited systematic learning activities have begun transforming them into specific talents. Still, we can observe them in older children and adults through the facility and speed with which individuals acquire new knowledge and skills. The easier or faster the learning process, the higher the underlying natural abilities we will assume. Many scholars have stressed this link between natural abilities and learning pace. For instance, Gottfredson (1997) states: "Although researchers disagree on how they define intelligence, there is virtual unanimity that it reflects the ability to reason, solve problems, think abstractly, and acquire knowledge." (p. 93). Carroll (1997) similarly affirms: "Experts have largely neglected what seems to be an obvious conclusion to be drawn from the evidence from IQ tests: that IQ represents the degree to which, and the rate at which, people are able to learn . . ." (p. 44).

Talents (T)

The concept of talent is very straightforward: just think of "performance." Talented athletes excel in their particular sport, talented musicians possess an outstanding mastery of their chosen instrument, talented mechanics or electricians are among the top 10 percent in their trade in terms of mastery of the knowledge and skills in their occupation. With regard to school subjects, consider top academic grades—performance—and you find the talented students in mathematics, grammar, science, etc. Talents are observed more easily during the training phase; during that time, many occasions for normative assessments present themselves, including teachers' examinations, achievement tests, competitions, scholarships, and so forth. After individuals have completed their training, performance rankings usually disappear. How will you know if the plumber you have called is below or above average compared to his or her peers? How about the mechanic working on your car, the dentist repairing a filling, the accountant preparing your income tax return, the coach managing your child's hockey team? Most of the time, the only guideline will be word of mouth. Sport stands out as the rare major field in which talent assessment continues publicly throughout the career of its members; professional athletes deal with constant normative comparisons of their performances!

How can we map the diversity of human talents? One of the best-known category systems has its origin in Holland's RIASEC work-related classification of personality types: Realistic, Investigative, Artistic, Social, Enterprising, and Conventional (see Anastasi & Urbina, 1997, chapter 14). The RIASEC structure was adopted by the ACT, an educational testing and information organization, in the creation of its World-of-Work Map (ACT, 2008). Occupations are further subdivided into 26 smaller groups summarily identified within each of the RIASEC categories in the T area of Figure 7.1. Although quite broad, the World-of-Work Map does not mention three major talent fields: (a) pre-occupational academic subject matters, (b) games, and (c) sports. They are added to Figure 7.1 to complete the talent taxonomy. Note the lack of elitism in the DMGT's concept of talent. Contrary to most scholars, who tend to borrow their examples from eminent achievements in elite professions (e.g., inventors, internationally renowned artists, prize winners), I have defined the concept of talent in such a way that it ensures the presence of many individuals—the top 10 percent—in almost every human occupation.

The Talent Development Process (D)

The DMGT addresses the talent development process from two distinct perspectives: (a) a detailed map of the sub-components and facets involved, and (b) an operational definition of the process itself, to which is attached a set of six defining characteristics. This component introduces a neologism, "talentee," which aims to describe any individual who actively pursues a talent development program in *any* occupational field.

Mapping Talent Development

As shown in Figure 7.1, the DMGT proposes three main sub-components to describe the talent development process: Activities (DA), Investment (DI), and Progress (DP). The talent development process begins when a child, an adolescent, or an adult accesses (DAA), through identification or selection, a systematic, talent-oriented and long-term program of activities; at that point, the individual becomes a talentee. The talent development activities include a specific content (DAC), the curriculum, offered within a specific learning environment (DAF or format). That learning environment may be either unstructured (autodidactic learning) or structured (e.g., school, conservatory, sports organization). The DI sub-component focuses on the intensity of the talent development process in terms of time (DIT), money (DIM), or psychological energy (DIE). These three indices usually lead to longitudinal curves (evolution over weeks, months, years) showing increases or decreases over time, as well as comparison curves between talentees. The energy construct is probably less easy to operationalize. It could be assessed as passion, concentration during practice, or determination to achieve; it parallels to a large extent the "deliberate" in Ericsson's concept of deliberate practice (Ericsson, Krampe, & Tesch-Römer, 1993).

The progress (DP) of talentees from initial access to peak performance can be broken down into a series of stages (DPS); for example, "novice," "advanced," "proficient," and "expert." Sports and arts have adopted a geographically based system of stages: Local excellence is the lowest rung, followed by regional, provincial/state, national, and international excellence. Special access criteria and developmental activities characterize different levels or stages. The measurement of pace (DPP) constitutes the main quantitative representation of talentees' progress within and between developmental stages. Teachers or trainers can assess pace with both ipsative and normative measures. Talentees can measure their ipsative progress over time, trying to improve on previous achievements or "personal bests." But, within the context of talent development, normative assessments are the rule, namely how quickly talentees are progressing compared to average peers or peers who are pursuing a similar talent development program, at the same level of course. Finally, the long-term developmental course of talentees will be marked by a series of more or less crucial turning points (DPT): being spotted by a teacher or coach, receiving an important scholarship, suffering an injury, as well as positive (falling in love) or negative (death of a close one) personal events.

Defining Talent Development Operationally

The main elements of the mapping process described above can be synthesized in the following formal definition: Talent development is the systematic pursuit by talentees, over a significant period of time, of an enriched program of activities aimed at a specific excellence goal. In the specific case of academic talent development, this generic definition becomes: Academic talent development is the systematic pursuit by talentees, over a significant period of time, of an enriched K–12 curriculum aimed at a specific academic excellence goal. Either of these definitions summarizes six essential characteristics:

a. an enriched curriculum/training program;
b. a clear and challenging excellence goal;
c. selective access criteria;
d. systematic and regular learning/training activities;
e. regular performance-based assessment of progress; and
f. personalized—accelerated, of course—pacing.

Within the DMGT framework, the first defining characteristic—an enriched curriculum—constitutes the core of any talent development program. Within the regular school system, it is the K–12 curriculum that must be enriched *on a daily basis* for academic talentees to experience regular learning challenges. The second defining characteristic—a long-term excellence goal—again targets planned academic excellence with regard to the subject matters included in the regular curriculum. This long-term goal must be far enough in the future to necessitate substantial talentee investment. The third characteristic follows logically from the first two; indeed, because of its enriched curriculum and high excellence goals, academic talent development requires outstanding learning abilities. Recall that the qualifier "outstanding" is operationally defined as belonging to the top 10 percent on any valid measure of the targeted ability. The fourth characteristic—regular learning and practice—reminds us that an enriched school curriculum must propose real intellectual challenges on a *daily* basis. Vygotsky's concept of a "zone of proximal development" (1978) aptly conveys the need to maintain the students' pace at the cutting edge of their learning capacity: not too slow to force them to idle regularly, nor too fast to create feelings of helplessness. As part of these full-time enriched developmental activities, regular formative and normative academic assessments allow talentees and their teachers to ascertain adequate progress toward the predetermined academic excellence goal(s). Talentees should know regularly if their learning pace matches, falls behind, or exceeds expectations. Finally, grouping talentees together to offer an enriched curriculum does not mean that individual differences in learning aptitude have disappeared (Gagné, 2005). Consequently, those who progress significantly faster than their peers should be allowed to accelerate (Colangelo, Assouline, & Gross, 2004).

The Supporting Cast: Intrapersonal (I) and Environmental (E) Catalysts

Borrowed from chemistry, the concept of catalyst refers metaphorically to a facilitating—or sometimes hindering—role played by elements *indirectly* involved in a chemical transformation. In the case of talent development, the key ingredients are the gifted inputs—acting as building materials—and their talented outcomes. The DMGT distinguishes two major types of catalyst: (a) characteristics that define the talentees themselves, labeled "intrapersonal," and (b) characteristics that define the environment in which the talent development process will happen.

Intrapersonal (I) Catalysts

As shown in Figure 7.1, intrapersonal catalysts are subdivided into two main dimensions: (a) relatively stable physical and mental traits, and (b) more mobile goal-oriented processes. Physical (IF) traits include general appearance, racial or ethnic traits, disabilities (think of the Paralympic Games), chronic illnesses, etc. These "catalytic" physical traits differ qualitatively (through their role) from physical characteristics that directly impact the level of natural physical and mental abilities (e.g., height in the case of basketball or hand span as a determinant of a young musician's repertoire). Mental (IP) characteristics cluster around two main constructs: temperament and personality, which represent the nature and nurture poles respectively, or basic tendencies as opposed to behavioral styles. The goal-management dimension includes three sub-components: Awareness (IW), Motivation (IM), and Volition (IV). Being aware of one's strengths and weaknesses, both within the G and I components, plays a crucial role in the way talentees plan their developmental planning activities. Goal-oriented processes may be differentiated according to goal-identification activities (IM) as opposed to goal-attainment activities (IV): what we want to achieve and how we will go about reaching that goal. The IM sub-component includes the identification—and occasional reassessment—of an appropriate talent development goal. Talentees examine their values and their needs, as well as determining their interests or being swept by a passion. The loftier the goal, the more difficulties talentees will encounter in their efforts (IV) to reach it. High-level long-term goals require an intense dedication, as well as daily acts of will power to maintain practice through obstacles, boredom, and occasional failure.

Environmental (E) Catalysts

As part of the version 2.0 update of the DMGT, the E catalysts have been moved up, and partially *behind* the intrapersonal catalysts (see Figure 7.1). That important overlap signals the crucial *filtering* role that the I component plays with regard to environmental influences. The narrow arrow at the left indicates some limited direct E influence on the developmental process; but the bulk of environmental stimuli have to pass through the sieve of an individual's needs, interests, or personality traits. Talentees continually pick and choose which stimuli will deserve their attention.

The first distinct sub-component of the E component, called Milieu (EM), can be examined both at a macroscopic level (e.g., geographic, demographic, sociological) and a microscopic level (e.g., size of family, socio-economic status, neighborhood services). The second sub-component, Individuals (EI), focuses on the psychological influence of significant persons in the talentee's social environment. It includes parents or care-givers and siblings, but also the larger family, teachers and trainers, peers, mentors, and even public figures adopted as role models by talentees. The significant impact of interpersonal influences is probably easier to imagine than that of any other source of influence within the environment. Thus, it is not surprising that a good percentage of the professional literature on talent development, not only in academics, but also in arts, business, or sports, examines the potential influence of significant individuals in the immediate environment of gifted or talented youngsters. The third sub-component, Provisions (EP), covers all forms of talent development services and programs. The two traditional facets of enrichment and administrative provisions directly parallel the Content (DAC) and Format (DAF) facets of the DA sub-component earlier described. Here we adopt a broader outlook rather than examining provisions from the strict perspective of a given talentee's talent development course. Enrichment (EPE) refers to specific talent development curricula or pedagogical strategies; its best-known example is called "enrichment in density" or "curriculum compacting." Administrative (EPA) provisions are traditionally subdivided into two main practices: (a) part-time (e.g., clusters, pull-out classes) or full-time ability grouping; and (b) acceleration (e.g., early entrance to school, grade skipping, Advanced Placement). In summary, EM is a complex of *social* influences, EI is a complex of *psychological* influences, and EP is a complex of *educational* influences.

The Chance Factor

First introduced as one of five environmental sub-components, the role of chance has evolved to a *qualifier* of *any* causal influence. Chance represents the *degree of control* that talentees have over the various causal factors affecting their talent development. Atkinson (1978) stated that all human accomplishments could be ascribed to two crucial "rolls of the dice" over which no individual exerts any personal control: the accidents of birth and background. Indeed, we do not control the genetic endowment received at conception; yet that genetic endowment affects both our natural abilities (the G component) and our temperament, as well as other elements of the I component. Moreover, we do not choose or control the family into which we are born or the social environment in which we are raised. These two factors alone give a powerful role to chance in sowing the bases of a person's talent development possibilities. Because of this redefined role, the "chance" factor no longer appears in a visual representation of the DMGT. However, because of its popularity among DMGT "fans"—as well as my personal attachment to it—it retains a special spot in the background of components which it influences (see Figure 7.1).

PREVALENCE AND LEVELS

The question of prevalence represents a crucial definitional element in the case of all *normative* constructs, which, like giftedness and talent, target a small proportion of the whole population. Practically speaking, adopting a threshold of 10 percent instead of 1 percent—a tenfold difference in estimated prevalence—has a huge impact on selection practices and educational provision. There is no absolute answer to the "how many" question; nowhere will we find a magical number that automatically separates those labeled gifted or talented from the rest of the population. The choice of an appropriate threshold requires consensus among professionals. Nutritionists achieved such a consensus when they created the Body Mass Index (BMI) and set thresholds to separate normal weight from overweight and overweight from obesity (National Institutes of Health, 1998). But such a consensus does not exist in the gifted field, leaving room for diverse practical thresholds. Scholars' proposals range from the 1 percent adopted by Terman (1925) to the 20 percent advanced by Renzulli (1986) to create the talent pools in his Revolving Door Identification Model. What about the ratios used in school districts? In a survey of state policies, Mitchell (1988) noted that "states using intelligence and achievement test scores for identification generally use cut-off points which range between the 95th and 98th percentile levels" (p. 240) or between 2 percent and 5 percent.

The Metric-based (MB) System

The threshold for both giftedness and talent in the DMGT model is placed at the 90th percentile (Gagné, 1998). Two reasons underlie the choice of 10 percent: (a) it sits close to the mid-point of the observed range of suggestions; and (b) it allows us to use the metric system to create levels within the gifted/talented population. This choice for the basic threshold might appear unduly generous to some; but consider that it is counterbalanced by the creation of levels of giftedness or talent. There are five hierarchically structured levels; each new level comprises the top 10 percent (one decimal place) of the preceding level. Thus, within the top 10 percent of *mildly* gifted or talented persons, the four progressively more selective subgroups are respectively labeled *moderately* (top 1:100), *highly* (top 1:1,000), *exceptionally* (top 1:10,000), and *extremely* or *profoundly* (top 1:100,000) gifted or talented. This metric-based (MB) system is an intrinsic element of the DMGT.

Comments

First, the MB system of levels applies to every domain of giftedness and every field of talent. Because giftedness domains are not closely correlated, individuals gifted in one domain are not necessarily the same as those gifted in another. Consequently, the total number of gifted and talented individuals largely exceeds 10 percent. Some studies indicate that it might well be two or three times larger (Bélanger & Gagné, 2006). Second, according to the MB system, the vast majority—90 percent—of gifted/talented individuals belong to the lowest level; highly gifted/talented individuals are a rarity. For example, the prevalence of *exceptionally* gifted individuals (intellectually), those with IQs of 155 or more, is approximately 1:10,000. Since the DMGT defines the total gifted population as the top 10 percent (IQs ≥ 120) of the same-age general population, the prevalence of exceptionally gifted individuals *within the gifted population* does not exceed 1:1,000. It corresponds to one such student in 30 to 40 homogeneous groups of intellectually gifted students. Even full-time teachers of the gifted would, in the course of their 35-year professional career, encounter just a few. Consequently, when we present extreme examples of behavior to groups of parents or teachers, we risk conveying a distorted image of the "garden variety" of gifted and talented individuals. To present giftedness and talent as very exceptional phenomena may tempt school administrators to judge that such a rare population does not justify large investments of time and money to meet their educational needs.

THE BIOLOGICAL UNDERPINNINGS OF THE DMGT

The need to discuss the subject of biological underpinnings originated from frequent misinterpretations of the giftedness versus talent differentiation. These users of the DMGT oversimplified that differentiation by opposing the terms "innate" and "systematically developed." Judging natural abilities to be innate went far beyond recognizing that they had genetic roots. When we say that Mary is a "born" pianist, we are certainly not implying that she was able to play a concerto within weeks of beginning her piano lessons or that she became proficient with minimal practice. Describing her talent as innate only makes sense metaphorically to convey the idea that Mary progressed rapidly and seemingly effortlessly through her talent development program, at a much more rapid pace than her learning peers. The same applies to any natural ability. Intellectually precocious children do not suddenly manifest an exceptional vocabulary or logical reasoning processes; they develop these cognitive abilities by going through the same developmental stages as any other child. The difference resides in the ease and speed with which they will advance through these successive stages. The term "precocious" says it all: They reach a given level of knowledge and reasoning *before* the vast majority of learning peers. And the higher their intellectual giftedness, the earlier these successive stages will be reached. When the term "innate" is used to describe natural abilities inappropriately, we convey two false images: namely, (a) that the observed individual differences are immutable; and (b) that they are present at birth or, if not, that they appear suddenly with very little training.

If natural abilities cannot be considered "innate," what exactly is innate? Where does the "gift" in giftedness reside? To answer that question, we need to look at the biological underpinnings of human behavior. These underpinnings range in depth from gene activity at the deepest level to directly observable anatomical characteristics like height or body build. And there are extremely complex causal paths linking these various levels of biological structures and processes. Now that the human genome has been decoded, researchers have reoriented their efforts toward pinpointing specific genes responsible for various human abilities and other personality characteristics. But their scientific activities go well beyond the identification process itself to reconstructing the complete biological chain of impacts from the proteins encoded by the identified genes to the specific intervening physiological structures and processes, all the way to examining their impact on mental or physical abilities, as well as on the intrapersonal catalysts.

To illustrate these various levels of influence, from gene activity to behavioral expression, consider a "house" metaphor. In that house, the DMGT occupies the ground floor where directly observable and measurable behaviors manifest themselves. We often call these behaviors *phenotypes* to contrast them with gene-level, or *genotypic* activity. Underneath, we can imagine a series of basements representing progressively deeper biological substrates. At the deepest level, we find genotypic structures and processes (e.g., DNA, RNA, protein production). The next highest basement contains a large diversity of physiological and neurological processes that not only control a person's biological development from conception to death, but also ensure the proper functioning of body and brain. A number of such structures or processes have already been identified as influencing individual differences in cognitive processing. The highest basement includes anatomical structures (e.g., brain size, tallness, joint flexibility) associated with abilities and other personal characteristics. Where among these three subterranean levels do we find "innate" elements? Certainly not at the highest level; most of these anatomical structures result from extensive development and do not achieve maturity until adolescence or adulthood. If we go one basement down to the level of physiological processes, we might be in a gray zone where it becomes difficult to separate innate processes from those that result from development. What seems to be clear is that the lowest basement, the basement devoted to gene activity, is mostly, but not totally, under inborn control.

THE DYNAMICS OF TALENT DEVELOPMENT

The DMGT is a talent development model, *not* a model representing a person's total personal development. Consequently, only elements having a significant influence on a talentee's developmental process are included. Within the DMGT, natural abilities or aptitudes act as the "raw materials" or the constituent elements of talents. It follows from this relationship that talent necessarily implies the presence of well-above-average natural abilities; in most situations, one cannot become talented without first being gifted, or close to that top 10 percent threshold. The reverse is not true: High natural abilities may simply remain gifts, and not be translated into talents, as witnessed by the well-known phenomenon of academic underachievement among intellectually gifted children. There is also a dynamic association between specific gifts and talents; for instance, between physical abilities and sports, or between creativity and art. Because of their status as raw materials, gifts represent *generic* abilities that can be molded into quite distinct skills, depending on the field of activity adopted by a talentee. For example, manual dexterity can be molded into the particular skills of a pianist, a dentist, a typist, or a video-game player. Similarly, analytical reasoning, one of many cognitive natural abilities, can be molded into the scientific reasoning of a chemist, the game analysis of a chess player, or the strategic planning of an athlete.

In most talent development situations, each of the four causal components (G, I, E, D) contributes positively to the emergence of talents. And it is assumed that this positive contribution will become more intense as talentees attempt to reach higher talent goals. These contributions can vary considerably in intensity and continuity from one talentee to another. No two developmental paths look alike. Hence, talent development is a very complex process, a process where the four causal components modify their interactions over the course of a talentee's developmental path. Think, for instance, of the close supervision that many parents give to their children's homework in elementary school and its virtual disappearance by the time the students reach high school.

Within the K–12 educational system, it is not rare to observe academically talented students investing little more in their schooling than their high natural intellectual gifts. Most of these students never show much intrinsic motivation for learning, need almost no environmental support, and invest little time in their schooling beyond presence in the classroom and occasional pre-examination "cramming." Conversely, a few students with barely above-average natural intellectual abilities may reach the bottom rung of the MB system of levels—*mild* academic talent—thanks to intense dedication and effort (IV), long hours of deliberate study (DI), and continuous support from both parents and teachers (EI). These two examples illustrate diverse dynamic interactions between the four causal components. We could ask: "What makes a difference?" In other words, do some components generally—on average—exercise more powerful influences on talent emergence? Answers to that complex question are discussed in detail elsewhere (Gagné, 2003). But creating a causal hierarchy should not make us forget that in most situations, all components play a crucial role in the talent development process. In a nutshell, emergence of talent results from a complex choreography between the four causal components, a choreography unique to each individual.

SUMMING UP

In conclusion, four characteristics are specific to the DMGT. Jointly, they make the DMGT a distinct and unique conception of giftedness and talent. First, the DMGT clearly differentiates definitions of the field's two key concepts. The separation of potentialities/aptitudes from realizations/achievements is operationalized through a distinction between outstanding natural abilities (gifts) and outstanding systematically developed knowledge and skills (talents). This distinction leads to another clear definition, that of talent development, a progressive transformation of gifts in any one domain into talents in any occupational field. Only in the DMGT does the concept of talent become as important as that of giftedness to understand the development of outstanding knowledge and skills. Finally, differentiation between potentialities and realizations permits a much clearer definition of underachievement among gifted individuals; it simply becomes the *non*-transformation of high natural abilities into outstanding systematically developed skills.

Second, the introduction within the giftedness and talent definitions of prevalence estimates (top 10 percent) also constitutes a unique facet of the DMGT. Its metric-based system of five levels that applies to any giftedness domain or talent field helps to maintain a constant awareness of differences *within* the sub-populations of gifted and talented individuals. The availability of clear thresholds and labels could facilitate not only the selection and description of study samples, but also the comparison of results from different studies. Moreover, the MB system of levels should remind educators that the vast majority of gifted or talented individuals (90 percent) belong to the lowest—mild—category, and that only a tiny fraction of those identified as gifted or talented in their youth will ever achieve eminence in their chosen field.

Third, the DMGT's complex structure identifies causal factors of talent emergence, especially those located within the intrapersonal and environmental catalysts. But that comprehensive outlook maintains the individuality of each component, clearly specifying its precise nature and role within this talent development theory. The giftedness construct remains well circumscribed, and thus more easily operationalized. The catalysts are clearly situated outside the giftedness and talent concepts themselves. This sets the DMGT apart from many rival conceptions where disparate elements are included in the giftedness definition itself.

Fourth, most conceptions focus almost exclusively on intellectual giftedness (IG) and academic talent (AT), as well as academically based professions (e.g., scientists, lawyers, or doctors). The DMGT follows an orientation adopted explicitly by only a few past scholars (e.g., DeHaan & Havighurst, 1961; Gardner, 1983; Marland, 1972); namely, to broaden the concept of giftedness and acknowledge various manifestations. In that respect, the DMGT stands almost alone in bringing physical giftedness within the fold of the giftedness construct, defining that domain much more broadly than Gardner's bodily–kinesthetic intelligence. This openness should foster closer ties between professionals focusing on academic talent development and those who devote their energies to athletic talent development.

NOTE

1. The architecture of the DMGT comprises three hierarchical levels: (a) five components (G, T, D, I, E), each of them subdivided into (b) a diverse number of sub-components, which in turn are subdivided into (c) more specific facets. Three-letter symbols represent these elements: the first—or single—letter identifies the component; the second letter—or pair—identifies sub-components; and the third one—or trio—identifies a particular facet. These symbols make it easier to systematize the coding of biographical information. This approach, called DMGT-based analysis (Gagné, 2000), can be used to analyze the content of scientific publications, case-study materials, or any other type of information dealing with the talent development process.

REFERENCES

ACT. (2008). Retrieved August 28, 2008 from http://www.act.org/wwm/index.html

Anastasi, A., & Urbina, S. (1997). *Psychological testing* (7th ed.). Upper Saddle River, NJ: Prentice-Hall.

Atkinson, J. W. (1978). Motivational determinants of intellective performance and cumulative achievement. In J. W. Atkinson & J. O. Raynor (Eds.), *Personality, motivation, and achievement* (pp. 221–242). New York: Wiley.

Bélanger, J., & Gagné, F. (2006). Estimating the size of the gifted/talented population from multiple identification criteria. *Journal for the Education of the Gifted, 30*, 131–163.

Brody, L. E., & Stanley, J. C. (2005). Youths who reason exceptionally well mathematically and/or verbally: Using the MVT:D[4] model to develop their talents. In R. J. Sternberg & J. E. Davidson (Eds.), *Conceptions of giftedness* (2nd ed., pp. 20–37). Cambridge, UK: Cambridge University Press.

Carroll, J. B. (1997). Psychometrics, intelligence, and public perception. *Intelligence, 24*, 25–52.

Colangelo, N., Assouline, S., & Gross, M. U. M. (2004). *A nation deceived: How schools hold back America's brightest students.* Iowa City: The Connie Belin & Jacqueline N. Blank International Center for Gifted Education and Talent Development, The University of Iowa. Available at: http://www.accelerationinstitute. org/nation_deceived/]

Cross, T. L., & Coleman, L. J. (2005). School-based conception of giftedness. In R. J. Sternberg & J. E. Davidson (Eds.), *Conceptions of giftedness* (2nd ed., pp. 52–63). Cambridge, UK: Cambridge University Press.

DeHaan, R. F., & Havighurst, R. J. (1961). *Educating gifted children* (Revised ed.). Chicago: University of Chicago Press.

Ericsson, K. A., Krampe, R. T., & Tesch-Römer, C. (1993). The role of deliberate practice in the acquisition of expert performance. *Psychological Review, 100*, 363–406.

Feldhusen, J. F. (2005). Giftedness, talent, expertise, and creative achievement. In R. J. Sternberg & J. E. Davidson (Eds.), *Conceptions of giftedness* (2nd ed., pp. 64–79). Cambridge, UK: Cambridge University Press.

Gagné, F. (1985). Giftedness and talent: Reexamining a reexamination of the definitions. *Gifted Child Quarterly, 29*, 103–112.

Gagné, F. (1998). A proposal for subcategories within the gifted or talented populations. *Gifted Child Quarterly, 42*, 87–95.

Gagné, F. (2000). Understanding the complex choreography of talent development through DMGT-based analysis. In K. A. Heller, F. J. Mönks, R. J. Sternberg, & R. Subotnik (Eds.), *International handbook for research on giftedness and talent* (2nd ed., pp. 67–79). Oxford, UK: Pergamon Press.

Gagné, F. (2003). Transforming gifts into talents: The DMGT as a developmental theory. In N. Colangelo & G. A. Davis (Eds.), *Handbook of gifted education* (3rd ed., pp. 60–74). Boston: Allyn & Bacon.

Gagné, F. (2005). From noncompetence to exceptional talent: Exploring the range of academic achievement within and between grade levels. *Gifted Child Quarterly, 42*, 139–153.

Gagné, F. (2009). Building gifts into talents: Detailed overview of the DMGT 2.0. In B. MacFarlane & T. Stambaugh (Eds.), *Leading change in gifted education: The* festschrift *of Dr. Joyce VanTassel-Baska* (pp. 61–80). Waco, TX: Prufrock Press.

Gardner, H. (1983). *Frames of mind: The theory of multiple intelligences.* New York: Basic Books.

Gottfredson, L. S. (1997). Why g matters: The complexity of everyday life. *Intelligence, 24*, 79–132.

Marland, S. P., Jr. (1972). *Education of the gifted and talented: Report to the Congress of the United States by the U.S. Commissioner of Education.* (Government Documents, Y4.L 11/2: G36). Washington, DC: U.S. Government Printing Office.

Mitchell, B. M. (1988). The latest national assessment of gifted education. *Roeper Review, 10*, 239–240.

National Institutes of Health. (1998). *Clinical guidelines on the identification, evaluation, and treatment of overweight and obesity in adults: The evidence report* (NIH Publication No. 98-4083). Bethesda, MD: Author.

Renzulli, J. S. (1986). The Three-Ring Conception of Giftedness: A developmental model for creative productivity. In R. J. Sternberg & J. E. Davidson (Eds.), *Conceptions of giftedness* (pp. 53–92). New York: Cambridge University Press.

Terman, L. M. (1925). *Genetic studies of genius: Vol. I. Mental and physical traits of a thousand gifted children.* Stanford, CA: Stanford University Press.

U.S. Department of Education. (1993). *National excellence: A case for developing America's talent.* Washington, DC: U.S. Government Printing Office.

Vygotsky, L. S. (1978). *Mind in society: The development of higher psychological processes.* Cambridge, MA: Harvard University Press.

8

PROBLEMATIZING GIFTED EDUCATION

James H. Borland

THE NEED TO PROBLEMATIZE

Why do we exist as a field? Many, I believe, would say that the reason is to advocate for the creation and perpetuation of gifted programs, so that certain students can be identified as gifted and placed into these programs and be exposed to a differentiated curriculum. I propose that this represents a confusion of means with ends. It is the proper education of gifted students, not the creation or preservation of gifted programs, that is, or should be, our field's ultimate goal. If we view our purpose as a field as advocating for and working toward appropriate education for capable students, which is consistent with the larger goal of providing every student with an appropriate education, it becomes clear that creating and operating gifted programs is a means—only one means, and conceivably not the best means—toward achieving the larger goal.

There is, I believe, considerable benefit to be gained by stepping back and thinking radically, in the original sense of *radical*, meaning going to the root or origin, about what we ought to be doing and how we ought to be doing it. Put another way, I am suggesting a need to *problematize* gifted education. According to Suzanne Gallagher, "problematizing [is] the process of grasping an assumption, that is, a taken-for-granted way of thinking, and turning it into a question" (1999, p. 70). It involves bringing to the surface and identifying certain, often implicit, assumptions and beliefs and asking whether they really make sense and whether they admit of alternatives. I think we, as a field, would benefit from problematizing many of our beliefs and practices because we have grown too comfortable with certain "taken-for-granted" ways of thinking, and this has limited our vision and hampered our effectiveness as educators.

What form would this problematizing take? Let us start with what I think most individuals in the field would consider to be our *raison d'être*: creating gifted programs, identifying certain students as gifted, and placing those students in the programs so they can receive some form of curricular differentiation, usually educational enrichment. Although many would find that credo unexceptionable, it contains at least three beliefs that could usefully be problematized.

First, we could problematize the idea that educational enrichment is the best basis for a program for gifted students. We could then problematize the notion that gifted programs are necessary for gifted students. Finally, we could problematize the construct of the gifted student itself.

PROBLEMATIZING ENRICHMENT

The Paucity of Empirical Support for Enrichment Programs

If there is an archetypal gifted program in the United States, it is a part-time pull-out enrichment program in grades 3–5. Programs are most commonly found in the intermediate grades because identification is thought to be more problematic in the primary grades, because scheduling special programs is difficult when students move to a departmentalized system in middle school, and because honors and Advanced Placement classes are thought, rightly or wrongly, to provide adequate differentiation in high school. Programs are usually part-time and pull-out in format because full-time programs are thought to be more "elitist," since they completely eliminate heterogeneous grouping for students identified as gifted. And enrichment is the norm in such programs because many believe that gifted students need a "special" curriculum, something other than what is found in the core curriculum. Thus, enrichment, on a part-time basis, characterizes most gifted programs.

A serious problem with enrichment programs is that there is little evidence that they are effective. According to Slavin (1990), "well-designed studies of programs for the gifted generally find few effects of separate programs for high achievers unless the programs include acceleration" (p. 486). In other words, there is ample evidence that acceleration, as a means of differentiating the curriculum for high-ability students, does what it is intended to do: match content to the instructional needs of advanced students (see e.g., Colangelo, Assouline, & Gross, 2004; Coleman & Cross, 2001; George, Cohn, & Stanley, 1977; Southern & Jones, 1991). Similar evidence that enrichment is an effective means of meeting goals, other than the goal of providing enrichment, is exiguous at best.

Twenty years ago, Shore, Cornell, Robinson, and Ward, in their landmark *Recommended Practices in Gifted Education* (1991), wrote that since the time when "Passow (1958) remarked on the dearth of research on enrichment three decades ago . . . the situation has changed little." (p. 82). They concluded that, because of an absence of empirical support, the frequently recommended practice, that "[e]nrichment should be a program component," was not among those substantiated, wholly or in part, by research, but was instead among the practices "applicable to all children" (p. 286).

Two studies stand out as worthy of serious consideration. In a meta-analysis focusing on the effects of pull-out programs, Vaughn, Feldhusen, and Asher (1991) conclude that "pull-out models in gifted education have significant positive effects" (p. 92). However, this meta-analysis drew on only nine studies, although it examined outcomes related to four dependent variables. A worthy attempt to address the problem of the lack of efficacy studies was the study on learning outcomes conducted by the National Research Center on the Gifted and Talented (Delcourt, Loyd, Cornell, & Goldberg, 1994). The subjects of this study were either in gifted programs of one kind or another, including pull-out enrichment programs, or in no program at all. Students in the latter group included students identified as gifted, formally and informally, and others nominated by teachers as comparison subjects for the study. The authors conclude that the students in their sample who were in gifted programs academically outperformed both students given special provisions within heterogeneous classrooms and students receiving no provisions at all. The problem with this conclusion is that the students whose academic performance was superior were formally identified as gifted and placed in special programs. The students with whom they were compared were either students identified, formally or informally, as gifted, but not placed in programs; or students not identified as gifted at all (and thus obviously not in programs) who were nominated for the study by teachers. There is reason to suspect that the groups were not really comparable, that students formally identified and placed in gifted programs may be different in non-trivial ways from students who were not in programs and those who were not identified as gifted, and that these differences, as much as anything else, might have affected the outcomes.

Other Problems With Enrichment Programs

Lack of Scope and Sequence

Enrichment programs can be criticized on non-empirical grounds as well. For example, based on what I have observed in numerous pull-out programs, what passes for a curriculum lacks scope and sequence of learning activities. If a gifted program is justifiable, it must address identified educational needs in a logical sequence, not just consist of whatever entertaining activities a beleaguered teacher can invent with minimal support and resources. (See Chapter 20 by Brighton and Wiley on quality indicators for pull-out programs for examples of how such programs can be implemented in defensible ways.[1]) We would not tolerate this in any other aspect of public education. The idea of, say, a mathematics curriculum without a scope and sequence is absurd on the face of it.

Separation From the "Real" Curriculum

In addition, what passes for curriculum in pull-out programs is often totally divorced from the students' regular curriculum, leading to two separate but hardly equal experiences: the gifted program and "real" school. "Real" school consists of important work in the essential subject areas, work that is structured and sequenced and frequently evaluated. The gifted program, in contrast, is often marginal to real academic work and can be seen as non-essential by students, as an option, not a necessity. As a result, pull-out enrichment programs can lack academic rigor (Sawyer, 1988a, 1988b).

The Undifferentiated Differentiated Curriculum

Finally, there is a curious paradox inherent in most enrichment programs. Gifted programs purportedly exist to provide gifted students with differentiated curriculum, the need for which justifies the programs' existence. However, within these programs, there is typically little, if any, differentiation. All students experience the same enrichment at the same time, suggesting that they are all part of a monolithic population of generically gifted students. Assuming, perhaps erroneously, that I have sufficiently problematized enrichment as a basis for gifted programs to raise some questions as to its efficacy, does this simply mean that we need to make our programs stronger? Although that is one possible course of action, I suggest we go further and problematize the assumption that gifted education requires gifted programs.

PROBLEMATIZING GIFTED PROGRAMS

A number of years ago (Borland, 1996), I suggested that it might be a useful thought experiment to consider whether effective gifted education could be achieved without gifted programs. I have since come to see this less as a useful thought experiment and more as sound educational policy. Returning to the means–ends issue I raised above, I think we have to question the extent to which our most common means—gifted programs—achieves our desired end: effective education for students typically identified as gifted. I submit that, in this respect, gifted programs fall short.

Alternatives to Pull-out Enrichment Programs

To a great extent, I advanced this position above by arguing that enrichment, our most common form of programmatic differentiation, is of questionable efficacy. One might assert, however, that there are types of gifted programs which might be more effective. For example, the Enrichment Triad/Revolving Door approach (e.g., Renzulli & Reis, 1986), later expanded into the Schoolwide Enrichment Model (e.g., Renzulli & Reis, 1997), differs from typical enrichment programs in that students move in and out of the program as they become, or cease to be, gifted—operationally defined as the possession of above-average ability, creativity, and task commitment. Moreover, there is no single curriculum imposed on all students irrespective of their interests and needs; students investigate real-world problems of their own choosing, individually or in small groups. In addition, the Enrichment Triad Model has been based on and supported by actual research findings (see e.g., Gubbins, 1995).

There is much to recommend in this approach; however, one can raise some questions that, depending on how they are answered, may vitiate assertions that the existence of the Enrichment Triad/Revolving Door approach is sufficient to establish the desirability of gifted programs as the best means to the end of gifted education. For one thing, one could ask whether every student identified as gifted ought to be doing independent research; and whether other students, not identified as gifted, might not also be able to engage in such research and benefit from the experience. There is also a question regarding the extent to which programs that purport to be based on the Enrichment Triad/Revolving Door model really adhere to the model's essential tenets. With sufficient fidelity to the model as envisioned by Renzulli and Reis, the Enrichment Triad/Revolving Door model avoids some of the pitfalls of typical pull-out enrichment programs. The problem is that achieving this fidelity is not easy, and in too many schools, it is not achieved. And there is also the problem, in my view, of the separation of the program from the heart of the school curriculum (although Renzulli would certainly disagree; see Renzulli, 1987).

Acceleration as a Program

But what about acceleration, for which there is ample empirical support? Do the findings in favor of acceleration not suggest that gifted programs can lead to effective gifted education? I believe not. Few gifted programs specifically identified as gifted programs use acceleration as their primary means of meeting the needs of gifted students because, although it is strongly supported by research data, acceleration is controversial, misunderstood, and even feared (again, see e.g., Colangelo et al., 2004; Coleman & Cross, 2001; Southern & Jones, 1991).

Moreover, schools can, and do, employ acceleration without having gifted programs *per se*. Acceleration does not require identifying students as "gifted" or hiring special teachers or creating pull-outs or having any of the ordinary trappings of traditional gifted programs. If students are capable of working well beyond the level of their age peers in a subject area, they can simply be allowed to do so; there is no reason to have a gifted program as a gifted program *per se*. To sound a theme to which I will return later, acceleration is one example of how gifted education can be effected without either gifted programs or gifted students.

Having a Program in Order to Have a Program

I want to return to my experience evaluating and otherwise working with gifted programs in a number of schools and school districts over a period of nearly 40 years. When I conduct a program evaluation, one of the first things I do is to ask administrators why they have a gifted program. More often than not, this proves to be a surprisingly difficult question for them to answer. What the answer almost always boils down to is that they have a program in order to have a program. Educators assume that a gifted program is something they ought to have, but when pressed to delineate the specific educational needs the program exists to address, they often are at a loss.

I think this is why it is so rare to find a sound scope and sequence in most gifted programs. Few have taken the time to determine what certain students need that is not found in the core curriculum, and then used that knowledge to structure a gifted program.

A Part-time Versus a Full-time Solution

No matter how exemplary a gifted pull-out program might be, gifted students will spend a small percentage of their school time in it. The rest of the time, they are in heterogeneously grouped classrooms, at least in the elementary grades, where the overwhelming majority of gifted programs are found. This suggests that even the best pull-out programs are not comprehensive educational programs.

There are two alternatives to part-time gifted programs. One is full-time, homogeneously grouped gifted programs, which are uncommon outside large metropolitan areas, such as New York City, where they do predominate. However, this is not a real alternative for most highly able students because there is strong sentiment against such programs, deriving from a perception that because they group students homogeneously on a full-time basis, full-time programs are elitist. The other alternative is to focus on where gifted students spend the great majority of their time: the mixed-ability regular classroom. The only way gifted students can hope to receive an appropriate education in a heterogeneous classroom is for that classroom to be differentiated, as Tomlinson (e.g., 2001, 2004) and others have advocated. Nothing would bring about excellent education for gifted students (and other students as well) as much as effective differentiation.

Having worked with school districts that have undertaken efforts to create differentiated classrooms, I understand how difficult this goal is to achieve. It is not enough for administrators to declare that differentiation is *policy*; they must provide the resources and possess the patience required for differentiation to become *practice*. Convincing some teachers not to teach to the whole class all of the time or not to "teach to the middle" can be extremely difficult. In even the most successful situations, progress toward differentiation will inevitably be slow and incremental. Differentiation is difficult, but it is more difficult to conceive of effective education, education with professional integrity, without it.

Compared with creating a truly differentiated school district, implementing a gifted program is relatively easy. But, for me, this is a choice between an easier course of action with minimal, at best part-time, results; and an admittedly long, hard road with significant, comprehensive benefits for gifted students and, not coincidentally, other students as well, in a context that even educators outside the field of gifted education find philosophically palatable.

PROBLEMATIZING GIFTEDNESS

I want to take this line of reasoning a significant step further. If we problematize enrichment and pull-out programs for the gifted sufficiently to bring us to the point of questioning their axiomatic necessity, can we not go further and trouble the notion of the gifted student? In other words, can we consider the possibility of gifted education without gifted students (see also Borland 2003, 2005, 2009a)?

Giftedness as a Social Construct

Whereas enrichment is an educational practice and gifted programs are educational structural arrangements, giftedness as applied to students in schools is a social construct. That is to say, it is something that was not discovered but invented. Unlike, say, the planet Uranus, which has existed much longer than we have as a species, but remained undiscovered until William Herschel observed it in 1781 (see Holmes, 2008, for a fascinating account), gifted students as a distinct school sub-population only came into existence when certain historical forces in the second decade of the 20th century (including compulsory education laws, increased immigration, and especially the advent and widespread adoption of mental testing in schools) created a situation in which educators and psychologists felt a need for an organizing principle, a construct, that allowed them to make sense of observed phenomena (e.g., variance in scores on mental tests). Unlike heavenly bodies or subatomic particles or such things—things that exist whether humans are aware of them or not (with apologies to adherents of subjective idealism)— social constructs are human creations that reflect our attempt to make sense of the world around us.

According to this way of thinking, there were no students labeled gifted in our schools in the 19th century because the construct had not come into being. Certainly, there were students who were remarkably precocious, unusually clever, or academically able, but the understanding that they were representative of a group of students with certain defining characteristics that set them apart from other students and defined them as a discrete sub-population was not widely accepted among educators. Therefore, gifted students, as we know them today, did not exist. It was not until educators and psychologists felt the need for the construct that it was created and gifted students came into existence.

To state that giftedness among school students is a social construct is not, *ipso facto*, to deny its importance or legitimacy. Many of the important things we deal with in education and the social sciences are social constructs—such things as intelligence, creativity, disability, depression, and the like. What it does mean is that since we created the construct, we are responsible for its consequences. We therefore need to examine it critically in order to determine the extent to which it has served us well and whether we are better off as a result of its creation.

I believe that a critical analysis of the construct of the gifted student—problematizing if you like—is a healthy and useful undertaking. This first requires establishing criteria for judging the construct, and I propose three. The first is a logical criterion—to what extent does the construct of the gifted student make sense? The second is a pragmatic and utilitarian criterion—to what extent has the existence of the construct led to practices whose outcomes are positive and beneficial? And the third is a moral criterion—to what extent has the existence of the construct led to practices whose outcomes are morally defensible? I believe that, with respect to these three criteria, the construct of giftedness has failed us.

The Logical Criterion

For nearly a century, our profession's response to the fact that children differ in the ways in which they interact with the school curriculum (or curricula, including the informal and hidden curricula; see e.g., Martin, 1983) has been to believe that much of this difference is the result of the existence of distinct groups of children, including gifted children, who possess characteristics that separate them from the average. Once one accepts that there exist separate qualitatively different groups, the inevitable next steps are to try to fashion a workable definition of the populations whose existence has been posited, to develop and implement identification procedures to locate these populations, and then to develop and implement separate educational provisions to meet their needs. This is the course of action that was adopted and, I would argue, is why we have gifted children today.

There is an inescapable circularity in the reasoning here, especially with respect to giftedness. Sapon-Shevin writes:

> Participants agree—sometimes explicitly and sometimes tacitly—to a common definition and then act as though that definition represents an objectifiably identifiable category. In this way, the category assumes a life of its own, and members of the school organization learn common definitions and rules.
>
> (Sapon-Shevin, 1994, p. 121)

In other words, the category was created in advance of the identification of its members, and the identification of the members of the category is both predicated on the belief that the category exists and serves, in a circular fashion, to confirm the category's existence.

This simplistic dichotomization of humanity into two distinct, mutually exclusive groups, the gifted and the rest (the average? the non-gifted? the ungifted?), is so contrary to our experience of life in a variety of other spheres of human endeavor as to cause one to wonder how it has survived so long in this one. And are these two groups—the gifted and the rest—the discrete, discontinuous, structured wholes that this crude taxonomy implies? That is, is giftedness really its own thing, qualitatively different and apart from averageness or normality, making those who possess it markedly different, different in kind, from the rest of humanity? Can such a notion, expressed in those terms at least, really ring true for many people?

However implausible, these beliefs are implicit in the manner in which the word *gifted* is employed in both professional and everyday discourse. We routinely talk about "identifying *the* gifted." In other words, we treat giftedness as a thing, a reality, something that people, especially children, either have or do not have; something with an existence of its own independent of our conceiving or naming of it.

Even a casual examination of the field of gifted education illustrates how difficult this dichotomy is to put into consistent and ultimately defensible practice. I frequently talk to my students about something I facetiously call "geographical giftedness," the not-uncommon phenomenon whereby a gifted child, so-labeled by his or her school district, finds him- or herself no longer gifted after moving to another school system that uses a different definition of giftedness. Prior to a certain date, the student was a gifted child; after that date, he or she is "average." If we hold onto the notion of two discrete classes of humans, defined by measurable traits, into which children can be placed through correct educational assessment, we can explain this child's existential crisis only in terms of measurement error or one school system's adherence to an "incorrect" definition of giftedness.

But what is a "correct" definition of giftedness? Our failure, as a field, to answer that question is reflected in the multiplicity of definitions that have been proposed over the years. Sternberg and Davidson's (2005) anthology, *Conceptions of Giftedness*, sets forth 23 definitions of giftedness, which are remarkable for their variety and divergence, yet do not begin to exhaust the explicit definitions of giftedness, let alone the implicit ones and the operational definitions used by schools.

All of this strongly suggests that "the gifted" and "the average," rather than being pre-existing human genera, are labels for socially constructed groups that are constituted, both in theory and in practice, in ways that are far from consistent and, in many cases, anything but logical, systematic, or scientific. Giftedness has become (probably always was) what Stuart Hall (e.g., 1997), writing about race, calls a "floating signifier," a semiotic term

> [V]ariously defined as a signifier with a vague, highly variable, unspecifiable or non-existent signified. Such signifiers mean different things to different people: they may stand for many or even *any* signifieds; they may mean whatever their interpreters want them to mean.
>
> (Chandler, 2001, p. 33)

The Pragmatic and Utilitarian Criterion

I will give this criterion short shrift because, in previous sections of this chapter, I developed the argument that the practical application of the construct of giftedness in educational practice, leading to the creation of gifted programs, especially pull-out enrichment programs, has not resulted in beneficial educational outcomes.

The Moral Criterion

From the beginning, the practice of gifted education has been criticized on the grounds that it is at odds with education in a democracy and that it violates principles of equity that are, or ought to be, paramount in U.S. society. Gifted programs and their proponents have been called "elitist" and worse, and advocates of gifted education have been seen as the last-ditch defenders of tracking and other damaging educational practices (Oakes, 1985). Educators in this field have vigorously countered these charges, denying both that their goals are anti-egalitarian and that gifted programs are necessarily anti-democratic.

These defenses of the field, defenses in which I have participated (e.g., Borland, 1989), are sincere in that educators in the field of gifted education see their advocacy of gifted programs as a means of helping to realize the goal of an appropriate education for all children, regardless of exceptionality. They see gifted education as redressing a wrong, as a way of making the educational system meet the legitimate needs of an underserved minority. Moreover, professionals in gifted education believe that appropriate educational programs for students identified as gifted can be implemented without being elitist, racist, sexist, or blighted by socio-economic inequities.

If, as I believe, the intentions of educators in the field of gifted education are unexceptionable, I also think it is the case that the results of our efforts far too often betray the purity of our intentions. Sufficient evidence exists to suggest that the practice of gifted education is rife with inequities that have proven to be extremely difficult to eliminate. Racial inequalities in the identification of gifted students have been a constant throughout our history (see e.g., Borland & Wright, 1994; Ford, 1996; Ford & Harris 1999; Passow, 1989; VanTassel-Baska, Patton, & Prillaman, 1989), and they persist today.

With regard to socio-economic inequity, which, of course, in our society is not unrelated to racial and ethnic inequity, The National Educational Longitudinal Study of eighth-grade programs for gifted students (U.S. Department of Education, 1991) reveals the extent of the problem. Data from this study indicate that students whose families' socio-economic status places them in the top quartile of the population are about five times more likely to be in programs for gifted students than are students from families in the bottom quartile. Despite decades of efforts to eliminate racial and socio-economic imbalances in how gifted students are identified and educated, gifted programs have continued to serve middle- and upper-middle-class children to a degree disproportionate to their numbers in the population, while underserving poor children and children of color. It is worth repeating that this fact has nearly always been seen, within the professional field, as wrong and remediable. However, the persistence of the problem tempts one to question just how tractable the problem is within the field as it is currently established (see Borland & Wright, 2001, for a pessimistic speculation).

I think that two things are indisputably true. The first is that professionals in the field of gifted education, no less than any other group of educators, are opposed to racial and other forms of inequity, and are committed to fairness in access to education. Indeed, most would argue that educational equity is what brought them to the field in the first place. The second is that, despite the best of intentions, gifted education, as historically and currently practiced, mirrors, and perhaps perpetuates, vicious inequities in U.S. society.

Gifted Education Without Gifted Students

If problematizing the construct of gifted students leads to one degree or another of disenchantment with the construct, even leading to a dismissal of the construct as incoherent and meaningless, does that mean the end of gifted education? As I suggest above, this does not have to be the case. I am willing to entertain the idea that gifted education requires neither gifted programs nor gifted students and may even be more effective without them.

Differentiated classrooms in which students receive instruction tailored to their needs on a day-by-day, subject-by-subject basis would eliminate the classroom problems that afflict students currently placed in gifted programs without having to label students as gifted or (implicitly) ungifted and placing the former in enrichment programs of dubious quality. This is a tall order, but so are such things as closing the achievement gap and achieving universal literacy, goals that are dauntingly difficult but morally necessary. To paraphrase Robert F. Kennedy quoting George Bernard Shaw (http://en.wikiquote.org/wiki/George_Bernard_Shaw), in addition to looking at things as they are and asking, "Why?" (i.e., problematizing), we ought to be dreaming of things that never were and asking, "Why not?"

CONCLUSION

I have attempted in this chapter to undermine some of the most fundamental articles of faith in the field of gifted education: that enrichment works; that gifted education requires gifted programs; and, finally, that the notion of giftedness among school students makes sense and results in positive outcomes. Many, if not most, people in the field of gifted education, I suspect, would reject my arguments out of hand. That is well and good; intellectual disagreement and debate are healthy signs in any discipline or field of practice. What I would find disturbing would not be disagreement with my conclusions, but dismissal of the value of problematizing our most cherished notions.

A decade and a half ago, I wrote an article entitled "Gifted Education and the Threat of Irrelevance" (1996) in which I suggested that, as a field, we have a "fear of the big questions" (p. 133). By this I meant that we let others explore questions we find to be too controversial and thereby cede to others important intellectual territory that ought to be ours. We need to reclaim those "big questions" that others, including some not so friendly to our purposes, have laid claim to. Problematizing our most fundamental beliefs would be a good step in that direction.

NOTE

1. This statement was added by the editors.

REFERENCES

Borland, J. H. (1989). *Planning and implementing programs for the gifted.* New York: Teachers College Press.
Borland, J. H. (1996). Gifted education and the threat of irrelevance. *Journal for the Education of the Gifted, 19,* 129–147.
Borland, J. H. (2003). The death of giftedness. In J. H. Borland (Ed.), *Rethinking gifted education* (pp. 105–124). New York: Teachers College Press.
Borland, J. H. (2005). Gifted education without gifted children: The case for no conception of giftedness. In R. J. Sternberg & J. E. Davidson (Eds.), *Conceptions of giftedness* (2nd ed., pp. 1–19). New York: Cambridge University Press.

Borland, J. H. (2009a). Gifted education without gifted programs or gifted students: Differentiation of curriculum and instruction as an instructional model for gifted students. In J. S. Renzulli, E. J. Gubbins, K. S. McMillen, R. D. Eckert, & C. A. Little (Eds.), *Systems & models for the education of gifted & talented students* (2nd ed., pp. 105–118). Mansfield Center, CT: Creative Learning Press.

Borland, J. H. (2009b, February 17). Gifted kids deserve better: Time to fix the city's failed G&T plan. *New York Daily News*, p. 25.

Borland, J. H., & Wright, L. (1994). Identifying young, potentially gifted, economically disadvantaged students. *Gifted Child Quarterly, 38*, 164–171.

Borland, J. H., & Wright, L. (2001). Identifying and educating poor and under-represented gifted students. In Heller, K. A., Mönks, F. J., Sternberg, R. J., & Subotnik, R. F. (Eds.), *International handbook of research and development of giftedness and talent* (pp. 587–594). Oxford, UK: Pergamon Press.

Chandler, D. (2001). *Semiotics for beginners*. Retrieved September 3, 2011 from http://www.aber.ac.uk/media/ Documents/ S4B/semiotic.html

Colangelo, N., Assouline, S., & Gross, M. U. M. (2004). *A nation deceived. How schools hold back America's brightest students*. Iowa City: Connie Belin & Jacqueline N. Blank International Center for Gifted Education and Talent Development, The University of Iowa.

Coleman, L. J., & Cross, T. L. (2001). *Being gifted in school: An introduction to development, guidance, and teaching*. Waco, TX: Prufrock Press.

Cox, J., Daniel, N., & Boston, B. (1985). *Educating able learners*. Austin: University of Texas Press.

Delcourt, M. A. B., Loyd, B. H., Cornell, D. G., & Goldberg, M. D. (1994). *Evaluation of the effects of programming arrangements on student learning outcomes*. Charlottesville: The National Research Center on the Gifted and Talented, University of Virginia.

Ford, D. Y. (1996). *Reversing underachievement among gifted Black students*. New York: Teachers College Press.

Ford, D. Y., & Harris, J. J., III (1999). *Multicultural gifted education*. New York: Teachers College Press.

Gallagher, S. (1999). An exchange of gazes. In J. L. Kinchloe, S. R. Steinberg, & L. E. Villeverde (Eds.), *Rethinking intelligence* (pp. 69–84). New York: Routledge.

George, W. C., Cohn, S. J., & Stanley, J. C. (1977). *Educating the gifted: Acceleration and enrichment. Proceedings of the Ninth Annual Hyman Blumberg Symposium on Research in Early Childhood Education*. Baltimore: Johns Hopkins University Press.

Gubbins, E. J. (Ed.). (1995). *Research related to the Enrichment Triad Model*. (Research Monograph 95212). Storrs: The National Research Center on the Gifted and Talented, University of Connecticut.

Hall, S. (Ed.). (1997). *Representation: Cultural representations and signifying practices (Culture, media and identities, Vol. 2)*. Thousand Oaks, CA: Sage.

Holmes, R. (2008). *The age of wonder: How the romantic generation discovered the beauty and terror of science*. London: HarperPress.

Martin, J. (1983). What should we do with a hidden curriculum when we find one? In H. Giroux, & D. Purpel (Eds.), *The hidden curriculum and moral education* (pp. 122–139). Berkeley, CA: McCutchan.

Oakes, J. (1985). *Keeping track: How schools structure inequality*. New Haven, CT: Yale University Press.

Passow, A. H. (1958). Enrichment of education for the gifted. In N. B. Henry (Ed.), *Education for the gifted. Fifty-seventh yearbook of the National Society for the Study of Education: Part II* (pp. 193–221). Chicago: University of Chicago Press.

Passow, A. H. (1989). Needed research and development in educating high ability children. *Roeper Review, 11*, 223–229.

Renzulli, J. S. (1987). The positive side of pull-out programs. *Journal for the Education of the Gifted, 10*, 245–264.

Renzulli, J. S., & Reis, S. M. (1986). The Enrichment Triad/Revolving Door Model: A schoolwide plan for the development of creative productivity. In J. S. Renzulli (Ed.), *Systems and models for developing programs for the gifted and talented* (pp. 216–266). Mansfield Center, CT: Creative Learning Press.

Renzulli, J. S., & Reis, S. M. (1997). *The Schoolwide Enrichment Model: A how-to guide for educational excellence*. Mansfield Center, CT: Creative Learning Press.

Sapon-Shevin, M. (1994). *Playing favorites: Gifted education and the disruption of community*. Albany: State University of New York Press.

Sawyer, R. N. (1988a). In defense of academic rigor. *Journal for the Education of the Gifted, 11*, 5–19.

Sawyer, R. N. (1988b). Reply from Robert Sawyer. *Journal for the Education of the Gifted, 11*, 31–34.

Shore, B. M., Cornell, D. G., Robinson, A., & Ward, V. S. (1991). *Recommended practices in gifted education: A critical analysis*. New York: Teachers College Press.

Slavin, R. E. (1990). Achievement effects of ability grouping in secondary schools: A best-evidence synthesis. *Review of Educational Research, 60*, 471–499.

Southern, W. T., & Jones, E. D. (Eds.). (1991). *The academic acceleration of gifted children*. New York: Teachers College Press.

Sternberg, R. J., & Davidson, J. E. (Eds.). (2005). *Conceptions of giftedness* (2nd ed.). New York: Cambridge University Press.

Terman, L. M. (1925–1959). *Genetic studies of genius* (Vols. I–V). Stanford, CA: Stanford University Press.

Tomlinson, C. A. (2001). *How to differentiate instruction in mixed-ability classrooms* (2nd ed.). Alexandria, VA: Association for Supervision and Curriculum Development.

Tomlinson, C. A. (Ed.). (2004). *Differentiation for gifted and talented students*. Thousand Oaks, CA: Corwin Press.

U. S. Department of Education. (1991). *National educational longitudinal study 88. Final report: Gifted and talented education programs for eighth grade public school students*. Washington, DC: Office of Planning, Budget, and Evaluation, United States Department of Education.

VanTassel-Baska, J., Patton, J., & Prillaman, D. (1989). Disadvantaged gifted learners: At risk for educational attention. *Focus on Exceptional Children, 22*(3), 1–15.

Vaughn, V. L., Feldhusen, J. F., & Asher, W. J. (1991). Meta-analyses and review of research on pull-out programs in gifted education. *Gifted Child Quarterly, 35*, 92–98.

Section II

Identification of Giftedness

9

CONSIDERATIONS FOR IDENTIFICATION OF GIFTED AND TALENTED STUDENTS

An Introduction to Identification

Carolyn M. Callahan, Joseph S. Renzulli, Marcia A. B. Delcourt and Holly L. Hertberg-Davis

The term *identification*, when used in an educational context, is very broad and encompasses processes that might be in place for deciding which students will be offered particular services within a school or school district, which students might be selected for a special school (e.g., a residential program in the arts or in mathematics, science, and technology), or who is given the option of attending a summer Governor's School. Before any program personnel can determine who will be selected for participation, the definition of whatever construct is to be identified must be clear and agreed upon.

Because of the many conceptions of giftedness found in the theoretical and research literature, the first and most important decision that should be made regarding practical procedures for identification of gifted students is to select a conception or definition of giftedness to guide decision making. Once consensus is reached on a definition of giftedness, this definition provides guidance in determining who needs to receive special services and the method one will use to select those students. The process of identification will, of course, vary considerably depending on how a school district defines giftedness. But in any identification plan, regardless of the definition chosen, a common set of questions can be used to guide how decision makers respond to the recurring and problematic questions surrounding the identification of students for special programs and services. These questions reflect the practical, political, and psychometric complexities of the issue:

1. How do we ensure that we have given every student equal opportunity to be considered for the services?
2. How do we ensure we will gather the data that will allow for an appropriate match between the student and curricular and programming options?

3. Will this identification system be applicable to diverse school populations and groups of students that have been historically under-represented in programs for the gifted?
4. How will we "label" students identified for these programs?
5. Will the system be economical, but effective, in terms of the personnel time, group and individual testing costs, and other resources necessary to identify our students?
6. Will the system be flexible enough to accommodate talent potential across different domains such as music, art, drama, technology, and other nonverbal or mathematical talent areas that we have included in our definition?
7. Will the system be flexible enough to make changes if student performance warrants a re-examination of selection or rejection decisions?
8. Does the system reflect the regulations of the state department of education (especially in those cases where some level of financial reimbursement is provided by state agencies for each identified gifted student)?
9. Is the system legally defensible?
10. Is the system defensible to our constituents (parents, teachers, administrators)?

Regardless of the definition of giftedness espoused, adequate answers to these questions require acceptance of some fundamental tenets.

GUIDING PRINCIPLES

Axiom 1: There Is No Such Thing as a Perfect Identification System!

Every identification system reflects decisions about instruments and criteria used to screen, identify, and place students in educational programs. Instruments, both objective tests and human evaluations of performance, always contain some error. Further, the ways in which data from the various types of information are interpreted and weighed in the decision-making process are also subject to error.

Postulate 1. The Various Components of a Definition Should Lead to Independent, Distinct Identification Procedures

When the definition of "gifted" is translated into a process for identification, each aspect of giftedness should include tests, rating scales, observational protocols, etc., that are valid and reliable for assessing the construct under consideration. For example, tests of verbal intellectual ability are not appropriate for assessing specific academic abilities in mathematics.

Postulate 2. The Identification Process Should Be Flexible and Not Reflect a Decision That Cannot Be Reconsidered

Because the process cannot be perfect, identification processes and procedures should always include mechanisms for consideration of additional information, and for appeals to an alternative set of reviewers who have not already formed opinions about a student.

Postulate 3. Identification Procedures Should Contain Multiple, Specific Means by Which Students Can Enter the Pool for Consideration at Various Points in Their School Careers

A comprehensive and defensible identification plan will recognize developmental differences in children. The operational interpretation of this postulate is providing multiple pathways to bring student gifts and talents to the attention of a screening committee. Too often, only one screening mechanism is in place. In some cases, teachers are asked to nominate students. In other cases, a general ability test is used to screen students. Both of these options have limitations; hence, program personnel should consider several sources of data in determining who will receive further consideration. In addition, a child who may not have exhibited gifted behaviors in first grade may emerge as very talented in fourth grade and merit consideration for placement. Therefore, an exemplary practice is to allow for ongoing identification by designing a means through which students whose talents emerge after the first screening and identification take place can be given consideration for receiving gifted services.

Postulate 4. In Selecting Instruments for Assessing the Various Types of Giftedness, Reliability and Validity Are Critical, but Consideration of Norms—Both the Populations on Which the Test Was Normed and When the Norming Occurred—Are Also Very Important

Any instruments adopted—a test, a rating scale, an observational protocol, or a portfolio rating scale—should be examined for current psychometric data that verify their reliability and validity. For standardized, published instruments, the technical manuals will usually provide some data, but consultation with reviews of the tests in publications such as the *Mental Measurements Yearbook* will be very informative. If using rating scales or other protocols for which the psychometric data are not available, the data must be collected locally to defend the use of the instrument.

Axiom 2: What Is Good for the Goose Is Not Good for the Gander

While sharing information on what works or does not work can provide useful background, each and every program, school, and school district is unique. Careful consideration of the combination of demographics, values, and beliefs that led to the accepted definition of giftedness should guide the development of the identification process. Even when school districts have the same or similar definitions of giftedness, the population of the school district may differ substantially, suggesting that alternative instruments or criteria are warranted.

Axiom 3: Both Objective and Subjective Instruments Can and Should Provide Useful Data in the Identification Process

Standardized tests of cognitive ability and/or academic achievement are frequently used as primary sources of data in the identification process and are considered objective because they rely on direct reflections of student performance rather than the judgment of others. But some question the objectivity of these tests because the decision to use them is, in and of itself, a subjective (and sometimes questionable) act. Imagine, for example, using an IQ test to select students for an advanced music or drama program. Others question scores on such tests because of concerns about whether or not a one-hour "glimpse" into a young person's overall potential can be considered an objective appraisal of a student's total capacity for high-level performance. Almost all other criteria (e.g., teacher, parent, peer, or self ratings, portfolio or writing sample assessments, or grades earned in school subjects) are considered to be subjective as their use implies that the persons offering judgment may be open to personal bias, an idiosyncratic view of giftedness, or inconsistent grading standards. And yet, others will argue that these types of criteria enable us to see other signs of potential such as motivation, creativity, leadership and executive functions (initiation, execution, and completion of tasks), and intense interest in a topic not reflected in more objective cognitive ability tests.

Postulate 1. The Reliability and Validity of the Instrument Are More Important Than Whether or Not It Is Objectively Scored

Use a combination of types of instrument to make screening, selection, and placement decisions. Every instrument chosen, however, should be subject to consideration of the degree to which it meets the criteria for quality decisions relating to the category of giftedness being considered. Non-test assessments are often criticized for lack of objectivity, but careful training of the raters can mitigate bias and, when used with other instruments, they can provide valuable insights into student performance and potential in areas not assessed by standardized tests.

Axiom 4: People, Not Instruments, Make Decisions so it Is Critical That Decision Makers Have the Knowledge and Skills to Make Appropriate Choices

Regardless of the number or types of instruments used in a multi-criteria identification system, instruments only provide data—they do not make decisions. It is therefore important:

1. to establish criteria used to select persons who will be involved in the information-processing and decision-making process that reflect skills and background knowledge in interpreting test and non-test data; and
2. to provide orientation and training to those on selection committees on the specific tests and non-test instruments used, the standard error of measurement on those tests, the relative importance of data from the assessments, the criteria for decision making, and the services to be offered.

Cautionary measures should be taken to ensure that some criteria are not given too much weight at the expense of others. For example, a decision to use two or three cognitive ability and/or achievement measures (e.g., aptitude test, achievement test, and course grades), and only one measure of creativity (e.g., a creativity test or a teacher rating) may result in undervaluing the creativity criterion. This consideration is important in both the design of the identification system and in the interpretation and direction provided to the committee who will review students' records and subsequently make decisions.

Axiom 5: Avoid the Multiple Criteria Smokescreen and the Matrix Mirage

Most identification systems utilize a traditional nomination/screening/selection approach, and at least part of the multiple criteria screening process is usually based on non-test information (e.g., teacher nominations and/or ratings), with test and non-test data entered into a matrix with scores assigned to given levels of performance. There are two potential problems which may arise from this process. First, if only one process (teacher nomination or testing alone) qualifies a student for further screening, many potentially gifted students may be missed. If the nomination or screening process only determines which students will be eligible to take an individual IQ test or a more advanced cognitive ability test, and the test score alone is then used to determine placement, the test becomes the ultimate "gatekeeper." In that situation, a teacher nomination or a high rating is only used as a "ticket" to take an individual or a group ability test, but it is not used as "real data." Even when decision makers use a matrix to make decisions with the belief that adding all scores together gives them equal weight, they are deluding themselves and still missing the intent of using multiple criteria. Without going into great detail, this process is simply not warranted for statistical reasons. The matrix gives the appearance of fairness and equity using multiple criteria, but most often gives undue weight to one or two test scores. Not only is it not a good practice to add together test scores measuring different constructs and based on differing normative samples, it is likely that any highly positive attributes that might have been the basis for a teacher nomination or favorable information discovered in the screening process are not really influencing the decision making because of the lack of variability in those scores. (See Chapter 13 by Tonya Moon in this book for greater explanation of the issues in the use of matrices.) The danger here is, of course, that we may be systematically excluding high-potential students from different backgrounds, or students who have shown signs of high potential in areas other than the high verbal, mathematical, or analytic skills measured by standardized tests. What appears to be the use of multiple criteria ends up being a smokescreen for a more traditional cut-off score approach.

The multi-criteria smokescreen has other unintended side effects. Often, attempts to give the *impression* of a more flexible approach result in so much paperwork that it becomes inordinately time-consuming, expensive, and unwieldy. In other cases, the smokescreen could be used to give the *appearance* of concerns for equity when such concerns do not really exist.

Postulate 1. The Use of Multiple Criteria Is Important, but Exercise Caution in how Data Are Considered and Weighed in the Decision-Making Process

As noted before, the criteria for screening and identification must be carefully constructed to ensure development of student profiles that reflect the best possible picture of student talent and to guide the best match to educational programming.

Axiom 6: The Screening and Identification Process Is Not for Labeling

Traditionally, the process of identification has simply resulted in labeling all selected students as "the gifted," thereby relegating all others to a non-gifted category. In recent years, however, a large body of research has argued very forcefully against such a broad-stroke labeling process (Frasier, García, & Passow, 1995; Gardner, 1983; Renzulli & Reis, 1997; Sternberg, 1985; Winner, 1996); and in some cases, recommendations have been made to do away with any labeling altogether (Borland, 2004). A more current trend is to document specific student strengths by preparing student profiles (Field, 2009; Renzulli & Reis, 2007). This strength-based profile can be used for making more personalized decisions about the types of resources and activities recommended for talent development. Behavioral definitions (i.e., targeting specific strengths) are considered to be important because if we know and can document particular strengths, there is a greater likelihood that schools will attempt to cultivate these strengths in targeted students. This approach also helps to introduce an element of accountability into programming and it gives direction to efforts that schools should take in evaluating their programs (Delcourt, 2007).

Labeling of any kind is always a controversial issue. It would be "nice" to think that we can do away with any kind of labeling whatsoever, but the reality is that we cannot make accommodations for students if we do not recognize individual strength areas. And experience has shown that far too many schools claiming to "differentiate" for all students have, in reality, provided minimal or no advanced-level opportunities for high-potential students.

Postulate 1. In Considering Instruments for Inclusion in the Identification Process, Seek Instruments That Will Provide Data Leading to Appropriate Education Decisions Related to Services, Curriculum, and Instruction and Then Use Those Data

Congruence between identification and programming is so important that it might be viewed as "the golden rule" of gifted education. For example, identification for advanced courses in some subject areas such as mathematics is best accomplished through mathematics testing, examination of previous mathematics grades, teacher recommendations or ratings on mathematical skills, and perhaps even estimates of a student's motivation to work hard in mathematics. A problem arises, however, when students identified as mathematically talented are placed in what might be called an "all-purpose" gifted program. An even more important issue is how much flexibility and individualization is provided in such programs. If the program has a prescribed curriculum, or if individual teachers in the program prescribe most of the activities (e.g., the teacher's favorite Rain Forest Unit or play production), then we must raise the question of whether or not we are respecting the students' ability and prior knowledge, interest, learning styles, or preferred modes of expression that fall outside of these areas. In other words, the material covered in the special program may be different from the regular curriculum, but the prescriptive nature of what is to be learned remains essentially the same approach to teaching used in regular classrooms. Therefore, a related decision in developing an identification system is the selection of a pedagogical programming model that will be used to guide direct and indirect services to students regardless of how they are grouped or organized for special program services. While organizational models must be considered in order to match students with opportunities, the teaching/learning process within any predetermined organizational arrangement should be the focus of the decision making.

AN INTRODUCTION TO IDENTIFICATION: A SUMMARY

The axioms explored above and their related postulates point out the hazards in the "landscape" surrounding the always complicated and frequently controversial topic of identifying gifted and talented students for services in special programs. This discussion of the issues does not provide ready-made answers to the many challenges of identification system design, but an understanding of the historically encountered problems may be helpful in avoiding the pitfalls faced by so many persons who have set out on the journey of creating an efficient, effective, and equitable plan for identification. These axioms can prompt and frame thinking as the authors of the chapters which follow offer their points of view on identification.

DEFINITIONS AND TERMS IN THE IDENTIFICATION FIELD

Presentations of the various approaches to identifying gifted students in this book or in the other literature in the field of gifted education incorporate certain technical terms. In order to help you prepare for those encounters, we offer these explanations and definitions.

High-stakes Tests

When a decision is to be made about a student, a teacher, a school, etc., based in part or wholly on the results of a given test, we call that a high-stakes test. For example, when a student is given a test and the score is used to make a decision about an educational placement, that is considered a high-stakes test.

Reliability

The estimated reliability of a test or other assessment tool is a measure of the degree to which one might expect a student's score to vary if he or she took the test again. It is a measure of the stability of a test score across testing times, across different versions of a test, or both. The factors that affect the reliability of a test are random-error effects. For example, if a student feels ill during a test or is tired, she might not perform as well as she does on a different day. When we administer a test and make decisions about a student's educational program, we assume that the score will be reliable—that we would get about that same score if we gave the test tomorrow or next week. It is also important that rating scales and other instruments used in the identification process have inter-rater reliability. That is, we would expect two raters of a student's work to rate that work approximately the same so that whether or not a student is regarded as performing at a high level is not reflective of the bias of the rater.

Validity

A valid test or assessment instrument yields scores that serve the purpose for which we are going to use that score, and can be documented to be measuring what it claims to measure. If we are searching for valid measures of giftedness, they must match the definition of giftedness we are using and they must predict success in the placements we have in mind for the services to be offered. A test might be valid for identifying students using one definition of giftedness and for placement in some gifted programs, but not for others. For example, a test that is valid for use in identifying students for advanced work in language arts may not be valid for identifying students for advanced work in mathematics.

Ceiling Effects

On-grade-level testing (tests given to fourth grade students that measure the objectives of fourth grade) are often "too easy" for high-performing students who would be able to demonstrate much greater learning if the items on the test were more advanced. When students get all, or nearly all, items on a test correct, the test may have a ceiling effect, meaning that it did not allow the student to demonstrate learning beyond that level of the test.

Out-of-Level Tests

Out-of-level testing is using a more advanced test than is normally administered to a child of a given age or grade level so that a more accurate measure of the student's true level of performance can be made.

Regression to the Mean

A student who scores very high or very low on a given test on a given day is not likely to earn a score at the same level if the same test, or another test measuring the same construct or content, is subsequently administered to that student. The student's score is likely to be closer to the mean on the second testing. This occurs because of random error in tests.

Norming Sample

When standardized tests are created for the purpose of comparing students to one another on some factor, decisions must be made about those to whom they will be compared. Those selected for the comparison group are the norming sample.

Norms, Standard Scores, and Percentiles

Performance on a standardized test is presented in a score that represents a student's relative standing (compared to the sample used in the norming process or to the school district population). Such a score is often called a standard score, representing how far above or below the mean a student's score lies, or a percentile which indicates the percentage of the sample that scored at or below that student (e.g., when a student earns a score in the 98th percentile, 98 percent of the sample scored at or below that student).

GUIDING QUESTIONS TO CONSIDER REGARDING IDENTIFICATION

The chapters in this section of the book include a review of both traditional and non-traditional approaches to identifying and placing gifted students. To focus your reading, keep these questions in mind:

1. What definition of gifted would be best served by the approach described?
2. What are the advantages and disadvantages of using the approach or the instruments described?
3. Would students from all populations be well served by this approach?
4. Would you supplement this approach with any other strategy to ensure equity and fairness?

REFERENCES

Borland, J. H. (2004). *Issues and practices in the identification and education of gifted students from under-represented groups.* (Research Monograph 04186). Storrs: The National Research Center on the Gifted and Talented, University of Connecticut.

Delcourt, M. A. B. (2007). The effects of programming arrangements on the achievement and self-concept of gifted elementary school students. *Gifted Child Quarterly, 54,* 359–381.

Field, G. B. (2009). The effects of the use of Renzulli Learning on student achievement in reading comprehension, reading fluency, social studies, and science: An investigation of technology and learning in grades 3–8. *International Journal of Emerging Technologies in Learning, 4,* 29–39.

Frasier, M. M., García, J. H., & Passow, A. H. (1995). *A review of assessment issues in gifted education and their implications for identifying gifted minority students.* (Research Monograph 95204). Storrs: The National Research Center on the Gifted and Talented, University of Connecticut.

Gardner, H. (1983). *Frames of mind: The theory of multiple intelligences.* New York: Basic Books.

Renzulli, J. S., & Reis, S. M. (1997). *The Schoolwide Enrichment Model: A how-to guide for educational excellence.* Mansfield Center, CT: Creative Learning Press.

Renzulli, J. S., & Reis, S. M. (2007). A technology based program that matches enrichment resources with student strengths. *International Journal of Emerging Technologies in Learning, 2.* Retrieved October 1, 2008 from http://online-journals.org/ijet/article/viewArticle/126

Sternberg, R. J. (1985). *Beyond IQ: A triarchic theory of human intelligence.* New York: Cambridge University Press.

Winner, E. (1996). *Gifted children: Myths and realities.* New York: Basic Books.

10

TRADITIONAL PERSPECTIVES ON IDENTIFICATION

Susan K. Johnsen

Traditional approaches to identifying gifted and talented students rely heavily on norm-referenced and quantified information about individual students. Differences in performance are used to make decisions about classification and programming. Johnsen (2004) describes a recommended three-phase process for identifying gifted students. The first phase, *nomination or referral*, includes the process of creating a pool of all students who exhibit any or some of the characteristics that might indicate a special gift and/or talent. Nomination assessments may include teacher and parent checklists, group intelligence and achievement tests, portfolios of work, peer and self-nominations, teacher reports of students' learning, performance on problem-solving activities, and/or student background information.

During the next phase in the process, *screening/assessment*, a school committee selects some of the students for further screening, which may include individually administered measures or methods that allow for more clinical observations or the collection of other data needed for decision making. Sometimes all of the students are screened; in other cases, only 20–25 percent, depending upon state or local education agencies' rules and regulations. To ensure equal access, however, multiple sources and measures are used in decision making during the screening phase.

During the final phase of the identification process, *selection/placement*, the placement committee examines all data collected on each child during the previous two phases. The placement committee then determines which students are selected for gifted programming. The percentage of students placed in the program varies depending on the number of programming options and the number of students whose characteristics indicate a need for services. The committee may also design an individual plan for the student that identifies long- and short-term goals, classroom activities, and evaluation.

Every effort should be made to ensure consideration of students from special populations such as those with disabilities, English-language learners, and students from minority or lower-income backgrounds and from rurally isolated areas. While traditional approaches vary from one another and from the steps described above, all distinguish a group of students who will receive specialized services in gifted education from those who will not receive these services.

FACTORS INFLUENCING TRADITIONAL APPROACHES TO IDENTIFICATION

Traditional approaches to identifying gifted students are based primarily on federal and state definitions, standards-based practices, state rules and regulations, and/or program characteristics. At the core of these factors lies educators' explicit or implicit theoretical understanding of giftedness and gifted education. Each of these factors interacts with one another and ultimately affects the overall identification process.

Federal and State Definitions

The majority of states use some form of the federal definition of giftedness, which includes multiple domains: intellectually gifted (85 percent of states use this domain), creatively gifted (65 percent), performing/visual arts (62.5 percent), academically gifted (57.5 percent), specific academic areas (52.5 percent), and leadership (42.5 percent) (The Council of State Directors of Programs for the Gifted [CSDPG] & National Association for Gifted Children [NAGC], 2009). Only 29 of the states, however, actually require local education agencies (LEAs) to apply the state definition (CSDPG & NAGC, 2009). As a result, definitions not only vary across states, but also across LEAs within a state.

Standards-based Practices

Standards for identifying and assessing gifted students include selecting technically adequate instruments, using non-biased and equitable approaches, using multiple criteria and sources, and using guidelines for interpreting results (CEC–TAG & NAGC, 2006; NAGC, 1998, 2010). The Office for Civil Rights created a checklist for the assessment of gifted programs, which emphasizes the importance of equal access (Trice & Shannon, 2002). In addition, states have developed rules and regulations, with 26 requiring specific criteria or methods to be used in the identification process (CSDPG & NAGC, 2009). Even though 21 states recommend using multiple criteria and 23 recommend use of multiple sources of information (e.g., parents, teachers, and the student) (CSDPG & NAGC, 2009), only eight states require LEAs to follow a specific identification procedure. The freedom to develop not only a definition for gifted and talented students, but also the procedures for identifying them, creates even greater variation between states and local education agencies.

Program Characteristics

Another influence on identification procedures is the program's characteristics. What area(s) of giftedness is the program intended to serve? Is it student-interest driven? Is it content- or course-driven, such as Advanced Placement courses? The traditional identification procedure should focus on finding students who will benefit academically and socially from the program.

Louis, Subotnik, Breland, and Lewis (2000) describe how programs establish admission criteria based on both the program and the students' characteristics. For example, the Juilliard School's pre-college program uses auditions, cut-off scores on a standardized test, and referrals from a network of outstanding teachers who serve as talent scouts.

They look for students who have "a combination of innate musicality and musical intelligence, honed by years of dedicated practice under the guidance of a superb teacher" (Louis et al., p. 304). Hunter College Elementary School, which focuses on general intelligence, abstract reasoning, and non-intellective traits such as creativity, motivation, task commitment, and attention span, selects students based on an intelligence-test score, a set of four problem-solving activities, and observations of children's classroom interactions.

Implicit or Explicit Theoretical Understanding

Another major factor that influences the traditional approach is educators' implicit or explicit theoretical understandings of giftedness. If educators involved in establishing the identification procedures believe that intelligence is unitary, primarily innate, and stable, then they are more likely to select assessments that measure general intellectual functioning and expect that a student who has a high intelligence score is gifted across all domains and will be able to perform in any number of areas. If they believe that giftedness is more domain-related and diverse (e.g., independent abilities) (Guilford, 1967; Thorndike, 1931; Thurstone, 1938), then they are more likely to select alternative assessments such as performance checklists and/or products that measure specific domains. Furthermore, if they believe that giftedness is developmental and includes a set of interacting components such as general intelligence, domain-related skills, creativity, and non-intellective factors (Cattell, 1971; Gagné, 1999; Renzulli, 1978; Tannenbaum, 1991), then they would select multiple assessments that address each of the interacting components; for example, general intelligence tests, achievement tests, observations in the classroom over time, product portfolios, and other identification tools.

Not only do educators' understandings of giftedness influence the selection of assessments but also the criteria they set for decision making. Should students who receive gifted services perform in the top 2 percent, 5 percent, or 10 percent? Is the comparison to other students' performance made within the LEA or with a national sample? Is a high score required on an intelligence test and/or an achievement test? If educators believe in innate intelligence, a high score on an intelligence test would certainly be a part of the identification process and be heavily weighted in selecting students for placement. In contrast, if educators believe giftedness is multifaceted, then variations in assessment scores would be expected, and different decision criteria would be established. As Gagné notes in Chapter 7 in this book, if educators adopt a more disjunctive definition (e.g., a student might be gifted in visual arts, or in creativity, or in mathematics, etc.) and identify students in the top 10 percent within each area of giftedness, then an LEA might serve 30–40 percent of the population.

In practice, 15 states require intelligence tests (CSDPG & NAGC, 2009), which connotes a belief in the importance of aptitude. However, most states also require multiple measures, implying that giftedness may be exhibited in diverse ways. The number of students that may receive funding, however, is limited (e.g., 4 percent of a school district's population in Arizona; 5 percent in Arkansas; 1 percent in Nebraska; 3 percent in Washington) (CSDPG & NAGC, 2009). This limitation may influence the theory of giftedness embraced by educators as they create more exclusive definitions to meet state standards (e.g., serve only students who are academically able).

HOW THE TRADITIONAL IDENTIFICATION PROCESS SUPPORTS A DEFENSIBLE DEFINITION

Traditional approaches do not adhere to or support any one definition because of the variations in the factors that influence the identification process. However, the effects of the process have raised important issues in the field of gifted education. Two major issues are the under-representation of special populations and the dynamic nature of giftedness.

Under-representation

The under-representation of minority students in gifted education has been well documented (Daniels, 1998; Ford & Harris, 1994; Morris, 2002). Procedures that have been identified as potential bases for exclusion include selective referrals (Frasier, Garcia, & Passow, 1995; Peterson & Margolin, 1997), test bias (Frasier et al., 1995), over-reliance on traditional tests (Ford & Harmon, 2001; Maker, 1996), and educators' attitudes (Harris, Plucker, Rapp, & Martinez, 2009; Soto, 1997).

Selective Referrals

Teachers often develop their own conceptions of giftedness and nominate children who reflect these conceptions (Hunsaker, 1994; Neumeister, Adams, Pierce, Cassady, & Dixon, 2007; Plata & Masten, 1998). For example, teachers are more likely to give higher ratings to students who do not match gender stereotypes (Siegle & Powell, 2004), have interests in unusual areas (Siegle & Powell, 2004), are academically able (Guskin, Peng, & Simon, 1992; Hunsaker, Finley, & Frank, 1997), are from higher socio-economic status groups (Guskin et al., 1992), and are verbal and well-mannered (Dawson, 1997; Neumeister et al., 2007; Schack & Starko, 1990) than to nominate those who are economically disadvantaged (Peterson & Margolin, 1997) or English-language learners (Plata & Masten, 1998). Under-referral is a problem for parents as well (Frasier et al., 1995). For example, fewer minority parents request an evaluation of their child for possible gifted and talented programming (Scott, Perou, Urbano, Hogan, & Gold, 1992). Gifted students with disabilities are particularly vulnerable in traditional identification approaches because their patterns of strengths and weaknesses make them appear to have average abilities and achievement (Morrison & Rizza, 2007; Waldron & Saphire, 1990). In fact, Barnard-Brak, Johnsen, and Pond (2009) found that only 11.1 percent of students with disabilities who were potentially gifted were participating in programs for gifted and talented students.

Test Bias

Frasier et al. (1995) argued that "standardized tests discriminate against students whose linguistic and perceptual orientation, cognitive style, learning and response styles, economic status, and cultural or social background differed from the dominant norm group" (p. viii). Other researchers agree that special populations of gifted students perform poorly on norm-referenced, standardized intelligence tests (Ford, 1998; Ford & Harmon, 2001; Maker, 1996). Tests may indeed be biased if they do not address four major areas of concern (Ryser, 2004a): a representative normative sample that includes all groups; reduced language demands for students from linguistically different backgrounds; items and formats that are not biased against certain cultural and socio-economic groups; and usefulness in predicting all students' success in the gifted education program.

Over-reliance on Traditional Tests

While 21 states use multiple criteria, 26 states require traditional testing using one or more traditional assessments (intelligence or achievement tests) (CSDPG & NAGC, 2009). If biased, these tests might exclude special populations. Therefore, many researchers advocate the use of nontraditional or alternative assessments to allow students to show evidence of potential (Callahan, Hunsaker, Adams, Moore, & Bland, 1995; Ford, 1996; Frasier et al., 1995). Studies indicate that minority students perform better on these alternative forms of assessment than on traditional assessments (Borland & Wright, 1994; Pierce et al., 2007; Reid, Udall, Romanoff, & Algozzine, 1999; VanTassel-Baska, Johnson, & Avery, 2002).

Educators' Attitudes

Because educators are involved in most aspects of identification, their attitudes can influence the decisions relative to which students are referred, and also who is selected and served. In particular, cultural prejudice and indifference (Passow & Frasier, 1996), negative cultural perceptions toward giftedness (Morris, 2002), low teacher expectations (Alviderez & Weinstein, 1999; Johnsen & Ryser, 1994), and negative reactions toward non-English speaking students (Soto, 1997) and lower socio-economic status (SES) students (McBee, 2006) have been noted as potential sources of bias.

The Dynamic Nature of Giftedness

Traditional assessment has prided itself on delivering reliable and valid estimates of students' current abilities. These approaches rely on the notion that performance is stable and that scores on intelligence or achievement tests and other types of products will identify those students with exceptional gifts or talents. However, questions have arisen about the degree to which a one-point-in-time assessment is sufficient to identify learning potential, particularly with students from low-income backgrounds with limited school-related experiences (Banks & Neisworth, 1995). A dynamic assessment approach characterized by a test–teach–test sequence and a process orientation is one suggested alternative (Budoff, 1987; Campione, 1989; Lidz, 1991). Jitendra and Kameenieu (1993) describe five different models based on assumptions that interventions may affect learning potential. Each of the models focuses on the interaction between the student and the task. These models have been incorporated into identifying gifted and talented students with positive results (Borland & Wright, 1994; Maker, 1996). They have also been the basis for early identification and talent development models. In addition to early interventions and dynamic assessment, McCoach, Kehle, Bray, and Siegle (2001) have recommended examining achievement and academic performance longitudinally for identifying gifted students with learning disabilities who may experience greater difficulty as assignments become more reading-intensive.

RESOURCES NECESSARY FOR IMPLEMENTATION OF TRADITIONAL ASSESSMENT

Human Resources

To implement traditional assessment procedures fully, resources are needed to: (a) prepare *all* individuals who will be involved in the identification process (e.g., administrators, general education teachers, special education teachers, gifted education teachers, counselors, and psychologists); and (b) supply those individuals with support and valid assessment tools. Professional development should prepare all educators and parents to recognize the characteristics of gifted and talented students, to select and/or interpret assessment procedures, and to evaluate programming options. Teachers knowledgeable about specific characteristics of gifted and talented students are better able to contribute to the identification process (Johnsen & Ryser, 1994; Shaklee & Viechnicki, 1995). Without training and the knowledge of how to differentiate and challenge students, teachers often find it difficult to complete the required assessment forms and checklists reliably and validly. Sustained training with regular follow-up is more likely to have an impact on teacher ability to identify gifted and talented students (Johnsen, Haensly, Ryser, & Ford, 2002).

Parents/guardians also need information regarding diverse characteristics of gifted children, the identification process, and the benefits of participating in the gifted education program. Without such information, presented in a culturally sensitive format and in the parents' native language (Reyes, Fletcher, & Paez, 1996), parents/guardians may be reluctant to refer their children for assessment (Scott et al., 1992).

Material Resources

Material resources include technically adequate instruments. Specific criteria for evaluating the technical adequacy of instruments have been provided in the literature (Callahan & Caldwell, 1993; Callahan, Lundberg, & Hunsaker, 1993; Jolly & Robins, 2004) and in online resources such as the Buros Center for Testing (http://www.unl.edu/buros). Central to the criteria is an emphasis on selecting assessments that are valid (e.g., appropriate for the purpose, represents the domain or gifted area, represents the theory or underlying model, and predicts performance on other assessments and probability of success in the program) and reliable (e.g., consistently measures the trait and is stable over time). Other areas included for consideration are: age of the instrument, norming sample, types of scores, qualifications of the personnel needed to administer the assessments, and practical considerations (e.g., cost, time, required training). All assessments used in the identification process, including qualitative assessments, need to meet these technical standards to reduce error and ensure that the assessment is actually serving its purpose (Ryser, 2004b).

Assessment tools will vary, based on the program. Separate instrumentation should be used for different areas of giftedness (Callahan, et al., 1995). For example, if the purpose of the test is to identify students who would be successful in an accelerated mathematics program, assessments might include an achievement test that can discriminate between students who perform well in mathematics and those who do not perform well, a rating scale focused on characteristics related to mathematical problem solving, and above-grade-level mathematics projects produced by the student. Educators would also need to address these questions:

1. Does the achievement test have a ceiling (e.g., will the students be able to show what they know using this instrument)? Above-grade-level assessments have been recommended for gifted students because most on-level achievement tests do not include sufficiently advanced and difficult items to assess the highest level

of a gifted student's knowledge and skills (Lupkowski-Shoplik & Assouline, 1993; Stanley, 1976).

2. Do characteristics assessed on selected rating scales describe specific abilities in problem solving in mathematics and discriminate levels of performance in problem solving?

3. Do all students have an equal opportunity to develop above-grade-level mathematics projects? The classroom curriculum must be flexible so that students have the opportunity to create such projects. In cases where qualitative information is collected (e.g., rating scales, products, performances), not only do teachers need to offer opportunity, but standardized approaches (e.g., common directions and administration) are necessary to ensure that the assessment's technical qualities are adequate.

If a decision is made to include creativity or intelligence tests, then the educator needs to assess the validity of the instrument *in the domain of mathematics*. Will a creativity test provide information about producing new knowledge in mathematics? Will the intelligence test provide information about students' aptitude to learn mathematics?

BELIEFS AND VALUES UNDERLYING TRADITIONAL ASSESSMENT

Educators who use a traditional process rely heavily on quantitative and qualitative assessments in making decisions about classification and instruction. Objective measures such as intelligence tests and achievement tests are more frequently mandated than subjective measures such as students' work, behaviors, or characteristics (Brown et al., 2005). Students who meet cut-off scores on different instruments, or overall, are admitted into the program. What are the beliefs and values that underlie this process?

1. *Gifted students exist.* One of the underlying beliefs is that a gifted and talented group of students exists. These students have different sets of characteristics from their peers. This group can be identified or recognized by their outstanding performance or potential for performance. Depending upon the educators' conceptions of giftedness, this group may be defined broadly or narrowly.

2. *Some students are gifted and talented while others are not.* For the most part, giftedness is innate and resides within the individual, not necessarily in interaction with the environment. However, giftedness is complex and requires a variety of data to assess its presence appropriately. Gifted and talented students exhibit characteristics that can be identified and distinguish them from others. Identification is finding the appropriate assessments and delineating criteria and/or a cut-off point signaling the potential to benefit from gifted education programs and a separate curriculum.

3. *Gifted students should be identified so that they may receive services.* Similar to special education students, gifted students have the right to an appropriate education. They are a national resource, an investment in the future of the United States. It is the educators' responsibility to find students who excel and differentiate for them. Without services, these students are vulnerable and will not develop their talents and will waste valuable time.

4. *Technically adequate assessments are available for most areas of giftedness.* Current assessments are able to discriminate between students who are gifted and talented and other groups. Above-grade-level tests can be used to identify students who are advanced in academic areas. Intelligence tests can be used to examine aptitude and do predict academic achievement, number of years of education, and occupational status (Kaufman & Harrison, 1986; Neisser et al., 1996; Robinson & Chamrad, 1986). While fewer assessments are available in the areas of the visual and performing arts and leadership, promising approaches are emerging (Baum, Owen, & Oreck, 1996). More work is needed in developing the reliability and validity of qualitative assessments.

Along with the educators' implicit and explicit theory of giftedness, these beliefs are central to the traditional identification process. If there is no group or groups that can be defined by specific characteristics, then there is no need for identification.

PROGRAMMATIC AND CURRICULAR IMPLICATIONS OF TRADITIONAL ASSESSMENT

All gifted students are not the same by virtue of being identified as gifted and talented, but instruments used in the traditional assessment process often do not provide sufficient diagnostic information for individualized programming. Therefore, most programs must accommodate a variety of abilities and interests. This approach may not be problematic for educators who embrace a "general intellectual ability" conception of giftedness, but it is an issue for educators who view giftedness as domain-related. In the latter case, abilities and interests are perceived to be wide-ranging. This view is supported by evidence that students with talents in specific domain areas exhibit different characteristics: independence, intellectual competence, and academic propensity *in science* (Filippelli & Walberg, 1997); pitch, memory, reasoning, general intelligence, language, movement, and reactions in *conducting musicians* (Subotnik, 1997); visual memory, sensitivity to information specifying depth and perspective, and an ability to depict what is seen *in drawing* (Miller, 2005); and agility, flexibility, proportion, coordination, and rhythm *in dance* (Papierno, Ceci, Make, & Williams, 2005; Subotnik, 2002). If individual learning profiles are not aligned to learning opportunities, then academic underachievement becomes more likely (Benbow & Stanley, 1996; Bleske-Recheck, Lubinski, & Benbow, 2004; Colangelo, Assouline, & Gross, 2004; Stanley, 2000). Therefore, educators responsible for developing the program and curriculum need to collect curriculum-based assessments to determine each student's educational needs when traditional assessment procedures provide limited information about each student.

POLITICAL ISSUES ASSOCIATED WITH TRADITIONAL ASSESSMENT

Traditional assessment approaches raise political issues ranging from definitional challenges to federal mandates that may interfere with the identification process.

1. *No universal definition.* Because definitions, identification procedures, and selection criteria vary across states and within states, a student may be identified as gifted in one state and not in another, or even as gifted in one school and not in

another within the same school district. With no universal definition, it is difficult to build a body of research because samples vary across studies. Therefore, common evidence-based practices related to comprehensive identification procedures are limited.

2. *Exclusive, static definitions.* In addition to the lack of a universal definition, some states and schools establish criteria that identify a very small proportion of students (e.g., 1–2 percent). Most often, in these states, exclusive reliance on intelligence tests as a way of identifying potential results in narrow definitions and rigid criteria which increase the error of missing students who might be identified, and create the impression that giftedness is an innate rather than a developing ability. Students are identified as gifted or not gifted rather than along a developmental continuum. Consequently, students from lower-income backgrounds and other underserved groups are less likely to be identified, creating programs that may be viewed as elitist, since they serve only a small number of students from less diverse backgrounds. Programs using a narrow conception of giftedness may also risk legal issues concerning equal access. Further, such programs would not necessarily be viewed as essential since they are based on the premise that gifts are innate and do not need to be developed (e.g., "once gifted, always gifted").

3. *Ill-defined areas of giftedness.* Even with broader definitions, areas of giftedness are ill defined, making it difficult to find appropriate assessments. This limitation is particularly true in the areas of leadership and creativity, where the adequacy of paper-and-pencil tests has been questioned (Oakland, Falkenberg, & Oakland, 1996; Sternberg, 1986). Furthermore, limited research is available for the assessment of talent within domains. Most assessments examine general abilities and do not capture the student's potential to interact, to adapt, and to learn from instruction (Johnsen, 1997).

4. *System resistance to above-grade-level assessments.* Using above-grade-level assessments, highly recommended in the field of gifted education because they are more likely to discriminate among gifted students, may be a challenge because of high-stakes testing rules. In fact, state assessments have become the "template for . . . assessment" (Moon, Brighton, & Callahan, 2003, p. 59). Consequently, above-grade-level assessments are costly and therefore infrequently used to identify gifted and talented students. It is more likely that state-mandated tests are used inappropriately in the identification process (Callahan, Tomlinson, Hunsaker, Bland, & Moon, 1995).

5. *Response to Intervention models.* Response to Intervention (RtI) was introduced in the Individuals with Disabilities Education Act (IDEA) of 2004 as a mandated, alternative approach for identifying students with learning disabilities. Most models focus on students who are not progressing, rather than students who are above grade level (Rollins, Mursky, Shah-Coltrane, & Johnsen, 2009). Unfortunately, some standard protocol approaches require teachers to follow a scripted curriculum that provides for little variation for individual students (Johnsen, 2010). This curricular rigidity might limit the teacher's use of challenging or differentiated activities so that gifted students are less likely to be able to manifest gifts and talents during the identification process. A few states (e.g., Colorado and Ohio) do include gifted students within the first tier of an RtI process (Coleman & Hughes, 2009; Rollins et al., 2009). Response to Intervention models do have the potential

for identifying students who are gifted with learning disabilities, or those who are performing above grade level, with alternative, more dynamic assessments (Coleman & Johnsen, 2010), but for the majority of states, the focus is on those who are below grade level.

CONCLUSION

A traditional identification procedure using primarily quantitative assessments is the most widely used approach in the United States. Implementation of this approach, however, is quite diverse and is influenced by federal and state definitions, standards-based practices, state rules and regulations, program characteristics, and implicit or explicit conceptions of giftedness. For the most part, educators who use traditional approaches believe that gifted students exist and form a distinct group, that they can be identified with technically adequate assessments, and that they need to be served to develop their gifts and talents.

To implement this approach, all who are involved in the identification process need to receive professional development, including administrators, parents, special educators, and general educators. Without this development, the quality of the overall process is in jeopardy. Moreover, technically adequate assessments need to be selected to ensure adequate ceilings, alignment with the program, and recognition of all groups, particularly those from special populations. Since traditional assessment approaches do not generally provide sufficient diagnostic information for programming, a diverse group of gifted students is often served within a common program. To meet each student's interests, abilities, and skills more effectively, teachers need to gather more information to tailor the curriculum to each student.

Even when well implemented, the traditional approach presents challenges including under-representation of minority students and inability to consider the dynamic nature of giftedness. Therefore, decisions are made on what is assessed, what the student has acquired, rather than what the student might develop.

Politically, the process raises important issues; however, even though traditional approaches have serious challenges, they do recognize that gifted and talented students exist. Without the recognition that some students have distinct characteristics, is there a need for professional development, for services, or for resource support?

REFERENCES

Alviderez, J., & Weinstein, R. S. (1999). Early teacher perceptions and later student academic achievement. *Journal of Educational Psychology, 91*, 731–746.

Banks, S. R., & Neisworth, J. T. (1995). Dynamic assessment in early intervention: Implications for serving American Indian/Alaska Native families. *Journal of American Indian Education, 34*(2), 27–43.

Barnard-Brak, L., Johnsen, S. K., & Pond, A. (2009, August). *The incidence of potentially gifted students within a special education population.* Presentation at the Biennial World Conference on Gifted and Talented Children, Vancouver, Canada.

Baum, S. M., Owen, S. V., & Oreck, B. A. (1996). Talent beyond words: Identification of potential talent in dance and music in elementary students. *Gifted Child Quarterly, 40*, 93–101.

Benbow, C. P., & Stanley, J. C. (1996). Inequity in equity: How "equity" can lead to inequity for high-potential students. *Psychology, Public Policy, and Law, 2*, 249–292.

Bleske-Recheck, A., Lubinski, D., & Benbow, C. P. (2004). Meeting the educational needs of special populations: Advanced Placement's role in developing exceptional human capital. *Psychological Science, 15*, 217–224.

Borland, J. H., & Wright, L. (1994). Identifying young, potentially gifted, economically disadvantaged students. *Gifted Child Quarterly, 38*, 164–171.

Brown, S. W., Renzulli, J. S., Gubbins, E. J., Siegle, D., Zhang, W., & Chen, C-H. (2005). Assumptions underlying the identification of gifted and talented students. *Gifted Child Quarterly, 49*, 68–79.

Budoff, M. (1987). The validity of learning potential assessment. In C. S. Lidz (Ed.), *Dynamic assessment: An interactional approach to evaluating learning potential* (pp. 52–81). New York: Guilford Press.

Callahan, C. M. (2001). Beyond the gifted stereotype. *Educational Leadership, 59*(3), 42–46.

Callahan, C. M., & Caldwell, M. S. (1993). Establishment of a national data bank on identification and evaluation instruments. *Journal for the Education of the Gifted, 16*, 201–219.

Callahan, C. M., Hunsaker, S., Adams, S. M., Moore, S. D., & Bland, L. (1995). *Instruments used in the identification of gifted and talented students.* Storrs: The National Research Center on the Gifted and Talented, University of Connecticut.

Callahan, C. M., Lundberg, C., & Hunsaker, S. L. (1993). The development of the Scale for the Evaluation of Gifted Identification Instruments (SEGII). *Gifted Child Quarterly, 37*, 133–140.

Callahan, C. M., Tomlinson, C. A., Hunsaker, S., Bland, L., & Moon, T. R. (1995). *Instruments and evaluation designs used in gifted programs.* (Report No. 95132). Storrs: The National Research Center on the Gifted and Talented, University of Connecticut.

Campione, J. C. (1989). Assisted assessment: A taxonomy of approaches and an outline of strengths and weaknesses. *Journal of Learning Disabilities, 22*, 151–165.

Cattell, R. B. (1971). *Abilities: Their structure, growth, and action.* Boston: Houghton Mifflin.

Colangelo, N., Assouline, S., & Gross, M. U. M. (Eds.). (2004). *A nation deceived: How schools hold back America's brightest students.* Iowa City: The Connie Belin & Jacqueline N. Blank International Center for Gifted Education and Talent Development, The University of Iowa.

Coleman, M. R., & Hughes, C. E. (2009). Meeting the needs of gifted students within an RtI framework. *Gifted Child Today, 32*(3), 14–17.

Coleman, M. R., & Johnsen, S. K. (2010). *RtI for gifted students.* Waco, TX: Prufrock Press.

Council for Exceptional Children, The Association for the Gifted (CEC–TAG), & National Association for Gifted Children (NAGC). (2006). *Initial knowledge and skill standards for gifted and talented education.* Retrieved from http://www.cectag.org

Council of State Directors of Programs for the Gifted, & National Association for Gifted Children. (2009). *State of the states in gifted education 2008–2009: National policy and practice data.* Washington, DC: NAGC.

Daniels, V. I. (1998). Minority students in gifted and special education programs: The case for educational equity. *Journal of Special Education, 32*, 41–44.

Dawson, V. L. (1997). In search of the wild bohemian: Challenges in the identification of the creatively gifted. *Roeper Review, 19*, 148–152.

Filippelli, L . A, & Walberg, H. J. (1997). Childhood traits and conditions of eminent women scientists. *Gifted Child Quarterly, 41*, 95–103.

Ford, D. Y. (1996). Multicultural gifted education: A wake up call to the profession. *Roeper Review, 19*, 72–78.

Ford, D. Y. (1998). The underrepresentation of minority students in gifted education: Problems and promises in recruitment and retention. *The Journal of Special Education, 32*, 4–14.

Ford, D. Y., & Harmon, D. A. (2001). Equity and excellence: Providing access to gifted education for culturally diverse students. *Journal of Secondary Gifted Education, 12*, 141–148.

Ford, D. Y., & Harris, J. J., III (1994). *Multicultural gifted education.* New York: Teachers College Press.

Frasier, M. M., Garcia, J. H., & Passow, A. H. (1995). *A review of assessment issues in gifted education and their implications for identifying gifted minority students.* Storrs: The National Research Center on the Gifted and Talented, University of Connecticut.

Gagné, F. (1999). My convictions about the nature of abilities, gifts, and talents. *Journal for the Education of the Gifted, 22*, 109–136.

Guilford, J. P. (1967). *The nature of human intelligence.* New York: McGraw-Hill.

Guskin, S. L., Peng, C. J., & Simon, M. (1992). Do teachers react to "Multiple Intelligences"? Effect of teachers' stereotypes on judgments and expectancies for students with diverse patterns of giftedness/talent. *Gifted Child Quarterly, 36*, 32–37.

Harris, B., Plucker, J. A., Rapp, K. E., & Martinez, R. S. (2009). Identifying gifted and talented English language learners: A case study. *Journal for the Education of the Gifted, 32*, 368–393.

Hunsaker, S. L. (1994). Creativity as a characteristic of giftedness: Teachers see it, then they don't. *Roeper Review, 17*, 11–15.

Hunsaker, S. L., Finley, V. S., & Frank, E. L. (1997). An analysis of teacher nominations and student performance in gifted programs. *Gifted Child Quarterly, 41*, 19–24.

Jitendra, A. K., & Kameenui, E. J. (1993). Dynamic assessment as a compensatory assessment approach: A description and analysis. *Remedial and Special Education, 14*(5), 6–18.

Johnsen, S. K. (1997). Assessment beyond definitions. *Peabody Journal of Education, 72*(3&4), 136–152.

Johnsen, S. K. (2004). Making decisions about placement. In S. K. Johnsen (Ed.), *Identifying gifted students: A practical guide* (pp. 107–131). Waco, TX: Prufrock Press.

Johnsen, S. K. (2010). Assessing your school's RtI model in serving gifted students. In M. R. Coleman & S. K. Johnsen, *RtI for gifted students*. Waco, TX: Prufrock Press.

Johnsen, S. K., Haensly, P., Ryser, G., & Ford, R. (2002). Changing general education classroom practices to adapt for gifted students. *Gifted Child Quarterly, 46*, 45–63.

Johnsen, S. K., & Ryser, G. (1994). Identification of young gifted children from lower income families. *Gifted and Talented International, 9*(2), 62–68.

Jolly, J. L., & Robins, J. (2004). Technical information regarding assessment. In S. K. Johnsen (Ed.), *Identifying gifted students: A practical guide* (pp. 51–105). Waco, TX: Prufrock Press.

Kaufman, A. S., & Harrison, P. L. (1986). Intelligence tests and gifted assessment: What are the positives? *Roeper Review, 8*, 154–159.

Lidz, C. S. (1991). *Practitioner's guide to dynamic assessment.* New York: Guilford.

Louis, B., Subotnik, R. F., Breland, P. S., & Lewis, M. (2000). Establishing criteria for high ability versus selective admission to gifted programs: Implications for policy and practice. *Educational Psychology Review, 12*, 295–314.

Lupkowski-Shoplik, A., & Assouline, S. G. (1993). Identifying mathematically talented elementary students: Using the lower level of the SSAT. *Gifted Child Quarterly, 37*, 118–123.

McBee, M. T. (2006). A descriptive analysis of referral sources for gifted identification screening by race and socioeconomic status. *The Journal of Secondary Gifted Education, 17*(2), 103–111.

McCoach, D. B., Kehle, T. J., Bray, M. A., & Siegle, D. (2001). Best practices in the identification of gifted students with learning disabilities. *Psychology in the Schools, 38*, 403–411.

Maker, C. J. (1996). Identification of gifted minority students: A national problem, needed changes, and a promising solution. *Gifted Child Quarterly, 40*, 41–50.

Miller, L. K. (2005). What the Savant Syndrome can tell us about the nature and nurture of talent. *Journal for the Education of the Gifted, 28*, 361–373.

Moon, T. R., Brighton, C. M., & Callahan, C. M. (2003). State standardized testing programs: Friend or foe of gifted education? *Roeper Review, 25*, 49–60.

Morris, J. E. (2002). African American students and gifted education. *Roeper Review, 24*, 59–62.

Morrison, W. F., & Rizza, M. G. (2007). Creating a toolkit for identifying twice-exceptional students. *Journal for the Education of the Gifted, 31*, 57–76.

National Association for Gifted Children. (1998). *NAGC Pre-K–Grade 12 gifted programming standards.* Retrieved January 19, 2012 from http://www.nagc.org/index.aspx?id=546

National Association for Gifted Children. (2010). *NAGC Pre-K–Grade 12 gifted programming standards: A blueprint for quality gifted education programs.* Retrieved January 19, 2012 from http://www.nagc.org/index.aspx?id=1863

Neisser, U., Boodoo, G., Bouchard, T. J., Jr., Boykin, A. W., Brody, N., Ceci, S. J. et al. (1996). Intelligence: Knowns and unknowns. *American Psychologist, 51*, 77–101.

Neumeister, K. L., Adams, C. M., Pierce, R. L., Cassady, J. C., & Dixon, F. A. (2007). Fourth-grade teachers' perceptions of giftedness: Implications for identifying and serving diverse gifted students. *Journal for the Education of the Gifted, 30*, 479–499.

Oakland, T., Falkenberg, B. A., & Oakland, C. (1996). Assessment of leadership in children, youth, and adults. *Gifted Child Quarterly, 40*, 138–146.

Papierno, P. B., Ceci, S. J., Make, M. C., & Williams, W. M. (2005). The nature and nurture of talent: A bioecological perspective on the ontogeny of exceptional abilities. *Journal for the Education of the Gifted, 28*, 312–331.

Passow, A. H., & Frasier, M. M. (1996). Toward improving identification of talent potential among minority and disadvantaged students. *Roeper Review, 18*, 198–202.

Peterson, J. S., & Margolin, R. (1997). Naming gifted children: An example of unintended "reproduction." *Journal for the Education of the Gifted, 21*, 82–101.

Pierce, R. L., Adams, C. M., Speirs Neumeister, K. L., Cassady, J. C., Dixon, F. A., & Cross, T. L. (2007). Development of an identification procedure for a large urban school corporation: Identifying culturally diverse and academically gifted elementary students. *Roeper Review, 29*, 113–118.

Plata, M., & Masten, W. (1998). Teacher ratings of Hispanic and Anglo students on a behavior rating scale. *Roeper Review, 21*, 139–144.

Reid, C., Udall, A., Romanoff, B., & Algozzine, B. (1999). Comparison of traditional and problem-solving assessment criteria. *Gifted Child Quarterly, 43*, 252–264.

Renzulli, J. (1978). What makes giftedness? Reexamining a definition. *Phi Delta Kappan, 60,* 180–184.

Reyes, E. I., Fletcher, R., & Paez, D. (1996). Developing local multidimensional screening procedures for identifying giftedness among Mexican American border populations. *Roeper Review, 18,* 208–211.

Robinson, N. M., & Chamrad, D. L. (1986). Appropriate uses of intelligence tests with gifted children. *Roeper Review, 8,* 160–163.

Rollins, K., Mursky, C., Shah-Coltrane, S., & Johnsen, S. K. (2009). RtI models for gifted students. *Gifted Child Today, 32*(3), 20–30.

Ryser, G. R. (2004a). Culture-fair and nonbiased assessment. In S. K. Johnsen (Ed.), *Identifying gifted students: A practical guide* (pp. 41–49). Waco, TX: Prufrock Press.

Ryser, G. R. (2004b). Qualitative and quantitative approaches to assessment. In S. K. Johnsen (Ed.), *Identifying gifted students: A practical guide* (pp. 23–40). Waco, TX: Prufrock Press.

Schack, G. A., & Starko, A. J. (1990). Identification of gifted students: An analysis of criteria preferred by preservice teachers, classroom teachers, and teachers of the gifted. *Journal for the Education of the Gifted, 13,* 346–363.

Scott, M. S., Perou, R., Urbano, R., Hogan, A., & Gold, S. (1992). The identification of giftedness: A comparison of White, Hispanic, and Black families. *Gifted Child Quarterly, 36,* 131–139.

Shaklee, B. D., & Viechnicki, K. J. (1995). A qualitative approach to portfolios: The early assessment for exceptional potential model. *Journal for the Education of the Gifted, 18,* 156–170.

Siegle, D., & Powell, T. (2004). Exploring teacher biases when nominating students for gifted programs. *Gifted Child Quarterly, 48,* 21–29.

Soto, L. D. (1997). *Language, culture, and power: Bilingual families and the struggle for quality education.* Albany: State University of New York Press.

Stanley, J. (1976). The study of mathematically precocious youth. *Gifted Child Quarterly, 26,* 53–67.

Stanley, J. C. (2000). Helping students learn only what they don't already know. *Psychology, Public Policy, and Law, 6,* 216–222.

Sternberg, R. J. (1986). *Intelligence applied: Understanding and increasing your intellectual skills.* San Diego, CA: Harcourt Brace Jovanovich.

Subotnik, R. F. (1997). Talent developed: Conversations with masters in the arts and sciences: Vladimir Feltsman: Piano virtuoso and educational innovator. *Journal for the Education of the Gifted, 20,* 306–317.

Subotnik, R. F. (2002). Talent developed: Conversations with masters in the arts and sciences: Eliot Feld. *Journal for the Education of the Gifted, 25,* 290–302.

Tannenbaum, A. (1991). The social psychology of giftedness. In N. Colangelo, & G. A. Davis (Eds.), *Handbook of gifted education* (pp. 27–44). Boston: Allyn & Bacon.

Thorndike, E. L. (1931). *Human learning.* New York: Appleton-Century-Crofts.

Thurstone, L. L. (1938). *Primary mental abilities.* Chicago: University of Chicago Press.

Trice, B., & Shannon, B. (2002, April). *Office for Civil Rights: Ensuring equal access to gifted education.* Paper presented at the Annual Meeting of the Council for Exceptional Children, New York.

VanTassel-Baska, J., Johnson, D., & Avery, L. D. (2002). Using performance tasks in the identification of economically disadvantaged and minority gifted learners: Findings from Project STAR. *Gifted Child Quarterly, 46,* 110–123.

Waldron, K. A., & Saphire, D. G. (1990). An analysis of factors for gifted students with learning disabilities. *Journal of Learning Disabilities, 23,* 491–498.

11

THE USE OF TRADITIONAL ASSESSMENT TOOLS FOR IDENTIFYING GIFTED STUDENTS

Tracy C. Missett and Marguerite C. Brunner

The use of norm-referenced, standardized tests of intelligence and achievement in the process of identifying gifted students has a long tradition. Indeed, use of these tests continues to dominate the identification of giftedness in most states and school districts (Brown et al., 2005; Callahan, 2005; Sternberg, Jarvin, & Grigorenko, 2011).

Proponents of the use of intelligence tests contend that they are objective, valid means of assessing intellectual ability and the single most reliable predictors of academic achievement. However, reliance on traditional assessment tools—intelligence and achievement tests—as the sole data sources in identifying gifted students has received scrutiny (Borland, 2003; Gentry, Hu, & Thomas, 2008; Reis & Renzulli, 2011). Critics question the validity of these tests for measuring giftedness and argue that an emphasis on traditional assessment tools reflects outdated conceptions of giftedness. They further contend that traditional assessments contribute to the under-identification of minority, low socio-economic status (SES), and twice-exceptional students, as well as students with creative talents (Callahan, 2005; Chart, Grigorenko, & Sternberg, 2008; Gallagher & Gallagher, 1994). Still others note that relying solely on traditional test scores results in an arbitrary and indefensible use of cut-off scores for inclusion in gifted programs (Sternberg et al., 2011). These criticisms have led to expanded conceptions of giftedness along with new paradigms for identifying more diverse populations for gifted programs and services (Brown et al., 2005; Callahan, 2005; Reis & Renzulli, 2011; VanTassel-Baska, Johnson, & Avery, 2008). New paradigms call for the use of multiple criteria for identification, including a combination of portfolios, authentic and dynamic assessments, performance tasks, teacher rating scales, and other non-traditional assessments in combination with traditional assessments.

While moving the role of traditional assessment tools from center stage in the decision-making process has been encouraged, few argue that they have no place in conceptions of intellectual giftedness[1] or identification of students gifted in specific academic domains (Robinson, 2005; Sternberg et al., 2011), and they remain a prominent data source in identification procedures in most school districts. However, in order to evaluate the advantages, and limitations, of using traditional assessment tools for identifying gifted students, one must understand what these instruments purport to measure and for what purposes they are valid and reliable instruments. This understanding will aid educators in determining how and under what circumstances it is appropriate to use traditional assessment tools to identify gifted students.

WHAT INTELLIGENCE AND ACHIEVEMENT TESTS MEASURE

Intelligence, or general intellectual ability, is generally described as a multidimensional mental capability that involves and combines the ability to reason, think abstractly, comprehend complex ideas, learn quickly, and learn from experience (Gagné & St. Père, 2001; Sternberg et al., 2011; Tannenbaum, 2003). Intelligence quotient (IQ) tests purport to measure those constructs. Comprehensive achievement tests measure a broad range of accomplishment and knowledge in specific academic content areas (e.g., reading, language arts, mathematics, science, social studies), as well as basic skills and learning that are deemed to be important in education (Lohman, 2005; Sternberg et al., 2011). Measures of specific aptitudes and measures of achievement in specific content areas are also sometimes used for identification of students in one domain of talent. For example, the Differential Aptitude Test of Numerical Reasoning (DAT-N, 1990) might be used to screen students for placement in an accelerated mathematics program.

Lewis Terman, who is often credited as a founder of gifted education, developed one of the first intelligence tests used in the United States based on a translation of the scales developed by Binet and Simon in France (Stanford Revision of the Binet–Simon Scale, commonly known as the Stanford–Binet) (Assouline, 2003; Terman, 1916). He incorporated a new method of scoring this test, which ultimately was represented by an IQ score. The term IQ continues to describe scores on tests of intelligence. Terman believed that IQ tests measured innate abilities and were the single most valid indicator of a child's relative intelligence and likelihood of high academic achievement.

Current intelligence tests do not use the scoring process developed by Terman; rather, examinees' scores are derived by comparing their performance to others in a normative sample. The score distribution is purposefully constructed to reflect a population distribution along the normal bell curve, with a mean or average score of 100 and a standard deviation of 15 or 16 depending on the test (Lakin & Lohman, 2011; Robinson, 2005). Approximately 3 percent of test takers score above 130, with about the same percentage scoring below 70, often considered the threshold for cognitive disability or mental retardation. Individuals from all ethnicities, racial backgrounds, and socio-economic levels can be found in all ranges along the IQ and achievement continuum.

Most traditional intelligence tests measure not only general intellectual abilities, often referred to as g, but also specific abilities related to general intelligence. The purpose of administering these tests to students is to provide information about a student's relative academic aptitude or ability to learn, and to predict how students will achieve academically. The two most widely used individual tests of intelligence[2] are the Stanford–Binet Intelligence Scales, which includes sub-scales yielding scores in the areas of Fluid Reasoning, Knowledge, Quantitative Reasoning, Visual–Spatial Processing, and Working Memory abilities, and the Wechsler Intelligence Scale for Children (WISC, 2003) which produces scores on four broad measures comprising Verbal Comprehension, Working

Memory, Perceptual Reasoning, and Processing Speed. Commonly administered paper-and-pencil group tests include the Cognitive Abilities Test (CogAT, 2001), and the Otis–Lennon School Ability Test (OLSAT8; see Otis & Lennon, 2003). The OLSAT8 yields a total ability score as well as verbal and nonverbal scores, and the CogAT yields a composite score as well as scores for verbal, quantitative, and nonverbal sub-components. Commonly administered group achievement tests include the Iowa Tests of Basic Skills (ITBS)/Iowa Tests of Educational Development (ITED), the Metropolitan Achievement Test (MAT, 2000), and the Scholastic Assessment Test (SAT) (Assouline, 2003; Lohman, 2005; Sternberg et al., 2011).

VALIDITY AND RELIABILITY ISSUES

One would expect a student's IQ score, generally viewed to be a constant trait after a child attains the age of seven or eight, to be consistent over time. Most well-constructed standardized achievement and intelligence tests used by schools are reliable, particularly tests with a large number of items (Assouline, 2003; Lohman, 2005; Sternberg et al., 2011). Two types of validity are considered critical in assessing the value of traditional assessment tools used in the identification of gifted students—predictive validity and construct validity (Borland, 2008; Sternberg et al., 2011). Intelligence quotient (IQ) tests (the predictor) were originally devised to predict educational performance or achievement (the criterion) (Lakin & Lohman, 2011; Sternberg, Grigorenko, & Bundy, 2001). In addition, intelligence tests are judged on the degree to which they provide evidence of construct validity, whether the assessment actually measures the construct of intelligence or giftedness.

The Predictive Validity of IQ Tests

Although a vigorous debate exists in the field regarding the reliability and validity of traditional assessment tools (Borland, 2008), a few general principles are well supported in the literature. Intelligence quotient (IQ) scores correlate, probably more than any other measurable human trait, with a number of educational, occupational, economic, and social outcomes (Gottfredson, 2001; Sternberg et al., 2001; Sternberg et al., 2011). Those most relevant to the educational setting are addressed here.

Intelligence quotient (IQ) and academic achievement test scores are strongly correlated, particularly in the humanities, sciences, and social sciences, with IQ scores predicting school performance (grades) and scores on achievement tests. Intelligence quotient (IQ) scores remain reasonably stable over time, and are particularly stable by the time a child reaches the age of seven or eight.[3] Thus, a child's standing relative to others in his or her age cohort on measures of IQ varies little over the life of that individual. Correlations between IQ and achievement tests increase with age (Gottfredson, 2001; Robinson, 2005; Sternberg et al., 2011). It is likely that this increased relationship is attributable to the increasing overlap of traits being measured which make ability and achievement difficult to distinguish. In fact, some researchers posit that achievement and ability tests measure what are essentially different aspects of the same construct (Lohman, 2006; Sternberg et al., 2001). The SAT, for example, assesses traits associated with both intelligence and achievement and is used to predict success in college (Sternberg et al., 2011). Finally, two-way correlations between IQ and total years spent in education are strong as well. Critics who argue against the validity of using IQ tests to identify gifted students make those arguments on the basis of construct validity. In other words, they argue that IQ does not assess the criterion of interest, namely giftedness, because giftedness is more multidimensional than simply intelligence (Borland, 2008).

The literature on IQ also strongly supports the existence of significant differences among group means on intelligence measures (Gottfredson, 2001; Lohman, 2005; Sternberg et al., 2001). Because these differences continue to be a subject of intense interest and debate, it is appropriate to caution that group means have no direct implications for specific individuals within any group, and that other individual factors are believed to contribute significantly to ability and academic attainment.

While scores of males and females do not differ significantly on general measures of intelligence, differences do exist on certain tasks found within intelligence tests. Specifically, differences favor males on visual–spatial tasks and differences favor females on verbal tasks and tasks related to memory. Also, although females initially show greater strengths on tasks tapping quantitative abilities, this advantage reverses before puberty (Loehlin, 2004).

Significant differences are found in the mean scores of different ethnic groups as well, and those differences in scores on intelligence tests have been the foundation of much criticism of the use of traditional intelligence test scores for making placement decisions for programs for gifted and talented students (Loehlin, 2004; Sternberg et al., 2001). Most recent research suggests that Asian Americans have comparable or slightly higher mean IQ and achievement scores than Caucasian American students (Rushton & Jensen, 2006). African American mean scores are nearly one standard deviation below that of Caucasians on IQ tests and are slightly less than one standard deviation lower on tests of achievement. The mean IQ and achievement scores of Hispanics typically lie between those of Blacks and Whites. These differences are somewhat smaller, but still significant, for individuals from different ethnic groups but similar socio-economic backgrounds (Loehlin, 2004). Group differences clearly have implications for the identification of gifted students where scores on traditional assessment tools are used as the primary indicators of giftedness. In fact, the under-identification and under-representation of minority and ethnically diverse students in gifted programs remains an intractable problem in the field, and often the problem is attributed to the use of standardized, traditional tools (Ford, 2003; Gentry, Hu, & Thomas, 2008; Naglieri & Ford, 2003).

Group differences in mean IQ scores have led some to claim that IQ tests themselves are not valid because they are "biased" against, or unfair to, certain ethnic and minority groups (Borland, 2003; Ford, 2003; Naglieri & Ford, 2003). However, to the extent that intelligence tests are designed to (and do) predict school performance and achievement equally well for all groups, others argue that they are not biased against any group, regardless of existing differences in mean scores across groups, because they predict equally well for all groups (Loehlin, 2004; Robinson, 2005). As Robinson (2005) observed on the issue of bias, "it is life, not the tests, that is unfair to many children in our communities." (p. 282).

Unresolved Issues Related to Validity and Reliability

The research provides no definitive explanation for group differences in mean IQ scores (Borland, 2003; Gottfredson, 2001; Sternberg et al., 2001). Indeed, there is little consensus regarding the degree to which nature and/or nurture differentially impact on intelligence and achievement, nor is there consensus on the degree to which or how the environment affects intelligence (Sternberg et al., 2011). However, there is little debate that environment does have an impact on intelligence. For example, poor educational opportunities, poverty, malnutrition, early exposure to lead, and prenatal exposure to alcohol and drugs correlate with depressed scores on traditional assessments (Ford, 2010).

There is also a debate about the degree to which proper schooling can develop IQ scores, and whether large-scale intervention programs such as Head Start—which children typically enter at the age of three—can permanently raise IQ scores among low SES and minority children. A significant literature shows that "the general trend observed in these programs is that test scores increase over the course of the program itself, but that, after the intervening forces are withdrawn, the gains fade with time" (Sternberg et al., 2001, p. 12), and by the end of elementary school (age 11 or 12), improvements in IQ gained from Head Start fade (Aughinbaugh, 2001; Barnett & Hustedt, 2005; Robinson, 2005). Because of persistent group differences in mean IQ test scores and the consequent under-representation of diverse students in gifted programs, use of traditional assessment tools to identify gifted students is considered a major inhibitor in increasing diversity in gifted programs (Ford, 2003; Gentry et al., 2008). As a result, significant efforts have been made to devise assessments that are culturally sensitive and that identify equal numbers across groups, primarily through the use of nonverbal tests of ability (Lohman, Korb, & Lakin, 2008; Naglieri & Ford, 2003) and to use other indicators of talent outside of the test paradigm to assess potential. See Chapter 14 by Worrell in this book for a more extensive discussion of these instruments.

WHEN TO USE TRADITIONAL ASSESSMENT TOOLS

As views on intelligence and giftedness have broadened beyond IQ, and researchers in the field increasingly recognize the variety of ways in which children display giftedness, a new paradigm for identifying a diverse range of students appears appropriate and necessary (Borland, 2008; Callahan, 2005; VanTassel-Baska, Feng, & de Brux, 2007). Instead of relying solely on scores from traditional assessments, multiple criteria are urged, including portfolios, dynamic assessment, nonverbal tests of ability, creativity measures, and authentic assessment tools. However, these forms of assessment should themselves be valid and reliable indicators of the gifts and talents served in a gifted program (Callahan, 2005; Robinson, 2005).

That is not to say, however, that traditional assessment tools have no place in identifying students for gifted programs and services (Sternberg et al., 2011). Traditional assessment tools have been shown to be reliable and valid predictors of strong educational accomplishment, and in some contexts, are particularly appropriate. For example, traditional assessments are useful in estimating a student's readiness for the next level of instruction, and they have consistently been shown to be effective for students whose ability and performance are demonstrably well beyond those of their age peers and who would benefit from accelerative interventions (Colangelo et al., 2010; Robinson, 2005). Moreover, many researchers in the field argue that ability and achievement tests may be useful in the identification of twice-exceptional learners where significant discrepancies in achievement scores and ability scores are seen (Assouline, Nicpon, & Whiteman, 2010; Bianco, 2005; Kalbfleisch & Iguchi, 2008).

However, these instruments should inform decision making that is relevant or matched to the gifted curriculum and services offered, as well as the particular population of students being considered for these services. Thus, if a gifted program emphasizes verbal and language skills, placement decisions based on quantitative or nonverbal measures of ability cannot be defended (Callahan, 2005; Robinson, 2005). Moreover, Lakin and Lohman (2011) propose that educators look to a child's standing on traditional test scores relative to other students "who have had roughly similar opportunities to acquire the abilities measured by the test" (p. 616) rather than the child's standing relative to national norms. See Chapter 12 by Lohman in this book for details on using this approach. Current versions of both intelligence and achievements tests have gone to considerable lengths to ensure adequate representation of subgroups and to eliminate racial or ethnic or gender bias.

In conclusion, the use of traditional assessment tools in the conceptualization and identification of giftedness continues to find support in the research and in practice. However, there is also great support for the proposition that they should not be the only predictor of success or the only delimiter of the construct of giftedness, but rather that they should be supplemented with additional assessments better to capture what is currently viewed to be a multidimensional construct.

NOTES

1. In this chapter, reference is to identification of the intellectually gifted or those gifted in specific academic domains—not those who are identified as gifted in the arts or leadership.
2. The term "individual" is used to refer to assessments administered one-on-one, usually by a trained examiner or licensed clinical psychologist.
3. However, as discussed below, some research suggests that targeted academic interventions directed toward improving the cognitive and metacognitive skills of young children can lead to at least temporary gains in traditional assessments (Sternberg et al., 2001; Sternberg et al., 2011). Moreover, individuals who go on to develop certain emotional disorders experience diminishing cognitive capacities as they experience increased symptoms associated with the disorder.

REFERENCES

Assouline, S. G. (2003). Psychological and educational assessment of gifted children. In N. Colangelo & G. A. Davis (Eds.), *Handbook of gifted education* (pp. 124–145). Boston: Allyn & Bacon.

Assouline, S. G., Nicpon, M. F., & Whiteman, C. (2010). Cognitive and psychosocial characteristics of gifted students with written language disability. *Gifted Child Quarterly, 54*, 102–115.

Aughinbaugh, A. (2001). Does Head Start yield long-term benefits? *The Journal of Human Resources, 36*, 641–665.

Barnett, S., & Hustedt, J. T. (2005). Head Start's lasting benefits. *Infants and Young Children, 18*, 16–24.

Bennett, G. K., Seashore, H. G., & Wesman, A. G. (1990). *Differential Aptitude Tests* (5th ed.). Upper Saddle River, NJ: Pearson.

Bianco, M. (2005). The effects of disability labels on special education and general education teachers' referrals for gifted programs. *Learning Disability Quarterly, 28*, 285–293.

Borland, J. H. (2003). *Rethinking gifted education.* New York: Teachers College Press.

Borland, J. H. (2008). Identification. In J. A. Plucker & C. M. Callahan (Eds.), *Critical issues and practices in gifted education* (pp. 261–280). Waco, TX: Prufrock Press.

Brown, S. W., Renzulli, J. S., Gubbins, E. J., Siegle, D., Zhang, W., & Chen, C-H. (2005). Assumptions underlying the identification of gifted and talented students. *Gifted Child Quarterly, 49*, 68–79.

Callahan, C. M. (2005). Identifying gifted students from underrepresented populations. *Theory Into Practice, 44*, 98–104.

Chart, H., Grigorenko, E. L., & Sternberg, R. J. (2008). Identification: The Aurora Battery. In J. A. Plucker & C. M. Callahan (Eds.), *Critical issues and practices in gifted education* (pp. 281–301). Waco, TX: Prufrock Press.

Colangelo, N., Assouline, S. G., Marron, M. A., Castellano, J. A., Clinkenbeard, P. R., Rogers, K. et al. (2010). Guidelines for developing an academic acceleration policy. *Journal of Advanced Academics, 21*, 180–203.

Ford, D. (2003). *Desegregating gifted education: Seeking equity for culturally diverse students. Rethinking gifted education.* New York: Teachers College Press.

Ford, D. Y. (2010). Recruiting and retaining gifted students from diverse ethnic, cultural, and language groups. *Multicultural education: Issues and perspectives* (7th ed., pp. 371–392). Hoboken, NJ: Wiley.

Gagné, F., & St. Père, F. (2001). When IQ is controlled, does motivation still predict achievement? *Intelligence, 24*, 13–23.

Gallagher, J. J., & Gallagher, S. A. (1994). *Teaching the gifted child* (4th ed.). Boston: Allyn & Bacon.

Gentry, M., Hu, S., & Thomas, A. T. (2008). Ethnically diverse students. In J. A. Plucker & C. M. Callahan (Eds.), *Critical issues and practices in gifted education* (pp. 195–212). Waco, TX: Prufrock Press.

Gottfredson, L. S. (2001). What do we know about intelligence? *American Scholar, 65*, 15–30.

Kalbfleisch, M. L., & Iguchi, C. M. (2008). Twice-exceptional learners. In J. A. Plucker & C. M. Callahan (Eds.), *Critical issues and practices in gifted education: What the research says* (pp. 707–719). Waco, TX: Prufrock Press.

Lakin, J. M., & Lohman, D. F. (2011). The predictive accuracy of verbal, quantitative, and nonverbal reasoning tests: Consequences for talent identification and program diversity. *Journal for the Education of the Gifted, 34*, 595–623.

Loehlin, J. C. (2004). Group differences in intelligence. In R. S. Sternberg (Ed.), *Handbook of intelligence* (pp. 176–196). New York: Cambridge University Press.

Lohman, D. F. (2005). Review of Naglieri and Ford (2003). Does the Naglieri Nonverbal Ability Test identify equal proportions of high-scoring White, Black, and Hispanic students? *Gifted Child Quarterly, 49*, 19–28.

Lohman, D. F. (2006). Beliefs about differences between ability and accomplishment: "From folk theories to cognitive science." *Roeper Review, 29*, 32–40.

Lohman, D. F., & Haggen, E. P. (2001). *Cognitive Abilities Test.* Itaskca, IL: Riverside.

Lohman, D. F., Korb, K. A., & Lakin, J. M. (2008). Identifying academically gifted English-language learners using nonverbal tests. *Gifted Child Quarterly, 52*, 275–296.

Naglieri, J. A., & Ford, D. Y. (2003). Addressing underrepresentation of gifted minority children using the Naglieri Nonverbal Ability Test (NNAT). *Gifted Child Quarterly, 47*, 155–160.

Otis, A., & Lennon, R. (2003). *Otis-Lennon School Ability Test* (8th ed.). Upper Saddle River, NJ: Pearson.

Reis, S. M., & Renzulli, J. S. (2011). Is there still a need for gifted education? An examination of current research. *Learning and Individual Differences, 20*, 308–317.

Robinson, N. M. (2005). In defense of a psychometric approach to the definition of academic giftedness: A conservative view from a die-hard liberal. In R. J. Sternberg & J. E. Davidson (Eds.), *Conceptions of giftedness* (2nd ed., pp. 417–435). Boston: Cambridge University Press.

Rushton, J. P., & Jensen, A. R. (2006). The totality of evidence shows the race IQ gap still remains. *Psychological Science, 17*, 921–922.

Sternberg, R. J., Grigorenko, E. L., & Bundy, D. A. (2001). The predictive value of IQ. *Merrill-Palmer Quarterly, 47*, 1–41.

Sternberg, R. J., Jarvin, L., & Grigorenko, E. L. (2011). *Explorations in giftedness.* New York: Cambridge University Press.

Tannenbaum, A. J. (2003). Nature and nurture of giftedness. In N. Colangelo & G. A. Davis (Eds.), *Handbook of gifted education* (3rd ed., pp. 45–59). Boston: Allyn & Bacon.

Terman, L. M. (1916). *The measurement of intelligence: An explanation of and complete guide for the use of the Stanford revision and extension of the Binet-Simon Intelligence Scale.* Boston: Houghton Mifflin.

VanTassel-Baska, J., Feng, A. X., & de Brux, E. (2007). A study of identification and achievement profiles of performance task-identified gifted students over 6 years. *Journal for the Education of the Gifted, 31*, 7–34.

VanTassel-Baska, J., Johnson, D., & Avery, L. D. (2008). Using performance tasks in the identification of economically disadvantaged and minority gifted learners: Findings from Project STAR. *Gifted Child Quarterly, 46*, 110–123.

Wechsler, D. (2003). *Wechsler Intelligence Scale for Children* (4th ed.). The Psychological Corporation, San Antonio, TX.

12

IDENTIFYING GIFTED STUDENTS

Nontraditional Uses of Traditional Measures

David F. Lohman

How can schools make better use of information they routinely collect that can help them identify academically talented students? How can they use the same kinds and diversity of information they use for talent identification with middle-class, English-speaking students to identify academically talented English language learners (ELL) or students with low socio-economic status (SES)? How can educators avoid being misled by poorly normed tests or misusing scores from state achievement tests that have no norms?

At some point, these questions and underlying measurement issues must be considered when discussing talent identification and development programs (Lohman, in press; Lohman & Foley Nicpon, in press). Developing a good identification system requires attention to much more than whether a student's test scores exceed some pre-ordained cut-off score. Fortunately, there are several easy-to-implement procedures that can dramatically increase the effectiveness of talent identification. The goals of this chapter are to explain and illustrate these simple procedures. The common thread is the use of test scores and other information that schools commonly collect (or could collect). However, this information will be interpreted (or reinterpreted) in the local context. This means asking for or developing local norms on ability and achievement test scores. It also means taking into account the student's opportunity to learn when making inferences about talent. Neither of these steps is difficult, but each requires moving beyond entrenched beliefs about test score use. We begin with a discussion of test score scaling and its use in above-grade-level testing. Although this is an unconventional use of test scores, it is only a small step off the beaten path. Next, we introduce local norms: why they are important and how they can be obtained from testing companies or developed using a spreadsheet. Third, we go one step beyond local norms to subgroup norms or comparisons. These procedures offer the most defensible method for identifying academically talented low SES, ELL, and minority students. Finally, we show how to integrate these strands into a simple scheme for combining ability test scores, achievement test scores, and teacher ratings.

ABOVE-GRADE-LEVEL TESTING

Above-grade-level testing refers to the practice of assessing a gifted student with a test designed for older students. Sometimes gifted students are administered a higher level of a test in order to obtain a better estimate of their abilities than can be derived from an on-grade-level test that is too easy for them. At other times, however, the goal is to make a decision about acceleration for the student. In such cases, it can be helpful to know how the student's achievement in a domain compares with the achievement of older students. For example, a third grade student may be administered a mathematics achievement test at the level that is designed for seventh grade students. Here the goal is not to obtain a better estimate of the student's rank compared to other third grade students, but rather to estimate her rank compared to seventh graders on the seventh grade test.

Scores on achievement and ability tests that span multiple age or grade groups are typically placed on a common, developmental score scale. This is most easily done when the test consists of one long string of items ordered by difficulty. The scale score that the student obtains can be interpreted using norms for students at different age or grade levels. On the Cognitive Abilities Test (CogAT) (Lohman, 2011), scale scores are called "Universal Scale Scores" (USS); on the Iowa Tests of Basic Skills (ITBS) they are called "Scale Scores" (SS). Both of these scales are constructed by comparing the performance of adjacent age (or grade) groups on common subsets of items.

Whether above-grade-level achievement testing is appropriate or inappropriate depends on how the scores will be interpreted. For example, is the goal to obtain a better estimate of the student's ability when compared to other students of the same age? Inferences about *ability* assume that the student's opportunity to acquire the knowledge or skills presented in the test is similar to other students in the norm group. If the student is less familiar with some of the test content, then the above-grade-level achievement test could underestimate the student's ability. Or is the goal to decide whether a third grade student is likely to succeed in a seventh grade mathematics class? In this case, the appropriate norm group consists of seventh grade students in the class that the individual might attend. The test that gives the best information on ability compared to age-mates may not provide the best guidance for acceleration. Similarly, the test that best guides acceleration may not provide the best estimate of ability compared to age-mates.

USING LOCAL NORMS

Most test users rely exclusively on national norms when interpreting scores on ability and achievement tests. Often, they are not aware of the limitations of national norms and the extent to which other normative comparisons can assist them. In the field of gifted education, the exclusive use of national norms stems in part from early definitions of giftedness based on Stanford–Binet IQ scores. In the early years of ability testing, psychologists did not understand the extent to which IQ scores change with age and experience, and how the methods used to scale the Binet tests impacted the range of scores that the test produced (see Lohman & Foley Nicpon, in press). Psychologists also did not appreciate the extent to which performance on ability tests was improving across decades—especially for young children on the nonverbal items (Flynn, 1999; Thorndike, 1975).

Advantages of National Norms

Well-developed national norms on ability tests have a number of desirable characteristics. When national norms are used, the scores of test-takers are compared to a common standard defined by the performance of a representative national sample of children of the same age or grade. When the same test is administered to a new class of students and interpreted using the same national norms, variation in the abilities of different cohorts of students who are being considered for talent development programs are readily documented.

When national norms are developed, vagaries of performance due to sampling are typically removed by careful smoothing of score distributions across age or grade groups (for an explanation of the process, see Lohman, 2009). The accuracy and stability of scores obtained using good national norms are particularly important for interpreting score profiles across subtests or batteries within the test.

Limitations of National Norms

However, national norms can be misleading, especially on ability tests that do not require a high level of professional certification to administer. National norms on many group ability tests used in schools are seriously deficient. Some widely used tests have never been properly normed and give IQ scores that are 10 to 17 points too high; others have been normed but not recently, and on at least one widely used test, normative scores were incorrectly computed, vastly over-identifying the number of very high- and very low-scoring students (for details, see Lohman, Korb, & Lakin, 2008). In such cases, national norms are more harmful than helpful.

Advantages of Local Norms

The primary limitation of national norms is the failure to take into account local variations in ability or achievement. However, the need for special programming at the local level depends on the discrepancy between the individual student's current levels of cognitive or academic development and that of his classmates—not that of all other students in the nation. In some schools, the average student scores at the 20th national percentile (NPR). In such a school, a student who scores at the 70th NPR is probably significantly mismatched with her peers. Conversely, in some very high-achieving schools, a student who scores at the 95th NPR may not be seriously mismatched with the instructional challenges in the classroom. Because schools vary widely in the average ability and achievement of their students, policies that require all individuals in the district or state to attain the same level of excellence on a nationally normed test result in some schools in which no students are served by the program, and other schools in which a substantial fraction of the students are labeled "gifted." Local norms eliminate both of these problems.

Local norms also allow users to focus on how best to measure academic talent rather than on finding a test with national norms that give the desired percentage of "gifted" students—overall or within subgroups of the population. Often, tests that achieve these goals either have out-of-date (or inaccurate) norms or they measure only a limited aspect of scholastic aptitude. Poorly normed nonverbal tests that measure only figural reasoning abilities suffer on both counts.

Use of local norms, especially when presented as percentiles, also helps educators to avoid many of the problems that attend IQ scores and test scores merely reported on an IQ-like scale.[1] Chief among these problems is the common but erroneous belief that IQ tests measure innate abilities that should remain constant as the student matures. It is much easier for parents and teachers to believe that the student's local percentile rank on a reasoning test can be expected to change with experience and opportunity than for them to understand that IQ scores are similarly changeable.

Limitations of Local Norms

Local norms typically represent the performance of a particular sample of students only for the year in which the test was administered. Thus, they require census testing (i.e., testing all second grade students rather than testing only those individuals nominated for the program). Furthermore, because the normative scores are based on a small sample, the local percentile rank (PR) scores are less stable than national PRs. However, this may not be an issue if the goal is simply to identify and serve the top X percent of students in the class. Indeed, simple ranks (rather than percentile ranks) may be sufficient. Later discussion in this chapter will elaborate on this approach.

Multiple Perspectives

Fortunately, one does not have to interpret test scores using a single normative perspective. For example, some group-administered ability tests report both age and grade norms as well as local norms that are calculated from the data submitted by a given school or school district. A score that is not unusual from one perspective may be unusual when viewed from another perspective. Figure 12.1 shows an example from Form 7 of the Cognitive Abilities Test (CogAT) (Lohman, 2011). The columns for "Age Scores" and "Grade Scores" use national norms. The "Local Scores" column reports percentile ranks for the distribution of Standard Age Scores (SAS) in the local group that this tested. The value of each perspective depends on the inferences that will be made from the test scores. If the goal is to identify the most talented students in the school or district, then

CogAT® LIST OF STUDENT SCORES
Cognitive Abilities Test™ (CogAT®)

Class: Halladay
Building: Oak Elementary
District: Elm ISD
Form-Level: 7-9
Test Date: 10/2012
Norms: Fall 2011
Grade: 3 Page: 1

STUDENT NAME I.D. Number F-1 F-2 F-3 Code ABCDEF G H I J K L MNOPZ	Birth Date Level (Gender) Age Form Program	No. of Items	No. Att	Raw Score	USS	AGE SCORES SAS	AGE SCORES PR	AGE SCORES S	GRADE SCORES PR	GRADE SCORES S	LOCAL SCORES PR	LOCAL SCORES S	Student Profile APR Graph	Profile
Bagsby, Aiden 0000152007	12/03 9 (F) 06-02 7													
Verbal		62	62	57	190	115	79	7	82	7	95	8	79	
Quantitative		52	52	46	186	114	77	7	80	7	94	8	77	7A
Nonverbal		56	56	47	188	114	76	6	79	7	93	8	76	
Composite (VQN)					189	114	78	7	81	7	95	8		
Brigerton, Ryan 0000131196	07/04 9 (F) 08-03 7													
Verbal		62	62	19	139	79	6	2	9	2	23	3	6	
Quantitative		52	52	17	144	83	10	2	13	3	27	4	10	2A
Nonverbal		56	56	13	147	85	13	3	16	3	30	4	13	
Composite (VQN)					143	82	9	2	12	3	26	4		

Fig. 12.1 Example of a report showing national age scores, national grade scores, and locally normed scores on Form 7 of the Cognitive Abilities Test.
USS = Universal Scale Score; SAS = Standard Age Score; PR = Percentile Rank; S = Stanine.

local norms provide critical information. For example, scores on the Verbal Battery for the first student (Alden Bagsby) would not be considered remarkable when compared to all other children in the United States. Alden's national age percentile rank (APR) for the Verbal Battery is only 79 and the national grade percentile rank is only slightly higher at 82. However, the local percentile rank for the Verbal score is 95. He may well benefit from a greater challenge than he is currently experiencing in his classes.

Computing Local Norms

Rank Orders

Precise local norms are not needed for many school-based talent development programs. The problem is akin to identifying athletes for the junior or senior high varsity basketball or track team. All that is needed is some way to identify the most talented students in each domain in which programs are offered. For example, many programs distinguish between verbal and quantitative/spatial abilities. A rank ordering of students on each of these dimensions is all that is needed. Ranking works both when all students in a grade are tested (i.e., census testing) and when only a subset of students who were nominated for the program are tested. The middle panel of Table 12.1 shows an example in which scores for 20 students were rank ordered by sorting the data using a spreadsheet.

Table 12.1 Getting ranks

1. Get the data into an excel spreadsheet: a. CogAT SAS scores; b. Potential grouping variable (e.g., ELL).			2. To get local ranks, sort (rank order) the data by CogAT scores.			3. To get separate ranks for each ELL group, sort by ELL and then SAS.		
ID	CogAT	ELL	ID	CogAT	ELL	ID	CogAT	ELL
1	92	N	8	121	N	8	121	N
2	85	N	10	114	N	10	114	N
3	111	N	3	111	N	3	111	N
4	90	Y	15	107	N	15	107	N
5	105	N	5	105	N	5	105	N
6	102	Y	6	102	Y	11	100	N
7	72	Y	11	100	N	16	97	N
8	121	N	16	97	N	18	93	N
9	95	Y	9	95	Y	1	92	N
10	114	N	18	93	N	17	86	N
11	100	N	1	92	N	2	85	N
12	74	N	4	90	Y	20	78	N
13	81	Y	14	88	Y	12	74	N
14	88	Y	17	86	N	6	102	Y
15	107	N	2	85	N	9	95	Y
16	97	N	19	84	Y	4	90	Y
17	86	N	13	81	Y	14	88	Y
18	93	N	20	78	N	19	84	Y
19	84	Y	12	74	N	13	81	Y
20	78	N	7	72	Y	7	72	Y

Most test publishers offer reports that provide this information. Figure 12.2 shows a portion of one such report for scores on the CogAT Verbal Battery. In the full report, separate rankings for all students in each class (or building) are given for each of the three CogAT batteries.

If particular groups of students differ markedly in opportunity to develop the abilities measured by the test, then ranks should be computed separately within these groups. The panel on the right in Table 12.1 shows how ranks within a grouping variable (here ELL status) can be obtained by sorting on two variables: first on ELL status and second on the CogAT score of interest (SAS). Ranks within a specific group also can easily be obtained using the test publisher's online test analysis and interpretation tools.

Percentile Ranks (PRs)

Although a simple rank order may suffice for many purposes, true local norms require the estimation of percentile ranks. Two scores that have adjacent ranks may differ substantially in percentile rank. For example, suppose the three highest scores in a data set are IQs of 140, 120, and 119. Clearly, the difference between the first and second student is larger than the distance between the second and third students. Simple ranks discard this information; percentile ranks can preserve it.

The critical difference between ranks and percentile ranks (PRs) is that the PRs take into account where each score falls in the overall distribution of scores. The PR of any score is simply the percentage of cases in the distribution with the same or lower value. Percentile ranks will be unstable, however, unless the distribution has many cases or has known characteristics. If, as is the case with ability test scores, one can assume that scores are approximately normally distributed, then the distribution is well described by the mean (M) and standard deviation (SD). In this case, the computation of local percentile ranks requires only that one know the mean and SD of scores within the local group. Although one can use different kinds of test scores in this computation (e.g., on CogAT, one could use raw scores, USS scores, or SAS scores), it is helpful to use the nationally normed age-based scores (such as CogAT SAS scores) in these calculations. By design, SAS scores are made to be normally distributed in the population. This makes the assumption of a normal distribution for the local sample more plausible. Standard Age Scores (SAS) also use the power of the national norms to control for the effects of age. Then the percentile ranks of SAS scores are computed for the local population using the local mean and SD of SAS scores.

CogAT®	CLASS LIST RANKED BY TESTS Cognitive Abilities Test™ (CogAT®)						Class/Group: Ortega									Form: 6

Verbal	SAS	APR	GPR	Student Name	SAS	APR	GPR	Student Name	SAS	APR	GPR	Student Name	SAS	APR	GPR	Student Name
	139	99	99	Regis, Clare	109	71	78	Delarosa, Amanda	101	52	53	Washington, Shanika	84	16	26	Peters, Matt
	137	99	98	Russell, Jalen	109	71	70	Maclean, Darnell	99	48	53	Freed, Jenna				Card, Susan
	121	91	91	Chavez, Natalia	107	67	65	Dukes, Sanetra	95	38	40	Brown, Nara				
	115	83	86	Hwang, Jung	101	52	55	Atsushi, Eri	94	35	48	Fry, Michelle				
	110	73	78	Lee, Samuel	101	52	58	Garcia, Felipe	90	27	27	Hogan, Ryan				

Fig. 12.2 Portion of a class report showing student ranks on the Verbal Battery of CogAT.
SAS = Standard Age Score; APR = national Age Percentile Rank; GPR = national Grade Percentile Rank.

If all students in a grade are tested, then the mean and standard deviation are easily estimated. Table 12.2 shows an example that uses the "AVERAGE," "STDEV," and"NORMDIST" functions in Microsoft Excel to compute local PRs. The example has only 20 cases, but at least 50 cases approximately normally distributed are needed before computing local norms in this way. Administering the same test each year to a different cohort of students (e.g., all second grade students) will provide increasingly stable local norms by cumulating cases across years (recalculating the local mean and SD each year). Thus, the sample that has only 50 cases in the first year would have approximately 100 the second year, 150 cases the third year, and so on. Note that if one uses the national mean and SD for SAS scores (M = 100; SD = 16), rather than the local mean and SD, then one will obtain the National Age PRs that correspond to each SAS score. Indeed, performing this calculation provides a good check on the accuracy of the procedures.

Table 12.2 Getting local percentile ranks (PRs)

1. Get the data into Excel	3. To get local Percentile	4. To get within-ELL local PRs, use mean
2. Get the mean and standard deviation for all SAS scores (ignores ELL)	Ranks (PRs),use Excel function "NORMDIST"	and SD for each group (M = 93.8, SD – 13.4 for non-ELL; and M – 87.4, SD – 9.7 for ELL).
a. Use "AVERAGE" function for the mean	a. Insert local mean and SD (see column 1)	Using Mean– 100 and SD – 16 for all students gives National
b. Use "STDEV" function for SD	b. NORMDIST (X, 93.8, 13.4, TRUE) where "X" = CogAT score	PRs for CogAT (last column)

ID	CogAT	ELL	ID	CogAT	ELL	LPR	ID	CogAT	ELL	LPR	Within ELL LPR	NPR
8	121	N	8	121	N	98	8	121	N	98	95	91
10	114	N	10	114	N	93	10	114	N	93	88	81
3	111	N	3	111	N	90	3	111	N	90	83	75
15	107	N	15	107	N	84	15	107	N	84	75	67
5	105	N	5	105	N	80	5	105	N	80	71	62
6	102	Y	6	102	Y	73	11	100	N	68	58	50
11	100	N	11	100	N	68	16	97	N	59	49	43
16	97	N	16	97	N	59	18	93	N	48	38	33
9	95	Y	9	95	Y	54	1	92	N	45	36	31
18	93	N	18	93	N	48	17	86	N	28	22	19
1	92	N	1	92	N	45	2	85	N	26	20	17
4	90	Y	4	90	Y	39	20	78	N	12	9	8
14	88	Y	14	88	Y	33	12	74	N	7	5	5
17	86	N	17	86	N	28	6	102	Y	73	93	55
2	85	N	2	85	N	26	9	95	Y	54	78	38
19	84	Y	19	84	Y	23	4	90	Y	39	61	27
13	81	Y	13	81	Y	17	14	88	Y	33	52	23
20	78	N	20	78	N	12	19	84	Y	23	36	16
12	74	N	12	74	N	7	13	81	Y	17	25	12
7	72	Y	7	72	Y	54	7	72	Y	5	6	4

Mean = 93.8
SD = 13.4

Although local PRs can be computed in a spreadsheet such as Excel (as illustrated in Table 12.2), one can also obtain local norms from some test publishers simply by asking for them at the time the tests are scored (see Figure 12.1).

THE IMPORTANCE OF OPPORTUNITY TO LEARN (OTL)

Individual differences in rate (or depth) of learning can indicate talent. In any domain, students with an aptitude or talent for a particular kind of learning or performance will typically learn in a few trials what otherwise similar individuals take many trials to learn. Inferences about intellectual ability from test scores, classroom activities, projects, and other behavioral evidence are thus always judged relative to some larger group of individuals that we assume have had similar opportunities to develop the knowledge, skills, or other observed characteristics. For most rating scales, the comparison group is usually only roughly defined (e.g., "When compared to other second grade students that you have taught, how able is this individual?"). On ability and achievement tests, however, the norm groups consist of narrowly defined samples of students of the same age or in the same grade. On ability tests, age groups typically consist of other students in the norming sample who differ from the examinee by no more than a few months. The individual who is six months older than another student is expected to perform somewhat better on the same set of tasks. Some tests use even more narrowly defined comparison groups. For example, normative scores on the ITBS depend on the number of weeks that the student has been in a particular grade. This means that the same number-correct score maps onto different age or grade percentile ranks, depending on the student's age in years and months or the number of weeks she has been enrolled in a particular grade in school.

However, if for any reason the individual's experiences differ markedly from those of other students who are the same age or in the same grade, then these normative comparisons will either underestimate or over-estimate the individual's ability to learn. Clearly, the intellectual abilities of students who live in poverty, who have irregular or poor schooling, who have less experience with the language of instruction (or testing) than the students they are being compared to are often underestimated when their behavior is compared with that of other children who are the same age or in the same grade.

It is important to understand that, regardless of the adequacy of the norm group for making inferences about talent, performance on the test tells something useful about the student's current level of development of the knowledge and skills measured by the test. Thus, we may rightly say that a fourth grade ELL student is reading at the first-grade level on an English language reading test. For many instructional decisions, this interpretation may be the most important. However, the same student's reading ability may be at a much higher level in another language. *Reading ability* is a broader construct than *reading ability in English*. And the student's *verbal ability* may be higher than his ability to read in any language. This is the broadest construct and as such requires the largest inference. Judgments about intellectual talent rest on this third type of inference. Such inferences are valid only when the student's performance on some set of tasks can be compared to the performance of others who have had similar opportunities to develop the abilities, knowledge, or skills required by those tasks.

Since the earliest days of mental testing, psychologists have struggled with the problem of accounting for differences in opportunity to learn, especially those differences moderated by exposure to the language of testing. Two fundamentally different approaches have been taken:

1. adjustment or redevelopment of norms so that students' scores can be compared with the scores of other individuals who have had similar opportunities to learn the language in which the test is presented or the knowledge it presumes; or
2. attempts to reduce or eliminate the impact of language or culture on the test itself.

The second approach has long been the preferred option. The use of culture- and language-reduced or so-called "nonverbal" tests stretches from the form boards of Itard through Army Beta to the performance battery of the Wechsler scales, the Progressive Matrices test (Raven, 1938), the Nonverbal Battery of the Cognitive Abilities Test (Thorndike & Hagen, 1963), and the Universal Nonverbal Intelligence Test (Bracken & McCallum, 1998). The most important disadvantage of this approach is that the abilities measured by nonverbal tests—especially those that use only figural reasoning items—under-represent the construct of intelligence. The most salient advantage of this approach is that the scores of all students can be interpreted using the same set of norms. However, using common norms assumes that the effects of language and culture have indeed been eliminated.

In recent years, nonverbal tests have been widely administered to test ELL children being considered for inclusion in talent development programs. To understand how ELL children perform on such tests, it is helpful to distinguish between the *language loading* and the *cultural loading* of a test. Paradoxically, reducing the language demands may actually increase the cultural loading of the test. In a comparison of three of the most widely used group-administered nonverbal tests, Laing, Castellano, and Buss (2006) trained examiners, administered the Naglieri Nonverbal Ability Test (NNAT; Naglieri, 2003), the Standard Progressive Matrices (SPM; Raven, Court, & Raven, 1983), and Form 6 of the Cognitive Abilities Test (CogAT; Lohman & Hagan, 2001) to over 1,200 students (approximately half ELL) in grades K–6. Directions were given in English or Spanish, as appropriate. When scores for the three nonverbal tests were placed on a common scale (M = 100, SD = 16), ELL students scored an average of 10 points lower than non-ELL students on the NNAT, nine points lower on the CogAT Nonverbal Battery, and eight points lower on the SPM (Lohman et al., 2008). Restricting the analysis to Hispanic students eligible for free/reduced-price school lunches still showed ELL/non-ELL differences of approximately eight points. Thus, in spite of controls for ethnicity, location, and socio-economic status (SES), Spanish-speaking ELL students performed substantially lower than their non-ELL Hispanic classmates on all three nonverbal reasoning tests. The overt demands for language on all three nonverbal tests were minimal, yet familiarity with the culture still had a substantial effect.

The second example comes from the standardization of a Spanish adaptation of the WISC-IV (Wechsler, 2004) intended for Spanish-speaking students with no more than five years in the U.S. educational system. Since the target population for the test was Spanish-speaking students in the United States, the sample of bilingual individuals used to norm the test was selected to represent that population. Normative data were later analyzed by the number of years each student had attended U.S. schools relative to his or her total education. The perceptual reasoning tests (Block Design, Picture Concepts, and Matrix Reasoning) measure nonverbal/fluid reasoning. The verbal comprehension tests (Similarities, Vocabulary, and Comprehension) measure verbal, crystallized abilities using items that were translated into Spanish. Surprisingly, exposure to the U.S. educational system had large effects on the perceptual reasoning index (10 points) and only a small effect on the verbal comprehension index (2.2 points). Those students with the most exposure to U.S. schooling performed significantly better on the perceptual reasoning tests. As Weiss, Saklofske, Prifitera, and Holdnack (2006) note, "[T]his is an interesting finding because it is widely assumed that the lack of an adaptation and acculturation primarily affects crystallized knowledge." However, the assumption that typical nonverbal tests provide a culture-fair measure of innate ability is not supported by research—recent or dated. Indeed, as Anastasi and Urbina (1997) concluded in their summary of 70 years of research on the topic, "nonverbal tests are often more culturally loaded than verbal tests" (p. 344).

Note that in both of these examples presented above, the nonverbal tests measured primarily or exclusively figural reasoning abilities. However, some nonverbal tests use other kinds of picture-based tasks in order to represent a broader reasoning construct. For example, picture-based analogies can measure verbal or quantitative reasoning in addition to figural–spatial reasoning. Two recent examples are the Universal Nonverbal Intelligence Test (Bracken & McCallum, 1998) and the primary-level tests on Form 7 of CogAT (Lohman, 2011). Items in these tests not only reduce the demands of language, but they also measure the ability to reason with pictorially represented verbal and quantitative concepts. The broader measure of ability they provide predicts success better in school than unidimensional nonverbal tests that use only figural–spatial content (McCallum, Bracken, & Wasserman, 2001). Furthermore, ELL, low SES, and minority students in grades K–2 perform as well or better on picture–verbal and picture–quantitative tests than on figural reasoning tests (Lohman & Gambrell, in press).

MEASURING OPPORTUNITY TO LEARN

Measuring opportunity to learn requires finding some variable (or set of variables) that not only captures learning opportunities but that can be unambiguously coded for all students. In the *WISC IV–Spanish* study (Wechsler, 2004) for example, the number of years attending U.S. schools was used. Some researchers also add home language. More refined measures of ELL status are available in schools in which all ELL students are administered the same English Language Proficiency test each year. These tests allow schools to create groups that distinguish between students who have different levels of familiarity with, and competence in, American English. To determine economic opportunity, the most accessible measure for schools is whether the student qualifies for a free or reduced-price school lunch.

If students can be grouped using one or more measures of opportunity to learn, separate rank orders are easily created within the different OTL groups. If there are many students in each group, then separate percentile ranks (PRs) can also be calculated within each group. This is easily done if one can estimate the mean and SD of test scores for each group. For relatively small samples (fewer than 50 students), one can estimate different means for each OTL group, but then use the same SD for all groups. Again, accumulating cases across years allows one to estimate increasingly stable local PR scores for the students in each OTL group.

USING WITHIN-OTL SCORES

The need for precise estimates of ability is a direct consequence of trying to determine whether or not a student is truly "gifted." However, if the goal is merely to identify low SES or ELL students who might profit from special encouragement, projects, or enrichment, then there is no need for such precision.

One of the major stumbling blocks for effective talent identification among low SES and ELL students is the presumption that all talented individuals must receive the same kind of special instruction. In athletics, we would expect that some individuals who had little experience in swimming might have talent for the sport. But we would not think it reasonable immediately to expect them to swim at the same pace as students who had had many years of practice in the sport. Clearly, the inference of talent is distinguishable from a judgment about the current level of development of that talent. Thus, any attempt to identify talent within OTL groups must also be accompanied by a redesign of the programs that serve the students who will be identified as talented.

In considering how this might be done, it is helpful to keep in mind that encouraging interest and persistence in the pursuit of excellence is as important for talent development as the acquisition of academic knowledge and skills. Further, unlike their classmates whose parents may have greater resources, students from low SES and immigrant families often must rely on their school to provide special services and opportunities for talent development. If the school cannot make it happen, then it does not happen. Therefore, some form of enrichment may be most appropriate for many of these students whose academic development is similar to that of their classmates but who exhibit undeveloped talent. The scheme outlined in the next section is specifically designed for schools that must serve both those students who are considerably in advance of their peers and those who exhibit talent but are not currently mismatched with their peers.

COMBINING ABILITY TESTS, ACHIEVEMENT TESTS, AND TEACHER RATINGS

Many schools use multiple criteria to identify academically talented students. However, the various sources of evidence must be combined in some way. Often this is done by converting test scores, teacher ratings, and other information to point values. Points are then summed and students admitted accordingly. Although these methods are often easy to understand, they can easily mislead. Some of the potential problems are:

1. At best, converting a continuous score with many values to a point scale with few values discards information. Often, the information that is retained is distorted by the way points map onto the original score scale.
2. When adding or averaging scores, the final rank order is determined by the score with the greatest variability in point values, not the score that on average contributes the most points. The score with the greatest variability may not be the score one wishes to emphasize.
3. Unless different rankings are determined for different domains (e.g., verbal versus quantitative), students with uneven score profiles are often excluded. This is because adding or averaging diverse information discards the unique information in each measure.

4. Rating-scale data and other sources of information can be helpful. However, even when raters are well trained, such measures are usually less reliable and less valid than the test scores. Hence, even assigning ratings a lesser weight (or point value) can be problematic. For example, although one could certainly justify providing enrichment opportunities to a student rated (by a teacher) as highly creative, it would be difficult to defend a decision to deny the opportunity for advanced instruction to an individual who received lower ratings on creativity but obtained high ability and achievement test scores. Yet for every student who gains admission because of high teacher ratings, another individual with equally high achievement or ability test scores is denied admission because of lower teacher ratings. An effective way to overcome this dilemma is to use ratings (and other measures that are potentially less reliable and valid) to provide opportunity, but never to remove it.

Figure 12.3 shows a scheme that accomplishes this goal.[2] This particular version uses only CogAT scores and teacher ratings from the Scales for Rating the Behavioral Characteristics of Superior Students (SRBCSS; Renzulli et al., 2004).

The vertical dimension of Figure 12.3 distinguishes students who exhibit superior reasoning abilities in *either* the verbal domain *or* in the quantitative–nonverbal domain from those who exhibit strong but less stellar reasoning abilities in these domains. We have set two cut-off scores. One identifies those students who score at or above the 96th percentile rank; the other identifies those students who score at or above the 80th percentile rank (but below the 96th PR) on *either* verbal reasoning *or* quantitative–nonverbal reasoning. These percentile-rank criteria are commonly used in gifted programs. Although national norms can be used for this purpose, we strongly recommend that schools use local norms. Local norms can be obtained using the procedures outlined earlier in this chapter.

| | | Teacher Rating on Learning Ability, Motivation, or Creativity | |
		Low teacher ratings	High teacher ratings
CogAT Verbal OR Quantitative-Nonverbal Reasoning	($\geq 96^{th}$ PR)	II	I
	(80th–95th PR)	IV	III

Fig. 12.3 Combining ability (CogAT Verbal or Quantitative–Nonverbal) and teacher ratings (SRBCSS ratings of ability, motivation, or creativity). Two levels of ability and two levels of ratings are combined to provide four categories (see text for explanation).

The horizontal dimension of the matrix distinguishes between students who, when compared to other individuals nominated for the program, obtain relatively high teacher ratings and students who obtain lower teacher ratings. Teacher ratings are considered high if *any* one of the ratings for learning ability, motivation, or creativity is high. If teachers rate all students, then a high rating might be one that was obtained by the top 5 percent or 10 percent of students. However, it is often difficult to obtain reliable ratings for classes with many students. Another option, then, is to obtain teacher ratings on the much smaller subset of students whom teachers or others have nominated for the program or whose test scores are above the 80th PR. When only a subset of students is rated, then a much more lenient standard should be set. For example, one could distinguish between those students with ratings above the average of the group of nominated students and those with ratings that are below the average of this group. If there is no variability in the ratings of nominated students, then procedures for nominating students are too restrictive or raters are poorly trained. Of course, schools can implement a rule that is either more stringent or more lenient than *above* (or *below*) *average*.

Combining these two criteria gives four categories of assessment results.

- Students in Category I exhibit superior reasoning abilities on CogAT and are rated as highly capable, motivated, or creative by their teachers.
- Students in Category II also exhibit superior reasoning abilities but, when compared to other students, are not rated as highly by their teachers on any one of the three major scales of the SRBCSS. Programs that follow a traditional identification scheme (e.g., self-contained classrooms or schools) would accept individuals in both Category I and Category II. However, the progress of students in Category II should be monitored closely.
- Students in Category III exhibit somewhat lower but still strong reasoning abilities (80th to 95th PR) on CogAT, and are rated as highly capable, motivated, or creative by their teachers. These students would be included in school-wide enrichment programs that aim to serve a broader range of individuals than are served by traditional programs (Renzulli, 2005). Schools that serve many low SES individuals would find that many of their best students would fall into this category, especially when using national rather than local (i.e., school) test norms.
- Finally, students in Category IV exhibit good but not exceptional reasoning abilities (between the 80th and 95th PR), and are not rated as unusually capable, motivated, or creative by their teachers. Although good students, these individuals would not be provided with special programming on the basis of either their CogAT scores or teacher ratings. However, they should be reconsidered when information on achievement is available.

These procedures can be carried out on a spreadsheet or similar data management tool such as Riverside Publishing's Interactive Results Manager (iRM). Figure 12.4 shows a sample student roster in iRM that has CogAT Verbal (V) and Quantitative–Nonverbal (QN) local percentile ranks (LPRs), and three SRBCSS rating scales that have been classified as above or below the average of the group that was rated. Typically, ratings would be gathered only for students who had test scores above the 80th LPR. Figure 12.5 shows the number of students in each category, which is linked to a roster with names and scores.

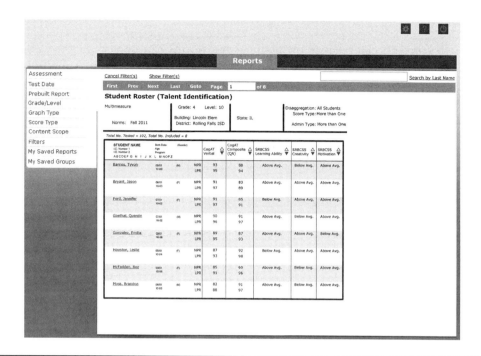

Fig. 12.4 A sample student roster.

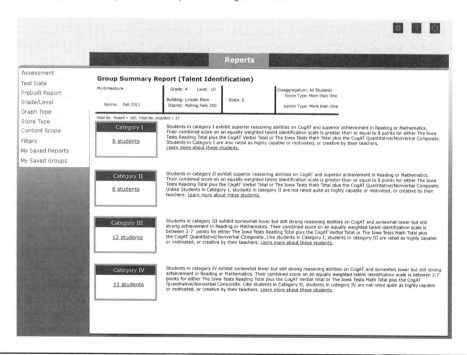

Fig. 12.5 Number of students in each category.

SUMMARY

Although conventional reliance on national test norms can be very helpful, effective talent identification at the local level often requires the use of local and subgroup normative perspectives. The value of these alternative perspectives increases as test scores for the student group, the school, or the district depart from the national mean. The need for alternative instruction depends primarily on the mismatch between a student's current level of cognitive and academic development and that of his classmates. Local norms for ability and achievement tests can often be obtained from the test publisher, but they can also easily be developed using commonly available spreadsheet programs. The simplest comparisons report local rank orders of students—for all students or for subgroups defined by some measure of opportunity to learn. Local percentile ranks can also be computed providing one has sufficient data to estimate them. Increasingly accurate local norms can be obtained by accumulating data across years.

Opportunity to learn (OTL) can be estimated by ELL status or by an index of family income such as eligibility for a free/reduced-price school lunch. By accounting for opportunity to learn, schools are better able to identify their most academically talented students than is possible using only figural reasoning, nonverbal tests. Low SES and minority students often score well below other students on nonverbal tests, especially when they have had limited exposure to tests that present unfamiliar tasks. More importantly, verbal and quantitative reasoning abilities are essential aspects of academic talent for all students. By accounting for opportunity to learn, one can measure these abilities for all students, thereby better identifying the most academically talented individuals in all groups. Providing appropriately challenging instruction for all students who might benefit from enrichment or acceleration requires a rethinking of the purpose of the gifted program—and perhaps beginning with a renaming of the program so that it encourages talent identification and development rather than simple certification of giftedness (Callahan, 2005).

NOTES

1. Examples include CogAT Standard Age Scores (SAS); Otis–Lennon School Ability Index (SAI); Naglieri Nonverbal Ability Index scores.
2. Elsewhere (Lohman & Renzulli, 2007), we show how to include achievement test scores as well.

REFERENCES

Anastasi, A., & Urbina, S. (1997). *Psychological testing* (7th ed.). Upper Saddle River, NJ: Prentice Hall.

Bracken, B. A., & McCallum, S. (1998). *Universal Nonverbal Intelligence Test—UNIT*. Itasca, IL: Riverside.

Callahan, C. M. (2005). Identifying gifted students from underrepresented populations. *Theory Into Practice, 44*, 98–104.

Flynn, J. R. (1999). Searching for justice: The discovery of IQ gains over time. *American Psychologist, 54*, 5–20.

Laing, P., Castellano, J., & Buss, R. (2006). Project Bright Horizon. Phoenix, AZ: Washington Elementary School District.Lohman, D. F. (2009). The contextual assessment of talent. In MacFarlane, B. & Stambaugh, T. (Eds.), *Leading change in gifted education: The festschrift of Dr. Joyce VanTassel-Baska* (pp. 229–242). Waco, TX: Prufrock Press.

Lohman, D. F. (2011). *Cognitive Abilities Test (Form 7)*. Rolling Meadows, IL: Riverside.

Lohman, D. F. (2012). Decision strategies. In S. L. Hunsaker (Ed.), *Identification: The theory and practice of identifying students for gifted and talented education services* (pp. 217–248). Mansfield Center, CT: Creative Learning Press.

Lohman, D. F., & Foley Nicpon, M. (2012). Ability testing and talent identification. In S. L. Hunsaker (Ed.),

Identification: The theory and practice of identifying students for gifted and talented education services (pp. 283–335). Mansfield Center, CT: Creative Learning Press.

Identification of students for gifted and talented services: Theory into practice.

Lohman, D. F., & Gambrell, J. L. (in press). Use of nonverbal measures in gifted identification. *Journal of Psychoeducational Assessment.*

Lohman, D. F., & Hagen, E. P. (2001). *Cognitive Abilities Test (Form 6).* Itasca, IL: Riverside.

Lohman, D. F., Korb, K., & Lakin, J. (2008). Identifying academically gifted English language learners using nonverbal tests: A comparison of the Raven, NNAT, and CogAT. *Gifted Child Quarterly, 52,* 275–296.

Lohman, D. F., & Renzulli, J. S. (2007). *A simple procedure for combining ability test scores, achievement test scores, and teacher ratings to identify academically talented children.* Retrieved January 16, 2012 from http://faculty.education.uiowa.edu/dlohman/

McCallum, R. S., Bracken, B. A., & Wasserman, J. D. (2001). *Essentials of nonverbal testing.* NY: Wiley.

Naglieri, J. A. (1996). *Naglieri Nonverbal Ability Test.* San Antonio, TX: Harcourt Brace Educational Measurement.

Raven, J. C. (1938). *Progressive matrices: A perceptual test of intelligence.* London, UK: Lewis.

Raven, J. C., Court, J. H., & Raven, J. (1983). *Manual for Raven's Progressive Matrices and vocabulary scales, section 4: Advanced Progressive Matrices, sets I and II.* London, UK: Lewis.

Renzulli, J. S. (2005). *Equity, excellence, and economy in a system for identifying students in gifted education: A guidebook.* (Research Monograph 05208). Storrs: The National Research Center on the Gifted and Talented, University of Connecticut.

Renzulli, J. S., Smith, L. H., White, A. J., Callahan, C. M., Hartman, R. K., Westberg, M. et al. (2004). *Scales for Rating the Behavioral Characteristics of Superior Students.* Mansfield Center, CT: Creative Learning Press.

Thorndike, R. L. (1975). Mr. Binet's test 70 years later. *Educational Researcher, 4,* 3–7.

Thorndike, R. L., & Hagen, E. (1963). *Cognitive Abilities Test.* New York: Houghton Mifflin.

Wechsler, D. (2004). *WISC IV–Spanish.* San Antonio, TX: Harcourt.

Weiss, L. G., Saklofske, D. H., Prifitera, A., & Holdnack, J. A. (2006). *WISC-IV advanced clinical interpretation.* Burlington, MA: Elsevier.

13

USES AND MISUSES OF MATRICES IN IDENTIFYING GIFTED STUDENTS

Considerations for Better Practice

Tonya R. Moon

Identification of gifted students remains one of the most controversial aspects of gifted programming. This controversy stems from the lack of a consistent definition of giftedness (Davis & Rimm, 1994), which makes identifying giftedness tricky; diversity in the ways in which giftedness is operationalized from school district to school district, sometimes referred to as the "geographic giftedness" phenomenon (Borland, 1989); and a lack of understanding of the technical aspect of measurement involved in the identification process.

While there are myriad ways in which school districts implement the process of gifted identification, one commonly used process includes the use of a gifted identification matrix. Scholars in the field have written extensively about the perils of using matrices in identifying students for gifted services (e.g., Callahan & McIntire, 1994; Feldhusen & Baska, 1985; Frasier & Passow, 1994; VanTassel-Baska, 2007). The purpose of this chapter is to provide a (mostly) non-technical discussion of the uses and misuses of matrices and to offer some guidance on appropriate practices that can be applied in a school setting.

COMMON PRACTICES INVOLVING A GIFTED IDENTIFICATION MATRIX

The form and formats of identification matrices vary widely; however, there are two common ways in which they are used (see Figure 13.1).

Scenario 1

One common identification procedure based on a matrix involves a student moving through a series of steps, often referred to as a two-stage identification process (see Figure 13.1). Stage One is generally a screening process that collects student data using several different types of standardized instrument (e.g., group-administered achievement tests or intelligence tests) and/or nominations or rating scales completed by a teacher and/or parent. In order to move to Stage Two in the identification process, a student must meet a predetermined minimum score on the Stage One screening instrument or instruments. For example, for a student to move to the second stage in the identification process, her performance on the screening instruments must meet one of several optional criteria:

1. a predetermined score on the intelligence test (e.g., IQ equal to or greater than 125); or
2. a predetermined overall performance score generated by assigning points to varying score ranges on the assessments administered (e.g. five points for an IQ score exceeding 130; three points for a reading achievement score between the 90th and 94th percentile).

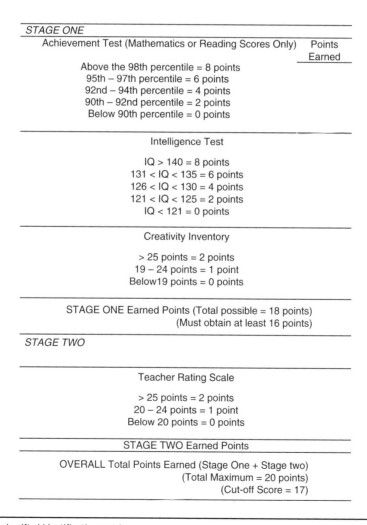

Fig. 13.1 A sample gifted identification matrix.

Stage Two of the screening process typically includes additional testing on other IQ or achievement tests such as an individually administered intelligence test, teacher and/ or parent questionnaires, or observations of the student in a class setting with points assigned to particular behaviors using a rating scale. Points are then summed and students are deemed eligible for the gifted program if they meet or exceed a predetermined cut-off score.

Scenario 2

In other instances, the identification process involves screening students with all of the identification instruments (e.g., achievement test, ability test, rating scale); recording each student's performance on every instrument; determining where the student's score fits within a pre-specified score range for that instrument and transferring that "final" score for each assessment to a matrix; summing the number of total points accumulated from each assessment; and finally selecting students based on whether or not their total scores meet or exceed a predetermined overall cut-off score (see Figure 13.2).

Issues With the Gifted Identification Matrix Processes

Both identification scenarios described above employ a matrix to allocate point values to assessment scores which are then summed to make a decision regarding gifted

	Points Earned
Group Achievement Test (Mathematics or Reading Scores Only)	
Above the 98th percentile = 8 points 95th – 97th percentile = 6 points 92nd – 94th percentile = 4 points 90th – 92nd percentile = 2 points Below 94th percentile = 0 points	
Intelligence Test	
IQ > 140 = 8 points 131 < IQ < 135 = 6 points 126 < IQ < 130 = 4 points 121 < IQ < 125 = 2 points IQ < 121 = 0 points	
Creativity Inventory	
46 – 50 points = 3 points 41 – 45 points = 2 points 36 – 40 points = 1 point Below 36 points = 0 points	
Teacher Rating Scale	
> 40 points = 4 points 35 – 39 points = 3 points 30 – 34 points = 2 points 25 – 29 points = 1 points Below 25 points = 0 points	
Total Points Earned	

Fig. 13.2 A sample gifted identification matrix.

placement. While it might initially seem that the scenarios above describe a highly systematic and fair approach to identifying gifted students, there are several issues which make the use of matrices questionable. While both scenarios above appear to utilize multiple assessments, an approach supported by recommended best practices (see American Educational Research Association [AERA], American Psychological Association [APA], & National Council on Measurement in Education [NCME], 1999), in Scenario 1, students must reach specific levels on initial assessments before they are allowed to move on to the next level, where they are presented with additional assessments. In the end, this becomes a "multiple hurdles" process, rather than a multiple criteria approach, which is the true intent of using multiple assessments. In Scenario 1 above, students have to obtain a certain level of proficiency on one set of assessments before being allowed to take the second set of assessments. In order to be considered for gifted services, a set level of performance must be demonstrated on both sets of assessments. Thus, in this situation, students who are identified for gifted services are those students who have performed well on both sets of assessments, and those who do not meet the pre-established criteria on both sets of assessments are automatically eliminated from consideration.

The second issue in both scenarios is that, regardless of a band of relatively different scores, students' performances on the assessments are narrowed down to one number. For example, in Figure 13.1 (above), any student who scores between the 95th and the 97th percentile receives the same point value (in this case, 6) on the achievement test. This practice of "throwing away" precise information is problematic for a number of reasons, the most egregious of which is the incorrect assumption that the percentile rank (PR) scale is an equal-interval scale. Indeed, percentile ranks are *not* an equal-interval scale, and thus, the difference between any two percentile ranks is *not* the same as between any other two percentile ranks. Using our example in Figure 13.1, to make the assumption that a student's performance at the 95th percentile is the same as another student's performance at the 97th percentile, and therefore assigning both students the same point value (2) is an inappropriate practice. Furthermore, the range of 92–94 is not equivalent to the range of 95–97. It requires a greater gain in actual standard scores or number of items answered correctly to move from the 95th percentile to the 98th, than it does to move from the 92nd to the 95th. Further, the norm group against which the students are being compared are likely not equivalent; therefore the 95th percentile on one test is not equivalent to the 95th percentile on a different test in reflecting student status relative to peers.

The third issue in both scenarios is that, in both, multiple assessments are combined without regard to what contribution each individual assessment is making to the overall operationalized definition of giftedness. Often, little regard is given to aligning the types of instruments used in the identification process with the district definition of giftedness. As a hypothetical example, assume that District A defines gifted students as: "students who show the potential for performing at a remarkably high level of accomplishment in the area of general intellectual ability or specific academic aptitude."

District A uses a gifted identification matrix and, as part of that process, administers an achievement test, a creativity test, and a teacher rating scale in Stage One; and then in Stage Two, a full-scale IQ assessment is given. While the district's definition of giftedness does not mention the construct of creativity, a creativity assessment is given in Stage One. In other words, the operationalized definition is not aligned with the guiding definition of giftedness.

The fourth issue with Scenarios 1 and 2 is the practice of combining assessments without a systematic evaluation of the benefit that each assessment contributes to improved decision making regarding student identification. By combining multiple assessments that measure *different* constructs (e.g., achievement, creativity, and teacher ratings), measurement error is increased. This often results in high rates of false positives (i.e., identifying a student as gifted when in fact the student is not gifted) and false negatives (i.e., not identifying a student as gifted when in fact the student is gifted). In other words, the combining of multiple assessments that measure different constructs results in a high probability that many of the students who *are* identified to receive gifted services should not be identified for those services; and many students who are *not* identified to receive gifted services should, in fact, receive the services.

The fifth issue with the use of the gifted identification matrix is that test scores receive the greatest weight in determining a student's overall score. Most districts use teacher and parent rating scales or inventories as data points in the matrix as a way to broaden the pool of potential students considered for gifted programs. In the end, however, greater weight is given to the test scores because of the range restriction associated with rating scales and inventories, thus making identification of a student who does not test well unlikely, despite the inclusion of rating scales.

The lack of systematically determining cut-off scores for identification is another problematic practice. Whenever students are classified as "gifted" or "not gifted" based on assessments used in an identification process, performance standards (i.e., cut-off scores) should be established. While setting cut-off scores is not without controversy, not establishing those cut-off points on sound empirical data has the potential to have long-term effects for students.

Two issues that are not unique to the use of matrices but relate to the process of identification in general are the potential biases that exist in rating scales or checklists completed by teachers and/or parents, and the lack of quality norms with standardized assessments. While not limited to matrices, bias can impact a student's opportunity to receive gifted services. For example, in some cultures, group needs take precedent over individual needs (Skogrand, Hatch, & Singh, 2005). Therefore, to advocate for one child over another would be counter to the more collaborative nature of the group. A parent might be unable to complete a required assessment simply because the parent does not have the necessary skills in the rating scale's required language. Additionally, teacher bias or lack of understanding of the traits of giftedness across cultural groups might influence the rating that a student is given.

Finally, with all instruments used in any identification process, the assumption that the norms for any standardized instrument are of equal quality is problematic. Norms allow a student's score to be compared to the test scores of a representative sample of examinees that also took the same assessment. The quality of an instrument's norms is dependent upon several factors. The larger the sample that participated in the norming process, the more confident one can be that the standard scores accurately reflect the student's true performance. The participants of the norming sample must be representative of the types of student with whom the assessment will be used. Seldom do school districts have the resources or foresight to establish norms for any teacher or parent rating scale, resulting in arbitrary designation of point values on teacher or parent rating scales or observational data collected on students. Thus, the assignment of matrix points to ranges on teacher rating scales is arbitrary and indefensible.

The length of time that has passed since the norms were created also affects the quality of norms. For example, norms that were collected 10 years ago may no longer fairly represent today's population of students. It is a requirement that norms for state-mandated achievement tests be updated every seven years; but few other assessments are subject to this standard, so students may be compared to students of another generation. The quality of norms is also dependent upon the inclusion of factors shown to affect performance on the task of interest. For example, if parental education has been shown to affect student achievement, then in the norming sample for a student achievement test there should be representation of various parental education levels to allow for equitable comparisons of students who come from a range of parental educational levels.

Considerations to Make the Use of Multiple Measures for Gifted Identification a Valid Approach

The intentions of those who adopt matrices for identifying gifted students are to reflect multiple measures of student performance and potential to obtain a comprehensive set of quantitative and qualitative data regarding a candidate for gifted services. Accurate and valid information about that student's status and needs should be derived from a variety of assessments and procedures. A comprehensive gifted identification system should:

1. Consider all components of the definition of giftedness as defined by the respective state and district. Multiple assessments should be used that reflect each category of giftedness outlined in the definition. If a gifted program is focused on advanced mathematics, the identification process should be based upon assessments that measure important determinants for being successful in advanced mathematics (e.g., current mathematics achievement, quantitative reasoning, problem-solving skills, interest in mathematics).
2. Use the most up-to-date version of any standardized assessment that is supported by strong psychometric data to inform the decisions that will be made about gifted placement.
3. Undertake careful study of the norms of all standardized assessments used in an identification process to ensure that they are up-to-date and representative of the types of students that are being targeted for gifted services.
4. Use multiple measures, including both standardized and non-standardized assessments, as well other data sources including:
   a. interviews with parents/guardians, teachers, other relevant professionals, and if appropriate, the student;
   b. direct observations of the student in a variety of settings and on more than one occasion;
   c. curriculum-based measures designed specifically to elicit the types of knowledge, skills, and understandings that are the focus of the gifted services;
   d. student portfolios.
5. Integrate these multiple sources of data in a technically defensible way. One consideration is to investigate the incremental validity of particular sources of data. For example, does the use of an interest survey provide a significantly better result for a decision about gifted programming than use only of a group-administered

achievement test and ability test? If it is found that the interest survey significantly aids in the decision, then using the interest form is said to have incremental validity.

6. Consider confidence intervals and standard error of measure, if appropriate, when making decisions about placement. Confidence intervals are included in test manuals and provide a range in which a student's test score would be likely to fall if he or she were tested over several occasions. This interval allows for test error to be considered in interpreting a score.

7. Adhere to recommended and accepted practices for the administration, scoring, interpretation, and reporting of standardized assessments. For more details, see *The Standards for Educational and Psychological Testing* (AERA et al., 1999).

8. Develop case studies/profiles of students. The purpose of the case study is to provide a deeper understanding of a student's particular strengths, interests, abilities, motivation, and/or learning profile. Case studies include student data across multiple sources of information representing the various areas of the gifted definition.

9. An identification and placement committee made up of professionals with a background in assessment and gifted education should discuss the information gathered from all data sources in a balanced way to determine if the student's current level of academic performance and skills suggests a need for modifications in educational programming and what those modifications should be.

REFERENCES

American Educational Research Association, American Psychological Association, & National Council on Measurement in Education. (1999). *The standards for educational and psychological testing.* Washington, DC: American Educational Research Association.

Borland, H. A. (1989). *Planning and implementing programs for the gifted.* New York: Teachers College Press.

Callahan, C. M., & McIntire, J. (1994). *Identifying talent in American Indian and Alaska Native students.* Washington, DC: U.S. Department of Education.

Davis, G. A., & Rimm, S. B. (1994). *Education of the gifted and talented* (3rd ed.). Needham Heights, MA: Allyn & Bacon.

Feldhusen, J. F., & Baska, L. K. (1985). Identification and assessment of the gifted and talented. In J. F. Feldhusen (Ed.), *Excellence in educating the gifted* (pp. 87–88). Denver, CO: Love.

Frasier, M. M., & Passow, A. H. (1994). *Toward a new paradigm for identifying talent potential.* (Research Monograph 94112). Storrs: The National Research Center on the Gifted and Talented, University of Connecticut.

Skogrand, L., Hatch, D., & Singh, A. (2005, July). Understanding Latino families, implications for family education. *Family Resources.* Retrieved August 6, 2011 from http://www.extension.org/sites/default/files/w/5/5e/utahfactsheet.pdf

VanTassel-Baska, J. L. (Ed.). (2007). *Alternative assessments with gifted and talented students.* Waco, TX: Prufrock Press.

14

IDENTIFYING GIFTED LEARNERS
Nonverbal Assessment
Frank C. Worrell

In education and psychology, assessment is a term that refers to the process of documenting and integrating information from a variety of sources to assist in making a decision. Sources of information can include observations, interviews, and tests of many types. Educational and psychological tests can be an important source of information in educational assessments if the tests are well constructed and the use of the test scores is supported by validity evidence (American Educational Research Association [AERA], American Psychological Association [APA], & the National Council on Measurement in Education [NCME], 1999). As should be clear, assessment is a broader term than testing. In the current chapter, the focus is primarily on nonverbal tests, but the tests are discussed in terms of the type of information that they yield for use when assessing children for placement in programs for gifted and talented students.

Identifying children who are gifted—that is, those for whom placement in a gifted and talented education program is most appropriate—depends on using tests that yield reliable and valid scores. Reliability refers to the consistency of the scores that the test yields. Test scores should be both internally consistent and consistent across administrations. Additionally, there should be appropriate validity evidence supporting the use of these scores for placing students in gifted and talented education programs. That is, there should be some evidence that the use of the scores results in more accurate classification decisions; or, in less technical terms, evidence indicating that students who are classified as gifted and talented on the basis of the test scores are more successful when placed in gifted programs than individuals who were not so classified.

Typically, assessing individuals who are being considered for gifted services involves the use of academic achievement and cognitive ability instruments, the majority of which require verbal responses. However, there are several circumstances in which verbal assessments may *not* be appropriate (DeThorne & Schaefer, 2004; Lohman, Korb, & Lakin, 2008; McCallum, 2003a). For example, individuals with speech, language, or hearing impairments may be disadvantaged in their ability to understand and respond to verbal queries. Similarly, individuals who do not speak, or are not fluent in, the language in which a test has been normed will not be able to demonstrate the full extent of their knowledge on a verbal measure. In circumstances like these, in which the use of a verbal instrument may obscure rather than showcase an examinee's knowledge and skills, the use of nonverbal instruments may be more appropriate. Although one can argue that assessment by a jury or panel in identifying gifted musicians, dancers, or sculptors is nonverbal, this chapter will focus on intellectual and academic giftedness, as these domains are the ones for which nonverbal assessments (as the term is commonly used) have been developed.

To frame the discussion of the use of nonverbal assessments for identifying students for placement in gifted services, I first offer a simple definition of giftedness and describe the skills and abilities typically assessed in the identification and placement process. Second, I distinguish between the two major types of nonverbal tests that are used and review, very briefly, two theoretical models of intelligence that have implications for interpreting scores from cognitive instruments including nonverbal tests. Third, I discuss the extant evidence related to using nonverbal instruments in identifying giftedness. Fourth, I highlight several articles useful for individuals who want to familiarize themselves with the major nonverbal instruments that can be used for identification. Finally, I conclude with comments on using nonverbal tests for identifying ethnic and racial minority students for gifted placement.

What is Giftedness?

There are many conceptions of giftedness in the literature (Heller, Mönks, Sternberg, & Subotnik, 2000; Sternberg & Davison, 1986, 2005). Whether one associates giftedness with concepts such as aptitude, expertise, genius, or talent, almost all the conceptions of giftedness converge on the notion of superior or outstanding performance in a specific domain. Thus, in this chapter, giftedness is defined as performance at the upper end of a distribution of scores in a specific domain relative to an appropriate peer group. This definition is deliberately non-specific with regard to what the upper end of the distribution should be (e.g., the top 1 percent or 5 percent), as these decisions vary by program, district, state, and available resources; but the definition does require specification of the domain, the appropriate peer group, and the performance indicator on which the scores are based (Lohman, 2005a). In this chapter, the scores of interest are scores from nonverbal tests.

In the context of identifying children and youth for academically oriented programs or services for gifted and talented students, the focus is on predicting outstanding academic performance or the potential for such. Thus, a primary interest is in identifying individuals who have the aptitude to process information more quickly, reason more accurately, and produce higher-quality products than peers in domains such as geography, mathematics, and physics. In order to identify gifted individuals in these domains, both academic achievement and cognitive ability (i.e., the ability to reason) need to be assessed. Nonverbal assessment of achievement has not received much attention in the extant literature. As Frisby (2003, p. 241) noted, school-based education typically "involves the understanding and expression of ideas transmitted through the medium of spoken and written language." Nonetheless, the necessity of assessing individuals with disabilities has led to the development of several nonverbal measures of achievement.

Although it is important for those who will be identifying students for gifted services to know that these measures are available, these instruments are most frequently used in assessing children with academic delays rather than academic gifts, and thus will not be discussed in this chapter. Readers interested in the nonverbal assessment of academic achievement can consult Frisby (2003).

The assessment of reasoning in academic settings is, in essence, the assessment of intelligence according to the psychometric tradition, and this type of intelligence is often the best single predictor of a broad range of academic achievement other than previous achievement in the same domain. Thus, whereas previous achievement in social studies, biology, and civics (for example) will be the best predictors of subsequent achievement in each of these subjects, respectively, intelligence is typically the second best predictor across all academic areas. Many scholars believe that intelligence includes the capacity to reason, solve problems , memorize, acquire knowledge, and adapt to one's environment, in conjunction with the speed with which one can engage in these tasks (Sattler, 2008).

Although debates continue about the nature of intelligence and the relative contributions of genes and the environment to the variability in intelligence, psychometric research has indicated that:

a. the capacities listed above—excluding adapting to one's environment—are determined in part by general intelligence or g (Spearman, 1927), the global score on most intelligence tests;
b. the relationship between intelligence and schooling is bi-directional; and
c. g predicts positive academic, behavioral, emotional, health, mortality, social, and vocational outcomes (Brody, 1997; Ceci & Williams, 1997; Deary, Whalley, & Starr, 2009; Gottfredson, 1997; Neisser et al., 1996; Terman & Oden, 1959).

With specific relevance to this chapter, these findings suggest that individuals who are classified as gifted will lose that designation without appropriate educational opportunities (all other factors being equal) and that gifted individuals (as a group) will have better average outcomes than their non-gifted peers.

Despite the widespread acceptance of g, there are theorists who argue that intelligence consists of much more than g, and some who argue that there is no g (Ceci, 1996; Neisser et al., 1996; see Sattler, 2008, for a review of the major frameworks and theories of intelligence). A comprehensive overview of intelligence theories is beyond the scope of this chapter, but in addition to g, a review of the Cattell–Horn conceptualization (Cattell, 1963; Horn, 1968; Horn & Cattell, 1967) is especially useful in thinking about identifying the academically gifted. Initially, these researchers postulated that there were two *types* of intelligence, fluid and crystallized, rather than a single general intelligence construct. Fluid intelligence consists of nonverbal facilities like processing speed and working memory; and crystallized intelligence consists of knowledge and skills that are acquired as one develops. Thus, fluid intelligence is hypothesized to be relatively culture-free (a hypothesis to which not all researchers ascribe), whereas crystallized intelligence is context- and culture-dependent, as it is learned. More recently, Horn and Blankson (2005) argued for eight general intelligence factors:

a. crystallized intelligence or acculturation knowledge (G_c);
b. fluid intelligence (G_f);

c. short-term memory (G_{sm});
d. long-term memory (G_{lm});
e. processing speed (G_s);
f. visual processing (G_v);
g. auditory processing (G_a); and
h. quantitative knowledge (G_q).

Both g and the Cattell–Horn conceptualization have important implications for gifted identification and nonverbal assessment.

Assessing Nonverbal Reasoning

A substantial number of instruments are used to assess cognitive and academic abilities (DeThorne & Schaefer, 2004; McCallum, 2003b; Naglieri & Goldstein, 2009; Sattler, 2008). Instruments most frequently used to assess cognitive abilities and reasoning have subtests intended to assess both verbal and nonverbal reasoning. "Tests are commonly called *nonverbal* if items present visual stimuli such as concrete objects or line drawings and require a nonverbal response such as assembling a puzzle, pointing to an answer, or filling in a circle under a picture." (Lohman, 2005d, p. 113). For example, the Wechsler Intelligence Scale for Children-Fourth Edition (WISC-IV; Wechsler, 2003) has four composite indices: Verbal Comprehension, Perceptual Reasoning, Working Memory, and Processing Speed. The core subtests that make up the Perceptual Reasoning (Block Design, Picture Concepts, and Matrix Reasoning) and the Processing Speed (Coding, Symbol Search) indices are labeled as nonverbal tests because the required responses are nonverbal. Similarly, the Stanford–Binet Intelligence Scales-Fifth Edition (SB-V; Roid, 2003a, 2003b) have five tests that are described as nonverbal (Fluid Reasoning, Knowledge, Quantitative Reasoning, Visual–Spatial Processing, and Working Memory).

However, *all* of the WISC-IV and SB-V subtests require the use of verbal instructions, which highlights two important issues. First, there are two types of nonverbal tests. Tests that require the use of language for administration, even if the responses to the items are nonverbal, are more accurately described as *language-reduced* tests (McCallum, 2003a; McCallum, Bracken, & Wasserman, 2001) as language plays an important role in their administration and can have an impact on the scores obtained. On the other hand, tests that are administered nonverbally and also require nonverbal responses are called *language-free* (Lohman, 2005d; McCallum, 2003a). Second, nonverbal tests are also measures of g, or general intelligence (Bracken & McCallum, 2001; Canivez & Watkins, 2010; Drombrowski, Watkins, & Brogan, 2009; McCallum, 2003b). Indeed, both global composite scores (g) and other indices (e.g., fluid reasoning [G_f], short-term memory [G_{sm}], processing speed [G_s]) are calculated and interpreted for the WISC-IV and the SB-V, as these tests are intended to measure g as well as some of the factors suggested by Horn and Blankson (2005), a consideration that will be described in more detail in the next section.

Should Nonverbal Tests Be Used to Assess Giftedness?

Several lines of evidence relate to the use of nonverbal tests in assessing giftedness. These involve examination of the processes measured by nonverbal tests, the importance of domain specificity, and the ability to predict giftedness into the future.

Most Tests Assess g

In the same way that we can abstract commonalities across subgroups—for example, African Americans, Asian Americans, European Americans, and Latinos are all American and all human—we can look for the commonalities required in reasoning and problem-solving tasks across a variety of domains (e.g., mathematics problem solving, reading comprehension, writing an essay, and recreating a design in a limited amount of time). The commonality of the reasoning processes required across these different tasks, many of which are used as subtests of cognitive instruments, is a simple way to think about g. In other words, "the g factor is what ever it is that a variety of tests have in common" (Jensen, 1980, p. 223). Tasks requiring more complex reasoning are typically more accurate reflections of g.

We can divide a test score into three components: common variance (g), unique variance or specificity, and error. Error variance is as its name says and is not useful, and g has already been defined. Unique variance refers to the components of reasoning that the test is assessing that are reliable, not error, and not g. These are the aspects of tests related to the specific factors described by Horn and Blankson (2005) such as short-term memory or quantitative reasoning.

Consider the language-reduced tasks on the WISC-IV and SB-V listed previously. Sattler (2008, p. 577) described scores on four of the SB-V language-reduced sub-scales as "good measures of g" with more than 50 percent of their variance attributed to g—Knowledge (63 percent), Quantitative Reasoning (66 percent), Visual–Spatial Processing (55 percent), and Working Memory (54 percent); however, Fluid Reasoning scores (49 percent) were described as a "fair measure of g," as only 49 percent of the variance was attributable to g. On the other hand, none of the WISC-IV nonverbal subtest scores were good measures of g; they were all classified as fair measures of g (Sattler, 2008, p. 285): Block Design (49 percent), Picture Concepts (37 percent), Matrix Reasoning (49 percent), Coding (26 percent), and Symbol Search (37 percent).

At the same time, some of these subtest scores had at least adequate specificity or unique variance (i.e., at least 15 percent of the variance in the scores are unique, and the scores have more unique variance than error variance) at all ages: Visual–Spatial Processing, Working Memory, Fluid Reasoning, Block Design, Picture Concepts, Matrix Reasoning, Coding, and Symbol Search. Quantitative Reasoning on SB-V did not have adequate specificity for most ages. There are two important points to be made here. First, scores may be better predictors at some ages than at others. Second, scores that are good measures of g may not have good specificity and vice-versa. In short, not all scores are created equal and the differences have implications for use in identifying giftedness (Lohman et al., 2008).

Nonverbal Tests Versus Verbal Reasoning

The distinction between nonverbal testing and nonverbal reasoning is important. As Lohman (2005d) pointed out, the nonverbal label on a test refers to the test stimuli and not the type of reasoning that the test items require. Thus, although a test may be called nonverbal, it may still require verbal reasoning. This point is perhaps most obvious in tests that use pictures of objects and require categorization or the use of analogies. Knowledge of the names of the objects and categories and the ability to reason verbally are required to solve these problems (Lohman 2005d). Conversely, a test may have verbal instructions, but may require the use of nonverbal reasoning to complete the tasks. Several types of cognitive abilities (e.g., verbal reasoning, nonverbal reasoning, spatial abilities) can be assessed and many tests assess several cognitive abilities. Thus, it is important to know what cognitive abilities a test is assessing and the amount of specificity in the test scores.

Of course, language is a symbol system, and one way to think about nonverbal tests is in terms of their use of symbol systems, including language, for reasoning. In developing the Universal Nonverbal Intelligence Test (UNIT), Bracken and McCallum (1998) wanted to provide a language-free test that included symbolic and non-symbolic subtests, memory subtests, and reasoning subtests. Thus, this instrument has subtests that require symbolic reasoning (e.g., Analogic Reasoning, which is based on matrix analogies using common objects) and non-symbolic reasoning (e.g., Cube Design, which is based on completing three-dimensional block designs using white and green blocks).

Domain Specificity

One concern about typical assessment for placement in gifted and talented students is lack of academic domain specificity. Most assessments take place in the elementary grades where students are typically assessed with cognitive instruments and placed in a program on the basis of the total score. Although strong performance in mathematics or language arts may have been one of the triggers for the gifted assessment, and the actual assessment may have included a standardized achievement battery, placement in the program, and even more importantly, curriculum planning are typically independent of the gifted classification decision. Thus, except in cases of academic acceleration, curricula in most gifted and talented programs in elementary and middle schools involve a broad range of enrichment activities, which may have no relationship to the talents of the students in the program.

Perhaps the problem lies in the question that schools and programs often ask. Rather than asking if a student is gifted—a question that suggests some general, innate capacity—the question would be better focused on identifying the academic domains in which the student performs very well. If the goal of identification is to develop talent in a domain, it is important to use instruments that predict future performance in the domain (Lohman 2005a, 2005b). Support for this hypothesis is displayed quite simply in Figure 14.1, taken from Lohman (2005a, p. 345). Lohman (2005a) reported average regression weights predicting reading scores on the Iowa Test of Basic Skills (ITBS; Hoover, Dunbar, & Frisbie, 2001). Predictors included the verbal reasoning, quantitative reasoning and nonverbal reasoning subtests of the Cognitive Abilities Test (CogAT; Lohman & Hagen, 2001). For both non-Hispanic White students and Hispanic students, verbal reasoning was a much stronger predictor of reading achievement than quantitative reasoning and nonverbal reasoning, and indeed, verbal reasoning was the only meaningful predictor.

Additional support for the importance of domain specificity comes from the longitudinal Study of Mathematically Precocious Youth (SMPY). In 2007, Park, Lubinski, and Benbow showed that 25 years after taking the SATs, individuals with higher verbal than quantitative scores assessed prior to age 13 were more likely to complete master's and doctoral degrees in the humanities, whereas individuals with higher mathematics scores were more likely to complete degrees in STEM (science, technology, engineering, and mathematics) fields. These differences were also reflected in tenure-track appointments, as well as in the number of literary publications (higher verbal group) and STEM

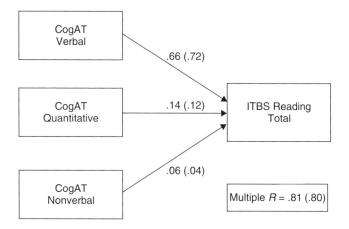

Fig. 14.1 Average regression weights across grades 1–6 for the prediction of ITBS Reading Total scores from CogAT Verbal, Quantitative, and Nonverbal reasoning abilities.
First weight is for non-Hispanic White students; the second weight (in parentheses) is for Hispanic students. The multiple correlations were R = .81 and .80 for White and Hispanic students, respectively.
D. F. Lohman. "An Aptitude Perspective on Talent: Implications for Identification of Academically Gifted Minority Students." *Journal for the Education of the Gifted*, 28 (2005): 345.

patents (higher mathematics group). Recent theorizing suggests that spatial ability makes a unique contribution to identifying gifts in some STEM fields (Lubinski, 2010; Lubinski & Benbow, 2006), such as engineering. And in several studies of reading achievement, phonemic awareness, a domain-specific measure of reading, predicted future reading achievement better than full-scale IQ test scores (e.g., Scarborough, 1998).

Unfortunately, some data suggest that the problem is not that simple, as there are some studies indicating that g and verbal ability have similar predictive validity for reading outcomes. For example, the correlations of full-scale IQ scores on the WISC-IV with reading ($r = .78$) and oral language ($r = .75$) scores on the Wechsler Individual Achievement Test (WIAT) are as high or higher than the correlations of these achievement scores with the WISC-IV Verbal Comprehension Index ($r = .74$ and $r = .75$, respectively). Results from the SB-V are similar. Of course, both the WISC-IV and the SB-V are individually administered tests, which are designed to result in optimal performance, and the full-scale scores on these instruments contain both verbal and nonverbal components.

Predicting Giftedness Over Time

Lohman and Korb (2006) discussed the oft-seen circumstance in which individuals who qualify for a gifted program on the basis of a test score do not qualify a year later. One reason for this is called regression to the mean, which occurs when test scores are not perfectly correlated (i.e., r < 1.0). Of course, test scores are never perfectly correlated, in part because they always include error as mentioned previously. Moreover, scores further away from the mean, such as the extremely high scores used for gifted identification, show greater regression to the mean than scores closer to the mean. Even with a between-test correlation of .975, 21 percent of the individuals who were in the top 2 percent of scores at Time 1 would not be in the top 2 percent at Time 2 (Lohman & Korb, 2006). One way to reduce the effect of regression to the mean is particularly pertinent here as it has implications for the selection of gifted students. This involves requiring the use of multiple scores in placing students in gifted programs and "combining scores that estimate different aptitudes needed for the development of future competence" in the domain of interest (Lohman & Korb, 2006, p. 477).

Summary

If one believes that g is the sole or only important predictor of academic performance, and there is evidence suggesting that the scores on a nonverbal test are good measures of g, one should certainly use nonverbal measures. Moreover, as mentioned previously, there are individuals for whom, and circumstances in which, nonverbal tests will provide information that cannot be obtained from a verbal measure. In circumstances such as these, nonverbal tests should be used, not as the assessment of giftedness, but as part of a comprehensive assessment procedure. However, in light of the previous discussion, the question "Should nonverbal tests be used to assess giftedness?" is probably not the correct question to ask. Other questions are also important in determining if a nonverbal test should be used. What is the evidence supporting the relationship of scores on the nonverbal test with scores in the gifted domain in which one is assessing the student? And what are the other skills and aptitudes that are related to performance in the domain?

Major Nonverbal Tests

Several resources are useful in assessing nonverbal tests and their utility. The first is the *Handbook of Nonverbal Assessment* (McCallum, 2003b). The handbook contains chapters on six of the major nonverbal measures of cognition used with children: the Comprehensive Test of Nonverbal Intelligence, Second Edition (CTONI-2; Hammill, Pearson, & Wiederholt, 2009), the Leiter International Performance Scale Revised (Leiter-R; Roid & Miller, 1997), the Naglieri Nonverbal Ability Test (NNAT; Naglieri, 1997, 2003a, 2003b), the Raven Progressive Matrices (Raven, Raven, & Court, 1998a, 1998b, 1998c, 1998d, 2000), the Test of Nonverbal Intelligence, Third Edition (TONI-3; Brown, Sherbenou, & Johnsen, 1997), and the Universal Nonverbal Intelligence Test (UNIT; Bracken & McCallum, 1998). The handbook also contains chapters on a nonverbal measure of intelligence in adults, and nonverbal measures of achievement, behavior, personality, psychopathology, and neuropsychological functioning.

In addition to providing information on administration, scoring, and interpretation, the McCallum (2003b) handbook also contains sections on the development of the instruments (e.g., description of the normative sample, type of items), the psychometric properties of the scores, and the strengths and weaknesses of the instruments. However, as the chapters are written for the most part by the instruments' authors, readers should not accept any claims uncritically. McCallum (2003a), who is a co-author of the UNIT, pointed out that the UNIT and the Leiter-R were the only two multidimensional nonverbal measures in the set, as the other instruments all use matrix analogy-type items across subtests. He suggested that the other instruments are only useful for screening purposes: "When psychoeducational assessments are conducted for 'high stakes' placement, eligibility, or diagnostic decision-making reasons, broader, more comprehensive measures of intelligence are more appropriate (i.e., Leiter-R; UNIT)." (McCallum, 2003a, p. 16).

The second highlighted piece is an article in the *American Journal of Speech-Language Pathology* (DeThorne & Schaefer, 2004), which describes 16 nonverbal measures of intelligence—both language-reduced and language-free—for use with children, all evaluated using a set of explicit criteria. The 16 scales are described in terms of:

a. the age range that can be assessed with the instrument;
b. whether the instrument yields a verbal score;
c. the average time length of administration by the examiner;
d. whether manipulatives are used in administration;
e. whether the instructions are verbal, nonverbal, or both;
f. names and a brief description of each of the nonverbal subtests on the instruments;
g. the cost of the instrument;
h. the normative sample;
i. the reliability of scores;
j. the availability of validity evidence in support of the scores' use; and
k. reviews of the instruments (when available).

Third, in the *Practitioner's Guide to Assessing Intelligence and Achievement*, Naglieri and Goldstein (2009) included a discussion of several instruments with nonverbal subtests not included in the other two reference works, including the Cognitive Assessment System (CAS; Naglieri & Das, 1997), the Wechsler Nonverbal Scale of Ability (Wechsler & Naglieri, 2006), and the Woodcock-Johnson III Tests of Cognitive Abilities (Woodcock, McGrew, & Mather, 2001). One other instrument with nonverbal subtests, the Differential Ability Scales, Second Edition (DAS; Elliott, 2007), is described in Sattler (2008). The fourth piece (Lohman, 2005d) is written specifically for the field of gifted education, and includes a cogent summary and critique of nonverbal ability tests, and several recommendations for consideration.

Identifying Gifted Students From Diverse Populations

One important consideration with regard to the use of nonverbal tests in the assessment of gifted youth is the identification of groups that are typically under-represented in programs for the gifted and talented. One explanation put forward for this under-representation is selection or identification problems related to bias in scores on traditional assessment instruments like the WISC-IV and SB-V. Nonverbal tests have been proposed as one way to counter that bias. Indeed, Naglieri and Ford (2003, p. 157) reported that "samples of White and minority children perform similarly on" the NNAT (Naglieri, 2003a), and that "similar percentages of White, Black, and Hispanic children . . . earned NNAT standard scores of 125" (Naglieri & Ford, 2003, p. 158).

The specific claims with regard to the accuracy of this interpretation of NNAT scores have been debated in the literature (see Lohman, 2005c; Naglieri & Ford, 2005). However, the claim also raises broader validity concerns that the field of gifted education has been reluctant to address. First, intelligence tests were devised to predict academic functioning, and that remains their primary purpose. Second, there is a consensus that the scores on major tests of intelligence are *not* biased predictors of achievement for ethnic and racial minority groups (Frisby & Braden, 1999; Neisser et al., 1996). Thus, differences in academic achievement among demographic subgroups in the population will be reflected in the scores of verbal and nonverbal measures that are valid predictors of academic functioning. Unfortunately, despite some closing of the achievement gap, there are still substantial racial and ethnic group differences in academic achievement, with African Americans, American Indians, and Latinos having lower scores than some Asian American and European Americans (KewalRamani, Gilbertson, Fox, & Provasnik, 2007). These differences exist in letter, number, and shape recognition in four-year olds, and in reading and mathematics scores, as well as other subject areas, in elementary, middle, and high school.

Thus, the scores on any test which purports to predict academic achievement in children and adolescents in the United States that do not reflect the actual differences in achievement in the society are probably biased.

> Nonverbal reasoning tests reduce, but do not eliminate differences in mean scores between groups, and they are not the best way to identify those students who either currently exhibit or are most likely to achieve academic excellence. When used alone, they increase bias while appearing to reduce it.
>
> (Lohman, 2005d, p. 134)

Scores that are more accurate predictors of academic achievement will be more similar in terms of test-score gaps to the achievement gaps that actually exist. This claim also holds for identifying gifted English language learners (Lohman et al., 2008).

CONCLUSION

Nonverbal tests were designed to assess skills and aptitudes with minimal or no use of language. Several of these measures have been well developed, have national norms, and provide ample evidence of reliability of scores and validity of inferences from scores. Nonverbal tests are very useful in assessing individuals with language, speech, or hearing concerns, or individuals for whom a test in their first language is not available. However, as with verbal tests, a nonverbal test should never be used as the sole criterion in the identification of gifted students (Lohman & Lakin, 2008).

REFERENCES

American Educational Research Association, American Psychological Association, & the National Council on Measurement in Education. (1999). *Standards for educational and psychological testing.* Washington, DC: American Educational Research Association.

Bracken, B. A., & McCallum, R. S. (1998). *Universal Nonverbal Intelligence Test.* Austin, TX: Pro-Ed.

Bracken, B. A., & McCallum, R. S. (2001). Assessing intelligence in a population that speaks more than two hundred languages: A nonverbal solution. In L. A. Suzuki, J. G. Ponterotto, & P. J. Meller (Eds.), *Handbook of multicultural assessment: Clinical, psychological, and educational applications* (2nd ed., pp. 405–431). San Francisco: Jossey-Bass.

Brody, N. (1997). Intelligence, schooling, and society. *American Psychologist, 52,* 1046–1050. doi:10.1037/0003-066X.52.10.1046

Brown, L., Sherbenou, R. J., & Johnsen, S. K. (1997). *Test of Nonverbal Intelligence* (3rd ed.). Austin, TX: Pro-Ed.

Canivez, G. L., & Watkins, M. W. (2010). Exploratory and higher-order factor analyses of the Wechsler Adult Intelligence Scale-Fourth Edition (WAIS-IV) adolescent sample. *School Psychology Quarterly, 25,* 223–235. doi:10.1037/a0022046

Cattell, R. B. (1963). Theory of fluid and crystallized intelligence: A critical experiment. *Journal of Educational Psychology, 54,* 1–22.

doi:10.1037/h0046743

Ceci, S. J. (1996). *On intelligence: A bioecological treatise on intellectual development.* Cambridge, MA: Harvard University Press.

Ceci, S. J., & Williams, W. M. (1997). Schooling, intelligence, and income. *American Psychologist, 52,* 1051–1058. doi:10.1037/0003- 066X.52.10.1051

Deary, I. J., Whalley, L. J., & Starr, J. M. (2009). *A lifetime of intelligence: Follow-up studies of the Scottish Mental Surveys of 1932 and 1947.* Washington, DC: American Psychological Association.

DeThorne, L. S., & Schaefer B. A. (2004). A guide to child nonverbal measures. *American Journal of Speech-Language Pathology, 13,* 275–290. doi:10.1044/1058-0360(2004/029)

Drombrowski, S. C., Watkins, M. W., & Brogan, M. J. (2009). An exploratory investigation of the factor structure of the Reynolds Intellectual Assessment Scales (RIAS). *Journal of Psychoeducational Assessment, 27,* 494–507. doi:10.1177/0734282909333179

Elliott, C. D. (2007). *Differential Ability Scales-Second Edition: Administration and scoring manual.* San Antonio, TX: Harcourt.

Ford, D. Y. (1995). Desegregating gifted education: A need unmet. *Journal of Negro Education, 64,* 52–62. doi:10.2307/2967284

Ford, D. Y. (1998). The underrepresentation of minority students in gifted education: Problems and promises in recruitment and retention. *The Journal of Special Education, 32,* 4–14. doi:10.1177/002246699803200102

Frisby, C. L. (2003). Nonverbal assessment of academic achievement with special populations. In R. S. McCallum (Ed.), *Handbook of nonverbal assessment* (pp. 241–258). New York: Kluwer.

Frisby, C. L., & Braden, J. (Eds.). (1999). Bias in mental testing [Special issue]. *School Psychology Quarterly, 14*(4).

Gottfredson, L. S. (1997). Why g matters: The complexity of everyday life. *Intelligence, 24,* 79–132. doi:10.1016/S0160-2896(97)90014-3

Hammill, D. D., Pearson, N. A., & Wiederholt, J. L. (2009). *Comprehensive Test of Nonverbal Intelligence* (2nd ed.). Austin, TX: Pro-Ed.

Heller, K. A., Mönks, F. J., Sternberg, R. J., & Subotnik, R. F. (Eds.). (2000). *International handbook of giftedness and talent* (2nd ed., rev. reprint). San Francisco: Elsevier.

Hoover, H. D., Dunbar, S. B., & Frisbie, D. A. (2001). *The Iowa Test of Basic Skills, Form A.* Itasca, IL: Riverside.

Horn, J. L. (1968). Organization of abilities and the development of intelligence. *Psychological Review, 75,* 242–259. doi:10.1037/h0025662

Horn, J. L., & Blankson, N. (2005). Foundations for better understanding of cognitive abilities. In D. P. Flanagan & P. L. Harrison (Eds.), *Contemporary intellectual assessment: Theories, tests, and issues* (pp. 41–68). New York: Guilford.

Horn, J. L., & Cattell, R. B. (1967). Age differences in fluid and crystallized general intelligences. *Acta Psychologica, 26,* 107–129. doi:10.1016/0001-6918(67)90011-X

Jensen, A. R. (1980). *Bias in mental testing.* New York: The Free Press.

KewalRamani, A., Gilbertson, L., Fox, M., & Provasnik, S. (2007). *Status and trends in the education of racial and ethnic minorities* (NCES 2007-039). Washington, DC: National Center for Education Statistics, Institute of Education Sciences, & U.S. Department of Education.

Lohman, D. F. (2005a). An aptitude perspective on talent: Implications for identification of academically gifted minority students. *Journal for the Education of the Gifted, 28,* 333–360.

Lohman, D. F. (2005b). *Identifying academically talented minority students.* Storrs: The National Research Center on the Gifted and Talented, University of Connecticut.

Lohman, D. F. (2005c). Review of Naglieri and Ford (2003): Does the Naglieri Nonverbal Ability Test identify equal proportions of high-scoring White, Black, and Hispanic students? *Gifted Child Quarterly, 49,* 19–28. doi:10.1177/001698620504900103

Lohman, D. F. (2005d). The role of nonverbal ability tests in identifying academically gifted students: An aptitude perspective. *Gifted Child Quarterly, 49,* 111–138. doi:10.1177/001698620504900203

Lohman, D. F., & Hagen, E. P. (2001). *Cognitive Abilities Test (Form 6).* Itasca, IL: Riverside.

Lohman, D. F., & Korb, K. A. (2006). Gifted today but not tomorrow? Longitudinal changes in ability and achievement during elementary school. *Journal for the Education of the Gifted, 29,* 451–484.

Lohman, D. F., Korb, K. A., & Lakin, J. M. (2008). Identifying academically gifted English-language learners using nonverbal tests: A comparison of the Raven, NNAT, and CogAT. *Gifted Child Quarterly, 52,* 275–296. doi:10.1177/0016986208321808

Lohman, D. F., & Lakin, J. (2008). Nonverbal test scores as one component of an identification system: Integrating ability, achievement, and teacher rating. In J. L. VanTassel-Baska (Ed.), *Alternative assessments with gifted and talented students* (pp. 41–66). Waco, TX: Prufrock Press.

Lubinski, D. (2010). Spatial ability and STEM: A sleeping giant for talent identification and development. *Personality and Individual Differences, 49,* 344–351.
doi:10.1016/j.paid.2010.03.022

Lubinski, D., & Benbow, C. P. (2006). Study of Mathematically Precocious Youth after 35 years: Uncovering antecedents for the development of math-science expertise. *Perspectives on Psychological Science, 1,* 316–345.

McCallum, R. S. (2003a). Context for nonverbal assessment of intelligence and related abilities. In R. S. McCallum (Ed.), *Handbook of nonverbal assessment* (pp. 3–22). New York: Kluwer.

McCallum, R. S. (Ed.). (2003b). *Handbook of nonverbal assessment.* New York: Kluwer.

McCallum, R. S., Bracken, B. A., & Wasserman, J. D. (2001). *Essentials of nonverbal assessment.* Hoboken, NJ: Wiley.

Naglieri, J. A. (1997). *Naglieri Nonverbal Ability Test—Multilevel form.* San Antonio, TX: The Psychological Corporation.

Naglieri, J. A. (2003a). *Naglieri Nonverbal Ability Test—Individual form.* San Antonio, TX: The Psychological Corporation.

Naglieri, J. A. (2003b). Naglieri Nonverbal Ability Tests: NMAT and MAT-EF. In R. S. McCallum (Ed.), *Handbook of nonverbal assessment* (pp. 175–189). New York: Kluwer.

Naglieri, J. A., & Das, J. P. (1997). *Cognitive Assessment System.* Itasca, NY: Riverside.

Naglieri, J. A., & Ford, D. Y. (2003). Addressing underrepresentation of gifted minority children using the Naglieri Nonverbal Ability Test (NNAT). *Gifted Child Quarterly, 47,* 155–160.
doi:10.1177/001698620304700206

Naglieri, J. A., & Ford, D. Y. (2005). Increasing minority children's participation in gifted classes using the NNAT: A response to Lohman. *Gifted Child Quarterly, 49,* 29–36.
doi:10.1177/001698620504900104

Naglieri, J. A., & Goldstein, S. (Eds.). (2009). *Practitioner's guide to assessing intelligence and achievement.* Hoboken, NJ: Wiley.

Neisser, U., Boodoo, G., Bouchard, T. J., Jr., Boykin, A. W., Brody, N., Ceci, S. J. et al. (1996). Intelligence: Knowns and unknowns. *American Psychologist, 51,* 77–101.
doi:10.1037/0003-066X.51.2.77

Park, G., Lubinski, D., & Benbow, C. P. (2007). Contrasting intellectual patterns predict creativity in the arts and sciences: Tracking intellectually precocious youth over 25 years. *Psychological Science, 18,* 948–955.

Raven, J., Raven, J. C., & Court, J. H. (1998a). *Manual for Raven's Progressive Matrices and Vocabulary Scales, Section 1: General overview.* San Antonio, TX: The Psychological Corporation.

Raven, J., Raven, J. C., & Court, J. H. (1998b). *Manual for Raven's Progressive Matrices and Vocabulary Scales, Section 2: The Coloured Progressive Matrices.* San Antonio, TX: The Psychological Corporation.

Raven, J., Raven, J. C., & Court, J. H. (1998c). *Manual for Raven's Progressive Matrices and Vocabulary Scales, Section 4: The Advanced Progressive Matrices.* San Antonio, TX: The Psychological Corporation.

Raven, J., Raven, J. C., & Court, J. H. (1998d). *Manual for Raven's Progressive Matrices and Vocabulary Scales, Section 5: The Mill Hill Vocabulary Scale.* San Antonio, TX: The Psychological Corporation.

Raven, J., Raven, J. C., & Court, J. H. (2000). *Manual for Raven's Progressive Matrices and Vocabulary Scales, Section 3: The Standard Progressive Matrices.* San Antonio, TX: The Psychological Corporation.

Roid, G. H. (2003a). *Stanford-Binet Intelligence Scales for Children-Fifth Edition: Examiner's manual.* Itasca, IL: Riverside.

Roid, G. H. (2003b). *Stanford-Binet Intelligence Scales for Children-Fifth Edition: Interpretive manual.* Itasca, IL: Riverside.

Roid, G. H., & Miller, L. J. (1997). *Leiter International Performance Scale-Revised (Leiter-R) manual.* Wood Dale, IL: Stoelting.

Sattler, J. M. (2008). *Assessment of children's cognitive functions* (5th ed.). San Diego, CA: Author.

Scarborough, H. S. (1998). Predicting the future achievement of second graders with reading disabilities: Contributions of phonemic awareness, verbal memory, rapid naming, and IQ. *Annals of Dyslexia, 48,* 115–136.

Spearman, C. E. (1927). *The abilities of man.* New York: Macmillan.

Sternberg, R. J., & Davidson, J. E. (Eds.). (1986). *Conceptions of giftedness.* New York: Cambridge University Press.

Sternberg, R. J., & Davidson, J. E. (Eds.). (2005). *Conceptions of giftedness* (2nd ed.). New York: Cambridge University Press.

Terman, L. M., & Oden, M. H. (1959). *The gifted group at mid-life: 35 years' follow-up of the superior child. Genetic studies of genius* (Vol. V). Stanford, CA: Stanford University Press.

VanTassel-Baska, J., & Stambaugh, T. (Eds.). (2007). *Overlooked gems: A national perspective on low-income promising learners.* Proceedings from the National Leadership Conference on Low-income Learners. Washington, DC: National Association for Gifted Children, & the Center for Gifted Education, The College of William and Mary.

Wechsler, D. (2003). *Wechsler Intelligence Scale for Children-Fourth Edition: Administration and scoring manual.* San Antonio, TX: The Psychological Corporation.

Wechsler, D., & Naglieri, J. A. (2006). *Wechsler Nonverbal Scale of Ability.* San Antonio, TX: Pearson.

Woodcock, R. W., McGrew, K., & Mather, N. (2001). *Woodcock-Johnson Test of Cognitive Abilities and Tests of Achievement.* Rolling Meadows, IL: Riverside.

Worrell, F. C. (2003). Why are there so few African Americans in gifted programs? In C. C. Yeakey & R. D. Henderson (Eds.), *Surmounting the odds: Education, opportunity, and society in the new millennium* (pp. 423–454). Greenwich, CT: Information Age.

Worrell, F. C. (2009). What does gifted mean? Personal and social identity perspectives on giftedness in adolescence. In F. D. Horowitz, R. F. Subotnik, & D. J. Matthews (Eds.), *The development of giftedness and talent across the lifespan* (pp. 131–152). Washington, DC: American Psychological Association. doi:10.1037/11867-00

15

NOT JUST A TEST

Utilizing Non-test Assessments in Identifying Gifted and Talented Students

Tonya R. Moon

Scholars have recommended for many years that the collection of data to be used in the identification of gifted and talented students be based on both objective and subjective assessments of student potential and student achievements. The concept of using "multiple criteria" in making identification decisions rests on the assumption that there will be multiple instruments and data collection strategies used to assess students. The phrase "multiple criteria" suggests that the processes through which data on student characteristics are gathered are varied—not just that multiple tests will be used to gather that data. Accordingly, in the data-gathering process, school officials should consider supplementing test data with an array of non-test approaches to learning about the potential of students. These approaches might include curricular-based assessments, performance-based assessments, and teacher and parent ratings of students.

PERFORMANCE-BASED ASSESSMENTS AS A VIABLE OPTION FOR IDENTIFICATION PROCEDURES

Nontraditional assessments in which students create their own responses to a task, produce products, or demonstrate skill and knowledge through a medium other than a traditional test is considered performance-based assessment. Performance assessments, product assessments, and portfolios are all considered types of performance-based assessment.[1] Appropriately constructed performance-based assessments (PBAs) provide an opportunity to understand not only what students know and understand in specific content areas, but how they can translate, apply, and evaluate that knowledge and skill. When properly constructed, PBAs require the use of higher-order thinking skills, including problem-solving skills. Further, high-quality PBAs are not constrained by test ceilings.[2]. That is, students can demonstrate knowledge, skill, and understanding at a level not constrained or delimited by the task.

Just as selecting a test begins with translating a definition of gifted into operational terms, designing an identification system that incorporates PBAs must begin with the definition of giftedness that guides the gifted program in question. This definition will guide the development of specifications for the task that reflect the discipline or area of giftedness being considered (e.g., mathematics, language arts) and the cognitive processes believed to represent gifted behaviors (e.g., problem solving, communication) to be assessed. It will also provide the parameters for determining the necessary psychometric characteristics of the task (e.g., reliability, validity, and generalizability) that must be determined before it can be used. For example, if the domain of language arts is being considered, a performance assessment that requires students to create a story or poem reflecting the events of the past week in school might be considered. The task scoring rubric would reflect the specific language arts criteria, both in terms of content knowledge and the skills that are considered gifted behaviors in language arts in the definition.

RESEARCH SUPPORTING THE USE OF PERFORMANCE-BASED ASSESSMENTS

While limited, a small body of empirical work supports the use of PBAs for classroom use and identification purposes with gifted students. Moon, Brighton, Callahan, and Robinson (2005) reported that students found PBAs more meaningful, interesting, and motivating than traditional assessments (e.g., multiple-choice tests). VanTassel-Baska, Feng, and de Brux (2007), Pfeiffer, Kumtepe, and Rosado (2006), and Sarouphim (2001) all report that performance-based assessments identify as gifted higher percentages of African American students and students from low-income backgrounds than do traditional identification tools. Borland and Wright (1994) found that PBAs in conjunction with other types of data helped identify young, potentially gifted, economically disadvantaged students. In short, while the field of gifted education has only recently investigated the use of such instruments, there is a growing body of evidence to suggest its strengths and potential for success in identifying a broad range of students for gifted services.

Disadvantages of Performance-based Assessments

The disadvantages associated with the use of PBAs as part of a gifted program's identification process rest predominantly on establishing technical adequacy, limitations with the range of content assessed, limited knowledge regarding their usability for gifted identification, and costs associated with development and scoring. Practical issues that must be addressed prior to using PBAs as part of a gifted identification system involve considerations such as time and cost in administering and scoring as well as the training of evaluators. Of course it is also critically important that the instruments used in the identification process closely reflect the definition of giftedness and the program goals and services for which students are being identified.

Portfolios

Portfolios are considered to be a collection of a student's work that demonstrates either (a) the student's growth, or (b) the student's best work (a.k.a., showcase). As such, portfolios are not assessments at all, but rather a collection of previously completed assessments. Best Work Portfolios are commonly used in the process of identification for placement in gifted programs. This type of portfolio is generally composed of pieces, of which some might include samples from PBAs, that are representative of the student's best work; included also is a student reflection on the pieces, as well as teachers' comments related to the pieces. In addition, portfolios may include student performances on outside assessments such as standardized achievement tests.

OTHER TYPES OF ASSESSMENTS FOR CONSIDERATION AS ONE COMPONENT OF AN IDENTIFICATION PROCESS

Rating Scales

Rating scales are among the most widely used instruments for screening and identifying students for gifted programs (Pfeiffer & Petscher, 2008). Popular rating scales for identifying gifted students are the Scales for Rating the Behavioral Characteristics of Superior Students (SRBCSS, Renzulli et al., 1997), the Gifted and Talented Evaluation Scales (GATES; Gilliam, Carpenter, & Christensen, 1996), the Purdue Academic Rating Scales (PARS; Feldhusen, Hoover, & Sayler, 1989), and the Gifted Rating Scales (GRS; Pfeiffer & Jarosewich, 2003). Many school divisions use locally constructed teacher and parent rating scales. Recent research has raised concerns about the use of rating scales for identifying students, in particular minority students, for gifted services. Neumeister, Adams, Pierce, Cassady, and Dixon (2007) found that even experienced teachers did not fully perceive or recognize the culturally situated giftedness of minority students. In the study by Neumeister et al. (2007), teachers appeared to rely on mainstream cultural values to nominate students as gifted. Peterson (1999) also suggested that the under-representation of minority students might be a result of "pivotal players" (i.e., teachers) (p.354).

According to the position statement of the National Association for Gifted Children (National Association for Gifted Children [NAGC], n d a), rating scales (and observations and interviews) should only play a supplemental role in the gifted identification process because of the potential bias and prejudices inherent in all individuals. The position statement also recommends that only structured tools with inclusive and clear criteria be used, and that all individuals who will rate students receive training in the appropriate use of the instruments as well as the variations in the manifestations of giftedness among different subgroups of students. Relying solely or heavily on teacher rating scales for nominating or identifying students for gifted services may play a large role in the under-representation of minority students in gifted programs.

FINAL COMMENTS

Expertise in using assessments for identification and placement of gifted students and use of "comprehensive assessment alternatives" is recommended practice (NAGC, n d b). No single type of instrument or procedure exists that is sufficient for identifying gifted and talented students or for monitoring the development of their talent. But the use of alternative assessment tools, be they student performance assessments, checklists, or rating scales, requires documentation of their technical soundness for the purpose of identifying talent; and rigorous training procedures must be in place for those individuals who evaluate student responses on alternative assessments or rate student behaviors on rating scales. Finally, staff development is necessary to inform those working directly with students and evaluating them about what talent potential looks like across ethnic and socio-economically varied groups.

NOTES

1. For a detailed description and examples of performance-based assessments, see Chapter 44 in this book by Tonya R. Moon.
2. A test or assessment ceiling exists when a student actually has the potential to demonstrate greater learning or higher-level performance than the assessment tool allows. For example, on some standardized achievement tests given on-grade-level, high-performing students answer all or nearly all items correctly and could answer more advanced-level questions. But those questions are not on the test, so the true level of achievement cannot be assessed.

REFERENCES

Borland, J., & Wright, L. (1994). Identifying young, potentially gifted, economically disadvantaged students. *Gifted Child Quarterly, 38,* 164–171.

Callahan, C. M., Tomlinson, C. A., Hunsaker, S. L., Bland, L. C., & Moon, T. R. (1995). *Instruments and evaluation designs used in gifted programs.* Storrs: The National Research Center on the Gifted and Talented, University of Connecticut.

Feldhusen, J. F., Hoover, S. M., & Sayler, M. F. (1989). *Identification of gifted students at the secondary level.* Monroe, NY: Trillium Press.

Gilliam, J. E., Carpenter, B. O., & Christensen, J. R. (1996). *Gifted and Talented Evaluation Scale (GATES).* Waco, TX: Prufrock Press.

Moon, T. R., Brighton, C. M., Callahan, C. M., & Robinson, A. E. (2005). Reliable and valid performance assessments for the middle school classroom. *Journal for Secondary Gifted Education, 16*(2/3), 119–133.

Moon, T. R., Callahan, C. M., & Tomlinson, C. A. (2003). Effects of state testing programs on schools with high concentrations of student poverty—Good news or bad news? *Current Issues in Education* [online], *6*(8). Available at: http://cie.ed.asu.edu/volume6/index.html

National Association for Gifted Children. (n d a). *The role of assessment in the identification of gifted children.* (Position statement). Retrieved January 23, 2009 from http://www.nagc.org/uploadedFiles/assessment%20pos%20paper%20final.pdf

National Association for Gifted Children. (n d b). *Using tests to identify gifted students.* (Position statement). Retrieved March 9, 2009 from http://www.nagc.org/index.aspx?id=404

Neumeister, C., Adams, C., Pierce, R., Cassady, J., & Dixon, F. (2007). Fourth grade teachers' perceptions of giftedness: Implications for identifying and serving diverse gifted students. *Journal for the Education of the Gifted, 30,* 479–499.

Peterson, J. S. (1999). Gifted—Through whose cultural lens? An application of the postpositivistic mode of inquiry. *Journal for the Education of the Gifted, 22,* 354–383.

Pfeiffer, S. I., & Jarosewich, T. (2003). *Gifted rating scales.* San Antonio, TX: Pearson.

Pfeiffer, S. I., Kumtepe, A., & Rosado, J. (2006). Gifted identification: Measuring change in a student's profile of abilities using the gifted rating scales. *The School Psychologist, 60,* 106–111.

Pfeiffer, S. I., & Petscher, Y. (2008). Identifying young gifted children using the gifted rating scales—Preschool/kindergarten form. *Gifted Child Quarterly, 52,* 19–29.

Renzulli, J. S., Smith, L. H. L., White, A. J., Callahan, C. M., Hartman, R. K., & Westberg, K. L (1997). *Scales for Rating the Behavioral Characteristics of Superior Students.* Mansfield Center, CT: Creative Learning Press.

Sarouphim, K. M. (2001). DISCOVER: Concurrent validity, gender differences, and identification of minority students. *Gifted Child Quarterly, 45,* 130–138.

VanTassel-Baska, J., Feng, A. X., & de Brux, E. (2007). A study of identification and achievement profiles of performance task-identified gifted students over 6 years. *Journal for the Education of the Gifted, 31*(1), 7–34.

16

RESPONSE TO INTERVENTION (RtI) APPROACHES TO IDENTIFICATION PRACTICES WITHIN GIFTED EDUCATION

Mary Ruth Coleman

There are many ways to view gifted education. Your philosophy of education guides your beliefs about who is "gifted" and how the needs of students with gifts and talents should be addressed. The choice of a Response to Intervention (RtI) framework for identification and services flows logically from a philosophy that gifted education can only flourish within a culture that supports excellence for all learners (Brown & Abernathy, 2009). Anchors of this philosophy within RtI would include the following beliefs:

- nurturing potential as well as responding to crystallized abilities is important (Coleman & Shah-Coltrane, 2011);
- data can show the patterns of a student's strengths and needs (Pereles, Baldwin, & Omdal, 2011);
- a range of supports and services will be needed to address the strengths of students (Johnsen, 2011); and
- collaboration and teamwork provide the best path to identifying and addressing students' strengths and needs (Hughes & Rollins, 2009).

Within this philosophical framework, identification practices focus on using data to recognize patterns of strengths and needs in order to match students with appropriate supports and service. But let us take a step back for a moment and explore briefly what RtI is, and then look more closely at what using an RtI framework would mean for identification practices in gifted education.

RESPONSE TO INTERVENTION: AN INTRODUCTION

The RtI system, sometimes called Response to Intervention or Instruction, is a multi-tiered system of support relying on data about a student's strengths and needs to develop an evidence-based instructional plan (Kirk, Gallagher, Coleman, & Anastasiow, 2009). While there are many ways that RtI is currently being implemented, there are some key attributes of the approach on which most people agree. RtI implementation usually includes:

- a multi-tiered system of supports and services (three tiers is the most common arrangement);
- a focus on early interventions (i.e., support can be provided prior to formal identification);
- the use of screening, monitoring of progress, and assessment information for data-driven decision making;
- the use of collaborative problem solving to plan for students' needs;
- the reliance on evidence-based approaches (sometimes called standard protocols) to address students' needs; and
- strong partnerships with families (Coleman & Hughes, 2009).

Perhaps the most familiar depiction of RtI is the triangle showing the three tiers (see Figure 16.1). The tiers form an array of supports and services that increase in intensity as the strengths and needs of the student increase.

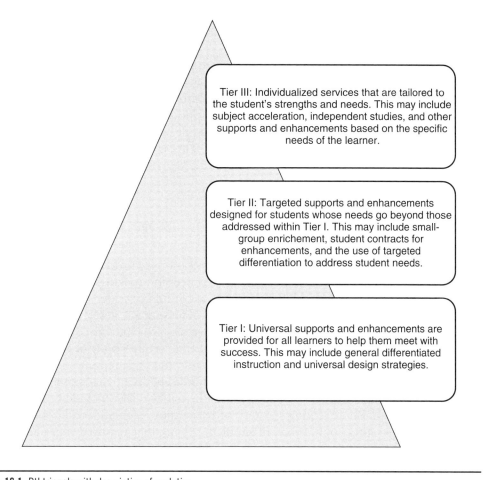

Fig. 16.1 RtI triangle with description of each tier.

The triangle shown here has no lines between the tiers to show that access to supports and services is fluid and is based on each student's needs. A student can, and usually does, receive supports and services across the tiers to address his or her specific pattern of strengths and needs. Matching a student to these supports and services is done through collaborative planning and data-driven decision making. Generally, supports provided at Tiers I and II do not require formal identification, while the services in Tier III do. This varies from district to district, as there is no "right" way to set up the tiers. It is up to individual districts or states to determine the specific configuration of supports and services. Ideally, identification practices are directly related to the services provided and are aligned to provide the maximum success for students (Coleman, 2003). Given this expectation of alignment, it is logical to assume that as the supports and services change, there will be implications for how students are identified within an RtI framework.

IMPLICATIONS OF AN RTI APPROACH FOR GIFTED EDUCATION IDENTIFICATION

While several states and districts are beginning to include gifted education in their RtI models, this is still an emerging effort (Rollins, Mursky, Shah-Coltrane, & Johnsen, 2009). Given the emerging nature of these practices, the *implications* discussed below are not conclusive; they are offered as food for thought as we re-examine identification practices in light of an RtI approach.

From an RtI perspective, identification is not an "in" or "out," "all" or "nothing" placement proposition. It is much more dynamic because it uses data to recognize a student's strengths and needs, and then matches these to appropriate supports and services across the tiers. In fact, the major shift in the identification paradigm within RtI is moving from "identifying whether the student is gifted or not" to "identifying the supports and services needed to help the student thrive." This is not a simple proposition. To understand this shift, we need to look at each of the key aspects of RtI to see its implications for gifted education (see Table 16.1).

COMPONENTS OF RTI AND THEIR IMPLICATIONS FOR GIFTED EDUCATION IDENTIFICATION

Imbedded in the paradigm shift concerning identification is a process shift relying on the collaborative planning approach and data-driven decision making. With the focus on using a data-driven decision-making approach, we should consider what kinds of data can be useful to the team. A student's aptitude, achievement, performance, observed characteristics and behaviors, motivation, and interests can all be sources of information about the student. This information can be compiled to create a body of evidence showing the student's strengths and needs across academic and social/emotional domains.

To illustrate, consider Amanda, a student with strengths in mathematics. A body of evidence showing Amanda's strengths in mathematics might include her progress-monitoring reports documenting mastery of basic knowledge and skills; some work samples demonstrating applications of problem solving that required more advanced and complex understandings; observational records of engagement during math-talks that reflect her deep understanding or unusual perspective on the mathematical concepts under discussion; and formal assessment data showing her mathematical aptitude

Table 16.1 Components of RtI and their implications for gifted education identification

Component of RtI	Description	Implications for Gifted Identification
Tiered Framework of Supports and Services	Multiple levels of support are available and Tiers I and II can be accessed prior to formal identification.	Focus is on matching students with appropriate supports and services across the tiers versus an "all" or "nothing" label of the student as "gifted."
Early Intervention	Supports and enhancements are made available prior to formal identification, as soon as the strengths and needs are seen.	Not a one-size-fits-all approach. Opportunities to nurture potential exist within Tiers I and II.
		A body of evidence can be developed based on a student's response to high-end learning experiences within Tiers I and II.
		Formal identification is not an "all" or "nothing" proposition as a student's strengths can be addressed within Tiers I and II.
Screening, Progress Monitoring, Assessment (decision making)	Universal screening of all learners for strengths is in place; periodic progress monitoring is used to document mastery of foundational knowledge and skills; and comprehensive assessments are completed as needed for data-driven decision making.	With universal screening, the initial student search is broad, including all students.
		Progress-monitoring data show both the level and rate of mastery and can be used as part of curriculum compacting.
		Comprehensive assessments that include formal as well as informal data help to round out the body of evidence used in the identification process.
Collaborative Planning	Teams including educational professionals, related service providers, and family members review data showing the students' strengths and needs to determine appropriate supports and services.	Identification involves judgment used to match students with appropriate supports and services, and is not driven by isolated cut-off points and formulaic algorithms that determine placement decisions.
		Teams can consider the students' strengths and needs in the context of school, family, and community.
		Guidelines are needed to bring consistency to the process used in decision making.
Evidence-based Instructional Approaches	Instructional approaches that have a track record of success build on a combination of research and theory; practitioner wisdom; and family/community values.	The availability of a set of evidence-based practices that have been selected for the classroom, school, and/or district will help teachers address the strengths and needs of their students.
		Confidence in instructional practice should be increased when students demonstrate success. Evidence of success can be used as part of the body of evidence showing strengths.
Family Partnerships	Family involvement in collaborative planning and support for the students' success.	Family involvement and support leads to more positive outcomes for students.
		Culturally resonant practices can be put in place with family input.

and achievement. The collaborative planning team (including Amanda and her parents) would use this body of evidence to select appropriate supports and services for her across the tiers. These supports and services might include a choice of mathematics games and challenges during unstructured time in the general classroom (Tier I); curriculum compacting for mathematics chapters and computer-based enrichment opportunities in mathematical problem solving (Tier II), and subject acceleration in mathematics provided in a cross-grade-level collaboration (Tier III).

So, will Amanda be identified as gifted in mathematics? Probably so, as she is receiving intensive services including subject acceleration in mathematics and shows a sustained need for this type of support. Formal identification as gifted should be considered when a student shows advanced abilities and achievement that likely require sustained support at the most intense level. In Amanda's case, identification is fairly straightforward. But what happens within an RtI approach for students whose patterns of strengths and needs are more complex? Three special cases that are challenging for identification are discussed next: early nurturing of potential, students who are twice exceptional, and students who are underachieving.

Nurturing Potential

One of the major challenges facing gifted education is the under-representation of students from culturally/linguistically different backgrounds and from economically disadvantaged families (Coleman & Shah-Coltrane, 2011; Ford, 2007). The RtI approach may help us to address this challenge in two ways. The first is through the early nurturing of potential within Tiers I and II which can be done prior to formal identification (Coleman & Shah-Coltrane, 2011). The idea that potential is fundamental to giftedness is not new (Marland, 1972) and several models of gifted education include a focus on nurturing potential. The value-added of an RtI approach is its explicit framework for collaboration between general and gifted education. This framework includes clear expectations for universal supports and enhancements at Tier I, and targeted supports and enhancements at Tier II which can be delivered prior to formal identification. Thus, students whose potential has not yet crystallized into performance can be given high-end learning experiences to nurture their growth. The second area of promise for addressing under-representation is in the use of a body of evidence to document strengths and needs. Because this approach looks at multiple types of information, from multiple sources, over multiple time periods, it provides a rich data set that can reveal patterns of strength that may be missed if single-score or time-bound methods are used. While we do not yet know if these approaches will help us redress the under-representation of children of color and poverty identified for gifted education services, the framework of RtI certainly holds promise.

Twice-Exceptional Learners

Students with both areas of disability and areas of giftedness often pose a special challenge to identification (Baum & Owen, 2004). How can we recognize both the strengths and the areas of challenge simultaneously? Again, RtI approaches offer some interesting opportunities with data-driven collaborative problem solving (Pereles, Omdal, & Baldwin, 2009). Within the RtI collaborative problem-solving approach, a team can review the specific pattern of strengths and needs that shows up in the data without having to over-focus on the educational labels the student will need in order to access services (Pereles, Baldwin, & Omdal, 2011). Interventions and enhancements can be given in Tiers I and II to support and enrich learning. The team can recommend and provide a differentiated curriculum in Tier I and then select appropriate additional services as comprehensive evaluation evolves. Response to the differentiated curriculum and the additional services will provide more data on the student's strengths and needs, which will verify the services and can be of help to the team with the selection of services at Tier III or determine that no further services are needed. Because services are seen as more flexible and progress monitoring is in place, adjustments can be made more easily if things are not working. Response to Intervention (RtI) seems to offer a new path to the identification of students with dual exceptionalities (Pereles et al., 2011).

Students Who Are Underachieving

Identification decisions are difficult to make when highly able students are not working up to their educational potential. Is a student who has a high IQ score gifted even if his performance in school is mediocre or dismal? Should a student identified as gifted be "de-gifted" if her performance takes a down turn and she is failing in her classes? Because the RtI approach shifts the focus from wondering whether the student is truly gifted to looking at the supports and services the student needs to thrive, these questions seem a little easier to answer. When students are not performing at their expected levels of success, a problem-solving team would certainly need to create an intervention plan. This process, based on data (including measures of aptitude), would entail looking at possible causes for the underachievement and selecting supports and enhancements to help turn the situation around. The student and family are partners in this planning process, so all individuals can share the responsibility for implementing the plan. The collaborative nature of the work helps to ensure that the student will not fall through the cracks and that support will be available. Family partnerships, a strong point of RtI, hold promise for helping to ensure that all students will get the support they need to reach their potential.

CONCLUSIONS

While this chapter may have given the impression that RtI approaches can solve all of our identification dilemmas, this is certainly not the case. Response to Intervention (RtI) is not a silver bullet and it is not without its own set of challenges. These challenges include the misuse of progress monitoring to hold students back rather than to document mastery; an over-focusing on data derived from measuring things that are easier to measure (e.g., low-level knowledge and basic skills) to the exclusion of more complex outcomes that are appropriate for students with gifts and talents; and a delaying of formal identification as gifted while a slower "RtI" process is unfolding. In spite of the remaining challenges, RtI approaches do hold promise, but we still have much to learn as we explore the identification of students with gifts and talents within an RtI framework.

REFERENCES

Baum, S. M., & Owen, S. V. (2004). *To be gifted and learning disabled.* Mansfield Center, CT: Creative Learning Press.

Brown, E. F., & Abernathy, S. H. (2009). Policy implications at the state and district level with RtI for gifted students. *Gifted Child Today, 32*(3), 52–57.

Coleman, M. R. (2003). The identification of students who are gifted. *ERIC Clearing House Digest E644, June 2003.* Arlington, VA: ERIC Clearinghouse on Disabilities and Gifted Education.

Coleman, M. R., & Hughes, C. E. (2009). Meeting the needs of gifted students within an RtI framework. *Gifted Child Today, 32*(3), 14–17.

Coleman, M. R., & Shah-Coltrane, S. (2011). Remembering the importance of potential: Tiers 1 and 2. In M. R. Coleman & S. K. Johnsen (Eds.), *RtI for gifted students* (pp. 43–62). Waco, TX: Prufrock Press.

Ford, D. Y. (2007). Diamonds in the rough: Recognizing and meeting the needs of gifted children from low SES backgrounds. In J. VanTassel-Baska & T. Stambaugh (Eds.), *Overlooked gems: A national perspective on low-income promising learners* (pp. 37–41). Washington, DC: National Association for Gifted Children.

Hughes, C. E., & Rollins, K. (2009). RtI for nurturing giftedness: Implications for the RtI school-based team. *Gifted Child Today, 32*(3), 31–39.

Johnsen, S. K. (2011). Assessing your school's RtI model in servicing gifted students. In M. R. Coleman & S. K. Johnsen (Eds.), *RtI for gifted students* (pp. 103–118). Waco, TX: Prufrock Press.

Kirk, S., Gallagher, J., Coleman, M. R., & Anastasiow, N. (2009). *Educating exceptional children* (13th ed.). Belmont, CA: Wadsworth/Engage.

Marland, S. P., Jr. (1972). *Education of the gifted and talented: Report to the Congress of the United States by the U.S. Commissioner of Education and background papers submitted to the U.S. Office of Education,* 2 vols. (Government Documents, Y4.L 11/2: G36). Washington, DC: U.S. Government Printing Office.

Pereles, D. A., Omdal, S., & Baldwin, L. (2009). Response to Intervention and twice-exceptional learners: A promising fit. *Gifted Child Today, 32*(3), 40–51.

Pereles, D. A., Baldwin, L., & Omdal, S. (2011). Addressing the needs of students who are twice-exceptional. In M. R. Coleman & S. K. Johnsen (Eds.), *RtI for gifted students* (pp. 63–86). Waco, TX: Prufrock Press.

Rollins, K., Mursky, C. V., Shah-Coltrane, S., & Johnsen, S. K. (2009). RtI models for gifted children. *Gifted Child Today, 32*(3), 20–30.

Section III
Service Delivery Options and Programming
Models for Gifted Students

17

CONTEXTS FOR INSTRUCTION
An Introduction to Service Delivery Options and Programming Models in Gifted Education
Holly L. Hertberg-Davis and Carolyn M. Callahan

SERVICE DELIVERY OPTIONS

We define *service delivery options* in this textbook as individual options for providing services to gifted students. Generally, service delivery options refer to and describe organizational structures such as the settings and/or student groupings utilized to provide advanced instruction to identified students. Pull-out programs, acceleration, and cluster grouping are three examples of service delivery options. These service delivery options provide general guidance for where, and to some extent how often and with whom, gifted students will be educated, but usually do not describe the specific types of educational experiences or curriculum that students will encounter within these structures (Advanced Placement courses, considered to be accelerated courses, are notable exceptions). Individual service delivery options rarely articulate a complete programming diet adequate for meeting the academic and affective needs of a broad range of gifted students, but rather need to be combined in thoughtful ways into a spectrum of services.

PROGRAMMING MODELS

Programming models, on the other hand, are organized, articulated, holistic approaches to delivering services to gifted students. Programming models generally describe the multiple *settings* in which gifted students receive advanced instruction, the multiple types of student *groupings* they will encounter, and in many cases, the *types of curricular experiences* in which students will engage (e.g., The Schoolwide Enrichment Model, The Levels of Service Model). Programming models also specify appropriate methods for identifying students for the services described and provide guidelines for effective implementation of the program. Most programming models are designed to constitute a school's entire gifted program.

CHOOSING APPROPRIATE SERVICE DELIVERY OPTIONS AND PROGRAMMING MODELS

As with all steps in the process of designing a defensible program for gifted students, choosing which service delivery option or gifted programming model to use in a school is a philosophical, financial, and context-driven decision. Choosing, for example, to utilize a pull-out classroom as part of a school's gifted program reflects the belief that grouping gifted students together for instruction for at least part of the day or week enhances their learning and/or their affective development. On the other hand, if a school subscribes to the belief that students need to be educated in heterogeneous settings, utilizing cluster grouping combined with differentiation of curriculum and instruction in the regular classroom might be an appropriate service delivery choice.

Ultimately, programming decisions must be made based upon the school's definition of giftedness and the resulting needs of the population of identified students. Typically, this is best accomplished through offering a spectrum of services or full implementation of a programming model, rather than through offering a single service delivery option. The three programming models presented in this section—The Schoolwide Enrichment Model, Total School Cluster Grouping, and The Levels of Service Model—all reflect the "spectrum of services" philosophy. Each programming model takes a balanced approach to offering gifted services, focusing both on the needs of students currently performing at high levels and on the needs of students whose talents have yet to be developed, and providing opportunities for identified gifted students to learn together sometimes and in more homogeneous settings at other times. With some common characteristics and some notably distinct features, all of these models have the potential to allow students with unusually high levels of performance in a discipline or across disciplines to receive appropriately advanced instruction, while also providing learning experiences designed to encourage students' talents to emerge.

The service delivery options and programming models we have included in this section are by no means exhaustive of all approaches in the field. Due to space restrictions, we could not provide full consideration to all approaches and have focused on in-depth descriptions of the most frequently offered options. However, we have provided a list of resources for learning about other approaches (e.g., The Autonomous Learner Model [Betts, 1985]; and The Catalyst Model [Landrum, 2001]) in the *Recommended Readings by Topic* section of this textbook).

Questions are presented below to help frame your thinking as you read the chapters in this section:

1. What philosophical assumptions about gifted students and how to serve them underlie this model or service option?
2. How well will this service delivery option or programming model match the cognitive and affective needs of the students identified under the various definitions of giftedness that were offered in Section II of the text?
3. For what "types" of gifted students might this service delivery option or programming model provide the best fit? For what "types" of gifted students might this approach not be appropriate?
4. What research evidence has been offered about the effectiveness of this option or model in serving students identified under the definitions of giftedness presented in Section II?

5. What additional services or approaches might students identified under our definition of giftedness need beyond those provided through this service delivery option or programming model?
6. What resources (e.g., financial, personnel, space) are necessary for full and effective implementation of this option or model? To what degree do these needs match the resources available within our school or district?

A FINAL NOTE

It is certainly true that the service delivery options chosen or programming models offered to gifted students are important, but it is critical to remember that the structures, settings, and grouping configurations we provide for gifted students are meaningless unless accompanied by appropriately differentiated curriculum and instruction. For a full treatment of appropriate curriculum and instruction for gifted learners, see Section IV of this volume.

REFERENCES

Betts, G. (1985). *Autonomous Learner Model for the gifted and talented.* Greeley, CO: Autonomous Learning.

Landrum, M. S. (2001). An evaluation of the Catalyst Program: Consultation and collaboration in gifted education. *Gifted Child Quarterly, 45,* 139–151.

18

EVIDENCE TRUMPS BELIEFS

Academic Acceleration Is an Effective Intervention for High-ability Students

Nicholas Colangelo, Susan G. Assouline, and Maureen A. Marron

Education researchers and practitioners have long acknowledged the enormous range of individual differences among students in terms of cognitive ability and academic achievement. Within a single grade, some students struggle to master basic academic content, whereas others begin a new school year already knowing a large portion of that year's curriculum (Reis et al., 1993). Various school reform efforts (e.g., the No Child Left Behind Act of 2001) rightly focus on increasing academic achievement among struggling students. At the same time, however, students who demonstrate exceptional academic ability often are not appropriately challenged by their school's curriculum and are failing to make increases in achievement (Duffet, Farkas, & Loveless, 2008; National Science Foundation, 2010; Plucker, Burroughs, & Song, 2010). Educational equity requires that all students have opportunities to develop their abilities (Benbow & Stanley, 1996) and may take the form of remedial efforts for some students and accelerated curricula for others. Without such efforts, the talents and abilities of the United States' highest achieving students are left undeveloped.

Academic acceleration is a simple, effective intervention that allows high-ability students to progress through an educational program at a rate faster or at an age younger than typical (Pressey, 1949). The term "acceleration" is used interchangeably to refer to acceleration as a service delivery model (in which students receive services at a younger than expected age) and as a curriculum model (in which students receive curricular material at a faster pace) (Schiever & Maker, 2003). The goal of acceleration—and a core feature of gifted education—is to provide an appropriate and equitable education to high-ability students by matching the level, complexity, and pace of the curriculum with a student's level of cognitive and academic development.

Despite the consistency of the research supporting the effectiveness of acceleration, school officials routinely avoid it. In 2004, we (Colangelo and Assouline) published

A Nation Deceived: How Schools Hold Back America's Brightest Students (Colangelo, Assouline, & Gross, 2004), a two-volume report that synthesized 50 years of research on acceleration, in which we identified academic and social issues as major factors explaining this striking disparity between the research on acceleration and the practice of it. Educators fear negative academic effects: Students will learn curricular material but not adequately comprehend it, and subsequent academic progress will be stunted. Concern over social development causes even greater resistance to acceleration; many fear that removing students from the traditional trajectory of a specific grade for a specific age may result in undesirable short-term or long-term consequences, regardless of students' ability to handle the academic side effectively.[1] Prior to the publication of *A Nation Deceived*, acceleration had become the classic casualty of belief trumping evidence. In *A Nation Deceived*, we discounted mistaken beliefs and myths about acceleration with research evidence, provided accessible information to educators, started a new dialog about the role of acceleration in the education of gifted students, and encouraged the practice of acceleration.

Additional evidence of the disparity between acceleration research and practice comes from the *State of the States in Gifted Education 2010–2011* (National Association for Gifted Children [NAGC] & Council of State Directors of Programs for the Gifted [CSDPG], 2011). The most recent results of this national survey indicate that acceleration policies are infrequent at the state level and highly variable at the district level: Only eight states have a state policy explicitly allowing acceleration; 12 states have a policy that formally relegates the decision to local education agencies (LEAs); 23 states have no policy, thus leaving any decisions about acceleration to LEAs by default. Even among the eight states explicitly allowing acceleration, not all forms of acceleration are uniformly embraced: Two of these states do not allow early entrance to kindergarten and two states leave decisions about early entrance to kindergarten to LEAs.

CATEGORIES OF ACCELERATION

The two *categories* of acceleration are *content-based* and *grade-based* (Institute for Research and Policy on Acceleration [IRPA], National Association for Gifted Children [NAGC], & The Council of State Directors of Programs for the Gifted [CSDPG], 2009; Rogers, 2004; Southern & Jones, 2004). The primary distinguishing feature between content-based and grade-based acceleration is whether the accelerative intervention shortens the number of years that a student spends in the K–12 system. Each category of acceleration can be classified further into forms and types. *Forms* are ways of varying the level, pace, and complexity of the curriculum. Some forms of acceleration have an additional level of specification: the *type*. *Types* are specific variations of practicing a particular form of acceleration. The distinctions between categories, forms, and types are subtle, yet informative, especially in terms of curriculum and service delivery models.

Content-based acceleration strategies provide students with advanced content, skills, or understandings before typical age- or grade-level instruction in that content area (Southern & Jones, 2004). Students typically remain with age and grade peers for most of the school day, but receive higher-grade-level instruction in an advanced-grade classroom. Content-based acceleration can also refer to allowing students to work on higher-grade-level instruction in their regular classrooms in lieu of on-grade-level instruction.

The *forms* of content-based acceleration include single-subject acceleration, curriculum compacting, dual enrollment, credit by examination, Advanced Placement courses and International Baccalaureate programs, and talent search programs.

Some forms of content-based acceleration can be classified into *types*. For example, single-subject acceleration can mean any of the following representative (but not exhaustive) types (IRPA, NAGC & CSDPG, 2009):

1. A third grade student performing above grade level in reading goes to a fourth grade teacher daily for instruction in reading and returns to the third grade classroom for instruction in other subject areas.
2. A musically gifted sixth grade student enrolls in a high school instrumental music course and returns to the sixth grade classroom for instruction in other subject areas.
3. A group of fifth grade students performing above grade level in mathematics is transported to a junior high-school building every morning for a seventh grade pre-algebra class and then transported back to their home school for instruction with their fifth grade classmates for the remainder of the day.
4. A high school mathematics teacher travels to a middle school to provide instruction to a group of middle school students who perform above grade level in mathematics. The students remain with their classmates for the remainder of the day, and the teacher returns to the high school.

Grade-based acceleration strategies typically shorten the number of years a student spends in the K–12 system (Rogers, 2004; Southern & Jones, 2004). In practice, a student is placed on a full-time basis in a higher grade level than typical (given the student's age) to provide access to appropriately challenging learning opportunities. Although grade-based acceleration is commonly known as "grade skipping," there are other *forms* of grade-based acceleration, including early entrance to school (kindergarten or first grade), grade telescoping, and early entrance to college. Early entrance to kindergarten does not shorten the number of years that the student spends in the K–12 system, but it does shorten the waiting time to start school.

The forms of grade-based acceleration can be classified into types. For example, the *types* of early entrance to college can include any of the following representative (but not exhaustive) scenarios (IRPA, NAGC, & CSDPG, 2009):

1. A student is granted a diploma after spending only five semesters in high school by accumulating credits through dual-credit coursework taken while in middle school, and by satisfying some high school graduation requirements in educational options other than traditional courses. The student then enrolls in college as a full-time student.
2. A student leaves high school without the traditional diploma, entering university full-time.
3. A student participates in an "early entrance to college" program.

ACCELERATION: AN EMPIRICAL SUCCESS STORY

At one level, it is easy to understand the reluctance to accelerate. Parents and educators try to make the best decisions for students, but they have no guarantee that what they do today will be of benefit in the students' futures. Acceleration is not a frequent or familiar practice in traditional education settings; it can be difficult in any group or social setting to be the person who does something different. Although decisions to accelerate often go against prevailing practices and attitudes, parents and educators can feel confident about acceleration because of the consistent base of research results from studies employing a variety of methodologies across different populations of students. Research demonstrates the efficacy of grade-based and content-based acceleration in academic and social–emotional outcomes for high-ability students in the short and long term: Grade-accelerated students outperform their chronologically older classmates on academic achievement tests, and grade- and content-accelerated students show approximately equal levels of social and emotional adjustment (see Assouline, Colangelo, Lupkowski-Shoplik, Forstadt, & Lipscomb, 2009; Colangelo et al., 2004; Kulik, 2004; Kulik & Kulik, 1992; Lipscomb, 2003; Lubinski, Benbow, Webb, & Bleske-Rechek, 2006; Lubinski, Webb, Morelock, & Benbow, 2001; Rogers, 2010; Sayler, 1996; Sayler & Brookshire, 1993; Southern & Jones, 1991; Wells, Lohman, & Marron, 2009).

Academic Effects of Acceleration

Research on acceleration tends to be in the form of case studies, instrument evaluations (Lipscomb, 2003), meta-analyses (Kulik & Kulik, 1992; Rogers, 2004, 2010), retrospective and prospective longitudinal studies (Subotnik & Arnold, 1993, 1994; Swiatek & Benbow, 1991), and studies of talent search program participants (Lubinski et al., 2001; Lubinski et al., 2006). A meta-analysis synthesizes the results of a group of studies on the same issue (Gall, Gall, & Borg, 2007) and permits conclusions about the magnitude of the effect of an intervention through the effect size metric.[2] Meta-analyses yield some of the strongest evidence for the effectiveness of acceleration (Kulik, 2004; Rogers, 2010).

In Kulik's (2004) meta-analysis, the median effect size was 0.80, a large impact, which implies that the accelerated students scored almost one grade equivalent above bright, non-accelerated students. Rogers's (2010) best-evidence synthesis (a form of meta-analysis) of 234 studies assessed academic, social, and psychological outcomes of various forms of acceleration. On academic outcomes, Rogers found a strong, positive overall effect size of 0.68 for acceleration. Rogers concludes that "there is a powerful academic effect to be gained from engaging in a variety of forms of acceleration, either grade-based or subject-based and either as an in-school option or an out-of-school option" (p. 2).

Longitudinal studies, many from the Study of Mathematically Precocious Youth (SMPY) project, provide a reassuring, consistent, and optimistic message about accelerated students' futures. Over the longer term, accelerated students attain advanced degrees, produce scholarly works, and contribute professionally at rates well above societal baselines (Lubinski et al., 2001; Lubinski et al., 2006). Other researchers (e.g., Adelman, 1999, 2006) have linked success in college to certain forms of content-area acceleration (and a rigorous curriculum more generally).

Social Effects of Acceleration

Concerns about the possible negative social effects of acceleration cause many educators and parents to reject acceleration (Colangelo et al., 2004). The concern stems, in part, from the misconception that acceleration refers exclusively to grade-based acceleration.

Additionally, some people are swayed by hearing about highly publicized cases of maladjusted accelerated students (e.g., the case of William Sidis, reported in Montour, 1977), while overlooking the many representative examples.

One complication in understanding social and emotional effects is lack of agreement on operational definitions. *Social effects* can refer to a multitude of constructs, including interpersonal relationships, emotional well-being, self-esteem, attitudes about school, and hopes and aspirations for the future. Thus, the evidence tends to be piecemeal. Another complication is that the measurement of social outcomes tends to be more subjective and less reliable than the measurement of academic outcomes.

Despite these limitations, Rogers (2010) assessed social and psychological outcomes of acceleration in her meta-analysis and reported small, but positive, effect sizes for social outcomes (ES = 0.14) and psychological adjustment (ES = 0.21). Kulik (2004) reported equivocal results when comparing accelerated students with bright but not accelerated students on *attitude toward school* and *attitude toward particular academic subjects*. Some studies in Kulik's meta-analysis indicated that accelerated students liked school in general and a particular subject if it was within the area of acceleration, whereas other studies indicated a slight downturn in attitudes. Kulik attributed the downturn to students not being accustomed to expending effort on school work. Accelerated students tend to have elevated educational ambitions (the desire to attain an advanced degree), higher career aspirations, and a greater willingness to commit to longer periods of preparation (often necessary to complete advanced degrees) than non-accelerated students. Accelerated students participate in extracurricular activities to the same extent as non-accelerated students (Kulik, 2004).

Trends in the data suggest that accelerated students show a slight decline in *self-acceptance* (Kulik, 2004; Robinson, 2004), but, importantly, this dip is *slight* and (usually) *temporary*. Serious, long-term negative effects have not been identified (Neihart, 2007). These findings are consistent with the Big-Fish-Little-Pond effect (Gross, 1998; Marsh, Chesser, Craven, & Roche, 1995; Marsh & Parker, 1984), in which the top achievers in a heterogeneous classroom orient to the possibility that they may not be the top achievers in a homogeneous setting. Most likely this is a useful reality check because bright students with realistic self-esteem may be better suited for future challenges than bright students with inflated self-esteem.

Social Effects of Grade-based Acceleration

According to Rogers (2010), "the most consistently positive effects across academic, psychological, and social outcomes were found for grade skipping" (p. 2). Other researchers reported that grade-skipped students had good perceptions of their social relationships and their emotional development, that they tended to have fewer serious behavior problems in school than regular students (Richardson & Benbow, 1990; Robinson, 2004), and that they have high self-esteem and internal locus of control (Richardson & Benbow, 1990).

Social Effects of Early Entrance to School

Discussions about early entrance to kindergarten can be emotionally laden as some critics contend that children are pushed into high-pressure academics before they have experienced childhood. However, some children are academically and socially ready for school, and allowing them to enter school early gives them the freedom to be themselves.

Early entrants adjust well academically and socially (Gagné & Gagnier, 2004; Robinson, 2004). Robinson (2004) reported slight positive, but not statistically significant, effects for socialization and affect. Although researchers typically hope for statistically significant differences in their studies, a finding of no difference between early entrants and traditional-age kindergarten children is a good outcome. Early entrants should fit in with their older peers and be at the same social level. It is not defensible to expect early entrants to demonstrate social maturity or adjustment beyond that exhibited by their older-age same-grade peers.

Robinson (2004; Robinson & Weimer, 1991) recommends that candidates for early entrance be no more than three months away from the school district's designated cut-off birth date, and that they undergo a psychological evaluation that includes assessment of academic readiness, emotional regulation, social skills, and social maturity. The performance of young students on ability and achievement measures is more variable than that of older students; however, with a thorough evaluation, decisions about early entrance can be made with confidence.

Social Effects and Early Entrance to College

Early entrance to college is typically viewed as an easier decision to make than early entrance to school because the student's accumulated years of academic experience and social development can indicate maturity, motivation, and readiness.

Adjusting to college is a challenge for many first-year students (Brody, Muratori, & Stanley, 2004; Muratori, 2007), so naturally there is concern about adjustment among early entrants. The evidence regarding the social–emotional adjustment of early college entrants is generally positive (Shepard, Foley Nicpon, & Doobay, 2009), although it is not uniform (Robinson, 2004). Early entrants generally are satisfied that they left high school early (Muratori, 2007; Robinson, 2004), and they are successful in college, particularly those who entered early through a structured program that provides social support for the transition to college life and its academic demands (Muratori, 2007; see also Brody et al., 2004).

Long-term Social Effects

Lubinski (2004) reports that adults who were accelerated in middle school and high school recall their pre-college experience more positively than intellectual peers who were not accelerated. Students who were accelerated did not regret their acceleration, and a small percentage wished they had been accelerated more (Lubinski, 2004). The positive recollections about acceleration from adults are good indicators that the long-term social effects of acceleration are beneficial to the individual. What happens if the intervention takes the form of *not* accelerating students who are academically ready for acceleration? The students reported that a slow-paced curriculum led to boredom and discontent (Lubinski, 2004).

ACCELERATION IN SPECIAL POPULATIONS: RADICAL ACCELERATION

Radical acceleration is "any combination of procedures that results in a student graduating from high school three or more years earlier than is customary" (Gross, 2004, citing Stanley, 1978, p. 87). Radical acceleration is appropriate for only the most highly gifted students, such as those who have an IQ that is three or more standard deviations above the average IQ. The measured IQ of profoundly gifted students represents a highly significant deviation from the normal IQ of 100. An age-appropriate regular curriculum is not sufficiently challenging for profoundly gifted students, and they may underachieve and exhibit negative social interactions if they remain in educational and social settings not suited to their learning needs (Gross, 2004). Gross (2004) finds positive outcomes for students who radically accelerate, including success in college and positive social interactions with older classmates. Educators and the public seem more comfortable with the forms of acceleration that are less visible to others and deviate less from typical school placements (such as Advanced Placement classes for high school students, and content acceleration for elementary school students); hence the challenges of accommodating profoundly gifted students include the visibility of the acceleration and finding the right amount of acceleration.

ACCELERATION IN SPECIAL POPULATIONS: TWICE-EXCEPTIONAL STUDENTS

Students who are twice exceptional are identified as gifted *and* are diagnosed with a disability in one or more areas such as learning (e.g., specific learning disability: dyslexia, dysgraphia, written language disability, mathematical disability), emotional/behavioral (e.g., anxiety, depression), or physical domains (e.g., visual or auditory difficulties) (NAGC, 2009). Students who are gifted and also on the autism spectrum (autism spectrum disorder [ASD]) are twice exceptional.

Twice-exceptional students require educational programming that addresses both their area of strength and their area of weakness. Several misconceptions can make it difficult for students to obtain the right balance of accelerated and non-accelerated instruction (Assouline, Foley Nicpon, & Huber, 2006): these include the primary misconception that a student with a disability cannot also be gifted; and a secondary misconception that a student with a disability cannot be served by acceleration in the area of the student's strength. Assouline et al. (2006) recommend a comprehensive evaluation of the student's academic ability, aptitude, and achievement, as well as an assessment of social–emotional development to understand the cognitive, social, and academic profiles of twice-exceptional students (Assouline, Foley Nicpon, & Doobay, 2009), because students who appear to be similar on the surface might have very different educational programming needs.

THE DEFENSIBILITY OF ACCELERATION

Our review of the research confirms that acceleration is an empirically effective intervention for high-ability students, with positive academic, social, and psychological short-term and long-term outcomes. For some students, acceleration should be the intervention of choice over other service delivery options and curriculum approaches, such as enrichment and differentiation. Key considerations include how many and what types of acceleration opportunities will be of benefit to an individual student.

Acceleration and Enrichment

It is unfortunate that a false dichotomy between acceleration and enrichment has characterized the field, when the question for educators should be *how much* of each approach will benefit which student (e.g., the question of "educational dose," as recently discussed by Wai, Lubinski, Benbow, & Steiger, 2010).[3] Enrichment provides "richer, more varied educational experiences, a curriculum that has been modified or added to in some way" (Schiever & Maker, 2003). The goal of enrichment programs is to add depth and breadth to the regular curriculum through resource rooms, special-interest clubs, Saturday classes, summer programs, etc. Enrichment programs do not necessarily strive to move a student through the curriculum more quickly or to provide access to accelerated curriculum. Some argue that the more closely enrichment matches a student's interests and talents, the more it approaches acceleration (see discussion in Stanley, 1978).

Acceleration and Differentiation

Some schools adopt differentiation as an approach to serving the needs of *all* students. Differentiation refers to a classroom in which "the teacher proactively plans and carries out varied approaches to content, process, and product in anticipation of and response to student differences in readiness, interest, and learning needs" (Tomlinson, 2005, p.7). The program goals of differentiation are to respond to the diversity and mixed academic ability in a classroom by offering multiple avenues for learning. However, in a recent survey (Duffett et al., 2008), 81 percent of teachers reported that struggling students received the most one-on-one attention; only 5 percent reported that advanced students received the most attention. It seems unlikely that high-ability students receive an appropriately differentiated curriculum when they receive so little attention from teachers. Moreover, the range of individual differences and academic needs may be too great for one teacher to accommodate, and the academic needs of the student may exceed the teacher's ability to prepare accelerated content.

Although the principle of differentiation is consistent with the goals of gifted education, Hertberg-Davis (2009) notes varied reasons for how differentiation can fail to fulfill the needs of gifted students, including:

> lack of sustained teacher training in the specific philosophy and methods of differentiation, underlying beliefs prevalent in our school culture that gifted students do fine without any adaptations to curriculum, lack of general education teacher training in the needs and nature of gifted students, and the difficulty of differentiating instruction without a great depth of content knowledge . . .
>
> (Hertberg-Davis, 2009, p. 252)

Acceleration is about appropriate educational placement based on the developmental readiness of the student. The more closely enrichment and differentiation match interests and talents, the more they approximate to acceleration. If enrichment and differentiation do not include a faster pace and a higher level of work, they will not be as effective as acceleration (Borland, 2009; Stanley, 1978).

Acceleration and School Reform Models

Acceleration compares favorably to school reform models. In an evaluation of more than 200 studies of the achievement effects of multiple school-reform models (Boreman, Hewes, Overman, & Brown, 2002, reported in Kulik, 2004), only Direct Instruction, the

School Development Program, and Success for All had some demonstrated effectiveness. However, the Success for All effect size represents not quite one month of growth; whereas the acceleration meta-analyses (see above) report large effect sizes that correspond to nearly one academic year of growth. In other words, the reform models cannot compete with the effects of acceleration as an intervention.

WHAT RESOURCES ARE NEEDED TO MAKE ACCELERATION HAPPEN?

Daurio (1979) identified reasons why acceleration was not used as an educational intervention: opposition to the use of tests to identify promising talent at young ages; selectively biased recall of adjustment problems following acceleration; and confusion over definitions of enrichment and acceleration. Several decades later, hints of these reasons remain impediments to acceleration (Colangelo et al., 2004).

What are some practical steps toward encouraging the practice of acceleration in schools?

- Offer professional development opportunities to demonstrate how the practice of acceleration can meet the needs of high-ability students.
- Form collaborations with school personnel to handle the logistics of acceleration, including scheduling and transportation issues.
- Form collaborations with school personnel to discuss the alignment of curriculum and to ensure that students can maintain their accelerated standing as they progress through the school system.
- Recognize that many acceleration options come with no financial cost (e.g., content-based acceleration) or limited financial cost (e.g., Advanced Placement courses).
- Encourage the use of above-level tests to identify students who may benefit from acceleration.
- Present data on academic and social–emotional outcomes and promote the use of objective assessments to increase decision makers' comfort with the process.
- Advocate for changes in school acceleration practices and policies using *Guidelines for Developing an Academic Acceleration Policy* (IRPA, NAGC, & CSDPG, 2009) to formalize the educational opportunities available for students.

The advantages of acceleration—a simple and economical intervention—for high-ability students are significant. A major obstacle to the practice and implementation has been incorrect beliefs about negative effects of acceleration. It is time for evidence to trump beliefs.

RESOURCES

- The Institute for Research and Policy on Acceleration (IRPA), a unit of the Belin-Blank Center at The University of Iowa (www.accelerationinstitute.org), advocates for academic acceleration of high-ability students. The institute provides research, clinical advice, support for writing acceleration policy, and acceleration testimonials.

- *Guidelines for Developing an Academic Acceleration Policy.* The recommendations in this publication provide schools with assistance in writing policy so that opportunities for accelerated learning are formalized. The document is the result of the collaborative efforts of IRPA, the National Association for Gifted Children (NAGC), and the Council of State Directors of Programs for the Gifted (CSDPG) (http://www.accelerationinstitute.org/Resources/Policy_Guidelines/).
- Decision-making guides for identification of students for acceleration, and implementation of the acceleration process. The Iowa Acceleration Scale (IAS) (3rd edition) (Assouline et al., 2009) is a tool to help schools make objective and effective decisions for grade acceleration in grades K–8. The IAS guides a child-study team (educators, teachers, parents, and other professionals) through a discussion of the student's academic and social characteristics. The IAS pays particular attention to non-academic and social–emotional factors, including the child's interpersonal skills, emotional maturity, and motivation to accelerate, as well as the attitudes of the receiving teacher and the school.

NOTES

1. *Time Magazine* published an article on academic acceleration and *A Nation Deceived* on September 27, 2004. *A Nation Deceived* has been widely circulated in print and electronically. Volume I is available in Arabic, Chinese, French, German, Hindi, Japanese, Korean, Russian, and Spanish. All versions are available for downloading at no cost at www.accelerationinstitute.org.
2. Effect size is the standardized difference between two means. Effect sizes can indicate "no impact" (ES = 0.0), a "small impact" (ES = 0.20), a "medium impact" (ES = 0.50), or a "large impact" (ES = 0.80).
3. To quote Borland (2009, p. 113), "In educational circles, acceleration is like the Battle of New Orleans; the war is over, but some people do not know it yet and keep on fighting."

REFERENCES

Adelman, C. (1999). *Answers in the tool box: Academic intensity, attendance patterns, and bachelor's degree attainment.* Washington, DC: U.S. Department of Education.

Adelman, C. (2006). *The tool box revisited: Paths to degree completion from high school through college.* Washington, DC: U.S. Department of Education.

Assouline, S., Colangelo, N., Lupkowski-Shoplik, A., Forstadt, L., & Lipscomb, J. (2009). *Iowa Acceleration Scale manual: A guide for whole-grade acceleration K-8* (3rd ed.). Scottsdale, AZ: Great Potential Press.

Assouline, S. G., Foley Nicpon, M., & Doobay, A. (2009). Profoundly gifted girls and autism spectrum disorder: A psychometric case study comparison. *Gifted Child Quarterly, 53,* 89–106.

Assouline, S. G., Foley Nicpon, M., & Huber, D. M. (2006). The impact of vulnerabilities and strengths on the academic experiences of twice- exceptional students: A message to school counselors. *Professional School Counseling, 10*(1), 14–24.

Benbow, C. P., & Stanley, J. C. (1996). Inequity in equity: How equity can lead to inequity for high-potential students. *Psychology, Public Policy, and Law, 2,* 249–292.

Borland, J. H. (2009). Gifted education without gifted programs or gifted students: An anti-model. In J. S. Renzulli, E. J. Gubbins, K. S. McMillen, R. D. Eckert, & C. A. Little (Eds.), *Systems & models for developing programs for the gifted & talented* (2nd ed., pp. 105–118). Mansfield Center, CT: Creative Learning Press.

Brody, L. E., Muratori, M. C., & Stanley, J. C. (2004). Early entrance to college: Academic, social, and emotional considerations. In N. Colangelo, S. Assouline, & M. U. M. Gross (Eds.), *A nation deceived: How schools hold back America's brightest students* (Vol. II, pp. 97–108). Iowa City: The Connie Belin & Jacqueline N. Blank International Center for Gifted Education and Talent Development, The University of Iowa.

Colangelo, N., Assouline, S., & Gross, M. U. M. (2004). *A nation deceived: How schools hold back America's brightest students* (Vol. I). Iowa City: The Connie Belin & Jacqueline N. Blank International Center for Gifted Education and Talent Development, The University of Iowa.

Daurio, S. P. (1979). Educational enrichment versus acceleration: A review of the literature. In W. C. George, S. J. Cohn, & J. C. Stanley (Eds.), *Educating the gifted: Acceleration and enrichment* (pp. 13–63). Baltimore: Johns Hopkins University Press.

Duffet, A., Farkas, S., & Loveless, T. (2008). *High achieving students in the era of NCLB.* Washington, DC: Thomas B. Fordham Institute.

Gagné, F., & Gagnier, N. (2004). The socio-affective and academic impact of early entrance to school. *Roeper Review, 26,* 128–138.

Gall, M. D., Gall, J. P., & Borg, W. R. (2007). *Educational research: An introduction* (8th ed.). Boston: Pearson.

Gross, M. U. M. (1998). Fishing for the facts: A response to Marsh and Craven, 1997. *Australian Journal of Gifted Education, 7,* 10–23.

Gross, M. U. M. (2004). Radical acceleration. In N. Colangelo, S. Assouline, & M. U. M. Gross (Eds.), *A nation deceived: How schools hold back America's brightest students* (Vol. II, pp. 87–96). Iowa City: The Connie Belin & Jacqueline N. Blank International Center for Gifted Education and Talent Development, The University of Iowa.

Hertberg-Davis, H. (2009). Myth 7: Differentiation in the regular classroom is equivalent to gifted programs and is sufficient: Classroom teachers have the time, the skill, and the will to differentiate adequately. *Gifted Child Quarterly, 53,* 251–253.

Institute for Research and Policy on Acceleration, National Association for Gifted Children, & The Council of State Directors of Programs for the Gifted. (2009). *Guidelines for developing an academic acceleration policy.* Iowa City, IA: Authors.

Kulik, J. A. (2004). Meta-analytic studies of acceleration. In N. Colangelo, S. Assouline, & M. U. M. Gross (Eds.), *A nation deceived: How schools hold back America's brightest students* (Vol. II, pp. 13–22). Iowa City: The Connie Belin & Jacqueline N. Blank International Center for Gifted Education and Talent Development, The University of Iowa.

Kulik, J. A., & Kulik, C. C. (1992). Meta-analytic findings on grouping programs. *Gifted Child Quarterly, 36,* 73–77.

Lipscomb, J. M. (2003). *A validity study of the Iowa Acceleration Scale.* (Unpublished doctoral dissertation). University of Iowa, Iowa City.

Lubinski, D. (2004). Long-term effects of educational acceleration. In N. Colangelo, S. Assouline, & M. U. M. Gross (Eds.), *A nation deceived: How schools hold back America's brightest students* (Vol. II, pp. 23–38). Iowa City: The Connie Belin & Jacqueline N. Blank International Center for Gifted Education and Talent Development, The University of Iowa.

Lubinski, D., Benbow, C. P., Webb, R. M., & Bleske-Rechek, A. (2006). Tracking exceptional human capital over two decades. *Psychological Science, 17,* 194–199.

Lubinski, D., Webb, R. M., Morelock, M. J., & Benbow, C. P. (2001). Top 1 in 10,000: A 10-year follow-up of the profoundly gifted. *Journal of Applied Psychology, 86,* 718–729.

Marsh, H. W., Chesser, D., Craven, R., & Roche, L. (1995). The effects of gifted and talented programs on academic self-concept: The big fish strikes again. *American Educational Research Journal, 32,* 285–319.

Marsh, H. S., & Parker, J. W. (1984). Determinants of student self-concept. Is it better to be a relatively large fish in a small pond even if you don't learn to swim as well? *Personality and Social Psychology, 47,* 213–231.

Montour, K. M. (1977). William James Sidis, the broken twig. *American Psychologist, 32,* 265–279.

Muratori, M. C. (2007). *Early entrance to college.* Waco, TX: Prufrock Press.

National Association for Gifted Children. (2009). *Twice-exceptionality.* (Position Statement). Washington, DC: Author.

National Association for Gifted Children, & The Council of State Directors of Programs for the Gifted. (2011). *State of the states in gifted education 2010–2011: National policy and practice data.* Washington, DC: Authors.

National Science Foundation (2010). *Preparing the next generation of STEM innovators: Identifying and developing our nation's human capital.* Washington, DC: Author.

Neihart, M. (2007). The socioaffective impact of acceleration and ability grouping: Recommendations for best practice. *Gifted Child Quarterly, 51,* 330–341.

Plucker, J. A., Burroughs, N., & Song, R. (2010). *Mind the (other) gap! The growing excellence gap in K–12 education.* Bloomington, IN: Center for Evaluation and Education Policy, Indiana University.

Pressey, S. L. (1949). *Educational acceleration: Appraisals and basic problems* (Bureau of Educational Research Monographs No. 31). Columbus: Ohio State University Press.

Reis, S. M., Westberg, K. L., Kulikowich, J., Caillard, F., Hébert, T., Plucker, J. et al. (1993). *Why not let high ability students start school in January? The curriculum compacting study.* Storrs: The National Research Center on the Gifted and Talented, University of Connecticut.

Richardson, T. M., & Benbow, C. P. (1990). Long-term effects of acceleration on the social-emotional adjustment of mathematically precocious youths. *Journal of Educational Psychology, 82,* 464–470.

Robinson, N. M. (2004). Effects of academic acceleration on the social-emotional status of gifted students. In N. Colangelo, S. Assouline, & M. U. M. Gross (Eds.), *A nation deceived: How schools hold back America's brightest students* (Vol. II, pp. 59–68). Iowa City: The Connie Belin & Jacqueline N. Blank International Center for Gifted Education and Talent Development, The University of Iowa.

Robinson, N., & Weimer, L. (1991). Selection of candidates for early admission to kindergarten. In W. T. Southern, & E. Jones (Eds.), *The academic acceleration of gifted children* (pp. 29–50). New York: Teachers College Press.

Rogers, K. B. (2004). The academic effects of acceleration. In N. Colangelo, S. Assouline, & M. U. M. Gross (Eds.), *A nation deceived: How schools hold back America's brightest students* (Vol. II, pp. 47–58). Iowa City: The Connie Belin & Jacqueline N. Blank International Center for Gifted Education and Talent Development, The University of Iowa.

Rogers, K. B. (2010). Academic acceleration and giftedness: The research from 1990 to 2008, a best-evidence synthesis. In N. Colangelo, S. Assouline, D. Lohman, & M. A. Marron (Eds.), *Proceedings of the 2008 Wallace Symposium poster session on academic acceleration.* Iowa City: The University of Iowa.

Sayler, M. F. (1996, April). *Differences in the psychological adjustment of accelerated eighth grade students.* Paper presented at the Annual Meeting of the American Educational Research Association, New York.

Sayler, M. F., & Brookshire, W. K. (1993). Social, emotional, and behavioral adjustment of accelerated students, students in gifted classes, and regular students in eighth grade. *Gifted Child Quarterly, 37,* 150–154.

Schiever, S. W., & Maker, C. J. (2003). New direction in enrichment and acceleration. In N. Colangelo & G. A. Davis (Eds.), *Handbook of gifted education* (3rd ed., pp. 163–173). Boston: Allyn & Bacon.

Shepard, S., Foley Nicpon, M., & Doobay, A. (2009). Early entrance to college and self-concept: Comparisons across the first semester of enrollment. *Journal of Advanced Academics, 21,* 40–57.

Southern, W. T., & Jones, E. D. (Eds.). (1991). *The academic acceleration of gifted children.* New York: Teachers College Press.

Southern, W. T., & Jones, E. D. (2004). Types of acceleration: Dimensions and issues. In N. Colangelo, S. Assouline, & M. U. M. Gross (Eds.), *A nation deceived: How schools hold back America's brightest students* (Vol. II, pp. 5–12). Iowa City: The Connie Belin & Jacqueline N. Blank International Center for Gifted Education and Talent Development, The University of Iowa.

Subotnik, R., & Arnold, K. (Eds.). (1993). Longitudinal studies in gifted education [Special issue]. *Roeper Review, 15.*

Subotnik, R., & Arnold, K. (1994). Longitudinal study of giftedness and talent. In R. F. Subotnik, & K. A. Arnold (Eds.), *Beyond Terman: Contemporary studies of giftedness and talent.* Norwood, NJ: Ablex.

Stanley, J. C. (1978). Identifying and nurturing the intellectually gifted. In W. C. George, S. J. Cohn, & J. C. Stanley (Eds.), *Educating the gifted: Acceleration and enrichment* (pp. 172–180). Baltimore: The Johns Hopkins University Press.

Swiatek, M. A., & Benbow, C. P. (1991). Ten-year longitudinal follow-up of ability-matched accelerated and unaccelerated gifted students. *Journal of Educational Psychology, 83,* 528–538.

Tomlinson, C. A. (2005). *How to differentiate instruction in mixed-ability classrooms* (2nd ed.). Upper Saddle River, NJ: Pearson.

Wai, J., Lubinski, D., Benbow, C. P., & Steiger, J. H. (2010). Accomplishment in science, technology, engineering, and mathematics (STEM) and its relation to STEM educational dose: A 25-year longitudinal study. *Journal of Educational Psychology, 102,* 860–871.

Wells, R., Lohman, D. F., & Marron, M. A. (2009). What factors are associated with grade acceleration? An analysis and comparison of two U.S. databases. *Journal of Advanced Academics, 20,* 248–273.

19

COGNITIVE AND AFFECTIVE OUTCOMES OF PULL-OUT PROGRAMS

Knowns and Unknowns

E. Jean Gubbins

Program developers spend a considerable amount of time reflecting on two critical questions: "Who are the gifted and talented students in our school district?" and "What are the most effective screening and identification techniques?" Once they have answered those questions and know and understand the educational needs of their identified students, they must ask: "How do we serve them?" and more specifically, "Where do we serve them?" Questions with a focus on the physical grouping and location of students (e.g., full-time classes, pull-out programs, resource programs, special schools, within-class programs, magnet programs) are referring to service delivery models.

DEFINITIONS OF PULL-OUT PROGRAMS

The nomenclature associated with service delivery models varies considerably in the literature and program documents. One service delivery model frequently used in elementary schools, the pull-out program, is the focus of this chapter. Pull-out programs are also referred to as "resource programs," "resource rooms," or "magnet programs." While the use of pull-out programs is fairly common, a consistent definition of the model is lacking. On a very literal level, "pull-out" means removing specific students from general education classrooms and bringing them together in another location for instruction. The number of times that students leave the classroom, the total amount of time per week out of the classroom, the number of students per class, and the use of multi-grade or single-grade classes vary. Looking across just six definitions (Cox & Daniel, 1984; Davis, Rimm, & Siegle, 2011; Gubbins et al., 2002; Moon, 1995; Olszewski-Kubilius & Limburg-Weber, 2010; Rogers, 2002), variability can be identified in:

a. time frame (from less than an hour a week to a full day or more a week);
b. the types of activities in which students engage, with some making no mention of instructional activities, others offering general descriptions such as enrichment activities or extension activities, and still others specifying content, process skills, or an instructional strategy (thinking-skills building, creative problem solving, independent learning, or independent projects); and
c. who provides instruction.

Details are few or even non-existent regarding what a pull-out program should or could be. The only commonality associated with the term is the specification that identified gifted and talented students leave the general education classroom for a period of time. In addition, pull-out programs are sometimes referred to as "enrichment programs" which implies curricular modifications. Hence, it is somewhat difficult to discern the cognitive and affective outcomes that could reasonably be attributed to pull-out programs (Landrum, 2006).

ONE PRACTITIONER'S PERSPECTIVE: POSITIVE AND NEGATIVE CHARACTERISTICS OF PULL-OUT PROGRAMS

One way to start unraveling the impact of this service delivery model is to begin with an analysis of the potential positive and negative characteristics across the various dimensions of a service delivery model from a practitioner's perspective. Table 19.1 provides an experiential and practical analysis of positive and negative attributes associated with pull-out programs for elementary students.

Although the 11 dimensions on Table 19.1 are important in program development regardless of the programming options selected, they are not the main purpose of this chapter. They are included because they are critical in the decision-making process when selecting a service delivery model. These dimensions should be reviewed carefully to ensure that the potential positive characteristics emerge as the pull-out program plans are developed (if that is the one of the service delivery options selected).[1] The potential negative characteristics serve as cautions to guide decision making as well.

As suggested in Table 19.1, pull-out programs are efficient ways to manage personnel, resources, schedules, and program components, as all responsibilities rest with a limited number of people within the school or district. All design and implementation issues can be resolved with advice and suggestions from the personnel most closely associated with the program. Of course, the responsibility for design and implementation issues can rest at any level from a central office administrator to program teachers. Relegating decision making to teachers alone does not capitalize on the expertise of all district administrators and teachers, and may result in conflict from inconsistencies in philosophy about educational practice in the district. After reviewing the 11 practitioner's criteria for pull-out programs and the related potential positive and negative characteristics, it is important to consider the research base on the cognitive and affective benefits.

RESEARCHERS' PERSPECTIVES: COGNITIVE AND AFFECTIVE OUTCOMES OF PULL-OUT PROGRAMS

Prevalence of Pull-out Programs

There is considerable literature available about pull-out programs, but the confusion surrounding the term does make it somewhat difficult to verify if the researchers are

Table 19.1 One practitioner's perspective: Potential positive and negative characteristics of pull-out programs

Dimension of Planning	Positive Characteristics	Negative Characteristics
Screening and Identification	Gifted and talented teachers with background knowledge in the field are available to offer input into designing and implementing defensible screening and identification systems.	General education teachers who have received limited professional development about the services in the program are asked to nominate or evaluate students to receive those services.
Program Model	Research-based program model guides program development, implementation, and evaluation.	A pull-out model may not support or extend the district's philosophical perspectives for educating all students.
Program Content	Students are engaged in challenging curricular opportunities designed by teachers who have a specific background and training in developing curriculum and providing instruction for gifted students.	Program content may not be directly assessed by district- or state-level tests with the result that no data is available on the program's impact on student learning.
	Program content may be extensions of curricula in general education classrooms, parallel to school's curricula, unrelated to current grade-level curricula, or interest-based, independent investigations.	If program content is not codified, it is unlikely to be consistent across teachers and unlikely to be shared with general education teachers within and across schools.
		Content, concepts, and skills may not be directly transferable to classroom curricula.
Professional Development	Teachers are more likely to have advanced-level expertise in developing and delivering appropriate curriculum for gifted and talented students (attained through coursework, certification classes, conferences, and workshops).	Classroom teachers who are responsible for providing instruction when the gifted students are not attending classes offered in the pull-out program may not have developed expertise in gifted and talented education, due to lack of access to formal and informal professional development activities. They may come to regard the education of gifted students as the sole purview of the resource-room teacher.
Learning Environment	Program teachers and classroom teachers work collaboratively to ensure that gifted and talented students are involved with challenging curricula in both learning environments.	Students are required to make up missed classroom work while attending the pull-out program.
Communication	Effective oral and written communications about the program and progress of students are the responsibility of gifted and talented teachers directly involved with all phases of the program. It is in their best interest to share program information with administrators, teachers, and parents.	Without consistent and comprehensive communications with classroom teachers, knowledge about students' progress, interests, and productivity will be compromised.
		Gifted and talented program progress reports may not be integrated with the school's report cards.

Economic	Student assignment can be based on the number of identified students at each grade level. Gifted and talented teachers' schedules can be scheduled to include time to meet with each class and to serve as a resource for classroom teachers by co-teaching of classes, demonstration lessons, or project development.	In a district with multiple gifted and talented teachers implementing the pull-out model, additional economic resources may be required to employ a district coordinator. If the gifted and talented teachers' schedules do not allow time to act as a resource to classroom teachers, then fewer students benefit from the teachers' expertise and knowledge, and there is less likelihood of shared responsibility for educating gifted learners.
Resources	Technology and non-technology resources are purchased specifically to meet the needs of gifted and talented students and program content.	Resources for the pull-out program may not mirror those in classrooms, which may raise questions about equitable distribution of limited resources.
Time Commitment	Students participate in the pull-out program a set number of hours per week and manage program and classroom responsibilities effectively. Identified students have the opportunity to work with intellectual peers.	May disrupt the teachers' and students' schedule to such an extent that identified gifted and talented students withdraw from the pull-out program. Teachers may resent that the identified gifted and talented students do not participate and contribute to all their classes.
Cognitive Benefits	Students respond positively to challenging curricular options. Students make achievement gains in relevant content areas.	There is a lack of curriculum planning between the gifted and talented program teachers and classroom teachers, resulting in duplication of content instead of curricular enhancement and extensions.
Affective Benefits	Students interact with other students with similar interests. Students are challenged to work at high levels. Students interact with their intellectual peers and develop social connections through their program involvement.	Identified students sense a change in class rank when they meet with other identified gifted and talented students. The challenge level of the program content may be stressful. Identified gifted and talented students may prefer to interact socially with all students in their general education classroom and miss such opportunities when they are involved in the pull-out program.

truly addressing pull-out programs or some variant of the term (Gallagher & Gallagher, 1994). Pull-out programs have been the predominant method of delivering services in elementary schools for many decades (Cox & Daniel, 1984; Gubbins et al., 2002; Schroth, 2008; Swiatek & Lupkowski-Shoplik, 2003). Even though the Council of State Directors of Programs for the Gifted and the National Association for Gifted Children used the term "resource room" instead of "pull-out programs" for their 2008–2009 survey (CSDPG & NAGC, 2009), some educators view the terms as synonymous (Olszewski-Kubilius & Limburg-Weber, 2010). The survey revealed that regular classrooms, followed by resource rooms, were the most common service delivery models for grades 3–6. The continued popularity of pull-out programs as one administrative model to serve gifted and talented students is not without supporters and detractors among researchers. It is important to consider the findings of several research studies when designing or redesigning a program for gifted and talented students.

Cognitive Outcomes

Research syntheses, retrospective studies, case studies, and national database studies provide perspectives on the effectiveness of elementary school pull-out programs. Combing through the literature on pull-out programs is complicated by the fact that, in research studies on the impact of gifted programs on students, the exact service delivery model utilized is frequently not detailed; or the sole focus of the research study is on the impact of ability grouping; or confusion abounds in conflating the service delivery model and the curricular goals (enrichment). However, the findings of studies investigating both pull-out programs *and* ability grouping are highlighted in this chapter as both bodies of research offer valuable insights for program developers.

Research Syntheses

Best-evidence syntheses and meta-analyses conducted in the early 1990s through to the early 2000s (Kulik, 1992, 2003; Rogers, 1991, 2002; Vaughn, Feldhusen, & Asher, 1991) offered a positive view of the impact of pull-out programs and ability-grouping practices. Rogers (1991, 2002) found that enrichment (pull-out) programs, when involving curriculum extension, had significant impact on student achievement.

Kulik (1992) examined the impact of several forms of ability grouping on gifted students, cautioning that the effects of grouping depend on the extent of curricular and other adjustments for highly talented learners. He outlined guidelines for the types of curricular experiences that should be included in pull-out programs:

- Highly talented youngsters profit greatly from work in accelerated classes. Schools should therefore try to maintain programs of accelerated work.
- Highly talented youngsters also profit greatly from an enriched curriculum designed to broaden and deepen their learning. Schools should therefore try to maintain programs of enrichment (p. 45).

Vaughn et al. (1991) focused their meta-analyses and other studies on pull-out programs and determined that they have small to medium positive effects on academic achievement, and on critical and creative thinking. They recommended that program developers be proactive and address potential criticisms of pull-out programs, including the lack of connectedness with the general education curricula, the limited percentage of time per week for program involvement, and the failure to match the pace, depth, and breadth of the curricula to the students' needs. All of these criticisms must be studied carefully as program plans evolve and discussions begin about how to meet students' academic needs.

Researchers emphasized that pull-out programs or ability grouping *alone* yield few, if any, achievement differences. Students must be provided with opportunities to engage with intellectual peers in accelerated content (Assouline, Blando, Croft, Baldus, & Colangelo, 2009; Colangelo, Assouline, & Gross, 2004; VanTassel-Baska & Little, 2010; VanTassel-Baska & Wood, 2009) or challenging curricular options through interest-based investigations or independent studies (Olszewski-Kubilius & Limburg-Weber, 2010; Renzulli & Reis, 1985, 1997).

Delcourt, Cornell, and Goldberg's (2007) study of the cognitive and affective learning outcomes of gifted elementary school students involved in different service delivery models (i.e., separate class, separate school, pull-out program, and within-class program) offered further research support for pull-out programs. They determined that students from within-class programs received the lowest scores on norm-referenced achievement tests in mathematics problem solving, reading comprehension, science, and social studies when compared to gifted peers in separate class, separate school, or pull-out programs. They stated that:

> [C]hildren in special schools, separate schools, separate class programs, and pullout programs showed substantially higher levels of achievement than both their gifted peers not in programs and those attending within-class programs that did not focus on differentiating the curriculum.
>
> (Delcourt et al., 2007, p. 377)

This research, along with that of Tieso (2002), who investigated the effects of grouping and curricular practices on mathematics achievement, confirms the interdependence of the service delivery model, grouping strategy, and the differentiation and modification of curricula to meet students' academic needs: "quantitative analyses indicated that a differentiated mathematics unit used in combination with flexible grouping practices improved the academic achievement of students with middle and high levels of prior knowledge when compared with the comparison subgroups (middle or high)" (Tieso, 2002, p. 32). Kulik (2003) concurred when he demonstrated that experimental studies provided strong evidence that grouping programs are often very effective when they are used to provide appropriate curricular materials for students with different educational needs. Studies also provide strong evidence that grouping contributes little to educational improvement efforts when it is used as an end in itself (Kulik, 2003, p. 275).

When students are grouped purposefully based on their academic needs, the program content must be differentiated with well-defined learner outcomes rather than a series of unrelated activities; otherwise, the time outside general education classrooms is not warranted.

Retrospective Studies, Case Studies, and National Database Studies

Cognitive outcome data from retrospective studies, case studies, and national databases provide additional perspectives on the effectiveness of pull-out programs. Two researchers conducted retrospective studies of students involved in gifted programs. Westberg

(1999) interviewed several of her former students 15 years after they participated in a pull-out program and found that their early interest in specific topics and completion of individual and small-group investigations of real problems influenced their creative productive work long after they finished college and graduate school. Hébert (1993) also conducted retrospective, in-depth case studies of gifted and talented students involved in gifted programs from first or second grade through secondary school. Ten highly productive students participated in one district's program based on the Enrichment Triad Model (Renzulli, 1977), which provided an elementary pull-out program (2–4 hours per week), middle school "talent pool" classes, secondary school interdisciplinary studies, and Advanced Placement or college-level courses. Students revealed that their early experiences with independent and small-group investigations of real problems influenced their post-secondary plans, promoted their search for creative outlets of their projects (e.g., stringer for local newspaper, creator of high school sports publication, participant in science fairs, producer of literary magazine), and helped them plan and implement any type of research assignment. These students' creative productive experiences in the pull-out program and their subsequent influence on their potential careers were also supported by Delcourt's earlier research (1988) with high school students.

Murphy (2009) prepared several essays on the impact of gifted education on student achievement. In one essay, he used the Early Childhood Longitudinal Study, Kindergarten Cohort (ECLS-K) and found that reading and mathematics programs significantly influenced student achievement. When he controlled for unmeasured student characteristics, the impact of gifted program participation on mathematics achievement remained significant, while the impact on reading achievement became statistically insignificant. Adelson (2009) also analyzed the ECLS-K data on school personnel-reported reading and mathematics gifted programs to determine the effects on school achievement, student achievement, and academic attitudes. Analysis of the variables of interest revealed that gifted programming did not have an impact on reading or mathematics achievement at the school or student level. As there were no details provided in the national database about the specific programming practices, Adelson (2009) warned:

> In light of inconsistent policies and programming practices nationwide, these results indicate that school personnel who report that they are providing a gifted program in mathematics or reading may not be providing an effective program in terms of achievement or academic attitudes.
>
> (Adelson, 2009, abstract)

The ECLS-K research studies by Murphy and Adelson present contrasting perspectives on the impact of gifted and talented programs, which may be due, in part, to the use of different statistical models or differing definitions of "program."

Typically, cognitive outcomes are the goals of gifted and talented programs as educators search for alternative ways to enhance and extend the curricular opportunities offered within general education classrooms (Davis et al., 2011; Gallagher & Gallagher, 1994; Van-Tassel-Baska, 1998, 2005). But, of course, they also want to consider the whole child as the challenge level of curricula is raised in pull-out programs. How students perceive their academic abilities and how they view themselves (self-concept) may also be affected by involvement in pull-out programs. A review of researchers' findings provides a brief snapshot of what is known and unknown about the affective impact of pull-out programs.

Affective Outcomes

Affective outcomes are important considerations when students are recognized publicly for their abilities, leaving their classrooms for the pull-out program euphemistically named "Challenge," "Explore," "Aspire," or "Leap." Feldhusen and Nimlos-Hippen (1992) compared the self-concept of gifted and non-gifted peers, noting that sixth grade gifted students in pull-out or self-contained programs have more positive self-concepts. Hoge and Renzulli (1991, 1993) reviewed several studies to determine if identified students held more positive self-concepts than their less gifted peers, or if identified gifted students' self-esteem was lower, due to fear of never living up to others' expectations. Although these researchers did not focus on service delivery models, their findings are useful in assessing affective outcomes. Hoge and Renzulli (1991) concluded that "the direct comparisons of gifted and nongifted students revealed that the gifted students showed no deficits in self-esteem" (p. 28). In fact, gifted students indicated somewhat higher levels of general and academic self-esteem. Other studies revealed that there is some support for the social comparison theory, whereby students "compare their academic outcomes with those of other students and . . . these social comparisons will be a salient basis in the formation of academic self-concept" (Marsh, Chessor, Craven, & Roche, 1995, p. 314).

Students' perceptions of and reactions to program involvement provide critical insights into the affective outcomes of gifted and talented programs. Adams-Byers, Squiller Whitsell, and Moon (2004) interviewed and surveyed students ($n = 44$) during a residential summer program and asked them to reflect on their perceptions of involvement with various service delivery models (e.g., full-time schools, homeschooled, no gifted/talented program, pull-out, and self-contained programs) during the school year. Opportunities to learn with gifted and talented peers who understand each other and think alike was a positive reaction to participation, but the researchers also noted the lowering of self-esteem. Marsh et al. (1995) and Seaton, Marsh, and Craven (n.d.) consistently demonstrated through multiple research studies that students involved in academically selective environments have lower academic self-concepts than students with similar abilities in non-selective environments. This phenomenon is known as the Big-Fish-Little-Pond Effect (BFLPE) (Marsh et al., 1995).

The BFLPE is described as follows: Identified gifted and talented students may be the top one to three high-performing students in general education classrooms, where they are acknowledged and praised by teachers and students for their academic prowess. They might be the "go-to" students when complex problems are presented or they may be the leaders in discourse about mathematical concepts. However, when these students are regrouped for a pull-out program, they join a group of 10–15 other high-performing students who are very cognizant of the performance of others. If students continually compare their performance to that of others in their new academic group instead of focusing on individual growth and achievements, their sense of academic self could be affected negatively. Marsh et al. (1995) proposed that "students with an individual mastery orientation—as opposed to an ego/competitive orientation—are more likely to use skill development and improvement over time as a basis for their academic self-concepts" (pp. 314–315). They contend that programs promoting the pursuit of self-selected areas of interest may be more effective in eliminating or reversing BFLPE than competitive programs encouraging social comparison. Students involved in multiple learning experiences, in which they have input into what and how they learn, will "derive increasing understanding of their own talents and capabilities, and from that understanding they can build a personal commitment to develop their talents" (Feldhusen, 1998, p. 4). Care should be exercised in not equating lower self-esteem with poor self-esteem.

Neihart (2007) echoes the contrasting results of analyzing self-concept. She reviewed studies indicating that students in full-time gifted classrooms had lower self-concepts than students involved in part-time options, while other studies she reviewed (Vaughn et al., 1991) indicated that placement in a pull-out program did not affect self-concept, positively or negatively.

VanTassel-Baska, Feng, Quek, and Struck (2004) studied the perceptions of teachers, program coordinators, and students after two years of involvement in gifted programs. Program involvement positively affected how these well-motivated students approached learning, as they experienced enhancement of self-confidence, communication skills, and thinking skills. Moon, Feldhusen, and Dillon (1994) also reported that students involved in an enrichment program were self-confident and it "helped them clarify and confirm their abilities" (p. 43). Students were interviewed when they were in high school and reflected on their pull-out program based on the Purdue Three-Stage Model, which fostered basic thinking skills, promoted self-concepts by interacting with other gifted children, developed intellectual and creative abilities through involvement with challenging content, and helped students become independent and effective learners. Study findings included verification of the program's positive impact on students and achievement of program goals. Participating students developed more adequate self-concepts, which prompted the authors to comment: "For some students, the development of self-concept appears to have been by far the most important benefit of the program, especially when viewed from the perspective of the parents" (Moon et al., 1994, p. 43).

Neihart (2007) examined the socio-affective impact (e.g., attitude toward subject matter, development of career interests, healthy social relationships, and high motivation) of peer ability grouping. She concurred with the findings of many researchers that grouping high-ability students for acceleration has a positive impact on achievement, and recognized that the socio-affective impact of peer ability grouping was not researched as widely. Although she did not center her review of research on pull-out programs, there are connections between findings on pull-out programs and those related to peer ability grouping. She concluded that: "various forms of ability grouping have differential effects for gifted students. Peer ability grouping seems to have positive socio-affective effects for some gifted students, neutral effects for others, and detrimental effects on a few" (p. 334). Similarly, Rogers (1993) stated: "What seems evident about the spotty research on socialization and psychological effects when grouping by ability is that no patterns of improvement or decline can be established" (p. 10). Neihart's earlier insights (1999) from the research literature about gifted and talented students remain accurate:

Some researchers found the gifted to be advanced in their social adjustment and development, and other studies observed certain subgroups of gifted students to have more difficulties socially. Hence, empirical research indicates that the gifted are a diverse group when it comes to social competence.
(Neihart, 1999, "Giftedness and Social Competence," paragraph 3)

Although there is a dearth of research on the affective outcomes of pull-out programs, it is important to consider the potential effects on students' sense of self as they try to balance the academic and social demands of their general education classrooms and the pull-out program.

CONCLUSIONS

There are "knowns and unknowns" regarding the cognitive and affective outcomes of pull-out programs. Some research indicates positive cognitive (i.e., achievement) and positive affective (i.e., self-concept) outcomes associated with pull-out programs, while other studies indicate that the impact of these programs is not what program developers would hope for. It is important to remember that a pull-out program is just a mechanism used to organize a group of identified gifted and talented students in a location where they are involved in various curricular and instructional experiences. What goes on in that location is not always patently obvious from the research studies. While phrases such as critical thinking, problem solving, creative thinking, and curricular extension are typically linked with pull-out programs, these phrases are labels rather than descriptions of actual curricular experiences.

Pull-out programs can involve students for as little as 5 percent of the school week or as much as 20 percent, which, according to Gallagher (2000), could be a "nontherapeutic educational dosage" (p. 10). What happens during the other 80–95 percent of the time? It is essential to plan and monitor the curricular and instructional strategies to meet the cognitive and affective needs of gifted and talented students both inside and outside of the regular classroom. Pull-out programs are not a panacea for meeting these needs; they are a partial solution that must be combined with other services (e.g., mentorships, academic competitions, independent study) offered within and outside general education classrooms. Rogers (2002) warned that:

> [P]ull-out programs are not enough . . . the pull-out can probably never be considered sufficient differentiation for gifted or talented children. Their needs are every day in almost every academic area. A pull-out experience once or twice a week will not suffice.
>
> (Rogers, 2002, p. 259)

Given these warnings about the limitations of pull-out programs, it is important for program developers to analyze the positive and negative characteristics outlined in Table 19.1 (above). Capitalizing on the positive characteristics and resolving the negative characteristics will make pull-out programs a viable option for meeting the cognitive and affective needs of gifted and talented students.

NOTE

1. The development of a gifted "program" is ideally the creation of multiple options for providing for the needs of gifted and talented learners. Hence, a pull-out program may be one of several options including acceleration, full-time schools, or within-classroom enrichment that may be offered within one program.

REFERENCES

Adams-Byers, J., Squiller Whitsell, S., & Moon, S. M. (2004). Gifted students' perceptions of the academic and social/emotional effects of homogeneous and heterogeneous grouping. *Gifted Child Quarterly, 48*, 7–20.

Adelson, J. L. (2009). *Examining the effects of gifted programming in mathematics and reading using the ECLS-K.* (Unpublished doctoral dissertation). University of Connecticut, Storrs.

Assouline, S. G., Blando, C. A., Croft, L. J., Baldus, C. M., & Colangelo, N. (2009). Promoting excellence: Acceleration through enrichment. In J. S. Renzulli, E. J. Gubbins, K. McMillen, R. D. Eckert, & C. A. Little (Eds.), *Systems & models for developing programs for the gifted & talented* (pp. 1–17). Mansfield Center, CT: Creative Learning Press.

Cohen, J. (1988). *Statistical power analysis for the behavioral sciences* (2nd ed.). Hillsdale, NJ: Erlbaum.

Colangelo, N., Assouline, S., & Gross, M. U. M. (Eds.). (2004). *A nation deceived: How schools hold back America's brightest students* (Vol. I). Iowa City: The Connie Belin & Jacqueline N. Blank International Center for Gifted Education and Talent Development, The University of Iowa.

Council of State Directors of Programs for the Gifted, & The National Association for Gifted Children. (2009). *State of the states in gifted education 2008–2009: National policy and practice data.* Washington, DC: Authors.

Cox, J., & Daniel, N. (1984, Sept./Oct.). The pull-out model. *Gifted Child Today, 34,* 55–61.

Davis, G. A., Rimm, S. B., & Siegle, D. (2011). *Education of the gifted and talented* (6th ed.). Upper Saddle River, NJ: Pearson.

Delcourt, M. A. B. (1988). *Characteristics related to high levels of creative productive behavior in secondary high school students.* (Unpublished doctoral dissertation). University of Connecticut, Storrs.

Delcourt, M. A. B., Cornell, D. G., & Goldberg, M. D. (2007). Cognitive and affective learning outcomes of gifted elementary school students. *Gifted Child Quarterly, 51,* 359–381.

Delcourt, M. A. B., Loyd, B. H., Cornell, D. G., & Goldberg, M. D. (1994). *Evaluation of the effects of programming arrangements on student learning outcomes.* (Research Monograph 94018). Storrs: The National Research Center on the Gifted and Talented, University of Connecticut.

Feldhusen, J. F. (1998). Programs for the gifted few or talent development for the many? Retrieved January 19, 2012 from http://www.jstor.org/stable/20439330Feldhusen, J. F., & Nimlos-Hippen, A. L. (1992). An exploratory study of self-concepts and depression among the gifted. *Gifted Educational International, 8,* 136–138.

Gallagher, J. J. (2000). Unthinkable thoughts: Education of gifted students. *Gifted Child Quarterly, 44,* 5–12.

Gallagher, J. J., & Gallagher, S. A. (1994). *Teaching the gifted child.* Boston: Allyn & Bacon.

Gubbins, E. J., Westberg, K. L., Reis, S. M., Dinnocenti, S. T., Tieso, C. L., Muller, L. M. et al. (2002). *Implementing a professional development model using gifted education strategies with all students.* (Research Monograph 02172). Storrs: The National Research Center on the Gifted and Talented, University of Connecticut.

Hébert, T. P. (1993). Reflections at graduation: The long-term impact of elementary experiences in creative productivity. *Roeper Review, 16,* 22–28.

Hoge, R. D., & Renzulli, J. S. (1991). *Self-concept and the gifted child.* (RBDM9104). Storrs: The National Research Center on the Gifted and Talented, University of Connecticut.

Hoge, R. D., & Renzulli, J. S. (1993). Exploring the link between giftedness and self-concept. *Review of Educational Research, 63,* 449–465.

Kulik, J. A. (1992). *An analysis of research on ability grouping: Historical and contemporary perspectives.* (RBDM9204). Storrs: The National Research Center on the Gifted and Talented, University of Connecticut.

Kulik, J. A. (2003). Grouping and tracking. In N. Colangelo & G. A. Davis (Eds.), *Handbook of gifted education* (3rd ed., pp. 268–281). Boston: Allyn & Bacon.

Landrum, M. S. (2006). Identifying student cognitive and affective needs. In J. H. Purcell, & R. D. Eckert (Eds.), *Designing services and programs for high ability learners: A guidebook for gifted education* (pp. 1–14). Thousand Oaks, CA: Corwin Press.

Marsh, H. W., Chessor, D., Craven, R., & Roche, L. (1995). The effects of gifted and talented programs on academic self-concept: The big fish strikes again. *American Educational Research Journal, 32,* 285–319.

Moon, S. (1995). The effects of an enrichment program on the families of participants: A multiple-case study. *Gifted Child Quarterly, 39,* 198–203.

Moon, S. M., Feldhusen, J. F., & Dillon, D. R. (1994). Long-term effects of an enrichment program based on the Purdue Three-stage Model. *Gifted Child Quarterly, 38,* 38–48.

Murphy, P. R. (2009). *Essays on gifted education's impact on student achievement.* (Unpublished doctoral dissertation). Florida State University, Tallahassee.

Neihart, M. (1999). The impact of giftedness on psychological well-being. Retrieved January 19, 2012 from http://talentdevelop.com/articles/TIOGOPW.html

Neihart, M. (2007). The socioaffective impact of acceleration and ability grouping: Recommendations for best practice. *Gifted Child Quarterly, 51,* 330–341.

Olszewski-Kubilius, P., & Limburg-Weber, L. (2010). *A research-based primer on terminology and educational options for gifted students* (display article). Retrieved January 19 2012 from http://www.ctd.northwestern.edu/numats/about/displayArticle/?id=2&pf=0

Renzulli, J. S. (1977). *The Enrichment Triad Model: A guide for developing defensible programs for the gifted and talented.* Mansfield Center, CT: Creative Learning Press.

Renzulli, J. S., & Reis, S. M. (1985). *The Schoolwide Enrichment Model: A how-to guide for educational excellence.* Mansfield Center, CT: Creative Learning Press.

Renzulli, J. S., & Reis, S. M. (1997). *The Schoolwide Enrichment Model: A how-to guide for educational excellence* (2nd ed.). Mansfield Center, CT: Creative Learning Press.

Rogers, K. B. (1991). *The relationship of grouping practices to the education of the gifted and talented learner.* (RBDM9102). Storrs: The National Research Center on the Gifted and Talented, University of Connecticut.

Rogers, K. B (1993). Grouping the gifted and talented: Questions and answers. *Roeper Review, 16,* 8–12.

Rogers, K. B. (2002). *Re-forming gifted education: How parents and teachers can match the program to the child.* Scottsdale, AZ: Great Potential Press.

Seaton, M., Marsh, H. W., & Craven, R. G. (nd). Big-Fish-Little-Pond Effect under the grill: Tests of its universality, a search for moderators and the role of social comparison. Retrieved January 19, 2012 from http://www.self.ox.ac.uk/documents/SeatonMarshCraven.pdf

Schroth, S. T. (2008). Levels of service. In J. A. Plucker, & C. M. Callahan, (Eds.), *Critical issues and practices in gifted education: What the research says* (pp. 321–333). Waco, TX: Prufrock Press.

Southern, W. T., & Jones, E. D. (2004). Types of acceleration: Dimensions and issues. In N. Colangelo, S. Assouline, & M. U. M. Gross (Eds.), *A nation deceived: How schools hold back America's brightest students* (Vol. 2, pp. 5–12*).* Iowa City: The Connie Belin & Jacqueline N. Blank International Center for Gifted Education and Talent Development, The University of Iowa.

Swiatek, M. A., & Lupkowski-Shoplik, A. (2003). Elementary and middle school student participation in gifted programs: Are gifted students underserved? *Gifted Child Quarterly, 47,* 118–130.

Tieso, C. L. (2002). *The effects of grouping and curricular practices on intermediate students' math achievement.* (Research Monograph 02154). Storrs: The National Research Center on the Gifted and Talented, University of Connecticut.

VanTassel-Baska, J. (1998). *Excellence in educating the gifted* (3rd ed.). Denver, CO: Love.

VanTassel-Baska, J. (2005). Gifted programs and services: What are the nonnegotiables? *Theory Into Practice, 44,* 90–97.

VanTassel-Baska, J., Feng, A. X., Quek, C., & Struck, J. (2004). *Psychology Science, 46,* 363–378.

VanTassel-Baska, J., & Little, C. A. (2010). *Content-based curriculum for high-ability learners.* Waco, TX: Prufrock.

VanTassel-Baska, J., & Wood, S. M. (2009). The integrated curriculum model. In J. S. Renzulli, E. J. Gubbins, K. McMillen, R. D. Eckert, & C. A. Little (Eds.), *Systems & models for developing programs for the gifted & talented* (pp. 655–692). Mansfield Center, CT: Creative Learning Press.

Vaughn, V. L., Feldhusen, J. F., & Asher, J. W. (1991). Meta-analyses and review of research on pull-out programs in gifted education. *Gifted Child Quarterly, 35,* 92–98.

Westberg, K. L. (1999, Summer). What happens to young, creative producers. *NAGC: Creativity and Curriculum Divisions' Newsletter,* pp. 3, 13–16.

20

ANALYZING PULL-OUT PROGRAMS

A Framework for Planning

Catherine M. Brighton and Kristofor Wiley

Pull-out programs represent the most common service delivery model outside the general education classroom (Council of State Directors of Programs for the Gifted [CSDPG] & National Association for Gifted Children [NAGC], 2009; Swiatek & Lupkowski-Shoplik, 2003). The purpose of this chapter is to offer recommendations for defensible use of the pull-out-program model based on consideration of potential benefits and liabilities.

DEFINING TERMS

Given the variety of groupings employed in gifted education programs, it is important to clarify the parameters for a typical pull-out program. Borland (2003) defined gifted pull-out programs as part-time services delivered by a special teacher, in a separate setting, with other students identified as gifted, typically focused on some form of enrichment or extension, although not necessarily related to what is occurring within the general education setting. During some period(s) of time each week, target students are "pulled out" of their primary educational setting to receive these services.

The pull-out model has been, and continues to be, among the most common delivery models in the field of gifted education. Twenty-five years ago, Cox, Daniel, and Boston (1985) conducted the Richardson Study, a national, comprehensive survey to determine the landscape of gifted programs across the United States. The findings suggested that nearly 80 percent of gifted programs surveyed included pull-out components. More than two decades later, pull-out programs are still prevalent. The *State of the States in Gifted Education 2008–2009* report (CSDPG & NAGC, 2009) states that in early elementary settings, resource rooms (one common name for a pull-out program) were the second most frequently used model, following regular classroom instruction, among states reporting the use of models for delivering instruction to the gifted. The report identified resource rooms as the most commonly used model at the upper elementary level; in middle schools, resource rooms were the third most commonly used model after the regular classroom and cluster grouping models. Resource rooms were, however, relatively uncommon in high school settings. These recent findings show that the conclusions of the Richardson Study are still reflected in the types of programming offered in gifted education classrooms. The pull-out model is a dominant presence at the elementary and middle school levels. As a result, the scope of this chapter will be limited to pull-out programs in K–8 settings.

A FRAMEWORK FOR ANALYSIS

More than two decades ago, Belcastro (1987, cited in Vaughn, Feldhusen, & Asher, 1991) proposed criteria which he believed all gifted programs should meet in order to be defensible:

a. curricular offerings should be integrated with the regular curriculum;
b. the students are selected based on a system for fair identification of students;
c. students receive daily program experience;
d. students receive instruction with intellectual peers;
e. the pace of instruction matches students' learning rates;
f. curriculum is reflective of complex and higher-level content and thinking processes; and
g. instruction is delivered by excellent teachers.

While developed more than 20 years ago, these recommendations closely align with the National Association for Gifted Children's *2010 Pre-K–Grade 12 Gifted Programming Standards* (NAGC, 2010). To supplement Belcastro's criteria, we offer three additional NAGC standards for guiding best practice in implementing a pull-out model:

• Implementation of interventions to develop cognitive and affective growth should be based on research of effective practices.
• Educators are responsible for assessing the quantity, quality, and appropriateness of the programming and services provided for students with gifts and talents by disaggregating assessment data and yearly progress data.
• Educators regularly plan and implement multiple grouping arrangements including clusters, resource rooms, special classes, or special schools.

In sum, these indicators serve as yardsticks for determining the degree to which a pull-out program incorporates best-evidence practice.

To consider more precisely how to create the best fit between these 10 evaluation criteria and the pull-out model, it makes sense to consider three specific contexts for pull-out models, each of which has different assumptions, degrees of intensity, and implications for practice.

Scenario 1: A Within-school Enrichment Approach

Duckburg Elementary School operates a reading/language arts resource room; the teacher, Mrs. Jones, holds an elementary teaching credential with a gifted endorsement. Students in third to fifth grades who show high capability or potential in reading/language arts are excused from the general education homeroom during that block two days a week to attend the resource room with other identified students to participate in advanced-level literature groups. Mrs. Jones collaborates with the regular classroom teachers to ensure that she provides evidence of mastery of the key concepts taught that day in the general education classrooms. Since she can do this more quickly with the identified students, she uses their remaining time to focus on advanced content and engage in deep discussion.

Scenario 2: An Accelerative Approach

Mr. Smith is a gifted specialist at Springdale Elementary School. The school district determined that it is critical to provide appropriately challenging services in mathematics, so students in third, fourth and fifth grades identified as highly capable in mathematics leave the regular classroom during mathematics instruction every day to attend class with Mr. Smith. Because he is solely responsible for their mathematics instruction, he provides all of the instructional feedback and quarterly report-card grades in this subject. Mr. Smith utilizes the same textbook series used in the general classroom, but allows individual students to cover the material at their own pace, often moving from a text at one grade level to one at the next grade in the middle of the school year. In addition to an advanced mathematics degree, Mr. Smith has an endorsement in gifted education and has received extensive training in differentiated instruction. He recognizes that the students in this class, while equally in need of advanced mathematics instruction, are not a homogeneous group. Therefore, Mr. Smith makes every effort to differentiate the curriculum and instruction within the class to meet the various learning needs, strengths, and preferences of his students.

Scenario 3: A Center-based Enrichment Approach

Daleville Public School operates a full-day pull-out center at a city-center school building. Students who are identified as gifted spend one day per week at the Gifted Education Center, where their curriculum and instruction is based on the Schoolwide Enrichment Model (SEM) (see Chapter 21 in this book by Renzulli and Reis). The teachers have worked closely with the home schools of the students to compact the general curriculum. Students are grouped and regrouped within and across grade levels depending on level of readiness in the area of instruction. Teachers construct activities to extend or enrich the curriculum in the home school. For example, if the students are reading poetry in third grade, non-fiction in fourth grade, and science fiction in fifth grade language arts, the teachers will offer a unit on biographies of poets, historians, and fiction writers in the context of studying how to become a writer—learning about where and how ideas are generated, how poets compose and revise, how historians do research, etc. Or they may study journalism as an additional area of writing, extending the language arts curriculum with sports writers, editors, columnists, or reporters coming in to discuss their craft, the way they do research, etc. Students are provided with specific assignments to complete in their home schools during the time freed up as a result of curriculum compacting, as they work up to and complete their SEM Type III projects. Home school teachers and the librarian/media center staff receive descriptions of the assignments from the Gifted Education Center and assist students as necessary. On any given day, some 120 students in first through eighth grades attend the center and are served by a team of six teachers holding gifted endorsements from their state.

APPLYING THE CRITERIA

Integration With Regular Curriculum

While most service delivery models are defined by the curriculum they deliver, pull-out models are characterized not only by the quality of educational experiences offered within them, but also by the relationship between this curriculum and the curriculum they require participants to miss when absent from the regular classroom. In Scenario 1, the pull-out curriculum is matched topically to the curriculum missed, as when a student is pulled out of fourth grade reading instruction to participate in an advanced literature group. Because the pull-out occurs during reading/language arts time, the gifted resource teacher must ensure that the skills and concepts from the general education lesson are mastered prior to supplementing them with more complex activities. This approach allows both for quick and precise extension for higher-readiness students, and for the general classroom teacher to focus on the needs of a smaller group of students on days when students are pulled out.

Scenario 2 describes what pull-out services might look like utilizing an accelerative approach. In the event that gifted education services can be scheduled during every instructional period of a subject (e.g., Mr. Smith teaches the advanced mathematics class every day at the same time as the typical mathematics instruction), this opens up the option of accelerating the identified students, as they no longer need to interface with the general classroom in that subject. Implementing this approach requires systematic transitions between grade levels and school levels. Students who learn at an accelerated pace should be guaranteed access to higher-level materials for the rest of their academic careers in the district.

Scenario 3 explores the more complicated option of releasing identified students from a full day of regular instruction to attend a pull-out program that delivers an alternative curriculum. In this model, students' competency in the skills and knowledge of the general curriculum are documented, and (in the specific example provided) the regular classroom curriculum is extended through reading related and reinforcing literature and working as practicing professionals to write their own poems, biographies, non-fiction, or science fiction work. By grouping by language-arts readiness (first in reading and then in writing skills) and then by interest, the teachers can provide focused skill instruction at an appropriate level, tied to the writing of professionals in the students' areas of interest.

Systematic and Fair Identification of Gifted Students

The topic of identification is addressed elsewhere in this textbook (see Section II), but there are some specific considerations related to the pull-out model that warrant discussion here. A non-negotiable best practice for a gifted program is to have direct alignment among the operational definition (what it means to be gifted in this community), the identification procedures (how students are determined to be eligible for services), the service delivery models (the structures surrounding how and where students are served), and the direct services offered to students (the curriculum, instruction, and classroom assessment related to the specific area/s served). Given the wide variability in how pull-out programs are conceptualized and implemented, varying from single-subject and cross-disciplinary enrichment to accelerative options, the need for a seamless link between the definition, identification procedures, and type of pull-out program becomes imperative.

Appropriate criteria for identifying students to take part in the advanced literature program in Scenario 1 might include reading achievement scores two standard deviations higher than grade-level expectations and demonstrated interest in the area of reading and literature. In Scenario 2, students demonstrating advanced achievement in the area of mathematics coupled with an assessed fit for acceleration (see Colangelo, Assouline, and Marron's Chapter 18 in this book) might indicate alignment between identification and that program model. Identification for participation in the full-day program in Scenario 3 should be based on the Three-Ring Conception of Giftedness model specified by Renzulli and Delcourt in Chapter 5.

Daily Program Experience

As indicated, pull-out programs vary widely in terms of the amount of time that students spend within them. Some pull-out models include daily access to gifted education services, while others provide once-a-week opportunities. The objection of Belcastro (1987) and others to pull-out programs that meet less frequently is that gifted students are gifted all of the time, and pull-out programs are only a "part-time solution to a full-time problem" (Cox et al., 1985). However, the reality is that the frequency with which a pull-out program is offered may be restricted by funding issues, staffing shortages, or space limitations. In those cases, it is important to ensure that the curricular and instructional experiences within the general education classroom are appropriate for the advanced needs of gifted students.

In the case of the program described in Scenario 1, the twice-weekly advanced literature supplements to the general education program can work in conjunction with cluster grouping, within-class groupings, and/or differentiated learning experiences to address learners' needs in multiple ways throughout the school week. Scenario 2 meets the criteria by providing focused, daily advanced instruction in the subject area in which identified students need services. In the full-day Scenario 3, curriculum compacting frees students for daily engagement independently or in small groups, with supervision by the teacher, media specialist, reading teacher in the school, aides, or parent volunteers.

Placement With Intellectual Peers

A benefit of the pull-out model is the opportunity for students to interact with intellectual peers during instruction. Delcourt, Cornell, and Goldberg's study on learning outcomes (2007) suggests that students in pull-out programs exhibit greater affective benefits than peers served in homogeneous settings (special schools, separate classes), particularly concerning perceptions of academic competence, preference for challenging tasks, sense of acceptance by peers, internal orientation for success, and positive attitudes toward learning. Rogers (1991) also claims that the enrichment pull-out model produces "small but positive" effects on student self-esteem. She later expands this notion: "Affectively, students in pull-out programs are more positive about school, have more positive perceptions of giftedness, and are more positive about their program of study at school than are gifted students not participating in pull-out programs" (Rogers, 2007, p. 389). These findings suggest that there are affective benefits when students are provided with opportunities to learn with their intellectual peers.

Pace of Program Matched With Students' Learning Rates

There is a dichotomy at work in the ability of a pull-out program to match the pace of a student's learning. On the one hand, trained pull-out teachers are at an advantage due to the relative academic homogeneity of the group, making it a more streamlined process to adjust the pace of instruction and level of rigor. On the other hand, the part-time nature of the pull-out model means that, even if program pace is well-matched to student ability, that is only true for a fraction of the students' instructional time. It is crucial in these scenarios that provisions such as cluster grouping, push-in services, or differentiated instruction are available within the regular classroom.

Complex and Higher-level Curriculum

A simultaneous advantage and criticism of pull-out programs is that without a standardized curriculum, designing and implementing an enriched program of study is open-ended. Van Tassel-Baska (cited in Vaughn et al., 1991) raised concerns about the large inconsistencies in quality among curricula used in pull-out programs, the lack of vertical and horizontal articulation of concepts across grade and school levels, and the short periods of time available to develop complex ideas even if the curricula were available for their use. Likewise, the U.S. Department of Education's report, *National Excellence: A Case for Developing America's Talent* (1993), noted that a significant flaw in the pull-out model is the lack of consistently rigorous curriculum and instruction, making it highly variable to determine defensibility in regard to this criterion across different contexts.

That said, that very freedom from standardized assessment allows for the possibility of profound curriculum for students. In the presence of an appropriate evaluation system, resource teachers in pull-out classrooms can address themes and implement instructional models which prove difficult to enact under the rigors of current assessment requirements. In the past several years curricula have been developed and tested that can be integrated into the instruction in pull-out classrooms (See, for example, Chapter 31 in this book by VanTassel-Baska.) In all of the scenarios noted above, it is strongly recommended that a strong curricular scope and sequence be developed by teachers with content-area expertise, and expertise in the needs of advanced learners. The effectiveness of this curriculum in leading students toward program goals should be evaluated systematically and adjustments made accordingly (for in-depth information on evaluating gifted programs, see Chapter 43 of this volume by Callahan).

Implementation by Excellent Teachers

The NAGC's *Pre-K–Grade 12 Gifted Programming Standards* (2010) specify the importance of highly qualified educators working with identified gifted students. The standards clearly state that teachers "must understand the characteristics and needs of the population for whom they are planning curriculum, instruction, assessment, programs, and services" (2010, no page). Further, there is ample evidence that teachers of gifted learners must possess advanced content knowledge in the disciplines in which they teach. Only 20 U.S. states require teachers in specialized gifted education programs to hold a certificate or endorsement in gifted education, and only five states require that teachers of the gifted receive annual professional development to refine their knowledge bases (CSDPG & NAGC, 2009). While legislation may lag behind good sense, it is critical that teachers whose responsibility it is to educate gifted learners have training in how to meet the academic needs of these students. Arguably, this would include teachers within gifted education programs and general education teachers, as gifted students often spend the majority of their time in the regular education classroom.

Assess the Quantity, Quality, and Appropriateness of the Programming and Services Provided

The Association for the Gifted (a division of the Council for Exceptional Children) (CEC–TAG) and NAGC (2009) authored a joint position statement regarding the importance of holding schools accountable for the growth of advanced students. This statement further endorses the use of growth models to measure gifted students' growth over annual time blocks, offering recommendations such as "[m]odels need to expand their focus to take into consideration teacher and program effects on all students' performance," and "measurement of academic success [is determined by] how much student achievement improves based on individual student gains" (2009, no page). Pull-out program effects should be evaluated systematically in order to document the degree to which these models have accomplished their program goals.

Regularly Use Multiple Forms of Grouping Including Clusters, Resource Rooms, Special Classes, or Special Schools

As can be seen in the preceding sections, the pull-out model is a flexible approach that can, if designed and implemented in defensible ways, be a component of a full continuum of services to meet the needs of gifted learners. As suggested by this criterion, using a full complement of grouping configurations amplifies the power of the pull-out program, and ameliorates the noted weaknesses of part-time service. In the case of Scenario 1, as noted above, additional secondary services like cluster grouping, push-in services, and differentiated instruction can work hand-in-hand with pull-out programs to ensure that students' needs are met throughout the school day and week. When a district is prepared to offer a spectrum of services to a variety of students and/or to coordinate pull-out program services thoughtfully with regular classroom instruction, the pull-out model can provide learning opportunities not available in the regular education classroom.

ADDITIONAL CAVEATS

Outside of the theoretical criteria for evaluation established above, there are more pragmatic considerations for administrators of gifted programs. One reason that pull-out programs are popular is their relatively easy inclusion as part of a broad spectrum of service delivery options. Another is that they carry certain functional advantages. Implementation can begin small, serving a handful of students in existing facilities with part of one teacher's day. For a district or school experimenting with the landscape of gifted services, this progressive stance can be comforting. On the other hand, it is easy to be convinced that this often part-time solution is sufficient, and general educators may feel as if meeting the needs of gifted learners is addressed elsewhere. It is crucial, when utilizing any form of the pull-out model in which gifted students spend the majority of their instructional time within the general education classroom, that the teachers of those classrooms are also held responsible for meeting their needs through differentiated instruction.

BUILDING EXEMPLARY PULL-OUT PROGRAMS: A SUMMARY

In this chapter, criteria for providing exemplary services using a pull-out program were explained and illustrated using three possible scenarios. Promising possibilities are revealed with caveats for consideration in designing such a program. A summary of considerations and questions to ask in planning are provided in Table 20.1.

REFERENCES

Belcastro, F. P. (1987). Elementary pull-out program for the intellectually gifted—boon or bane? *Roeper Review, 9*, 208–212.

Belcastro, F. P. (1998). *A survey of types of gifted programs offered in Iowa public school districts.* (ERIC Document Reproduction Service No. ED 432 110).

Borland, J. H. (2003). *Rethinking gifted education.* New York: Teachers College Press.

Council for Exceptional Children–The Association for the Gifted, & The National Association for Gifted Children. (2009). *Growth in achievement of advanced students.* (Position Paper). Washington, DC: Authors.

Council of State Directors of Programs for the Gifted, & National Association for Gifted Children. (2009). *State of the states in gifted education 2008–2009: National policy and practice data.* Washington, DC: Authors.

Cox, J., Daniel, N., & Boston, B. O. (1985). *Educating able learners: Programs and promising practices.* Austin: University of Texas Press.

Delcourt, M., Cornell, D., & Goldberg, M. (2007). Cognitive and affective learning outcomes of gifted elementary school students. *Gifted Child Quarterly, 51*, 359–381.

National Association for Gifted Children. (2009). *Grouping.* (Position Paper). Washington, DC: Author.

National Association for Gifted Children. (2010). *2010 Pre-K–Grade 12 gifted programming standards: A blueprint for quality gifted education programs.* Washington, DC: Author.

Passow, A. H. (1982). Differentiated curricula for the gifted/talented. In *Curriculum for the gifted/talented: Selected*

Table 20.1 Guiding principles, recommendations, and questions to ask in planning pull-out programs

Yardstick	Recommendation	Focus question(s)
Integration with regular curriculum	Work in tandem and with specific coordination with the general education program.	What provisions are in place to ensure consistent communication between general and gifted education teachers? In what ways can the frequency and quality of communication be increased? To what degree are general education classrooms reflective of high-quality instruction and practice?
Systematic and fair identification of students	Ensure that identification procedures align with the service provided and program goals.	How does the district conceptualize giftedness and how is this reflected in the types of services offered in the district? To what degree are the goals of the program reflected in the identification procedures?
Ensure a daily program experience	Provide daily program experiences either singly or in conjunction with general education classrooms.	How frequently are identified students receiving services? To what degree are general education classrooms partners in delivering services during non-resource windows of time?
Provide placement with intellectual peers	Provide a variety of intellectual peer placements so that students see themselves in multiple ways.	What considerations are made regarding peer placements in general education and resource-room groupings? In what ways does this facilitate or restrict students' affective development and self-efficacy?
Match the pace of program with students' learning rates	Use data to ensure a good fit of program pace and complexity with student needs.	What are the provisions related to acceleration in the core curricula? To what degree are transitions between school levels smooth and pre-planned? To what degree can enrichment and acceleration co-exist in resource models in this context?
Provide complex and higher-level curriculum	Regardless of which curriculum model is used, ensure that services meet Passow's (1982) "Would, Could, Should" defensibility criteria. That is, the curriculum should be something only gifted students would do, could do, or should do.	To what degree do services provided in pull-out programs meet Passow's criteria? If there are students who would participate and benefit from the services if given the opportunity to do so, does the school respond by changing the program or admitting the student? Are services provided in the resource room qualitatively different from what is offered in general education?
Utilize highly qualified teachers	Ensure that resource teachers are highly qualified (and provided with ongoing training) in the characteristics and needs of gifted students, differentiated instruction, and the content.	To what degree is the current resource-room faculty considered highly qualified in terms of knowledge of gifted learners? Curriculum and instruction for gifted learners? The discipline(s) in which they teach? What is the provision for ongoing professional learning in regard to these areas?
Use research-based effective practices and utilize assessment data to document growth	Employ practices with evidence of effectiveness in order to justify their use. Consistently collect data related to program goals.	To what degree are the practices of the pull-out program aligned with a documented model or approach? To what degree are these adopted approaches supported by evidence of effectiveness? What locally developed data collection plans exist to inform program decisions? What can be put into place to document evidence of program success more carefully?
Collect and	Set focused program goals and ensure that the program	What tools are used to document student and program outcomes? To what

disaggregate assessment data and yearly progress data	is faithful to those goals.	degree are these tools aligned with stated program goals? How frequently are these measures collected? What additional pieces of data would be useful to document the effectiveness of the program?
Consistently use multiple forms of grouping including clusters, resource rooms, special classes, or special schools	Select the grouping options likely to be most successful considering the school context and ensure that there exist qualitatively different services beyond the grouping itself.	To what degree are varied groupings employed in this context? How is the pull-out program viewed in light of the larger spectrum of services? What more could be put into place to ensure a broader continuum of services for all students in the community?

proceedings of the First National Conference on Curriculum for the Gifted and Talented (pp. 4–20). Ventura, CA: Ventura Superintendent of Schools.

Rogers, K. B. (1991). *The relationship of grouping practices to the education of the gifted and talented learner: Executive summary.* (ERIC Document Reproduction Service No. ED343330).

Rogers, K. B. (2007). Lessons learned about educating the gifted and talented: a synthesis of the research on educational practice. *Gifted Child Quarterly, 51,* 382–396.

Swiatek, M. A., & Lupkowski-Shoplik, A. (2003). Elementary and middle school student participation in gifted programs: Are gifted students underserved? *Gifted Child Quarterly, 47,* 118 130.

U.S. Department of Education. (1993). *National excellence: A case for developing America's talent.* Washington, DC: Office of Educational Research and Improvement. (ERIC Document Reproduction Service No. ED372580).

Vaughn, V., Feldhusen, J., & Asher, W. (1991). Meta-analyses and review of research on pull-out programs in gifted education. *Gifted Child Quarterly, 35,* 92–98.

21

THE SCHOOLWIDE ENRICHMENT MODEL

A Focus on Student Creative Productivity, Strengths, and Interests

Joseph S. Renzulli and Sally M. Reis

How can we develop the potential of our academically able children? What services should be provided to students who are identified for gifted and talented programs, as opposed to those for all students? How can we help children learn to think creatively and value opportunities for creative, self-selected work? These questions lie at the core of the Schoolwide Enrichment Model (SEM), developed to encourage and develop creative productivity in young people. In this chapter, a chronology of how the SEM model was developed, a description of the original Enrichment Triad Model, and a summary of pertinent research highlights are presented (Renzulli & Reis, 1994). A description of the model is followed by an explanation of Renzulli Learning, a new SEM service delivery resource that uses a computer-generated profile of each student's academic strengths, interests, learning styles, and preferred modes of expression.

The SEM promotes engagement using three types of enjoyable, challenging, and interest-based enrichment experiences. Separate studies on the SEM have demonstrated its effectiveness in schools with widely differing socio-economic levels and program organization patterns (Reis & Renzulli, 2003; Renzulli & Reis, 1997). The SEM was developed using Renzulli's Enrichment Triad Model (Renzulli, 1977; Renzulli & Reis, 1985, 1997) as a core and has been implemented in thousands of schools across the United States and internationally (Burns, 1998). The effectiveness of the SEM has been studied in over 30 years of research and field-tests, suggesting that the model is effective at serving high-ability students and providing enrichment in a variety of educational settings.

A BRIEF HISTORY AND THEORETICAL UNDERPINNINGS OF THE SEM

The original Enrichment Triad Model (Renzulli, 1977), the curriculum core of the SEM, was developed in the mid-1970s and initially implemented as a gifted and talented programming model in school districts in Connecticut and the northeast of the United States. The model, field-tested in several districts, proved to be quite popular and requests increased from all over the United States for visitations to schools using the model and for information about how to implement it. Thus began over 30 years of field-testing, research, and dissemination.

Present efforts to develop giftedness are based on a long history of theoretical or research studies dealing with human abilities (Sternberg, 1984, 1988, 1990; Sternberg & Davidson, 1986; Thorndike, 1921). A few additional general conclusions from the most current research on giftedness (Sternberg & Davidson, 2005) provide a critical background for this discussion of the SEM. The first is that giftedness is not a unitary concept, but there are many manifestations of gifts and talents, and therefore, single definitions cannot adequately explain this multifaceted phenomenon. The confusion about present theories of giftedness has led many researchers to develop new models for explaining this complicated concept. Most agree that giftedness is developed over time and that culture, abilities, environment, gender, opportunities, and chance contribute to the development of gifts and talents (Sternberg & Davidson, 2005).

The SEM focuses on the development of both academic and creative–productive giftedness. Creative–productive giftedness describes those aspects of human activity and involvement where a premium is placed on the development of original material and products that are purposefully designed to have an impact on one or more target audiences. Learning situations designed to promote creative–productive giftedness emphasize the use and application of information and thinking skills in an integrated, inductive, and real-problem-oriented manner. Our focus on creative productivity complements our efforts to increase academic challenge when we attempt to transform the role of the student from that of a learner of lessons to one of a first-hand inquirer who can experience the joys and frustrations of creative productivity (Renzulli, 1977).

Why is creative–productive giftedness important enough to lead to questioning of the traditional approach that has been used to select students for gifted programs on the basis of test scores? Some research (Neisser, 1979; Reis & Renzulli, 1982; Renzulli, 1978, 1986, 2005) tells us that there is much more to identifying human potential than the abilities revealed on traditional tests of intelligence, aptitude, and achievement. Accordingly, the SEM integrates opportunities for both academic giftedness and creative–productive giftedness.

THE THREE-RING CONCEPTION OF GIFTEDNESS

The SEM is based on Renzulli's (1978) "three-ring" conception of giftedness, which defines gifted behaviors rather than gifted individuals (see Chapter 5 by Renzulli and Delcourt in this book and visit http://www.gifted.uconn.edu/sem/semart13.html for a diagram and more detail). This conception encompasses three interrelated components and is described as follows:

> Gifted behavior consists of behaviors that reflect an interaction among three basic clusters of human traits—above average ability, high levels of task commitment, and high levels of creativity. Individuals capable of developing gifted behavior are those possessing or capable of developing this composite set of traits and applying

them to any potentially valuable area of human performance. Persons who manifest or are capable of developing an interaction among the three clusters require a wide variety of educational opportunities and services that are not ordinarily provided through regular instructional programs.

(Renzulli & Reis, 1997, p. 8)

Longitudinal research supports the distinction between academic giftedness and creative–productive giftedness; for example, Perleth, Sierwald, and Heller (1993) found differences between students who demonstrated creative–productive as opposed to traditional academic giftedness. Renzulli's research has suggested that gifted behaviors can be developed *in certain people, at certain times, and under certain circumstances* (Renzulli & Reis, 1997).

These questions have led us to advocate *labeling the services students receive rather than labeling the students*, for we believe that emphasis should shift from the traditional concept of "being gifted" (or not being gifted) to a concern about the *development of gifted and creative behaviors* in students who have high potential for benefiting from special educational opportunities, as well as the provision of some types of enrichment for all students. This change in terminology may also provide the flexibility in both identification and programming endeavors that encourages the inclusion of "at risk" and underachieving students in our programs. Our ultimate goal is the development of a total school enrichment program that benefits all students and concentrates on making schools places for talent development for all young people.

THE ENRICHMENT TRIAD MODEL

The Triad Model (Renzulli, 1977), the curricular basis of the SEM, was originally designed as a gifted program model to encourage creative productivity on the part of young people by exposing them to various topics, areas of interest, and fields of study; and to further train them in *applying* advanced content, process-training (such as critical and creative thinking skills) and methodology training to self-selected areas of interest using three types of enrichment. The original Triad Model with three types of enrichment was implemented in programs designed for academically talented and gifted students. For a diagram of the Enrichment Triad Model, see http://www.gifted.uconn.edu/sem/semexec.html under "An Overview of the Enrichment Triad Model."

Type I Enrichment

In the Enrichment Triad Model, Type I enrichment is designed to expose students to a wide variety of disciplines, topics, occupations, hobbies, persons, places, and events that would not ordinarily be covered in the regular curriculum. In schools using this approach, an enrichment team of parents, teachers, and students often organizes and plans Type I experiences by contacting speakers, organizing mini-courses, or arranging other activities of potentially high interest to students that either complement or extend the regular curriculum. Type I enrichment is mainly designed to stimulate new interests leading to Type II or III follow-up on the part of students who become motivated by Type I experiences. Type I enrichment can be provided for general groups, or for students who have already expressed an interest in the topic area.

Type II Enrichment

Type II enrichment includes materials and methods designed to promote the development of thinking and feeling processes. Some Type II enrichment is general, and usually provided to groups of students in their classrooms or in enrichment programs. This general Type II training includes the development of:

a. creative thinking and problem solving, critical thinking, and affective processes;
b. a wide variety of specific learning-how-to-learn skills;
c. skills in the appropriate use of advanced-level reference materials; and
d. written, oral, and visual communication skills.

Other Type II enrichment is specific, as it cannot be planned in advance, and usually involves advanced instruction in an interest area selected by the student. For example, students who become interested in botany after a Type I on this topic would pursue advanced training in this area by reading advanced content in botany; compiling, planning, and carrying out plant experiments; and undertaking more advanced research methods training for those who want to go further and pursue a Type III in that area.

Type III Investigations

Type III enrichment involves students who become interested in pursuing investigation of a self-selected area and are willing to commit the time necessary for advanced content acquisition and process training in which they assume the role of a first-hand inquirer. Type III products can be completed by individuals or small groups of students and are always based on students' interests. Type III enrichment enables students to:

- apply interests, knowledge, creative ideas, and task commitment to a self-selected problem or area of study;
- acquire advanced-level understanding of the knowledge (content) and methodology (process) used within particular disciplines, artistic areas of expression, and interdisciplinary studies;
- develop authentic products that are primarily directed toward bringing about a desired impact upon a specified audience;
- develop self-directed learning skills in the areas of planning, organization, resource utilization, time management, decision making, and self-evaluation; and
- develop task commitment, self-confidence, and feelings of creative accomplishment.

THE SCHOOLWIDE ENRICHMENT MODEL

The SEM (Renzulli & Reis, 1997) has three major goals designed to challenge and meet the needs of high-potential, high-ability, and gifted students; and at the same time, provide challenging learning experiences for all students. These goals are:

a. to maintain and expand a continuum of special services that will challenge students with demonstrated superior performance or the potential for superior performance in any and all aspects of the school and extracurricular program;

b. to infuse into the general education program a broad range of activities for high-end learning that will challenge all students to perform at advanced levels, and allow teachers to determine which students should be given extended opportunities, resources, and encouragement in particular areas where superior interest and performance are demonstrated;

c. to preserve and protect the positions of gifted education specialists and any other specialized personnel necessary for carrying out these goals.

With the Enrichment Triad Model as its theoretical and curricular basis, the SEM identifies a talent pool of approximately 10–15 percent of above-average-ability/high-potential students through a variety of measures, including achievement tests, teacher nominations, assessment of potential for creativity and task commitment, as well as alternative pathways of entrance (self-nomination, parent nomination, etc.). High achievement and/or intelligence quotient (IQ) test scores automatically include a student in the talent pool, enabling those students who are underachieving in their academic school work to be included (see http://www.gifted.uconn.edu/sem/semart04.html for more information on SEM identification).

The SEM has three service delivery components that provide services to students, including the Total Talent Portfolio, Curriculum Modification and Differentiation, and Enrichment (see http://www.gifted.uconn.edu/sem/semhand.html under "Schoolwide Enrichment Model"). These three services are delivered through the regular curriculum, a continuum of special services (see http://www.gifted.uconn.edu/sem/semhand.html under "Continuum of Special Services"), and a series of enrichment clusters.

The Total Talent Portfolio

In the SEM, teachers help students to understand more fully dimensions of their learning, their abilities, interests, and learning styles. This information, focusing on their strengths rather than deficits, is compiled in a management form called the "Total Talent Portfolio" that can be used subsequently to make decisions about talent development opportunities in general education classes, enrichment clusters, and/or in the continuum of special services (see http://www.gifted.uconn.edu/sem/semhand.html under "Dimensions of the Total Talent Portfolio"). The major purposes of the Total Talent Portfolio are:

a. to collect information about students' strengths on a regular basis;
b. to *classify* this information into the general categories of abilities, interests, and learning styles;
c. periodically to *review and analyze* the information in order to make decisions about providing opportunities for enrichment experiences in the general education classroom, the enrichment clusters, and the continuum of special services; and
d. to use this information to make decisions about acceleration and enrichment in school and in later educational, personal, and career decisions.

This expanded approach to identifying talent potentials is essential if we are to make genuine efforts to include a broader, more diverse group of students in enrichment programs. This approach is also consistent with the more flexible conception of *developing* gifts and talents that has been a cornerstone of the SEM, addressing concerns for promoting more equity in special programs.

Curriculum Modification and Differentiation Techniques

The second service delivery component of the SEM is a series of curriculum modification techniques that can:

a. adjust levels of required learning so that all students are challenged;
b. increase the number of in-depth learning experiences; and
c. introduce various types of enrichment into regular curricular experiences.

The procedures that are used to carry out curriculum modification include curriculum differentiation strategies, such as curriculum compacting, and increased use of greater depth in regular curricular material (Reis et al., 1993; Renzulli, 1994). Curriculum compacting is an instructional differentiation technique designed to make appropriate curricular adjustments for students in any content area and at any grade level, through:

a. defining the goals and outcomes of a particular unit or segment of instruction;
b. determining and documenting which students already have mastered most or all of a specified set of learning outcomes; and
c. providing replacement strategies for material already mastered through the use of instructional options that enable a more challenging and productive use of the student's time.

An example of how compacting is used is best represented in the form, "The Compactor" that serves as both an organizational and record-keeping tool (see http://www.gifted.uconn.edu/siegle/CurriculumCompacting/section3.html). Teachers should fill out one compactor form per student, or one form for a group of students with similar curricular strengths. Completed compactor forms should be kept in students' academic files, and updated on a regular basis.

Enrichment Learning and Teaching

The third service delivery component of the SEM, based on the Enrichment Triad Model, is enrichment learning and teaching that has roots in the ideas of a small but influential number of philosophers, theorists, and researchers such as Jean Piaget (1975), Jerome Bruner (1960, 1966), and John Dewey (1913, 1916). The work of these theorists, coupled with our own research and program development activities, have given rise to the concept we call enrichment learning and teaching. The best way to define this concept (Renzulli & Reis, 1997) is in terms of the following four principles:

1. Each learner is unique, and therefore, all learning experiences must be examined in ways that take into account the abilities, interests, and learning styles of the individual.

2. Learning is more effective when students enjoy what they are doing, and therefore learning experiences should be constructed and assessed with as much concern for enjoyment as for other goals.
3. Learning is more meaningful and enjoyable when content (i.e., knowledge) and process (i.e., thinking skills, methods of inquiry) are learned within the context of a real and present problem; therefore, attention should be given to opportunities to personalize student choice in problem selection, consideration of the relevance of the problem for individual students at the time the problem is being addressed, and authentic strategies for addressing the problem.
4. Some formal instruction may be used in enrichment learning and teaching, but a major goal of this approach to learning is to enhance knowledge and thinking skills acquired through formal instruction with student-determined applications of knowledge and skills that result from students' own construction of meaning.

The ultimate goal is to replace dependent and passive learning with independent and engaged learning. Although all but the most conservative educators will agree with these principles, much controversy exists about how these (or similar) principles might be applied in everyday school situations. A danger also exists that these principles might be viewed as yet another idealized list of glittering generalities that cannot be manifested easily in schools that are entrenched in the deductive model of learning. Developing a school program based on these principles is not an easy task. Over the years, however, we have achieved success by gaining faculty, administrative, and parental consensus on a small number of easy-to-understand concepts and related services, and by providing resources and training related to each concept and service delivery procedure.

RESEARCH RELATED TO THE SEM

The effectiveness of the SEM has been studied through more than 20 years of research and field-testing (Gubbins, 1995; Olenchak, 1990; Olenchak & Renzulli, 1989; Reis & Renzulli, 2003; Renzulli & Reis, 1994). This research suggests that the model effectively serves high-ability students in a variety of educational settings, and in schools serving diverse ethnic and socio-economic populations. These studies also suggest that the pedagogy of the SEM can be applied to various content areas, implemented in a wide variety of settings, and used with diverse populations of students including twice-exceptional students (high-ability students with learning disabilities) and those who underachieve. Additionally, the research suggests that the use of the SEM results in more use of advanced reasoning skills and thinking skills, and students who are involved in SEM activities achieve at higher levels on traditional achievement tests than students who continue to use regular curricular or remedial activities. A summary and table of relevant research and pertinent references is available at http://www.gifted.uconn.edu/sem/rrsem.html.

SCHOOL STRUCTURES OF SEM

The Regular Curriculum

The regular curriculum consists of everything that is a part of the predetermined goals, schedules, learning outcomes, and delivery systems of the school. The regular curriculum might be traditional, innovative, or in the process of transition, but its predominant feature is that authoritative forces (i.e., policy makers, school councils, textbook adoption committees, state regulators) have determined that the regular curriculum should be the "centerpiece" of student learning. The regular curriculum is influenced by the implementation of SEM through differentiating the challenge level of required material, using curriculum compacting and the enrichment recommended in the Enrichment Triad Model (Renzulli, 1977). Although our goal in the SEM is to influence rather than replace the regular curriculum, the application of certain SEM components and related staff development activities has often resulted in substantial changes in both the content and instructional processes of the entire regular curriculum.

The Enrichment Clusters

The enrichment clusters, a second component of the SEM, are non-graded groups of students who share common interests, and who come together during specially designated time blocks during the school day to work with an adult who shares their interests, and who has some degree of advanced knowledge and expertise in the area. The enrichment clusters usually meet for a block of time weekly during a semester. All students complete an interest inventory developed to assess their interests, and an enrichment team of parents and teachers tally all of the major families of interests. Adults from the faculty, staff, parents, and community are recruited to facilitate enrichment clusters based on these interests, such as creative writing, drawing, sculpting, archeology, and other areas. Training is provided to the facilitators who agree to offer the clusters. The main rationale for participation in one or more clusters is that *students and teachers want to be there*. All teachers (including music, art, physical education, etc.) are involved in teaching the clusters, and their involvement in any particular cluster is based on the same type of interest assessment that is used for students in selecting clusters of choice. Enrichment clusters promote real-world problem solving, focusing on the belief that "every child is special if we create conditions in which that child can be a specialist within a specialty group" (Renzulli, 1994, p. 70).

Enrichment clusters are organized around interdisciplinary themes or cross-disciplinary topics (e.g., a theatrical/television production group that includes actors, writers, technical specialists, costume designers). The clusters are modeled after the ways in which knowledge utilization, thinking skills, and interpersonal relations take place in the real world. Thus, all work is directed toward the production of a product or service. Cluster facilitators do not prepare a detailed set of lesson plans or unit plans in advance; rather, three key questions are addressed by the facilitator and students:

1. What do people with an interest in this area (e.g., film making) do?
2. What knowledge, materials, and other resources do they need to do it in an excellent and authentic way?
3. In what ways can the product or service be used to have an impact on an intended audience?

Enrichment clusters incorporate the use of advanced content, providing students with information about particular fields of knowledge. The methods used within a field are also considered advanced content by Renzulli (1988a), involving the use of knowledge of the structures and tools of fields, as well as knowledge about the methodology of particular fields. Enrichment clusters are not intended to be the total program for talent development in a school, or to replace existing programs for talented youth. Rather, they are one component of the SEM that can stimulate interests and develop talent in the entire school population.

They can also serve as staff development opportunities as they provide teachers with an opportunity to participate in enrichment teaching, and subsequently to analyze and compare this type of teaching with traditional methods of instruction. In this regard, the model promotes a spill-over effect by encouraging teachers to become better talent scouts and talent developers, and to apply enrichment techniques to general education classroom situations. Research indicates that enrichment clusters result in increased use of advanced thinking and research skills in gifted and other students in both clusters and regular classroom settings (Reis, Gentry, & Maxfield, 1998).

The Continuum of Special Services

A broad range of special services is the third school structure addressed in the model, as represented at http://www.gifted.uconn.edu/sem/semhand.html. Although the enrichment clusters and the SEM-based modifications of the regular curriculum provide a broad range of services to meet individual needs, a program for total talent development still requires supplementary services that challenge our most academically talented young people. These services, which cannot ordinarily be provided through enrichment clusters or the regular curriculum, typically include: individual or small-group counseling, acceleration, direct assistance in facilitating advanced-level work, arranging for mentorships with faculty members or community persons, and making other types of connections between students, their families, and out-of-school persons, resources, and agencies.

Direct assistance also involves setting up and promoting student, faculty, and parental involvement in special programs such as Future Problem Solving (an international education program focused on creative thinking skills), state and national essay competitions, mathematics contests, and many others. Another type of direct assistance consists of arranging out-of-school involvement for individual students in summer programs, on-campus courses, special schools, theatrical groups, scientific expeditions, and apprenticeships at places where advanced-level learning opportunities are available. Provision of these services is one of the responsibilities of the SEM teaching specialist or an enrichment team of teachers and parents. Most SEM teaching specialists spend two days a week in a resource capacity to the faculty, and three days providing direct services to students.

NEW DIRECTIONS IN THE SEM

Renzulli Learning™ (see http://www.renzullilearning.com/default.aspx) is the newest component of the SEM. It is an interactive online program that aids in the implementation of the SEM by matching student interests, expression styles, and learning styles with a vast array of educational enrichment activities and resources, designed to enhance and challenge high-potential students' learning processes. Field (2009) studied the use of Renzulli Learning with students in both an urban and a suburban school. In this 16-week experimental study, both gifted and non-gifted students who participated in this enrichment program and used Renzulli Learning for 2–3 hours each week demonstrated significantly higher growth in reading comprehension than control-group students who did not participate in the program. Students also demonstrated significantly higher growth in oral reading fluency and in social studies achievement than those students who did not participate (Field, 2009).

Components of Renzulli Learning include the Renzulli Profiler, the Renzulli Enrichment Database, and the Total Talent Portfolio. The Renzulli Profiler is an interactive assessment tool that identifies students' talents, strengths, interests, and preferred learning and expression styles to provide a comprehensive student learning profile. The Renzulli Enrichment Database includes thousands of carefully screened, grade-level appropriate, child-safe enrichment opportunities that are regularly monitored, updated, enhanced, and expanded. Each student's Profile (interests, learning styles, and product styles) is linked with the Renzulli Enrichment Database to generate a customized list of activities designed to appeal to that student's grade level, interests, and abilities, as well as his or her learning and expression styles.

A secondary self-directed search enables students and teachers to enter a set of one or more self-selected keywords to locate specific database entries either from their own individual activity list or from the entire database. This feature is particularly useful for selecting a particular topic for project work or for in-depth study. A global search capability enables students and teachers to access the entire Enrichment Database, across all interests, expression styles, learning styles, or even grade levels. This permits students with above-grade capabilities to locate and pursue new activities and threads of interest, all within the safety of a pre-screened information environment. It also helps teachers to identify possible projects and other curriculum enhancements within the same space that their students explore.

The Total Talent Portfolio (TTP) provides a complete record of the student's online learning activities and academic progress, and an online portfolio to save students' best work. The TTP enables students to create and post writings, internet links, images, and other work on projects or areas of interest.

Renzulli Learning™ also offers a series of management tools for teachers, administrators, and parents, designed to help them follow individual students' learning progression, analyze group usage patterns, and formulate lesson plans and classroom organization. It gives teachers the virtual equivalent of multiple "teaching assistants" in their classrooms—each and every day—to implement the SEM. Teachers can monitor students' progress by accessing their profiles and viewing all of the activities and assessments that they have completed. Teachers using this system can even submit their own ideas for activities and interact with other teachers, enrichment specialists, curriculum coordinators, and administrators from around the United States. Finally, parents can view their child's progress, his or her profile, and choice of enrichment activities and projects.

NON-NEGOTIABLES FOR IMPLEMENTING THE SEM

The many changes taking place in general education have resulted in some unusual reactions to the SEM that might best be described as the good news/bad news phenomenon. The good news is that many schools are expanding their conception of giftedness and are more willing than ever to extend a broader continuum of services to larger proportions of the school population. The bad news is that the motivation for these changes is often based on mistaken beliefs:

a. that we can adequately serve high-potential students without some form of grouping;
b. that we do not need special program teachers;
c. that special program teachers are best utilized by going from classroom to classroom with a "shopping cart" of thinking skill lessons and activities.

The non-negotiables for implementing the SEM clearly contradict these beliefs.

1. The first non-negotiable is that anyone who tries to implement an SEM program has read our book entitled *The Schoolwide Enrichment Model: A How-to Guide for Educational Excellence* (Renzulli & Reis, 1997). A thorough knowledge of the goals and components is essential.
2. Although we have advocated a larger talent pool than traditionally has been the practice in gifted education, and a talent pool that includes students who gain entrance on *both* test *and* non-test criteria (Renzulli, 1988b), we firmly maintain that the concentration of services necessary for the development of high-level potentials cannot take place without *identifying and documenting individual student abilities.* Targeting and documenting does not mean that we will simply play the same old game of classifying students as "gifted" or "not gifted," and let it go at that. Rather, targeting and documenting are part of an ongoing process that produces a comprehensive and always evolving Total Talent Portfolio documenting student abilities, interests, and learning styles. All information in the TTP should be used to make individual programming decisions about present and future activities, and about ways in which we can enhance and build upon documented strengths. This information enables educators to recommend enrollment in advanced courses or special programs (e.g., summer programs, college courses), and provides direction in developing specific interests and resulting projects within topics or subject-matter areas with potential for advanced learning.
3. Enrichment specialists must devote a *majority* of their time to working directly with talent pool students, and this time should primarily be devoted to facilitating individual and small-group investigations (i.e., Type IIIs). Some of their time with talent pool students can be devoted to stimulating students' interest to conduct Type IIIs through *advanced* Type I experiences and *advanced* Type II training, focusing on learning the research skills necessary to carry out investigations in various disciplines.
4. Schoolwide Enrichment Model programs must have specialized, trained personnel who work directly with talent pool students, to teach advanced courses and to coordinate enrichment services in cooperation with a schoolwide enrichment team. The old cliché, "something that is the responsibility of everyone ends up being the responsibility of no one," has never been more applicable than when it comes to enrichment or gifted education specialists. The demands made upon general education classroom teachers, especially during these times of mainstreaming, heterogeneous grouping, and accountability testing leave precious little time to challenge our most able learners and to accommodate interests that clearly are

above and beyond the regular curriculum. In a study completed by researchers at The National Research Center on the Gifted and Talented, Westberg, Archambault, Dobyns, and Salvin (1993) found that in 84 percent of general education classroom activities, *no differentiation was provided for identified high-ability students.* Accordingly, time spent in enrichment programs with specialized teachers is even more important for high-potential students.

Related to the last non-negotiable are the issues of teacher selection and training and the scheduling of special program teachers. Providing unusually high levels of challenge requires advanced training in the discipline(s) that one is teaching, in the application of process skills, and in the management and facilitation of individual and small-group investigations. It is these characteristics of enrichment specialists and the services they provide rather than the mere grouping of students that have resulted in achievement gains and high levels of creative productivity on the parts of special program students.

CONCLUSION

The current emphasis on testing connected to federal legislation, the standardization of curriculum, and the drive to increase achievement scores have produced major changes in education during the last two decades. The absence of opportunities to develop creativity in all young people, and especially in talented students, is troubling. In the Schoolwide Enrichment Model, students are encouraged to become partners in their own education and develop a passion and joy for learning. As students pursue creative enrichment opportunities, they learn to acquire communication skills and to enjoy creative challenges. The SEM provides the opportunity for students to develop their gifts and talents and to begin the process of lifelong learning, culminating, we hope, in creative productive work of their own selection as adults.

REFERENCES

Bruner, J. S. (1960). *The process of education.* Cambridge, MA: Harvard University Press.
Bruner, J. S. (1966). *Toward a theory of instruction.* Cambridge, MA: Harvard University Press.
Burns, D. E. (1998). *SEM network directory.* Storrs: Neag Center for Gifted Education and Talent Development, University of Connecticut.
Dewey, J. (1913). *Interest and effort in education.* New York: Houghton Mifflin.
Dewey, J. (1916). *Democracy and education.* New York: Macmillan.
Field, G. B. (2009). The effects of using Renzulli Learning on student achievement: An investigation of internet technology on reading fluency, comprehension, and social studies. *International Journal of Emerging Technologies in Learning, 4,* 29–39.
Gubbins, E. J. (Ed.). (1995). *Research related to the Enrichment Triad Model.* (Research Monograph 95212). Storrs: The National Research Center on the Gifted and Talented, University of Connecticut.
Neisser, U. (1979). The concept of intelligence. In R. J. Sternberg & D. K. Detterman (Eds.), *Human intelligence* (pp. 179–189). Norwood, NJ: Ablex.
Olenchak, F. R. (1990). School change through gifted education: Effects on elementary students' attitudes toward learning. *Journal for the Education of the Gifted, 14,* 66–78.
Olenchak, F. R., & Renzulli, J. S. (1989). The effectiveness of the Schoolwide Enrichment Model on selected aspects of elementary school change. *Gifted Child Quarterly, 32,* 44–57.
Perleth, C. H., Sierwald, W., & Heller, K. A. (1993). Selected results of the Munich Longitudinal Study of Giftedness: The multidimensional/typological giftedness model. *Roeper Review, 15,* 149–155.
Piaget, J. (1975). *The development of thought: Equilibration of cognitive structures.* New York: Viking.

Reis, S. M., Gentry, M., & Maxfield, L. R. (1998). The application of enrichment clusters to teachers' classroom practices. *Journal for the Education of the Gifted, 21*, 310–324.

Reis, S. M., & Renzulli, J. S. (1982). A case for the broadened conception of giftedness. *Phi Delta Kappan, 64*, 619–620.

Reis, S. M., & Renzulli, J. S. (2003). Research related to the Schoolwide Enrichment Triad Model. *Gifted Education International, 18*(1), 15–40.

Reis, S. M., Westberg, K. L., Kulikowich, J., Caillard, F., Hébert, T. P., Plucker, J. A. et al. (1993). *Why not let high ability students start school in January? The curriculum compacting study.* (Research Monograph 93106). Storrs: The National Research Center on the Gifted and Talented, University of Connecticut.

Renzulli, J. S. (1977). *The Enrichment Triad Model: A guide for developing defensible programs for the gifted and talented.* Mansfield Center, CT: Creative Learning Press.

Renzulli, J. S. (1978). What makes giftedness? Re-examining a definition. *Phi Delta Kappan, 60*, 180–184, 261.

Renzulli, J. S. (1986). The Three-Ring Conception of Giftedness: A developmental model for creative productivity. In R. J. Sternberg & J. E. Davidson (Eds.), *Conceptions of giftedness* (pp. 53–92). New York: Cambridge University Press.

Renzulli, J. S. (1988a). The multiple menu model for developing differentiated curriculum for the gifted and talented. *Gifted Child Quarterly, 32*, 298–309.

Renzulli, J. S. (Ed.). (1988b). *Technical report of research studies related to the enrichment triad/revolving door model* (3rd ed.). Storrs: Teaching the Talented Program, University of Connecticut.

Renzulli, J. S. (1994). *Schools for talent development: A practical plan for total school improvement.* Mansfield Center, CT: Creative Learning Press.

Renzulli, J. S. (2005). The Three-Ring Conception of Giftedness. In R. J. Sternberg & J. E. Davidson (Eds.), *Conceptions of giftedness* (2nd ed., pp. 246–279). New York: Cambridge University Press.

Renzulli, J. S., & Reis, S. M. (1985). *The Schoolwide Enrichment Model: A comprehensive plan for educational excellence.* Mansfield Center, CT: Creative Learning Press.

Renzulli, J. S., & Reis, S. M. (1994). Research related to the Schoolwide Enrichment Model. *Gifted Child Quarterly, 38*, 2–14.

Renzulli, J. S., & Reis, S. M. (1997). *The Schoolwide Enrichment Model: A how-to guide for educational excellence* (2nd ed.). Mansfield Center, CT: Creative Learning Press.

Sternberg, R. J. (1984). Toward a triarchic theory of human intelligence. *Behavioral and Brain Sciences, 7*, 269–287.

Sternberg, R. J. (1988). Three facet model of creativity. In R. J. Sternberg (Ed.), *The nature of creativity* (pp. 125–147). Boston: Cambridge University Press.

Sternberg, R. J. (1990). Thinking styles: Keys to understanding student performance. *Phi Delta Kappan, 71*, 366–371.

Sternberg, R. J., & Davidson, J. E. (Eds.). (1986). *Conceptions of giftedness.* New York: Cambridge University Press.

Sternberg, R. J., & Davidson, J. E. (Eds.). (2005). *Conceptions of giftedness* (2nd ed.). New York: Cambridge University Press.

Thorndike, E. L. (1921). Intelligence and its measurement. *Journal of Educational Psychology, 12*, 124–127.

Westberg, K. L., Archambault, F. X., Jr., Dobyns, S. M., & Salvin, T. J. (1993). *An observational study of instructional and curricular practices used with gifted and talented students in regular classrooms.* (Research Monograph 93104). Storrs: The National Research Center on the Gifted and Talented: University of Connecticut.

22

CLUSTER GROUPING PROGRAMS AND THE TOTAL SCHOOL CLUSTER GROUPING MODEL

Marcia Gentry and C. Matthew Fugate

Faced with increased pressure for students to perform on state-mandated tests, many educators have shifted their focus to students who are achieving at or below academic standards (Brighton, Hertberg, Moon, Tomlinson, & Callahan, 2005; Moon, Brighton, Jarvis, & Hall, 2007; Richardson, 2009). At the same time, budget cuts have caused many schools to eliminate programs for gifted students, opting instead to move these students into general education classrooms (Hertberg-Davis, 2009; Teno, 2000). As a result, most gifted students spend the majority of their time in classrooms led by teachers with little or no training in how to meet their academic needs (Council of State Directors of Programs for the Gifted [CSDPG] & National Association for Gifted Children [NAGC], 2009), and with little motivation to attend to the learning of those already performing at high levels. If gifted students are placed in heterogeneous classrooms in which the focus is on test performance rather than meeting their academic needs, achievement and motivation can rapidly decrease (Delcourt, Loyd, Cornell, & Goldberg, 1994; Moon et al., 2007).

Support for the effectiveness of differentiation as a strategy for working with gifted learners is widespread among scholars in gifted education (Ahlfeld, 2010; Cox, 2008; Latz, Speirs Neumeister, Adams, & Pierce, 2009; Oliver, 2007; Renzulli & Reis, 1991; Sisk, 2009; VanTassel-Baska, 2006; Westberg, Archambault, & Brown, 1997; Westberg, Archambault, Dobyns, & Slavin, 1993). When teachers differentiate instruction, they make learning personal, meaningful, and relevant for the students in their classrooms, affecting how they view school and themselves as learners (Cox, 2008; Oliver, 2007). Yet a lack of differentiation continues to be an ongoing problem in schools (Bernal, 2003; Hertberg-Davis, 2009; Latz et al., 2009; Renzulli & Reis, 1991; VanTassel-Baska, 2006). Westberg et al. (1993) studied 46 third and fourth grade classrooms across the United States in five subject areas. For 84 percent of the time that students spent in classrooms, no differentiation occurred in curricular instruction. VanTassel-Baska (2006) found a broad lack of training offered to teachers in gifted pedagogy. When training did occur it was with "no empirical framework for enhancing teacher competence tied to the goals of the program or its effectiveness with learners" (p. 205). She also found that most training offered to teachers lacked expectations for classroom implementation.

Many reasons are offered to explain why differentiation has not been effectively implemented by teachers, including lack of administrative support. Principals are the educational leaders of their schools, and teachers' willingness to differentiate is closely tied to the administrators' attitudes toward differentiation (Hertberg-Davis & Brighton, 2006). Other reasons include a lack of effective professional development in differentiation strategies which hinders teacher buy-in; the pressure to adhere to prescribed curricula out of fear that scores on state-mandated tests will fall; student behavior problems and concerns about classroom management; resistance to altering long-established styles of teaching; lack of adequate planning time; and a fear that parents will misunderstand or disagree with differentiation practices (Latz et al., 2009; Sisk, 2009; VanTassel-Baska, 2006; Westberg et al., 1993).

Total School Cluster Grouping (TSCG) offers an approach to cluster grouping that addresses many of these concerns. Total School Cluster Grouping uses talent development approaches typically found in gifted education programs to improve the achievement and performance of all children in a school, and at the same time address the needs of gifted students. This model fits seamlessly with the Three-Ring Conception of Giftedness (Renzulli, 1978) and the Schoolwide Enrichment Model (Renzulli & Reis, 1997; see Chapter 21 of this volume) by focusing on how educators can enhance every student's strengths, skills, and confidence using grouping strategies and enriched curriculum. The goals of TSCG (Gentry & Mann, 2008) include:

- providing full-time services for high-achieving, high-ability elementary students;
- helping all students improve achievement and educational self-efficacy;
- helping teachers more effectively and efficiently to meet the diverse academic needs of their students; and
- weaving gifted education and talent development "know-how" into the fabric of all educational practices in the school.

A LOOK AT GENERAL CLUSTER GROUPING

Generally, cluster grouping is defined as placing a group of gifted, high-ability, or high-achieving students together in a general education classroom with other students and a teacher who is qualified to provide appropriately challenging curriculum and instruction (Gentry, 1999). Often, a specific, arbitrary number of gifted students is recommended for the cluster, with the remainder of the class defined as heterogeneous in achievement levels. Gentry (1999) identified three, non-negotiable components of traditional cluster grouping programs:

- groups of students identified as gifted and talented or high-achieving are placed in classrooms with students of other achievement levels;
- curriculum and instruction for high-achieving students is differentiated by the teacher;
- successful teachers of students in the high-achieving cluster classroom have a background and/or interest in working with gifted students.

Cluster grouping has become a widely recommended and implemented programming strategy for meeting the needs of high-achieving or gifted students in elementary classrooms. The current popularity of cluster grouping is a result of increased implementation of inclusive classrooms, budget cuts, heterogeneous grouping policies, accountability for students' academic performance, and the widespread elimination of gifted programs (CSDPG & NAGC, 2009; Purcell, 1994; Renzulli, 2005;).

RESEARCH ON CLUSTER GROUPING

Research on cluster grouping can be found in the literature dating back to the 1960s. However, much of this work was based primarily on anecdotal accounts of grouping programs, relying on student and teacher perceptions. Only recently have researchers studied the effects of cluster grouping on student achievement and classroom practices using experimental, quasi-experimental, and qualitative research methods (e.g., Gentry & Owen, 1999). The current research suggests that cluster grouping meets the needs of high-ability students (Brown, Archambault, Zhang, & Westberg, 1994; Coleman & Cross, 2005; Davis & Rimm, 2004; Gentry & Owen, 1999; Hoover, Sayler, & Feldhusen, 1993; Kulik, 2003; LaRose, 1986; Renzulli, 1994; Rogers, 2002). By allowing these students the opportunity to work and learn together, achievement, interest, and motivation are increased through the combination of intellectual challenge, advanced subject matter, and the use of high-level thinking skills (Bernal, 2003; Feldhusen, 1998).

Full-time Grouping

Because the focus and purpose of many clustering programs center on students identified as gifted in a specific classroom, little attention is paid to the composition and practices that take place in other classrooms at the same grade level. However, considering that cluster grouping places all of the highest-achieving students in one classroom, it most certainly affects all of the students and teachers in other classrooms throughout the school (Gentry & Mann, 2008) and raises issues around full-time grouping.

A review of the analyses of full-time grouping produces conflicting results, conclusions, and opinions. Ability grouping is seen as either "good" or "bad," with results ranging from the opinion that tracking is the cause of America's failing schools (e.g., Oakes, 1985) to conclusions that without ability grouping, both high- and low-ability students would be harmed (Kulik, 2003; Loveless, 1998). Educators face calls to eliminate all ability grouping and move to full-inclusion programs, increased class sizes with decreased resources, and increased accountability for student performance (Gentry & Mann, 2008, Hertberg-Davis, 2009). Within these constraints, teachers are expected to meet the individual needs of all students in large, heterogeneous classrooms; yet most educators understand that what makes grouping "good" or "bad" is what goes on within the groups (Kulik, 2003).

Ability grouping alone does not result in differential student achievement; curricular and instructional differentiation is necessary to support appropriate learning for all students at their different developmental levels regardless of grouping arrangement (Castle, Deniz, & Tortora, 2005; Kulik, 2003; Swiatek & Lupkowski-Shoplik, 2003). Kulik (2003) recommended that if teachers used a variety of flexible grouping strategies with curriculum that is appropriately adjusted to meet their students' needs, then high-, average-, and low-achieving students would all have the opportunity for academic growth. Additionally, researchers have found several major benefits to cluster grouping:

- Student achievement increases when cluster grouping is used (Brulles, 2005; Gentry, 1999; Gentry & Owen, 1999; Pierce et al., 2007).
- Gifted students develop a realistic perception of their abilities compared to their peers (Marsh, Chessor, Craven, & Roche, 1995).
- Teachers are able to address the unique social and emotional needs of gifted learners (Peterson, 2003).
- Gifted students have the opportunity to interact regularly with their intellectual peers (Delcourt & Evans, 1994; Rogers, 1991; Slavin, 1987).
- Gifted students are afforded full-time services without additional costs (Bernal, 2003; Gentry & Owen, 1999; Hoover et al., 1993; LaRose, 1986).
- Highly qualified teachers with both interest and experience in working with gifted students help to ensure effective differentiation of the curriculum, more so than if the students had been distributed among several teachers (Bryant, 1987; Kennedy, 1995; Kulik & Kulik, 1992; Rogers, 2002).
- Removing the highest achievers from other classrooms allows other achievers to emerge and gain recognition of their abilities (Gentry & Owen, 1999; Kennedy, 1989).
- Students are provided with an appropriate level of challenge (Kulik, 2003; Rogers, 2002).
- Teachers are given the ability to address individual strengths and weaknesses with a more focused range of ability levels (Moon, 2003).
- Over time, fewer students are identified as low achievers and more students are identified as high achievers (Gentry, 1999).
- Cluster grouping reduces the range of achievement levels that must be addressed in the classrooms of all teachers (Coleman, 1995; Delcourt & Evans, 1994; Gentry, 1999; Rogers, 1993).

In discussing their meta-analyses findings on grouping practices, Kulik and Kulik (1992) concluded:

> If schools eliminated grouping programs with differentiated curricula, the damage to student achievement would be great, and it would be felt broadly. Both higher and lower aptitude students would suffer academically from the elimination of such programs. The damage would be truly great if, in the name of de-tracking, schools eliminated enriched and accelerated classes for their brightest learners. The achievement level of such students would fall dramatically if they were required to move at the common pace. No one can be certain that there would be a way to repair the harm that would be done.
>
> (Kulik & Kulik, 1992, p. 73)

TOTAL SCHOOL CLUSTER GROUPING

Researchers agree that gifted education pedagogy, if seen as an interconnected part of the educational process, has the potential to benefit all students (Reis, Gentry, & Park, 1995; Renzulli, 1994; Tomlinson & Callahan, 1992; U.S. Department of Education, 1993; VanTassel-Baska, 2009). An appropriately designed cluster program uses gifted education strategies and shifts the focus of the curriculum to address the academic needs of all students more than typical classroom practice (Gubbins et al., 2002). Hence, Total School Cluster Grouping (Gentry & Mann, 2008) was designed to go several steps beyond general cluster grouping, fostering thoughtful consideration of the appropriate placement and performance of every student in the school, including students identified as gifted and talented, high-ability, high-potential, or high-achieving.[1] In Total School Cluster Grouping, the system involves all teachers in attending to each and every child in the school, with the focus on improving the achievement of all students.

This model differs from general cluster grouping in the following ways:

- Identification occurs annually based upon student performance, with the expectation that achievement will increase as students grow, develop, and respond to appropriately differentiated curriculum.
- Achievement levels are identified for every child (i.e., low, low-average, average, above-average, high).
- Classrooms with high-achieving students contain no above-average achievers. These students are clustered into the other classrooms, which gives them the opportunity to learn without the highest achievers present.
- Some classrooms may contain clusters of learners who have special needs, with support provided to the general education teacher.
- Teachers may flexibly group students between classes or among grade levels as well as use a variety of flexible grouping strategies within their classrooms.
- All teachers receive professional development in gifted education strategies and have the opportunity for additional training through advanced workshops, conferences, and coursework.
- The teacher working with the high-achieving cluster is often selected by his or her colleagues and is committed to working with this cluster. (Gentry & Mann, 2008)

Finally, high-achieving students placed in heterogeneous classrooms may perform well below their potential, yet still be viewed as excelling when compared to their classmates, when in truth they are capable of responding to much more challenging curriculum and expectations (Hertberg-Davis, 2009; Kulik & Kulik, 1992; Loveless, 2008; Rogers, 1991). In TSCG, students have the opportunity to observe the performance levels of, and interact with, their intellectual peers, with many finding themselves challenged academically for the first time. At the same time, students in other classrooms who may have sat quietly while "the smart kids" answered the questions, may feel a new freedom to engage in and contribute to the learning process.

RESEARCH ON TOTAL SCHOOL CLUSTER GROUPING

Gentry & Owen (1999) examined the effects of cluster grouping on the achievement and identification of all students, and on teachers' practices. They reported that, when compared to similar students in a longitudinal, quasi-experimental study, student achievement increased among all students in the cluster-grouped school. Standardized achievement scores in mathematics, reading, and the total battery on the Iowa Test of Basic Skills (Hieronymus, Hoover, & Lindquist, 1984) improved for two entire graduation years of students between second and fifth grades. Additionally, the cluster-grouped students who began with lower total achievement than their comparison school counterparts ended with significantly higher total achievement than the comparison school students. The gains in achievement and differences in achievement were both statistically and practically significant. Additionally, more students in the treatment school were identified as above-average or high achievers; whereas fewer students were identified as low achievers in each successive year of the five-year study. Since publication of this research, many districts have implemented TSCG, but few have published the results of their efforts. As a result, only anecdotal information, like the work published by Teno (2000), exists regarding the efficacy of their implementation.

A key component to the success of TSCG is effective professional development. Gentry and Owen (1999) found that training in various instructional strategies normally found in gifted classrooms, such as integrating higher-order thinking skills or compacting the curriculum, gave teachers the confidence to explore and implement these strategies. As a result, teachers felt they had the educational support necessary to become instructional leaders in their schools (Gentry & Keilty, 2004).

IMPLEMENTATION OF THE TOTAL SCHOOL CLUSTER GROUPING MODEL

The Total School Cluster Grouping Model provides an organizational framework that places students into classrooms on the basis of achievement, flexibly groups and regroups students for instruction based on needs and interests, and provides appropriately challenging learning experiences for all students.

Identification Procedures and Guidelines

In Total School Cluster Grouping, the identification of students for placement into clusters occurs yearly. Students are identified as achieving in one of five achievement categories, using a combination of student classroom performance (as identified by their teachers) and achievement test data (see Table 22.1). Additionally, teachers are given the freedom flexibly to group and regroup students based on individual student interests and growth,

Table 22.1 Categories of achievement in Total School Cluster Grouping

Achievement Level	Definition
High Achieving	Excel at mathematics *and* reading when compared to age peers.
Above-average Achieving	Excel at mathematics *or* reading, or pretty good at mathematics and reading, but not as advanced at both as those students identified as high-achieving.
Average Achieving	Achieve in the middle when compared to others in their grade level *at their school*. This may be ongrade level or below grade level, depending on the average achievement level for the school population.
Low-average Achieving	May struggle in mathematics or reading, or slightly behind their peers in both areas but with extra support, are not "at risk" of failing.
Low Achieving	These are the students for whom school fails. They constantly struggle and are seen as "at risk" for failing. The longer these students attend school, the further behind they fall.

M. Gentry and R. L. Mann. *Total School Cluster Grouping and Differentiation.* Mansfield Center, CT: Creative Learning Press, 2008, p. 9.

even after class placements have been made. Achievement category identification is based on the relative performance of the students within the specific school population.

When considering placement for students with special needs, identification should match their achievement levels. For twice-exceptional students—those who are identified as both gifted and having special educational needs—placement in the high-achieving cluster is recommended so that their strengths can become the educational focus. It is important to understand that:

- categories are for assistance in student placement and are not definitive, permanent labels, or indicators of expectations;
- mathematics and reading achievement are used as the basis for identification as these subjects comprise the majority of the elementary curriculum, and students who excel in these subjects will need the most radical differentiation;
- identification for classroom placement takes place yearly, and students will likely improve as they grow, learn, develop, and progress through the grade levels in the school.

Identification and placement in this model are based on a holistic and flexible approach; therefore, cut-off scores and matrices should not be used. Cut-off scores place too much emphasis on only one measure, and matrices focus on a rigid set of criteria with multiple measures added together for identification. The identification and placement process used in TSCG can be labor-intensive, involving several steps, but using balanced information from both teachers and test results to make thoughtful classroom placement decisions makes the effort worthwhile.

Guidelines for the Identification Process

First, before examining test data, teachers must identify the classroom performance of their students. Because some students who test well do not necessarily perform accordingly in class, and those who perform well in class do not always test well, classroom performance should be the only consideration at this stage, whether or not the teachers have access to testing data. Contrary to other models, TSCG test data should only be used to include students in cluster groups. It should never be used to exclude them from the group. A student with a low test score can still be identified by his or her performance in class as high-achieving.

Once teachers have identified the classroom achievement levels of their students, examination of testing data can begin. This is an important step because teachers may fail to identify high-achieving students due to poor organizational skills, because they fail to complete assigned work, or because they have behavior issues. Yet these students may very well have the potential to achieve at high levels. Placing these underachievers in the high-achieving cluster classroom might be the first step to unlocking their achievement. Because there is no limit to the number of spaces in the high-achieving cluster in TSCG, the temptation *not* to identify an underperforming student is removed.

Test data will help to determine cluster placement. Using local norms of above the 90th percentile in both mathematics and reading is suggested for automatic inclusion in the high-achieving cluster. Other high achievers will be identified by their teachers regardless of their test scores. To identify students as above-average achievers, educators can use a local norm of above the 90th percentile in mathematics *or* reading, or above the 70th percentile in mathematics *and* reading.

	TOTAL	Classroom 1	Classroom 2	Classroom 3	Classroom 4	Classroom 5
High Achieving	11	3	2	3	2	1
Above Average	28	6	5	5	6	6
Average	50	10	10	10	9	11
Low-average	23	4	5	4	5	5
Low	8	1	2	2	3	0
Special Education	5	1	1	1	0	2
TOTAL	125	25	25	25	25	25

Fig. 22.1 Grade-level identification data and numbers from *this* year.

Developing Class Lists

Using all of the information gathered during the identification process, the development of class lists ensues. Grade-level teachers work together with administrators to develop a template for classroom placement. The template is based on the aggregated numbers of students from the different classrooms and their identification categories. It will change from year to year and between different grade levels depending on the students in that particular grade level or year. A table like the one shown in Figure 22.1 (above) can be used to create a template of the numbers of students to assign to each class for the coming year. Figure 22.1 shows the identification categories of five heterogeneous classrooms from the current school year, with a total column for the entire grade level, after teachers have engaged in the identification process. Based on this total, the group members work to create a template that will guide the placement of students for the next school year. This proposed template is shown in Figure 22.2.

The proposed template in Figure 22.2 is in no way designed to be rigid or provide specific numbers of students for each category, as these numbers will come from the

	TOTAL (from Fig. 22.1)	Classroom 1	Classroom 2	Classroom 3	Classroom 4	Classroom 5
High Achieving	11	11				
Above Average	28		7	7	7	7
Average	50	10	10	10	10	10
Low-average	23	3	4	8	8	0
Low	8	0	0	0	0	8
Special Education	5	1[*]	4	0	0	0
TOTAL	125	25	25	25	25	25

[*] Twice-exceptional child, with learning disability and gifted.

Fig. 22.2 Proposed grade-level placement template for *next* year, based on data in Figure 22.1.

identification process and will vary widely from school to school and from year to year. Once the placement template has been developed, teachers and administrators can begin to use the student data cards to create class lists collaboratively. During this class-list development session, rich conversations will ensue about individual children—with whom they work well, what their needs are, and which teacher might be best for them. Additionally, teachers will discuss parents, children who should be separated for specific reasons, and other topics pertinent to developing a class list that will enable next year's teacher to do her best work possible.

The goals of the development of class lists are to:

- reduce the number of achievement groups each teacher has in his or her classroom while still maintaining some heterogeneity;
- cluster the high-achieving students in one classroom (in larger schools, there may be more than one classroom with high-achieving students);
- place a group of above-average achieving students in each of the remaining teachers' classrooms;
- cluster students needing special services in classrooms (if appropriate) with resource-personnel assistance to the classroom teacher;
- honor parental requests for specific teachers when possible, and if it follows building or district policy;
- evenly distribute students with behavior problems among all classrooms so that no teacher has more than his or her fair share of difficult students.

In some years, there may not be a "normal" distribution of achievement levels within a grade level. Keep program placements flexible and remember that there is no preconceived notion about how many students can or must be identified as "gifted." For students who enroll in a school after the first day, temporary placements can be made based on a quick assessment of mathematical and reading skills, with a permanent placement determined once a complete school record is obtained and further assessments can be made.

Teacher Selection and Appointment

One perceived challenge in the initial implementation of TSCG involves which teachers teach which classrooms of students. Gentry and Owen (1999) developed some basic "truths" in this area. Teachers in the high-achieving cluster(s) must have the desire to work with these students and the commitment to differentiating the curriculum in an appropriately challenging manner. They must also commit to further professional development (e.g., workshops, coursework, licensure, or degree programs) in working with gifted students. Finally, teaching the high-achieving cluster is not a lifetime appointment; rather, teacher assignments should be made for a minimum of three years, giving the teachers a chance to learn about and implement successful strategies and to enjoy working with their particular groups of students. At the end of three years, or sooner if teacher/student mismatch or attrition occurs, the appointment is revisited, and other teachers with an interest in, and commitment to, working with these students are considered.

Considerations

To be successful, TSCG requires that all teachers know their students, exhibit a willingness to collaborate, and engage in continued professional development. Additionally, TSCG should reflect the community and the culture of the school in which it is implemented. As previously stated, strong administrative leadership is crucial, as it affects the entire school. Teachers will need time to facilitate student identification and the creation of class lists. Additionally, it is important for the administrators to work closely with parents and the community to ensure understanding and support.

As with any program adopted by schools, having a firm plan in place can help in the evaluation of the effectiveness and efficacy of the model. This does not have to involve burdensome collection of new data, but rather can be based on data that are readily available. However, data from all students must be examined, not just those from high-achieving students. Additionally, educators should maintain records of identification categories of students in order to facilitate analyses and comparisons over time. Another important consideration is whether the students identified as high-achieving proportionally represent the demographic student population of the district and school in which the program exists. Students from low-income families, from certain ethnic groups, and with learning disabilities have long been underidentified for gifted program services (Gentry, 2009; Gentry, Hu, & Thomas, 2008; Yoon & Gentry, 2009). Because there are no limits placed on the number of students identified as high-achieving, if it is discovered, during evaluation of the model, that the program is not developing in a manner that is representative of the population it serves, then school personnel should intervene, providing appropriate enrichment and levels of service (see Chapter 23 by Schroth of this book) to develop the potentials of students from the under-represented groups. It may be possible to develop a high-achieving cluster of children who show potential by providing them with the extra support in order to help them achieve.

SUPPORTING THE SUCCESS OF THE TOTAL SCHOOL CLUSTER GROUPING MODEL

The following checklist should be used to maintain fidelity to the model.

- Every teacher is using gifted education practices.
- Differentiation occurs in every classroom.
- Regrouping is allowed to occur among classes and grade levels.
- Test scores are being used for inclusive purposes in designating yearly identification categories.
- No language about "low" or "high" classes exists, as each classroom is a cluster classroom.

Reaching out to Parents

A major concern raised by educators in the implementation of TSCG is how to explain the model to parents. Concerned parents can be a valuable asset in the development of a successful program if questions raised by parents serve to increase accountability and overall program quality. Open communication with families, particularly throughout the beginning stages, is vital. Schools can develop brochures, and host parent meetings and presentations to help them understand and become advocates for the program. Communications should stress key points about the model, including the research base supporting the model, teacher training to enhance ability to differentiate instruction, the identification process, and the flexibility of student grouping.

Professional Development

Just as there should be an expectation of differentiation to meet the needs of students, a "one-size-fits-all" approach to professional development is insufficient to meet the needs of the teachers and staff. Training in grouping, differentiation, and meeting the needs of high-ability learners should be made available to all teachers and should be continuous and needs-based (Gentry & Mann, 2008). Through a carefully planned continuum of professional development, gifted education strategies will be present in all classrooms, lessening the perception of a "gifted class" that engages in "better" learning activities. Instead, the climate of the entire school becomes one of talent development committed to a focus on student strengths, talents, and interests.

The Role of the Teacher

The role of the teacher in TSCG is to facilitate, mediate, implement, and inspire. Hence, fostering and maintaining a positive classroom environment that allows students to focus on each other's strengths and interests rather than on their differences in achievement is key. Risk-taking becomes possible when students understand that they are in a safe and positive learning community where the teacher maintains high expectations for every student. This understanding has profound effects on student performance, and in turn, students are more likely to achieve. Through ongoing participation in professional development and reflection, teachers learn to implement challenging, research-based strategies that meet the diverse needs of their students.

CONCLUSIONS

In an ever-changing educational landscape that is increasingly focused on accountability, and at the same time suffering from decreasing budgetary resources, it has become necessary for educators to find better ways to meet the needs of all students, regardless of their achievement level. The Total School Cluster Grouping Model gives entire school communities a research-based model of programming and instruction that provides tools and training in effective gifted pedagogical practices that teachers can use in every classroom. Implementation of this model takes work and a commitment to evaluating and changing the program continuously to fit the needs of the school context most effectively. Leveraging the benefits that this model has for all students and teachers can help create a positive school climate and learning environment.

NOTES

1. In the literature these terms are often used interchangeably. For the remainder of this chapter, we will use high-achieving in order to include all students working at the specified level regardless of whether they have been formally identified as gifted by the school.

REFERENCES

Ahlfeld, K. (2010). Hands-on learning with a hands-off approach for professional development. *School Library Monthly, 26*(6), 16–18.

Bernal, E. M. (2003). To no longer educate the gifted: Programming for gifted students beyond the era of inclusionism. *Gifted Child Quarterly, 47,* 183–191.

Brighton, C. M., Hertberg, H. L., Moon, T. R., Tomlinson, C. A., & Callahan, C. M. (2005). *The feasibility of high-end learning in a diverse middle school.* (Research Monograph 05210). Storrs: The National Research Center on the Gifted and Talented, University of Connecticut.

Brown, S. B., Archambault, F. X., Zhang, W., & Westberg, K. (1994, April). *The impact of gifted students on the classroom practices of teachers.* Paper presented at the Annual Conference of the American Educational Research Association, New Orleans.

Brulles, D. (2005). *An examination and critical analysis of cluster grouping gifted students in an elementary school.* (Unpublished doctoral dissertation). Arizona State University, Metro Phoenix.

Bryant, M. A. (1987). Meeting the needs of gifted first grade children in a heterogeneous classroom. *Roeper Review, 9,* 214–216.

Castle, S., Deniz, C. B., & Tortora, M. (2005). Flexible grouping and student learning in a high-needs school. *Education and Urban Society, 37,* 139–150.

Coleman, L. J. & Cross, T. L. (2005). *Being gifted in school: An introduction to development, guidance, and teaching* (2nd ed.). Waco, TX: Prufrock Press.

Coleman, M. R. (1995). The importance of cluster grouping. *Gifted Child Today, 18,* 38–40.

Council of State Directors of Programs for the Gifted, & National Association for Gifted Children. (2009). *State of the states in gifted education 2008{hy}2009: National policy and practice data.* Washington, DC: Authors.

Cox, S. (2008). Classroom techniques: Differentiation instruction in the elementary classroom. *Educational Digest, 73*(9), 52–54.

Davis, G. A., & Rimm, S. W. (2004). *Education of the gifted and talented* (5th ed.). Englewood Cliffs, NJ: Prentice-Hall.

Delcourt, M. A. B., & Evans, K. (1994). *Qualitative extension of the learning outcomes study.* Storrs: The National Research Center on the Gifted and Talented, University of Connecticut.

Delcourt, M. A. B., Loyd, B. H., Cornell, D. G., & Goldberg, M. D. (1994). *Evaluation of the effects of programming arrangements on student learning.* (Research Monograph 94108). Storrs: The National Research Center on the Gifted and Talented, University of Connecticut.

Feldhusen, J. F. (1998). Developing students' talent. In D. J. Treffinger, & K. W. McCluskey (Eds.), *Teaching for Talent Development* (pp. 27–34). Sarasota, FL: Center for Creative Learning.

Gentry, M. (1999). *Promoting student achievement and exemplary classroom practices through cluster grouping: A research-based alternative to heterogeneous elementary classrooms.* (Research Monograph 99138). Storrs: The National Research Center on the Gifted and Talented, University of Connecticut.

Gentry, M. (2009). Myth 11: A comprehensive continuum of gifted education and talent development services: Discovering, developing, and enhancing young people's gifts and talents. *Gifted Child Quarterly, 53,* 262–265.

Gentry, M., Hu, S., & Thomas, A. T. (2008). Ethnically diverse students. In J. A. Plucker, & C. M. Callahan (Eds.), *Critical issues and practices in gifted education* (pp. 195–212). Waco, TX: Prufrock Press.

Gentry, M., & Keilty, W. (2004). Ongoing staff development planning and implementation: Keys to program success. *Roeper Review, 26,* 148–156.

Gentry, M., & Owen, S. V. (1999). An investigation of total school flexible cluster grouping on identification, achievement, and classroom practices. *Gifted Child Quarterly, 43,* 224–243.

Gentry, M., & Mann, R. (2008). *Total School Cluster Grouping and differentiation: A comprehensive, research-based plan for raising student achievement and improving teacher practices.* Mansfield Center, CT: Creative Learning Press.

Gubbin, E. J., Westberg, K. L., Reis, S. M., Dinnocenti, S., Tieso, C. M., Muller, L. M. et al. (2002). *Implementing a professional model using gifted education strategies with all students.* (Research Monograph 02172). Storrs: The National Research Center on the Gifted and Talented, University of Connecticut.

Hertberg-Davis, H. L. (2009). Myth 7: Differentiation in the regular classroom is equivalent to gifted programs and is sufficient: Classroom teachers have the time, the skill, and the will to differentiate adequately. *Gifted Child Quarterly, 53,* 251–253.

Hertberg-Davis, H. L., & Brighton, C. M. (2006). Support and sabotage: Principals' influence on middle school teachers' responses to differentiation. *The Journal of Secondary Gifted Education, 17,* 90–102.

Hieronymus, A. N., Hoover, H. D., & Lindquist, E. F. (1984). *Iowa Test of Basic Skills* (Form G). Chicago: Riverside.

Hoover, S., Sayler, M., & Feldhusen, J. F. (1993). Cluster grouping of elementary students at the elementary level. *Roeper Review, 16,* 13–15.

Kennedy, D. M. (1989). Classroom interactions of gifted and non gifted fifthgraders. (Unpublished doctoral dissertation). Purdue University, West Lafayette, IN.

Kennedy, D. M. (1995). Teaching gifted in regular classrooms: Plain talk about creating a gifted-friendly classroom. *Roeper Review, 17,* 232–234.

Kulik, J. A. (2003). Grouping and tracking. In N. Colangelo & G. Davis (Eds.), *Handbook of gifted education* (pp. 268–281). Boston: Allyn & Bacon.

Kulik, J. A., & Kulik, C.-L. C. (1992). Meta-analytic findings on grouping programs. *Gifted Child Quarterly, 36,* 73–77.

LaRose, B. (1986). The lighthouse program: A longitudinal research project. *Journal for the Education of the Gifted, 9,* 224–232.

Latz, A. O., Speirs Neumeister, K. L., Adams, C. M., & Pierce, R. L. (2009). Peer coaching to improve classroom differentiation: Perspectives from project CLUE. *Roeper Review, 31,* 27–39.

Loveless, T. (1998). The tracking and ability grouping debate. Retrieved January 30, 2012 from http://www.edexcellence.net/publications/tracking.html

Loveless, T. (2008). An analysis of NEAP data. In S. Farkas, A. Duffett, & T. Loveless (Eds.), *High-achieving students in the era of NCLB* (pp. 13–48). Washington, DC: Thomas B. Fordham Institute.

Marsh, H. W., Chessor, D., Craven, R., & Roche, L. (1995). The effects of gifted and talented programs on academic self-concept: The big fish strikes again. *American Educational Research Journal, 32,* 285–319.

Moon, S. M. (2003). Personal talent. *High Ability Studies, 14,* 5–21.

Moon, T. R., Brighton, C. M., Jarvis, J. M., & Hall, C. J. (2007). *State standardized testing programs: Their effects on teachers and students.* (Research Monograph 07228). Storrs: The National Research Center on the Gifted and Talented, University of Connecticut.

Oakes, J. (1985). *Keeping track: How schools structure inequality.* New Haven, CT: Yale University Press.

Oliver, C. L. (2007). Goldilocks/baby bear approach to differentiation. *Understanding Our Gifted, 19*(2), 3–6.

Peterson, J. S. (2003). An argument for proactive attention to affective concerns of gifted adolescents. Journal of Secondary Gifted Education, 14, 62–71.

Pierce, R. L., Cassady, J. C., Adams, C. M., Dixon, F. D., Speirs Neumeister, K. L., & Cross, T. L. (2007, April). *Cluster grouping and the academic achievement of gifted students.* Paper presented at the Annual Convention of the American Educational Research Association, Chicago.

Purcell, J. (1994). *The status of programs for high-ability students.* (CRS94306). Storrs: The National Research Center on the Gifted and Talented, University of Connecticut.

Reis, S. M., Gentry, M., & Park, S. (1995). Extending the pedagogy of gifted education to all students: The enrichment cluster study. (Tech. Rep.). Storrs: The National Research Center on the Gifted and Talented, University of Connecticut.

Renzulli, J. S. (1978). What makes giftedness? Reexamining a definition. *Phi Delta Kappan, 60,* 180–184, 261.

Renzulli, J. S. (1994). *Schools for talent development: A comprehensive plan for total school improvement.* Mansfield Center, CT: Creative Learning Press.

Renzulli, J. S. (2005). A quiet crisis is clouding the future of R & D. *Education Week, 24*(38), 32–33, 40.

Renzulli, J. S., & Reis, S. M. (1991). The reform movement and the quiet crisis in gifted education. *Gifted Child Quarterly, 35,* 26–35.

Renzulli, J. S., & Reis, S. M. (1997). *The Schoolwide Enrichment Model: A comprehensive plan for educational excellence* (2nd ed.). Mansfield Center, CT: Creative Learning Press.

Richardson, J. (2009). Quality education is our moon shot: An interview with Secretary of Education Arne Duncan. *Phi Delta Kappan, 91*(1), 24–29.

Rogers, K. B. (1991). *The relationship of grouping practices to the education of the gifted and talented learner.* Storrs: The National Research Center on the Gifted and Talented, University of Connecticut.

Rogers, K. B. (1993). Grouping the gifted and talented: Questions and answers. *Roeper Review, 16,* 8–12.

Rogers, K. B. (2002). *Re-forming gifted education.* Scottsdale, AZ: Great Potential Press.

Sisk, D. (2009). Myth 13: The regular classroom teacher can "go it alone." *Gifted Education Quarterly, 53,* 269–271.

Slavin, R. E. (1987). Ability grouping and student achievement in elementary schools: A best-evidence synthesis. *Review of Educational Research, 57,* 293–336.

Swiatek, M. A., & Lupkowski-Shoplik, A. (2003). Elementary and middle school student participation in gifted programs: Are gifted students underserved? *Gifted Child Quarterly, 47,* 118–130.

Teno, K. M. (2000). Cluster grouping elementary gifted students in the regular classroom: A teacher's perspective. *Gifted Child Today, 23,* 44–53.

Tomlinson, C. A., & Callahan, C. M. (1992). Contributions of gifted education to general education in a time of change. *Gifted Child Quarterly, 36*, 183–189.

U.S. Department of Education. (1993). *National excellence: A case for developing America's talent.* Washington, DC: U.S. Government Printing Office.

VanTassel-Baska, J. (2006). A content analysis of evaluating findings across 20 gifted programs: A clarion call for enhanced gifted program development. *Gifted Child Quarterly, 50*, 199–215.

VanTassel-Baska, J. (2009). Myth 12: Gifted programs should stick out like a sore thumb. *Gifted Child Quarterly, 53*, 266–268.

Westberg, K. L., Archambault, F. X., & Brown, S. W. (1997). A survey of classroom practices with third and fourth grade students in the United States. *Gifted Education International, 12*, 29–33.

Westberg, K. L., Archambault, F. X., Dobyns, S., & Slavin, T. (1993). The classroom practices observation study. *Journal for the Education of the Gifted, 16*, 29–56.

Yoon, S. Y., & Gentry, M. (2009). Racial and ethical representation in gifted programs. *Gifted Child Quarterly, 53*, 121–136.

23

THE LEVELS OF SERVICE MODEL

Stephen T. Schroth

INTRODUCTION

When a student enters school, his or her caregivers assume that the child will be provided with instruction appropriate to advance his or her cognitive, affective, and psychomotor needs (Callahan, 2001; Feldhusen & Moon, 1992; Sapon-Shevin, 1994). Gifted children often come to school with academic readiness levels that are significantly advanced compared to those of their age peers, or learn material at a rate that outpaces their colleagues. Parents of gifted children, and those interested in their education, often seek ways to assure that they are provided with opportunities to grow academically just as other students do. However, in an era in which increased attention has been brought to closing the achievement gap, many have questioned the value of providing services for gifted students. However, research consistently demonstrates that gifted students who receive *any* level of services achieve at higher levels than their gifted peers who receive none (Delcourt, Loyd, Cornell, & Goldberg, 1994; Kulik, 2003). School leaders and others responsible for providing instruction and other programming to gifted children thus must negotiate the delicate balance of providing pathways to equity while simultaneously developing excellence (Sapon-Shevin, 1996).

Deciding how to meet the needs of gifted learners begs certain questions, including: Can we provide appropriate services to gifted students while providing opportunities for all learners? Do particular gifted program models promise better student outcomes than others? Are certain gifted program models more effective with certain populations of gifted students than others? In an effort to provide equitable and excellent services to all students, Treffinger (1998) created the Levels of Service (LoS) model. The model is predicated upon the belief that one of gifted education's most significant contributions is empowering and enabling students to develop and use their talents (Treffinger, 1998; Treffinger, Young, Nassab, & Wittig, 2004).[1] Concentrating efforts on providing programming and services to gifted children, rather than on finding the "right" definition or identification process, is believed to have the greatest impact and is the focus of the LoS model framework. The model seeks to recognize, respect, and nurture *all* students'

226

strengths by providing a spectrum of services to meet the needs of a variety of learners (Treffinger et al., 2004). Programming experiences are geared toward one of four levels: all students, many students, some students, or a few students. While it requires a high level of fidelity to the key concepts and principles undergirding the approach, the LoS model presents a viable and attractive option for school leaders who seek a program model that benefits all students in a school. Understanding the LoS model and the interplay of its various components is thus very important for its implementation.

FOUR LEVELS OF SERVICE

The LoS model focuses on selecting programming approaches for children that best meet their individual needs. To this end, the LoS model provides what are termed four separate *levels of service.* Somewhat similar to the Schoolwide Enrichment Model (Renzulli & Reis, 1997), the LoS model provides services for the entire student population at Level I, which is also called Services for All Students, and specialized services by Level IV, also known as Services for a Few Students. Each level of service has *keys to success* that assist teachers and administrators in making sure that students are being provided with appropriate instructional activities by the LoS model.

Level I: Programming for All Students

As indicated by its name, Level I programming provides instructional activities, experiences, and events geared toward developing the interests and talents of all students every day, in every classroom. Although the regular classroom teacher is chiefly responsible for planning, arranging, and delivering Level I services, these services often involve other individuals, such as curriculum specialists, guest lecturers, parents, and administrators. Level I activities are planned experiences that are applicable and beneficial to all students, and hence, are often delivered in a whole class or small-group setting. They are presented over a specific, albeit brief, time frame and use readily accessible resources. Teachers initiate Level I services and include all students for whom they think the activities are appropriate. Level I activities are structured by the model developers to play a vital role in providing equitable and excellent instruction to all students (Treffinger, 1998; Treffinger et al., 2004). By emphasizing hands-on experiences involving applying, producing, sharing, and describing rather than rote memorization and passive learning, Level I activities provide a foundation for success in activities at the higher levels.

In order to assure consistency and quality throughout the LoS model, it is vital that teachers and administrators adhere to the Level I "keys for success."

Key I-1: Build a foundation and tools for thoughtful, self-directed learning by providing students with transferable skills, tools, and processes that will apply to any content area. This foundation will be best supported if students are given specific tools and guidelines for creative and critical thinking, exposure to problem-solving methods, opportunities to engage in decision making, debriefing episodes where learning can be processed and work evaluated, exposure to a broad array of technologies and learning media, and a chance to set goals for learning and project deadlines.

Key I-2: Offer a variety of activities that expose students to new interests and promote discovery. Through such variety, students will learn to explore and pursue their own interests; become comfortable playing with ideas; more readily seek out resources including parents, siblings, and community members for assistance; and listen better to peers and others for areas suitable for exploration.

Key I-3: Get to know students' personal characteristics. While a great deal of formal and informal student data are already collected in schools, these data must be analyzed to allow for curriculum compacting, better use of information related to students' learning styles, gathering of resources that promote active participation, and assisting students to analyze their own interests, strengths, and talents.

Key I-4: Create and maintain a stimulating classroom environment. Use information gathered about students and activities to create a learner-friendly space, one that provides opportunities for students to work individually or in small groups, on a variety of activities, creating an assortment of products, while learning how to use an array of learning resources.

All four of these keys are interrelated and overlap to unlock learning in a successful classroom.

Level I activities can play out in a variety of ways in the classroom. A regular classroom activity might be subtly changed to lay the foundation for thoughtful, self-directed learning, as when a daily question session is added to the class routine, asking students to demonstrate productive thinking, predicting or forecasting, decision making, and/or the communication of their own ideas. Teachers can get to know their students' personal characteristics in different ways, perhaps using a learning styles inventory and then reviewing the results with students. Finally, teachers and students can create and maintain stimulating classroom environments by developing criterion checklists for rating independent study projects. Although many of these techniques are subtle, all are purposeful and designed to stimulate student thinking and maximize student learning. Thoughtful and explicit teaching and modeling of independent learning skills will have the added benefit of allowing students to transfer these skills to other fields.

Level II: Programming for Many Students

Building upon skills and interests garnered in Level I, Level II of the LoS model provides a broad range of services for the many students (and potentially all) who are able to participate in them. As with Level I services, many Level II activities take place in the regular classroom, but some may also occur elsewhere. Level II activities focus on enrichment and extension of experiences and provide students with opportunities to develop their talents, strengths, interests, and potentials. Activities provided as a part of Level II services are often longer in duration or require deeper involvement than those in Level I and may evolve from a student's personal interests or experiences. Unlike Level I services, students must actively choose to participate in Level II activities.

As with Level I, the LoS model provides keys for success for Level II to assist teachers and administrators in adhering to the LoS model.

Key II-1: Assume the role of guide as students discover and clarify their personal strengths, interests, and areas of curiosity. Effective teachers use student interest inventories and other anecdotal evidence to determine activities, provide opportunities for students to dig deeper into curricular topics that are especially appealing, use curriculum compacting and scaffolding to differentiate instruction, provide explicit direction about what students do well, and begin to build portfolios that document student strengths, interests, endeavors, and products.

Key II-2: Provide voluntary or invitational opportunities for students to express their motivation, competence, and dedication through hands-on experiences. Teachers might inventory enrichment activities available in their school and emphasize certain ones to individual students; make students aware of special activities, events, or programs in the area; hold individual or group talent planning conferences with students; and/or nominate students to participate in activities.

Key II-3: Provide easy avenues to enter and exit activities so that students can freely continue explorations but are not required to do so. Teachers who desire to make this process as seamless as possible might provide open enrollment for activities, clarify expectations accompanying any activity, hold group discussions about when it is appropriate to join or drop an activity, allow students to make appropriate decisions about discontinuing an activity without penalty, while simultaneously challenging students to look past easy, low-effort options.

Key II-4: Use a variety of school and other resources to enrich and enhance students' learning experiences, encouraging the involvement of all school personnel, developing working relationships with community organizations, and networking with students, staff, parents, and volunteers who have specific skills, talents, hobbies, or expertise to share.

Key II-5: Create opportunities for students to analyze their interests and talents and then apply self-directed learning skills to high-quality projects. Teachers might support the product development through learning contracts that assist students in making appropriate decisions regarding their work, assisting students to share their work with a variety of audiences, beginning the process of allowing students to evaluate their own work as well as that of their peers, and providing opportunities to use the equipment and technology best suited to their projects.

Level II services take place in a variety of ways in classrooms, schools, and communities, depending upon the personalities of (and resources available to) teachers, and the unique talents and interests of individual students. A Level II experience might entail a school sponsoring an inventing program where 80 percent of students develop a prototype of an idea of their own invention, or offering optional mini-courses one afternoon each week that allow students to select activities that appeal to them. There is no single way of providing Level II services; rather, there are many avenues to allow students opportunities to engage in activities building upon their talents and interests. Encouraging students to think about and select opportunities that they wish to pursue is powerful, allowing them to build the tenacity and resiliency necessary to success (see, e.g., Callahan & Miller, 2005; Renzulli, 2005; Sternberg, 2002).

Level III: Programming for Some Students

Students' needs are met in a variety of settings—many outside the classroom—for Level III activities. As such, Level III activities focus on in-depth studies providing a high degree of challenge for the small number of students who are ready for and motivated by such experiences. The number and variety of Level III opportunities offered are directly related to student needs, which in turn are determined by student talents, competencies, interests, and abilities. The selection process for participation in Level III services entails gathering data documenting the student characteristics essential for effective performance in the specific activity. Level III services are very different from those provided at Levels I and II, as they extend beyond the general curriculum and are linked directly to certain skills, goals, objectives, and indicators of success. Level III activities often extend beyond the school day and the school building, and may involve regularly scheduled small-group or individual activities.

Within the LoS model, Level III programming has as its objective the utilization of the skills and talents of those most able to provide advanced learning opportunities. While many teachers may be able to nurture talent and cultivate growth in most children, Level III calls for those with a high degree of skill within their talent domain, as well as access to additional resources and experts, to deliver services to those children who will benefit from them.

There are four keys to success which assist in ensuring that Level III programming is implemented with integrity.

Key III-1: Be alert for, and note carefully, a student's sustained interests, specific talent strengths, and emerging levels of expertise.

Key III-2: Design opportunities targeted to specific student needs and then communicate expectations clearly.

Key III-3: Deliver differentiated services that respond to a student's unique personal strengths and talents via individual or group experiences are representative of success.

Key III-4: Expand and extend the array of services offered by drawing upon staff, parents, community members, and other mentors to guide students in learning experiences related to their talent strengths. This goal can be achieved through training regarding team building and action planning, creating curriculum enhancement teams to stimulate innovation, using a community resource pool to develop opportunities for mentoring, and linking learning with out-of-school events.

Level III services are highly individualized and require a high degree of teacher buy-in and acceptance. Training and professional development most likely will be necessary to obtain this result. Teachers can be assisted in understanding classroom "talent spotting" through comparisons to musical ensembles or athletic teams, where many participate but few perform at the highest levels. Similarly, the quality of opportunities designed to meet student needs might be improved through increased team planning. Additionally, in-service training on strategies such as curriculum compacting might be necessary. Finally, to expand and extend upon the services offered at a school, teachers might need to form partnerships with a local art museum or university to gain access to a wider range of expertise and perspectives in serving students with particular skills and talents. Since Level III activities are created on the basis of observed student needs—such as a special mathematics program for students who excel at mathematics—teachers must be adept at identifying those students who have talents that outstrip the school's regular offerings.

Level IV: Programming for a Few Students

Level IV services are one-of-a-kind experiences tailored to exceptional learners who have soared beyond the school's customary curricular offerings. Activities provided as a part of Level IV services are advanced and challenging, emphasizing productive thinking and original inquiry within a specific talent area or domain. Level IV services comprise unique projects that involve rigorous content, processes, and products which outstrip those offerings provided to a student's peers of similar chronological age. Level IV services might include early admission to kindergarten, grade skipping, dual enrollment in a college or university, accelerated content, or advanced research. Because Level IV services are geared to an exceptionally high-achieving student's talents and skills, they tend to be unique and specific to that student.

Three keys to success have been created to assure quality implementation of Level IV programming.

Key IV-1: Document and analyze the programming needs of students with demonstrated competence, commitment, and passion for their interest areas. This can be accomplished through knowing and understanding personal creativity characteristics, using fair and appropriate assessments, and understanding how to interpret test scores.

Key IV-2: Plan authentic opportunities that stimulate and enable students to reach new levels in terms of creative products or performances. Level IV programming provides opportunities to investigate real problems, share original products with others, and initiate mentorships and collaborations with adults.

Key IV-3: Provide a supportive environment that encourages students to self-initiate inquiry into ideas and topics of interest, including establishing goals and timelines for projects, teaching realistic self-evaluation skills, and providing access to teachers and mentors skilled in working with exceptional students.

In a regular classroom setting, Level IV programming may meet the needs of an exceptionally skilled child by accepting a high school student's published poems in lieu of other assignments in an English class. Out-of-classroom experiences might include allowing students to use creative problem-solving skills to redesign a middle school's after-school clubs and programming.

DESIRED STUDENT OUTCOMES

The four levels of the LoS model are designed with clear student outcomes in mind (Treffinger et al., 2004). Specifically, the LoS model has identified three broad categories of successful adult behavior that are used as the basis for desired student outcomes. The three broad categories of human behavior are exhibited by *happy/effective persons, independent learners,* and *creatively productive persons* (Treffinger et al., 2004). Each category suggests the specific desired student outcomes in Table 23.1.

Table 23.1 Desired student outcomes for three categories of successful adult behaviors

Healthy/Effective Persons	Independent Learners	Creatively Productive Persons
• Competent and able to demonstrate mastery of basic ideas	• Setting goals and defining tasks or project outcomes	• Seeing many possibilities or connections
• Awareness of personal learning styles and preferences and their implications for learning and productivity	• Identifying methods and resources for meeting goals	• Looking at problems in varied or original ways
• Personal and social effectiveness	• Carrying out appropriate actions and activities	• Sustaining and enhancing existing strengths
• Sound and fair thinking and reasoning	• Pursuing projects and products passionately and vigorously	• Innovating by formulating new possibilities and directions
• Effective functioning in team or group settings	• Monitoring, managing, and modifying actions as necessary	• Communicating ideas and sharing products with others
• Identification and implementation of effective leadership practices	• Using a variety of tools and technologies to design, produce, and share products	• Expressing and acting on principles, values, and convictions
• Confidence in personal abilities, commitments, and judgments	• Evaluating accomplishments and planning new directions	• Committing to improving the quality of life for self and others
• Commitment to lifelong learning and talent development		• Pursuing goals and purposes despite obstacles

D. J. Treffinger, G. C. Young, C. A. Nassab, and C. V. Wittig. *Enhancing and Expanding Gifted Programs: The Levels of Service approach.* Waco, TX: Prufrock Press, 2004, p. 11.

The three categories, and the desired student outcomes they suggest, do not exist in a vacuum (Treffinger et al., 2004). Instead, the categories are interrelated, with a broad degree of overlap and common characteristics. Further, the desired student outcomes do not come about separately, but instead are the result of participation in a talent development program such as the LoS model.

These desired student outcomes are complemented and buttressed by institutional goals that are essential to, and interconnected with, talent development, including that of gifted children (Treffinger et al., 2004). These institutional goals, vital to the success of the LoS model, insofar as they summarize the approach necessary on the part of a school environment to assure student success, include:

A. placing student success and productivity at the forefront of policies, procedures, and actions;
B. making deliberate efforts to seek, recognize, respond to, and enhance the development of students' strengths, talents, and interests;
C. offering appropriate and challenging learning opportunities and experiences for all students;
D. creating, maintaining, and supporting a culture for teaching and learning that values, promotes, and rewards excellence;
E. creating, supporting, and enhancing an environment or climate conducive to developing, recognizing, and celebrating individuals' talents;
F. recognizing and honoring individuality, helping all students to be aware of their learning styles and preferences, and providing opportunities for them to study, explore, learn, and perform in their best ways;

G. incorporating creative thinking, critical thinking, problem solving, and decision making on a daily basis;

H. encouraging independent, responsible self-direction and teaching the skills required for independent, self-directed learning;

I. inspiring individuals to become aware of, and to make optimal use of, their own strengths, talents, and interests—for their own benefit and the benefits of others;

J. using many and varied resources, such as people, places, and materials, to expand learning opportunities and enrichment of all learners;

K. spotting talent on a daily basis, always being alert for signs of strengths, talents, and interests in every person; and

L. engaging in ongoing dialog, learning, and communication to sustain commitments to innovation and continuous development..

These institutional goals (Treffinger et al., 2004, p.12), like the desired student outcomes, are interrelated and overlapping.

WHO IS BEST SERVED BY THE LEVELS OF SERVICE MODEL?

Gifted education has long been obsessed with and distracted by questions regarding definitions of giftedness. Numerous different definitions of giftedness exist, many of them incompatible with other characterizations of the concept. Some theorists advocate for a fairly restrictive view of giftedness, one based upon obtaining certain scores on IQ tests or other measurements of intelligence (Stanley, 1980). Others call for a more inclusive definition, taking into consideration other factors such as performance, motivation, and creative thinking (Callahan & Miller, 2005; Renzulli, 2005; Sternberg, 2002). Still others oppose designating any child as gifted, based on concerns for equity (Borland, 2005; Sapon-Shevin, 1994).

The LoS model circumvents these arguments by focusing on providing services for all children, emphasizing program offerings rather than definitions of giftedness (Treffinger, 1998; Treffinger et al., 2004). By allowing all students to participate in Level I services and most to partake in Level II, the LoS model avoids issues of defining giftedness. Because Level III and Level IV services are matched specifically to student needs, these likewise avoid the conundrum of defining giftedness while simultaneously meeting Passow's (1982) definition of defensible curriculum for the gifted—that which other students could not do, should not do, and would not do (Callahan & Caldwell, 1997).

TEACHER TRAINING FOR THE LEVELS OF SERVICE MODEL

Although the LoS model is elegant in its simplicity and eloquent in its calls for appropriate challenge for all learners, it demands a high level of teacher awareness of, and competence in, a variety of instructional, curricular, assessment, and grouping strategies, as well as a good deal of administrative support. Prior studies have suggested that teachers need a great deal of professional development and training in order to implement a program bringing strategies traditionally associated with gifted education to the regular education classroom (see e.g., Gubbins et al., 2002). Indeed, many regular classroom teachers and administrators are resistant to acceleration, grade skipping, or other services that are a part of the LoS model (Schroth & Helfer, 2009). For school leaders interested in adopting the LoS model, extensive professional development materials to assist with planning and implementation do exist (see, e.g., Treffinger, Young, Nassab, Selby, & Wittig, 2008). Administrators considering adopting the LoS model would be well advised to plan on providing training for teachers charged with delivering it.

CONCLUSION

The LoS model provides a programmatic model that promises to provide appropriate and challenging instruction to all students. Drawing upon some of the best practices of gifted education, the LoS model eschews debates about defining giftedness and battles concerning identification, instead focusing on the delivery of services to students. While it requires skilled delivery of instruction, careful monitoring of assessment data, and able planning of curricular activities, the LoS model presents a useful programmatic model for those interested in offering both equity and excellence to students. The LoS model requires careful attention to professional development, planning, coordination of services, and evaluation, and to that end, a list of helpful resources are provided in Recommended Readings by Topic at the end of this book.

NOTE

1. Throughout the description of the model, Treffinger (1998) and Treffinger et al. (2004) are the sources for the specifics of program description and examples. Specific repetitive references to Treffinger (1998) and Treffinger et al. (2004) have not been listed. When additional references are used to document the model, those are added to the text.

REFERENCES

Borland, J. H. (2005). Gifted education without gifted children: The case for no conception of giftedness. In R. J. Sternberg (Ed.), *Conceptions of giftedness* (2nd ed., pp. 1–19). New York: Cambridge University Press.

Callahan, C. M. (2001). Fourth down and inches. *The Journal of Secondary Gifted Education, 12*, 148–156.

Callahan, C. M., & Caldwell, M. S. (1997). *A practitioner's guide to evaluating programs for the gifted*. Washington, DC: The National Association for Gifted Children.

Callahan, C. M., & Miller, E. M. (2005). A child-responsive model of giftedness. In R. J. Sternberg (Ed.), *Conceptions of giftedness* (2nd ed., pp. 38–51). New York: Cambridge University Press.

Colangelo, N., Assouline, S., & Gross, M. U. M. (2004). *A nation deceived: How schools hold back America's brightest students*. Iowa City: The Connie Belin & Jacqueline N. Blank International Center for Gifted Education and Talent Development, The University of Iowa.

Delcourt, M. A. B, Loyd, B. H., Cornell, D. G., & Goldberg, M. D. (1994). *Evaluation of the effects of programming arrangements on student learning outcomes*. Storrs: The National Research Center on the Gifted and Talented, University of Connecticut.

Feldhusen, J. F., & Moon, S. M. (1992). Grouping gifted students: Issues and concerns. *Gifted Child Quarterly, 36*, 63–67.

Gubbins, E. J., Westberg, K. L., Reis, S. M., Dinnocenti, S., Tieso, C. L., Muller, L. M. et al. (2002). *Implementing a professional development model using gifted education strategies with all students*. (Research Monograph 02172). Storrs: The National Research Center on the Gifted and Talented, University of Connecticut.

Kulik, J. A. (2003). Grouping and tracking. In N. Colangelo & G. A. Davis (Eds.), *Handbook of gifted education* (2nd ed., pp. 268–281). Boston: Allyn & Bacon.

Passow, A. H. (1982). The relationship between the regular classroom and differentiated curricula for the gifted/talented. In *Curricula for the gifted/talented: Selected proceedings of the First National Conference on Curricula for the Gifted and Talented* (pp. 1–20). Ventura, CA: Ventura County Superintendent of Schools.

Renzulli, J. S. (2005). The Three-Ring Conception of Giftedness: A developmental model for promoting creative productivity. In R. J. Sternberg (Ed.), *Conceptions of giftedness* (2nd ed., pp. 246–279). New York: Cambridge University Press.

Renzulli, J. S., & Reis, S. M. (1997). *The Schoolwide Enrichment Model: A how-to guide for educational excellence* (2nd ed.). Mansfield, CT: Creative Learning Press.

Sapon-Shevin, M. (1994). *Playing favorites: Gifted education and the disruption of community.* Albany: State University of New York Press.

Sapon-Shevin, M. (1996). Beyond gifted education: Building a shared agenda for school reform. *Journal for the Education of the Gifted, 19,* 194–214.

Schroth, S. T., & Helfer, J. A. (2009). Practitioners' conceptions of academic talent and giftedness: Essential factors in deciding classroom and school composition. *Journal of Advanced Academics, 20,* 384–403.

Stanley, J. C. (1980). On educating the gifted. *Educational Researcher, 9,* 8–12.

Sternberg, R. J. (2002). Beyond *g*: The theory of successful intelligence. In R. J. Sternberg & E. L. Grigorenko (Eds.), *The general factor of intelligence: How general is it?* (pp. 447–479). Mahwah, NJ: Erlbaum.

Treffinger, D. J. (1986). *Blending gifted education with the total school program.* Buffalo, NY: DOK.

Treffinger, D. J. (1998). From gifted education to programming for talent development. *Phi Delta Kappan, 79,* 752–755.

Treffinger, D. J., Young, G. C., Nassab, C. A., & Wittig, C. V. (2004). *Enhancing and expanding gifted programs: The Levels of Service approach.* Waco, TX: Prufrock Press.

Treffinger, D. J., Young, G. C., Nassab, C. A., Selby, E. C., & Wittig, C. V. (2008). *The talent development planning handbook: Designing inclusive gifted programs.* Thousand Oaks, CA: Corwin Press.

24

PARENTS AND THE DEVELOPMENT AND EDUCATION OF GIFTED STUDENTS

Nancy M. Robinson

Even the great impact a school program can make on a gifted student's development and *joi de vivre* pales in comparison with the impact of the family from the moment of conception. Leaving aside the influences of parents' genetic contributions and health on that of their offspring, there are myriad ways in which parents influence intellectual, emotional, social, and motivational development, as well as the other resources and opportunities their children encounter. Before looking to the home–school partnership, consider a few of the most important ways that parents—deliberately, unconsciously, or through pure luck—play their roles.

SETTING THE STAGE AT HOME

Warm Engagement: Rearing Gifted Children Is Labor Intensive!

In a landmark study of talented high school students who persevered in developing their talents (Csikszentmihalyi, Rathunde, & Whalen, 1996), one of several key factors identified as significant in their talent development was the warm engagement of their families. Responsive and stimulating experiences are important for gifted children, as they are for all children (Freeman, 1991), but effective parenting of gifted children takes extra time (Snowden & Christian, 1999). Parents of gifted children spend much more time than comparison parents on reading, playing, making up rhymes and songs, going on interesting jaunts, etc. (Karnes, Shwedel, & Steinberg, 1984). Unexpectedly, one investigator (Thomas, 1984) found that fathers of early readers worked on average 10 fewer hours a week than did other fathers. (A silver lining in economic downturns?) Indeed, although more studies have involved mothers than fathers, fathers' engagement is critical in supporting the long-term achievement not only of gifted sons (Hébert, Pagnani, & Hammond, 2009), but of gifted daughters as well (O'Shea, Heilbronner, & Reis, 2010).

Gifted children claim significantly more of their parents' time than do other children for a number of reasons. Some of the demand comes directly from the children's constant search for input, their internal urge for mastery and exercise of increasingly complex ideas, their constant questions, their passion for being read to, and the asynchrony of the level of their thinking and their own reading skills. And early interests may be no fleeting matter. Among a group of toddlers who were precocious speakers, those who showed the most interest in being read to at the age of two were the best readers at the age of six (Dale, Crain-Thoreson, & Robinson, 1995).

Gifted children may also seek adult company for conversations, game playing, and daily activities because their age-mates are not sufficiently interesting. Indeed, so long as the gifted child's social circle is restricted to age-mates, a circumstance much more common in middle-class European American communities than in other cultures (Rogoff, Morelli, & Chavajay, 2010), the search for others who resemble them in mental age, who "talk their language," may lead them to seek (unattainable) older children and (more attainable) adults for company (Gross, 1989). In other words, the initiative for parent input often comes from the children themselves.

But warmly engaged parents also, on their own initiative, talk more to their children (Fowler, 1990; Freeman, 1991, 2000; Robinson, Dale, & Landesman, 1990). In one of the few studies to observe very young children's actual interactions with their mothers, White and Watts (1973) reported that mothers of the most competent children not only talked a great deal to their children, but "performed excellently the functions of designer and consultant . . . they design a physical world . . . beautifully suited to nurturing . . . burgeoning curiosity . . . These mothers . . . get an enormous amount . . . of teaching in 'on the fly'" (pp. 243–244).

Such parents take the time to structure their children's explorations without prematurely providing answers (Campbell & Mandel, 1990; Moss, 1992; Moss & Strayer, 1990), undertake more joint decision making (McDowell, 1992), and engage in more complex, abstract, and informational conversation than, generally, do parents of more typically developing children. In addition, they extend the children's experiences outside of school through family and group activities and excursions such as library trips. Children whose talents lie outside the limits of standard school subjects—in the arts, for example, or in physical skills—are especially dependent on parents for chauffeuring, and locating and funding learning opportunities. Indeed, the encouragement of children's talents often falls heavily on the shoulders of parents, with obvious disadvantages to children whose parents have many other responsibilities and/or few resources at their disposal.

Parental Resources

Children identified as gifted come much more frequently from advantaged homes and from Caucasian and Asian families than would be expected on a strictly proportional basis (Robinson, 2003). Indeed, this fact is an enormous political issue that continually threatens to scuttle programs for gifted students, who already seem to have "more than their share" of life's advantages. Yet the situation clearly reflects the social reality that life's advantages of all kinds are in fact distributed in grossly unfair ways. Here is further proof that children's optimal development depends in large part on optimal conditions of upbringing that are much more likely to occur in families with the resources of educational background and aspirations (as well as the time and inclination to devote them to children), together with first-rate health care and nutrition, with income stability, and so on. One of the most telling research findings to substantiate this view comes from a study by Turkheimer, Haley, Waldron, D'Onofrio, and Gottesman (2003), showing that in impoverished families, more than half the variance in children's IQs is accounted for by environmental factors, while heritability accounts for approximately 0 percent; but that just the opposite is true in affluent families. One can conclude that where families provide the basic wherewithal for healthy child development, the genes will play their role, but that in stressed families lacking these resources, genetic effects can be overwhelmed by adverse situations.

Even among families at or close to the poverty line, however, those who provide the most positive child-rearing conditions can also produce high-achieving children. Two studies by Robinson and colleagues (Robinson, Lanzi, Weinberg, Ramey, & Ramey 2002; Robinson, Weinberg, Redden, Ramey, & Ramey, 1998), following a very large group of children who had been enrolled in Project Head Start, found that those in the top 3 percent in achievement in first and/or third grade tended to come from families with slightly more education, a little more money, somewhat more child-centered parenting attitudes and—the most significant difference—fewer children. The secrets of success lie not in background variables, but in those experiences that impinge directly on children's lives—and chief among these are the actual interactions between parents and children.

High Expectations and the Encouragement of Independence Set the Stage for Achievement

Another of the insights underlined by the study by Csikszentmihalyi et al. (1996) was that high-achieving high school students' families, while remaining warmly engaged, also expected their children to do their reasonable best in conducting their lives and achieving their goals. In such families, a fair amount of independence is expected—when children are able to get their own drinks of water or dress themselves, for example, they are expected to do so. Such families fit the pattern that Baumrind (1971) described as "authoritative"—those who do not expect blind obedience, but who give and expect respect, and provide the kind of structure and predictability with which children thrive. Having parents who promote a child's independence and his or her struggles to master the difficult sets the stage for both high achievement (Adolph, Shrout, & Vereijken, 2003) and high motivation to achieve—the desire to gain one's goals and the wherewithal to stick with the protracted effort to get there (Trudewind, 1982; Windecker-Nelson, Melson, & Moon, 1997; Winterbottom, 1958).

Parents of gifted youngsters are more likely than other parents to value their children's independence (Karnes et al., 1984). In their landmark longitudinal study of gifted individuals, Terman and Oden (1947) observed that the parents of the most successful men had encouraged initiative and independence when their sons were young. In another landmark study, this one focused on world-class achievers, Bloom (1985) described parents during the early years as child-centered and involving the children informally in areas of family interest, but also as instilling in them self-discipline, the importance of doing one's best, and the satisfaction of accomplishment.

Part of encouraging independence is giving children space to learn from their own mistakes; engaged families need not be overprotective. Interestingly, in a study of toddlers with precocious language skills, those with the most advanced mastery of personal pronouns were also those who were most courageous in trying out complex language patterns, right or wrong (Dale & Crain-Thoreson, 1993).

Believing One Can Get Smarter Is More Important Than Being Smart

Another critical aspect of parenting—and teaching—style is the extent to which adults instill in children the firm belief that their own efforts can pay off in enhanced ability (as a thinker, a problem solver, a learner, or in any other activity they elect to try). The work of Carol Dweck, a social psychologist at Stanford University, and her colleagues (e.g., Dweck, 2006; Elliott & Dweck, 1988; Mueller & Dweck, 1998) has unlocked a potent tool, particularly for bright children used to having everything come easily to them. It can change performance-driven children into learning-driven children who, rather than giving up when things become difficult, persevere in the confidence that hard work pays off. Believing that one's ability is malleable as an outcome of effort can be powerfully encouraged if adults praise children, not for being smart, but for their investment in an activity.

When accomplishment is recognized by remarks such as, "That shows how hard you worked on it," or, "You hung in until you got the answer," this promotes a learning orientation, a preference for challenge over simplicity, the freedom to focus on the problem at hand, and the perseverance that is needed to hone expertise. On the other hand, telling children that they are smart when they perform well makes them want to avoid situations in which they might not perform so well, since this would make them seem to others—and to themselves—not so smart after all.

Setting the Stage for Creativity

The parenting strategies discussed thus far are also consistent with the development of creative modes of thinking—willingness to take risks that involve seeing problems in a new light, or combining ideas in novel ways, or producing inventions or paintings or poetry. Families whose children ultimately turn out to be creatively productive adults also provide the independence and space that children need to think for themselves, and the freedom from having to "perform" to prove one's worth. Indeed, creativity may be surprisingly predictable from childhood to adulthood (Cramond, Matthews-Morgan, Bandalos, & Zuo, 2005), although high ability also plays a role (Wai, Lubinski, & Benbow, 2005).

Child rearing by watchful but independence-promoting parents can be healthy and exuberant, of course; many creative individuals had creative parents themselves. On the other hand, sometimes this creativity-promoting space is inadvertent and may, indeed, even arise from tragedy, as may happen after a divorce or the death of a parent, or even in abusive relationships in which children retreat into their own space, sometimes a fantasy existence, as a form of self-protection (Albert, 1980; Goertzel, Goertzel, Goertzel, & Hansen, 2003; Olzewski, Kulieke, & Buescher, 1987; Olzewski-Kubilius, 2002; Simonton, 1998). While these findings certainly do not lead to a parenting prescription for family discord or dissolution—far from it!—they do demonstrate that a stress-free childhood is not necessarily good preparation for a happy or productive life.

Special Needs of Gifted Children

Gifted children are as diverse a group as exists anywhere—differing in family background and family composition, in temperament, in aspects of talent and interests, and in the evenness and range of their abilities. While there is absolutely no evidence to substantiate the stereotype that gifted children are, as a group, less socially skilled or more prone to mental health issues than are typically developing children, there are a number of aspects of their lives that do require somewhat different parenting skills. Here are some issues and a few hints:

- Asynchronies: Gifted children seldom grow all of a piece. Most (not all) are somewhat less mature socially than they are mentally, for example; and among their mental abilities, some abilities are usually more advanced than others. Although it may be startling when a preschooler who is reading at the third grade level dissolves in a meltdown when encountering an unfamiliar word, parents have an easier time handling such discrepancies than do teachers.

- Exaggerated aspirations: Although we have mentioned the importance of parents holding reasonably high expectations for their children's behavior, sometimes the children expect too much—in part because they can envision higher goals than their age-mates can, in part because they are used to having things come easily. See the discussion of Dweck's work (above) for ways to shift children from performance goals to learning goals. High goals are, of course, valuable in life, and the negative aspects of "perfectionism" are generally more connected with the feeling that you are not living up to the expectations of others, than not living up to your own (Hewitt & Fleck, 1991).

- Hypersensitivity and hyperintensity: A number of psychologists (Dabrowski, 1967; Piechowski, 1997) maintain that gifted children are especially sensitive—socially, physically, temperamentally—and need help in learning to cope. The prevalence of such super-sensitivity is yet to be well established, but clearly it does occur in some gifted children, making parenting more difficult.

- Debating skills: Parents of highly verbal children who are impressive for reasoning beyond their years are at risk of engaging in ongoing verbal combat that is helpful to no one. Despite their protests, such children are almost always much happier when parents are able to follow predictable routines and to set limits calmly, firmly, and authoritatively.

- Friends: As noted previously, gifted children who have restricted access to friends of their own mental maturity often turn to parents to serve as proxies. Parents need to take care to communicate "who's the kid and who's the grownup," but to step in as needed to provide the companionship that lonely children crave.

- Fears and obsessions: Gifted children's fears are like those of children older than they are (Jersild & Holmes, 1935; Klene, 1988; Wolman, 1978), as are their concerns about world events to which other children pay little heed. However, they often lack the emotional experience—the calluses—to be able to put such information in context, and to weather their worries with the knowledge that "this, too, shall pass." Sometimes, flooding them with information about the situation to the point of boredom will help them to turn away from their ruminations, but mostly, sympathetic recognition and reassurance about their own safety are the best responses parents have to offer.

- Boredom: Once they have mastered a skill or acquired a bit of knowledge, gifted children are less likely than age-mates are to be satisfied with repetition—although, especially in school, this is likely to constitute a major part of their day. As we have seen, in the home they demand considerable adult attention to keep the input and challenges coming. By the same token, they usually need their parents' help at school to assure an optimal educational match. Parents can teach their children responsibility for self-advocacy, for finding their own challenges, and for engaging in ongoing projects and activities on their own, but will also likely need to become involved at school as well.
- Exceptionally high ability: Children who are "profoundly" or "severely" gifted may be so different from both typically developing (and even most other gifted) children of their own age that they are truly out of sync; their parents need out-of-the-ordinary problem-solving strategies.

Spotting Giftedness in Children: Parents Know!

Three longitudinal projects about young, gifted children in our lab at the University of Washington recruited participants through parent nomination in response to local on-air invitations and newspaper articles. Like other studies that have recruited such subjects (e.g., Louis & Lewis, 1992), almost all the children volunteered by their parents did indeed fit the descriptions—toddlers who were precocious in language (Robinson et al., 1990), preschoolers and children in kindergarten who were precocious in mathematics (Robinson, Abbott, Berninger, & Busse, 1996), or preschoolers who might be advanced in any of a number of ways (Robinson & Robinson, 1992). Several findings are notable:

- Parents were accurate: Their initial descriptions of their children's thinking and problem solving corresponded very well with scores on standardized measures, even at these very young ages, and even though the children's talents ranged from mildly to extremely advanced.
- This fact, in reverse, also served to underscore the validity of the standardized measures: The scores actually reflected well the children's observable behavior at home, as rated by the parents and substantiated by their treasured anecdotes (Pletan, Robinson, Berninger, & Abbott, 1995) .
- The children tended to maintain their advancement as a group and, in some cases, actually were more advanced at the end of the study than its beginning (Robinson, Abbott, Berninger, Busse, & Mukhopadhyay, 1997; Robinson & Robinson, 1992). The parents were onto "something real."

To Label or not to Label

Many parents are reluctant to use the label "gifted" when talking about their children and even more reluctant to share the label with the children themselves (Cornell, 1989, 1990; Foster, 2000; Wingert, 1997). Some investigators found that those who do use the label freely tend to have children with more maladjusted behavior (Cornell, 1989; Freeman, 1991) or to be more critical of their children (Wingert, 1997). It is difficult to distinguish, in such a situation, the chicken and the egg, since parents may be more comfortable blaming problems on a child's giftedness than on some other etiology. Sometimes there are other differences between those who do use the label and those who do not; in Freeman's study, for example, the labelers' children were, as a group, of significantly higher IQ, perhaps more "different" than the others.

Colangelo and Brower (1987), in fact, looking at families of students in seventh to ninth grades who had been identified as gifted at least five years before, found no long-term negative effects of labeling on children or other family members including siblings. Similarly, Chamrad, Robinson, Treder, and Janos (1995), in a study of a large number of families with two children, of whom none, one, or two had been labeled "gifted," found few differences among the groups, but those differences were all positive: having a gifted sibling has some advantages for their relationship and for the adjustment of the non-labeled sibling.

Whatever a parent's feelings about use of the label "gifted," it clearly constitutes a necessary part of the process of seeking admission to special programs and to negotiating schools' willingness to meet the needs of the students. Children may also find the label helps them to understand and accept the differences they experience with their age-mates, and further, to adapt to specialized programs and experiences that at first seem quite challenging because they can no longer succeed with so little effort! Parents and counselors can be helpful in making neither too much nor too little of the term, but helping children to relish the difference between the new comparison group and the old one.

MAKING THE HOME–SCHOOL PARTNERSHIP WORK

Parents see the participation of their children in gifted educational programs to be mostly positive and valuable, and in cases in which such programs are terminated, view the loss with consternation. Some see even those programs designed specifically for gifted children as under-challenging, however. Negotiating options that provide an optimal match for the level and pace of children's learning, as well as a match for their interests and their social skills, makes significant demands on parents' skills. They (as well as educators) need to be well informed about local options that do—or could be made to—exist. They also need to stay abreast of changes over time, both in their child and in the settings that point toward the need for in-school adjustments or alternate routes such as homeschooling, independent schools, mentors, and special classes for children talented in areas outside the core of school curricula.

Parents and Schools Share Responsibility

Although it is natural that parents be more deeply invested in the welfare of their children than anyone else, clearly it is in everyone's best interests that effective partnerships be developed between home and school. More than half of the load may fall on the parents to make those partnerships work, however, and may require informed preparation, patience, empathy, and negotiating skill. Both parents and educators need to listen carefully to one another and to keep their eye on the goal: a student who is energized, challenged, learning at a rate and level commensurate with ability, acquiring academic skills to support continued growth, and happy to be doing so.

Views of the Child May Differ and Both May Be Right!

Many parents are disheartened by their perception that the teacher "doesn't know my child at all." This may be an accurate perception, but one that is entirely understandable for the following reasons.

- The setting: A child's behavior may be very different under a restricted behavior code in a class of 30, housed all day with a single adult in one room of approximately 900 square feet, than at home, with the opportunity for solitary play and an almost-always-available adult, and perhaps interesting older siblings as well.
- Temperament: A quiet, compliant child may easily be overlooked, even by a conscientious teacher who is responding to so many divergent needs. A boisterous rebel gets tended to!
- Boredom and repetition: Some repetition is inevitable, but even very good-hearted children eventually become irritable and sometimes misbehave when things move, as said one student, "like a slow-motion movie *all day long*."
- A gifted child may be deliberately hiding: Many bright children make huge sacrifices to be "just like everyone else," especially when they feel very different from others (Janos, Marwood, & Robinson, 1985). To avoid loneliness and "nerdiness," some are careful not to stand out. This is particularly true for boys during the early teens and for girls of all ages.
- No chance to be "who they are": The curriculum may simply offer little opportunity for a teacher to see the more advanced learning of which a child is capable or to observe a child's special interest or expertise, especially given today's emphasis (in 2012) on content standards and bringing all children up to grade-level performance. Many kindergarten teachers, for example, remain unaware that some children "just looking" at picture books are actually reading them.
- Creativity interpreted as non-conformity and high aspirations interpreted as perfectionism: Qualities valued by parents may be hard to deal with in a diverse group.
- Performance goals versus learning goals: A child accustomed to learning effortlessly and always being at the top of the class may refuse challenges even when the teacher offers them, not wanting to risk seeming not so bright. (See discussion of Dweck's work, above.)
- A mild and/or unsuspected learning disability or attention deficit disorder which actually does put a damper on the acquisition of some academic skills, thereby masking the child's more advanced intellectual ability.
- Even special programs may not provide a good fit for an individual gifted child because the level of demand is inappropriately low or high, there is too little differentiation within what is mistakenly seen as (but never is) a "homogeneous" class, or for some other reason specific to the child.

Given this situation, parents can be very helpful by listening receptively when a teacher describes a child's behavior at school. In return, the parent can share a picture of the child's behavior and special interests outside of school, with documentation such as a photo of a project, some writing the child has completed independently, a list of books recently read, a painting, or a recording of a recital performance. If a child is expressing unhappiness about school when at home, this too can be shared without being critical of the teacher. If a psychologist has evaluated the child's mental ability and/or academic skills, such information can also support the picture that the parent paints for the teacher and, under some circumstances, parents may want to obtain such an independent evaluation. Each party may be in for some surprises!

Considering a Smorgasbord of Possibilities: Preparation and Flexibility Are Key to Successful Negotiations

When a parent concludes that the current school situation is a poor fit for his/her child, research into local options as well as brainstorming about possibilities that might work is in order. Valuable resources for this purpose are Karen Rogers's *Re-forming Gifted Education* (2002) as well as the chapters in Sections IV and V in this volume that describe accelerative/enriching substitutions or adaptations that can, in combination or in sequence, make for a better fit. Homeschooling for all or part of the day, when parents are free to provide it, should not be overlooked (see also Chapter 25 by Hood in this book).

The secret is, in general, not to be too closely wedded to any single option, but rather to present the idea of *experiments*, one or more of which may be worth *trying*. The notion of an experiment lightens the onus on the teacher, provides a chance for collaboration, feedback, and fine-tuning, and opens the way for more such experiments along the way. Parental offers to spend time in the classroom (not necessarily with his/her own child) or to provide necessary materials or resources may be appropriate. If special programs are available, parents need to be careful to meet application deadlines. *Remember that the request is not for a "better" educational program for this child than others, but an "appropriate" one, a "better fit."*

If the results of teacher conferences do not seem to be improving the situation, then the next step may be a (calm and reasoned) discussion with the counselor, the principal, a gifted specialist within the school district, or a psychologist, depending on the situation. Often, school psychologists are so burdened with testing children who are struggling in school that a psychologist in the community may be more helpful in providing an objective view of the child's abilities and needs.

Once agreements are reached and plans made, it is helpful to write and share a memorandum of what the parent understands to be in place, complete with dates for future conferences and assessment of how things are going. Unless part of the picture is a child's disability, a legally binding document such as a 504 Plan or an Individual Educational Plan (IEP) is not usually required.

Successful negotiations are not those in which there are winners and losers, but those in which goals are reached—in this case, optimizing the opportunity for the gifted student to find joyful engagement and zest in learning, courage in the face of challenge, healthy talent development, and improved academic progress. When both parents and teachers are able to focus on this shared goal, their own differences often can be negotiated, compromises reached, "experiments" committed to, and personal issues minimized. (See Fisher & Ury, 1981, before embarking on this path.) When educators and parents are at loggerheads, the student is the major loser; when they work together, everyone "wins."

In addition, collaborative advocacy among multiple parents can establish alliances to explore new options. It is a fact of life that such things do not happen on their own, and that parents who are politically adept and forward-looking for children—their own and others—are the moving force behind nearly every effective school change. Some resources for this purpose, beyond the scope of the current chapter, are the article database of The Davidson Institute for Talent Development (www.davidsongifted.org) and the advocacy and legislation site of the National Association for Gifted Children (www.nagc.org).

RESOURCES FOR PARENTS

Useful websites include, as mentioned, www.davidsongifted.org, www.nagc.org, and hoagiesgifted.com. The National Association for Gifted Children (NAGC) publishes a magazine, *Parenting for High Potential*, and several publishers, notably Great Potential Press, as well as Prufrock Press, and Free Spirit Publishing, have developed books specifically for parents of gifted children.

REFERENCES

Adolph, K. E., Shrout, P. E., & Vereijken, B. (2003). What changes in infant walking and why. *Child Development, 74,* 475–497.

Albert, R. S. (1980). Family positions and the attainment of eminence: A study of special family positions and special family experiences. *Gifted Child Quarterly, 24,* 87–95.

Baumrind, D. (1971). Current patterns of parental authority. *Developmental Psychology Monographs, 4*(1), Part 2.

Bloom, B. S. (Ed.). (1985). *Developing talent in young people.* New York: Ballantine.

Campbell, J. R., & Mandel, F. (1990). Connecting math achievement to parental influences. *Contemporary Educational Psychology, 15,* 64–74.

Chamrad, D. L., Robinson, N. M., Treder, R., & Janos, P. M. (1995). Consequences of having a gifted sibling: Myths and realities. *Gifted Child Quarterly, 39,* 135–145.

Colangelo, N., & Brower, P. (1987). Labeling gifted youngsters: Long-term impact on families. *Gifted Child Quarterly, 31,* 75–78.

Cornell, D. G. (1989). Child adjustment and parent use of the term "gifted." *Gifted Child Quarterly, 33,* 59–64.

Cornell, D. G. (1990). High ability students who are unpopular with their peers. *Gifted Child Quarterly, 34,* 155–160.

Cramond, B., Matthews-Morgan, J., Bandalos, D., & Zuo, L. (2005). The Torrance Tests of Creative Thinking: Alive and well in the new millennium. *Gifted Child Quarterly, 49,* 283–291.

Csikszentmihalyi, M., Rathunde, K., & Whalen, S. (1993). *Talented teenagers: The roots of success and failure.* New York: Cambridge University Press.

Dabrowski, K. (1967). *Personality shaping through positive disintegration.* Boston: Little, Brown.

Dale, P. S., & Crain-Thoreson, C. (1993). Pronoun reversals: Who, when, and why? *Journal of Child Language, 20,* 573–589.

Dale, P. S., Crain-Thoreson, C., & Robinson, N. M. (1995). Linguistic precocity and the development of reading: The role of extra-linguistic factors. *Applied Psycholinguistics, 16,* 173–187.

Dweck, C. S. (2006). *Mindset: The new psychology of success.* New York: Random House.

Elliott, E. S., & Dweck, C. S. (1988). Goal: An approach to motivation and achievement. *Journal of Personality and Social Psychology, 54,* 5–12.

Fisher, R., & Ury, W. L. (1981). *Getting to yes.* Boston: Houghton Mifflin.

Foster, J. F. (2000). *A case study approach to understanding the gifted experience: Children's and parents' perceptions of labeling placement.* (Unpublished doctoral dissertation). University of Toronto, Toronto, Canada.

Fowler, W. (1990). *Talking from infancy: How to nurture and cultivate early language development.* Cambridge, MA: Brookline Books.

Freeman, J. (1991). *Gifted children growing up.* London, UK: Cassel.

Freeman, J. (2000). Families: The essential context for gifts and talent. In K. A. Heller, F. J. Mönks , R. J. Sternberg, & R. F. Subotnik (Eds.), *International handbook of giftedness and talent* (2nd ed., pp. 573–585). Oxford, UK: Elsevier.

Goertzel, M., Goertzel, V., Goertzel, T., & Hansen, A. (2003). *Cradles of eminence: Childhoods of more than 700 famous men and women.* Scottsdale, AZ: Great Potential Press.

Gross, M. U. M. (1989). The pursuit of excellence or the search for intimacy? The forced-choice dilemma of gifted youth. *Roeper Review, 11*, 189–194.

Hébert, T. P., Pagnani, A. R., & Hammond, D. R. (2009). Paternal influence on high-achieving gifted males. *Journal for the Education of the Gifted, 33*, 241–274.

Hewitt, P. L., & Fleck, G. L. (1991). Perfectionism in the self and social contexts, conceptualization, assessment, and association with psychopathology. *Journal of Personality and Social Psychology, 60*, 456–470.

Janos, P. M., Marwood, K. A., & Robinson, N. M. (1985). Friendship patterns in highly intelligent children. *Roeper Review, 46*, 46–49.

Jersild, A. T., & Holmes, F. B. (1935). *Children's fears.* New York: Columbia University Press.

Karnes, M. B., Shwedel, A. M., & Steinberg, D. (1984). Styles of parenting among parents of young, gifted children. *Roeper Review, 6*, 232–235.

Klene, R. (1988, August). *The occurrence of fears in gifted children.* Paper presented at the Annual Meeting of the American Psychological Association, Atlanta.

Louis, B., & Lewis, M. (1992). Parental beliefs about giftedness in young children and their relation to actual ability level. *Gifted Child Quarterly, 36*, 27–31.

McDowell, J. A. (1992). *Interactional styles of preschool gifted and nongifted children with their mothers.* (Unpublished doctoral dissertation). New Mexico State University, Las Cruces.

Moss, E. (1992). Early interactions and metacognitive development of gifted preschoolers. In P. S. Klein & A. Tannenbaum (Eds.), *To be young and gifted* (pp. 278–318). Norwood, NJ: Ablex.

Moss, E., & Strayer, F. F. (1990). Interactive problem-solving of gifted and non-gifted preschoolers with their mothers. *International Journal of Behavioral Development, 13*, 177–197.

Mueller, C. M., & Dweck, C. S. (1998). Praise for intelligence can undermine children's motivation and performance. *Journal of Personality and Social Psychology, 75*, 33–52.

O'Shea, M., Heilbronner, N. N., & Reis, S. M. (2010). Characteristics of academically talented women who achieve at high levels on the Scholastic Achievement Test—Mathematics. *Journal of Advanced Academics, 21*, 234–271.

Olszewski, P., Kulieke, M., & Buescher, T. (1987). The influence of the family environment on the development of talent: A literature review. *Journal for the Education of the Gifted, 11*, 6–28.

Olszewski-Kubilius, P. (2002). Parenting practices that promote talent development, creativity, and optimal adjustment. In M. Neihart, S. M. Reis, N. M. Robinson, & S. M. Moon (Eds.), *The social and emotional development of gifted children: What do we know?* (pp. 205–212). Waco, TX: Prufrock Press.

Piechowski, M. (1997). Emotional giftedness: The measure of intrapersonal intelligence. In N. Colangelo & G. A. Davis (Eds.), *Handbook of gifted education* (pp. 366–381). Needham, MA: Allyn & Bacon.

Pletan, M. D., Robinson, N. M., Berninger, V. W., & Abbott, R. D. (1995). Parents' observations of kindergart[e]ners who are advanced in mathematical reasoning. *Journal for the Education of the Gifted, 19*, 30–44.

Robinson, N. M. (2003). Two wrongs do not make a right: Sacrificing the needs of academically talented students does not solve society's unsolved problems. *Journal for the Education of the Gifted, 26*, 251–273.

Robinson, N. M., Abbott, R. D., Berninger, V. W., & Busse, J. (1996). The structure of abilities in math-precocious young children: Gender similarities and differences. *Journal of Educational Psychology, 88*, 341–352.

Robinson, N. M., Abbott, R. D., Berninger, V. W., Busse, J., & Mukhopadhyay, S. (1997). Developmental changes in mathematically precocious young children: Longitudinal and gender effects. *Gifted Child Quarterly, 41*, 145–158.

Robinson, N. M., Dale, P. S., & Landesman, S. J. (1990). Validity of Stanford-Binet IV with young children exhibiting precocious language. *Intelligence, 14*, 173–186.

Robinson, N. M., Lanzi, R. G., Weinberg, R. A., Ramey, S. L., & Ramey, C. T. (2002). Factors associated with high academic competence in former Head Start children at third grade. *Gifted Child Quarterly, 46*, 281–294.

Robinson, N. M., & Robinson, H. B. (1992). The use of standardized tests with young gifted children. In P. S. Klein & A. Tannenbaum (Eds.), *To be young and gifted* (pp. 141–170). Norwood, NJ: Ablex.

Robinson, N. M., Weinberg, R. A., Redden, D., Ramey, S. L., & Ramey, C. T. (1998). Factors associated with high academic competence among former Head Start children. *Gifted Child Quarterly, 42*, 148–156.

Rogers, K. D. (2002). *Re-forming gifted education: How parents and teachers can match the program to the child.* Scottsdale, AZ: Great Potential Press.

Rogoff, B., Morelli, G. A., & Chavajay, P. (2010). Children's integration in communities and segregation from people of differing ages. *Perspectives on Psychological Science, 5*, 431–440.

Simonton, D. K. (1998). Gifted child—genius adult: Three life-span developmental perspectives. In R. Friedman & K. B. Rogers (Eds.), *Talent in context: Historical and social perspectives on giftedness* (pp. 151–175). Washington, DC: American Psychological Association.

Snowden, P. L., & Christian, L. G. (1999). Parenting the young gifted child: Supportive behaviors. *Roeper Review, 21*, 215–221.

Terman, L. M., & Oden, M. H. (1947). *Genetic studies of genius, Vol. IV: The gifted child grows up.* Stanford, CA: Stanford University Press.

Thomas, B. (1984). Early toy preferences of four-year-old readers and nonreaders. *Child Development, 55,* 424–430.

Trudewind, C. (1982). The development of achievement motivation and individual differences: Ecological determinants. In W. W. Hartup (Ed.), *Review of child development research* (Vol. 6, pp. 669–703). Chicago: University of Chicago Press.

Turkheimer, E., Haley, A., Waldron, M., D'Onofrio, B. D, & Gottesman, I. I. (2003). Socioeconomic status modifies heritability of IQ in young children. *Psychological Science, 14,* 623–628.

Wai, J., Lubinski, D., & Benbow, C. P. (2005). Creativity and occupational accomplishments among intellectually precocious youths: An age 13 to age 33 longitudinal study. *Journal of Educational Psychology, 97(3),* 484–492.

White, B. L., & Watts, J. C. (Eds.). (1973). *Experience and environment: Major influences on the development of the young child* (Vol. I). Englewood Cliffs, NJ: Prentice Hall.

Windecker-Nelson, E., Melson, G. F., & Moon, S. M. (1997). Intellectually gifted preschoolers' perceived competence: Relations to maternal attitudes, concerns, and support. *Gifted Child Quarterly, 41,* 133–144.

Wingert, H. D. (1997). *The label "gifted": Parent beliefs, transmission of beliefs and impact on the child.* (Unpublished doctoral dissertation). Simon Fraser University, British Columbia, Canada.

Winterbottom, M. (1958). The relation of need for achievement in learning experience in independence and mastery. In J. Atkinson (Ed.), *Motives in fantasy, action, and society* (pp. 437–453). Princeton, NJ: Van Nostrand.

Wolman, B. (1978). *Children's fears.* New York: Grosset and Dunlap.

25

EFFECTIVENESS AND IMPLICATIONS OF HOMESCHOOLING FOR GIFTED STUDENTS

Lorie Hood

For over a century, researchers have explored issues surrounding gifted and talented individuals and those who support them, establishing a knowledge base relating to cognitive and affective development, curricular and programmatic options, parenting and teacher-related issues, special populations of gifted students, etc. (Plucker & Callahan, 2008). However, despite the fact that homeschooling, in one form or another, has been part of the education of our citizens since the inception of the United States, very little is known about homeschooling gifted students.

HOMESCHOOLING: A BRIEF HISTORY

Schooling children in the home has been an option for much of our nation's history (Gordon, 1994). In fact, early laws governing education compelled parents and "masters" to educate children and did not provide for schools or teachers (McMullen, 2002). Early in our nation's history, nearly every child was taught at least part-time in the home, and those who received training or education outside the home did so through an apprenticeship or private tutor (Keddie, 2007; McMullen, 2002). In the early 19th century, proponents of public education hoped that a public system of education would "bring about unity and equality for students" (McMullen, 2002, p. 77). Thomas Jefferson believed such a system "would help sustain democracy by bringing everyone together to share values and learn a common history" (McMullen, 2002, p 77). However, compulsory education laws were not universally adopted until the early 20th century. As a result, until the early 1900s, most children were "homeschooled."

As an alternative to traditional schooling, homeschooling has had a significant resurgence over the last 15 years. The number of homeschooled children increased by 29 percent between 1998 and 2003, and is now growing at the rate of 11 percent per year (Cloud & Morse, 2001). Ray (2010) reported that over 2 million children were being homeschooled in the United States in 2010. Despite this reported growth and the growth in groups advocating for the use of homeschooling, the research base from which to draw information about demographics, relative achievement rates, trends or practices in homeschooling is almost non-existent. Partly this is due to a lack of consistency in data-gathering processes across states, and partly this is due to reluctance on the part of homeschoolers to report information that would increase government oversight and regulation (Kunzman, 2008). The only ongoing, comprehensive research currently being conducted on homeschooling is authored by Ray (2000, 2004, 2010), president of a homeschool advocacy group (National Home Education Research Institute). Thus, beyond a single government survey conducted by The National Household Education Surveys Program (NHES), which looked at broad trends across states, there is little unbiased data on homeschooling in the United States (Kunzman, 2008). In fact, aside from Kunzman and Ray, no other broad-based, empirical studies exist in the research literature on homeschooling. Given the overall lack of research on homeschooling in general, "it should not be surprising that even less empirical data are available on the subset of homeschooling gifted children. In fact, it appears that not a single, comprehensive study of gifted homeschoolers has been published" (Kunzman, 2008, p. 254). However, anecdotal evidence, the available partial empirical data on homeschooling, and what the current research tells us about gifted students may combine to yield some insight into the subset of gifted homeschooled students.

REASONS FOR HOMESCHOOLING

Homeschoolers and homeschool advocates cite special learning needs, inadequate curriculum, and state testing for the recent resurgence in homeschooling (Moorse, 2001). In a survey of parents' reasons for homeschooling their children, the NHES found that 17 percent of the parents who responded cited dissatisfaction with the academic instruction available to their children (National Center for Education Statistics [NCES], 2009). While only 2 percent of parents surveyed in the NCES study identified "child has other special needs" as the most important reason for homeschooling, much of the anecdotal evidence on homeschooling and empirical evidence on the gifted suggest that homeschooling may be a viable alternative for gifted students (Dauber & Benbow, 1990; Montgomery, 1989; Shyers, 1992; Taylor, 1986).

ACADEMIC NEEDS OF GIFTED STUDENTS

Gifted children differ from their non-gifted peers in the ways in which they learn best. Not only do gifted children need to learn at a faster pace and at a higher level, they are also driven to learn in greater depth (Gross, 1993; U.S. Department of Education, 1994). In a traditional classroom, a gifted student may be accommodated in terms of level and pace; however, it is nearly impossible to allow a gifted student who is driven to learn about a specific topic the time he or she would need to exhaust that topic. Class periods, bells, and curricular directives that orient teachers to cover many subjects within a school day require a student in a non-homeschool situation to stop learning about one topic and move on to the next whether he or she is ready to move on or not (Gatto, 1991). Homeschooling offers a student the freedom to explore without limits.

The available flexibility of homeschooling allows for forms of pedagogy and curriculum that resonate with gifted education: intense, in-depth focus on a particular subject or project; accelerated pacing; individual mentoring; "real-world" internships; and accessing programs and coursework within a broader community (Kunzman, 2008, p. 257).

In the home environment, students and parents have the flexibility to learn without interruption, focus on one topic in depth, and even focus on one subject to the exclusion of others (Ensign, 1997). Often, gifted homeschooled students will work on a subject for several months simply because they are "turned on" by new insight, excited about the material, or motivated by success. One mother of a highly gifted six-year-old girl reported that her daughter moved through six grade levels in mathematics in less than a year to the exclusion of other topics, only to set mathematics aside and do the same thing with writing for another five months. "In a public school," the mother reported, "there is no way she would have been allowed to do this. No one had to tell her to work on math or writing; she did it because she was excited and motivated about learning." Homeschool proponents would say that this child was self-motivated because she was able to learn about what she wanted. Experts in gifted education would say the advanced academic needs of this child were being met by allowing her to move at her own pace and level, as well as learn in depth (Colangelo, Assouline, & Gross, 2004; Ensign, 1997; Gross, 1993, 2000).

Another way in which the structure of homeschooling has potential to accommodate the academic needs of the gifted learner is the opportunity to begin "school" early. In *A Nation Deceived* (Colangelo et al., 2004), starting school early is touted as "an easy yes" for gifted students. Gifted five- year-olds often enter kindergarten performing addition and subtraction and reading at a second or third grade level. However, most state laws require a child to be five years of age prior to the September of their kindergarten year, regardless of a student's achievement level. In a homeschool environment, when to "begin school" is a moot point.

Subject acceleration is another way to accommodate a gifted child's learning needs (Colangelo et al., 2004; Rogers, 2004). Like any child, gifted children are not uniform in their development or in their interests (Gross, 1993; Kearney, 1996). Where one child may be gifted across subjects, another may show precocity in only one domain. With a homeschool model, the adaptation of curriculum is as simple as following the child. It is the ultimate form of individualization. While subject acceleration allows a gifted learner to move up in one or more subject areas, a radically accelerated child moves up one or more entire grade levels. The gifted student may move at a pace and level appropriate for that individual child—a gifted child advocate's dream. Despite the research base that uniformly supports radical acceleration of highly and profoundly gifted students (see Chapter 18 in this book by Colangelo, Assouline, and Marron for a summary of this research), teachers and administrators are still reluctant to allow children to skip more than one grade. Homeschooling allows students to be radically accelerated and form psychosocially healthy relationships based on common interests and intellectual and developmental age (Gross, 1989).

Gifted students are more likely to form positive and lasting friendships with older students, with whom they share a commonality of intellectual and psychosocial development, than with age-peers who are likely to be still at a stage of emotional development which the gifted student passed through some years before.

(Gross, 1994)

SOCIAL AND EMOTIONAL NEEDS OF GIFTED STUDENTS

While radical acceleration addresses the needs of gifted students to form relationships and learn with intellectual and social peers either in schools or a homeschooling environment, it does nothing to address asynchronous development. Based on the work of Hollingworth (1931, 1939), Vygotsky (1962), Dabrowski (1972), and Terrassier, (1985), the Columbus Group (1991, as cited by Codd, n.d.) defines asynchronous development as:

> [D]evelopment in which advanced cognitive abilities and heightened intensity combine to create inner experiences and awareness that are qualitatively different from the norm. The uniqueness of the gifted renders them particularly vulnerable and requires modification in parenting, teaching and counseling in order for them to develop optimally.
>
> (Columbus Group, 1991, as cited by Codd, n.d., under "A New Definition of Giftedness—Defining Giftedness from Within")

Asynchronous development is a challenge for gifted students as well as the people who parent or educate them. While a six-year-old may be reading at an eight grade level and prefer interacting with older children, he or she may still throw temper tantrums like a four–year-old. In addition, according to this theory of development, as the level of giftedness increases, so does the asynchrony (Cohen, 1999; Gross, 2000).

Asynchrony is as much part of being gifted as is advanced cognitive ability, and as such, is something gifted individuals and those who support them must accommodate. While there is no perfect environment for the asynchronous child, studies show that homeschooled students often form relationships with a wider age range of students than their publicly schooled peers (Montgomery, 1989). However, it takes considerable time, effort, and organization to ensure that a child has adequate opportunity for, and access to, appropriate social activities within a homeschool context (Ensign, 1997). Some parents of homeschooled children form cooperative homeschooling groups (homeschool co-ops), which provide a group learning environment and may present opportunities for gifted students to form relationships with those of comparable intellectual ability or similar interests. In addition to co-ops, parents who homeschool have formed athletic groups, social groups, and other extracurricular group activities in an attempt to provide social opportunities for their children. Thus, homeschooling potentially offers two vitally important things to the gifted student: the ability to move at an academically appropriate pace and level; and the opportunity to form relationships with a wide age range of other students.

TYPES OF HOMESCHOOLING

Unschooling, as defined by its founder John Holt, is a child-centered approach that uses a child's natural curiosity about the world around her to stimulate learning and create "curriculum." John Holt, considered one of the most influential people in the modern homeschooling movement, believed that the public school system squelched children's natural curiosity with too much structure and authoritarianism (Davis, 2006). Holt established the concept of "unschooling" in the 1970s and 1980s, an approach which fosters a view of children as natural learners, capable of learning everything they need under the supervision of an adult. By allowing the day to unfold naturally, a parent can use events, such as a thunderstorm or a trip to the grocery store, as logical "lessons." A child's curiosity or even fear about a thunderstorm could easily be used to stimulate a science lesson. Likewise, a trip to the grocery store could become a learning experience about mathematics or nutrition.

> In an era of increased standardized testing, top-down curricula, and the mandates of the federal No Child Left Behind Act, 'Unschooling' is attractive to some parents, who say learning should be a more organic, curiosity-inspired exercise. Advocates say it allows children to become passionate about, and invested in, their own learning.
>
> (Davis, 2006, p. 5)

Distance learning is another approach to creating a homeschooling curriculum that is often sought out by homeschoolers as a means of accommodating acceleration and enrichment for gifted students (e.g., Adams & Cross, 2000; Brody, 2004; Southern & Jones, 2004). There are several programs specifically created to support the gifted: The Duke University Talent Identification Program (Duke TIP; http://www.tip.duke.edu/), the Davidson Institute for Talent Development(www.davidsongifted.org), the Johns Hopkins Center for Talented Youth (http://cty.jhu.edu), the Summer Institute for the Gifted (http://www.cgp-sig.com), the Education Program for Gifted Youth (EPGY) at Stanford University (http://epgy.stanford.edu/) all offer distance learning opportunities. Distance learning may provide opportunities to study advanced subjects beyond the expertise of the students' parents (Wallace, 2009), and may provide the flexibility in terms of pace and level particularly appropriate for gifted students (Adams & Cross, 2000).

In addition to programs specifically created for gifted learners, online courses for credit from traditional institutions— i.e., junior college, university and stand-alone, remote homeschool institutions—may also provide instructional resources. A student could enroll in a college-level physics course and take it from home on his or her computer without disrupting the homeschool environment. However, Kunzman (2008, p. 258) raises concerns with regard to virtual learning: "A homeschool experience dominated by 'virtual classrooms' and electronic communication provides a decidedly different form of socialization than either a school building or a homeschool community group offers, one that is arguably lacking in important facets of interpersonal skills."

Critics of homeschooling contend that children who are homeschooled lack adequate socialization. The limited research on homeschooling suggests no lack of, or delay in, social development associated with homeschooling (McDowell, as cited by Kim, 2005, para. 2; Montgomery, 1989), yet socialization is still a concern for many. "The 'socialization question' as it is known among homeschoolers, is actually an omnibus inquiry which usually leads to more specific questions" (Arai, 1999, p. 2). Critics of homeschooling argue that children who are never exposed to traditional schooling will lack the coping skills to deal with real-world problems once they leave the protection of their family (Luffman, 1997; Menendez, 1996; Stough, 1992). However, Webb (1989), one of the few researchers who has examined aspects of the adult lives of wholly or partly home-educated people, found that all who had attempted higher education were successful and that their socialization was often better than that of their schooled peers.

One strategy used by homeschooling parents to address the potential isolation of being schooled at home is dual enrollment or educating children part-time in the home and part-time in a traditional classroom. A gifted learner in need of acceleration could attend public school with age-peers for non-accelerated classes and choose a distance option or homeschool curriculum for his or her accelerated subjects. Another means by which homeschoolers can mitigate the effects of a single-student classroom is by joining a homeschooling co-op.

> Homeschoolers frequently enjoy a network of support groups and learning co-ops. Advocates point to the makeup of these homeschool groups— which are frequently multi-age—as providing more flexibility for varying interests and abilities, with little or no attention paid to "age/grade level" classifications.
>
> (Kunzman, 2008, p. 257)

Other types of dual enrollment for the gifted high school student is dual enrollment in college and traditional school, or dual enrollment in college combined with homeschooling. Whatever the configuration, homeschoolers potentially find balance with dual enrollment. Witte (2007, no page) stated that "for our son, dual enrollment became the centerpiece of a homeschool curriculum that balanced radical academic acceleration with the asynchronous development needs of a young adolescent." For parents who feel unprepared to teach their own child due to time constraints or an inability to teach at ther child's ability level, there are many packaged options for homeschool curricula. Indeed, one of the criticisms of those who oppose homeschooling in general is that "only a licensed teacher should be entrusted with academic instruction" (Kunzman, 2008, p. 257). With regard to gifted students, one concern is "whether parents will be capable of providing instruction in specialized or advanced subject matter" (Kunzman, 2008, p. 257). These concerns are in some cases valid; packaged homeschool curricula have been developed, but have not been subjected to research scrutiny.

Despite major gaps in the research base on homeschooling in general, and the complete lack of formal studies on homeschooling gifted students, combining the available research has provided some insight to support homeschooling as a possible option for educating gifted students. However, research on homeschooling gifted students is nonexistent. High-quality, empirical research data are needed to guide decision making about options and opportunities. Studies are needed to provide:

- broad-based and basic information on the demographics of those who homeschool;
- data on the percentage of homeschoolers choosing to homeschool to meet the needs of one or more gifted students;
- comparisons of homeschooled, gifted students' achievement rates to the achievement rates of gifted students who are educated in an institutional setting;
- comparisons of the social and emotional development of gifted homeschooled children to that of gifted students in traditional settings;
- delineation of the trends and practices in homeschooling of gifted students;
- evaluation of the quality and appropriateness of available homeschooling curricula for gifted learners.

It is hoped that this chapter will serve as a catalyst to stimulate those who support gifted students, whether as parents, researchers, advocates, or in another capacity, to consider carefully the available data as well as the lack of empirical research when deciding whether homeschooling is an appropriate option for the gifted student they are supporting.

REFERENCES

Adams, C. M., & Cross, T. L. (2000). Distance learning opportunities for academically gifted students. *Journal of Secondary Gifted Education, 11*, 88–96.

Arai, A. B. (1999). Homeschooling and the redefinition of citizenship. *Education Policy Analysis Archives, 7*(27). Retrieved 9/20/2011 from http://www.epaa.asu.edu/ojs/article/download/562/685

Brody, L. E. (2004). Meeting the diverse needs of gifted students through individualized educational plans. In D. Boothe, & J. C. Stanley (Eds.), *In the eyes of the beholder: Critical issues for diversity in gifted education* (pp. 129–138). Waco, TX: Prufrock Press.

Cloud, J., & Morse J. (2001, August 27). Home sweet school. *Time.* Retrieved from http://www.time.com/time/magazine/article/0,9171,1000631,00.html

Codd, M. (1991). Why do we need to define giftedness? Rhode Island Advocates for Gifted Education (RIAGE). Retrieved 9/17/2011 from http://www.riage.org/articles/why-do-we-need-to-define-giftedness/

Cohen, H. (1999). Asynchrony: Homeschooling an exceptionally gifted child. *California HomeSchooler Magazine, 7*(3). Retrieved 9/16/2011 from http://www.ctd.northwestern.edu/resources/topics/displayArticle/?id=168

Colangelo, N., Assouline, S., & Gross, M. U. M. (2004). *A nation deceived: How schools hold back America's brightest students.* Iowa City: The Connie Belin & Jacqueline N. Blank International Center for Gifted Education and Talent Development, University of Iowa.

Dabrowski, K. (1972). *Psychoneurosis is not an illness.* London, UK: Gryf.

Dauber, S. L., & Benbow, C. P. (1990). Aspects of personality and peer relations of extremely talented adolescents. *Gifted Child Quarterly, 43*, 10–14.

Davis, M. R. (2006). 'Unschooling' stresses curiosity more than traditional academics. *Education Week, 26*(16), 8.

Ensign, J. (1997). *Homeschooling gifted students: An introductory guide for parents.* (ERIC Digest No. 543). Reston, VA: ERIC Clearinghouse on Disabilities and Gifted Education. (ERIC Document Reproduction Service No. ED 414 683).

Gatto, J. T. (1991). *Dumbing us down: The hidden curriculum of compulsory schooling.* Philadelphia: New Society.

Gordon, W. M. (1994). The law of homeschooling. NOPLE Monograph Series No. 52. Retrieved from ERIC database (No. ED 370 211).

Gross, M. U. M. (1989). The pursuit of excellence or the search for intimacy? The forced-choice dilemma of gifted youth. *Roeper Review, 11*, 189–194.

Gross, M. U. M. (1992). The use of radical acceleration in cases of extreme intellectual precocity. *Gifted Child Quarterly, 36*, 91–99.

Gross, M. U. M. (1993). *Exceptionally gifted children.* London, UK: Routledge.

Gross, M. U. M. (1994). Radical acceleration: Responding to academic and social needs of extremely gifted adolescents. *The Journal of Secondary Gifted Education 5*(4) Summer 1994. Retrieved 9/19/2011 from http://www.davidsongifted.org/db/Articles_id_10117.aspx

Gross, M. U. M. (2000). Issues in the cognitive development of exceptionally and profoundly gifted individuals. In K. A. Heller, F. J. Mönks, R. J. Sternberg, & R. F. Subotnik (Eds.), *International Handbook of Giftedness and Talent* (pp. 179–192). Oxford, UK: Pergamon Press.

Hollingworth, L. S. (1931). The child of very superior intelligence as a special problem in social adjustment. *Mental Hygiene, 15*(1), 3–16.

Hollingworth, L. S. (1939). What we know about early selection and training of leaders. *Teachers College Record, 40*, 575–592.

Kearney, K. (1996). Highly gifted children in full inclusion classrooms. *Highly Gifted Children, 12*(4). Retrieved 9/18/2011 from http://www.davidsongifted.org/db/Resources_id_11313.aspx

Keddie, C. S. (2007). Homeschoolers and public school: Proposals for providing fairer access. *Journal of Legislation and Public Policy, 10*(3). Retrieved 9/11/2011 from http://www.law.nyu.edu/journals/legislation/issues/volume10number3/index.htm

Kim, M. (2005, May 26). Researchers say socialization no longer an "issue." *Christian Post.* Retrieved from http://www.christianpost.com/article/20050526/7552_Researchers_Say_Socialization_No_Longer_an_"Issue". htmKunzman, R. (2008). Homeschooling. In J. A. Plucker, & C. M. Callahan (Eds.), *Critical issues and practices in gifted education: What the research says* (pp. 253–260). Waco, Texas: Prufock Press.

Luffman, J. (1997). A profile of home schooling in Canada. *Education Quarterly Review, 4*(4), 30–47.

McMullen, J. G. (2002). Behind closed doors: Should states regulate homeschooling? *South Carolina Law Review, 54*(75), 75–109.

Menendez, A. J. (1996). *Homeschooling: The facts.* Silver Spring, MD: Americans for Religious Liberty.

Montgomery, L. (1989). The effect of home schooling on leadership skills of home schooled students. *Home School Researcher, 5*(1), 1–10.

Moorse, K. (2001). *When schools fail: Is homeschooling right for your highly gifted child?* Retrieved 8/27/2011 from http://www.hoagiesgifted.org/schools_fail.htm.

National Center for Higher Education. (2002). *Statistical analysis report: Higher education.* (NCES 97-584). Retrieved 9/19/2011 from http://nces.ed.gov/pubs/97584.html.

Plucker. J. A., & Callahan, C. M. (Eds.). (2008). *Critical issues and practices in gifted education: What the research says.* Waco, Texas: Prufrock Press.

Ray, B. D. (2000). Home schooling: The ameliorator of negative influences on learning. *Peabody Journal of Education, 7*(1&2), 71–106.

Ray, B. D. (2004). Homeschoolers on to college: What research shows us. *Journal of College Admission, 185,* 5–11, Retrieved from www.nheri.org/Research-Facts-on-Homeschooling.html

Ray, B. D. (2010). Academic achievement and demographic traits of homeschool students: A nationwide study. *Academic Leadership Journal.* Retrieved 9/19/2011 from www.academicleadership.org .

Rogers, Karen B. (2004). *Re-forming gifted education: Matching the program to the child.* Scottsdale, AZ: Great Potential Press.

Shyers, L. E. (1992). A comparison of social adjustment between home and traditionally schooled students. *Home School Researcher, 8*(3), 1–8.

Southern, W. T., & Jones, E. D. (2004). Types of acceleration: Dimensions and issues. In N. Colangelo, S. Assouline, & M. U. M. Gross (Eds.), *A nation deceived: How schools hold back America's brightest students* (Vol. 2, pp. 5–12). Iowa City: The Connie Belin & Jacqueline N. Blank International Center for Gifted Education and Talent Development, University of Iowa.

Stough, L. (1992). *Social and emotional status of home schooled children and conventionally schooled children in West Virginia.* (M. S. thesis). University of West Virginia. Retrieved from ERIC database (No. ED 353 079).

Taylor, J. W. (1986). *Self-conception in homeschooling children.* (Doctoral dissertation). Andrews University. Retrieved 9/11/2011 from thsc.birddogsw.com (AB Arai education policy analysis archives, 1999).

Terrassier, J-C. (1985). Dyssyncrony–uneven development. In J. Freeman (Ed.), *The psychology of gifted children* (pp. 265–274). New York: Wiley.

U.S. Department of Education (1994). *Prisoners of time. Report of the National Education Commission on Time and Learning.* Washington, DC: U.S. Government Printing Office.

Vygotsky, L. S. (1962). *Thought and language.* Cambridge, MA: MIT Press.

Wallace, P. (2009). Distance learning for gifted students: Outcomes for elementary, middle, and high school aged students. *Journal for the Education of the Gifted, 32*(3), 295–320.

Webb, J. (1989). The outcomes of home-based education. Employment and other issues. *Educational Review, 41,* 121–133.

Witte, G. (2007, Spring). Dual enrollment: The right challenge. *Digest of Gifted Research, Duke University Talent Identification Program, 7*(3). Retrieved from www.davidsongifted.org/db/Articles_id_10449.aspx

Section IV
Curricular and Instructional Decisions

26

DEFENSIBLE CURRICULUM FOR GIFTED STUDENTS

An Introduction

Holly L. Hertberg-Davis and Carolyn M. Callahan

For many years, curriculum was considered to be appropriately differentiated for gifted learners when it emphasized the development of higher-level and creative thinking skills, solving real-world problems addressed to multiple audiences, exploring key concepts of the field, and conducting in-depth, independent investigations (Feldhusen, VanTassel-Baska, & Seeley, 1989; Maker & Nielson, 1995; National/State Leadership Training Institute on the Gifted and Talented [N/SLTI–G/T], 1979; Renzulli, 1977; Van-Tassel-Baska, 1992, 1994). In 1979, the curriculum committee of the N/SLTI–G/T developed a list of seven principles of a curriculum for the gifted which served for many years as the definitive criteria for what makes curriculum for the gifted unique. Curricula should:

1. Focus on, and be organized to include, more elaborate, complex, and in-depth study of major ideas, problems, and themes that integrate knowledge within and across systems of thought.
2. Allow for the development and application of productive thinking skills to enable students to re-conceptualize existing knowledge and generate new knowledge.
3. Enable [gifted learners] to explore constantly changing knowledge and information and develop the attitude that knowledge is worth pursuing in an open world.
4. Encourage exposure to, selection of, and use of specialized and appropriate resources.
5. Promote self-initiated and self-directed learning and growth.
6. Provide for the development of self-understanding and understanding of one's relationship to persons, societal institutions, nature, and culture.
7. Involve evaluations of the curricula, conducted in accordance with prior stated principles, stressing higher-level skills, creativity, and excellence in performance and products.

While the qualities and principles outlined above (N/SLTI–G/T, 1979) unquestionably describe a powerful and challenging curriculum, the assignation of them to a curriculum for the gifted suggests two things:

1. that it is possible to describe a "standard" curriculum for the gifted that can appropriately meet the needs of *all* gifted students; and
2. that these principles designate a curriculum that is *inappropriate* for students who are not labeled as gifted.

Throughout the late 1980s and early 1990s, discussions in the literature of both general education and gifted education called these two assumptions into question (e.g., Oakes, 1985; Sapon-Shevin, 1994; Shore & Delacourt, 1996; Tomlinson, 1996). Critics argued that students identified as gifted receive special learning opportunities that could benefit all students (Oakes, 1985; Sapon-Shevin, 1994), increasing pressure on members of the field of gifted education to justify that the curriculum presented to gifted students is indeed uniquely suited to those learners and inappropriate for others (Borland, 1989).

The field of gifted education has responded to this pressure by seeking to define, as Tomlinson (1996) termed it, its own "instructional identity," attempting to answer the question "What distinguishes curriculum for the gifted from curriculum for other students?" Current curriculum theory in gifted education is largely based upon the assumption that the same principles that undergird good curriculum for gifted students also undergird good curriculum for *all* learners—what varies are such things as pacing, complexity, depth, or "fuzziness" of problems (see chapters in this volume by Kaplan [28], Renzulli [27], Tomlinson [29], and VanTassel-Baska [31]). Qualities of curriculum that were traditionally thought of as being the territory of gifted programs—emphasis on higher-level thinking skills, concept-based instruction, "real-world" investigations—are now regarded as descriptors of an appropriate curriculum for all (Hockett, 2009). Additionally, most curriculum theory acknowledges that gifted learners are themselves a heterogeneous group with diverse needs (see Chapter 32 of this volume by Callahan), and therefore curriculum and instruction must be flexible and responsive to individual learning differences.

The Parallel Curriculum Model (Tomlinson et al., 2002, 2009) presents a distillation of widely agreed-upon principles of high-quality curriculum and instruction for all learners, including the gifted. According to Tomlinson et al. (2009, pp. 36–37), high-quality curriculum and instruction:

- [should] have a clear focus on the essential facts, understandings, and skills of the discipline;
- provide opportunities for students to develop in-depth understandings;
- are organized to ensure that all student tasks are aligned with the goals of in-depth understanding;
- are coherent (organized, unified, sensible) to the student;
- are mentally and affectively challenging and engaging to the learner;
- recognize and support the need of each learner to make sense of ideas and information, reconstructing older understandings with new ones;
- are fresh, rich, surprising, and joyful;
- provide appropriate choices for the learner;

- allow for meaningful collaboration;
- are focused on products that matter to students;
- connect with students' lives and worlds;
- seem real, purposeful, and useful;
- deal with profound ideas;
- call on students to use what they learn in interesting and important ways;
- aid students in developing a consciousness of their thinking;
- help learners become competent problem solvers;
- involve students in setting their learning goals and assessing their progress;
- stretch the student.

The chapters that follow describe curricular models designed to provide appropriate learning experiences for gifted learners that fit the above descriptors—curriculum and instruction that focus on rich content promoting genuine understanding of the key concepts and principles underlying a field of study, that allow students to develop the skills and habits of mind of practicing professionals and independent learners, that continually push students forward from their current levels of comfort, and that are flexible enough to address the wide variety of needs that appear even in a population of gifted students.

While many of the underlying assumptions about what constitutes an appropriate curriculum for gifted students in these chapters are similar, each model provides unique and valuable answers to the question: *What distinguishes a curriculum for the gifted from curriculum for other students?* As you read, consider the following questions:

- What are the assumptions about giftedness and gifted learners undergirding this curriculum model? What types of gifted students are best served with this curricular model?
- To what degree would this curriculum model provide an appropriate fit for the students identified under your definition of giftedness?
- What research evidence is there of the effectiveness of this model?
- What training and background do teachers need to implement this model effectively?
- How does this model address best practices for serving gifted students and maximizing their learning potential?

REFERENCES

Borland, J. H. (1989). The limits of consilience: A reaction to Françoys Gagné's "My convictions about the nature of abilities, gifts, and talents." *Journal for the Education of the Gifted, 22,* 137–147.

Feldhusen, J., VanTassel-Baska, J., & Seeley, K. (1989). *Excellence in educating the gifted.* Denver, CO: Love.

Hockett, J. A. (2009). Curriculum for highly able learners that conforms to general education and gifted education quality indicators. *Journal for the Education of the Gifted, 32,* 394–440.

Maker, C. J., & Nielson, A. B. (1995). *Teaching models in education of the gifted.* Austin, TX: Pro-Ed.

National/State Leadership Training Institute on the Gifted and Talented. (1979). *Inservice training manual: Activities for developing curriculum for the gifted and talented.* Los Angeles: Author.

Oakes, J. (1985). *Keeping track: How schools structure inequality.* New Haven, CT: Yale University Press.

Renzulli, J. S. (1977). The Enrichment Triad Model: A plan for developing defensible programs for the gifted and talented. *Gifted Child Quarterly, 21,* 227–233.

Sapon-Shevin, M. (1994). *Playing favorites: Gifted education and the disruption of community.* Albany: State University of New York Press.

Shore, B. M., & Delacourt, M. A. B. (1996). Effective curricular and program practices in gifted education and the interface with general education. *Journal for the Education of the Gifted, 20*, 138–154.

Tomlinson, C. A. (1996). Good teaching for one and all: Does gifted education have an instructional identity? *Journal for the Education of the Gifted, 20*, 155–174.

Tomlinson, C. A., Kaplan, S. N., Renzulli, J. S., Purcell, J., Leppien, J., & Burns, D. (2002). *The Parallel Curriculum Model: A design to develop high potential and challenge high-ability learners.* Thousand Oaks, CA: Corwin Press.

Tomlinson, C. A., Kaplan, S. N., Renzulli, J. S., Purcell, J., Leppien, J., & Burns, D. (2009). *The Parallel Curriculum Model* (2nd ed.). Thousand Oaks, CA: Corwin Press.

VanTassel-Baska, J. (1992). *Planning effective curriculum for gifted learners.* Denver, CO: Love.

VanTassel-Baska, J. (1994). *Comprehensive curriculum for gifted learners* (2nd ed.). Boston: Allyn & Bacon.

27

THE MULTIPLE MENU MODEL
A Guide for Developing Differentiated Curriculum
Joseph S. Renzulli

A major goal of all curriculum is making the material personally significant to the students, transforming attitudes and conduct significantly.

(Phillip A. Phenix, January 1987)

Anyone who sets out to develop curriculum will come face to face with two unavoidable realizations. First, developing curriculum is a difficult and demanding process. It involves far more thought and work than "slapping together" information and activities, no matter how exciting these activities may be. An extraordinary amount of effort is necessary to produce material that reflects established curricular principles and creates authentic, relevant, and personally meaningful instructional activities.

Second, present day curriculum writers (2012) generally agree about underlying principles for developing curriculum. Most of these principles, invariably phrased as "should" statements, point out the need for:

a. identifying the curriculum standards to be addressed in the unit of instruction;
b. focusing instruction on abstract concepts;
c. selecting content and process skills to introduce to students and to use in developing student activities; and
d. determining the assessment devices to judge student performance and acquisition of knowledge.

These same "should" lists typically call for cooperative efforts between content scholars and teachers or instructional specialists in designing the curriculum. However, these principles are far too general to provide the specific guidance necessary for the practical job of writing curricular units of instruction. Knowing, for example, that a curricular unit should focus on higher-level thinking skills and advanced content is valuable, but this knowledge does not tell curriculum writers how to identify appropriate content or skills, how to examine various instructional sequences and activity options, or how to prepare a blueprint for fitting together the pieces that will allow content and process to work together in a harmonious and effective fashion. The Multiple Menu Model attempts to address these issues by providing a management plan to guide curriculum developers in selecting content and strategies from a number of options or "menus" drawn from theories of knowledge, instruction, and curricular design.

UNDERSTANDING THE RATIONALE OF THE MULTIPLE MENU MODEL

To design effective curriculum, the curriculum writer must first understand how knowledge within a discipline is constructed. Disciplines have evolved as discrete entities over centuries as the result of the different and evolving kinds of questions that researchers within each discipline ask, and the different research methodologies they develop to answer them. The Multiple Menu Model was created to help curriculum designers use the information on how knowledge develops to create engaging and authentic units of instruction. When curriculum designers understand how knowledge develops, choices about which content and which instructional approaches to use in a unit become explicit.

A Brief Theory of Knowledge

The theory of knowledge underlying the Multiple Menu Model is based on the three levels of knowing first suggested by the American psychologist and philosopher, William James (1885). These levels include knowledge-of, knowledge-about (also referred to as knowledge-that), and knowledge-how.

Knowledge-of

This entry level of knowing might best be described as an awareness level. Knowledge-of consists of being acquainted with, rather than familiar with, a topic. James (1885) referred to this level as "knowledge by acquaintance" to distinguish it from more advanced levels, which he referred to as "knowledge by systematic study and reflection." For example, a "lay" person may be knowledgeable of a field of study called astrophysics and might even know something about what astrophysicists study; however, it would be inaccurate to say that this person is knowledgeable about astrophysics in any way other than on a very superficial awareness level. Knowledge-of involves remembering (storage of knowledge), recollecting (retrieval of knowledge), and recognizing, but does not ordinarily include more advanced processes of the mind.

Knowledge-about

Knowledge-about represents a more advanced level of understanding than merely remembering or recalling information, including more advanced elements of knowing such as distinguishing, translating, interpreting, and being able to explain a given fact, concept, theory, or principle. Being able to explain a given fact, concept, theory, or principle may involve the ability to demonstrate it through physical or artistic performance (e.g., demonstrating a particular dance movement) or through a combination of verbal and manipulative activities (e.g., demonstrating how a piece of scientific apparatus works).

Among the most important decisions a curriculum developer makes is to determine how much knowledge-about to include in a unit, lesson, or lesson segment, and the depth or complexity of coverage. It is at this knowledge-about level that learners must begin to deal with the underpinnings of the discipline. In order to move from acquaintance with facts to mental facility and practical use of content in a field, students will need to understand key concepts that organize the discipline, essential principles that govern the concepts, and ways in which practicing professionals in the field do their work. Teachers who do not have an extensive background in the knowledge area in which they plan to develop curricular units will need to acquire the knowledge. They could take formal courses, study the topic independently, or team up with content specialists in the area in which they plan to develop curricular units. A carefully selected introductory college textbook in a content field is usually the most economical way to begin acquiring the knowledge base necessary for curriculum development in a given field.

Knowledge-how

This level of knowing represents types of knowledge that enable individuals to apply investigative methodology to generate knowledge and make new contributions to their respective fields of study. Most knowledge experts consider the appropriate use of methodology to be the highest level of competence in a content field, and representative of the kind of work pursued by researchers, writers, and artists making new contributions to the sciences, humanities, and the arts. Engagement in learning at this level of knowledge which places students in the role of practicing professionals is typically missing from curricular units of instruction, yet seems to generate the most excitement from students.

The three levels of knowing also exist on a continuum from the simple to the complex. The curriculum developer is responsible for determining the degree of complexity appropriate for a given age or ability group. In the final analysis, the curriculum developer's understanding of the content field and instructional techniques, an understanding of cognitive and developmental psychology, and experience of working with students at varying grades and instructional levels will determine the level of knowledge and content appropriate for a particular age group.

In the Multiple Menu Model, the theory of knowledge represented by James's three levels is used in harmony with Alfred North Whitehead's (1929) concepts of romance, technical proficiency, and generalization. For example, according to Whitehead, a young person might develop a romance with (or interest in) the field of medicine while still at the knowledge-of level. This person might pursue the romance (interest) to the point of technical proficiency and become a practitioner in one of the medical professions. Most professionals within a field reach their maximum involvement at the level of technical proficiency; a few, however, go on to the generalization level. These persons say, in effect, "I want to add new information and contribute new knowledge to the field of medicine." This third level is consistent with one of the major goals of special programming for high-ability students.

APPLYING THEORY TO THE CONSTRUCTION OF THE MULTIPLE MENU MODEL

The Multiple Menu Model was developed as a way for educators to design curricular units that place a premium on both the organization and pursuit of knowledge, and the application of investigative methodologies as they pertain to a particular discipline or field of study. It requires teachers to identify a discipline's principles and concepts and to reflect carefully on how they can share the meaning of these ideas with the young people with whom they work. It encourages the curriculum writer to offer students opportunities to apply the research methodologies that practicing professionals use in their fields of study. The curriculum writer needs to consider all of these elements because they help students develop deep understandings of the subject matter, ground student learning in meaningful and authentic contexts, and equip students with the skills used by practicing professionals so they can apply them in learning new information. This type of curricular planning helps students pursue the depth and complexity of a discipline and its content, rather than learning only surface-level content knowledge.

Because of the accelerated rate at which knowledge is expanding, the Multiple Menu Model is structured to address the selection of content and the selection of procedures in ways that maximize the transfer of learning to new situations. The model concentrates on the various structural elements of a discipline and focuses instruction on the basic principles, functional concepts (Ward, 1960), and methodologies within that discipline. Teachers should view principles and concepts as tools that help the learner understand any and all of the selected topics of a content field. Information of this type is referred to as "enduring knowledge," as opposed to time-sensitive topics or transitory information. For example, understanding the concept of reliability is central to the study of psychological testing; reliability, therefore, may be considered an enduring element of that field. The specific reliability of any given test, however, is more timely or transitory in nature because it changes over time (and from test to test) and is information that learners can always "look up" and understand if they have a basic comprehension of the more enduring concept of reliability.

In a similar fashion, the Multiple Menu Model deals with content selection by focusing on representative topics (Phenix, 1964). These topics consist of any and all of the content in a field that the curriculum developer might choose as the focus of a unit, lesson, or lesson segment. For example, a teacher might choose *The Merchant of Venice* as a representative literary selection to illustrate the key concept of a tragic hero. The teacher may also integrate other selections that employ this key concept into the unit of study, and a second or third selection might be necessary if an instructional objective is to compare and contrast tragic heroes. It is not necessary to cover an extensive list of selections if one or a few representative literary selections can convey the concept. Similarly, a teacher can cover the biological topic of tropism by selecting phototropism as the major focus of a unit and then making reference to other tropisms (geo-, hydro-, chemo-, and thigmo-) based on the same general principle. Students should, of course, have the opportunity to follow up on related topics if they develop a specific interest.

The Multiple Menu Model emphasizes process objectives that have broader transfer value such as application, appreciation, self-actualization, and improved cognitive structures. In other words, this model views representative topics as *vehicles* for process development, not ends in and of themselves. The structural dimensions and key concepts mentioned above provide the learner with tools for examining any topic in a given discipline. The learner develops, practices, applies, and gains an appreciation of a particular segment of knowledge by studying a representative topic. The student may then use the same strategies to examine other topics.

This model also emphasizes appropriate use of methodology within content fields. All content fields can be defined, in part, by the research methods and investigative techniques used to add new knowledge to that field, and most knowledge experts consider the appropriate use of methodology to be the highest level of competence in a content field. Indeed, research scientists, composers, authors, and academics who are making new contributions to their fields typically operate at this level. Although this level requires an advanced understanding of a field and sometimes requires the use of sophisticated equipment, young students can successfully learn and apply some of the entry-level methodologies associated with most fields of knowledge (Bruner, 1960). A focus on the acquisition and application of methodology encourages more active learning and an active involvement with a content field.

In the sections which follow, an overview of each menu is provided that includes an outline of the menu options, examples, and directions for application. For details on the items included at each level of the model, see *The Multiple Menu Model* by Renzulli, Leppien, and Hays (2000).

THE STRUCTURE OF THE KNOWLEDGE MENU

The Multiple Menu Model provides curriculum developers with a set of practical planning guides or menus to help them combine authentic knowledge with instructional techniques. Each menu represents the knowledge segments that will form the basis for a curricular unit, lesson, or lesson segment, and the various instructional techniques that will enable the knowledge to be taught in an interesting and effective manner.

Using the Knowledge Menu

The Multiple Menu Model focuses on inquiry, asking curriculum developers to select the most important concepts and ideas to share with learners. The Knowledge Menu requires educators to examine a discipline from four perspectives: its location and organization within the larger context of knowledge, its underlying principles and concepts, its methodology, and its most representative topics and contributions to the universe of knowledge and wisdom. These perspectives become the components of the instructional unit. The first three sections or perspectives of the Knowledge Menu are considered "tools." The final section represents the topics within any field to which the tools may be applied as one goes about the process of "studying" a topic.

Section I—Structure of Knowledge: Helping Students Understand the Location, Definition, and Organization of a Field of Knowledge

Teachers designing curriculum units based on the Multiple Menu Model must first locate the targeted discipline in the larger domain of knowledge in order to provide students with an overview of the unique perspectives that each discipline or field of study offers in understanding complex phenomena. Next, teachers should examine with their students the characteristics of the discipline and its subdivisions to learn why people study a particular area of knowledge and what they hope to contribute to human understanding. This first dimension of the Knowledge Menu helps students examine questions such as:

- "What is sociology?"
- "What do sociologists study and why?"
- "How is sociology similar to and different from other disciplines; e.g., psychology and anthropology?"
- "What, then, is social psychology or social anthropology?"
- "How does each fit into the larger picture and purpose of social sciences?"

These questions about the structure of the discipline help students gain an understanding not only of where the discipline is located, but also the discipline's connectedness with other disciplines.

Relationships within a discipline and between disciplines can be best illustrated by using teacher and student graphic organizers, or Knowledge Trees, such as the example provided in Figure 27.1.

Curriculum writers can also organize a series of instructional activities that provide an overview and address introductory questions about the specific field of study such as the following:

1. How is this field of study defined?
2. What is the overall purpose or mission of this field of study?
3. What are the major areas of concentration of each subdivision?
4. What kinds of questions are asked in the subdivisions?
5. What are the major sources of data in each subdivision?
6. How is knowledge organized and classified in this field or subdivision?
7. What are the basic reference resources in the field or subdivision?
8. What are the major professional journals?

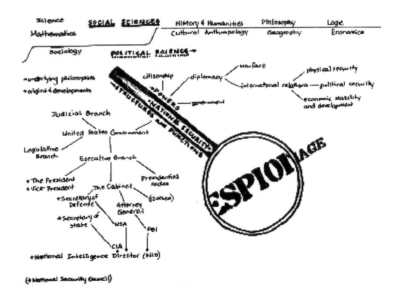

Fig. 27.1 Knowledge tree for unit on espionage.

Reprinted with permission from Real Patriot Games by Ann Murdock. © 2006, Creative Learning Press.

9. What are the major data bases? How can we gain access to them?
10. Is there a history or chronology of events that will lead to a better understanding of the field or subdivision?
11. Are there any major events, persons, places, or beliefs that are predominant concerns of the field, or best-case examples of what the field is all about?
12. What are some selected examples of "insiders' knowledge" such as field-specific humor, trivia, abbreviations and acronyms, "Meccas," scandals, hidden realities, or unspoken beliefs?

Introductory activities should motivate students to study a particular field and help them develop an interest. For example, a fourth grade teacher effectively introduced her students to the study of anthropology by bringing in pictures, artifacts, and stories from another culture. She then showed a video of a group of cultural anthropologists researching the ways members of a culture view their world. Through the video, she was able to prompt students to explore the following questions, escalating the level of interest in anthropology, and setting the stage for future learning:

• What is human about human beings, and how do we get those qualities?
• What are the common characteristics of different cultures?
• How does a culture change to accommodate different ideas and beliefs?
• What is valued in a culture?

She asked her students to look through the artifacts and speculate on the stories they might tell about a culture and how their own culture tells something about their beliefs, values, and traditions. Eventually, she wanted the students to use the skills of an anthropologist to study a culture, and to consider their own culture, and how the culture helps define who they are.

The outcome of this particular segment of the Knowledge Menu should lead students into an examination of the questions listed above, in each case with regard to a specific field or subdivision of the field around which a curricular unit is being developed. Not every question needs to be explored, nor should this section of the Knowledge Menu necessarily be considered a major focus of the unit of study. Rather, the purpose is to help learners see the "big picture" and the interrelationships that might exist between a field or discipline in general and its various subdivisions. This section of the Knowledge Menu is also designed to provide an overview of the field of study. A teacher might deal with the question, "What are the major areas of concentration of each subdivision?" in a relatively superficial way during the early stages of a unit, but when the last section of the Knowledge Menu (Representative Topics) is reached, this topic may become a focus of interest in the study of a particular subdivision.

Section II—Identifying the Basic Principles and Functional Concepts: Helping Students Get the Big Idea

The second dimension of planning the instructional unit focuses on identifying and selecting the most important ideas in a particular field of study that need to be explored by the students. Every field of knowledge is built on a set of basic principles and key concepts which help facilitate comprehension, information processing, and communication of information representative of the essence of the field. These principles and concepts consist of themes, patterns, main features, sequences, and structures that define an area of study. Some of these principles and concepts are applicable to several subdivisions within a given field, but ordinarily the subdivisions have a few concepts unique to that branch of knowledge. Indeed, subdivisions of major fields of knowledge probably come into being because of unique concepts (as well as other factors) that result in the establishment of a field's individual identity.

Basic principles are generally agreed-upon truths that have been arrived at through rigorous study and research. Principles are often stated as relationships among concepts: they concisely summarize a great deal of information; and they have the potential to provide information applicable to diverse situations. Principles may be factual and concrete (e.g., in order to survive, a civilization must be able to answer the basic biological needs of its members: food, drink, shelter, and medical care); or abstract and open to various interpretations (e.g., each culture views the physical environment in a unique way, prizing aspects of it that may be different from those prized by others). When carefully worded, these statements can be used by teachers as the organizational framework of a curricular unit. Principles help learners to probe the "big ideas" of a discipline and help teachers get to the heart of the content. When teachers carefully consider these principles as the central organizers of the unit, they are better equipped to explain to students the relevance of the content.

Functional concepts (Ward, 1960) are the intellectual instruments or tools with which a subject-area specialist works. In many ways, these concepts serve as the vocabulary of a field and the vehicles by which scholars communicate precisely with one another. Concepts are powerful organizers of meaning that help to label and make sense of large quantities of information within a field of knowledge. Unlike facts, which are limited to specific situations, concepts are broad enough to apply to many sets of conditions. A good way to identify the functional concepts of a field is to examine the glossary from a basic textbook in that field or highlighted words in a teacher's instructional manual.

Brandwein (1987) explains the difference between constructing curriculum that focuses on topics, and those that are designed around conceptual ideas:

> A concept opens up a variety of experience, of intelligible content. It leads to analysis and synthesis. It is not concepts but encyclopedic "topics" that tend to be rigid and confined in sequence. A topic can be "lectured." A concept is "sought" and perhaps "caught" in good time. One can "finish" a topic; a concept grows. In fact, in teaching say[,] history or economics, a topical sequence is extremely rigid, for it states inflexibly the body of knowledge that is meant to be "covered." A conceptual sequence, on the contrary, allows for variety, for comparison, and contrast, for exploration and discovery. It depends on problem-posing that varies within the idiosyncratic modes of inquiry.
>
> (Brandwein, 1987, p. 36)

In this section of the Knowledge Menu, curriculum writers determine which basic principles and functional concepts will become the focus of the instructional unit. Teachers must ask themselves important questions as they begin the curriculum planning process: "What is it that I am trying to teach an understanding of? What is it about cultures (for example) that I want my students to understand?" After selecting these principles and concepts, the curriculum writer can then begin to create a series of learning experiences that will help students uncover the meaning behind these conceptual ideas. The learning experiences should motivate students to explore, discover, examine, question, and scrutinize the principles and concepts so that they render meaning for the students; they should not simply mention or cover the concepts in some artificial manner. Developing a unit in which students construct an understanding of a discipline's principles and concepts helps students to apply and transfer understanding to other topics and other disciplines.

Section III—Knowledge About Methodology: Helping Students Act Like Practicing Professionals

The third section of the instructional unit focuses on designing instructional activities that engage students in exploring research methods common to a particular field of study (e.g., in a study of plants, activities that lead students to use methods and procedures used by a botanist). There are two types of methodologies: general and specific. General methodologies deal with the research methods used by practitioners to seek answers to questions that make contributions to a discipline. Specific how-to methodology is more domain-specific and assists the researcher in completing the more comprehensive tasks outlined above. For example, a student might learn how to conduct a survey in order to locate and construct appropriate data-gathering instruments needed for a research study.

This section of the Knowledge Menu is especially important because it affects the more active instructional techniques a teacher can select to use in his or her unit. By providing students with the know-how of investigative methodology, teachers increase the probability of more inductive or "hands-on" learning experiences. Once students have learned basic information about a field or topic and the procedures for doing some kind of research related to that topic, they can proceed to the application level—the level considered by many to be the highest level of involvement in a field of study. Student investigations may be limited in scope and complexity, and they frequently may follow prescribed scenarios such as the ones typically found in laboratory manuals or how-to books. Nonetheless, including even junior-level investigative activities in a curriculum forces teachers to go beyond the omnipresent didactic mode of instruction—the subject of so much criticism of education (Goodlad, 1984).

It is here that teachers can design learning experiences that will engage students in the methodologies of the discipline being studied. The goal is to place students in situations in which they acquire, manage, and produce information in an organized and systematic fashion by applying the thinking and research processes used to create this knowledge in the first place. When students have acquired a mature understanding of the methodology of the field, they are no longer passive recipients of information; they are able to begin the process of gaining and then generating knowledge within the field.

Section IV—Knowledge About Specifics (Representative Topics): Helping Students Apply Basic Concepts and Principles

In the last dimension of the Knowledge Menu, teachers help students apply the "tools" from Sections I, II, and III to selected representative topics in order to acquire an understanding of a specific discipline's content. Unlike traditional instruction, which asks teachers to cover an entire text by the end of the year or semester, the Multiple Menu Model asks teachers to winnow out from all the possible topics in a field the few that truly represent the field's principles and concepts. By narrowing the scope of information to be taught, a teacher can focus on finding interesting and dynamic issues that maximize student interest, motivation, and enthusiasm about a particular field of study. For example, there are thousands of studies in psychology that deal with principles of animal learning, but an unusually interesting study (e.g., Skinner's famous experiments on classical conditioning with pigeons) might have more motivational power than less dramatic studies, especially if presented through an engaging film or demonstration. Examples of representative topics from six fields of knowledge are listed in Table 27.1.

The following example illustrates how a teacher used carefully selected representative works to teach literary analysis skills both efficiently and in great depth. This teacher explored a concept in literature—tragic heroes—through intensive examination of three prototypical examples (e.g., *The Merchant of Venice, Joan of Arc,* and *The Autobiography of Malcolm X*). Selecting more than one exemplar of the concept allowed for both in-depth analysis and opportunities for students to compare and contrast authors' styles; historical perspectives; ethnic, gender, and cultural differences; and a host of other comparative factors that single selections would prohibit. The aim of the instruction in the beginning stages of the unit was to assist students in understanding the concept of tragic heroes and why it was being studied. One of the main purposes of the first three sections of the Multiple Menu Model is to learn *how* to study tragic heroes; therefore *who* should be studied (i.e., which tragic hero) was less important as long as the hero was representative of the concept. An emphasis on *how* rather than *who* also legitimized a role for students. The pay-off in transfer of learning was to follow up the in-depth coverage with more advanced learning that focused on factors that define the concept of tragic heroes (e.g., characteristics, themes, patterns, etc.). To build on this cognitive understanding of the tragic hero and to apply literary analysis skills, students formed small interest groups to compile categorical lists and biographical summaries of tragic heroes in sports, politics, science, civil rights, religion, the women's movement, arts and entertainment, and other areas in which students expressed special interest. In these small groups, students began to understand the concept in literature known as the tragic hero.

Once students have learned how to analyze a particular concept and after they have explored categorical representatives of the concept, students may show an interest in exploring this area in greater detail (e.g., investigating the lives or exploits of tragic heroes and heroines). The beauty of this approach is that students first gain the "tools" for studying a topic; they can then apply those tools to their own interest area.

Table 27.1 Examples of representative topics

Field	Representative Topics
Botany	Applying the principles of botany in understanding the problems of deforestation in the rain forests.
Geography or History	Applying the concept of regionalization to world geography or world history. In history, students can apply the concept of regionalization in analyzing the South of the United States, or students can apply the concept of regionalization and its effect on voting behavior in a particular area.
Mythology	Exploring how various myths (from various cultures) and descriptions of their main characters reveal cultural belief systems of the past that were largely mysterious.
Cytology	Applying knowledge of the principles and concepts of cells to engage in debates on genetic testing, closing, mutations, etc.
Microbiology	Examining the relationship between the dumping of animal waste and the health of a stream.

THE INSTRUCTIONAL TECHNIQUES MENUS

Engaging students in learning requires a number of critical instructional decisions. Viewed broadly, the Instructional Techniques Menus require educators to consider carefully how learning will take place as students interact with the content. The types of decisions that teachers make regarding which instructional techniques they will use to assist learners in the acquisition and application of knowledge are as important in the curriculum planning process as selecting the content for the instructional unit. The deeper the pool of strategies from which a teacher can select, the more variety he or she can offer students as they set about making meaning from these organized learning experiences. The Instructional Techniques Menus focus on pedagogy, organization, and the sequence of lessons. Specifically, they offer a range of options for engaging students in the process of "uncovering" the authentic content of the Knowledge Menu.

The Instructional Objectives and Student Activities Menu

This combined menu of instructional objectives and student activities is designed to provide a taxonomy of processes and behaviors to be used by learners as they construct knowledge about a discipline. This menu reminds the curriculum designer that in a well-balanced curriculum, activities must address both content and process objectives. The balance provides learners with practice in the spectrum of encoding and recoding activities associated with learning new information. By clarifying the process skills and sharing the objectives of the activities, students learn to identify and control their own thinking patterns and behaviors.

The first category of the menu, *Assimilation and Retention*, deals with information input or pick-up processes. At this level, teachers need to decide how the students will acquire information about a particular event, topic, or concept: Will students take notes as they read a particular book? Will students need to make observations of a particular event and record the information on a chart? The second category, *Information Analysis*, focuses on a broad range of thinking skills that describe the ways in which information can be processed in order to achieve greater levels of understanding. At this level, teachers consider how their students will interact with the information: Will students be asked to compare and contrast pieces of information, tabulate data they have gathered, make predictions based on data they have collected, or summarize information? In the *Information Synthesis and Application* category which deals with the output or products of the thinking process, teachers make decisions to suggest avenues in which students can create new ways of using the information they have gathered or analyzed: Will students use the information to create a new model or explanation, produce a book, make a presentation, or develop a new theory? Evaluation is also an output process, but in this case the focus is on the review and judgment of information in terms of aesthetic, ethical, and functional qualities. Teachers engaging students at this level might generate activities that help students judge the quality of a solution or determine whether something is meritorious. The four categories on this menu are not intended to be used in a linear and sequential fashion. In the real world of thinking and problem solving, one must often cycle back to lower levels of information input and analysis activities in order to improve the scope and quality of the products and judgments.

Instructional Strategies Menu

The next menu, the Instructional Strategies Menu, provides a broad range of teaching strategies representing ways in which teachers organize learning situations (e.g., discussion, dramatization, independent study). A variety of carefully selected instructional strategies from this menu provides students with multiple ways to engage with knowledge and employ the full range of their intellectual abilities and learning styles. The strategies range from highly structured teaching methods to those in which greater degrees of self-directedness are placed upon the learner and may be used in combination with one another.

As is the case with the menus discussed earlier, teachers should make an effort to achieve a balance in the use of these strategies. They should also work to develop curricular experiences for students that favor the less structured end of the instructional strategies continuum. This recommendation is consistent with the emphasis that educators place on both self-directed learning and creative productivity. Finally, teachers should attempt to match certain strategies with particular types of knowledge. Thus, for example, the simulation or role-playing strategy might fit more appropriately with content dealing with a controversial issue, and the programmed instruction strategy would work well with content designed to teach computer operation skills.

Instructional Sequences Menu

The Instructional Sequences Menu is based on the work of major learning theorists (e.g., Ausubel, 1968; Gagné & Briggs, 1979). Ausubel placed considerable stress on meaningful learning, which involves relating the content of the lesson to the student's knowledge base, experiential background, and capacity to learn. He argued that "the most important single factor influencing learning is what the learner already knows. Ascertain this and teach him accordingly." (Ausubel, Novak, & Hanesian, 1968, p. vi). The specific aspects of their work that are reflected in this menu are the organization and sequence of events that help maximize the outcomes of a pre-planned learning activity. This menu differs from the others in that the items are likely to be followed in a sequential fashion. According to Gagné and Briggs (1979), an important consideration in sequencing instruction is to organize material in such a way that the learner has mastered necessary prerequisites. Prerequisites are broadly interpreted to include a favorable attitude toward the material to be learned as well as essential terminology, functional concepts, and basic factual information. It is for this reason that the Instructional Sequences Menu begins with an item that highlights the need for gaining attention and developing motivation. Gagné and Briggs (1979) also emphasize the value of relating present topics to relevant previously learned material and, whenever possible, integrating present topics into a larger framework that will add greater meaning to the topic at hand. This concern is dealt with, in part, through the strategies recommended in the first section of the Knowledge Menu on locating the discipline. Finally, Gagné and Briggs recommend that transfer not be left to chance; instead, curriculum developers should provide links between information learned and other situations in which such information may be applied. In a similar fashion, Ausubel's (1968) theory of meaningful learning maintains that learning is enhanced when students are provided with a preview or overview of the material to be taught and the ways in which the material is organized. These "advance organizers" can be most easily dealt with by making students aware of content and process objectives at the beginning of an instructional sequence, and by connecting specific information back to the concepts and principles selected as the organizing frameworks for the unit. The Instructional Sequences Menu progresses from gaining attention and developing interest and motivation, through informing students about the purposes of the lesson, relating the topic to previously learned material, combining instructional strategies and providing options/suggestions for advanced follow-up, assessing performance, and providing an advanced organizer for subsequent areas of study.

Instructional Products Menu

The Instructional Products Menu deals with the outcomes of learning experiences that the teacher presents. Two kinds of outcomes are likely to emerge during the learning process and are planned for explicitly: concrete products and abstract products. Concrete products are physical constructions which young people create as they investigate the representative topics and interact with the principles, concepts, and methodology of the discipline. These physical constructions may include products such as essays, videos, dramatizations, and experiments. Abstract products include observed behaviors such as increased self-confidence and leadership characteristics in addition to less obvious, but equally important, products such as problem-solving strategies and appreciation of the structures and functions of knowledge. Note that the two kinds of products are mutually reinforcing. As students produce new kinds of concrete products, they will also demonstrate new abstract products, such as methodological skills and self-assurance. Likewise, as self-confidence and leadership opportunities increase, it is likely that students will create additional physical products as well. Curriculum writers can use the items in this menu to generate a variety of concrete and abstract products that will help the learner demonstrate the type of learning that has occurred.

CURRICULUM BY DESIGN: PUTTING IT ALL TOGETHER

As was mentioned at the outset, developing high-quality curriculum is a very challenging task and one that must be guided by a strong theoretical background if the final product is going to be more than a hodgepodge of activities and a jumble of factual information. But curriculum developers are pragmatists and must come up with tangible, practical outcomes. The Multiple Menu Model uses the major underlying theories of knowledge and instruction to create "templates" respecting sound theory, but at the same time provides guidance for the practical tasks of selecting and sequencing content and deciding upon objectives, activities, and outcomes.

The goal of the Multiple Menu Model is to achieve balance and coordination between knowledge and instructional technique, and to proceed from the abstract to the practical in the process of curriculum development. The complexity of the task defies simplification, but a certain amount of efficiency can be introduced into curriculum development by specifying the options that are available with regard to content and process, and by pointing out procedures that can be used for blending together factors that need to be considered simultaneously in the process.

Although the several options that make up the structure of this model are presented in the respective menus, two other conditions are necessary for the effective use of this or any other planning guide. First, the curriculum developer must understand the concepts presented in the menus. The appropriate use of an instructional activity such as extrapolating, or an instructional strategy such as simulation will elude us without practical understanding of both the concepts and how we can put them to work in a learning situation.

The second condition for successful use of this model involves some plan or guide for synthesizing the respective menus at the practical or output level (i.e., actually writing curricular material). Although there is still some controversy about whether knowledge (content) or instructional technique (process) should be the focus of curriculum planning, this model has chosen to place knowledge at the center. At the same time, however, the planning guides built into the model have been structured to encourage curriculum developers to consider each of the Instructional Techniques Menus in conjunction with the preparation of content. Taken collectively, the several menus and planning guides direct consideration of a broad range of options and interrelate the many factors that must be considered to achieve balance and comprehensiveness in curriculum development.

REFERENCES

Ausubel, D. P. (1968). *Educational psychology: A cognitive view*. New York: Holt, Rinehart and Winston.

Ausubel, D. P., Novak, J. D., & Hanesian, H. (1968). *Educational psychology: A cognitive view* (2nd ed.). New York: Holt, Rinehart and Winston.

Brandwein, P. (1987). On avenues to kindling wide interests in elementary school: Knowledges and values. *Roeper Review, 10*, 32–40.

Bruner, J. S. (1960). *The process of education*. Cambridge, MA: Harvard University Press.

Gagné, R. M., & Briggs, L. J. (1979). *Principles of instructional design* (2nd ed.). New York: Holt, Rinehart and Winston.

Goodlad, J. I. (1984). *A place called school: Prospects for the future*. New York: McGraw-Hill.

James, W. (1885). On the functions of cognition. *Mind, 10*, 27–44.

Phenix, P. H. (1964). *Realms of meaning*. New York: McGraw-Hill.

Phenix, P. H. (1987, January). *Views on the use, misuse, and abuse of instructional materials*. Paper presented at the Annual Meeting of the Leadership Training Institute on the Gifted and Talented, Houston, Texas.

Renzulli, J. S., Leppien, J. H., & Hays, T. (2000). *The Multiple Menu Model*. Storrs, CT: Creative Learning Press.

Ward, V. S. (1960). Systematic intensification and extensification of the school curriculum. *Exceptional Children, 28*, 67–71, 77.

Whitehead, A. N. (1929). The rhythm of education. In A. N. Whitehead (Ed.), *The aims of education*. New York: Macmillan.

28

DEPTH AND COMPLEXITY

Sandra N. Kaplan

BACKGROUND

References to depth and complexity applied to gifted education can be traced throughout time within the literature. These references address depth and complexity as a curricular concept, instructional technique, and/or programmatic feature. Increased variety and depth of subjects, to accommodate the "apt student with more indepthful subject matter" was advocated in the 1962 document *The Gifted Student: A Manual for Program Improvement* (Southern Regional Project for Education of the Gifted, 1962). Martinson (1968) addressed the need to respond to the "complex array of multiple interests" that gifted students manifest by addressing the inclusion of new and appropriate fields of knowledge (depth) beyond fact, detail, and repetition. The California Department of Education (1971) advocated that "the gifted learners (mathematics) curriculum as a whole achieve depth, provide selective emphasis, and promote in children a desire for complexities beyond the requirements of the standard curriculum," and generally provide "movement in depth" and progression to deeper understanding as an element of enrichment in any subject. Complexity has been defined recently by Rogers (2002, p. 89) as a content modification strategy "providing more difficult and intricately detailed content."

Funded by a 1994 U.S. Department of Education Javits Grant awarded to the California Department of Education, the Open GATE initiative provided the impetus for representatives from the state department of education and field experts in gifted education to tackle the issue in relation to the expectations that should be held to educate gifted and high-achieving students in the state. Within the context of this discussion, the Open Gate committee addressed the question: What is depth and complexity as it relates to differentiating curriculum for gifted and high-achieving students? The original answer to this question, outlined in the publication *Differentiating the Core Curriculum and Instruction to Provide Advanced Learning Opportunities* (California Department of Education [CDE] & California Association for the Gifted [CAG], 1994) together with the additional research and development supported by Javits Grants awarded to the University of Southern California (1996, #R206A970006; and 2004, #S206A040072-07), and the professional development opportunities provided by the CAG have been instrumental in redefining and refining the dimensions of depth and complexity as they are presented in their current forms.

The Prompts of Depth and Complexity

The collection of prompts (see Figure 28.1) distinguished by their affiliation to either the category of depth or that of complexity were derived from a variety of sources: recognized sophisticated and rigorous advanced curricula provided to gifted learners; analysis of the expectations of the disciplines and the anticipated expertise held by disciplinarians (leaders in those disciplines); and the conventional wisdom of educators of the gifted concerning the academic needs of gifted students. The differences between depth and complexity have been defined in terms of purpose.

The prompts of depth presented in their original and sequential form require the learner to recognize the simple versus difficult, concrete versus abstract, and explicit versus implicit differences in the application of the labeled set of depth prompts. The prompts associated with complexity require understanding of the intricacies of subject matter. The complexity set of prompts demands that the learner examine content in multiple dimensions in order to comprehend it.

FACILITATING THE UNDERSTANDING OF DEPTH AND COMPLEXITY

The original discussion about strategies for differentiation was narrative in nature and included Acceleration and Novelty in addition to Depth and Complexity. These became the basic features to modify the standard-based curriculum for gifted and high-achieving students. The explicit descriptions of the prompts and their accompanying graphic forms (see Figure 28.1) were derived by asking and answering this question: How can the narrative of depth and complexity be transformed into professional development experiences that facilitate the teachers' competencies to affect students' learning of these prompts?

While the prompts are primarily verbally and visually displayed, some teachers have transformed the prompts into graphic organizers (see Figure 28.2) or retrieval charts, thus allowing students to use the configuration of the prompt as a template to answer a question or complete a task.

The concept of prompts as a distinctive cognitive organizational symbol or structure that becomes a "mechanism of thought and/or action" (Ausubel & Fitzgerald, 1961) has been discussed and practiced for years. Ausubel & Fitzgerald articulate these cognitive structures as a prior experience to facilitate the transfer of the cognitive structure to influence new learning. Prompts also have been fundamental in promoting reflection and thus knowledge integration. Davis (2003) describes direct prompts as instrumental to focus student attention on specific types of reflection because they are specific and contextualized.

The translation of theory to practice by teachers is hampered by numerous factors. Noted among these are the positive learning responses of students to the teacher's presentations of a concept or skill which reinforce and often justify the teacher's decision to repeat that successful learning experience rather than provide for differing or new forms of learning experiences. To mediate this situation, a "depth and complexity" scope and sequence have been formulated (see Figure 28.3) to provide students with increasing

ICONS	PROMPT	KEY QUESTIONS	THINKING SKILLS	RESOURCES
	LANGUAGE OF THE DISCIPLINES	What terms or words are specific to the work of the _____? (disciplinarian) What tools does the _____ use? (disciplinarian)	• categorize • identify	• texts • biographies
	DETAILS	What are its attributes? What features characterize this? What specific elements define this? What distinguishes this from other things?	• identify traits • describe • differentiate • compare/contrast • prove with evidence • observe	• pictures • diaries or journals • poetry
	PATTERNS	What are the reoccurring events? What elements, events, and ideas are repeated over time? What was the order of events? How can we predict what will come next?	• determine relevant vs. irrelevant • summarize • make analogies • discriminate between same and different • relate	• time lines • other chronological lists
	TRENDS	What ongoing factors have influenced this study? What factors have contributed to this study?	• prioritize • determine cause and effect • predict • relate • formulate questions • hypothesize	• journals • newspapers • graphs • charts

ICONS	PROMPT	KEY QUESTIONS	THINKING SKILLS	RESOURCES
	UNANSWERED QUESTIONS	What is still not understood about this area, topic, study, or discipline? What is yet unknown about this area, topic, study, or discipline? In what ways is the information incomplete or lacking in explanation?	• recognize fallacies • note ambiguity • distinguish fact vs. fiction and opinion • formulate questions • problem solve • identify missing information • test assumptions	• multiple and varied resources • comparative analyses of auto-biographical and current nonfiction articles, etc.
	RULES	How is this structured? What are the stated and unstated causes related to the description or explanation of what we are studying?	• generalize • hypothesize • judge credibility	• editorials • essay • laws • theories
	ETHICS	What dilemmas or controversies are involved in this area, topic, study, or discipline? What elements can be identified that reflect bias, prejudice, and discrimination?	• judge with criteria • determine bias	• editorials • essays • autobiographies • journals
	BIG IDEAS, GENERALIZATIONS, PRINCIPLES, AND THEORIES	What overarching statement best describes what is being studied? What general statement includes what is being studied?	• prove with evidence • generalize • identify the main idea	• quotations • discipline-related essays
	OVER TIME	How are ideas related between the past, present, and future? How are these ideas related within or during a particular time period? How has time affected the information? How and why do things change or remain the same?	• relate • sequence • order	• time lines • text • biographies • autobiographies • historical documents
	DIFFERENT POINTS OF VIEW	What are the opposing viewpoints? How do different people and characters see this event or situation?	• argue • determine bias • classify	• biographies • autobiographies • mythologies and legends vs. non-fiction accounts • debates

ICONS	PROMPT	KEY QUESTIONS	THINKING SKILLS	RESOURCES
	Interdisciplinary	How are these subject areas related? What idea connects these areas?	• Relate • Justify • Associate • Correlate	• print and non-print references • Fiction and non-fiction

Fig. 28.1 Defining the prompts of depth and complexity.

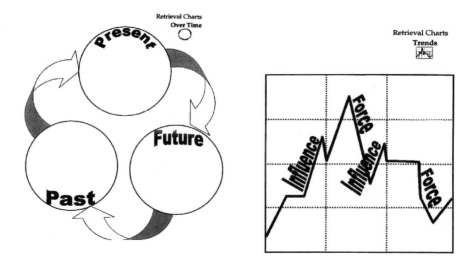

Fig. 28.2 Using the prompts of depth and complexity as graphic organizers.

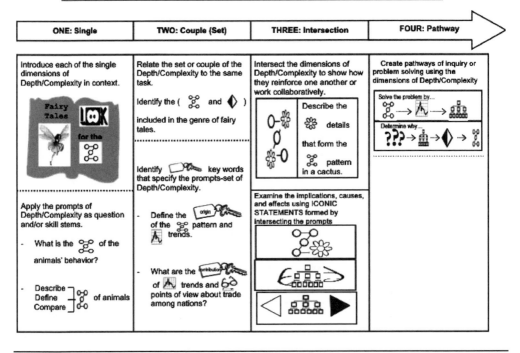

Fig. 28.3 Constructing a scope and sequence to teach the prompts of depth and complexity within and across grade levels.

levels of sophisticated understanding of the prompts and their application. This scope and sequence were designed to promote comprehensive and multiple opportunities to operationalize the prompts within and across areas of study, with the intent also to provide teachers with directionality for teaching the prompts over various time periods. Critical to the use of the scope and sequence is determining how the scope and sequence govern decisions to teach the prompts within a class, across grade levels, or within a curriculum or program. Such decisions are contingent on the alignment of the prompts of depth and complexity to decisions as to what curricular elements constitute differentiated curriculum and the developmental appropriateness of the differentiated curriculum to the learners.

Application of the Prompts of Depth and Complexity

The pacing, integration, and pedagogy used to introduce the prompts of depth and complexity are fundamental to the students' assimilation and application of this material (see Table 28.1). Determining when to introduce the prompts of depth and complexity

Table 28.1 Aligning the prompts of depth and complexity to different stages of student development

Stages of Development	Pacing Exemplars	Integration Exemplars	Pedagogical Exemplars
Students without any previous awareness of the prompts	Introduce individually the prompts from those that are simple to those that are more sophisticated (e.g., language of the discipline to big ideas)	Integrate each prompt individually with previously taught content to reduce the anxiety filter or the need for the students to address the new prompt with newly introduced content or skills. Introduce a new prompt only as students demonstrate verbal or written evidence of understanding and applying the prompt previously introduced.	Use teacher-directed modeling or demonstrations to identify, define, and integrate the prompt with content for students to observe. Provide multiple practice experiences that utilize the prompt with acquired content knowledge from various disciplines.
Students with prior knowledge of the prompts	Determine the students' readiness to identify and relate a prompt to a stated question or task: Which prompt would best assist you in understanding the reasons why an author would repeatedly present an idea or action of a character?	Apply the prompts as singletons or sets to comprehend, investigate, and/or analyze new subject matter. Relate the introduction of the newly introduced individual or set of prompts with critical, creative, logical or problem-solving skills: How can details provide evidence to prove a particular point of view?	Initiate the comprehension and usability of the prompt as a stimulus for inquiry: Look at the patterns illustrating trade routes on the map. What questions do these patterns cause you to ask and investigate?
Students who have evidenced mastery of the meaning and application of both the prompts of depth and complexity	Define learning experiences that enable the students to apply the prompts as sets and pathways to problem solve and/or conduct independent studies.	Relate the various prompts to the disciplines and the work of the disciplinarians: Where in the study of astrophysics would the use of trends and change of time become relevant?	Provide the outline for conducting a project, action research and/or independent study as the source for applying the prompts.

depends on the learners and the context. Importantly, the use of the prompts should provide the students with the opportunities to move from teacher-dependent to student-directed learning experiences.

The primary purpose underlying the prompts of depth and complexity is their relationship to fostering the acquisition and assimilation of subject matter and the mastery of skills. To this end, there is a series of steps that the teacher traverses in order to accomplish the goal of developing a curriculum unit or lesson.

1. Translation of the standard into a differentiated objective (see Figure 28.4) by selecting the prompts responsive both to the intent of the standard, the assessed needs, interests, and abilities of the gifted population, and the dimensions of a differentiated curriculum.
2. Selection of a pedagogical practice to implement the objective is dependent on identifying the relationship between the how (or instructional strategy) and the what (or subject matter) of the objective (see Table 28.2). The pedagogical practices are purposefully decided based on the roles the teacher and students will assume,

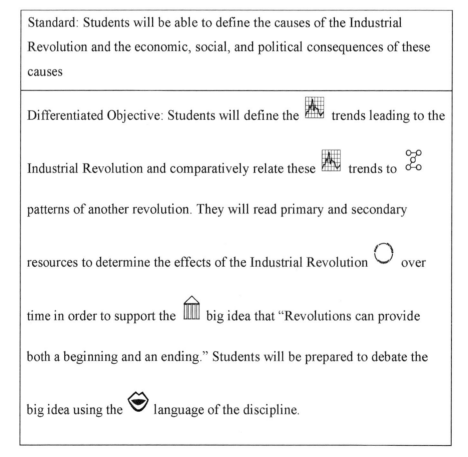

Fig. 28.4 Integrating the prompts of depth and complexity in the formation of an objective.

Table 28.2 Relationship of depth and complexity to pedagogical practices

TEACHER/STUDENT ROLES	INSTRUCTIONAL MODE	AFFECTIVE OUTCOME
Teacher-directed responsibility	Direct instruction	Student dependency and "appreciation" of modeling and practice
Teacher and student shared responsibility	Deductive and inductive reasoning	Student and teacher collaboration in the teaching/learning act
Student-directed responsibility	Inquiry	Student independence in learning how to learn

the instructional mode the teacher and students will emphasize, and the affective as well as the cognitive nature of the outcome.

The following is a template that illustrates how teachers can plan an inquiry lesson incorporating the prompts of depth and complexity. While it is recognized that there is no one right way to integrate the prompts into a lesson, the template serves as a guide as the teacher assumes the role of a curriculum designer or developer.

LESSON PLANS

This articulated lesson shows how a standard-based lesson is differentiated to include a range of depth and complexity prompts (see Figure 28.5). An important feature of the lesson is to note how the prompts of depth and complexity provide the "scaffolding" for students engaging in an academically rigorous lesson. In his theory of the zone of proximal development, Vygotsky (1978) stated the value of providing scaffolding as a means to move students from the known to the unknown and the familiar to the unfamiliar in order to achieve an intended goal. In this lesson, the prompts function as scaffolding (see Figure 28.6) providing the linguistic and non-linguistic cues or stimuli to scaffold the students within their zone of proximal development.

THE EVIDENCE

A pre- and post-tested quantitative study (unpublished) with gifted and non-gifted children in the second to fourth grades was conducted (in 2009) to discern the effects of a selected set of depth and complexity prompts (language of the discipline, details, patterns, points of view, ethics, and big ideas) on understanding social studies and language arts content areas in an urban Title 1 elementary school (serving students aged 5–11). The results indicate positive effects for students in terms of overall improvement in understanding the content areas using the selected set of depth and complexity prompts. While both gifted and non-gifted students showed improvement in using the prompts between the pre-test and the post-test, the academic gains of gifted students were greater in both content areas using these prompts: details, patterns, points of view, ethics, and big ideas. Non-gifted students showed more growth using the prompts of language of the discipline and patterns in the language arts content area. The differences between the gifted and non-gifted responses could be attributed to the fact that the language of the discipline and patterns are skills more readily mastered by gifted students in the area of reading. Teachers reacted to this specific result by commenting that one of the

LESSON PLAN

Date:_____

Subject:_____

Model of Teaching: **Inquiry – GROUP INVESTIGATION**

Standard:

Objective:

Syntax	Activity	Integration
Present the Puzzlement	Present a set of pictures depicting a problem, scene, situation, individual and/his/her work that stimulates curiosity about a selected standards-based topic: Ask students to look at the **details** of the picture.	Details
Solicit Questions from Students	Introduce the key words: *attribute, conditions,* etc. as STEMS to formulate questions about the picture set. Examples: a) Why are the people so unhappy (*conditions*?) b) What is the *purpose* or *value* of the object they are holding?	 Attributes Conditions Function Value
Research	Instruct students to identify **details** from the defined research materials and sources to answer their questions. Investigate trends that emerge from analysis of the research.	Details Trends
Share/ Summarize	Introduce a retrieval chart to record students' answers to their questions. | Question			
Answer			| Identify **patterns** reflective of the information recorded on the chart.	Patterns Rules
Recycle	Ask students what other **questions** they have that are still **unanswered** and record these questions for future study. Summarize findings to identify a **point of view**.	Unanswered Questions Points of View

Fig. 28.5 Integrating the prompts of depth and complexity in an inquiry lesson (group investigation model of teaching).

characteristics of giftedness has been advanced language development and decoding or recognizing and analyzing patterns.

A historic perspective on differentiation indicates that both the past and the present seem to advocate for principles such as depth and complexity to constitute an appropriate curriculum for the gifted. It should be clear that the concept of depth and complexity

(a)

Literary Critical Analysis Lesson-Model of Teaching: Advance Organizer

Grades: All grades

Standard(s): Language Arts – Literary Response and Analysis

Objective:

Students will define the ❀ details and ☍ patterns used in the presentation of literary elements (character, setting, problem, resolution) as a means of evoking or sustaining reader *interest* and *attention* in a story. Students will discuss and chart their responses.

Syntax	Learning Experiences
Motivation	Provide students with the formal definition of *interest*: a degree of attraction toward something.
	Form an Interest Measure as depicted on this chart:
	Interest Measure
	no interest / some interest / much interest
	Use the Interest Measure to discuss this set of topics:
* please see the end of the lesson for full-size printouts	Music Aliens Snow in the desert Friends Oceanography
	Introduce the concept of <u>Motivation</u> as a "push and pull theory:" *push* meaning the inner drive to express self and make sense of the world and *pull* meaning the environmental stimuli or factors that define or influence our behavior.

(b)

	Instruct students to read the passage to determine what feature of the passage "pushes" or "pulls" their motivation to attend to and become interested in this passage.
	A Spooky Night
	Jack was out one spooky October night, skipping through the park.
	Jack heard a strange sound coming from behind a tree, and decided to go and investigate. Jack slowly crept up to the tree.
	All of a sudden, a shiny cat jumped out singing 'Joy to the World'. The strangest thing about the cat was the red and yellow striped sock it wore on its head.
	The only thing that Jack could say was "Gezundheit!"
	Present these pictures to the students:
	Instruct students to view the pictures and respond to the question: Which picture captures your interest and attention?
	Discuss why one picture versus the other **grabs attention** or **interest**.
Introduce the Advance Organizer	Present the students with this big idea. 🏛
	"Change to the opposite of probability" grabs interest and attention. (Aristotle)
	Discuss the meaning of the big idea. 🏛 Discuss the use of language of the discipline ◠ in the context of the big idea. 🏛

(c)

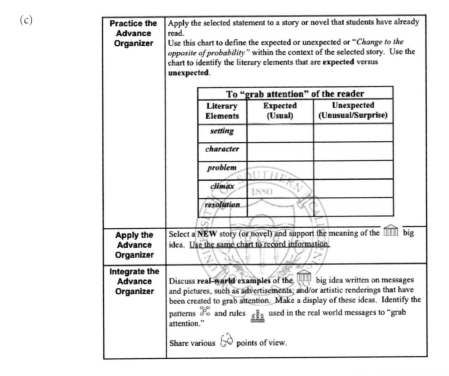

	Apply the selected statement to a story or novel that students have already read.
Practice the Advance Organizer	Use this chart to define the expected or unexpected or *"Change to the opposite of probability"* within the context of the selected story. Use the chart to identify the literary elements that are **expected** versus **unexpected**.

To "grab attention" of the reader		
Literary Elements	**Expected (Usual)**	**Unexpected (Unusual/Surprise)**
setting		
character		
problem		
climax		
resolution		

Apply the Advance Organizer	Select a **NEW** story (or novel) and support the meaning of the ▥ big idea. Use the same chart to record information.
Integrate the Advance Organizer	Discuss real-world examples of the ▥ big idea written on messages and pictures, such as advertisements, and/or artistic renderings that have been created to grab attention. Make a display of these ideas. Identify the patterns ⚬⚬ and rules ⛪ used in the real world messages to "grab attention." Share various 👁 points of view.

Fig. 28.6 Integrating the prompts of depth and complexity into an advance organizer model of teaching.

as integral features of a differentiated curriculum is not new. What is new is the presentation of the prompts of depth and complexity and the specific ways in which they have been developed and utilized in response to the needs, interests, and abilities of gifted students and the design of a differentiated curriculum.

REFERENCES

Ausubel, D. P, & Fitzgerald, D. (1961). Meaningful learning and retention: Intrapersonal cognitive variables. *Review of Educational Research, 31,* 500–510.

California Department of Education. (1971). *Principles, objectives and curricula for programs in the education of mentally gifted minors: Kindergarten through grade twelve.* Sacramento, CA: Office of State Printing.

California Department of Education, & the California Association for the Gifted. (1994). *Differentiating the core curriculum and instruction to provide advanced learning opportunities.* Sacramento: California Department of Education.

Davis, E. A. (2003). Prompting middle school science students for productive reflection: Generic and directed prompts. *The Journal of the Learning Sciences, 12,* 91–142.

Martinson, R. A. (1968). *Curriculum enrichment for the gifted in the primary grades.* Upper Saddle River, NJ: Prentice-Hall.

Moll, L. C. (1990). *Vygotsky and education: Instructional implications and applications of sociohistorical psychology instruction.* New York: Cambridge: University Press.

Rogers, K. B. (2002). *Re-forming gifted education: How parents and teachers can match the program to the child.* Scottsdale, AZ: Great Potential Press.

Southern Regional Project for Education of the Gifted. (1962). *The gifted student: A manual for program improvement.* Atlanta, GA: Southern Regional Education Board.

Vygotsky, L. S. (1978). *Mind in society: The development of higher psychological processes.* Cambridge, MA: Harvard University Press.

29

DIFFERENTIATED INSTRUCTION

Carol Ann Tomlinson

The idea of differentiated instruction is an old one. The writings of Confucius note that learners differ in their gifts and talents and that to teach them well, the teacher must start where the individuals are. A century or more ago, one-room schoolhouses across the United States almost inevitably called on teachers to differentiate instruction in a single classroom that typically housed students between the ages of six and 16. Teachers in multi-age classrooms have, for decades, by intent and necessity practiced differentiation. More recently, models such as Universal Design for Learning and Response to Intervention (RtI) guide teachers in planning for and teaching with student differences in the forefront of their work. It is likely that most parents practice some sort of differentiation as they discover how remarkably different two or three or four children in the same family can be. All of these examples are rooted in the observations that, inconvenient as it might be, humans vary as learners, and that to help them develop as fully as possible, the adults in their lives need to know them and respond to them, at least to some meaningful degree, on the learners' own terms. What this chapter will refer to as "differentiated instruction" is a more contemporary framework based on those same observations and rooted in research from multiple facets of education. This chapter will provide an overview of differentiation and the roles it might play in education of high-ability and high-potential learners.

DIFFERENTIATED INSTRUCTION

As is often the case with the vocabulary of education, the term "differentiated instruction" is used in a variety of ways. In this chapter, the term will be used to refer to an instructional model that provides guidance for teachers in addressing student differences in readiness, interest, and learning profile, with the goal of maximizing the capacity of each learner (e.g., Tomlinson, 1999, 2001, 2004; Tomlinson & Imbeau, 2010; Tomlinson & McTighe, 2006). The model positions instruction as one of the key elements in a classroom system of interdependent parts—learning environment, curriculum, assessment, and instruction. It emphasizes the importance of the quality of each element in student success.

Figure 29.1 (below), a concept map of differentiation, provides a visual representation of the key elements in the model of differentiation. It indicates that:

- Differentiation, at its core, is a teacher attempting to study and respond appropriately to learner variance.
- A teacher's implementation of differentiation is shaped by his/her mindset or beliefs about ability and potential.
- Differentiation is guided by key principles and practices such as community, quality curriculum, ongoing assessment to inform instruction, flexible grouping, respectful tasks, and teaching up.
- Teachers can modify or differentiate content (what students are expected to learn), process (how students gain access to, explore, and express what they are expected to learn), products (how students demonstrate what they have learned after extended periods of learning), and learning environment (both the physical and affective nature of the classroom), based on student needs.
- The student needs for which teachers may differentiate instruction include readiness, interest, and learning profile.
- There are a variety of instructional strategies that can be effective tools in helping teachers plan for and address learner variance.

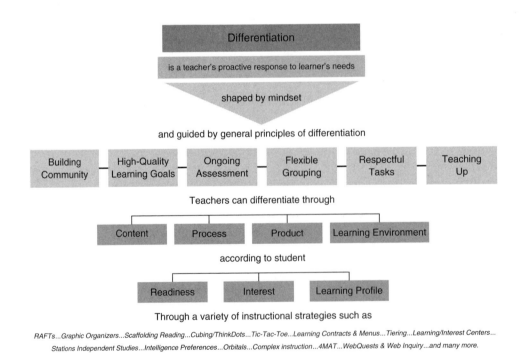

Fig. 29.1 A concept map of a model of differentiated instruction.

Carole Ann Tomlinson. *The Differentiated Classroom: Responding to the Needs of All Learners.* Alexandria, VA: ASCD, 1999, p. 15.

© 1999, ASCD. Reprinted with permission.

Differentiation is *not* a specific set of instructional strategies, but rather a way of thinking about teaching and learning that places students in the foreground of teacher thinking and planning. Built on the premise that each learner needs and deserves a teacher who values them enough to work diligently at maximizing that student's possibilities, differentiation asks teachers to consider ways in which they can shape all key classroom elements separately and collectively to benefit the varied students they teach.

EVIDENCE SUPPORTING DIFFERENTIATED INSTRUCTION

The model of differentiation discussed in this chapter is not so much a single entity as a synthesis of practices from a variety of educational specialties. For that reason, evidence for the practices the model commends comes from a variety of sources. Following is a capsule of some (but by no means all) research on various aspects of the model as well as a sampling of findings from examination of impacts of the full model of differentiation.

Research on Impacts of Addressing Student Readiness

The term "readiness" is not a synonym for ability, but rather a measure of a learner's current proximity to particular learning goals. Theories from psychology and neuroscience propose that a student learns best when tasks are moderately challenging for that student—neither unreasonably demanding nor too familiar. When tasks are too stringent, students become frustrated. When tasks are too easy, students are bored. In both instances, learning is diminished. Students learn best when tasks are at a degree of difficulty that moderately challenges a particular learner, and when a support system is present to help the student succeed at a new and slightly higher level of proficiency (e.g., Csikszentmihalyi, Rathunde, & Whalen, 1993; Howard, 1994; Jensen, 1998; National Research Council, 1999; Sousa & Tomlinson, 2010; Vygotsky, 1962, 1978; Willis, 2006).

Studies related to the match between learner readiness and learning tasks suggest:

- When teachers diagnose students' readiness relative to learning goals and provide work appropriate for students' readiness needs, achievement increases. Further, when students work in classrooms that support achievement of new learning at a high rate of success, students feel better about themselves and the subject in addition to increasing their learning (Fisher et al., 1980).
- Students learn more effectively when the structure of a particular task matches a student's level of development (Hunt, 1971).
- Students under-challenged by tasks demonstrate low involvement in learning activities and lessening of concentration. Students whose skills are inadequate for the level of challenge required by tasks demonstrate low achievement as well as a diminished sense of self-worth (Csikszentmihalyi et al., 1993).
- Students in multi-age classrooms where teachers differentiate instruction perform better than students in single-grade classrooms on 75 percent of measures used (Miller, 1990) and show benefits compared to peers in single-grade classrooms in study habits, social interaction, cooperation, and attitude toward school, as well as achieving at or above the level of single-grade counterparts (Gayfer, 1991; Veenman, 1996).

A study of 57 non-graded classrooms found achievement results favoring the non-graded classrooms in 58 percent of settings reviewed, found non-graded classrooms at least as effective as graded ones in 33 percent of settings reviewed, and favored graded classrooms in only 9 percent of settings reviewed. Mental health components favored the non-graded classrooms as well. Researchers noted that effects become more positive the longer students stay in such settings (Anderson & Pavan, 1996).

Research Related to Impacts of Addressing Student Interest

"Interest" refers to a student's proclivity or inclination for a topic or subject. Theory related to the role of interest in learning proposes that when a student finds learning interesting, learning is more likely to feel rewarding and the learner is more likely to function autonomously. When teachers help students to discover and pursue their interests, their engagement with learning and their productivity increase. In fact, when students experience "flow," or the sense of being absorbed by what they are doing, they are more likely to work harder and to invest in developing the skills necessary to complete the work successfully. In short, interest feeds motivation, which in turn, supports the habits of mind and work that lead to success (Amabile, 1983; Bruner, 1961; Collins & Amabile, 1999; Csikszentmihalyi, 1990; Sousa & Tomlinson, 2010).

Among research findings supporting attention to student interests are the following:

- Giving students freedom to choose what to work on, questions to pursue, and topics for study establishes the foundation for creative achievement (Collins & Amabile, 1999).
- When teachers engage students in discussing the pleasure of their work in classrooms where learners feel free to exchange ideas and share interests, student motivation can be sustained over extended periods of time (Hennessey & Zbikowski, 1993).
- Student interest is key to building ongoing motivation to pursue tasks at increasing levels of complexity, and satisfaction with earlier tasks is often critical in keeping students engaged with work that is temporarily not interesting to them (Csikszent-mihalyi, 1990).
- When students are interested in what they study, there are positive influences on learning in both the short and long term (Hébert, 1993; Renninger, 1990).

Research Related to Impacts of Addressing Student Learning Profile

The term "learning profile" was coined by the author of this chapter to serve as an umbrella label for four related but generally separate bodies of theory and research focused on differences in the ways that individuals learn. "Learning style" is *not* a synonym for "learning profile," but rather one of four elements that comprise "learning profile." The four bodies of theory and research deal with the differences in approach to learning that may result from learning style, intelligence preference, culture, and gender. What all four sets of writings have in common is a conclusion that individuals approach learning in different ways and these differences can have an impact on student success.

Various theorists propose that:

1. classroom elements (e.g., light, temperature, sound, etc.) can influence student attitudes about learning and their degree of learning success (Dunn, 1996);

2. students' neurological patterns (e.g., language systems, motor systems, sequencing systems, etc.) shape how they learn, and when a classroom is a poor fit for a student's approaches to learning, the student is likely to struggle with school (Levine, 2002);

3. intelligence is manifest in varied spheres, and while the manifestations are fluid, students benefit from instruction that addresses a student's preferences while extending the range of preferences as well (Gardner, 1983; Sternberg, 1985);

4. gender can impact on the way a student approaches learning in the classroom (Eliot, 2009; Gilligan, 1982; Gurian, 2001; Salomone, 2003; Saxe, 2005; Tannen, 1990);

5. culture shapes one's perspectives, points of view, frames of reference, modes of communication, sense of identity, and cognitive style (Storti, 1999; Trumbull, Rothstein-Fish, Greenfield, & Quiroz, 2001).

While it is not appropriate to generalize to a culture, classrooms that favor the cultural patterns of one group and are inhospitable to those of other groups are likely to have negative impacts on the learning of students from the less favored groups (Banks, 1993, 1994; Delpit, 1995; Lasley & Matczynski, 1997). Particular classrooms may also be more beneficial to students from some economic classes than others (Garcia, 1995). It is important to provide a range of materials, processes, and procedures for learning so that students from many backgrounds find classrooms effective places to learn (Educational Research Service, 2003).

Among research findings related to addressing student learning profiles in the classroom are the following:

- Positive learning effects result from addressing students' learning profiles for elementary students, secondary students, students with emotional difficulties, and students with learning disabilities—as well as for Native American, Hispanic, African American, Asian American, and Caucasian students (Dunn & Griggs, 1995).
- Significant attitude and achievement gains for students from a wide range of cultural groups are manifest when learning styles are accommodated (Sullivan, 1993).
- When students' cultural differences are ignored or misunderstood in the classroom, the academic success of students from many "minority" groups is likely to be undermined (Delpit, 1995).
- Students at the primary, elementary, middle, and high school level achieve significantly better than peers in control groups when classroom instruction is matched to their preferred learning patterns (i.e. analytical, creative, practical) (Grigorenko & Sternberg, 1997; Sternberg, 1997; Sternberg, Torff, & Grigorenko, 1998).

A number of experts and scholars in psychology and neuroscience question some aspects of the specific concept of learning style (not the category of learning profile as a whole). The criticism centers *not* so much on whether it is likely that individuals do approach learning differently, but rather on the use of instruments that lack reliability and validity to assess learning style (and hence, the meaningfulness of research results); the misguided practice of assigning students to learning style categories without regard to the variability of learning approaches within an individual; the uneven and sometimes inaccurate use of terminology related to learning style; use of laboratory rather than classroom findings to support theories; and misunderstanding of how the brain learns (Coffield, Moseley, Hall, & Ecclestone, 2004; Pashler, McDaniel, Rohrer, & Bjork, 2008). Reynolds (1997) also suggests that labeling students by learning style can result in discrimination; for example, the inference that students from some cultural groups, for example, are not effective abstract thinkers, thereby justifying decisions not to place them in learning contexts that require this sort of thought. Other experts in psychology and neuroscience find validity in some learning styles approaches (e.g., Lisle, 2006, for a visual–auditory–kinesthetic model) as well as benefit in providing students with options for multi-modal teaching and learning and multiple avenues to learn and express learning (Olshansky, 2008; Willis, 2006).

Research Related to Other Aspects of the Model

In addition to research that supports addressing student readiness, interest, and learning profile in the classroom, other elements in the model of differentiation discussed in this chapter that are related to learning and achievement are also grounded in research. These include:

- the impact of teacher and student mindset regarding the role of ability (Dweck, 2000);
- the importance of teacher–student connections and support (Allen, Gregory, Mikami, Hamre, & Pianta, 2010; Hattie, 2009; Langer, 2000);
- benefits of collaborative versus competitive environments and the importance of classroom cohesion or community (Hattie, 2009);
- focus on understanding and meaningful conceptualization rather than predominately on memorization of information (Donovan, Bransford, & Pellegrino, 1999; Mason, Schroeter, Combs, & Washington, 1992; Wenglinsky, 2002);
- teacher clarity about learning outcomes and clarity in communicating outcomes (Hattie, 2009; Rosenshine & Stevens, 1986);
- setting rich and challenging learning goals for all students (Hattie, 2009; Mason et al., 1992; Wenglinsky, 2002);
- helping students to see relevance and purpose in what they are learning (Anderson, Reder, & Simon, 1996; Pintrich & Schunk, 1996);
- flexible use of small learning groups (Hattie, 2009; Lou et al., 1996);
- use of varied instructional materials for small groups based on the needs of learners in those groups (Kulik & Kulik, 1991; Lou et al., 1996);
- flexible pacing based on learner needs (Ben Ari & Shafir, 1988);
- use of formative evaluation to understand student progress and address student needs (Hattie, 2009);
- use of a wide variety of instructional strategies to scaffold student growth with key knowledge and skill (Borko, Mayfield, Marion, Flexer, & Cumbo, 1997; Cotton, 2000; Palincsar, 1984).

Research on the Model of Differentiation as a Whole

While there is considerable research on specific aspects of the model, only recently have studies examined outcomes when multiple elements in the model are applied, or when the full model of differentiation is used. Among such studies, positive achievement outcomes were reported for:

- five high-achieving, urban, African American first graders with previously low writing achievement (Geisler, Hessler, Gardner, & Lovelace, 2009);
- first graders in Colombia who showed greater gains in oral reading and comprehension than peers in a non-differentiated treatment (Marulanda, Giraldo, & Lopez, 2006);
- students in a Chicago high school who received more differentiation and earned higher ACT Math, English, Reading, and Composite scores than peers in classes that received less differentiation (Rasmussen, 2006); and
- fifth graders in five urban elementary schools randomly assigned to an enriched reading program with differentiation (versus a traditional non-enriched, non-differentiated approach to teaching reading), who scored significantly higher in reading fluency and comprehension than students in the non-treatment classes (Reis, McCoach, Little, Muller, & Kaniskan, 2010).

Three reports of implementing schoolwide differentiation show positive achievement gains across subject areas, grades, and performance levels for students in two elementary and two high schools (Beecher & Sweeny, 2008; Burris & Garrity, 2008; Tomlinson, Brimijoin, & Narvaez, 2008).

There is a need for additional research on the differentiation model as a whole to provide further understanding of the relative importance of each of the model's components on the academic and affective growth of students throughout a spectrum of learners, including highly able and high-potential learners. Such research would also provide insight into teachers' understanding and implementation of the model.

TRAINING AND BACKGROUND NECESSARY FOR EFFECTIVE IMPLEMENTATION OF DIFFERENTIATION

In many ways, this model of differentiation is simply a description of effective, student-focused teaching. Its elements, for example, reflect indicators of expert-level performance in Danielson's (2007) frameworks for teaching and in many research findings related to effective teachers (Stronge, 2007). In that way, the model is an "aspirational" one. In other words, it aims to provide teachers with guidance that can help them systematically grow toward expertise in their profession. Simultaneously, it recognizes that teachers, like students, vary in readiness, interest, and mode of learning, and will therefore begin using the model at varied entry points, progress with its use at varied rates, and require different support systems in developing proficiency in implementing its elements.

The model asks teachers to understand that they teach content to human beings—in other words to be students of *who* they teach as well as *what* they teach. The goal is to connect content and learners, not simply to cover content. To that end, the model requires teachers to attend to four interrelated classroom elements: learning environment, curriculum quality, assessment to inform instruction, and use of multiple instructional strategies and routines to address learners' diverse needs. In each of these areas, some teachers will work at a greater level of competence and confidence, while others will work at more rudimentary levels. Growth in each area and in understanding the interconnectedness of the areas plays a considerable role in a teacher's progression from novice to expert.

According to this model, the learning environment contributes significantly to a student's trust of the teacher, peers, and the learning process. For that reason, the environment needs to be one in which the teacher sees human variability as both normal and desirable, and in which each student feels safe to take the risk of learning. Such an environment is more likely the outcome when:

- students feel accepted and valued as they are;
- students feel challenged to work hard and extend their academic reach;
- the teacher exhibits a growth-mindset belief that hard work is the prescription for learning success rather than inherent ability;
- the teacher connects with students as individuals;
- the teacher exemplifies respect for all students;
- students learn to respect and support one another in the learning process and to work as a community or team of learners;
- the teacher has a clear vision of a classroom in which there is a focus on both individual needs and group needs;
- students come to understand and contribute to the goal of creating a classroom that works for each person in it;
- students share responsibility for classroom operations with the teacher;
- the "geography" of the classroom is designed to support attention to student needs; and
- the teacher works with students to orchestrate a classroom in which routines and procedures allow for individual variance as well as the needs of the class as a whole.

In terms of curriculum, the model asks teachers to:

- use, modify, or create curriculum that helps students focus on understanding content;
- ensure that the curriculum engages students;
- show students the connections between what they are learning and their own lives;
- be clear on precisely what students should know, understand, and be able to do as the result of a segment of learning;
- ensure that students are clear on the essential learning goals;
- show students connections between the knowledge, understanding, and skill designated as essential; and
- "teach up"—that is, teach high-quality, rich curriculum to all students and scaffold students in achieving and exceeding high-level goals, rather than "teaching down" to students they perceive to be less capable and to students whose ceiling of achievement is higher than teachers anticipate.

In regard to assessment, differentiation guides teachers to:

- use pre-assessment of student readiness, interest, and learning profile to understand both the range of students in a class and the needs and strengths of individuals;
- use formative assessment persistently to monitor students' progress toward and beyond designated learning outcomes;

- ensure that pre-assessments and formative assessments of readiness are aligned with specified learning outcomes;
- involve students in analyzing assessment outcomes so they understand themselves better as learners and contribute more dynamically to their own success; and
- use information from formative assessments to shape instructional planning.

Instruction that is effectively differentiated stems from a student-focused environment, high-quality curriculum, and assessment used to guide teacher planning as well as to respond to learners' particular needs. Such instruction is: carefully aligned with essential learning outcomes; informed by ongoing assessment; responds to student readiness, interest, and learning profile at key points in an instructional cycle; uses flexible grouping based on thoughtfully balanced individual, small-group, and whole-class work; ensures that all students have "respectful tasks" (that is, the tasks focus on the same essential understandings, require all students to work at high levels of thought, and are equally appealing to students); and employs a variety of instructional and management strategies to attend to student variance, selected with the nature of the subject and learning goals in mind.

Teachers who become proficient with differentiation generally value students as individuals, enjoy studying their students, find their content worthwhile and enriching, find it rewarding to grow as a person and a professional, and have or find persistent, intelligent support in consistently extending their craft. Teachers progress with implementation of differentiation most markedly when they work with colleagues to understand, plan for, and use the principles and practices of differentiation; and when high-quality professional development on differentiation is sustained over an extended period of time and centered in the classroom (Tomlinson et al., 2008; Wenglinsky, 2002).

It is also important for teachers to learn to work together effectively in generalist/specialist teams in many of the same ways as physicians work as teams of general practitioners and specialists. A specialist in gifted education, for example, can help classroom teachers grow in their knowledge about, understanding of, and adaptations for both high-performing and high-potential learners. Students whose teachers have sustained professional development on working with varied populations of learners academically outperform students whose teachers do not (Wenglinsky, 2002).

PROVISIONS FOR CHALLENGING GIFTED LEARNERS THROUGH DIFFERENTIATION

Differentiated instruction, as described in this chapter, encourages appropriate challenge for high-performing and high-potential learners on several levels. First, the model is based on attributes of curriculum and instruction that have long been described as important in the education of gifted learners; for example, concept- or theme-based curriculum, complex thought, application of understanding to authentic contexts, student-focused challenge, teacher use of a wide range of instructional strategies, a student voice in the learning process, flexible pacing, use of resources at varied levels of complexity, and attention to learner interests. Classrooms where these characteristics are consistently evident provide a solid foundation for meaningful learning for advanced learners.

Second, the model advocates use of a range of instructional strategies to address variation in learner readiness, interest, and learning profile. Many of these strategies are advocated for use with high-ability learners in the literature of gifted education, including: simulations, the Complex Instruction model, curriculum compacting, interest centers, learning contracts, and independent study. The purpose of these strategies is generally either:

a. to support student understanding and application or transfer of learning;
b. to provide a framework within which students can work at appropriate levels of challenge while maintaining a shared focus on the key concepts and principles of the topic or discipline they are studying; or
c. both of these.

Virtually any strategy that benefits the growth of high-ability or high-potential learners can and should have a role in an effectively differentiated classroom.

Third, while allowing for many approaches to providing challenge, this model of differentiation provides a specific mechanism for continual adaptation of challenge level to a student's performance. "The Equalizer" (Figure 29.2) is analogous to an equalizer or tuner on a piece of sound equipment. Teachers can adjust task complexity to be appro-

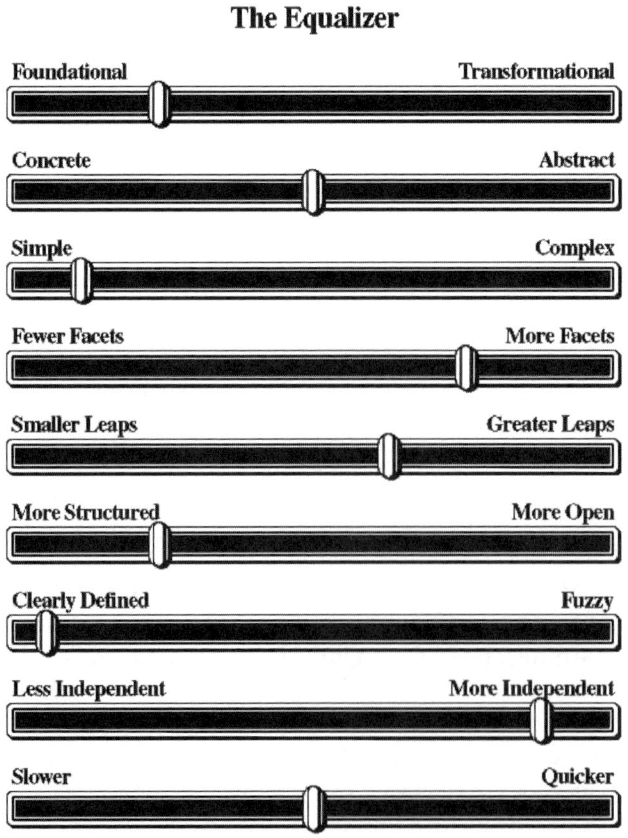

The Equalizer

Fig. 29.2 The Equalizer: A guide for adapting challenge to learner readiness.

Carole Ann Tomlinson and Caroline Cunningham Eidson. *Differentiation in Practice: A Resource Guide for Differentiating Curriculum, Grades K–5.* Alexandria, VA: ASCD, 2003, p. 185.

priately challenging by using The Equalizer to vary the "degree of difficulty" of a task by adjusting its level of concreteness or abstractness, specificity or openness, complexity, pace, and so on—with the goal of ensuring that students work in their "zones of proximal development"— that is, that students consistently work with tasks that are a bit too difficult for them, but also with a support system that enables them to succeed at the new level of challenge (Vygotsky, 1978) or at a level of "moderate challenge" (Howard, 1994; Jensen, 1998; Sousa & Tomlinson, 2010).

Fourth, the model advocates adapting knowledge and skills requirements for students based on pre-assessment and formative assessment information (Tomlinson & McTighe, 2006), while creating tasks and assessments based on the essential understandings of content at varied challenge levels to ensure appropriate challenge for a broad range of learners. That approach allows advanced learners to move ahead at a personally appropriate pace in mastery of facts and skills, while exploring enduring understandings about content in greater depth and breadth than may be appropriate for some other students.

All four aspects of the model not only allow for advanced levels of challenge, they also take into account the variability of particular individuals within any population—including gifted students—across content areas, learning contexts, and personal circumstances.

DIFFERENTIATION AND EXTENDED LEARNING OPPORTUNITIES FOR GIFTED LEARNERS

The population of students we call "gifted" is remarkably diverse, and becomes even more so when we consider students who have high but unrecognized capacity, and those with dual exceptionalities. In this respect, the model of differentiation is especially well suited for use with this population.

First, classes that are specially designed for advanced learners (e.g., pull-out classes, as well as Advanced Placement, Honors, or International Baccalaureate classes, and even special schools for gifted learners) include students with quite divergent strengths, motivations, backgrounds, interests, and approaches to learning. Those classes will be more likely to maximize the capacity of students in them when teachers are sensitive and responsive to that reality. Second, when teachers in such classes develop both the skill and will to differentiate instruction effectively, it is likely that they will be both more willing and able to serve a broader range of students. That would be an asset in terms of identification of, and service to, students who are often underserved—including highly able students with additional exceptionalities and students who come from less privileged backgrounds than is sometimes typical of classes and programs for high-ability learners. Third, when general education teachers work from a knowledge of and a desire to know more about students with advanced performance and potential, and in partnership with specialists in gifted education, both high-performing and high-potential learners would be more effectively served in a setting that accounts for a major portion of the school day of most gifted learners.

Even in the most effectively differentiated classrooms, there will sometimes be students who are so precocious that their needs cannot be adequately addressed in that setting and perhaps not even in the context of the school. The goal of differentiation is not to have one teacher meet all students' needs all the time and in all subjects, but rather markedly to extend the ability of teachers to teach more students more effectively in increasingly diverse classrooms and schools. Whether in general or special classroom settings, increasingly effective differentiation would lead to extended equity of access to excellent learning opportunities for more students, as teachers become increasingly proficient in valuing students as individuals, studying students in order to teach them better, creating a community of learners, working from high-quality curricula, using assessment to inform instructional plans and to strengthen student ownership of learning, and using a range of instructional strategies and teaching/learning processes to address students' particular readiness needs, interests, and approaches to learning.

To some educators, achieving that agenda sounds too ambitious. To others, it simply sounds like a call to insist on and foster good teaching. To the latter group, growing excellent teachers for all learners seems more necessary than optional. In summarizing his research on the qualities of effective teachers, Stronge (2007) reflects that teaching is an extremely complex undertaking and cautions that to see it as less trivializes it. He concludes that "the successful teacher understands and can successfully navigate complexity" (p. 101). With gifted education's emphasis on the needs of individuals, complex curriculum, and student-centered instruction, practitioners in that field appear well positioned both to implement differentiation artfully and to provide partnership and leadership for other educators in doing so as well.

REFERENCES

Allen, J., Gregory, A., Mikami, J., Hamre, B., & Pianta, R. (2010). *Predicting adolescent achievement with the CLASS-S observation tool.* A CASTL Research Brief. Charlottesville: Curry School of Education, University of Virginia.

Amabile, T. (1983). *The social psychology of creativity.* New York: Springer-Verlag.

Anderson, R., & Pavan, B. (1993). *Nongradedness: Helping it to happen.* Lancaster, PA: Technomic.

Anderson, J., Reder, L., & Simon, H. (1996). Situated learning and education. *Educational Researcher, 25,* 5–11.

Banks, J. (1993). *Multicultural education: Issues and perspectives* (2nd ed.). Boston: Allyn & Bacon.

Banks, J. (1994). *Multiethnic education: Theory and practice* (3rd ed.). Boston: Allyn & Bacon.

Beecher, M., & Sweeny, S. (2008). Closing the achievement gap with curriculum enrichment and differentiation: One school's story. *Journal of Advanced Academics, 19,* 502–530.

Ben Ari, R., & Shafir, D. (1988). *Social integration in elementary school.* Ramat-Gan, Israel: Institute for the Advancement of Social Integration in the Schools, Bar-Ilan University.

Borko, H., Mayfield, V., Marion, S., Flexer, R., & Cumbo, K. (1997). Teachers' developing ideas and practices about mathematics performance assessment: Successes, stumbling blocks, and implications for professional development. *Teaching and Teacher Education, 13,* 259–278.

Bruner, J. (1961). The act of discovery. *Harvard Educational Review, 31,* 21–32.

Burris, C., & Garrity, D. (2008). *Detracking for excellence and equity.* Alexandria, VA: Association for Supervision and Curriculum Development.

Coffield, F., Moseley, D., Hall, E., & Ecclestone, K. (2004). *Should we be using learning styles? What research has to say to practice.* London, UK: The Learning and Skills Research Centre.

Collins, M., & Amabile, T. (1999). Motivation and creativity. In R. J. Sternberg (Ed.), *Handbook of creativity* (pp. 297–312). New York: Cambridge University Press.

Cotton, K. (2000). *The schooling practices that matter most.* Portland, OR & Alexandria, VA: Northwest Regional Educational Laboratory & Association for Supervision and Curriculum Development.

Csikszentmihalyi, M. (1990). *Flow: The psychology of optimal experience.* New York: Harper & Row.

Csikszentmihalyi, M., Rathunde, K. R., & Whalen, S. (1993). *Talented teenagers: The roots of success and failure.* New York: Cambridge University Press.

Danielson, C. (2007). *Enhancing professional practice: A framework for teaching.* Alexandria, VA: Association for Supervision and Curriculum Development.

Delpit, L. (1995). *Other people's children: Cultural conflict in the classroom.* New York: The New Press.

Donovan, M., Bransford, J., & Pellegrino, J. (1999). *How people learn: Bridging research and practice.* Washington, DC: National Academy Press.

Dunn, R. (1996). *How to implement and supervise a learning styles program.* Alexandria, VA: Association for Supervision and Curriculum Development.

Dunn, R., & Griggs, S. (1995). *Multiculturalism and learning style: Teaching and counseling adolescents.* Westport, CT: Praeger.

Dweck, C. (2000). *Self-theories: Their role in motivation, personality, and development.* Philadelphia: Psychology Press.

Educational Research Service. (2003). *What we know about culture and learning.* Arlington, VA: Author.

Eliot, L. (2009). *Pink brain, blue brain: How small differences grow into troublesome gaps and what we can do about it.* New York: Houghton Mifflin Harcourt.

Fisher, C., Berliner, D., Filby, N., Marliave, R., Cahen, L., & Dishaw, M. (1980). Teaching behaviors, academic learning time, and student achievement: An overview. In C. Denham & A. Lieberman (Eds.), *Time to learn* (pp. 7–32). Washington, DC: National Institutes of Education.

Garcia, G. (1995). Equity challenges in authentically assessing students from diverse backgrounds. *Educational Forum, 59,* 64–73.

Gardner, H. (1983). *Frames of mind: The theory of multiple intelligences.* New York: Basic Books.

Gayfer, M. (1991). *The multi-grade classroom: Myth and reality, a Canadian study.* Toronto: Canadian Education Association.

Geisler, J., Hessler, R., Gardner, R., & Lovelace, T. (2009). Differentiated writing interventions for high-achieving urban African American elementary students. *Journal of Advanced Academics, 20,* 214–247.

Gilligan, C. (1982). *In a different voice: Psychological theory and women's development.* Cambridge, MA: Harvard University Press.

Grigorenko, E., & Sternberg, R. (1997). Styles of thinking, abilities, and academic performance. *Exceptional Children, 63,* 295–312.

Gurian, M. (2001). *Boys and girls learn differently: A guide for teachers and parents.* San Francisco: Jossey-Bass.

Hattie, J. (2009). *Visible learning: A synthesis of over 800 meta-analyses relating to achievement.* New York: Routledge.

Hébert, T. (1993). Reflections at graduations: The long-term impact of elementary school experiences in creative productivity. *Roeper Review, 16,* 22–28.

Hennessey, B., & Zbikowski, S. (1993). Immunizing children against the negative effects of reward: A further examination of intrinsic motivation training techniques. *Creativity Research Journal, 6,* 297–307.

Howard, P. (1994). *An owner's manual for the brain.* Austin, TX: Leorian Press.

Hunt, D. (1971). *Matching models in education.* Ontario, Canada: Institute of Studies in Education.

Jensen, E. (1998). *Teaching with the brain in mind.* Alexandria, VA: Association for Supervision and Curriculum Development.

Kulik, J., & Kulik, C. (1991). *Research on ability grouping: Historical and contemporary perspectives.* Storrs: The National Research Center on the Gifted and Talented, University of Connecticut. (ERIC Document Reproduction Service No. ED 350 777).

Langer, J. (2000). Excellence in English in middle and high school: How teachers' professional lives support student achievement. *American Educational Research Journal, 38,* 837–880.

Lasley, T., & Matczynski, T. (1997). *Strategies for teaching in a diverse society: Instructional models.* Belmont, CA: Wadsworth.

Levine, M. (2002). *A mind at a time.* New York: Simon & Schuster.

Lisle, A. M. (2006, September). *Cognitive neuroscience in education: Mapping neuro-cognitive processes and structures to learning styles, can it be done?* Paper presented at the British Educational Research Association Annual Conference, University of Warwick. Retrieved July 29, 2010 from http://www.leeds.ac.uk/educol/documents/157290.htm

Lou, Y., Abrami, P., Spence, J., Poulsen, C., Chambers, B., & d'Apollonia, S. (1996). Within-class grouping: A meta-analysis. *Review of Educational Research, 66,* 423–458.

Marulanda, M., Giraldo, P., & Lopez, L. (2006, March). *Differentiated instruction for bilingual learners.* Paper presented at the Annual Conference of the Association for Supervision and Curriculum Development, San Francisco.

Mason, D., Schroeter, D., Combs, R., & Washington, K. (1992). Assigning average-achieving eighth graders to advanced mathematics classes in an urban junior high. *Elementary School Journal, 92,* 587–599.

Miller, B. (1990). A review of the quantitative research on multi-grade instruction. *Research in Rural Education, 7,* 3–12.

National Research Council. (1999). *How people learn: Brain, mind, experience and school.* Washington, DC: National Academy Press.

Olshansky, B. (2008). *The power of pictures: Creating pathways to literacy through art.* San Francisco: Jossey-Bass.

Palincsar, A. (1984, April). *Working in the zone of proximal development.* Paper presented at the Annual Meeting of the American Educational Research Association, New Orleans.

Pashler, H., McDaniel, M., Rohrer, D., & Bjork, R. (2008). Learning styles: Concepts and evidence. *Psychological Science in the Public Interest, 9*, pp 106–119.

Pintrich, P., & Schunk, D. (1996). *Motivation in education: Theory, research, and application.* Columbus, OH: Prentice Hall.

Rasmussen, F. (2006). *Differentiated instruction as a means for improving achievement as measured by the American College Testing (ACT).* (Unpublished doctoral dissertation). School of Education, Loyola University of Chicago, IL.

Reis, S., McCoach, D., Little, C., Muller, L., & Kaniskan, R. (2010). The effects of enrichment pedagogy and differentiated instruction on reading achievement in five elementary schools. *American Educational Research Journal, 20*, 1–40.

Renninger, K. (1990). Children's play interests, representations, and activity. In R. Fivush & J. Hudson (Eds.), *Knowing and remembering in young children* (Emory Cognition Series, Vol. 3, pp. 127–165). New York: Cambridge University Press.

Reynolds, M. (1997). Learning styles: A critique. *Management Learning, 28*(2), 115–133.

Rosenshine, B., & Stevens, R. (1986). Teaching functions. In M. C. Wittrock (Ed.), *Handbook on research in teaching* (3rd ed., pp. 376–391). New York: Macmillan.

Salomone, R. (2003). *Same, different, equal: Rethinking single-sex schooling.* New Haven, CT: Yale University Press.

Saxe, L. (2005). *Why gender matters: What parents and teachers need to know about the emerging science of sex differences.* New York: Broadway Books.

Sousa, D., & Tomlinson, C. (2010). *Differentiation and the brain: How neuroscience supports the learner-friendly classroom.* Bloomington, IN: Solution Tree.

Sternberg, R. (1985). *Beyond IQ: A triarchic theory of human intelligence.* New York: Cambridge University Press.

Sternberg, R. J. (1997). What does it mean to be smart? *Educational Leadership, 55*(7), 20–24.

Sternberg, R., Torff, B., & Grigorenko, E. (1998). Teaching triarchically improves student achievement. *Journal of Educational Psychology, 90*, 374–384.

Storti, C. (1999). *Figuring foreigners out: A practical guide.* Yarmouth, ME: Intercultural Press.

Stronge, J. (2007). *Qualities of effective teachers* (2nd ed.). Alexandria, VA: Association for Supervision and Curriculum Development.

Sullivan, M. (1993). A meta-analysis of experimental research studies based on the Dunn and Dunn learning styles model and its relationship to academic achievement and performance. (Unpublished doctoral dissertation). St. John's University, Jamaica, NY.

Tannen, D. (1990). *You just don't understand: Women and men in conversation.* New York: Ballentine.

Tomlinson, C. (1999). *The differentiated classroom: Responding to the needs of all learners.* Alexandria, VA: Association for Supervision and Curriculum Development.

Tomlinson, C. (2001). *How to differentiate instruction in mixed-ability classrooms* (2nd ed.). Alexandria, VA: Association for Supervision and Curriculum Development.

Tomlinson, C. (2004). *Fulfilling the promise of the differentiated classroom: Strategies and tools for responsive teaching.* Alexandria, VA: Association for Supervision and Curriculum Development.

Tomlinson, C., Brimijoin, K., & Narvaez, L. (2008). *The differentiated school: Making revolutionary changes in teaching and learning.* Alexandria, VA: Association for Supervision and Curriculum Development.

Tomlinson, C., & Imbeau, M. (2010). *Leading and managing a differentiated classroom.* Alexandria, VA: Association for Supervision and Curriculum Development.

Tomlinson, C., & McTighe, J. (2006). *Integrating differentiated instruction and understanding by design: Connecting content and kids.* Alexandria, VA: Association for Supervision and Curriculum Development.

Trumbull, E., Rothstein-Fish, C., Greenfield, P., & Quiroz, B. (2001). *Bridging cultures between home and school: A quick guide for teachers.* Mahwah, NJ: Erlbaum.

Veenman, S. (1996). Effects of multigrade and multi-age classes reconsidered. *Review of Educational Research, 66*, 323–340.

Vygotsky, L. (1962). *Thought and language.* Cambridge, MA: MIT Press.

Vygotsky, L. (1978). *Mind in society: The development of higher psychological processes.* Cambridge, MA: Harvard University Press.

Wenglinsky, H. (2002). How schools matter: The link between teacher classroom practices and student academic performance. *Education Policy Analysis Archives, 10*(12). Retrieved October 31, 2011 from http://www.indiana.edu/~educy520/sec6342/week_07/wenglinsky02.pdf

Willis, J. (2006). *Research-based strategies to ignite student learning.* Alexandria, VA: Association for Supervision and Curriculum Development.

30

THE CLEAR CURRICULUM MODEL

Amy Azano

The CLEAR (**C**hallenge **L**eading to **E**ngagement, **A**chievement, and **R**esults) Curriculum Model[1] is a synthesis of key curricular elements from three distinct models in gifted education:

a. the differentiated instruction model (Tomlinson, 1995, 1999);
b. the Schoolwide Enrichment Model (SEM) (Renzulli & Reis, 1985, 2000); and
c. the depth and complexity model developed by Kaplan (2005).

The key curricular elements are then imposed on the standards of learning that characterize a subject area as a means of providing high-end learning clearly tied to the essential elements of the disciplines. CLEAR is a framework for designing high-quality, authentic curriculum appropriate for diverse learners, including students identified as gifted and those capable of advanced work. This chapter provides an overview of the CLEAR Curriculum Model and a description of the features embedded in the model. Additionally, it provides examples from two research-based units designed using the CLEAR Curriculum.

CONCEPTUAL FRAMEWORK

This section provides a brief overview of the specific, extrapolated components from the models comprising the theoretical foundation for the CLEAR Curriculum: differentiated instruction (Tomlinson, 1995, 1999), the Schoolwide Enrichment Model (Renzulli & Reis, 1985, 2000), and depth and complexity (Kaplan, 2005). (See Chapter 29 in this volume on differentiated instruction, Chapter 21 on the Schoolwide Enrichment Model, and Chapter 28 on depth and complexity in this volume.)

Differentiation

Differentiation, both in Tomlinson's work (1995, 1999, 2001) and in the CLEAR Curriculum, honors the individuality of learners. As a philosophy, differentiation is the belief that students should be at the center of their own learning and learning environment. The CLEAR Curriculum upholds this principle as a touchstone for quality instruction. Specifically, the CLEAR Curriculum incorporates multi-modal forms of continuous assessment to elicit student data critical for curricular and instructional planning and adjustment. The underlying assumption is that gifted or high-end learners are not a homogeneous group, but are quite different from one another in specific levels of background knowledge, understanding, interests, and learning profile in any given discipline or even within a unit of study. Formative assessments provide practical information to teachers about students' learning experiences and needs, what they have learned in prior units and lessons, and hence, their current readiness status. Subsequently, when assessments are analyzed and used to inform instruction, teachers can vary learning opportunities to respond to students' interests, learning profiles, and readiness levels.

Flexible grouping (whole group, small group, and independent), activities that foster independence and clearly defined learning goals are additional features incorporated from this model into the CLEAR Curriculum.

Schoolwide Enrichment Model

The Schoolwide Enrichment Model (see Renzulli, 1977; Renzulli & Reis, 1985, 2000) emphasizes creative productivity, opportunities for students to work with the tools and methods of practicing professionals in a field, and the importance of student engagement in long-term, "real-world" projects in an area of interest. This model also champions differentiation, specifically through learner-selected topics of investigation. The "real-world" projects emanating from the investigations into topics of high interest to individual students provide the opportunity for students to engage in activities beyond those expected of a student of a certain age or grade level. The particular value of advanced and meaningful work is evident in units based on the CLEAR Curriculum (examples are provided in later sections of this chapter).

Additionally, Renzulli's contributions to the field of gifted education have broadened definitions and understandings of what it means to be gifted. Congruent with this core principle of SEM, the CLEAR Curriculum incorporates varied learning challenges for students who express academic and creative–productive giftedness. This is most evident in the units' standards-based and performance-based assessments.

Depth and Complexity

These concepts—depth and complexity—are used in the CLEAR Curriculum to build layers of challenge and meaning onto standards-based learning opportunities. The CLEAR Curriculum integrates elements of depth (big ideas, language of the discipline, details, patterns, rules) and complexity (multiple perspectives, interdisciplinary connections, unanswered questions, ethical issues, changes over time) (Kaplan, 2005) to help students explore content. Most evident from this model are the integration of icons to differentiate and guide instruction. Icons in the CLEAR Curriculum units (see Figure 30.1) draw attention to the particular content focus, learning objective, or instructional configuration of an activity or lesson. Some icons were taken directly from Kaplan's work, while others were created specifically for the CLEAR Curriculum to complement the depth and complexity model.

DISCIPLINE EXPLORATION	
 LANGUAGE	**Language of the Discipline.** The task helps students achieve greater depth of understanding by coming to know and apply the vocabulary of professionals in the academic discipline.
 TOOLS http://siri.uvm.edu/graphics/Tools/Wrench.gif	**Tools of the Discipline.** The task helps students achieve greater depth of understanding by coming to know and apply the ways of thinking and working of professionals in the academic discipline.
 REAL WORLD	**Real-world Application.** The task requires students to apply the language and tools of the discipline in an environment or activity similar to what an expert in the field would.

SUBJECT ANALYSIS	
 DETAILS	**Details.** The task helps students achieve greater depth of understanding by studying the essential details relevant to what they are learning.
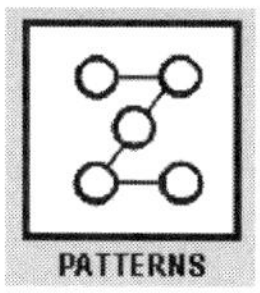 PATTERNS	**Patterns.** The task helps students achieve greater depth of understanding by analyzing the patterns and trends that can be identified in what they are learning.

Fig. 30.1 Example of icons.

Each of the three curriculum models represents dominant thinking in the field of gifted education. Few debate the benefits of differentiated instruction, of talent development and authentic knowledge, or of challenging curriculum; the CLEAR curriculum makes feasible the application of these key elements to existing curricular standards in conjunction with the four components of the classroom dynamic: content, process, product, and learning environment. Each of the models provides key elements adapted and integrated into one approach. While the models all provide direction in all four areas of curriculum development, their strengths are integrated into a new paradigm. Depth and complexity serve as the primary guide to selection of *content*, differentiation to considerations of *process* and *learning environment*, and the Schoolwide Enrichment Model guide *process* and *product elements of the model*. While individually these models lack equally rich focus on all components, the CLEAR Curriculum combines them to bring evenly balanced emphasis to all four, and draws its strength from the merging of the "best" of each of those models. The icons (see Table 30.1) used throughout the CLEAR units illustrate how these integrated elements construct a comprehensive curriculum for gifted learners.

Table 30.1 Categories of icons

Lesson Organization	Whole class
	Small group
	Independent work
	Anchor activity
Discipline Exploration	Big idea
	Language of the discipline
	Tools of the discipline
	Real-world application
Subject Analysis	Details
	Patterns
	Rules
	Perspectives
	Over time
	Unanswered questions
	Ethics
Focus of Student Differences	Differentiation by readiness
	Differentiation by interest
	Learning profile

DESCRIPTION OF THE MODEL

Distilled from the three models described, the CLEAR Curriculum identifies five foundational elements (see Figure 30.2): (1) **C**ontinual Formative Assessment; (2) Clear **L**earning Goals; (3) Data-driven Learning **E**xperiences; (4) **A**uthentic Products; and (5) **R**ich Curriculum. Each of these elements is considered crucial for encouraging engagement, achievement, and growth among diverse gifted learners.

Continual Formative Assessment

CLEAR Curriculum unit activities are informed by and adjusted according to ongoing formative assessment of students. Assessment data are collected and utilized not only to evaluate student growth, but also to provide a profile of student readiness levels, needs,

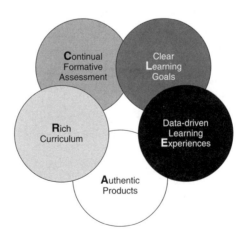

Fig. 30.2 Foundational elements of CLEAR Curriculum.

interests, and preferred ways of learning and expressing their learning. Assessment is regarded as an important tool for allowing teachers to get to know students and tailor further instruction to meet their unique needs.

Clear Learning Goals

CLEAR Curriculum units are designed around learning goals that are meaningful, important, and clear. Goals are consistent with the *Pre-K–Grade 12 Gifted Programming Standards* (National Association for Gifted Children [NAGC], 2010) and also reflect state and national standards, as well as the key knowledge, skills, and understandings central to the area of study of each unit.

Data-driven Learning Experiences

Underlying the CLEAR Curriculum are the assumptions that learners: (1) vary in their readiness levels, interests, and learning profiles; and (2) learn best and most efficiently when their diverse needs are addressed in the construction and/or modification of learning activities. As such, learning experiences within CLEAR Curriculum units are differentiated to meet the needs of a variety of high-achieving learners, including the gifted. Continual collection of data through formative assessments allows teachers to assign students to learning experiences appropriate for their needs.

Authentic Products

As would be expected in a model incorporating elements of the SEM, underlying the CLEAR Curriculum is the assumption that learning is made most meaningful when students (1) develop the skills and knowledge needed by professionals in the field of study; and (2) apply the knowledge and skills they have acquired in real-world and relevant contexts. CLEAR Curriculum units guide students in developing and carrying out projects on topics of their own choosing, using the methods and tools of experts in the field.

Rich Curriculum

The CLEAR Curriculum is designed to take students beyond mere factual, rote knowledge to deep understandings of the essential knowledge, skills, and "big ideas" of a unit of study. High-level challenge is built into the units through having students utilize the vocabulary and language of the discipline; investigate the patterns, rules, varied perspectives, unanswered questions, and ethical issues within a unit of study; make connections across disciplines; and understand how unit concepts and ideas have changed over time.

CLEAR CURRICULUM IN ACTION

Two language arts units (designed for students who are gifted in language arts or show potential for outstanding performance in language arts) were developed for the "What Works in Gifted Education" study.[2] The curriculum developers[3] relied on the core components of the CLEAR Curriculum. A poetry unit, "The Magic of Everyday Things," and a research unit, "Exploration and Communication," were developed for third grade gifted students. As language arts units, both are aligned with the *Standards for the English Language Arts* (National Council of Teachers of English [NCTE] & International Reading Association [IRA], 1996) and include lesson plans requiring approximately 45 minutes of instruction. Because gifted classrooms vary widely from one setting to another (from self-contained classes that meet daily to pull-out classes meeting weekly to within-classroom cluster groups which meet at the discretion of classroom teachers), the units also vary widely in the total time needed for implementation (from four weeks to four months). The units are designed to challenge gifted and high-ability students and are differentiated to address a broad range of skill levels within that population.

The overarching objective of the research unit is for students to explore a variety of non-fiction texts and expand their skills in research, writing, and the use of reading comprehension strategies. The unit also provides a dual focus of exploration and communication in research. Additionally, the unit is differentiated by interest so that students channel their interests in an area, person, or topic worthy of research.

The poetry unit is designed to help students discover the extraordinary—the "magical"—in ordinary experience. The unit gives students multiple opportunities to enhance their word knowledge, comprehension strategies, and writing skills. Throughout the unit, students learn how to critique poems while also developing their own anthology of poems.

In addition to the philosophical foothold of differentiation, Schoolwide Enrichment, and depth and complexity, the units are anchored by the five foundational elements of the CLEAR Curriculum as illustrated in Figures 30.3 and 30.4.

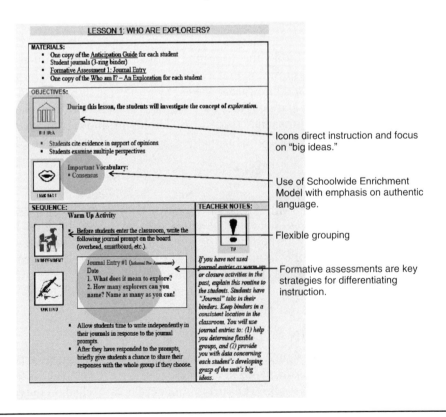

Fig. 30.3 CLEAR components (1).

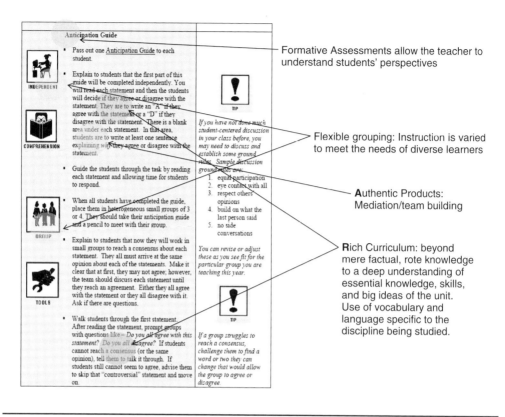

Fig. 30.4 CLEAR components (2).

Formative Assessments and Data-driven Learning Experiences

These two components of the CLEAR Curriculum work in tandem to provide differentiated instruction for individual learners. Each unit included four formative assessments to be used at regular intervals throughout the units to assess student understanding of recently taught concepts. Both units provide varied formative assessments (exit cards, journal entries, multiple-choice responses), along with guidance for teachers in using the assessment data collected with the assessments to inform instruction. Figure 30.5 is an example of an exit card administered to students following an activity near the beginning of the research unit.

Additionally, the following information is provided for teachers about how to use the data from the formative assessment:

> Journal entries and exit cards are informal assessment tools that can assist you to determine instructional groups throughout the unit. Students' responses will also help [you] tailor the kinds of questions you pose to particular students in order to further their thinking, and may also help determine the type and level of resources you make available to students.
>
> This exit card will help you assess your students' current knowledge about the research process and current capacity to think through the concepts that guide the unit. Make notes about each student's developing levels of understanding at this

FORMATIVE ASSESSMENT 3:

At the end of Lesson 4, have students respond to the following questions in their journals:

Exit Card

Choose either question #1 or #2 to answer on your card. Everyone must answer question 3. Please put your name on your card.

#1: Before you begin looking for the answers to your research question, what should you do first?

#2: What is a SOURCE?

#3: How does what you already know about a topic [your prior knowledge] help you in getting more information about it?

Fig. 30.5 Sample exit card.

point in the unit. Are there students who seem to have a sophisticated grasp of the concepts so far and could be ready for an additional challenge (advanced materials, more advanced questions about the research process to think about as they work, etc.) as they tackle their independent projects? Are there students who might need to be taken aside to have concepts reinforced or to be provided [with] additional background knowledge before they are ready to move on with independent research? This is a good time to address any misconceptions and to identify students who may require additional challenge or support. Students' work in the Research Handbooks during this lesson may also provide useful information about their progress so far.

(CLEAR Curriculum, Lesson 4, Research unit)

While several of the formative assessments included in the units were process-oriented and open-ended such as the exit card above, others were less subjective. After a poetry lesson on rhyme and rhythm, students were asked to complete an assessment in which they had to identify the word that did not rhyme from a list of words (see excerpted items in Figure 30.6).

4.	secret	meet	meat	secrete
5.	high	under	cry	untie
6.	eight	undulate	commiserate	community
7.	steak	stake	create	shake
8.	towel	show	stow	toe

Fig. 30.6 Sample items from formative assessment.

After students completed the assessment, teachers were provided with further direction on how the data should be used to differentiate the next activity according to students' readiness levels:

Using the Assessment Data:
   Use the assessment data to plan which words you will assign to particular students. Try to match each student to two or more words that are challenging for him or her—i.e.[,] not too easy or too difficult given current readiness level.
   (CLEAR Curriculum, Lesson 13, Poetry unit)

Examples of differentiated instruction varied depending on the given lesson. What follows are two examples—one differentiated by interest and the other by readiness level.
   Example of differentiating by interest:

Tell students it is their turn to brainstorm all the areas they are interested in. Instruct students to turn to the next blank page in their journals. Encourage students to jot down people, places, events that are interesting to them. Prompt them to think about things that they have learned or books that they have read on topics that they'd like to know more about. Give students some time to really think, talk, and record. Also provide some time for students to turn to their neighbors and share their lists so far.
   (CLEAR Curriculum, Lesson 2, Research unit)

Example of differentiating by readiness:

Students will be assigned one of three versions of the task, based on their readiness as assessed through Exit Card 1.
   Students in Group A will each be provided with an excerpt from Elizabeth Bishop's poem "The Fish." Their job will be to find as many concrete nouns and as many abstract nouns as they can in the excerpt. They should mark each kind of noun to keep track.
   Students in Group B will be provided with a set of vocabulary cards and two blank columns, with headings "concrete" and "abstract." Students will sort the words from their list into the two columns.
   Students in Group C will be given a set of vocabulary cards and a list similar to the one provided to Group B. In this case though, each column includes a definition and several examples to help students sort their words.
   (CLEAR Curriculum, Lesson 2, Poetry unit)

Clear Learning Goals

Clear learning goals and unit objectives are not only explained in great detail at the beginning of each unit, but they are also reinforced at the start of each lesson. Moreover, they are emphasized throughout various lesson activities. With a focus on "big ideas," units were developed with goals, performance assessments, and summative assessments in mind. The units use scaffolding strategies to extend the learner from his or her prior knowledge in poetry and research. In the poetry unit, students begin the unit (and each lesson) by *listening* to poems. In doing so, they learn an appreciation for the language, the meter, the rhyme and rhythm, and the *art* of poetry. From there, however, students are taught specific strategies for demystifying that "art." They learn the specific skills (e.g., using concrete language to describe abstract ideas) needed for writing poetry like canonical poets. With an emphasis on clear learning goals, students are able to move beyond their initial concepts of poetry to the point of critically analyzing poems and developing complete poetry anthologies.

Figure 30.7 illustrates clearly defined learning objectives for a lesson introducing the concept of metaphor.

Throughout the lesson, however, the teacher is directed to make these objectives explicit for students. While students advance through the various activities, the lesson plan again focuses the teacher's attention on the big ideas of the lesson (see Figure 30.8).

OBJECTIVES:

- Students will understand that:

Poets use metaphor to connect readers to important ideas through imagery.

Poetry helps readers see the extraordinary in the ordinary.

- Students identify literary devices, including **metaphor**

- Students identify the main idea of a selection

- Students generate ideas for writing

- Students participate as knowledgeable, reflective, creative, and critical members of a literary community

Important Vocabulary:

- Imagery

- Metaphor

- *Poetry for appreciation* word bank and comprehension vocabulary on website

Fig. 30.7 Sample of lesson objectives.

- Consider *Dreams* without the metaphors for life: Hold fast to dreams/For if dreams die/*Life is really bad*/Hold fast to dreams/For when dreams go/*Life is terrible*. In this version, the poet is *telling* readers straight out what he wants to say. But what good poets do is *show*, through the use of strong imagery, instead of *tell*. A good image sticks in the reader's mind, so the important message also sticks.

Fig. 30.8 Focus on big ideas.

Authentic Products

With a focus on teaching the skills and knowledge needed by professionals in a discipline, students learn to think and act like real poets and researchers. For the research unit, students learn how to craft a research question from a topic of personal interest. In the experimental study investigating the efficacy and effectiveness of the units, research topics selected by students ranged from historical figures to sporting events to exotic animals and places. In conducting research, they learned the skills of professional researchers: gathering reliable information, cross-referencing sources, understanding perspective, and so on. Students learned the "Big 6" research steps and, ultimately, presented a fully developed project at a research gala. This final product allowed them to experience not only the process of conducting research, but the ultimate goal of disseminating that work to wider audiences.

For the poetry unit, students practice reading and writing like poets. They learn to write in various poetic forms (e.g., the cinquain), to recognize and implement imagery and other literary devices, and become versed at figurative language. For their performance assessments, students compile their favorite works into a poetry anthology, and many teachers in the experimental study hosted poetry readings and provided students with an authentic audience for their work.

Rich Curriculum

With the current focus on accountability in education, it seems that assessment often trumps learning. While the CLEAR units utilize many forms of assessment (formative, summative, and performance), they also embody the components essential to a rich curriculum. Perhaps a nebulous term, "rich curriculum" in the context of the CLEAR Curriculum connotes *deep* understanding of complex issues and the *real-world* implications of those issues.

With a rich curriculum, students learn the tools and language needed in a discipline of study. This allows students to assume the identity of those practicing real-world skills. In units built on the CLEAR Curriculum, emphasis should be on assuming the professional persona in a field. Learners should not merely memorize their multiplication tables, but—as mathematicians (or economists, statisticians, computer scientists, etc.)—investigate the patterns implicit in that work. They should approach science concepts as biologists, chemists, and horticulturists. In the CLEAR poetry unit, students *became* poets. They emulated famous poets, systematically examined the craft of poetry, and performed their poems for classmates and larger audiences. Participating teachers commented that students who initially expressed a dislike for poetry not only enjoyed the unit but, ultimately, referred to themselves as poets. Additionally, they participated in writing workshops—something *real* writers do regularly. Figure 30.9 illustrates how a rich curriculum enabled students to deepen their understanding of poetry by allowing them time to reflect on their work. Additionally, the workshop time afforded teachers the opportunity to hold individual conferences with students. In making connections beyond simply the task at hand, the lesson is differentiated so that students who are ready can make connections across poems and organize their anthologies thematically.

In the research unit, students grappled with complex topics. As the unit is introduced, the teacher is directed to use the question "Who discovered America?" as an example of

Poet's Workshop

WRITING

- Today's lesson is a chance for students to process the many models and concepts to which they have been introduced by allowing extended time for Poet's Workshop.

- Before you allow students to start work, introduce them to the updated Poet's Workshop Conversation Sheet II. This sheet includes reference to metaphor, personification, and point of view.

TOOLS

- Remind students that they have now been introduced to the following forms, models, and devices:

  - So much depends...
  - The Magic Box
  - The Memory Box
  - Postcards (optional)
  - Cinquain
  - Metaphor
  - Personification
  - Point of view

INDEPENDENT

I

INTEREST

- Explain to students that they may work on any poem using these models and devices, on an unfinished poem from another lesson, or on a new poem. Hand each student a Workshop Rubric Guide to help them focus on key areas. *Remind students that they have already seen the various parts of this rubric and should now be quite familiar with the criteria.*

- Remind students that they should write final copies of their poems (after the prewriting, drafting, and conference process) in their anthology books, which is their final collection of poetry.

TIP

While students are working independently in Poet's Workshop, this is a great opportunity for you to (a) hold individual conferences with students or offer individual help, or (b) collect a group of students for a 'mini lesson' on a particular concept or model if they need additional explanation, practice, or extension.

R

READINESS

As you are working with individual students on their anthologies, you might alert some students to the notion that many poets use a theme to unite different poems in an anthology. Some students might be ready to think about developing their work around a coherent theme, such as poems about family or poems about the experience of feeling like an outsider.

Fig. 30.9 Workshop lesson plan.

a complicated research question with many possible answers. With this question serving as a model, students learn to be critical of assumptions and to explore ethical concepts about research, perspective, audience, bias, and plagiarism. Plagiarism is an example of a real-world application evident in the unit. The following is an example of how this concept was explored in the CLEAR unit:

Discussing Plagiarism:
 Put the dictionary definition of plagiarism on the overhead or write its contents on the board. Talk about the pronunciation of the word, and its definition. After discussing the definition, ask: How can plagiarism affect your research?

Have a substantial discussion about plagiarism and why it is unethical. Make sure students have a strong grasp of what it means to plagiarize.

(CLEAR Curriculum, Lesson 10, Research unit)

SUPPORT FOR THE CLEAR CURRICULUM

The purpose of the "What Works in Gifted Education" project is to evaluate the CLEAR Curriculum Model by assessing the effects of the poetry and research units. After the work was developed and piloted, the units were implemented in 110 classrooms. Qualitative data collection included observations, interviews, teacher logs, and surveys. In response to questions relating to multiple domains of fidelity of implementation, these data were collected to understand the feasibility of implementing units in a naturalistic setting. Additionally, researchers conducted multilevel data analyses of researcher-developed assessments and performance assessments to examine achievement difference between treatment and comparison groups. The analyses showed a significant difference favoring the treatment group over the comparison group on outcome measures for both units, after controlling for entry-level achievement as measured by the Iowa Tests of Basic Skills.

CONCLUSION

Derived from the philosophies inherent in the differentiated instruction model (Tomlinson, 1995, 1999), the Schoolwide Enrichment Model (SEM) Renzulli & Reis, 1985, 2000), and the depth and complexity model (Kaplan, 2005), the CLEAR Curriculum Model identifies five foundational elements (continual formative assessments, clear learning goals, data-driven learning experiences, authentic products, and rich curriculum) that encourage engagement and promote achievement for diverse gifted learners.

This curricular model builds layers of challenge and opportunities for more in-depth study authentic to the work of professionals within a discipline. This is especially critical for today's students who have access to information at a volume never before encountered. As such, it is imperative that teachers help students to differentiate between information and wisdom, between facts and truth, and teach them how to use their "active" and "ethical" intelligences. The CLEAR Curriculum Model provides opportunities for gifted and high-potential learners to explore unanswerable questions, to engage in relevant and meaningful academic pursuits, and to consider the implications of complex issues on their self-concept, community, and culture.

NOTES

1. The CLEAR Curriculum Model was developed as part of a Jacob K. Javits research grant authored by Carolyn M. Callahan, Tonya R. Moon, Holly L. Hertberg-Davis, and Catherine M. Brighton.
2. The "What Works in Gifted Education" study, conducted at the National Research Center on the Gifted and Talented, is funded by a Jacob K. Javits research grant.
3. Jane Jarvis and Maureen Murphy conceptualized and drafted the poetry and research units, respectively.

REFERENCES

Kaplan, S. (2005). Layering differential curricula for gifted and talented. In F. Karnes & S. Bean (Eds.), *Methods and materials for teaching gifted students* (pp. 107–132). Waco, TX: Prufrock Press.

National Association for Gifted Children. (2010). *Pre-K–Grade 12 gifted programming standards: A blueprint for quality gifted education standards.* Retrieved August 10, 2011 from http://www.nagc.org/index.aspx?id=546

National Council of Teachers of English, & International Reading Association. (1996). *Standards for the English language arts.* Urbana, IL: National Council of Teachers of English.

Renzulli, J. S. (1977). *The Enrichment Triad Model. A guide for defensible programs for the gifted and talented.* Wethersfield, CT: Creative Learning Press.

Renzulli, J. S., & Reis, S. (1985). *The Schoolwide Enrichment Model: A comprehensive plan for educational excellence.* Mansfield Center, CT: Creative Learning Press.

Renzulli, J. S., & Reis, S. (2000). The Schoolwide Enrichment Model. In K. A. Heller, F. J. Mönks, R. J. Sternberg, and R.F. Subotnik (Eds.), *The international handbook of giftedness and talent* (2nd ed., pp. 367–382). Oxford, UK: Elsevier.

Renzulli, J., Smith, L., White, A., Callahan, C., Hartman, R., & Westberg, K. (2002). *Scales for rating the behavioral characteristics of superior students.* Mansfield Center, CT: Creative Learning Press.

Tomlinson, C. A. (1995). *How to differentiate instruction in mixed-ability classrooms.* Alexandria, VA: Association for Supervision and Curriculum Development.

Tomlinson, C. A. (1999). *The differentiated classroom: Responding to the needs of all learners.* Alexandria, VA: Association for Supervision and Curriculum Development.

Tomlinson, C. (2001). *How to differentiate instruction in mixed-ability classrooms* (2nd ed.). Alexandria, VA: Association for Supervision and Curriculum Development.

Tomlinson, C., & Callahan, C. (1992). Contributions of gifted education to general education in a time of change. *Gifted Child Quarterly, 36,* 183–189.Tomlinson, C. A., Kaplan, S. N., Renzulli, J. S., Purcell, J., Leppien, J., & Burns, D. (2002). *The parallel curriculum.* Thousand Oaks, CA: Corwin Press.

31

THE INTEGRATED CURRICULUM MODEL

Joyce VanTassel-Baska

OVERVIEW OF THE MODEL

The Integrated Curriculum Model (ICM), as the title suggests, represents an attempt to unite multiple curricular approaches in the design and implementation of strategies for working with learners in schools. Too often, gifted learners end up with a curriculum diet composed of morsels of acceleration, morsels of project work, and morsels of higher-level thinking opportunities. The ICM organizes these features into one package, allowing gifted learners and others to experience a more integrated pattern of learning. This integrated approach also reflects two fundamental findings of recent research on learning. Studies have documented that:

a. better transfer of learning occurs when higher-order thinking skills are embedded in subject matter (Minstrell & Kraus, 2005; National Research Council [NRC], 2000; Perkins & Salomon, 1989); and
b. teaching concepts in a discipline is a better way to produce long-term learning than teaching facts and rules (Marzano, 1992).

Our understanding of creativity also has shifted toward the need for strong subject-matter knowledge as a prerequisite (Amabile, 1996). Because the ICM is organized around the subject-matter standards, it uses the content core as a basis for modification and integration.

The Integrated Curriculum Model (ICM) was first proposed in 1986, based on a review of the research literature on what worked with gifted learners, and further expounded upon in subsequent publications (VanTassel-Baska, 1986; VanTassel-Baska et al., 1998; VanTassel-Baska & Little, 2011). The model is composed of three interrelated dimensions responsive to different aspects of the gifted learner:

1. *Emphasizing advanced content knowledge that frames disciplines of study.* Honoring the talent search concept, this facet of the model ensures that careful diagnostic–prescriptive approaches are employed to enhance the challenge level of the

315

curriculum base. Curricula based on the model would represent advanced learning in any given discipline.

2. *Providing higher-order thinking and processing.* This facet of the model promotes student opportunities for manipulating information at complex levels by employing generic thinking models like Paul's Elements of Reasoning (Paul & Elder, 2001) and more discipline-specific models like Sher's Nature of the Scientific Process (Sher, 2003). This facet of the ICM also promotes the utilization of information in generative ways, through project work and/or fruitful discussions.

3. *Organizing learning experiences around major issues, themes, and ideas that define understanding of a discipline and provide connections across disciplines.* This facet of the ICM scaffolds curricula for gifted learners around the important aspects of a discipline and emphasizes these aspects in a systemic way (Ward, 1981). Thus, themes and ideas are selected based on careful research of the primary area of study to determine the most worthy and important ideas for curriculum development, a theme consistent with reform of curriculum specifications in key areas (American Association for the Advancement of Science [AAAS], 1990; Perkins, 1992). The goal of such an approach is to ensure deep understanding of disciplines, rather than misconceptions.

These three relatively distinct curriculum dimensions have proven successful with gifted populations at various stages of development and in various domain-specific areas, and taken together, form the basis of the Integrated Curriculum Model (VanTassel-Baska, 1986, 1998; VanTassel-Baska & Little, 2011; VanTassel-Baska & Stambaugh, 2006). Figure 31.1 portrays these interrelated dimensions of the ICM model.

Recent reviews of curricular interventions for the gifted have found the greatest effectiveness prevailing in an accelerative approach, guided by the content modification features exemplified in the ICM (Johnsen, 2000; VanTassel-Baska & Brown, 2007). The fusion of these approaches is central to the development of a coherent curriculum responsive to the diverse needs of talented students while also providing rich challenges for all.

THEORETICAL UNDERPINNINGS

The theoretical support for the ICM comes primarily from learning theory and development. One source is the work of Vygotsky (1978), particularly his concept of the zone of

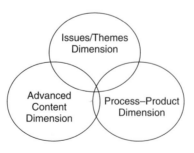

Fig. 31.1 Dimensions of the Integrated Curriculum Model (ICM)

J. VanTassel-Baska, J. *Curriculum Planning and Instructional Design for Gifted Learners* (2nd edition). Denver, CO: Love, 2003.

proximal development where learners must be exposed to material slightly above their current levels of performance in order to feel challenged by the learning experience. This idea was expanded on by Csikszentmihalyi (1991) in his concept of *flow* in which gifted learners demonstrated a broader and deeper capacity to engage in learning than did typical students (Csikszentmihalyi, Rathande, & Whalen, 1993).

A second aspect of this theory of learning is the view of interactionism, whereby the learner increases learning depth by interacting with others in the environment to enhance understanding of concepts and ideas. Ideas are validated and understood through the articulation of tentative connections made based on a stimulus such as a literary artifact, a film, a piece of music, or a problem. Learning increases as interactions provide the scaffolding necessary to structure thinking about the stimulus (Vygotsky, 1978).

A theory of constructivism whereby learners construct knowledge for themselves is also central to the instructional emphases within the ICM. Students must be in charge of their own learning in respect to each dimension of the model, whether it be content acceleration, project-based learning opportunities such as Problem-based Learning (PBL), or discussion-laden experiences in which concepts, issues, and themes are explored.

Another theoretical influence on the model was the work of Adler and his Paedeia Program (1984) that posited the importance of rich content representing the best products of world civilization coupled with the relevant cognitive skills to study them, appropriately linked to the intellectual ideas and philosophy that spawned the work of the disciplines.

Finally, the theory of multiculturalism espoused by Banks (1994a, 1994b, 2001) and more recently by Ford (2005; Ford & Harris, 1999) speaks to the aspect of the ICM concerned with students making a better world through deliberate social action, whether through the resolutions brought to policy makers as a result of PBL work, or the studies of technology use in researching issues, or the concerns about censorship in the history of great literature. Moreover, this theoretical orientation also provides a major emphasis on the works of minority authors both in the United States and abroad as well as an attempt to acknowledge multiple perspectives in student understanding of any content area, especially history.

APPLICATION

Current work in the ICM has continued to focus on a merger with the curriculum reform principles advocating world-class standards in all traditional curricular areas (VanTassel-Baska & Little, 2011). The major shift in thinking is from a model that looks only at the optimal match between the characteristics of the learner and the curriculum, to a model based on performance in various domains, thereby letting the level of functioning, rather than a predictive measure, determine who is ready for more advanced work in an area. Thus, differentiation for any population is grounded in differential standards of performance at a given period of time. Standards are constant; time is the variable.

Such an approach holds promise for gifted students in that the level and pace of curriculum *can* be adapted to their needs when the existing state standards call for the kind of focus that curriculum makers for gifted students have long advocated—higher-level thinking, interdisciplinary approaches, and an emphasis on student-centered learning. While gifted students need high but realizable expectations for learning at each stage of development, other students can also benefit from working to attain such standards in this model. By the same token, gifted students can also benefit from a developmental and personal perspective on fostering their abilities at a close-up level, an emphasis requiring organizational models such as tutorials, mentorships, and small clusters to support it.

What Types of Students Are Best Served Using the ICM?

The ICM was designed for students who have strong intellectual abilities and/or strong academic aptitudes in the areas in which curriculum units have been designed: science, social studies, and language arts. In the last several years, however, the research on effectiveness that has been conducted suggests that more students benefit from the curriculum beyond the population for whom it was intended (e.g., Swanson, 2006). Research on the units of study which used the ICM as the organizing framework have increasingly shown that the benefits of the units for all students is significant in respect to achievement and motivation.

Because the units are content-based, students who are strong in only one discipline can benefit greatly from experiencing them. For example, strong readers can grow from exposure to the language arts units even if they are not identified as gifted, as the readings in the unit can be used with strong readers, and the other differentiation features of the units serve to enrich their understandings in key ways. Because the units employ opportunities for open-ended learning, higher-level opportunities to learn, and the use of multicultural literature, they work very well with promising learners from low-income backgrounds and children of color. Moreover, the consistent use of instructional scaffolds becomes a critical aspect in elevating the level of learning for all. In summary, the model has been useful in designing curriculum that can be used with all learners, although research suggests the greatest growth has occurred for promising learners, high-level readers, and the gifted in relevant subject areas of the curriculum.

The ICM as a Mirror of Best Practice in Serving the Gifted

The ICM is designed to reflect best practice for serving the gifted across the dimensions of curriculum, instruction, and assessment. Within the realm of curriculum modification, we need to attend to content, process, and product variables that allow gifted learners to thrive, and weave those variables together in a curriculum package. In instruction, we need to employ inquiry models, grounded in constructivist orientations, in order to elevate student thought and action. In assessment, we need to use off-grade-level and nontraditional instruments that assess the authentic learning of the gifted learner, including off-grade-level tests, performance-based measures, product assessment, and portfolios.

Best practice for differentiation in curriculum features modification of the core curriculum by making it more advanced or accelerated, by providing greater complexity and depth, by making it more creative and open-ended, and by elevating the degree of abstraction and challenge (see Kaplan, 2009; Maker & Schiever, 2009; Tomlinson, 2009). The ICM has built in these research-based differentiation approaches through an emphasis on the use of advanced content and higher-level processes that lead to product generation, and a focus on an overarching concept or theme. All curriculum organized under its auspices provides students with a strong template for rigorous learning by deliberately incorporating the differentiation features found in the literature to aid in that process. Task demands are complex, students study topics in depth to the point of doing an original research project in each unit, and learners enter the content at a higher level than their age/grade dictates through both careful diagnostic assessment and the use of more advanced materials.

Best practice for instruction for gifted learners focuses on use of inquiry in multiple modalities from problem-based learning to project-based learning to shared inquiry approaches through discussion (VanTassel-Baska & Brown, 2007). Moreover, general learning research supports the use of higher-level thinking strategies, metacognition, teaching to conceptual understanding, and using concept maps as viable ways to elevate learning for all students (NRC, 2000). The ICM also offers teachers learning scaffolds that elevate student thinking, problem solving, and concept development. These scaffolds are used consistently across curriculum subject areas and grade levels to promote automaticity so that all students exposed to the units can transfer understandings and thinking skills to new situations. The units based on the ICM deliberately employ all of these research-based approaches in a consistent manner across subjects and levels to ensure the learning results that the units have attained for students (see below).

Research suggests that assessment for the gifted in respect to learning must use multiple assessment approaches, be off-grade-level, and stress authenticity in product within and across disciplines (VanTassel-Baska, 2008). The ICM units include performance-based assessments for both pre- and post-testing on the content, conceptual understanding, and higher-level skills taught in a given unit of study. Thus in science, the pre/post assessment measures learning in the scientific research process. Language arts assessments provide data on achievement of skills in literary analysis and interpretation, and persuasive writing; and in social studies, the concept under study, the use of reasoning, and the content topic are assessed. A rubric for each assessment provides a product assessment model. Other formative assessments in each unit provide ongoing diagnostic information for teaching.

Examples of Curriculum and Instructional Modifications, Using the ICM

Table 31.1 provides examples of the translation of the major dimensions of the ICM into differentiated approaches in each major content domain. Each of these sketchy translations has been developed into full units of study with both pre- and post-assessments to assess student learning. The examples demonstrate the ways in which accelerated learning, higher-level processes of thinking, problem solving, and research are incorporated; the types of generative products that students create; and the conceptual foundation included in the units of study. The product tasks column includes examples of measures relating to content, process, product, and concept learning. Teachers may assess students within a unit on critical thinking, concept development, content acquisition, and product sophistication using the tools provided.

RESEARCH ON THE EFFECTIVENESS OF THE INTEGRATED CURRICULUM MODEL

Over the past decade, quasi-experimental and experimental designs have been used to examine the outcomes of exposing gifted learners, promising learners from low-income and minority backgrounds, and typical learners to ICM units of study. Studies of the

Table 31.1 The Integrated Curriculum Model by subject area and dimensions of sample unit study

Content area: Topic	Accelerative approaches	Higher-level thinking/ problem solving	Product tasks	Concept/theme
Science:Botany/ plants	Pre-testing and compacting, study of botany at primary level	Reasoning model, scientific investigation skills, questions	Logs, experimental designs, PBL resolution project and presentation	Systems: understanding the elements, boundaries, interactions, inputs and outputs of cells, plants, and terrariums
Language Arts: Autobiographies of writers	Reading selections calibrated two grade levels above	Reasoning model, literature web, persuasive writing, research project	Autobiographical project, with talent development markers	Change: the ways that change is everywhere, related to time, caused by people or nature, etc.
Mathematics: Study of animal populations	Advanced mathematical skills in graphing, statistics, and estimation	Problem-based learning	Problem resolution in oral and written form for a real-world audience	Models that are conceptual and physical applied in order to understand phenomena
Social Studies: Ancient Egypt	Emphasis on the systems of ancient civilizations that made them great	Emphasis on historical analysis, document study, and trends	Research paper on an historical issue	Patterns of change over time as chronicled by historical events within and across cultures

science and language arts units used quasi-experimental research designs to compare the pre-test and post-test performance of students in classrooms where these units were taught to the performance of similar students who were not taught using the units. Gifted students in classrooms utilizing the ICM science units outperformed gifted students in comparison classrooms on tests measuring the ability to apply the scientific method and demonstrate scientific reasoning skills (see Feng, VanTassel-Baska, Quek, O'Neil, & Bai, 2005; VanTassel-Baska, Bass, Ries, Poland, & Avery, 1998) and science concepts, content, and process (Kim et al., in press). Gifted students in grades 2—8 in classrooms utilizing ICM language arts units showed significantly greater gains in literary analysis and persuasive writing (VanTassel-Baska, Zuo, Avery, & Little, 2002) and critical thinking skills (VanTassel-Baska, Bracken, Feng, & Brown, 2009) than gifted students in control classrooms. In a comprehensive study conducted to examine the efficacy of the social studies units (again using a quasi-experimental design) with students from Title 1 schools in grades 3–8, results suggested that significant and important learning gains were accrued for students in selected classrooms on the dimensions of content mastery, concept development, and higher-level thinking (Little, Feng, VanTassel-Baska, Rogers, & Avery, 2007).

The Role of Selecting High-quality Teachers

Multiple studies on the effectiveness of the ICM units indicate that a teacher's ability to implement the units thoughtfully impacts on student learning (e.g., Little et al., 2007).

Just as the roles of curriculum, instruction, and assessment are central to the differentiation process, so too is the teacher. In the absence of a well-trained teacher, differentiation of materials is insufficient to affect student growth. Access to high quality, well-trained teachers in specific subject areas who can provide challenge and nurturance for our best learners is clearly a critical issue in implementing the ICM and the units of study which use it as an organizing framework. Without thoughtful teachers, the best curricula will lie dormant in classrooms. Teachers who have only strong management skills without knowledge of the content will fail to excite the gifted.

What are the critical requirements for identifying high-quality teachers who can implement the ICM effectively? First, teachers need to be lifelong learners themselves, open to new experiences, and able to appreciate the value of new learning and how it applies to the classroom. Second, they need to be passionate about at least one area of knowledge in which they have expertise, and be able to communicate that passion and its underlying expertise to students. This would imply deep knowledge in the subject area of the unit to be taught, coupled with the ability to use the skills associated with that knowledge domain at a high level. Third, they need to be good thinkers, able to manipulate ideas at the analysis, synthesis, and evaluation levels with their students within and across areas of knowledge. Such facility would imply that they themselves were strong students with strong reasoning skills. Fourth, teachers using ICM units effectively must be capable of processing information in a simultaneity mode, meaning that they must be able to address multiple objectives at the same time, recognize how students might manipulate different higher-level skills in the same task demand, and easily align lower-level tasks within those that require higher-level skills and concepts. In addition, they must be creative engineers, able to restructure lessons and shape learning opportunities based on available student data, including the results of performance-based assessments in the units of study.

Data confirming the significant role of teacher training in providing differentiated instruction for the gifted (Hansen & Feldhusen, 1994; Tomlinson et. al., 1994) and the availability of coursework in the education of the gifted (Parker & Karnes, 1991), provide a strong rationale for placing gifted students with teachers who have received at least 12 university hours of professional training. The benefits to gifted learners become greater when a differentiated curriculum is handled by those sensitive to the nature and needs of such students. Training in the direct implementation of curricular materials to be used is also necessary to prepare teachers effectively for implementation of curriculum based on the ICM. Depending on the experience of the teachers involved, about two to four days of training in the various approaches employed in the curriculum materials have generally supported initial implementation.

The Role of Professional Development in Implementing the ICM

An age of meaningful accountability calls out for school contexts in which teacher learning is as paramount a concern as student learning. Therefore, a key area of need within a system of curriculum and instruction is an effective plan for professional development and a follow-up evaluation mechanism. Guskey (2000) has argued that our accountability system for judging the efficacy of professional development is weak, and has suggested that we need to consider several areas for assessing effectiveness. These include the following: participants' reactions, participants' learning, organizational support for change, use of knowledge and skills, and student learning outcomes.

Professional development research has guided the professional development approaches employed in working with the ICM. These include selecting content topics that respond to real, as opposed to perceived, need. Thus, in implementing reform-based principles, it is necessary to ascertain those principles that teachers routinely employ already, and those they need to develop. A recent analysis of classroom data (VanTassel-Baska et al., 2008) suggested that teachers of the gifted need more training in the use of individualization techniques, critical thinking, problem solving, and meta-cognition, as the pattern of data suggests the greatest discrepancy between observed and desired teacher behavior in these dimensions. Thus, workshops on the implementation of appropriate curricular units should stress these skills.

A second research-based best practice in professional development involves emphasizing student learning in key areas as the goal of instruction, and using student-learning data as the best evidence of effective staff development work. At The College of William & Mary, the Center for Gifted Education's professional development model encourages teachers to collect student data on the models taught through staff development, and to use these data to make adjustments in their teaching. Only then can the claim of effective professional development be made.

A third area of research-based professional development practice involves the follow-up mechanisms that are in place in schools to encourage active experimentation with new teaching strategies and models (e.g., Guskey, 2002). Clearly, many schools are not positioned to engage in meaningful professional development practices, given the limited organizational support for such activity. Principals and teacher teams must be actively engaged in ensuring that practices learned are tried out and supported in everyday practice. Evidence suggests that teachers should practice a strategy or model and see how students react, before they make judgments about it. If students respond favorably, then teachers are more apt to adopt positive attitudes and beliefs about using a new model for learning (Guskey, 2000). Our experience with professional development suggests similar findings. Results from teacher implementation data in science, for example, consistently showed that teacher enthusiasm for problem-based learning rose as they saw their students' motivation increase with use of the pedagogy (VanTassel-Baska et al., 1998).

Another key finding from the professional development literature suggests that training on practices that are embedded in content and materials to be used in the classroom aids student learning, and, thus, enhances the likelihood that teachers will continue employing the practice (Kennedy, 1999). This strategy has been extensively employed in National Science Foundation (NSF) projects over the past two decades, as well as in the curricular implementation workshops through the Center for Gifted Education. A major emphasis in such training involves the teaching of a core model, practice, feedback, and then a demonstration of how and where it may be found in a unit of study or inserted into one. Closely linked to this demonstration is showing how the model is aligned to the teaching of the content area under discussion based on the demands of state standards. Thus, teachers leave a workshop with a contextual base for the use of the technique.

Moreover, recent studies on professional development support the use of research-based learning strategies, such as those employed in ICM curriculum, to promote student achievement and positively affect teacher behaviors (Johnson, Kahle, & Fargo, 2006; VanTassel-Baska et al., 2008). In specific studies using gifted samples, Gentry & Keilty (2004) and Gubbins et al. (2002) found that cluster teachers needed support in compacting the curriculum and systematically employing higher-level skills and strategies in their teaching. Matthews and Foster (2005) found that the resource teacher model of professional development was efficacious when it was dynamic and ongoing.

Finally, research-based best practice in professional development supports the need for a match between the sophistication of the learning and the duration of training opportunities. In-depth summer training options appear to work well as a first-stage effort when the learning to be accrued is complex, because they offer more intensive time away from the classroom. However, more follow-up training opportunities are required onsite to ensure faithful implementation of such practices, coupled with further in-depth and advanced training opportunities during the actual implementation of the curriculum innovation. Training in the direct implementation of curricular materials to be used is also necessary to prepare teachers effectively for implementation of curriculum based on the ICM. Depending on the experience of the teachers involved, about two to four days of training in the various approaches employed in the curriculum materials have generally supported initial implementation.

The Role of Instructional Leadership in Implementing the ICM

Instructional leadership is critical for successful implementation of the ICM. Our studies have consistently shown the importance of having the support of school and district leadership in the implementation process which translates into permission and encouragement of teachers. In order for an innovation to be valued, it must be monitored for effective implementation. Leaders send signals about the degree of value placed on any given innovation. Thus, school leaders must deliberately monitor classrooms on a regular basis to ensure that the ICM is being implemented well. Since most of the ICM strategies focus on higher-level skill and concept development approaches, some training for administrators is warranted to ensure that desired teacher practices are understood well enough to be effectively monitored. Instructional leaders must also be sensitive to the need for policy change (Swanson, 2007). In any innovation, there will be continued need for support from a community that values the innovation, forward progress on converting the innovation to school, district and even state policy, and the mechanisms and will to collect research data on its effectiveness at all levels of the schooling enterprise. This process also implies that there is a leader in place over time to shepherd these changes through a system designed to continue the status quo rather than support innovation.

Leaders must also be motivational and even inspirational in schools in order to lift the spirits of teachers and students who are engaged in the difficult work of enhancing learning. Thus, principals must be aware of the need for honoring the culture and symbolically rewarding the efforts that go on within it (Peterson, 2001). A high priority must be placed on accolades for enhanced learning. One school district, for example, rotates board meetings to each school in the district, and asks the principal of each school to stage a performance demonstrating student learning using ICM unit activities as the basis for the performance.

FINAL LESSONS

As schools and districts consider implementation of the ICM, it may be helpful to consider the lessons we have learned over the past 20 years of curriculum design, development, field-testing, and efficacy research in our quest to upgrade curriculum and instructional quality for the gifted learners in our schools. These lessons include the need to use curriculum design templates that organize curriculum effectively for use in schools and classrooms; the need to employ teaching and learning models as scaffolds to elevate thinking and conceptual development; and the need to use curriculum designed for the gifted with other populations who can access it—typically learners who have not yet been identified as gifted, but who are promising in a given academic area. Lessons learned from professional development continue to suggest the need for follow-up learning at key points to ensure fidelity of implementation; advanced training as readiness dictates; and the ongoing support of leadership in schools and districts to ensure that the model is institutionalized. In the final analysis, we have learned that curriculum differentiation itself matters in enhancing the learning of gifted students if it is enacted thoughtfully and in the spirit intended.

BIBLIOGRAPHY

Adler, M. (1984). *The Paideia Program.* New York: MacMillan

Amabile, T. (1996). *Creativity in context.* Boulder, CO: Westview Press.

American Association for the Advancement of Science. (1990). *Science for all Americans: Project 2061.* New York: Oxford University Press.

Banks, J. (1994a). *An introduction to multicultural education.* Boston: Allyn & Bacon.

Banks, J. (1994b). *Multiethnic education: Theory and practice* (3rd ed.). Boston: Allyn & Bacon.

Banks, J. (2001). *Cultural diversity and education: foundations, curriculum, and teaching.* Boston: Allyn & Bacon.

Csikszentmihalyi, M. (1991). *Flow: The psychology of optimal experience.* New York: Harper Perennial.

Csikszentmihalyi, M., Rathunde, K. R., & Whalen, S. (1993). *Talented teenagers: The roots of success and failure.* New York: Cambridge University Press.

Feng, A., VanTassel-Baska, J., Quek, C., O'Neil, B., & Bai, W. (2005). A longitudinal assessment of gifted students' learning using the Integrated Curriculum Model: Impacts and perceptions of the William and Mary language arts and science curriculum. *Roeper Review, 27,* 78–83.

Ford, D. (2005). Integrating multicultural and gifted education: A curricular framework. *Theory into Practice, 44*(2), 125–138.

Ford, D., & Harris, J. J. (1999). *Multicultural gifted education* (Education and Psychology of the Gifted Series). New York: Teachers College Press.

Gentry, M., & Keilty, B. (2004). Rural and suburban cluster grouping: Reflections on staff development as a component of program success. *Roeper Review, 26,* 147–155.

Gubbins, E. J., Westberg, K. L., Reis, S. M., Dinnocenti, S. T., Tieso, C. L., Muller, L. M. et al. (2002). *Implementing a professional development model using gifted education strategies with all students.* (Research Monograph 02172). Storrs: The National Research Center on the Gifted and Talented, University of Connecticut.

Guskey, T. (2000). *Evaluating professional development.* Thousand Oaks, CA: Corwin Press.

Guskey, T. R. (2002). Does it make a difference? Evaluating professional development. *Educational Leadership, 59*(6), 45–51.

Hansen, J., & Feldhusen, J. (1994). Comparison of trained and untrained teachers of the gifted. *Gifted Child Quarterly, 38,* 115–123.

Johnsen, S. K. (2000, Summer). What the research says about curriculum. *Tempo, 25*–30.

Johnson, C. C., Kahle, J. B., & Fargo, J. D. (2006). Effective teaching results in increased science achievement for all. *Science Education, 91,* 371–383. doi: 10.1002/sce.20195

Kaplan, S. (2009). The Kaplan grid. In J. Renzulli (Ed.) *Systems and models in gifted education.* Waco, TX: Prufrock Press.

Kennedy, M. (1999). Form and substance in mathematics and science professional development. *NISE Brief, 3*(2), 1–7.

Kim, K. H., VanTassel-Baska, J., Bracken, B. A., Feng, A., Stambaugh, T., & Bland, L. (in press). *Project Clarion: Three years of science instruction in Title I schools among K–third grade students.*

Little, C. A., Feng, A. X., VanTassel-Baska, J., Rogers, K. B., & Avery, L. D. (2007) A study of curriculum effectiveness in social studies. *Gifted Child Quarterly, 51,* 272–284.

Maker, J., & Schiever, J. (2009). *Curriculum development and teaching strategies for gifted learners.* Austin, TX: Pro-Ed.

Marzano, R. (1992). *Cultivating thinking in English.* Urbana, IL: National Council for Teachers of English.

Matthews, D., & Foster, J. (2005). A dynamic scaffolding model of teacher development: The gifted education consultant as catalyst for change. *Gifted Child Quarterly, 49*, 222–230.

Minstrell, J., & Kraus, P. (2005). Guided inquiry in the science classroom. In J. Bransford, A. Brown, & R. Cocking (Eds.), *How students learn: History, mathematics, and science in the classroom* (pp. 475–477). Washington, DC: National Academy Press.

National Research Council. (2000). *How people learn.* Washington, DC: Author.

Parker, J., & Karnes, F. (1991). Graduate degree programs and resource centers in gifted education: An update and analysis. *Gifted Child Quarterly, 35*, 43–48.

Paul, R., & Elder, L. (2001). *Critical thinking: Tools for taking charge of your learning and your life.* Upper Saddle River, NJ: Prentice Hall.

Perkins, D. (1992). Selecting fertile themes for integrated learning. In H. H. Jacob (Ed.), *Interdisciplinary curriculum: Design and implementation* (pp. 67–75). Alexandria, VA: Association for Supervision and Curriculum Development.

Perkins, D., & Salomon, G. (1989). Are cognitive skills context bound? *Educational Research, 18*(1), 16–25.

Peterson, K. (2001, June). *Shaping school culture for quality teaching and learning.* Presentation to the National Leadership Institute, The College of William & Mary, Williamsburg.

Sher, B. T. (2003). Adapting science curricula for high-ability learners. In J. VanTassel-Baska, & C. Little (Eds.), *Content-based curriculum for high-ability learners* (pp. 191–218). Waco, TX: Prufrock Press.

Swanson, J. (2006). Breaking through assumptions about low-income, minority gifted students. *Gifted Child Quarterly, 50*, 11–24.

Swanson, J. (2007). Policy and practice: a case study of gifted education policy implementation. *Journal for the Education of the Gifted, 31*, 131–164.

Tomlinson, C. A. (2005). *How to differentiate instruction in mixed-ability classrooms* (2nd ed.). Upper Saddle River, NJ: Pearson.

Tomlinson, C., Tomchin, E., Callahan, C., Adams, C., Pizzat-Timi, P., Cunningham, C. et al. (1994). Practices of preservice teachers related to gifted and other academically diverse learners. *Gifted Child Quarterly, 38*, 106–114.

VanTassel-Baska, J. (1986). Effective curriculum and instructional models for talented students. *Gifted Child Quarterly, 30*, 164–169.

VanTassel-Baska, J. (2003). *Curriculum planning and instructional design for gifted learners* (2nd ed.). Denver, CO: Love.

VanTassel-Baska, J. (2008). *Assessment for gifted students.* Waco, TX: Prufrock Press.

VanTassel-Baska, J., Bass, G., Ries, R., Poland, D., & Avery, L. D. (1998). A national study of science curriculum effectiveness with high-ability students. *Gifted Child Quarterly, 42*, 200–211.

VanTassel-Baska, J., Bracken, B., Feng, A., & Brown, E. (2009). A longitudinal study of reading comprehension and reasoning ability of students in elementary Title I schools. *Journal for the Education of the Gifted, 33*(1), 7–37.

VanTassel-Baska, J., & Brown, E. (2007). Toward best practice: An analysis of the efficacy of curriculum models in gifted education. *Gifted Child Quarterly, 51*, 342–358.

VanTassel-Baska, J., Feng, A., Brown, E., Bracken, B., Stambaugh, T., French, H. et al. (2008). A study of differentiated instructional change over three years. *Gifted Child Quarterly, 52*, 297–312.

VanTassel-Baska, J., & Little, C. (2011). *Content-based curriculum for the gifted.* Waco, TX: Prufrock Press.

VanTassel-Baska, J., & Stambaugh, T. (2006). *Comprehensive curriculum for the gifted.* Boston: Pearson.

VanTassel-Baska, J., Zuo, L., Avery, L. D., & Little, C. A. (2002). A curriculum study of gifted student learning in the language arts. *Gifted Child Quarterly, 46*, 30–44.

Vygotsky, L. S. (1978). *Mind in society: The development of higher psychological processes.* Cambridge, MA: Harvard University Press.

Ward, V. (1981). *Educating the gifted: An axiomatic approach.* Ventura County, CA: Leadership Training Institute on the Gifted and Talented.

Section V

Specific Populations

32

HETEROGENEITY AMONG THE GIFTED

Not an Oxymoron

Carolyn M. Callahan and Holly L. Hertberg-Davis

It is a common, and easily understandable, belief that gifted students are a homogeneous population; however, thoughtful reflection will quickly lead to a very different perspective. While the screening and identification of gifted students does somewhat reduce the degree to which the resulting group varies, variability is not entirely erased. Like all students, identified gifted students still exist along continua of aptitudes and achievement (albeit within a smaller range) in areas of interest and passion, in preferred learning modes, and in the area of social and emotional adjustment. Individual differences among gifted learners and the means of responding appropriately to those differences have been addressed in chapters on definition, identification, service delivery options, and curriculum. However, there are additional important group characteristics, dimensions of beliefs and behavior, and potentially overlooked issues which need attention when planning educational programs for subgroups of gifted students.

For many reasons, consideration must be given to the potential differences among those identified as gifted, and to the possibility that some gifted students may not be easily identified for reasons that can be attributed to cultural differences, to differences in opportunity to learn, to handicapping or disabling conditions that might mask giftedness, or to biases in the process of identification. Indeed, as will become apparent, every gifted student falls into one of these subgroups; some are members of multiple subgroups. A student may (simply?) be a gifted male; another may be a gifted African American male who is twice exceptional.

It must be noted at the outset of this discussion that recognition of potential differences in the values, opportunities, characteristics, or behaviors that may typify a subgroup does carry with it two potential dangers. The first is overgeneralization and stereotyping. Just as including the item "enjoys reading advanced texts" on a behavior checklist used in screening for academic talent may lead to the false premise that *all* gifted students enjoy reading advanced texts and will always be seen carrying a heavy tome, so, too, a discussion of the issues faced by some gifted males may falsely lead to the generalization that *all* gifted males face those same issues. The second danger is a sense of being over-whelmed by all the subtleties one is expected to attend to in designing curriculum and instruction for the gifted. But rest assured, awareness of potential differences among subgroups of gifted students will ring true to lessons already learned about subgroups in the general population, with a layer of uniqueness. Most likely, awareness will lead to more effective decision making and greater insights into successful instructional plan-ning, and, consequently, greater accomplishments by students.

DIFFERENCES AMONG THE IDENTIFIED POPULATION OF GIFTED STUDENTS

There are many ways of thinking about the subgroups of students who are identified as gifted. The subgroups identified in this section are groups defined by gender or achieve-ment/underachievement patterns, geography, ethnicity, or cultural differences. Each of these groups is characterized by documented differences that affect engagement, achieve-ment, and ultimate probability of members achieving their full potential. The chapters in this section provide in-depth consideration of reasons why special attention should be paid to these specific populations of identified gifted students.

DIFFERENCES THAT MAY PRECLUDE IDENTIFICATION

While there are differences among subgroups of students identified as gifted, there are also differences among students in the general population whose talents are never addressed because we fail even to recognize that talent. Considerable attention has been directed at the under-representation of these students in programs for the gifted. Among the groups most often recognized as deserving of special attention for identification, talent development, and subsequent adjustments in curriculum are African American, Latino/Latina, and twice-exceptional learners. The authors of the chapters which follow provide insights into the ways we can come to see the possibility for these gifted children if they are recognized as such.

Of course, the scope of an introductory textbook is limited and we recognize there are other groups who have not received their due in this section (e.g., gay, lesbian, bi- and trans-sexual students; second language learners; and students with physical disabilities such as those with visual impairment and hearing loss). Their omission should not be interpreted as lack of recognition of the importance of considering the special needs of these students, or the importance of considering the issues they face as we plan gifted programs.

QUESTIONS TO GUIDE YOUR READING

1. What are some common themes across the groups of students discussed in these chapters? How are they alike?
2. What are the unique characteristics of each group?
3. Of the many suggestions made by the authors for modifying identification, pro-gram options or curricula, which seem most important?
4. Of groups not included (e.g., gifted second language learners), what would you surmise are some of the particular issues to consider in providing adequate educa-tional programs for these students?

33

GIFTED MALES

Understanding Their Challenges and Honoring Their Potential

Thomas P. Hébert

To better understand the lives of gifted males, spend some time in a park watching adolescent males play basketball. Observe closely and listen to their conversations. You will hear young men expressing warmth for each other in indirect ways, with lots of good-natured teasing. Through their animated conversation, you will hear unspoken masculine rules that govern adolescence. They may also report on their views of the girls in their schools. You may learn the latest trends in popular culture and technology and pick up current statistics on prominent athletes. You will certainly hear an assessment of what is wrong with school, which teachers challenge them, and which of their buddies are slacking off academically. You may even get a glimpse into the dreams and aspirations of these young men as they enjoy a game of hoops together.

In listening to these rich conversations, adults come to understand that growing up gifted and male involves complex challenges as well as advantages for success. Research on gifted males indicates that they have differing needs and strengths, and includes reports of best practices for promoting the success of this special population. This chapter will examine the issues central to the intellectual and psychosocial development of gifted males, including negotiating masculinity, the role of athleticism, identity development, underachievement, and the failure of schools to respond to the interests and learning styles of males. An exploration of best practices for promoting success is also presented, including father–son engagement, mentoring, management of athletics and extracurricular activities, counseling approaches, and instructional strategies aligned with the interests and learning preferences of gifted males.

NEGOTIATING MASCULINITY

Every young man is expected to understand society's image of what is masculine. These expectations are established at birth and continue to influence the development of

331

males throughout life. Negotiating societal rules about the meaning of masculinity is a challenge all boys face. Gifted males must determine not only what it means to be a man, but also what it means to be an intelligent male with special talents with which to contribute to society and realize full development of their potential.

Masculine gender expectations are socially constructed, rigidly enforced, and significant in shaping men's lives. Gifted boys seeking to understand how to become men receive messages from their peers and older males that there are certain rules that must be followed in becoming a man. Pollack (1998) refers to these rules as the "Boy Code"— a set of outdated and constricting assumptions, models, and societal rules that dictate what it means to be a man. One feature of this set of beliefs is that vulnerability, weakness, and the more gentle and caring emotions that are considered feminine must be camouflaged in order to survive boyhood. Pollack (1998, p. 14) highlights examples of this Boy Code in the preschool boy who shrugs and attempts to smile after he is hit in the eye with a baseball, as he struggles to blink back tears of pain; in the fifth grader whose parents have recently divorced who becomes the boisterous class clown; and in the teenager who responds to his school counselor's concerns about his academic troubles with a shrug of the shoulders and a "So what?"

The Boy Code may drive gifted males to mask their true identities and manage their image in order to play according to these rules. They may feel compelled to live semiauthentic lives while concealing their true selves. Such pressure to disconnect from their vulnerable inner selves may force gifted males to present a false image of invincibility. This image may be so convincing that it eventually becomes a barrier to authentic communication or intimacy and may ultimately become impossible to shed, leaving gifted boys vulnerable to difficulty in school and emotionally hollow, angry, or depressed (Hébert, 2002; Neu & Weinfeld, 2007; Pollack, 1998).

This issue becomes complex for psychologically androgynous gifted young men. Psychological androgyny, defined as a "person's ability to be at the same time aggressive and nurturant, sensitive and rigid, dominant and submissive, regardless of gender" (Csikszentmihalyi, 1996, p. 71), has been identified as a characteristic of gifted individuals. Researchers have reported that psychologically androgynous men have broader notions of appropriate or inappropriate male behavior, and their androgynous thinking does not threaten or diminish their sense of masculinity or their identity as men. Gifted young men who think this way and live their lives accordingly may be perfectly comfortable with themselves (Wilcove, 1998); however, this comfort with self may not completely protect them from peers who operate according to the Boy Code and reject sensitivity, empathy, and emotional expression from other males.

As a result, gifted males may find themselves the victims of bullying. A groundbreaking study by Peterson and Ray (2006) examined gifted middle school students and bullying and found that at all grade levels, a higher percentage of gifted males than gifted females were bullied. They indicated that 73 percent of males reported being bullied at some point between kindergarten and eighth grade. With research studies underscoring the significance of this issue, adults must appreciate the challenges that gifted young men face in negotiating their masculinity, and support them in discovering their authentic selves and developing comfort with their identities as gifted males.

THE ROLE OF ATHLETICISM

Consider this scenario. A young man begins his day at the breakfast table reaching for a box of cereal. A photo of an Olympic athlete greets him from the cover of that box. Shortly afterward, as he travels to school, he notices several cars with bumper stickers advertising parental pride in their son's involvement on the school soccer team. Arriving at his high school, he enters the building and is greeted by the large trophy case of athletic awards in the foyer. The discussion at lunch with the other young men at his table revolves around the results of the state university's success in defeating their arch-rival on Saturday. After a full day of classes he is reminded again of sports as he watches a television teenage situation comedy in which the handsome quarterback wins the heart of an adoring cheerleader.

The subtle messages that adolescent gifted males receive throughout a day illustrate the all-encompassing quality of U.S. society's athletic culture. These messages may influence their development in numerous ways. Questions to consider include: How does participation in sports affect psychosocial development? How do educators and parents help gifted males prosper in the culture of athletics and cope with the pressure to achieve in the masculine domain of sports? How do families and schools support non-athletic boys in a culture that places high value on athletic prowess? Finally, for the gifted young men grappling with multi-potentiality throughout adolescence, how do multi-talented scholar–athletes decide on appropriate outlets for developing both their academic and athletic talents?

Athletics offers many more benefits than strictly providing males with engagement in competition and outlets for expressing themselves through motion and energy release. Through interviews with athletes, Neu and Weinfeld (2007) noted that the high school and collegiate males they spoke with highlighted multiple benefits from involvement in sports. The athletes indicated that through sports, they developed positive personal qualities and learned important life lessons including self-efficacy, resiliency, perseverance, self-regulation, goal setting, self-esteem, and the ability to work with others through teamwork. In addition, the athletes interviewed pointed out that they developed an attribute known as "coachability"—the ability to listen, receive constructive feedback, and change behavior as a result of instruction. Neu and Weinfeld noted that these same characteristics are highly valued in careers beyond athletics and can enhance gifted males' ability to improve themselves and their communities.

Since involvement in sports can serve important developmental functions, it is critical that young men who choose to participate in sports engage in high-quality athletic experiences, thereby increasing the likelihood that they will benefit academically, athletically, and personally. The influence of the coach who designs these experiences cannot be underestimated. High school athletics have long played an important and beneficial role in the lives of young male athletes (Hébert, 1995; Kleiber & Kirshnit, 1990), and under the leadership of effective coaches, school athletic programs provide environments where kinesthetic talents are nurtured and developmental issues are addressed.

Within the culture of every high school are various athletic subcultures, each with its own value system. In his ethnography of an urban high school, Hébert (1995) discovered such a subculture, a swimming team, where gifted males not only excelled as athletes but also achieved academic excellence under their coach's guidance. Through experiences with their coach, the gifted males derived many benefits. Along with physical fitness, they learned the importance of remaining committed to a task, the value of having a passion, the rewards of cooperative teamwork, the importance of striving for excellence, the value of having a supportive mentor, and the sweet taste of achieving success.

According to many adolescents, nothing is worse than being an uncoordinated, non-athletic male in America's sports-dominated culture. Young men not blessed with athletic ability struggle to maintain peer approval in other ways. Educators and parents can help young men who want to participate in sports, but lack the ability, by engaging their passion for sports through different outlets. Non-athletes can apply their intellectual talents to the world of athletics in creative ways. Talented mathematicians might assist coaches in maintaining statistics for the school's sports programs. A student-designed television sports program shared in the school cafeteria might gain gifted non-athletic males significant peer group approval. Local newspapers could provide prestigious opportunities for volunteer sports reporters.

It is also important to acknowledge that there are gifted males who lack any interest in sports, and they too struggle to feel and appear masculine under the Boy Code without having to feign an interest in something they truly do not care about. In addition to concerns for non-athletic males or those not interested in sports, challenges also exist for the multi-talented male. For gifted males who excel in multiple domains—whether in music, academics, student government, drama, or other areas—the school's athletic field often becomes one more significant arena in which they feel compelled to prove themselves to peers, teachers, and families. In addition to the pressure that gifted young men may feel to be involved in sports, their extracurricular overload may lead to time-management problems and struggles with prioritizing their commitments. Many gifted males grapple with multi-potentiality early in their school careers, and for them, everything they do emerges as golden accomplishments. Coaches, club advisors, teachers, and administrators often recruit these multi-talented scholar–athletes to become involved in their own special projects or sports. Such well-meaning adults often fail to realize the high level of stress they may create in gifted males who feel driven to please everyone.

IDENTITY DEVELOPMENT

Researchers and theorists of gifted education who explore issues of identity development argue that despite their special talents, gifted adolescents, like all adolescents, struggle with identity development (Coleman & Cross, 2001; Hébert & Kelly, 2006). Coleman and Cross maintained that gifted students faced more conflict in their lives as young people because their advanced development and specific talents increased societal expectations. For gifted males (and females), in addition to being an adolescent, have to be *gifted* adolescents, a role that others do not have to manage.

Social context plays a crucial role in identity formation, as gifted males face the challenge of shaping an emerging identity while simultaneously juggling conflicting social demands. These conflicting demands include the message that gifted males are different and their differences lead to being praised and criticized for their strengths. Another message is the expectation that their exceptional talents should produce outstanding results at all times. In other words, they are expected never to fail or even just be average. In addition, they are expected to be constant achievers, and they may discover that others see them as "gifted students," but not as distinct individuals. When they eventually succeed at getting others to regard them as intelligent males, they hear messages such as "Dude, you really are a cool guy after all!" (Coleman & Cross, 2001; Hébert & Kelly, 2006).

In a study of six high-achieving males in a multi-ethnic urban high school, Hébert (2000a) uncovered a key role played by identity formation of gifted males. A strong belief in self emerged as the most influential factor shaping the success of the young men. They had constructed solid identities that provided them with the energy, drive, and tools they needed to face life's challenges in an urban setting. Their clearly defined aspirations were aligned with their personal qualities, strengths, and talents. They saw their aspirations as attainable because they possessed the motivation and drive to achieve.

Several qualities merged in these young men that supported their identity formation: sensitivity, multicultural appreciation, and an inner will. The study identified several factors that influenced this strong belief in self. Relationships with supportive adults who respected the students as capable young men were significant; strong emotional support from families was important to them; and involvement in talent development opportunities such as extracurricular activities, sports, and rigorous summer school experiences appeared to reinforce belief in self.

Similar results were found in subsequent studies conducted by Hébert on special populations of gifted males in different contexts. A strong belief in self was found to be significant in shaping the experiences of a group of gifted university males pursuing careers in elementary education. Their identities incorporated a sincere caring quality and they appreciated the empathic qualities within themselves because they realized these characteristics enabled them to be better professionals (Hébert, 2000b).

In addition, Hébert (2002) examined gifted African American first-generation college males in a predominantly White university and found that their firm belief in self, combined with strong internal motivation, played an important role in shaping their identity as achievers.

Aware of deeply ingrained racism in institutions and individuals they encountered throughout their adolescence, they remained unfazed and focused on their goals as they pursued college degrees on a campus where racist incidents occurred. Notably, in all three of Hébert's studies, significant adults who served as mentors to these gifted males reinforced their strong identities.

UNDERACHIEVEMENT AND SELECTIVE ACHIEVEMENT IN GIFTED MALES

Most educators agree that underachievement—broadly defined as a discrepancy between intellectual potential and academic performance—is a major problem in our schools. Researchers suggest this phenomenon is also a critical issue for gifted males (Peterson & Colangelo, 1996; Reis & McCoach, 2000). The underlying problems that influence underachievement in gifted students are well documented and include personality, family, community and school environment, social and cultural factors, and curriculum.

Individual personality factors play a role in the achievement orientations of young people. For example, an internal locus of control commonly referred to as an inner drive is evident in the personalities of achievers, while underachievers often explain their lack of academic success on external factors such as their environment or lack of parental support (Siegle & McCoach, 2005). A gifted male may blame his lack of achievement on the absence of the latest technology at home:

If my dad took me to the mall and bought me a new laptop, I would be more motivated to start the school year fresh. I'm sure my attitude would change. There's something about new tech stuff that gets me all psyched. That might sound weird, but it's using cool technology that makes a difference for me.

Rather than taking charge of his academic efforts, he blames his dismal school record on external circumstances he cannot control (Siegle & McCoach, 2005).

Research has indicated that family dynamics may also impact on students' efforts in school (Hébert, 2001; Rimm, 2008). For example, sibling rivalry may contribute to a gifted male's loss of academic motivation. Consider the gifted student whose older sister is the valedictorian in his high school. He smiles sheepishly and shrugs as he explains:

Nobody knows me as Mitchell, everyone in this high school knows me as Margaret's little brother. It's been like that since I was in elementary school. It will be nice when she graduates from here, but I bet I'll still be known as Margaret's younger brother.

When a young man decides that another member of the family is the academic superstar and he cannot compete, he may cease to try, finding other outlets for self-expression and purposefully underachieving in academics.

Community values may also influence how academic achievement is viewed within schools. Consider the experience of a mathematically precocious male who leaves a school district where the NASA space industry drives the economic base of the community, and transfers to a high school in a smaller rural community where the schools' athletic programs dictate the social life of the community. The gifted mathematician who thrived in a high school where mathematics and science competitions were celebrated, and students competed for admission to highly selective colleges and universities, finds himself lost and frustrated in a community and school culture that centers on athletic participation and prowess. His academic strengths may not be recognized or supported appropriately and his academic skills may atrophy over time.

The peer group in any school setting exerts a powerful influence on attitudes toward academic achievement. When peers determine that academic excellence is not masculine, school life for gifted males becomes complicated. Consider the experiences of gifted minority males capable of excelling in Honors or Advanced Placement courses whose involvement in such programs is disparaged by their male counterparts. They question whether it is worth the risk to achieve academically. This issue is reflected in the poignant message delivered by an African American male in college:

Think of seafood dealers. They never have to put a lid on their seafood tanks because the crabs always keep each other in. Every time a crab tries to climb out of the tank, other crabs clutch it and bring it back. So the dealer never has to use a lid on the tank. I don't want to say that misery loves company, but with some brothers it's an understood solidarity. It's understood that you're not supposed to be different.

(Olenchak & Hébert, 2002, p. 206)

Finally, the school curriculum may exacerbate underachievement in gifted males. An increased focus on language arts and reading instruction has emerged as a result of the standards movement in education (Gurian & Stevens, 2005; Hébert & Pagnani, 2010). But allocating more time to the development of reading and writing skills comes at the price of allocating less time to other areas of the curriculum such as art or science. Many of the content areas that are streamlined are those that have traditionally motivated males and enabled them to excel. The result is that boys have fewer opportunities to strengthen their skills in their preferred academic domains. They find early on that schools have become "feminine" places that do not value their strengths; in response, they underachieve academically in curriculum that is no longer aligned with their interests and strengths (Gurian & Stevens, 2005; Norfleet James, 2007). Neu and Weinfeld (2007) captured this issue succinctly:

> Rather than developing good readers who can later become scientists, as schools intend, we are losing scientists who don't have a chance to focus their scientific talent and interest early in life and who quickly conclude that school is not a place where they can succeed.
>
> (Neu & Weinfeld, 2007, pp. 33–34)

Two studies on gifted males have identified selective achievers (Hébert & Schreiber, 2010; Speirs Neumeister & Hébert, 2003). Selective achievers are "intrinsically motivated individuals whose performance matches ability only in specific areas that satisfy their interests and personal goal orientations" (Hébert & Schreiber, 2010, p. 570). These two comprehensive case-study investigations identified similar patterns of behavior among gifted college-age males. The findings indicated that strong intrinsic motivation, combined with independence and resistance to conformity played an influential role in shaping the achievement patterns of these young men. The males in these studies demanded serious intellectual challenges associated with gaining practical knowledge that would help them reach their personal goals. They identified the personalities and teaching styles of educators as important factors in determining whether they would put forth effort. The young men emphasized the importance of gaining concrete and practical knowledge, while also demanding efficient ways of learning. The researchers in both studies concluded that educators who seek to understand what is occurring with selective achievers must refrain from jumping to quick conclusions and assigning the label "underachievers" or "slackers." Instead, they must examine closely the motivation behind the inconsistent achievement patterns. By examining the attitudes and motivation of gifted males who insist on engaging in learning according to their own rules, Hébert and his colleagues have drawn important distinctions between underachievement and selective achievement in gifted young men.

SCHOOLS NOT RESPONDING TO MALE INTERESTS AND LEARNING PREFERENCES

Jon Scieszka, a popular author of children's literature, edited an anthology of short stories, memoirs, poems, and comics by boy-friendly authors. In *Guys Write for Guys Read*, Scieszka's (2005) foreword includes a helpful message to his young male audience:

> Hey guys—now here is something for you to read. A bunch of pieces by a bunch of guys . . . all about being a guy. Some are memories. Some are stories. Some are just

pieces of art these guys drew when they were your age . . . I know you are going to find something in here, because these things are funny, action-packed, sad, goofy, gross, touching, stupid, true, and all very short.

(Scieszka, 2005, p. 11)

Scieszka's message provides a vivid example of how the learning interests and preferred learning modes of boys often differ from those of their female counterparts. His words should be a signal to educators that we need to re-evaluate the ways we teach male students. For many boys, reading is a major obstacle to achieving school success. Schools have reported a downward trend in boys' achievement in reading and writing even as the standards movement and mandated testing have increased schools' emphasis on teaching language arts (Gurian & Stevens, 2005). Educators have reported that boys often view reading as a feminine activity perhaps because they have little interest in the books chosen by their primarily female teachers and school administrators (Hébert & Pagnani, 2010).

Although male readers enjoy several genres, research has identified a serious disconnection between boys' reading preferences and academic language arts curricula (Cavazos-Kottke, 2006; Millard, 1997; Partington, 2006). Non-fiction, science fiction, fantasy, horror, action, and comedy may all appeal to young male readers, but this matters very little, when early educational experiences and language arts classes focus on the types of literature that typically cater to girls. For example, character-driven narrative fiction has been shown to have little appeal to boys, yet the majority of required reading books comes from this "dialogue and emotions" type of literature and boys are often asked to explore the feelings of the book characters, though they may have little ability or desire to do so (Partington, 2006).

Educators struggle to employ strategies that encourage boys' interest in writing and develop their skills as writers. Writing has become part of every subject; boys often complain that it is no longer enough to solve a mathematics problem; they now must write about how they solved it (Neu & Weinfeld, 2007). The challenges of engaging males in reading and writing are only two examples of schools' failure to respond to male interests and preferred modes of learning.

Schools often present an environment that prevents males from learning in ways that may be more natural for them. Boys' needs—for movement, authentic hands-on projects, research, and experiential activities—are often neglected in schools. In addition, many boys have a natural tendency to be physically active and competitive (Neall, 2002; Norfleet James, 2007). When such a preference in males collides with a discouraging school environment, males feel alienated from classrooms. Neu and Weinfeld (2007) captured the essence of the problem:

While outside of school, students are multitasking and interacting with a variety of technology; inside of school they are expected to maintain focus for long periods of time on information that is primarily presented in the same low-tech way that it has been for years—listening to a teacher talk or reading a book.

(Neu & Weinfeld, 2007, p. 13)

Scholars have called attention to the importance of the digital technologies that engage adolescent males daily and the critical need for teachers to understand what young people view as modern literacy (Alvermann, 2002). Boys today are exploring the world via the internet, doing their homework on computers, and using social networking to connect with friends near and far. Educators are faced with teaching a generation of multitaskers, students who are instant messaging, text messaging, downloading music, networking in online social spaces, blogging, and designing web pages while simultaneously doing their homework (Hébert & Pagnani, 2010). Learners will engage in materials that have intrinsic value to them and teachers must therefore transfer the after-school technology practices of adolescent males into their classrooms.

BEST PRACTICES TO SUPPORT THE DEVELOPMENT OF GIFTED MALES

A number of strategies have been suggested in the gifted education literature to support the intellectual and emotional development of high-ability males: father–son engagement, mentoring, teaching boys to balance athletics and extracurricular activities, masculine counseling approaches, and using boy-friendly teaching strategies in classrooms.

Father–Son Engagement

Hébert, Pagnani, and Hammond (2009) examined paternal influences in the lives of significant American men through a comprehensive analysis of biographies and autobiographies of 10 prominent men. The researchers examined the father–son relationship to understand how effective fathers supported their high-achieving sons, and found that the fathers in this study maintained an unconditional belief in their sons, providing encouragement and guidance while maintaining high expectations and fostering determination. Fathers also modeled a strong work ethic for their sons, the father–son relationships incorporated mutual admiration and respect, and the fathers consistently expressed pride in their sons' accomplishments.

The interwoven themes in this study are important in understanding positive father–son relationships. As evident in the study, a father who works hard to provide for his family presents an example for his son, who himself strives to work hard in school and subsequently in his chosen profession. From this shared work ethic, mutual admiration and respect grow between father and son. A son who recognizes that his father has confidence in him and believes him capable of high accomplishment will begin to think of himself as an achiever. When a father's guidance encourages his son and teaches him lessons that help him achieve success, it is not surprising that he would openly express pride in his son's accomplishments. The fathers of the men featured in the study provided a model of engagement that may serve as a foundation for effective parenting of gifted males. They reinforce Gurian's (1996) view of healthy fatherhood: The father is involved in his son's life early on, communicates to him a sense of heritage and tradition, allows him to shape his own identity, and assists him in making the transition from boyhood to manhood with independence and respect.

Mentoring

From the research on father–son relationships, it is evident that relationships with adult males can have a lasting influence on gifted males. This may be especially significant for intelligent young men who are raised in households headed by single mothers. Research on mentors for gifted students documents the numerous intellectual, motivational, and emotional benefits of mentoring relationships (Clasen & Clasen, 2003; Hébert & Speirs Neumeister, 2000). Moreover, the influence of a significant adult on young males may be critical in reversing underachievement (Hébert & Olenchak, 2000).

Mentors for gifted males must be open-minded and non-judgmental, providing consistent and individualized social and emotional support and advocacy. Successful mentoring interventions consist of strength and interest-based strategies for addressing achievement. Mentors will be most effective when they genuinely care for their protégés, believe in them as unique individuals with special talents and abilities, and can look beyond the typical adolescent behaviors of boys to celebrate their strengths as gifted young men.

Teaching Boys to Balance Athletics and Extracurricular Activities

In a research study examining gifted high-achieving university males involved in a fraternity, Hébert (2006) discovered that the participants had been scholar–athletes in high school. In the fraternity, they became associated with older gifted males who were establishing themselves as student leaders in their university. Following the advice of the older "brothers," they became involved in extracurricular activities and programs associated with the fraternity and other campus groups involved in community service, campus leadership, and student government.

These experiences served as outlets for talent development as the young men developed areas of strength beyond athletics. The older successful role models within the fraternity helped these gifted males juggle busy schedules, maintain academic excellence, and manage their time wisely. Educators in K–12 schools may want to consider a mentoring approach, with senior high school males sharing success stories, time-management strategies, and personal advice with younger gifted boys.

Masculine Counseling Approaches

Educators and counselors who work extensively with gifted males have found that important conversations with young men are much easier when mutually engaged in a hands-on activity. Hébert and Danielian (2008) designed a model for an overnight "male only" outdoor adventure for gifted adolescent males, facilitated by male teachers and chaperoned by fathers and other adult males. The experience includes trust-building and team-building activities, a group project in which the participants undertake improvements to the outdoor environment, time for physical competitions between boys and their chaperones, collaborative preparation of meals, time for sharing individual talents, and open forum time for man-to-man conversation. The experience concludes with a campfire and a meaningful movie that addresses the issues of growing up male.

Pollack (1998) captured the essence of this approach: "start with action and energy, throw in loyalty and laughter, and 'doing together.' Add covert verbal expressions of caring, earnestness, and hidden physical touching—and you get a good friend" (p. 195). This formula for authenticity among males can inform masculine counseling approaches to be used with gifted males. Experiences with outdoor adventure, guided by appropriate role modeling from teachers and chaperones, show boys how males can benefit from sharing their lives with each other in man-to-man conversations, either in open fora or as they are engaged in activities together.

Incorporating Boy-friendly Teaching Strategies

To address the educational needs of gifted males, teachers need to expand their repertoire of instructional methods and strategies to include boy-friendly techniques aligned with the interests and learning styles of young men. By incorporating more boy-friendly teaching strategies, educators will be able to address their students' diverse interests, talents, and strengths. Strategies that provide different ways for boys to demonstrate understanding of course content would include more hands-on, experiential, and project-based learning; simulations; oral presentations; panel discussions and debates; speeches, videotaped, or recorded presentations; art; cartooning and storyboarding; independent research projects; interviews with experts; musical compositions; performance arts; building models; conducting experiments; and utilizing current computer technologies. By providing strategies reflecting the interests of gifted males as well as alternative ways for them to demonstrate understanding, teachers enable boys to experience school success and become better prepared to meet the challenges that will unfold in their professional lives.

CONCLUSION

Examination of the issues central to the intellectual and psychosocial development of gifted males illustrates the unique challenges these young men face. With an understanding of the experiences of gifted boys and young men, educators and parents can be better prepared to implement the suggested strategies to promote success and honor the potential of this special population.

REFERENCES

Alvermann, D. E. (Ed.). (2002). *Adolescents and literacies in a digital world.* New York: Peter Lang.

Cavazos-Kottke, S. (2006). Five readers browsing: The reading interests of talented middle school boys. *Gifted Child Quarterly, 50,* 132–146.

Clasen, D. R., & Clasen, R. E. (2003). Mentoring the gifted and talented. In N. Colangelo & G. A. Davis (Eds.), *Handbook of gifted education* (3rd ed., pp. 254–267). Boston: Allyn & Bacon.

Coleman, L. J., & Cross, T. L. (2001). *Being gifted in school: An introduction to development, guidance, and teaching.* Waco, TX: Prufrock Press.

Csikszentmihalyi, M. (1996). *Creativity: Flow and the psychology of discovery and invention.* New York: HarperCollins.

Gurian, M. (1996). *The wonder of boys: What parents, mentors, and educators can do to shape boys into exceptional men.* New York: Penguin Putnam.

Gurian, M., & Stevens, K. (2005). *The minds of boys: Saving our sons from falling behind in school and life.* San Francisco: Jossey-Bass.

Hébert, T. P. (1995). Coach Brogan: South Central High School's answer to academic achievement. *Journal of Secondary Gifted Education, 7,* 310–323.

Hébert, T. P. (2000a). Defining belief in self: Intelligent young men in an urban high school. *Gifted Child Quarterly, 44,* 91–114.

Hébert, T. P. (2000b). Gifted males pursuing careers in elementary education: Factors that influence a belief in self. *Journal for the Education of the Gifted, 24,* 7–45.

Hébert, T. P. (2001). "If I had a new notebook, I know things would change": Bright underachieving young men lost in urban classrooms. *Gifted Child Quarterly, 45,* 174–194.

Hébert, T. P. (2002). Gifted Black males in a predominantly White university: Portraits of high achievement. *Journal for the Education of the Gifted, 26,* 25–64.

Hébert, T. P. (2006). Gifted university males in a Greek fraternity: Creating a culture of achievement. *Gifted Child Quarterly, 50,* 26–41.

Hébert, T. P., & Danielian, J. S. (2008). Educators supporting gifted adolescent males through outdoor adventure. *Gifted Education Communicator, 39*(4), 32–37.

Hébert, T. P., & Kelly, K. R. (2006). Identity and career development in gifted students. In F. A. Dixon & S. M. Moon (Eds.), *The handbook of secondary gifted education* (pp. 35–63). Waco, TX: Prufrock Press.

Hébert, T. P., & Olenchak, F. R. (2000). Mentors for gifted underachieving males: Developing potential and realizing promise. *Gifted Child Quarterly, 44,* 196–207.

Hébert, T. P., & Pagnani, A. R. (2010). Engaging gifted boys in new literacies. *Gifted Child Today, 33*(3), 36–45.

Hébert, T. P., Pagnani, A. R., & Hammond, D. R. (2009). An examination of paternal influence on high achieving gifted males. *Journal for the Education of the Gifted, 33,* 241–274.

Hébert, T. P., & Schreiber, C. A. (2010). An examination of selective achievement in gifted males. *Journal for the Education of the Gifted, 33,* 570–605.

Hébert, T. P., & Speirs Neumeister, K. L. (2000). Mentors in the elementary classroom: Supporting the intellectual, motivational, and emotional needs of high ability students. *Journal for the Education of the Gifted, 24,* 122–148.

Kleiber, D., & Kirshnit, E. E. (1990). Sport involvement and identity formation. In L. Diamant (Ed.), *Mind-body maturity: The psychology of sports, exercise, and fitness* (pp. 193–211). New York: Hemisphere.

Millard, E. (1997). *Differently literate: Boys, girls and the schooling of literacy.* London, UK: Falmer Press.

Neall, L. (2002). *Bringing out the best in boys: Communication strategies for teachers.* Stroud, UK: Hawthorne Press.

Neu, T. W., & Weinfeld, R. (2007). *Helping boys succeed in school.* Waco, TX: Prufrock Press.

Norfleet James, A. (2007). *Teaching the male brain: How boys think, feel, and learn in school.* Thousand Oaks, CA: Corwin Press.

Olenchak, F. R., & Hébert, T. P. (2002). Endangered academic talent: Lessons learned from gifted first-generation college males. *Journal of College Student Development, 43,* 195–212.

Partington, R. (2006). Why boy books? *CSLA Journal, 30*(1), 15–16.

Peterson, J. S., & Colangelo, N. (1996). Gifted achievers and underachievers: A comparison of patterns found in school files. *Journal of Counseling and Development, 74,* 399–407.

Peterson, J. S., & Ray, K. E. (2006). Bullying and the gifted: Victims, perpetrators, prevalence, and effects. *Gifted Child Quarterly, 50,* 148–166.

Pollack, W. (1998). *Real boys: Rescuing our sons from the myths of boyhood.* New York: Random House.

Reis, S. M., & McCoach, D. B. (2000). The underachievement of gifted students: What do we know and where do we go? *Gifted Child Quarterly, 44,* 152–170.

Rimm, S. B. (2008). *Why bright kids get poor grades: And what you can do about it.* Scottsdale, AZ: Great Potential Press.

Scieszka, J. (Ed.). (2005). *Guys write for guys read.* New York: Viking.

Siegle, D., & McCoach, D. B. (2005). *Motivating gifted students.* Waco, TX: Prufrock Press.

Speirs Neumeister, K. L., & Hébert, T. P. (2003). Underachievement versus selective achievement: Delving deeper and discovering the difference. *Journal for the Education of the Gifted, 26,* 221–238.

Wilcove, J. L. (1998). Perceptions of masculinity, femininity, and androgyny among a select cohort of gifted adolescent males. *Journal for the Education of the Gifted, 21,* 288–309.

34

IS THIS REALLY STILL A PROBLEM?

The Special Needs of Gifted Girls and Women

Sally M. Reis

Since Callahan's ground-breaking work (1979) on the special needs of gifted girls and women, researchers and journalists have explored the complex and diverse paths that gifted girls and women travel, the barriers they face and sometimes overcome, and the critical choices and decisions they make over time. There is no one profile of this diverse group of individuals who follow unique paths to develop their talents, as many face multiple challenges and only some actualize their potential. Their development usually occurs over decades, as life experiences interact with abilities to prepare them for subsequent life accomplishments.

THEORIES ABOUT TALENT DEVELOPMENT IN GIFTED GIRLS AND WOMEN

Despite the many publications about gifted girls and women, few researchers have proposed theories about the process of female talent development that span various domains and can be widely applied under a variety of circumstances. Three such theories have been offered, including Reis's theory of talent development (Reis, 1987, 1995a, 1995b, 1998), Arnold, Noble and Subotnik's (1996) theories about "remarkable women," and Kerr's (1985, 1997) writing on smart girls and women.

Reis's Theory of Female Talent Development

In two decades of research with gifted girls and eminent women who achieved eminence spanning two decades, Reis (1995a) proposed and investigated a theory of female talent development, suggesting that the cumulative and contextual experiences of talented women differ from those of men in intellectual, moral, personal, and work perceptions. An award-winning children's writer whom Reis studied wove memories of her Hispanic heritage and parenting into her literary work, incorporating the insights and creative experiences gained as a mother and reflections on her own childhood. Other gifted women in Reis's study made careful choices about the development of their talents, achieving at high levels through working steadily and slowly, while acknowledging, and sometimes even celebrating, detours in their lives, such as raising family, helping others, and working in service for the betterment of others at home or in the community. All felt a certain intensity in their lives, characterized by a need and sense of obligation to pursue their talents in an active way. Many compared their own lives to the lives of their contemporaries—other equally talented women who did not attain the same level of eminence, but who appeared to live much calmer, and in some cases, happier lives.

Based on this research with gifted women, Reis proposed a definition of talent development in women (1995a), subsequently refined in 2005 and again for this chapter: *Feminine talent development occurs when women with high intellectual, creative, artistic or leadership ability or potential achieve at high levels in an area they choose, [and] make contributions that they consider meaningful to society; these contributions are enhanced when these women develop personally satisfying relationships and pursue what they believe to be significant and consequential work, resulting in the betterment of some aspect of society or their personal work.*

Remarkable Women by Arnold, Noble, and Subotnik

Arnold, Noble, and Subotnik (1996) suggest that talent development in women may differ from that of men due to differences in psychological needs and drives, in issues faced at home and at work, and in access to resources that encourage the development of gifts. Their model of talent development defines gifted behavior differently from traditional models. Most striking is their inclusion of the personal sphere as an outlet for gifted behavior. They note, for example, that there is talent in nurturing children well, building strong primary relationships and making a home—particularly for the many women worldwide whose pasts are marked by dysfunction, lack of health services, and other obstacles. In addition to the personal sphere, Arnold, Noble, and Subotnik recognize giftedness more traditionally, stating that "the widest sphere of influence lies in the creation of ideas or products that change the course of a domain or a social arena" (1996, p. 435). Success in the public sphere is characterized as "leadership" or "eminence." The model also heavily stresses context, however, suggesting that what qualifies as gifted behaviors depends on a woman's individual background.

Women with many opportunities and fewer obstacles may be seen as gifted if they become eminent for outstanding contributions to a field, while a person of fewer opportunities (i.e., an Indian woman of lower caste) may be regarded as demonstrating gifted behavior if she overcomes obstacles to receive a degree or enter a challenging and productive career. That is, context in women's lives in this talent development model focuses on the effect of women's relative position to "the mainstream of their societies' achievement centers" (Arnold et al., 1996, p. 435), and the effect that position has on whether and to what degree they will develop their talents. Demographic variables such as race, wealth, and geographic location are key facilitators/inhibitors of talent development. In this model, adversity may either help or hinder the development of women's gifts—depending on the woman and the circumstances.

Other factors contributing to achievement included in the model are the individual's characteristics and the support and validation of at least one other person. Those characteristics of achieving women that allow them to overcome cultural and gender discrimination include cognitive and emotional flexibility, willingness to take risks and aim high, tolerance for making mistakes, persistence in the face of adversity, and the ability to resist the tendency to internalize limiting messages from the outside. Talent is important, according to this model, but it certainly is not the only factor that influences female achievement, for, as these authors believe, a high level of innate ability is insufficient to withstand cultural pressures that have caused untold numbers of women to discount or deny their gifts.

Kerr's Smart Girls and Women

Kerr's work (1985, 1997) on gifted girls and women differs in its reliance on biographical research. Kerr drew conclusions about how female talent develops through study of the lives of 33 eminent women in various domains, including Margaret Mead, Eleanor Roosevelt, Marie Curie, Maya Angelou, and Katherine Hepburn. In her review of the lives of successful actresses, scientists, activists, writers, and others, Kerr identified several themes. One of the most unique factors Kerr identified is time alone during girlhood. For some girls who later became eminent women, time alone was a choice; for others, a state forced upon them by circumstance. Kerr suggests that, regardless of the cause of isolation, periods of aloneness provided these young women with time for reflection and an appreciation for individual work. Individualized instruction likewise was common across this group. Kerr noted that, for these girls, being able to move through material at their own pace probably prevented boredom and allowed advanced development of skills in areas of particular talent. This individualized instruction was often provided within the larger environment of same-sex education, allowing for attention above and beyond that which might have been found within mixed-gender classrooms. Finally, not only did most of the women whom Kerr studied have mentors—but they had mentors who had achieved the highest level of their professions. She cautions that one should not draw the conclusion that these eminent women owed their success to their relationships with influential people; but rather, that their talent was significant enough to impress those at the peak of their individual fields.

In addition to external factors, Kerr found a number of internal characteristics common to eminent women. First, almost all of the women were talented and insatiable readers as girls, which may have facilitated their learning and provided the context for new ideas. Many also felt they were "different" or "special" from a young age, either due to their gifts, or for other reasons, including the feeling that they were physically unattractive. All but one found adolescence painful and troublesome, contributing to an increase in the time they spent alone and providing direct experience of the costs and benefits of standing apart. As they matured, the women formed identities that emerge from ideas and work, rather than defining themselves primarily by relationships with others; most of the women were able to avoid seeing themselves primarily in terms of their membership in a couple or a group. Instead, Kerr's eminent women connected to others such as mentors or partners without losing their own identities or goals. Finally, reinforcing the theme that work was an integral part of the lives and relationships of these women, Kerr found that many joined work and love by marrying or partnering with others who shared their passions. Georgia O'Keeffe and Alfred Stieglitz, Marie and Pierre Curie, and Gertrude Stein and Alice B. Toklas are a few such couples.

These theories provide a backdrop for examining some of the challenges facing gifted girls and women, the internal and external barriers they face, and strategies that can be used to help high-potential girls develop and actualize their gifts and talents.

CHALLENGES FACING GIFTED GIRLS AND WOMEN

Research has addressed gender differences in gifted children and youth, but little has focused on gender differences in the process of talent development. In a study of male and female academically talented students, Csikszentmihalyi, Rathunde, and Whalen (1993) found that the teens were "equally likely to continue in or become disengaged from the domain of the area of their talent by the end of high school" (p. 207), and concluded therefore, that other factors contributed to engagement in the development of areas of interest and talent for students of both sexes. The review of research summarized in this chapter focuses on those areas that appear differentially to affect the development of talents and gifts in academically talented girls.

Ability and Testing Differences

Scores on many standardized tests suggest that high school males still score higher in verbal and quantitative areas, but the gap has lessened during the last few decades (College Board, 2006). For example, analysis of recent Scholastic Aptitude Test (SAT) scores of 1.3 million high school students reveals a persistent gender gap favoring males on both the verbal and mathematics sections across all other demographic characteristics, including family income, parental education, grade-point average (GPA), coursework, rank in class, size of high school, and size of city. Males outscored females by 34 points in mathematics and outscored females by three points on the verbal test (College Board, 2006). Wai, Cacchio, Putallaz, & Makel (2010) recently found that test performance differences between seventh grade boys and girls have narrowed considerably over the past 30 years, but boys still outnumber girls by more than three to one on scores at extremely high levels of mathematical and scientific reasoning. At the same time, girls slightly outnumber boys at extremely high levels of verbal reasoning and writing ability. Thirty years ago, the ratio of seventh graders scoring 700 or above on SAT mathematics was about 13 boys to 1 girl. That ratio dropped dramatically in the 1990s, but since 1995, the gap has remained constant at about four to one. These gender gaps do not merely reflect differences in academic preparation, but also point to fewer opportunities for selective colleges and programs for the gifted and talented—particularly at the secondary level.

Lower scores may have a detrimental impact on girls' desire to enter graduate school and select certain careers (Reis, 1998; Reis & Callahan, 1989). Selection of majors, affirmation of academic interests, and even choice of career can also be affected by scores on the SAT II achievement tests, on which boys outperform girls on almost every test, as Rosser (1989) found that both boys and girls estimate their mathematical and English abilities closer to their SAT scores than to their grades. Because Rosser also found that girls planned to go to slightly less prestigious colleges than boys with equivalent GPAs, we may surmise that when girls score lower, they may lower their expectations and apply for admission at less prestigious colleges. When girls attribute their potential success to ability as measured by these assessments, they may have less confidence that they can excel in challenging coursework and careers.

While the overall trends are generally positive about gains made by girls on tests in general, and in mathematics and some areas of science specifically, little progress has been made in the area of technology and engineering. A National Science Foundation report (NSF, 2000) details the problem clearly, stating: "at all levels of education and in employment, women are less likely than men to choose science and engineering fields" (p. xi). Although the number of women receiving degrees has increased in some areas of science and mathematics, bachelor's degrees granted to women in computer science actually decreased from 37 percent in 1984 to 28 percent in 1996 (NSF, 2000). High school females still take fewer higher-level mathematics and science classes, and data from the 2003 SATs indicate that only 18 percent of those expressing an interest in pursuing engineering, and only 16 percent of those interested in computer or information sciences were female (Educational Testing Services [ETS], 2003).

Despite data showing differences in achievement tests favoring academically talented boys, research has consistently found that girls get higher grades in both elementary and secondary school (Reis, 1998). Girls' attainment of higher grades, when contrasted with their lower scores on some standardized tests, may contribute to talented female adolescents' beliefs that they are not as "bright" as boys and can only succeed by working harder. In fact, perceptions of ability may affect self-assessments, and subsequently, performance. Reis and Park (2002) selected two sub-samples from the National Education Longitudinal Study representing the highest achieving students in mathematics and in science. Comparisons indicate that there were more males than females in both sub-samples of high-achieving students (mathematics and science). The results also suggest that the best predictor for distinguishing between mathematically high-achieving males and females was locus of control. High-achieving males had both higher self-concept and higher standardized mathematics test scores than high-achieving females. Female students were more influenced by teachers and parents, and more likely than the male students to regard "hard work" as more important in their performance than "chance or luck" and more influenced by parents.

Earlier research on talented adolescent females also suggested that such girls begin to lose self-confidence in elementary school and continue to do so throughout their academic careers (American Association of University Women [AAUW], 1991; Arnold, 1993). For example, in one qualitative study of five gifted adolescents, not one participant attributed success in school to extraordinary ability (Callahan, Cunningham, & Plucker, 1994). Identification as gifted and acceptance of gifts and talents may also be problematic because of adverse social consequences (Callahan et al., 1994; Eccles, Midgley, & Adler, 1984; Kramer, 1991; Reis, 1998). Some researchers have also found that gifted girls deliberately underestimate their abilities in order to avoid being seen as physically unattractive or lacking in social competence (Kramer, 1991; Swiatek, 2001). Callahan et al. (1994) found that middle school gifted females avoided displays of outstanding intellectual ability and worked to conform to the norm of the peer group.

However, some high-ability adolescent girls view their abilities and talents more positively. For example, Ford (1992) studied gender differences in the American achievement ideology among gifted and non-identified African American male and female adolescents, exploring perceptions of social, cultural, and psychological determinants of achievement and underachievement. Both male and female gifted students expressed the greatest support for the achievement ideology, and gifted females believed they had the highest level of teacher feedback on their efforts. In a longitudinal study of academically talented adolescents who either achieved or underachieved in an urban high school, the majority of high-achieving, culturally diverse students were proud of their abilities and did not minimize their intelligence (Reis, Hébert, Díaz, Maxfield, & Ratley, 1995). The high-achieving gifted girls avoided dating, worked hard to achieve at high levels academically and to pursue their interests and abilities in school, and were determined to be independent. Several said they wanted a different life from that of their mothers, many of whom struggled financially. In a more recent qualitative study, participants' high abilities were a contributing factor to the success of first-generation college women's access to coursework and extracurricular experiences and making other high-achieving friends who helped to shape the participants' emerging professional identity (Speirs Neumeister & Rinker, 2006).

In summary, research about ability, achievement and underachievement over the last two decades suggests that some gifted girls lose, to varying degrees, their enthusiasm for learning and their courage to speak out and display their abilities. Research on gifted females also indicates a decline in self-confidence in elementary school and continuing declines through college and graduate school (Arnold, 1993; Bell, 1989; Cramer, 1989; Hany, 1994; Kramer, 1991; Leroux, 1988; Perleth & Heller, 1994; Subotnik, 1988). These girls may increasingly doubt their intellectual competence, perceive themselves as less capable than they actually are, and believe that boys can rely on innate ability while they must work harder to succeed. Earlier research suggested decreases in self-confidence as well as in intellectual competence, but more recent research with targeted groups of minority gifted girls has found less evidence of this decline in perceptions about abilities, suggesting that over time, some positive changes may have occurred.

SOCIAL AND EMOTIONAL DIFFERENCES

Research has also revealed various personality factors, personal priorities, and social and emotional issues as reasons why talented females either cannot or do not realize their potential (Callahan, 1979; Kerr, 1997; Noble, 1987, 1989; Reis, 1998). Not all gifted females experience any or all of these barriers, but research studies identify a combination of internal and external factors as potential inhibitors to talent development in this population: dilemmas about abilities and talents, personal decisions about family, ambivalence of parents and teachers toward developing high levels of potential, decisions about duty and caring (putting the needs of others first) as opposed to nurturing personal development, religious and social issues (Noble, 1987; Reis, 1998).

External Barriers

External barriers such as childhood family experiences and parental attitudes toward having and raising girls as opposed to boys appear to affect gifted women negatively. Children may learn the stereotypical behaviors of their sex at an early age and display particular behavior patterns and play preferences even during preschool years (Kirschenbaum, 1980; Paley, 1984). The contents and furnishings of girls' and boys' rooms have been found to be drastically different, with girls' rooms having more dolls and doll houses and boys' rooms having more vehicles, educational and art materials, and machines (Pomerleau, Bolduc, & Malcuit, 1990). Some studies have suggested that gender stereotyping in toys and play patterns contribute to lower mathematics and science scores for adolescent girls on achievement tests (Lummis & Stevenson, 1990; Olszewski-Kubilius, Kulieke, Shaw, Willis, & Krasney, 1990; Yee & Eccles, 1988). Parents' educational levels and occupations as well as the type and level of parental aspirations for children's educational and occupational goals have been found to be associated with later career aspirations and success (Reis, 1998).

A poll conducted by the American Association of University Women of students in grades 4 through to 10 found that as girls mature, their self-esteem drops dramatically (AAUW, 1991). Enthusiastic and assertive as eight- and nine-year-olds, they begin to lose confidence in their abilities at the age of 13 and 14, and emerge from high school with measurably lowered goals and future expectations. Sixty percent of the girls said they were happy with themselves in elementary school; 37 percent were still happy with themselves in middle school; and only 29 percent remained happy with themselves in high school. Family and school experiences were identified by the adolescents as having the greatest impact on the decline in self-esteem. Parents may send contradictory messages that they want their gifted daughters to get good grades in all subjects, but also to exhibit "appropriate" polite and even demure behavior, a clear finding derived from research (Reis, 1998). Stereotypical feminine behaviors often conflict with the personal attributes that gifted females need to succeed. Some parents require (or at a minimum, expect) their daughters to be polite, well-mannered, and consistently congenial; and they send messages about how girls should dress and how often they should speak out and in what situations (Reis, 1998). According to the stereotype, girls are not supposed to be too independent. Mothers seem to have a particular influence on their gifted daughters. Reis (1998) found that talented girls with career-oriented mothers tended to develop a variety of talents and interests early in life and feel less conflict about growing up and becoming independent, autonomous women. Some gifted girls studied by Reis (1998) whose mothers had been at home, however, struggled with ambition and expressed conflicting feelings about work and home. Lashaway-Bokina (1996) found similar results in her study of Latina American gifted females who had dropped out of high school. Many of the young women were initially content to stay at home with their mothers and watch soap operas in the afternoon. These gifted females encountered confusing messages about their own future and their relationship with their mothers, and regarded their own abilities and talent development with ambivalence. Love for their mothers caused them to feel unsure about the development of their own talents. Their academic abilities, if developed, would lead to an unequivocally different life from the one in which they currently lived, and in which their mothers would always live. Being different from their mothers and separating themselves, in a number of ways, from their families caused fear and tension in these young women. With time, some of the young women managed to reconcile some of their problems and return to high school.

The process of socialization begins at birth and continues throughout life, and the effects of environmental socialization are pervasive and overwhelming on gifted girls. Potential negative barriers for gifted girls include the external influences they experience each time they turn on the television, reach for a magazine, or overhear a conversation between friends. Attitudes and opinions about what girls should look and act like come from family and friends, from observations throughout life, television and other media, and print materials including books, magazines, and textbooks. Television shows including children's programs (e.g., Saturday morning cartoons), fiction and non-fiction books, and even classic children's movies may impart a negative message to both young girls and boys. Popular magazines also reinforce gender stereotyping regularly through a continued focus on appearance and relationships with boys which may lead to conflict between developing one's talent first and putting the needs of a relationship first (Reis, 1998).

School experiences in elementary, middle or high school, or even in college, may reinforce negative stereotypes for girls. Several books and articles over the last few decades detail the differences between test scores, classroom interactions, and textbook inclusion and portrayal of females (Foster, 1994; Jones, 1989; Krupnick, 1992; Sadker & Sadker, 1994). History books, for example, seldom focus attention on women of accomplishment or even on women's contributions, or her-stories. The negative school and university climate has been discussed as responsible for changes in the attitudes of girls and women relative to achievement in school. Classroom observational research indicates that boys participate more actively in school and receive more attention from teachers (Foster, 1994; Krupnick, 1992; Sadker & Sadker, 1994); a few male students receive more attention than all other students in mathematics classes; and the amount of teacher attention given to girls is lowest in science classes (Jones & Wheatley, 1990; Handley & Morse, 1984; Shepardson & Pizzini, 1992). Science and mathematics classes, in particular, seem to include multiple examples of stereotyping. Lee & Marks (1992) reported blatant examples of stereotyping negatively affecting girls in chemistry, and researchers have also found that college classrooms have numerous instances of silent sexism (Foster, 1982, 1994; Grant, 1988; Rubin & Borgers, 1990). Reis & Kettle (1995) studied grouping patterns in science, for example, and found that mixed-gender groups usually resulted in the boys dominating and conducting the hands-on science experiments. In all-female groups, however, girls were able to participate fully. It would appear from reports and research articles to be commonly acknowledged that an atmosphere of inequality continues to exist in many university and college classrooms. While the most obvious threats to opportunities for women and girls may appear to have lessened due to the success of the Women's Movement, the reality of confronting more subtle obstacles and clear barriers remains. Gifted females appear to have made some gains, but much work remains undone (Reis, 1998).

Internal Barriers Including Personality Factors/Personal Choices and Decisions

A number of personality factors, personal priorities, and decisions have emerged as internal barriers to accomplishment in gifted females (Arnold, 1993; Bell, 1989; Hany, 1994; Kramer, 1991; Perleth & Heller, 1994; Reis & Callahan, 1989; Subotnik, 1988). The factors may include personal choices about relationships; choices about nurturing the talents in oneself as opposed to putting the needs of others first; religious and social issues which consistently affect girls and women; poor planning; hiding abilities and differences; perfectionism; attributing success to luck rather than to ability; and poor choice of partners (Reis, 1998).

Research has suggested that being identified as gifted or talented may create social problems for some gifted girls and women (Bell, 1989; Buescher, Olszewski, & Higham, 1987; Eccles et al., 1984; Kerr, Colangelo, & Gaeth, 1988; Kramer, 1991; Reis, 1987, 1995a, 1995b; Reis, Callahan, & Goldsmith, 1996). If gifted girls believe it is a social disadvantage to be smart due to the negative reactions of peers, or fear their peers' disapproval, they may deliberately understate their abilities in order to avoid being seen as physically unattractive or lacking in social competence. In other words, they may "play dumb."

Multi-potentiality is another barrier that may confront this population, as girls and women with high potential and many interests have multiple academic, career, and leisure possibilities (Ehrlich, 1982). Gifted girls and women may also display multiple educational, vocational, and leisure interests at comparable intensities, as well as complex personalities. For some, having many choices is beneficial because they present a variety of options. Others, however, cannot find their niche, make it on their own, or choose a vocational path (Fredrickson, 1979; Greene, 2002; Kerr, 1981; Schroer & Dorn, 1986), particularly when the options conflict with stereotypes of acceptable behaviors or careers for women.

As noted earlier, internal barriers arise when females hide their intelligence or begin to doubt that they have advanced abilities. For example, in a study of female graduates of a school for gifted students, Walker, Reis, and Leonard (1992), found that three out of four did not believe they had superior intelligence. A related issue occurs when females achieve high levels of success, but do not really believe they have earned it. Labeled by Clance (1985) the "Great Impostor Syndrome," this pattern of behavior describes a low sense of self-esteem occurring when females attribute their successes to factors other than their own efforts, and view their outward image as a successful achiever as being undeserved or accidental. "I was lucky," "I was in the right place at the right time," "I really didn't do as well as it seems," and "I had a lot of help" are all statements made by talented females when complimented on their successes (Reis, 1998). This response is related to attributing successes to effort or external factors such as luck while failures are explained as internal faults or as an absence of certain abilities.

Weiner (1986) found that personal attributions can influence emotions, self-concepts and subsequent behaviors. In research by Arnold (1993) with high school valedictorians, for example, by the second year of college, over a quarter of the female high school valedictorians studied had lowered their self-rankings of their intelligence, indicating that they were merely average in intelligence; male valedictorians' self-rankings remained consistent or actually improved. For these women, the pattern persisted after college graduation—only one of the women placed herself in the highest category of intelligence; men, in sharp contrast, steadily increased their self-ratings. Confusion about effort and ability is critical in attribution theory, as some high-achieving students tend to attribute their successes to a combination of ability and effort and their failures to lack of effort (Weiner, 1986). On the other hand, some women who readily accept their failures often attribute their successes to external factors such as luck and their failures to lack of ability. As children approach adolescence, they begin making a distinction between effort and ability, and gender differences emerge. The academic self-efficacy of young males is generally enhanced, based on their belief in their ability and is maintained during failures because of their attribution of failure to lack of effort. The same does not appear to be true for young females, as girls may accept responsibility for failure, but not for success (Weiner, 1986). Researchers believe that although girls may perceive themselves to be bright, they interpret any failure quite negatively, believing that it is caused by lack of ability (Dweck, 1986). Developing a strong belief in one's ability in the elementary and middle school years is important because "by the end of elementary school, children's [perceptions] . . . of ability begin to exert an influence on achievement processes independent of any objective measures of ability" (Meece, Blumenfeld, & Hoyle, 1988, p. 521). Many gifted adolescent girls believe that possessing high ability means that they will achieve excellent grades without effort; hence, they often believe that if they must work hard, they lack ability (Dweck, 1986).

Teachers may contribute to confusion about effort and ability, for as early as first grade, teachers tend to "attribute causation of boys' successes and failures to ability and girls' successes and failures to effort" (Fennema, Peterson, Carpenter, & Lubinski, 1990). Siegle and Reis (1998) found that teachers rate adolescent gifted females higher than gifted males on effort. Schunk (1984) found that children who initially receive feedback complimenting their ability, rather than feedback complimenting their effort, developed higher ability attribution, self-efficacy, and skills. This finding indicates that parents and teachers should praise girls for their ability and be specific about talents and accomplishments, thereby helping them understand that success is due to a combination of abilities and effort.

Another internal barrier to accomplishment in gifted females is the perfectionism that can cause some talented girls and women to set unreasonable goals for themselves and strive to achieve at increasingly higher levels. It also can cause women to strive to achieve impossible goals and/or spend their lives trying to achieve perfection in multiple areas. In one study on perfectionism in gifted adolescents in a middle school, for example, Schuler (1999) found that perfectionism is a continuum with behaviors ranging from healthy and normal to unhealthy and dysfunctional, and that some gifted girls were very negatively affected by perfectionism.

The reasons for the successful accomplishments of some highly talented girls and women and the failure of others to realize their high potential in meaningful work are complex and depend upon many factors, including values, personal choices, and social–cultural forces. This brief discussion of internal barriers summarizes some of the reasons that some talented females fail to achieve at the highest levels of accomplishment.

DEVELOPING THE TALENTS AND GIFTS OF GIRLS: STRATEGIES THAT WORK

Clearly, gifted and talented girls and women face conflicts between their own abilities and the social structure of their environments, and they may also often encounter both external barriers and internal barriers. Of course, not all girls or women experience the same dilemmas and decisions, but common trends have emerged in research on this population including dilemmas about abilities and talents, personal decisions about family, and decisions about duty and caring (putting the needs of others first) as opposed to nurturing personal talents and gifts (Arnold, 1993; Reis, 1987, 1998; Reis & Callahan, 1989; Subotnik, 1988). To counter these influences, teachers and parents of talented girls and women should encourage them to display their strengths and be strong, competent, and proud of their accomplishments. Renzulli (1986) discussed the differences between schoolhouse giftedness and creative–productive giftedness, indicating that while we should nurture and develop both, individuals who make important creative accomplishments in the world display creative–productive giftedness. All too often, parents and teachers encourage smart girls to do well in school, be quiet and studious, and work to get good grades in all content areas—in other words, develop only schoolhouse giftedness. However, Reis's study of adult gifted and eminent women (1998) suggests that characteristics such as courage to speak out and challenge authority, and the ability to create and produce, are critical in the process of talent realization.

To that end, the following suggestions, identified in research conducted over two decades, have emerged as helpful to enable high-potential females realize their talents (Reis, 1998):

1. Help young girls identify strengths, abilities, and interests; enable them to understand their abilities and learn how to accept their gifts and talents. Focusing on interests enables identification of potential areas for college, graduate school, and work later in life.
2. Spotlight achievements of gifted girls and women in a variety of domains to help girls become comfortable accepting praise and achieving at high levels.
3. Encourage girls and young women to become involved in many different types of activities and provide exposure to travel opportunities, clubs, and sports.
4. Encourage female students to take as many STEM (science, technology, engineering, and mathematics) courses as possible to keep options open for future work, and reinforce successes in these areas.
5. Help gifted girls create a written plan for their future with specific educational and career goals, identified interests, safe risks (e.g., going away to college), dreams and hopes, and criteria for friends and romantic relationships. Include plans for participation in diverse extracurricular and sport activities as well as future dreams about travel, enriching experiences (e.g., museums), and participation in interest-based clubs. Also include the need to postpone serious romantic relationships until after one's education is complete unless a relationship is developed with someone who completely supports one's ambitions and dreams.
6. Seek to identify and break down both the external and internal barriers that may impede the success of gifted females. Consciously discuss and actively challenge obstacles and barriers to success by pointing out negative stereotypes across various environments.
7. Encourage relationships with other motivated gifted girls who want to achieve. Whenever possible, group gifted girls together in self-contained classes, in clusters of gifted girls within heterogeneous classes, in science and mathematics clubs, or in interest groups (e.g., Latin class, robotics, creative writing), or other support groups.
8. Expose girls to other gifted females through direct and curricular experiences: field trips, guest speakers, seminars, role models, books, DVDs, articles, and movies.
9. Consistently point out options for careers and continue a focus on ability and interest for future careers.
10. Stress self-reliance, independence, decision making, humor, safe risk taking, and an inclination for creative action, and expose gifted girls to competition whenever possible to prepare them better for competitive situations in academics and in work.
11. Educate males to assume equal partnership in relationships and support the talent development of those they love.
12. Express a positive attitude about talents in girls in all areas and provide an unequivocal source of support, avoiding criticism as much as possible.
13. Help gifted girls develop a secure sense of self by helping them understand and develop a belief in self and an understanding of their interests, talents, and abilities.

CONCLUDING THOUGHTS: IS THIS REALLY STILL A PROBLEM?

My research and this review of research convince me that, yes, problems continue to exist in the opportunities for and accomplishments of talented females. Progress has been made, but as Callahan (1979) wrote over three decades ago, men still write more books, win more awards, are elected to office more frequently, govern more countries and states, and hold more of the financial and entrepreneurial power in the United States and other countries. In 2000, for example, approximately 6 percent of the ambassadors to the United Nations were female; while the share has increased from 5.7 percent in 2000 to 12.5 percent in 2008, this is still a low percentage overall. We have never had a female president in the United States, we continue to have fewer women in leadership positions in the United States and the world, and women, while they have made progress, continue to lag behind in many indicators. For example, male faculty had an average patenting rate that was 4.4. times greater than that of female faculty in the life sciences, even after accounting for the effects of productivity, networks, field, and employer attributes (Ding, Murray, & Stuart, 2006). Interviews with these female scientists suggest that they have less access to the commercial sector, and they have less time to pursue patents due to the demands on their time with families, other university work, and even fears about collegiality with their peers.

Gifted females still face barriers and the productivity of some talented women continues to be lower than their male counterparts. Some gifted girls, as they grow up, begin to feel ambivalent about their future work and the constraints it places on their perceived responsibilities to loved ones. Dreams for future high-profile careers and important work are diminished; some begin to doubt what they previously believed they could accomplish, and some settle for less lofty goals to take time for relationships with partners, family, and children. Some women experience, at various stages of life, differing levels of "feminine modesty," leading to changes in self-perceptions of ability and talent, which subsequently affect their perceptions of their potential (Reis, 1998). Some fall in love in college, and suddenly and unexpectedly, the dreams of the person they love become more important to them than their own dreams. They may lower their aspirations to pursue a relationship, but manage to focus their considerable talents and achieve eminence in the new domain. Still others choose a relationship that enables them to pursue a career with vigor and single-minded devotion, while some remain single to accomplish the same goal. Some talented women born after the Women's Movement of the 1960s and 1970s were surprised to find that they had to make choices because of relationships or other factors, after consistently being told that they could have and do it all. They learned, often to their surprise, that they could not (Reis, 1998, 2005).

Gifted and talented women often create complex and individualistic paths. In my study of eminent women, some had partners and some did not. Some had children and some did not. Some live fast-paced lives characterized by restless energy and a constant need to work. Others work more peacefully and carefully, living quieter lives while achieving similar or higher levels of productivity. The processes of developing talents also varied. Many of these gifted women developed their talents over decades, drawing from a backdrop of earlier varied life experiences that prepared them for their future life accomplishments. Others made careful choices about the development of their talents, achieving at high levels earlier and working steadily in an area of passion. All had two commonalities, work they loved and meaningful relationships with partners, friends, lovers, or family members who supported this work. It is this commitment to meaningful work and important connections that educators who work with talented girls should remember and try to nurture. The inequity in the productivity of adult gifted women continues, and so, programs and services to help gifted girls develop their talents must also continue.

REFERENCES

American Association of University Women . (1991). *Shortchanging girls, shortchanging America: A call to action.* Washington, DC: The American Association of University Women Educational Foundation.

Arnold, K. D. (1993). Academically talented women in the 1980s: The Illinois Valedictorian Project. In K. Hulbert & D. Schuster (Eds.), *Women's lives through time: Educated American women of the twentieth century* (pp. 393–414). San Francisco: Jossey-Bass.

Arnold, K. D., Noble, K. D., & Subotnik, R. F. (1996). *Remarkable women: Perspectives on female talent development.* Cresskill, NJ: Hampton Press.

Bell, L. A. (1989). Something's wrong here and it's not me: Challenging the dilemmas that block girls' success. *Journal for the Education of the Gifted, 12,* 118–130.

Buescher, T. M., Olszewski, P., & Higham, S. J. (1987). *Influences on strategies adolescents use to cope with their own recognized talents.* (Report No. EC 200 755). Paper presented at the Biennial Meeting of the Society for Research in Child Development, Baltimore,.

Callahan, C. M. (1979). The gifted and talented woman. In A. H. Passow (Ed.), *The gifted and talented* (pp. 401–423). Chicago: National Society for the Study of Education.

Callahan, C. M., Cunningham, C. M., & Plucker, J. A. (1994). Foundations for the future: The socio-emotional development of gifted, adolescent women. *Roeper Review, 17,* 99–105.

Clance, P. R. (1985). The imposter phenomenon. *New Woman, 15*(7), 40–43.

College Board. (2006). College Board announces scores for new SAT® with writing section. Retrieved September 15, 2011 from http://www.collegeboard.com/press/releases/150054.html

Cramer, R. H. (1989). Attitudes of gifted boys and girls towards math: A qualitative study. *Roeper Review, 11,* 128–133.

Csikszentmihalyi, M., Rathunde, K., & Whalen, S. (1993). *Talented teenagers: The roots of success and failure.* New York: Cambridge University Press.

Ding, W. W., Murray, F., & Stuart, T. E . (2006). Gender differences in patenting in the academic life sciences. *Science, 313,* 665–667.
doi: 10.1126/science.1124832

Dweck, C. S. (1986). Motivation processes affecting learning. *American Psychologist, 41,* 1040–1048.

Eccles, J. S., Midgley, C., & Adler, T. F. (1984). Grade-related changes in the school environment: Effects on achievement motivation. In J. Nicholls (Ed.), *Advances in motivation and achievement* (Vol. 3, pp. 283–331). Greenwich, CT: JAI Press.

Educational Testing Services. (2003). *2003 college-bound seniors: A profile of SAT program test takers.* Princeton, NJ: Author.

Ehrlich, V. (1982). *Gifted children: A guide for parents and teachers.* Englewood Cliffs, NJ: Prentice-Hall.

Fennema, E., Peterson, P. L., Carpenter, T. P., & Lubinski, C. A. (1990). Teachers' attributions and beliefs about girls, boys, and mathematics. *Educational Studies in Mathematics, 21,* 55–69.

Ford, D. Y. (1992). The American achievement ideology as perceived by urban African-American students. *Urban Education, 27,* 196–211.

Foster, T. (1994, April). *An empirical test of Hall and Sandler's 1982 report: Who finds the classroom climate chilly?* Paper presented at the Annual Meeting of the Central States Communication Association, Oklahoma City.

Fredrickson, R. H. (1979). Preparing gifted and talented students for the world of work. *Journal of Counseling and Development, 64,* 556–557.

Grant, L. (1988). The gender climate of medical schools: Perspectives of women and men students. *Journal of the American Medical Women's Association, 43,* 109–110.

Greene, M. (2002). Gifted adrift? Career counseling of the gifted and talented. *Roeper Review, 25,* 66–72.

Handley, H. M., & Morse, L. W. (1984). Two-year study relating adolescents' self-concept and gender role perceptions to achievement attitudes toward science. *Journal of Research in Science Teaching, 21,* 599–607.

Hany, E. A. (1994). The development of basic cognitive components of technical creativity: A longitudinal comparison of children and youth with high and average intelligence. In R. F. Subotnik & K. D. Arnold (Eds.), *Beyond Terman: Contemporary longitudinal studies of giftedness and talent* (pp. 115–154). Norwood, NJ: Ablex.

Jones, M. G. (1989). Gender issues in teacher education. *Journal of Teacher Education, 40*, 33–38.

Jones, M. G., & Wheatley, J. (1990). Gender differences in teacher-student interactions in science classrooms. *Journal of Research in Science Teaching, 27*, 861–874.

Kerr, B. A. (1981). Career education strategies for the gifted. *Journal of Career Education, 7*, 318–324.

Kerr, B. A. (1985). *Smart girls, gifted women.* Columbus, OH: Ohio Psychology.

Kerr, B. A. (1997). *Smart girls: A new psychology of girls, women, and giftedness* (rev. ed.). Scottsdale, AZ: Great Potential Press.

Kerr, B., Colangelo, N., & Gaeth, J. (1988). Gifted adolescents' attitudes toward their giftedness. *Gifted Child Quarterly, 32*, 245–247.

Kirschenbaum, R. J. (1980). Combating sexism in the preschool environment. *Roeper Review, 2*, 31–33.

Kramer, L. R. (1991). The social construction of ability perceptions: An ethnographic study of gifted adolescent girls. *Journal of Early Adolescence, 11*, 340–362.

Krupnick, C. G. (1992). Unlearning gender roles. In K. Winston & M. J. Bane, (Eds.), *Gender and public policy: Cases and comment.* Boulder, CO: Westview Press.

Lashaway-Bokina, N. (1996). *Gifted, but gone: High ability, Mexican-American, female dropouts.* (Unpublished doctoral dissertation). University of Connecticut, Storrs.

Lee, V. E., & Marks, H. M. (1992). Who goes where? Choice of single-sex and coeducational independent secondary schools. *Sociology of Education, 65*, 226–253.

Leroux, J. A. (1988). Voices from the classroom: Academic and social self-concepts of gifted adolescents. *Journal for the Education of the Gifted, 11*, 3–18.

Lummis, M., & Stevenson, H. W. (1990). Gender differences in beliefs and achievement: A cross-cultural study. *Developmental Psychology, 26*, 254–263.

Meece, J. L., Blumenfeld, P. C., & Hoyle, R. H. (1988). Students' goal orientations and cognitive engagement in classroom activities. *Journal of Educational Psychology, 80*, 514–523.

National Science Foundation. (2000). *Shaping the future.* Washington, DC: Author.

Noble, K. D. (1987). The dilemma of the gifted women. *Psychology of Women Quarterly, 11*, 367–378.

Noble, K. D. (1989). Counseling gifted women: Becoming the heroes of our own stories. *Journal for the Education of the Gifted, 12*, 131–141.

Olszewski-Kubilius, P., Kulieke, M. J., Shaw, S., Willis, G. B., & Krasney, N. (1990). Predictors of achievement in mathematics for gifted males and females. *Gifted Child Quarterly, 34*, 64–71.

Paley, A. M. (1984). *Boys and girls.* Chicago: The University of Chicago Press.

Perleth, C., & Heller, K. A. (1994). The Munich longitudinal study of giftedness. In R. F. Subotnik, & K. K. Arnold (Eds.), *Beyond Terman: Contemporary longitudinal studies of giftedness and talent* (pp. 77–114). Norwood, NJ: Ablex.

Pomerleau, A., Bolduc, D., & Malcuit, C. (1990). Pink or blue: Environmental gender stereotypes in the first two years of life. *Sex Roles: A Journal of Research, 22*, 359–367.

Reis, S. M. (1987). We can't change what we don't recognize: Understanding the special needs of gifted females. *Gifted Child Quarterly, 31*, 83–88.

Reis, S. M. (1995a). Talent ignored, talent diverted: The cultural context underlying giftedness in females. *Gifted Child Quarterly, 39*, 162–170.

Reis, S. M. (1995b). Older women's reflections on eminence: Obstacles and opportunities. *Roeper Review, 18*, 66–72.

Reis, S. M. (1998). *Work left undone: Compromises and challenges of talented females.* Mansfield Center, CT: Creative Learning Press.

Reis, S. M. (2005). Feminist perspectives on talent development: A research based conception of giftedness in women. In R. J. Sternberg & J. E. Davidson (Eds.), *Conceptions of giftedness* (2nd ed., pp. 217–245). Boston: Cambridge University Press.

Reis, S. M., & Callahan, C. M. (1989). Gifted females: They've come a long way—or have they? *Journal for the Education of the Gifted, 12*, 99–117.

Reis, S. M., Callahan, C. M., & Goldsmith, D. (1996). Attitudes of adolescent gifted girls and boys toward education, achievement, and the future. In K. D. Arnold, K. D. Noble, & R. F. Subotnik (Eds.), *Remarkable women: Perspectives on female talent development* (pp. 209–224). Cresskill, NJ: Hampton Press.

Reis, S. M., Hébert, T. P., Díaz, E. I., Maxfield, L. R., & Ratley, M. E. (1995). *Case studies of talented students who achieve and underachieve in an urban high school.* (Research Monograph No. 95120). Storrs: The National Research Center on the Gifted and Talented, University of Connecticut.

Reis, S. M., & Kettle, K. (1994). *Project Parity evaluation.* (Unpublished manuscript). Neag Center for Gifted Education and Talent Development, University of Connecticut.

Reis, S. M., & Park, S. (2002). Gender differences in high-achieving students in math and science. *Journal for the Education of the Gifted, 25*, 52–74.

Renzulli, J. S. (1986). The Three-Ring Conception of Giftedness: A developmental model for creative productivity. In R. J. Sternberg & J. E. Davidson (Eds.), *Conceptions of giftedness* (pp. 53–92). New York: Cambridge University Press.

Rosser, P. (1989). *Sex bias in college admissions tests: Why women lose out.* Cambridge, MA: National Center for Fair and Open Testing.

Rubin, L. J., & Borgers, S. B. (1990). Sexual harassment in universities in the 1980s. *Sex Roles, 23,* 397–411.

Sadker, M., & Sadker, D. (1994). *Failing at fairness: How America's schools cheat girls.* New York: Simon & Schuster.

Schroer, A. C. P., & Dorn, F. J. (1986). Enhancing the career and personal development of gifted college students. *Journal of Counseling and Development, 64,* 567–571.

Schuler, P. A. (1999). *Voices of perfectionism: Perfectionistic gifted adolescents in a rural middle school.* (Research Monograph 99140). Storrs: The National Research Center on the Gifted and Talented, University of Connecticut.

Schunk, D. H. (1984). Sequential attributional feedback and children's achievement behaviors. *Journal of Educational Psychology, 75,* 511–518.

Shepardson, D., & Pizzini, E. (1992). Gender bias in female elementary teachers' perceptions of the scientific ability of students. *Science Education, 76,* 147–153.

Siegle, D., & Reis, S. M. (1998). Gender differences in teacher and student perceptions of students' ability and effort. *Gifted Child Quarterly, 42,* 39–47.

Speirs Neumeister, K. L., & Rinker, J. (2006). An emerging professional identity: Influences on the achievement of high ability, first-generation college females. *Journal for the Education of the Gifted, 29,* 305–338.

Subotnik, R. (1988). The motivation to experiment: A study of gifted adolescents' attitudes toward scientific research. *Journal for the Education of the Gifted, 11,* 19–35.

Swiatek, M. A. (2001). Social coping among gifted high school students and its relationship to self-concept. *Journal of Youth and Adolescence, 30,* 19–39.

Wai, J., Cacchio, M., Putallaz, M., & Makel, M. C. (2010). Sex differences in the right tail of cognitive abilities: A 30 year examination. *Intelligence, 38,* 412–423. doi:10.1016/j.intell.2010.04.006

Walker, B., Reis, S., & Leonard, J. (1992). A developmental investigation of the lives of gifted women. *Gifted Child Quarterly, 36,* 201–206.

Weiner, B. (1986). *An attributional theory of motivation and emotion.* New York: Springer-Verlag.

Yee, D., & Eccles. J. (1988). Parent perceptions and attributions for children's math achievement. *Sex Roles, 19,* 317–334.

35

TWICE-EXCEPTIONAL STUDENTS

Gifted Students With Learning Disabilities

M. Layne Kalbfleisch

The current knowledge base in the area of twice exceptionality, particularly regarding those students with learning disabilities, includes both empirical research from the neurosciences and lessons from practice, where clinical and educational programs have sprouted to provide support and an organizational identity for twice exceptionality. Twice exceptionality is not a diagnosis widely accepted and supported in mainstream education. Notably, little epidemiological data exist to provide incidence or precedence for it, because it extends across several populations of disability and because no central definition exists for giftedness. However, information from empirical and epidemiological research, case studies, assessment, and current models of practice provides the fundamental knowledge necessary to advocate for and serve these special gifted children, poised to contribute to the world in extraordinary ways with their unique skills and talents.

THEORY, DEFINITION, IDENTIFICATION AND PHILOSOPHY OF TWICE EXCEPTIONALITY

Two underlying constructs are fundamental to understanding of twice exceptionality: the construct of giftedness and the construct of learning disability. Despite the fact that each defy singular definition in and of themselves, understanding that someone can have both a measured high intelligence quotient (IQ) or distinctive talents and a processing disorder (auditory or visual), or a disability (such as an attention disorder, learning disability, or autism) that skews how that intelligence is demonstrated amounts to what we observe as twice exceptionality (Kalbfleisch & Iguchi, 2008). A description for the gifted child with a learning disability was noted in the early 1970s (Elkind, 1973), and the term "twice exceptional" emerged in the 1980s when Whitmore (1980, 1981) and Maker (Udall & Maker, 1983; Whitmore & Maker, 1985) authored books on intellectual giftedness in disabled persons. Tannenbaum and Baldwin (1983) extended the descriptor to "paradoxical learner," capturing one of the dynamic hallmarks of twice exceptionality—students who underperform on sensory or rote tasks, yet can perform and do achieve at high levels of skill and expertise in domains that are oriented toward the visual and performing arts, design, science, music, and mathematics (Kalbfleisch, 2004, 2009). Brody and Mills (1997) added to the definition, noting specifically that the disabling condition actively suppresses the capability of the individual, undermining their perception of themselves and their abilities.

West (1997) highlighted stories and traits specific to twice-exceptional dyslexics, demonstrating repeatedly in profiles of celebrated individuals such as Albert Einstein, Michael Faraday, and Winston Churchill, the heightened and even optimized capabilities involving visual, spatial, and creative skills and in domains that require these types of talent. Retrospectively, we have come to recognize some of the defining traits of twice exceptionality from descriptions such as this one from Nikola Tesla, who pioneered the basis of nuclear magnetic resonance:

> In my boyhood I suffered from a peculiar affliction due to the appearance of images, often accompanied by strong flashes of light, which marred the sight of real objects and interfered with my thought and action. They were pictures of things and scenes which I had really seen, never of those I had imagined. When a word was spoken to me the image of the object it designated would present itself vividly to my vision and sometimes I was quite unable to distinguish whether what I saw was tangible or not. This caused me great discomfort and anxiety . . . These certainly were not hallucinations . . . for in other respects I was normal and composed.
> (Tesla, 2010, under "Blog Archive 2010," September 9, para. 3)

A definition of twice-exceptional learners was developed by a joint commission of The National Research Center on the Gifted and Talented (NRC/GT), the Association for the Education of Gifted Underachieving Students (AEGUS), and the Bridges Academy. They reached a consensus to characterize twice exceptionality in this way:

> Twice-exceptional learners are students who give evidence of the potential for high achievement capability in areas such as specific academics; general intellectual ability; creativity; leadership; and/or visual, spatial, or performing arts and also give evidence of one or more disabilities as defined by federal or state eligibility criteria such as specific learning disabilities; speech and language disorders; emotional/behavioral disorders; physical disabilities; autism spectrum; or other health impairments, such as attention deficit hyperactivity disorder.
> (http://2enewsletter.com/2e_Newsletter_Issue_35.pdf)

Unfortunately, little is known about the *prevalence* of twice exceptionality—how many twice-exceptional people there are within the general population; or *incidence*—how many people are actually diagnosed or identified as twice exceptional, although the new National Institute for Twice-Exceptionality (NITE) at the Belin-Blank International Center for Gifted Education and Talent Development, University of Iowa reports estimates of up to 360,000 twice-exceptional students in schools across the United States (see "What is Twice Exceptionality?" in NITE section at http://www.education.uiowa. edu/html/belinblank/Clinic/NITE.aspx). Estimates are difficult because each disability population is tracked and monitored differently, and learning disability, like the word "gifted," can have multiple definitions. A recent review highlights efforts to examine empirically twice exceptionality (Foley Nicpon, Allman, Sieck, & Stinson, 2011).

Philosophically, twice exceptionality is best understood within the cache of issues outlined in discussions about underachievement (see Chapter 37 in this book by Siegle and McCoach). Hence, twice-exceptional students can display any number of the qualities identified by Silverman (1989) and McEachern and Bornot (2001) in any number of combinations:

- above-grade-level and extensive vocabulary;
- good listening comprehension skills;
- strong verbal expression, poor or illegible handwriting;
- struggles with spelling basic words;
- has difficulty sitting still (hyperactivity, impulsivity, inattentiveness);
- can become deeply immersed in special interests and creative activities;
- can reason abstractly and solve complex problems;
- may display sophisticated sense of humor;
- displays divergent thinking skills;
- uses novel problem-solving strategies;
- can be easily bored and frustrated with grade-level school work in subjects where they are strong;
- dislikes rote memorization;
- has a difficult time engaging in social aspects of the classroom;
- has low self-concept;
- experiences confusion caused by a mix of special abilities that can lead to frustration and a sense of isolation and unhappiness;
- may be perceived by teachers as more quiet, asocial, and less accepted by others than gifted students.

Moon and Reis (2004) list qualities that hamper the identification of giftedness in gifted students with disabilities: these include learned helplessness, frustration, lack of motivation, perfectionism, super-sensitivity, lack of organizational skills, low self-esteem, unrealistic self-expectations, disruptive classroom behavior, and potential demonstration of poor listening and concentration skills (when they are uninterested). These are individuals whose intelligence circumvents the linguistic and linear requirements of school. Thus, their talents often take root and find context in alternative settings. Because of their natural abilities in the visual domains, they may demonstrate affinity for STEM fields (science, technology, engineering, and mathematics) and the arts.

Because defining twice exceptionality has defied psychometric and empirical characterization up to this point, and because it can include co-morbidity with a number of disorders (specific learning disability, dyslexia, attention deficit disorders, and autism, to name the few highlighted in this chapter), the gifted education field at large has only been able to respond to the consequences of it, when the goal should be proactive identification and support to enable the success that should come from educational experience and learning, not in spite of it. This is critical because the social and emotional aspects of twice exceptionality are fundamentally important to the twice-exceptional individual's ability to achieve a well-adjusted life (Assouline, Nicpon, & Huber, 2006; Foley Nicpon, Doobay, & Assouline, 2010; Gardynik & McDonald, 2005; King, 2005; Neu, 2003).

Changes in understanding of twice exceptionality are emerging from developmental and cognitive neuroscience. Kalbfleisch (2004) emphasized the study of "talent" to reunite the literatures and methodologies of the study of intelligence and creativity in order to examine boundary conditions that might shed light on twice-exceptional individuals whose intelligence appears to yield creative abilities, unique ways of seeing the world, and distinctive problem-solving approaches. Gilger and Hynd (2008) advocated for a contemporary take on twice exceptionality that extends the medical model of disability.

Studies in Neuroscience

Neuroscience studies are beginning to report some of the core physiological aspects of twice exceptionality as it pertains to autism and dyslexia (Brar et al., 2009; Kalbfleisch & Loughan, 2011; Kalbfleisch, Loughan, & Roberts, in press). Findings from functional magnetic resonance imaging (MRI) are illustrating some of the physiological bases of what we observe as cognitive strengths in this population.

Twice Exceptionality in Autism Spectrum Disorder

Autism, like other developmental learning-related disorders, has no unified definition. In fact, as a spectrum disorder, it even varies by formal name, encompassing labels such as "pervasively developmentally-delayed not otherwise specified" (PDD-NOS), high-functioning autism (HFA), and Asperger's syndrome (the highest functioning form of autism). Gender ratios for autism range from 4 boys to 1 girl (Bryson, 1996) to 2.5 to 1 (Attwood, 1998; Gillberg & Billstedt, 2000). Recent prevalence data released by the Autism and Developmental Disabilities Monitoring (ADDM) Network estimates a prevalence rate of approximately 10 per 1,000 among the states participating in this network (Arizona, Georgia, Maryland, South Carolina) with increases of up to 72 percent (in the state of Maryland) between the years 2000 and 2004 (Rice et al., 2010). Experts across national health agencies concur that autism remains a significant public health issue (King & Bearman, 2009). The Centers for Disease Control (CDC) indicate that approximately 730,000 individuals between the ages of 0 and 21 have autism in the United States alone (CDC, 2010). If you follow the logic of the psychometric ability curve, 16 percent of these individuals (or up to 116,800 people) may be twice exceptional (based on a conservative estimate of a cut-off point of a full scale IQ of 120, and categorized as having HFA or Asperger's syndrome).

One neuroimaging study of children with HFA and Asperger's syndrome indicates that certain attentional control skills are not significantly different from age- and IQ-matched neurotypical children on a behavioral level (they are as fast and as accurate on a measure of cognitive control when asked to identify the direction of a center arrow that is either embedded in a sequence of arrows all going in the same direction or in mixed directions); but the functional neural anatomy that supports their performance differs markedly (Brar et al., 2009). This moves the discussion away from core deficits and indicates that cognitive strengths also bear investigating. The ways their brains compensate and draw on capacity may help us better to understand behaviors such as little affiliation for the social domain. One published Aspergerian who restores European cars for a living explains that human interaction complicates and interrupts his intellectual pursuits:

Many people with Asperger's have an affinity for machines. Sometimes I think I can relate better to a good machine than any kind of person. I've thought about why that is, and I've come up with a few ideas. One thought is that I control the machines. We don't interact as equals. No matter how big the machine, I am in charge. Machines don't talk back. They are predictable. They don't trick me, and they're never mean. I have a lot of trouble reading other people. I am not very good at looking at people and knowing whether they like me, or they're mad, or they're just waiting for me to say something. I don't have problems like that with machines. I feel an affinity with many different kinds of machines. I'll try to explain . . .

(Robison, 2008, p.151)

People with Asperger's syndrome are typically the autism subgroup that is affiliated with twice exceptionality, as the intellectual qualities that typify them are apparent visual–spatial ability, single-minded focus, deep knowledge on topics of specific interest, and exceptional memory (Neihart, 2000).

As a result of studying the relationship between IQ discrepancy (the distance between verbal IQ and performance IQ) and executive function in HFA, Kalbfleisch and Loughan (2011) suggested a preliminary neuropsychological model of twice exceptionality in HFA. Executive function, while defying unitary definition (Salthouse, 2005), can best be described as a suite of intellectual management capabilities primarily driven by the frontal lobes of the brain (Denckla, 1994, 1996; Roca et al., 2010). They found that HFA children whose intelligence falls within the above-average to superior range on the verbal scale and is more than 15 points above their performance scale may experience less difficulty with the metacognitive skills of planning, organizing materials, and the monitoring aspects of executive function. Identifying metacognitive ability as a potential source of strength—or, at least, one that is not as severely impacted—in the highest functioning children with HFA becomes a means for strategic support and intervention. The open question that this study generated, and the inherent paradox, is: What role does verbal ability play in the intellectual strengths of autism? While it may not translate as a domain-specific skill, it may underlie or support select skills of executive function. Further evidence for this hypothesis comes from a case study reporting the neuroimaging of nonverbal reasoning skill in 16-year-old monozygotic twin brothers, one with Asperger's syndrome and the other with HFA, whose only disparity is between their verbal IQ scores which are above average (brother with HFA) and superior (brother with Asperger's) and lie 23 points apart from one another (Kalbfleisch, Loughan, & Roberts, in press). In this study, each brother's functional neural anatomy of reasoning aligned directly with the gray matter changes that define each of these types of autism, suggesting at least a compensatory mechanism and, at best, a positive plasticity associated with the structural changes that neuroanatomically define these points on the autism spectrum. These are the first studies to define a relationship between IQ discrepancy and executive function in HFA, and to pose this as a means for psychometric quantification of twice exceptionality.

Twice Exceptionality of Dyslexia

Dyslexia is a learning disability that has its basis in the disruption of a number of processes that facilitate the integration of receptive language in the brain. This disruption results in a person's failure to execute successfully formal language skills such as reading and writing (Schulte-Körne & Bruder, 2010). The National Assessment of Education Progress (NAEP) report of 2005 specified that up to 31 percent of fourth grade students are not reading on-grade-level (Daane, Campbell, Grigg, Goodman, & Oranje, 2005). Dyslexia affects both genders, but girls are less likely to be identified because of their quiet behavior and classroom compliance. Prevalence rates are often reported between 5 percent and 20 percent. Approximated estimates are taken to be on the low end, as these numbers come from students who are identified and receiving services. Thus, children with twice-exceptional dyslexia may be unaccounted for in this context, because they are underachieving but not failing in school.

The consequences affiliated with twice-exceptional dyslexia are notable talents in the visual–spatial domain. A discrete example of this comes from a study of one family with severe dyslexia, extremely high IQ, and exceptional visual–spatial talent, who all, in addition to these shared features, exhibit a specific structural change in the parietal operculum (where the brain integrates sensory information from vision, hearing, and other senses), displaying irregular interconnectivity similar to that observed in Albert Einstein's brain (Craggs, Sanchez, Kibby, Gilger, & Hynd, 2006). This intriguing example creates an open question regarding the extent to which giftedness and disability are co-morbid in the classical sense and/or to what extent compensation for the disability influences neural plasticity in the brain.

Twice Exceptionality of ADHD

Attention deficit hyperactivity disorder (ADHD) is a psychiatric disability that can be co-morbid to many other disabilities (autism and dyslexia exhibit this relationship) (Germanò, Gagliano, & Curatolo, 2010; Semrud-Clikeman, Walkowiak, Wilkinson, & Butcher, 2010) and also coexist with giftedness (Kaufmann, Kalbfleisch, & Castellanos, 2000). The Centers for Disease Control report that ADHD is the most commonly diagnosed neuropsychiatric disorder in childhood, characterized by a 21.8 percent increase between 2003 and 2007, from 7.8 percent to 9.5 percent. In adolescents, this increase reached 42 percent (CDC, 2010; Fulton et al., 2009). Because ADHD is commonly co-morbid with other disabilities (Larson, Russ, Kahn, & Halfon, 2011), and in the past, has been confused with creative abilities and temperamental tendencies affiliated with giftedness (Baum, Olenchek, & Owen, 1998; Cramond, 1995; Lind, 1993; Tucker & Hafenstein, 1997), estimating its prevalence in twice exceptionality is quite difficult. The source of the ambiguity appears to be centered on the degree to which the person can focus and whether or not the focus produces results (Kalbfleisch, 2009).

One study examined how well ADHD boys, gifted boys, and twice-exceptional boys with ADHD could shift between various academic and divergent thinking tasks (Kalbfleisch, 2000). Results indicated that the twice-exceptional boys were the most severely impaired while shifting between reading and divergent thinking, but were not impaired while shifting between the divergent thinking tasks. Further analysis on the divergent thinking tasks indicated there were no significant differences in performance between subject groups, even though the brain efficiency measures indicated a significant group difference (Kalbfleisch & Cramond, 2001). One of the recommendations from this study was to find ways for process to be product—that is, the performance of an activity is assessed as the learning outcome—in twice-exceptional ADHD students.

To complement complexity and challenge, gifted students with ADHD need to realize their gifts with sufficient support and structure to minimize the impact of their disability (Kaufmann et al., 2000). These students are often highly verbal and demonstrate a more accurate display of their intellectual capacities through oral and performance means of displaying learning as opposed to producing output in the form of a written paper or expected material product.

HOW ARE TWICE-EXCEPTIONAL STUDENTS DIFFERENT FROM GIFTED STUDENTS?

We continue to bypass twice-exceptional children whose unique qualities prime them for natural performance in STEM fields (Moon & Reis, 2004). Neuroscience research illustrates that the neural systems underlying visual–spatial processing are recruited differently in twice-exceptional adults with dyslexia. This evidence helps explain why twice-exceptional students have unique abilities that translate as intellectual strengths and natural talent in scientific and artistic fields based in visual modeling, numerical processing, quantitative analysis, and spatial relationships. Somehow, these skills translate into excellent divergent thinking and problem-solving skills and exceptional memory (Kalbfleisch, 2004, 2009; Kalbfleisch & Banasiak, 2008; Kalbfleisch & Iguchi, 2008). Self-esteem and resiliency can be enhanced when a student pursues skills and intellectual interests outside of the classroom, or when classrooms can be structured to tap interests and strengths. The logic that tends to obstruct higher-level learning opportunities for the twice-exceptional revolves around their paradoxical abilities. Because they do not perform well on the rote tasks that tend to characterize "seat work" and demonstrate basic competency in a classroom, a teacher may be reluctant to release them for special programs or other opportunities in which they can build on their strengths and experience greater levels of authenticity and success in their learning.

The inclusiveness of today's modern and mainstream educational settings nearly guarantees that a teacher will encounter twice-exceptional students—some invisible; some showing their colors. Unfortunately, preservice teachers do not usually receive extensive education in either special or gifted education unless they seek it out explicitly. Training and professional development opportunities and requirements for training and certification also vary by state. Training in recognizing the profiles and skills of each of these kinds of students within both special education and gifted education philosophies and paradigms is the best preparation for a skill set to accommodate these students.

Kaufmann et al. (2000) provide strategies designed to differentiate and enrich curriculum and instruction for these students. While presented in the context of ADHD, most provide good starting points for improving learning processes and experiences for the twice exceptional. These strategies and models—e.g., the triarchic model of intelligence (Sternberg, Ferrari, Clinkenbeard, & Grigorenko, 1996), synectics (Gordon, 1960), creative problem solving (Isaksen & Treffinger, 1985), curriculum compacting (Reis, Burns, & Renzulli, 1993), bibliotherapy (Frasier & McCannon, 1999), independent study (Betts, 1991), mentorship (Clasen & Clasen, 1997), and combinations of these models grounded in highly specialized and specific content (Bianco, Carothers, & Smiley, 2009)—can be adapted to account for some of the learning deficits that present across twice exceptionality and create motivation and choice to draw on the intellectual curiosity and skill of these students. When adapting the models for working with the twice-exceptional student, consideration should be given to the need to learn concepts first and details later, creating a sequence of short-term goals that can be realized and rewarded, and to engage multiple senses and to emphasize the visual (Winebrenner, 2003).

The most recent model providing promise for systematic and comprehensive treatment for the affective and educational needs of twice-exceptional students is the Response to Intervention (RtI) model. Defined as the "practice of providing high-quality instruction and interventions matched to student need, monitoring progress frequently to make decisions about changes in instruction or goals and applying child response data to important educational decisions" (National Association of State Directors of Special Education [NASDSE], 2005, p.2; see also Nielsen & Higgins, 2005; VanTassel-Baska, 1991), RtI is based on the principles of problem solving and flexibility (Rollins, Mursky, Shah-Coltrane, & Johnsen, 2009), monitoring student progress, tiering instruction to differentiate according to ability and need, involving a team including parents and educators (Hughes et al., 2009). While the original proposition does not include contingencies for gifted education, progressive, forward-thinking school districts in Colorado, Idaho, New York, and Wisconsin have followed the lead of Montgomery County Public Schools (in Maryland) (Weinfeld, Barnes-Robinson, Jeweler, & Shevitz, 2002, 2006) in serving twice-exceptional learners. They have adapted RtI to twice exceptionality, creating a usable and applicable form (Colorado Department of Education, 2008; Perreles, Baldwin, & Omdal, 2009).

The field of gifted education's interest in twice exceptionality is shepherded by scholars with sensibilities for complementary areas of research that allow for a more complete picture of twice exceptionality. Neuroscientists and neuropsychologists focus on the twice-exceptional individual from the inside out, bringing increased clarity and shape to definitions. As educational researchers, administrators, educators, counselors, and parents apply and experiment with policies and models, responsible practice and opportunities for more substantive research, intervention, assessment, and evaluation improve. Combined, these efforts lay the foundation for great gains in the education, achievement, and quality of life for those who are, as the name suggests, twice exceptional.

REFERENCES

Assouline, S. G., Nicpon, M. F., & Huber, D. H. (2006). The impact of vulnerabilities and strengths on the academic experiences of twice exceptional students: a message to school counselors. *Professional School Counseling, 10*, 14–25.

Attwood, T. (1998). *Asperger's syndrome.* London, UK: Kingsley.

Baum, S. M., Olenchak, F. R., & Owen, S. V. (1998). Gifted students with attention deficits: fact and/or fiction? Or, can we see the forest for the trees? *Gifted Child Quarterly, 42*, 96–104. doi: 10.1177/001698629804200204

Betts, G. (1991). The autonomous learner model for the gifted and talented. In N. Colangelo, & G. Davis (Eds.), *Handbook of gifted education* (1st ed., pp. 142–153). Boston: Allyn & Bacon.

Bianco, M., Carothers, D. E., & Smiley, L. R. (2009). Gifted students with Asperger syndrome: Strategies for strength-based programming. *Intervention in School and Clinic, 44*, 206–215. doi: 10.1177/1053451208328827

Brar, J., Kalbfleisch, M. L., Chandrasekher, L., Warburton, S. M., Girton, L. E., Hailyu, A. et al. (2009, June). *Differences in response conflict in autism spectrum disorders.* Paper presented at an International Meeting on Organization of Human Brain Mapping, San Francisco.

Brody, L. E., & Mills, C. J. (1997). Gifted children with learning disabilities: A review of the issues. *Journal of Learning Disabilities, 30*, 282–297. doi:10.1177/002221949703000304

Bryson, S. E. (1996). Brief report: Epidemiology of autism. *Journal of Autism and Developmental Disorders, 26*, 165–168.
  doi:10.1007/BF02172005
Centers for Disease Control. (2010). Increasing prevalence of parent-reported attention-deficit/hyperactivity disorder among children— United States, 2003 and 2007. *Morbidity and Mortality Weekly Report, 59*, 1439–1443.
Clasen, D., & Clasen, R. (1997). Mentoring: A time-honored option for education of the gifted and talented. In N. Colangelo & G. Davis (Eds.), *Handbook of gifted education* (2nd ed., pp 218–229). Needham Heights, MA: Allyn & Bacon.
Colorado Department of Education. (2008). *Response to intervention: A practitioner's guide to implementation.* Denver, CO: Author.
Craggs, J. G., Sanchez, J., Kibby, M. Y., Gilger, J. W., & Hynd, G. W. (2006). Brain morphology and neuropsychological profiles in a family displaying dyslexia and superior nonverbal intelligence. *Cortex, 428*, 1107–1118.
  doi:10.1016/S0010-9452(08)70222-3
Cramond, B. (1995). *The coincidence of attention deficit hyperactivity disorder and creativity.* Storrs: The National Research Center on the Gifted and Talented, University of Connecticut.
Daane, M. C., Campbell, J. R., Grigg, W. S., Goodman, M. J., & Oranje, A. (2005). *Fourth-grade students reading aloud: NAEP 2002 special study of oral reading.* (NCES 2006-469). National Center for Education Statistics, Institute of Education Sciences, U.S. Department of Education. Washington, DC: Government Printing Office.
Denckla, M. B. (1994). Measure of executive function. In G. R. Lyon (Ed.), *Frames of reference for assessment of learning disabilities: New views on measurement issues* (pp. 117–142). Baltimore: Brookes.
Denckla, M. B. (1996). A theory and model of executive function: A neuropsychological perspective. In G. R. Lyon & N. A. Krasnegor (Eds.), *Attention, memory, and executive function* (pp. 263–278). Baltimore: Brookes.
Elkind, J. (1973). The gifted child with learning disabilities. *Gifted Child Quarterly, 17*, 96–97.
Foley Nicpon, M., Allman, A., Sieck, B., & Stinson, R. D. (2011). Empirical investigation of twice exceptionality: Where have we been and where are we going? *Gifted Child Quarterly, 55*, 3–17.
  doi:10.1177/0016986210382575
Foley Nicpon, M., Doobay, A. F., & Assouline, S. G. (2010). Parent, teacher, and self perceptions of psychosocial functioning in intellectually gifted children and adolescents with autism spectrum disorder. *Journal of Autism and Developmental Disorders, 40*, 1028–1038.
Frasier, M., & McCannon, C. (1999). Using bibliotherapy with gifted children. *Gifted Child Quarterly, 25*, 81–85.
  doi:10.1177/001698628102500207
Fulton, B. D., Scheffler, R. M., Hinshaw, S. P., Levine, P., Stone, S., Brown, T. et al. (2009). National variation of ADHD diagnostic prevalence and medication use: Health care providers and education policies. *Psychiatric Services, 60*, 1075–1083.
  doi:10.1176/appi.ps.60.8.1075
Gardynik, U. M., & McDonald, L. (2005). Implications of risk and resilience in the life of the individual who is gifted/learning disabled. *Roeper Review, 274*, 206–214.
  doi:10.1080/02783190509554320
Germanò, E., Gagliano, A., & Curatolo, P. (2010). Comorbidity of ADHD and dyslexia. *Developmental Neuropsychology, 355*, 475–493.
  doi:10.1080/87565641.2010.494748
Gilger, J. W., & Hynd, G. W. (2008). Neurodevelopmental variation as a framework for thinking about the twice exceptional. *Roeper Review, 30*, 214–228.
  doi:10.1080/02783190802363893
Gillberg, C., & Billstedt, E. (2000). Autism and Asperger syndrome: Coexistence with other clinical disorders. *Acta Psychiatrica Scandinavica, 1025*, 321–330.
  doi:10.1034/j.1600-0447.2000.102005321.x
Gordon, W. J. (1960). *Synectics.* New York: Harper & Row.
Hughes, C. E., Rollins, K., Johnsen, S. K., Pereles, D. A., Omdal, S., Baldwin, L. et al. (2009). Remaining challenges for the use of RTI with gifted education. *Gifted Child Today, 32*(3), 58–61.
Isaksen, S. G., & Treffinger, D. J. (1985). *Creative problem solving: The basic course.* Buffalo, NY: Bearly.
Kalbfleisch, M. L. (2000). *Electroencephalographic differences between males with and without ADHD with average and high aptitude during task transitions.* (Unpublished doctoral dissertation). University of Virginia, Charlottesville.
Kalbfleisch, M. L. (2004). The functional neural anatomy of talent. *The Anatomical Record, 277B*(1), 21–36.
Kalbfleisch, M. L. (2009). The neural plasticity of giftedness. In L. Shavanina (Ed.), *International handbook on giftedness* (pp. 275–293). New York: Springer Verlag.

Kalbfleisch, M. L., & Banasiak, M. E. (2008). ADHD. In J. A. Plucker, & C. M. Callahan (Eds.), *Critical issues and practices in gifted education* (pp. 15–30). Waco, TX: Prufrock Press.

Kalbfleisch, M. L., & Cramond, B. (2001, April). *ADHD and divergent thinking: EEG performance and Torrance Tests for Creative Thinking–Figural Forms.* Paper presented at the Meeting of the National Association for Gifted Children, Cincinnati.

Kalbfleisch, M. L., & Iguchi, C. (2008). Twice exceptional learners. In J. A. Plucker, & C. M. Callahan (Eds.), *Critical issues and practices in gifted education* (pp.707–720). Waco, TX: Prufrock Press.

Kalbfleisch, M. L., & Loughan, A. R. (2011). Impact of IQ discrepancy on executive function in high-functioning autism: Insight into twice exceptionality. *Journal of Autism and Developmental Disorders* [online]. doi 10.1007/s10803-011-1257-2

Kalbfleisch, M. L., Loughan, A. R., & Roberts J. M. (in press). Impact of autism diagnosis on neural systems of nonverbal fluid reasoning in adolescent male monozygotic twins: Implications for twice exceptionality and evidence from neuroimaging. *Developmental Neuropsychology.*

Kaufmann, F., Kalbfleisch, M. L., & Castellanos, F. X. (2000). *Attention deficit disorders and gifted students: What do we really know?* Storrs: The National Research Center on the Gifted and Talented, University of Connecticut.

King, E. W. (2005). Addressing the social and emotional needs of twice-exceptional students. *Teaching Exceptional Children, 38*(1), 16–20.

King, M., & Bearman, P. (2009). Diagnostic change and the increased prevalence of autism. *International Journal of Epidemiology, 38*(5), 1224–1234. doi:10.1093/ije/dyp261

Larson, K., Russ, S. A., Kahn, R. S., & Halfon, N. (2011). Patterns of comorbidity, functioning, and service use for US children with ADHD, 2007. *Pediatrics 127*(3), 462–470. doi:10.1542/peds.2010-0165

Lind, S. (1993). Something to consider before referring for ADD/ADHD. *Counseling & Guidance, 4,* 1–3.

McEachern, A. G., & Bornot, J. (2001). Gifted students with learning disabilities: Implications and strategies for school counselors. *Professional School Counseling, 5*(1), 34–41.

Moon, S., & Reis, S. M. (2004). Acceleration and twice-exceptional students. In N. Colangelo, S. Assouline, & M. U. M. Gross (Eds.), *A nation deceived: How schools hold back America's brightest students* (Vol. II, pp. 109–120*)*. Iowa City: The Connie Belin & Jacqueline N. Blank International Center for Gifted Education and Talent Development, The University of Iowa.

National Association of State Directors of Special Education. (2005). *Response to intervention: Policy considerations and implementation.* Alexandria, VA: Author.

Neihart, M. (2000). Gifted children with Asperger's syndrome. *Gifted Child Quarterly, 44,* 222–229. doi:10.1177/001698620004400403

Neu, T. (2003). When the gifts are camouflaged by disability: Identifying and developing talent in gifted students with disabilities. In J. A. Castellano (Ed.), *Special populations in gifted education: Working with diverse gifted learners* (pp. 151–162). Boston: Allyn & Bacon.

Nielsen, M. E., & Higgins, L. D. (2005). The eye of the storm: services and programs for twice-exceptional learners. *Teaching Exceptional Children, 38*(1), 8–16.

Perreles, D. A., Omdal, S., & Baldwin, L. (2009). Response to intervention and twice-exceptional learners: A promising fit. *Gifted Child Today, 32*(3), 40–51.

Reis, S. M., Burns, D., & Renzulli, J. S. (1993). *Curriculum compacting: The complete guide for modifying the regular curriculum for high ability students.* Mansfield Center, CT: Creative Learning Press.

Rice, C., Nicholas, J., Baio, J., Pettygrove, S., Lee, L. C., Van Naarden Braun, K. et al. (2010). Changes in autism spectrum disorder prevalence in 4 areas of the United States. *Disability and Health Journal, 3,* 186–201. doi:10.1016/j.dhjo.2009.10.008

Robison, J. E. (2008). *Look me in the eye: My life with Asperger's.* New York: Three Rivers Press.

Roca, M., Parr, A., Thompson, R., Woolgar, A., Torralva, T., Antoun, N. et al. (2010). Executive function and fluid intelligence after frontal lobe lesions. *Brain, 133,* 234–247. doi:10.1093/brain/awp269

Rollins, K., Mursky, C. V., Shah-Coltrane, S., & Johnsen, S. K. (2009). RTI models for gifted children. *Gifted Child Today, 32*(3), 20–30.

Salthouse, T. A. (2005). Relations between cognitive abilities and measures of executive functioning. *Neuropsychology, 19*(4), 532–545. doi:10.1037/0894-4105.19.4.532

Schulte-Körne, G., & Bruder, J. (2010). Clinical neurophysiology of visual and auditory processing in dyslexia: a review. *Clinical Neurophysiology, 121,* 1794–1809. doi:10.1016/j.clinph.2010.04.028

Semrud-Clikeman, M., Walkowiak, J., Wilkinson, A., & Butcher, B. (2010). Executive functioning in children with Asperger syndrome, ADHD-combined type, ADHD-predominantly inattentive type, and controls. *Journal of Autism and Developmental Disorders, 40*(8), 1017–1027.
doi: 10.1007/s10803-010-0951-9

Silverman, L. K. (1989). Invisible gifts, invisible handicaps. *Roeper Review, 12,* 37–42.
doi:10.1080/02783198909553228

Sternberg, R., Ferrari, M., Clinkenbeard, P., & Grigorenko, E. (1996). Identification, instruction, and assessment of gifted children: A construct validation of a triarchic model. *Gifted Child Quarterly, 40,* 129–137.
doi:10.1177/001698629604000303

Tannenbaum, A. J., & Baldwin, L. J. (1983). Giftedness and learning disability: A paradoxical combination. In L. H. Fox, L. Brody, & D. Tobin (Eds.), *Learning disabled gifted children: Identification and programming* (pp. 11–36). Baltimore: University Park Press.

Tesla, N. (2010, September 9). Thinking in pictures and Asperger Syndrome. Retrieved from http://inthemind-seyedyslexicrenaissance.blogspot.com/ (under Blog Archive, 2010).

Tucker, B., & Hafenstein, N. L. (1997). Psychological intensities in young gifted children. *Gifted Child Quarterly, 41,* 66–75.
doi:10.1177/001698629704100302

Udall, A. J., & Maker, C. J. (1983). A pilot program for elementary age learning disabled/gifted students. In L. H. Fox, L. Brody, & D. Tobin (Eds.), *Learning disabled/gifted children: Identification and programming* (pp. 223–242). Austin, TX: Pro-Ed.

VanTassel-Baska, J. (1991). Serving the disabled gifted through educational collaboration. *Journal for the Education of the Gifted, 14,* 246–266.

Weinfeld, R., Barnes-Robinson, L., Jeweler, S., & Shevitz, B. (2002). Academic programs for gifted and talented/learning disabled students. *Roeper Review, 24,* 226–233.
doi:10.1080/02783190209554185

Weinfeld, R., Barnes-Robinson, L., Jeweler, S., & Shevitz, B. (2006). *Smart kids with learning difficulties: Overcoming obstacles and realizing potential.* Waco, TX: Prufrock Press.

West, T. G. (1997). *In the mind's eye: Visual thinkers, gifted people with dyslexia and other learning difficulties, computer images, and the ironies of creativity.* Amherst, NY: Prometheus Books.

Whitmore, J. R. (1980). *Giftedness, conflict, and underachievement.* Boston: Allyn & Bacon.

Whitmore, J. R. (1981). Gifted children with handicapping conditions: A new frontier. *Exceptional Children, 48*(2), 106–114.

Whitmore, J. R., & Maker, C. J. (1985). *Intellectual giftedness in disabled persons.* Austin, TX: Pro-Ed.

Winebrenner, S. (2003). Teaching strategies for twice exceptional students. *Intervention in School and Clinic, 38,* 131–137.
doi: 10.1177/10534512030380030101

36

GIFTED STUDENTS WITH EMOTIONAL AND BEHAVIORAL DISABILITIES

Tracy C. Missett

Students who simultaneously show evidence of high performance or potential in a talent or ability and have a disability that impacts on their ability to achieve and learn are often referred to as "twice exceptional" and require attention in the academic setting (Assouline, Nicpon, & Whiteman, 2010; Bianco & Leach, 2010). Recognition that twice-exceptional students exist in U.S. classrooms was articulated over three decades ago by Maker (1977) who referred to these students as "gifted handicapped." Initially, educators viewed twice exceptionality as paradoxical, as it seemed implausible that intellectually gifted children could concomitantly have a learning disability. However, based on Maker's contention that intellectual giftedness and learning disabilities can and do coexist, researchers began to investigate the characteristics, identification, and curriculum needs of students with dual exceptionalities (Baum, Cooper, & Neu, 2001; Brody & Mills, 1997). The National Association for Gifted Children (NAGC) (2010) recognizes this population and advocates finding mechanisms for identifying twice-exceptional children so that educators can serve both their gifts and disabilities, and thereby prevent them from falling through the academic cracks.

Much of the research on twice-exceptional students has been devoted to "high incidence" disabilities including specific learning disabilities (SLD) in reading and writing (i.e., dyslexia and dysgraphia), attention deficit hyperactivity disorder (ADHD), and auditory and visual processing disorders. In addition, twice-exceptional students in the autism spectrum have generated increased recent research, public, and educational interest (Assouline, Nicpon, & Doobay, 2009). However, while it is recognized that students in the highest IQ ranges and with extraordinary creative talents can also have emotional and behavior disabilities (EBD), such students have been overlooked in the twice-exceptional literature (Bianco & Leach, 2010; Kalbfleisch & Iguchi, 2008). Consequently, educators are often at a loss in recognizing the characteristics and serving the academic needs of gifted students with EBD.

The purposes of this chapter are three-fold:

1. to describe the scant literature on the characteristics and learning profiles of gifted students with EBD;
2. to situate gifted/EBD students within the broader twice-exceptional literature and describe the difficulties that arise in identifying and serving them in both special education and gifted programs; and
3. to offer strategies that will address both areas of exceptionality to educators for working successfully with gifted students with EBD.

CASES OF TWICE-EXCEPTIONAL STUDENTS WITH EBD

Jason

Jason is a seventh grade student at Meadow Middle School. When he was in second grade, Jason scored at the 99th percentile on the ability and achievement tests used by the district for identifying gifted students. Based on these scores, Jason was selected for the Meadow School District's gifted program. While he had struggled with writing since entering the gifted program, by middle school, his handwriting was illegible, he was not completing any writing assignments, he struggled to complete work in all classes, and he was at risk for failing. Nevertheless, Jason read science fiction novels incessantly and participated enthusiastically and persuasively during classroom debates. By the time he entered the seventh grade, Jason had withdrawn from his family, was isolated socially from his peers who were uncomfortable around him, and refused to cooperate in group activities. On many days, Jason felt too sick to go to school or asked to go to the nurse's office for stomach aches and headaches, although visits to his pediatrician indicated no illnesses. His current teachers, who have never taken professional development classes on gifted students with disabilities, think he is lazy and assume a mistake had been made when Jason was selected for the gifted program. Because he is not disruptive in class, however, his teachers largely ignore him. Halfway through the seventh grade, Jason attempted suicide and was diagnosed with depressive disorder. He was prescribed a mood stabilizer and antidepressant, and he has begun intensive psychotherapy. Jason recently returned to school, started to participate in class, and began to complete his assignments.

Sally

Sally is in third grade. Since kindergarten, Sally has had trouble following classroom routines, taking direction from teachers, playing cooperatively with her classmates, and sitting still during class instruction. She regularly visits the principal and is removed from the classroom for disruptive behavior such as destroying property and throwing pencils at her classmates. Sally is a highly creative student in art and is one of the strongest oral advocates in class discussions. However, she tends to argue with her teacher and classmates when they disagree with her opinions. Her constant arguments and volatile behavior frustrate, even frighten, her teacher who does not feel adequately prepared to work with her in the classroom. Homework often results in fierce battles at home and Sally's parents do not know how to manage their daughter. Sally has been diagnosed with ADHD, but her teacher and parents are concerned that other disabilities may be present. While her principal has suggested a comprehensive educational and medical evaluation, Sally's parents cannot afford a psychiatric evaluation. They are also concerned that Sally will be stigmatized if she is found to have an emotional disability and would rather she be served through special education for ADHD.

CHARACTERISTICS OF EBD

Emotional and behavioral disabilities (EBD) is a categorical label used to indicate those students who have an inability to learn due to significant difficulties regulating emotions and/or behavior, which are key indicators (Kauffman, Simpson, & Mock, 2009) of mental health disorders including:

- mood disorders (these include depression and bipolar disorder and are characterized by pervasive sad moods or periods of elation);
- anxiety disorders (characterized by anxiety, fearfulness, and avoidance of ordinary activities because of anxiety or fear);
- oppositional defiance disorder (ODD—characterized by a pattern of disobedient, hostile, and defiant behavior toward authority figures);
- conduct disorders (characterized by overt, aggressive, disruptive behavior and covert antisocial acts such as lying, stealing, setting fires); and
- schizophrenia (a disorder characterized by psychotic behavior manifested by loss of contact with reality, distorted thought processes, and abnormal perceptions).

Under the federal Individuals with Disabilities Education Improvement Act of 2004 (IDEIA, 2004), EBD students entitled to special education services are designated "emotionally disturbed." These students are characterized by an inability to build or maintain satisfactory relationships with peers and teachers; inappropriate types of behavior or feelings under normal circumstances; a pervasive depressed mood; and/or a tendency to develop physical symptoms or fears associated with personal or school problems. In addition to these primary characteristics, children with EBD often have many of the same difficulties with memory, sensory integration, anxiety, attention, and written expression as other high-incidence populations that are more frequently described in the twice-exceptional literature. In fact, it is estimated that 80 percent of children with EBD, including those who are gifted/EBD, also have at least one co-morbid learning disability (Hallahan, Kauffman, & Pullen, 2009).

Manifestations of EBD fall along two dimensions of disordered behavior: externalizing and internalizing. Externalizing behaviors are aggressive, disruptive, overt, and rarely go unnoticed by parents and educators. Internalizing behaviors reflect internal emotional conflicts such as depression and anxiety and are often more difficult to detect (Hallahan et al., 2009). Jason is an internalizer. Sally is an externalizer. Both are gifted students with EBD.

Gifted Students with EBD

Although many students with EBD are gifted and show evidence of high potential, there is very little empirical research on this population (Bianco & Leach, 2010; Morrison, 2001; Rizzo & Morrison, 2003). However, a few common behavioral and cognitive profiles have emerged. First, gifted students with EBD are generally described as extremely intense and highly sensitive. Like Sally, many externalizers are intellectually confident, but also challenge authority, and are impatient and viewed as argumentative. Many are verbally precocious and may be seen as a "know it all." While they often think in highly critical, creative, and abstract ways, they can also be inflexible in their cognitive patterns. Like Jason, gifted internalizers are often seen as underachieving, lazy, excessively perfectionist, and overly sensitive. These characteristics tend to frustrate and alienate teachers and peers, leaving children with EBD isolated in the academic setting. While their academic profiles combine to reflect both strengths and weaknesses, typically their strengths receive little attention in comparison to their negative behaviors (Davis, Culotta, Levine, & Rice, 2011; Hallahan et al., 2009).

Several additional broad conclusions can be drawn about gifted students who manifest emotional disabilities. First, most gifted students who develop EBD show signs of emotional difficulties before their disabilities are fully manifest. Moreover, their cognitive strengths diminish with the increasing presentation of EBD symptoms (Antshel, 2008), making early identification and intervention for these students critical in order to serve both exceptionalities and reduce the adverse academic, social, and emotional impacts of ignoring either exceptionality (or both) (Davis et al., 2011). Second, across multiple specific investigations, researchers have found that intellectually gifted students exhibit comparable or lower rates of anxiety and depression than non-gifted populations, and high IQ likely serves as a protective factor against depression (Cross, Cassady, Dixon, & Adams, 2008; Mueller, 2009). However, intellectually gifted individuals appear to be at increased risk for bipolar disorder, especially milder forms of bipolar disorder including cyclothymia (a disorder related to bipolar disorder which is characterized principally by less incapacitating periods of elation and depression) (Koenen, Moffitt, Rogers, Martin, & Kubzansky, 2009; MacCabe et al., 2010). Third, the research also shows a higher association between high creative abilities and mood disorders, although most highly creative youth do not have mood disorders (Papworth et al., 2008). Finally, prevalence rates for intellectually gifted students with ODD and conduct disorder are not well-established and there is scant research on gifted students with these emotional disorders. However, recent research suggests that high IQ students (above 120) with ADHD have significantly higher rates of depressive disorder, conduct disorder, and ODD than high IQ students without ADHD (Antshel, 2008).

IDENTIFICATION ISSUES

Because there is a paucity of empirical evidence informing what we know about gifted students with EBD, most descriptions of and recommendations for them are derived from what is known about other twice-exceptional groups and EBD students generally. Thus, we draw largely from the more general literature when discussing mechanisms for identifying, and strategies for serving, gifted students with EBD.

Identification of Twice-exceptional Students

Broadly speaking, children with any learning disability (including EBD) typically present an uneven and variable profile of abilities, demonstrating difficulties with some types of learning, but ease with others. Historically, students with learning disabilities were identified for special education services based on a discrepancy between full scale intelligence quotient (IQ) and achievement scores (Assouline et al., 2010; Kalbfleisch &

Iguchi, 2008). For twice-exceptional students, these variable abilities made identification of either or both exceptionalities difficult due to the phenomenon of masking (Assouline et al., 2010; Bianco, 2005). With masking, "giftedness and disability merge to create an illusion of an average student," or it causes either or both exceptionalities to appear less extreme (Kalbfleisch & Iguchi, 2008, p. 713).

Since the reauthorization of the IDEIA in 2004, the use of the ability–achievement discrepancy measurement has diminished in importance and has largely been replaced by the Response to Intervention (RtI) approach (Assoulinc et al., 2010; Cheney, Flower, & Templeton, 2008). Response to Intervention is a problem-solving model the purpose of which is to reduce the number of children identified as learning disabled in favor of early intervention and remediation of learning and behavioral difficulties, and to base any identification of a disability on data-driven, collaborative decision making. With RtI, students are identified as learning disabled only when their response to effective classroom instruction is significantly weaker than that of their peers and interventions designed to remediate these weaknesses have failed. Identification of a disability under RtI falls largely on the classroom teacher rather than on discrepancies between ability and achievement tests (Davis et al., 2011; Hallahan et al., 2010).

Due to the problems associated with masking, elimination of the ability–achievement discrepancy measurement in favor of RtI has been received with caution by some (Assouline et al., 2010; Mather & Gregg, 2006; Ruban & Reis, 2005). These researchers argue that eliminating the discrepancy measure will make it increasingly difficult to identify twice-exceptional students because their disability may mitigate their overall academic progress, but their giftedness will disguise the severity of the disability. Thus, they argue that the ability–achievement discrepancy should not be the only feature for identifying gifted students with learning disabilities, but it should be a piece of information carefully considered by educators. This may be particularly true for twice-exceptional students with EBD whose challenging behaviors can mask their potential and strengths, and for whom RtI alone is likely to be inadequate as a mechanism for identifying their abilities (Davis et al., 2011).

Identification of Students with EBD

Students with EBD, particularly those characterized by externalizing behaviors, pose extraordinary challenges for teachers, parents, and peers. Thus, their behaviors do not often go unnoticed in the school setting. Nevertheless, while it is estimated that approximately 6 percent of school-aged children have a seriously impairing emotional disability (i.e., have EBD), less than 1 percent of students are identified as emotionally disturbed for special education purposes, even if they are classified for other co-morbid conditions such as ADHD or SLD. Of all disability groups, students with EBD are believed to be the most under-identified and underserved (Cheney et al., 2008; Hallahan et al., 2009). There is no compelling basis for concluding that twice-exceptional students with EBD fare any better in this regard.

Unidentified and unserved students with EBD, including those in the highest IQ ranges, face significant adverse educational outcomes. These include disproportionately high suspension, expulsion, failure, dropout, and incarceration rates, and a near total neglect of interventions designed to uncover and promote academic strengths (Hallahan et al., 2009). This is despite consistent evidence that early identification and interventions for this population vastly improve these outcomes, promote pro-social behaviors and stronger emotional functioning, and lessen the increasing negative impacts of EBD on school performance (Cheney et al., 2008; Lewis, Jones, Horner, & Sugai, 2010).

A number of explanations have been offered for the under-identification of students with EBD, including the reluctance to attach a "special education" label that is seen as socially stigmatizing, and the lack of resources available in the school setting to service these students (Hallahan et al., 2009). Similarly, only a small percentage of students with EBD receive mental health services for their disabling conditions, further limiting early academic or psychiatric interventions and identification (Hallahan et al., 2009). If a student has been recognized for his/her abilities, teachers are likely to conclude that the student is purposefully "acting out" and being lazy rather than experiencing symptoms from a disability (Davis et al., 2011). All of the above factors contribute to poor emotional, behavioral, and academic prospects for many EBD students (Hallahan et al., 2009) and likely contribute to underachievement among those who are also gifted (Davis et al., 2011; McCoach & Siegle, 2008).

Identification of Gifted Students with EBD

Even after a student has been identified with EBD, teachers tend to overlook their abilities and competencies in favor of focusing solely on negative behaviors and their remediation (Hallahan et al., 2009; Morrison, 2001). These tendencies are particularly in evidence when it comes to teacher referrals of students for gifted programs and services (Bianco, 2005). A growing body of literature indicates that general, special, and gifted education teachers are all much less likely to refer students with EBD labels to gifted programs despite clear evidence of high academic abilities and potential, simply because the student has an emotional disability label (Bianco & Leach, 2010). It is hypothesized that the negative emotional and behavioral profiles associated with EBD students contradict stereotypic conceptions of the gifted student who many expect to be "perfect," which in turn accounts for the reluctance on the part of teachers to refer EBD students for gifted programs. Moreover, as many EBD students, by definition, have difficulty establishing relationships with teachers, they are typically without advocates in their schools, and are the least desired students in the classroom (Bianco, 2005).

One promising approach that can serve as a complement to RtI in identifying the academic strengths of students with EBD, including twice-exceptional students, is a positive behavioral intervention support (PBIS) system (Davis et al., 2011). This is an evidence-based school-wide behavior system used to support positive behaviors among all students and reduce challenging behaviors, thereby promoting safe and healthy learning environments for all (Benner, Beaudoin, Chen, Davis, & Ralston, 2010). Positive behavioral intervention support has been used effectively not only to identify students at risk for EBD, but also to identify academic strengths and weaknesses and facilitate the development of interventions geared toward both (Cheney et al., 2008; Davis et al., 2011).

STRATEGIES FOR WORKING WITH GIFTED/EBD STUDENTS

To meet the needs of twice-exceptional students with EBD in the classroom most effectively, a two-pronged approach appears to be necessary. First, schools must implement multi-component methods to identify and provide appropriate academic interventions to students "at risk" for and experiencing EBD. Second, to make the implementation of these methods effective, schools must provide for teachers who work with EBD students extensive professional supports and professional development designed to educate them regarding the complex profiles and needs of this group (Davis et al., 2011).

Regarding the first prong, identification of gifted students with EBD is likely to be most successful if it is based on a comprehensive evaluation using a combination of psychometric data (i.e., ability and achievement test scores) in concert with RtI and PBIS methods (Davis et al., 2011). A comprehensive and multi-tiered identification approach will more likely allow a complete picture of student abilities to emerge, and facilitate the development of interventions designed to serve both exceptionalities (Assouline et al., 2010). Individualized Education Plans (IEPs) developed for students with EBD should document both gifts and areas of need affected by the disability, and they should require interventions tailored to both. Curriculum that engages and challenges all students should be of paramount concern and should take priority over a singular focus on behavior modification in those students struggling emotionally and behaviorally (Davis et al., 2011).

Moreover, early identification and interventions are critically important (Cheney et al., 2008). Not only does cognitive functioning weaken with the onset of any disability, including EBD, but failure to identify and intervene increases the risk of adverse life and academic outcomes (Davis et al., 2011; Hallahan et al., 2009). Additional identification procedures and interventions should then continue as soon as behaviors associated with gifts or disabilities become evident.

Teachers and personnel working with gifted/EBD students must also have appropriate district-wide supports (school administrators, counselors, psychologists, etc.) to utilize effectively the identification methods and intervention systems described. Effective staff training and professional development delineating all aspects of RtI and PBIS interventions are critical, as is a teacher's adherence to these planned interventions. In fact, recent research shows that when teachers implement PBIS systems with fidelity to their research-based design, the behavioral functioning and academic success of EBD students improve (Benner et al., 2010; Gresham, 2005).

Social and emotional support for teachers working with these students is also recommended. Because the behaviors of students with EBD typically demand such a disproportionate amount of a teacher's time, energy, and resources, some studies suggest that many teachers leave the profession due to "burnout" (Cheney et al., 2008) associated with this category of students. To prevent burnout and ensure success, a collaborative team-based approach is necessary, involving administrators, parents, school counselors, school psychologists, and teachers (special education, general education, and gifted education), all working together to address systematically the academic and emotional profiles of gifted students with EBD. Finally, regular, special, and gifted education teachers should receive training on the cognitive profiles of gifted/EBD students, and on the implementation of classroom interventions that focus on academic strengths as well as emotional/behavioral needs (Bianco & Leach, 2010).

REFERENCES

Antshel, K. M. (2008). Attention-deficit hyperactivity disorder in the context of a high intellectual quotient/giftedness. *Developmental Disabilities Research Reviews, 14,* 293–299.

Assouline, S. G., Nicpon, M. F., & Doobay, A. (2009). Profoundly gifted girls and autism spectrum disorder. *Gifted Child Quarterly, 53,* 89–105.

Assouline, S. G., Nicpon, M. F., & Whiteman, C. (2010). Cognitive and psychosocial characteristics of gifted students with written language disability. *Gifted Child Quarterly, 54,* 102–115.

Baum, S. M., Cooper, C. R., & Neu, T. W. (2001). Dual differentiation: An approach for meeting the curricular needs of gifted students with learning disabilities. *Psychology in the Schools, 38,* 477–490.

Benner, G. J., Beaudoin, K. M., Chen, P.-Y., Davis, C., & Ralston, N. C. (2010). The impact of positive behavioral supports on the behavioral functioning of students with emotional disturbance. *Journal of Behavior Assessment in Children, 1,* 85–99.

Bianco, M. (2005). The effects of disability labels on special education and general education teachers' referrals for gifted programs. *Learning Disability Quarterly, 28,* 285–293.

Bianco. M., & Leach, N. L. (2010). Twice-exceptional learners: Effects of teacher preparation and disability labels on gifted referrals. *Teacher Education and Special Education, 33,* 219–334.

Brody, L., & Mills, C. (1997). Gifted children with learning disabilities: A review of the issues. *Journal of Learning Disabilities, 30,* 282–296.

Cheney, D., Flowers, A., & Templeton, T. (2008). Applying response to intervention metrics in the social domain for students at risk for developing emotional or behavioral disorders. *The Journal of Special Education, 42,* 108–126.

Cross, T. L., Cassady, J. C., Dixon, F. A., & Adams, C. M. (2008). The psychology of gifted adolescents as measured by the MMPI-A. *Gifted Child Quarterly, 52,* 326–339.

Davis, M. R., Culotta, V. P., Levine, E. A., & Rice, E. H. (2011). *School success for kids with emotional and behavioral disorders.* Waco, TX: Prufrock Press.

Gresham, F. M. (2005). Response to intervention: An alternative means of identifying students as emotionally disturbed. *Education and Treatment of Children, 28,* 328–344.

Hallahan, D. P., Kauffman, J. M., & Pullen, P. C. (2009). *Exceptional learners: An introduction to special education.* Boston: Allyn & Bacon.

IDEIA. (2004). Individuals With Disabilities Education Improvement Act of 2004, Pub. L. No. 108-446, 20 U.S.C. §1462(h).

Kalbfleisch, M. L., & Iguchi, C. M. (2008). Twice-exceptional learners. In J. A. Plucker & C. M. Callahan (Eds.), *Critical issues and practices in gifted education: What the research says* (pp. 707–719). Waco, TX: Prufrock Press.

Kauffman, J. M., Simpson, R. L., & Mock, D. R. (2009). Problems related to underservice: A rejoinder. *Behavioral Disorders, 33,* 172–180.

Koenen, K. C., Moffitt, T. E., Rogers, A. L., Martin, L. T., & Kubzansky, L. (2009). Childhood IQ and adult mental disorders: A test of the cognitive reserve hypothesis. *American Journal of Psychiatry, 166,* 50–57.

Lewis, T. J., Jones, S. E. L., Horner, R. H., & Sugai, G. (2010). School-wide positive behavior support and students with emotional/behavioral disorders: Implications for prevention, identification and intervention. *Exceptionality, 18,* 82–93.

MacCabe, J. H., Lambe, M. P., Cnattingius, S., Sham, P. C., David, A. S., Reichenberg, A. et al. (2010). Excellent school performance at age 16 and risk of adult bipolar disorder: National cohort study. *British Journal of Psychiatry, 196,* 109–115.

McCoach, D. B., & Siegle, D. (2008). Underachievers. In J. A. Plucker & C. M. Callahan (Eds.), *Critical issues and practices in gifted education: What the research says* (pp. 721–734). Waco, TX: Prufrock Press.

Maker, C. (1977). *Providing programs for the handicapped gifted.* Reston, VA: Council for Exceptional Children.

Mather, N., & Gregg, N. (2006). Specific learning disabilities: Clarifying, not eliminating, a construct. *Professional Psychology: Research and Practice, 37*(1), 99–106.

Morrison, W. F. (2001). Emotional/behavioral disabilities and gifted and talented behaviors: Paradoxical or semantic differences in characteristics? *Psychology in the Schools, 38,* 425–431.

Mueller, C. E. (2009). Protective factors as barriers to depression in gifted and nongifted adolescents. *Gifted Child Quarterly, 53,* 3–14.

National Association for Gifted Children. (2010). *2010 Pre-K–Grade 12 gifted programming standards: A blueprint for quality gifted education programs.* Retrieved August 15, 2011 from http://www.nagc.org/index.aspx?id=546

Papworth, M. A., Jordan, G., Backhouse, C., Evans, N., Kent-Lemon, N., Morris, J. et al. (2008). Artists' vulnerability to psychopathology: Towards an integrative cognitive perspective. *Journal of Creative Behavior, 42,* 149–163.

Rizzo, M. G., & Morrison, W. F. (2003). Uncovering stereotypes and identifying characteristics of gifted students with emotional/behavioral disabilities. *Roeper Review, 25,* 73–77.

Ruban, L., & Reis, S. (2005). Identification and assessment of gifted students with learning disabilities. *Theory Into Practice, 44*(2), 115–124.

37

UNDERACHIEVING GIFTED STUDENTS

Del Siegle and D. Betsy McCoach

Teachers lament the students in their classes "who could do better." Parents agonize over the average or below-average grades their gifted children receive. In some cases, students are aware they are performing below expectations; in other cases, they view their performance as "just fine." The underachievement of gifted students is both puzzling and frustrating. If gifted students fail to realize their potential, the waste of talent not only deprives society of potential contributions, but also represents a personal loss of self-fulfillment for the underachieving individual.

WHAT IS GIFTED UNDERACHIEVEMENT?

Identifying gifted underachieving students can be difficult for many reasons. First, no universally accepted definition of giftedness exists. Theories of giftedness abound (Sternberg & Davidson, 2005) as do lists of criteria for identifying gifted students (Johnsen, 2005). Further, disagreement surrounds how to define underachievement, including the controversy over the value judgment surrounding the term. *Whose* standards, expectations, or values should be used to determine whether a student is underachieving?

Underachievement is usually described as a discrepancy between expected performance (ability or potential) and actual performance (achievement) that cannot be explained by a learning disability or the documented need for any other category of special education services (Baum, Renzulli, & Hébert, 1995a; Butler-Por, 1987; Dowdall & Colangelo, 1982; Emerick, 1992; Redding, 1990; Reis & McCoach, 2000; Rimm, 1997a, 1997b; Supplee, 1990; Whitmore, 1980; Wolfle, 1991). Emerick (1988) suggested this discrepancy might include any of the following combinations: high IQ score and low achievement test scores; high IQ score and low grades; high achievement test scores and low grades; high indicators of intellectual or creative potential and low creative productivity; or high indicators of potential and limited presence of appropriate opportunity for intellectual and creative development. The last category is particularly pertinent when considering students from poverty-stricken backgrounds and other underserved populations. Obviously, the students identified using these different discrepancy definitions are likely to be radically different.

The severity of the discrepancy required to label someone as a gifted underachiever is also a crucial consideration. First, given the phenomenon of regression to the mean, those with the highest measured ability are not likely to have an equally extreme achievement level. Second, ability and achievement are not perfectly correlated (Thorndike, 1963). Intelligence test scores explain only 25 percent of the variance in school grades (Neisser et al., 1996). This leaves 75 percent of the fluctuation in achievement test scores unaccounted for by IQ scores. Based on this relationship, a student with an IQ score of 145 (three standard deviations above the mean) would have a predicted achievement of only 1.5 standard deviations above the mean. Third, most people probably perform somewhat below their capacity or ability. Although it seems reasonable to expect gifted students to exhibit above-average achievement, it is unreasonable to expect their achievement to be as exceptional as their ability; hence the discrepancy between a student's ability and his or her achievement must be severe enough to warrant substantial concern.

Reis and McCoach (2000) proposed an operational definition of underachievement:

> Underachievers are students who exhibit a severe discrepancy between expected achievement (as measured by standardized achievement test scores or cognitive or intellectual ability assessments) and actual achievement (as measured by class grades and teacher evaluations). To be classified as an underachiever, the discrepancy between expected and actual achievement must not be the direct result of a diagnosed learning disability and must persist over an extended period of time.
>
> (Reis & McCoach, 2000, p. 157)

This definition works well for students identified as gifted using traditional measures (e.g., using test scores) who are not performing well on tasks assigned by their teachers. For example, students with high IQ or high achievement test scores would be considered underachievers if they did not complete homework assignments and received poor grades as a result. However, the definition would not fit all of Emerick's (1988) categories.

The use of grades as a measure of achievement is controversial. Some believe that students who learn new material each year and perform well on their achievement tests, but do poorly on classroom work, should be considered non-producers instead of underachievers (Delisle & Galbraith, 2002). This exemplifies a key issue in the definition of underachievement: Should achievement be measured by grades or by standardized measures of academic achievement? Grades are far less reliable than standardized measures of academic achievement; however, they do provide an indication of a student's classroom achievement. In addition, to some extent, grades also reflect student motivation and student behavior. The largest longitudinal study of underachievers conducted to date (McCall, Evahn, & Kratzer, 1992) documented the importance of classroom grades. Thirteen years after high school, the educational and occupational status of high school underachievers paralleled their high school grades, rather than their abilities. Further, underachievers appeared to have greater difficulty completing college and remaining in their jobs and marriages than other students.

Conversely, using standardized achievement test scores as a measure of performance can be problematic. Students with high ability and low standardized achievement test scores may be underachievers, or they may have undiagnosed learning disabilities.

Therefore, gifted students with low standardized achievement test scores should be screened for learning disabilities prior to classifying them as underachievers (Moon & Hall, 1998).

The value judgment attached to identifying someone as an underachiever is also an issue. Should individuals be identified as underachieving because they choose not to perform in areas that are not of interest to them? An academically talented student who is also a talented pianist might be classified as underachieving if he chooses to focus on developing his music talents at the expense of his school work. As mentioned earlier, Delisle and Galbraith (2002) made a distinction between underachievers and non-producers, referring to the latter as *selective consumers*. It is unreasonable to expect gifted students to achieve at the highest levels universally. First, gifted students may choose not to exert effort in areas not important to them, while expending effort to excel in areas they value or enjoy. Second, although giftedness is most often used to refer to general cognitive ability, each student possesses a unique constellation of traits and talents. Even highly gifted students may perform at near-average levels in an area of relative weakness. Thus, the gifted students who should be of greatest concern to educators and parents are those failing to achieve in *any* productive area.

CHARACTERISTICS OF GIFTED UNDERACHIEVERS

While there appear to be several different types of underachiever, factors commonly associated with underachievement include:

- low academic self-perceptions (Freedman, 2000; Matthews & McBee, 2007; Schunk, 1998; Supplee, 1990; Whitmore, 1980);
- low self-efficacy (Siegle & McCoach, 2005);
- low self-motivation; low effort toward academic tasks (Albaili, 2003; Baslanti & McCoach, 2006; Lacasse, 1999; McCoach & Siegle, 2003b; Matthews & McBee, 2007; Rayneri, Gerber, & Wiley, 2003; Weiner, 1992);
- external attributions (Carr, Borkowski, & Maxwell, 1991; Siegle & McCoach, 2005);
- low goal-valuation (Baslanti & McCoach, 2006; Freedman, 2000; Lacasse, 1999; McCall et al., 1992; McCoach & Siegle, 2003b; Matthews & McBee, 2007);
- negative attitude toward school and teachers (Colangelo, Kerr, Christensen, & Maxey, 1993; Ford, 1996; McCoach & Siegle, 2003b; Rimm, 1995); and
- low self-regulatory or metacognitive skills (Carr et al., 1991; Krouse & Krouse, 1981; Yu, 1996).

Many underachievers exhibit one or more of the characteristics listed above. However, very few underachievers display all of those characteristics. Interestingly, the variability on motivational and attitudinal measures within samples of underachievers tends to be higher than the variability for comparison groups of average or high achievers. For example, groups of gifted underachievers displayed significantly more variability on self-report measures of motivation, perceptions, and attitudes than gifted achievers (McCoach & Siegle, 2003b). The large variability suggests that underachievers may share some common characteristics, but they are not a homogeneous population.

GENDER

Gifted underachievers tend to be male. When teachers are asked to identify gifted underachievers, they nominate two to three times as many boys as girls. For over half a century and across numerous studies of underachievers, the ratio of male underachievers to female underachievers appears to be at least two to one (Baker, Bridger, & Evans, 1998; Gowan, 1955; McCall, 1994; McCoach, 2002; McCoach & Siegle, 2001; Matthews & McBee, 2007; Peterson & Colangelo, 1996; Richert, 1991; Siegle et al., 2006). It may be that males are more likely to draw attention to themselves and their underachievement by acting out in class, misbehaving, or engaging in aggressive or antisocial behaviors. Perhaps gifted females who underachieve go unnoticed because they are more passive. Perhaps educators and parents fail to recognize females' giftedness in the first place. These concerns warrant further research. Of course, it is equally plausible that more males really do underachieve in school. Recent research indicates that females have higher GPAs in high school (Cole, 1997; Duckworth & Seligman, 2006), enroll in college at greater rates (Conger & Long, 2010), have higher college GPAs (Conger & Long, 2010; Sheard, 2009), and have higher persistence and graduation rates (Conger & Long, 2010), suggesting that females do seem to outperform males academically.

FAMILY DYNAMICS

The limited empirical research conducted on the family characteristics of underachieving gifted students suggests certain types of home environment may be related to the development of students' underachievement patterns (Baker et al., 1998; Brown, Mounts, Lamborn, & Steinberg, 1993; Rimm & Lowe, 1988; Zilli, 1971). For example, inconsistent parenting techniques appear to occur more frequently in the homes of underachieving children (Rimm & Lowe, 1988). In 95 percent of the families of underachieving gifted students studied by Rimm and Lowe, one parent emerged as the disciplinarian, while the other parent acted as a protector. Often, conflict between parents increased as the challenger became more authoritarian and the rescuer became increasingly protective. Therefore, Rimm and Lowe (1988) emphasized the importance of parents maintaining consistency between themselves.

Other researchers found that parents of underachievers tend to be either overly lenient or overly strict (Pendarvis, Howley, & Howley, 1990; Weiner, 1992) or may vacillate between lenient and strict. In addition, bestowing adult status on a child at too young an age may contribute to the development of underachievement (Fine & Pitts, 1980; Rimm & Lowe, 1988).

The role of underachievement in family conflict has received some attention. In a qualitative study of gifted urban underachievers, the family dysfunction that characterized the lives of the gifted underachievers contrasted with the happier home lives of the gifted achievers (Reis, Hébert, Diaz, Maxfield, & Ratley, 1995). However, data from another study comparing families of underachievers and those of achievers suggest that families with underachieving gifted students were not any more likely to be dysfunctional than families with achieving gifted students (Green, Fine, & Tollefson, 1988). Regardless of students' achievement status, functional families were more satisfied with their adolescent's academic achievement than were dysfunctional families.

THE INFLUENCE OF PEERS

High-achieving peers are cited as having a positive influence on gifted students who begin to underachieve in high school and as contributing to reversal of underachievement in some students (Reis et al., 1995). Students also report having more positive feelings toward school and their classes when their learning is supported, encouraged, and valued by peers (Fredricks, Alfeld, & Eccles, 2010). Likewise, negative peer attitudes often relate to underachievement (Clasen & Clasen, 1995; Weiner, 1992). Underachieving students frequently report peer influence as the strongest force impeding their achievement, and they often identify peer pressure or the attitude of the other students, including friends, as the primary force against getting good grades (Clasen & Clasen, 1995).

Several studies with non-gifted students also suggest the importance of peer influences on achievement in secondary school. Students with friends who care about learning demonstrate better educational outcomes than those in less educationally oriented peer groups, and affiliating with peers who are engaged with and like school predicts increased engagement and motivation over time (Chen, 1997; Kindermann, 1993; Ryan, 2001). Students also seem to resemble their friends more closely at the end of the school year than they do at the beginning of the school year, and students' grades reportedly decrease between fall and spring if their friends have lower grades in the fall (Berndt, 1999). Even at the beginning of the year, students in the fourth and fifth grades tend to affiliate with classmates who share similar motivation orientations, and they reorganize their peer groups throughout the year to preserve their motivational composition (Kindermann, 1993). Although peer achievement levels do relate to students' academic achievement, it is unclear whether the choice to associate with other non-achievers is a cause or a result of gifted students' underachievement.

POSSIBLE CAUSES OF UNDERACHIEVEMENT

Experts posit many potential causes of underachievement. An unusual or unexpected event in a student's life, such as a move to a new school or a change in family structure such as divorce or a parent marrying, can alter achievement patterns (Rimm, 1995). Young people who experience excessive power at home may have difficulty adjusting to a school environment in which they have limited choices. As noted earlier, bestowing adult status on a child at too young an age may contribute to the development of underachievement (Fine & Pitts, 1980; Rimm & Lowe, 1988). Sometimes gifted students who hear conflicting messages from parents, conflicting messages from parents and teachers, or conflicting messages from gifted specialists and classroom teachers use these conflicting messages to justify low achievement. For example, children may overhear their parents expressing discontent over the way the school is addressing the child's gifted needs. A gifted specialist may share concerns about the failure of a classroom teacher to address the academic needs of the gifted. Each of these scenarios provides students with ammunition to use as an excuse for not producing their best work.

Classrooms do not always provide intellectually stimulating environments in which gifted and talented students can thrive. Many gifted elementary school students have already mastered 40—50 percent of the content of their current grade level prior to the start of the school year (Reis et al., 1993). Regular education classrooms have been found to undermine, rather than support, a passion for learning (Fredricks et al., 2010), a conclusion which may relate to findings that 61 percent of classroom teachers have not received training in meeting the needs of advanced students (Robinson, Shore, & Enerson, 2007). School-year GPA, data normally indicative of underachievement, is not a significant predictor of gifted students' achievement in a summer program designed to meet their intellectual needs (Matthews & McBee, 2007). Matthews and McBee concluded that "educational programs . . . designed specifically to address the academic and social needs of gifted students can be successful in reversing many underachievement behaviors" (p. 167). Yet the majority of gifted students spend 80 percent of their time in regular education settings instead of specialized programs designed to meet their unique needs (Westberg, Archambault, Dobyns, & Salvin, 1993).

Although students must learn to function within a competitive society, overly competitive situations can also be detrimental to students' achievement. Gifted students with a fixed theory of intelligence may be particularly at risk in competitive situations.

Holding a fixed theory of intelligence appears to turn students toward concerns about performing and looking smart. Holding a malleable theory appears to turn students toward concerns about learning new things and getting smarter. We have also seen that entity theorists' concerns about looking smart can prevent them [students] from seeking learning opportunities, even ones that could be critical to performing well in the future.

(Dweck, 2000, p. 23)

Gifted students with a fixed theory of intelligence (performance orientation) may not wish to risk their "giftedness" by performing poorly in competitive situations or on difficult tasks. For them, not performing is less risky than performing and failing. For some, this means not completing assignments or studying for tests. For others, it means procrastinating and then hiding behind statements such as "I could have done better if I had more time." There is a direct relationship between procrastination and underachievement (Rosario et al., 2009).

Gifted students holding a fixed theory of intelligence may not see effort as contributing to their achievement. Even though teachers view students' ability and effort as equally related to the quality of work produced by students, gifted students view their ability as more related to the quality of their work than their effort (Siegle & Reis, 1998). Students may believe success is more contingent on their natural ability than the effort they put forth, or they may simply report they were not being challenged, and therefore, did not need to work hard to produce quality work (Siegle & Reis, 1998). Both of these explanations could contribute to eventual underachievement.

As a result of finding that college students can believe that ability is important in doing well without developing a fixed entity view, Siegle, Rubenstein, Pollard, and Romey (2010) conclude:

[A]lthough some researchers have cautioned against recognizing student ability at the peril of diminishing the importance of effort, educators and parents should not be fearful of discussing the role ability plays in gifted students' performances, while also emphasizing the importance of hard work and perseverance.

(Siegle et al., 2010, p. 92)

Perhaps gifted achievers are able to appreciate the role that ability plays in high perform-ance without being paralyzed by it, while gifted underachievers view ability as a possible limiting factor in their success.

While some gifted students underachieve because they have not had opportuni-ties to develop their potential, others choose not to develop their potential. Achieve-ment, and thus the reverse, underachievement, often reflects an interaction of beliefs (Siegle & McCoach, 2002). Students who underachieve may espouse one of three problematic beliefs: They do not believe they have the skills to do well and are afraid to try and fail; they do not see the work they are being asked to do as meaningful; or they believe that the "deck is stacked against them" and any effort they put forth will be thwarted. When students hold any one of these beliefs they tend not to per-form well. Motivated students feel good about their abilities, find the tasks in which they are engaged meaningful, and feel supported and appreciated in their environment. When these three areas are measured, the lowest scoring one is often the single best predictor of achievement and satisfaction levels (McCoach, 2010; Siegle & McCoach, 2009). In other words, those who are motivated and achieve tend to believe they have the skills to do well (self-efficacy), find the work meaningful (goal valuation), and view their environment as supportive (environmental perceptions). The intensity of the atti-tudes in the three areas need not be equally strong; however, attitudes must be posi-tive in each area. Ultimately, the three attitudes direct a resultant behavioral strategy (self-regulation) that results in achievement. According to this model, if any one of the three components is lacking, regardless of the strength of the others, motivation is hindered.

POSSIBLE SOLUTIONS

Interventions designed to reverse underachievement fall into two general categories: counseling and instructional interventions (Butler-Por, 1993; Dowdall & Colangelo, 1982). Unfortunately, there is no magic solution to the problem of underachievement, and a combination of counseling and instructional interventions appears to be the most promising option. The best-known interventions involve part-time or full-time special classrooms (e.g., Butler-Por, 1987; Fehrenbach, 1993; Supple, 1990; Whitmore, 1980) and usually involve smaller student-to-teacher ratios, greater student choice, and less conventional teaching and learning activities.

When comparing students across five treatment conditions, Siegle et al. (2006) found that the grades of the total group increased over a 6–9-week period. However, for stu-dents in the self-efficacy and self-regulation treatment group (focusing on study skills, test-taking strategies, and time-management skills) interventions showed small or little grade improvement, even among students reporting problems in those areas. Students whose curriculum was compacted showed only slight gains. Treatments linked to mak-ing school more meaningful and increasing student connections to school produced the strongest gains in academic grades. The researchers concluded that developing trusting relationships with gifted underachievers, making school meaningful, and helping stu-dents see the importance of school appear to be the strongest strategies for improving gifted underachievers' grades. During this goal-valuation intervention, the teacher dis-cussed the students' interests, values, and future plans with them. Based on these con-versations, the teacher either (a) helped the student understand how the current school work was useful to the student now or in the future; or (b) tied the student's interests to the content being covered in school.

These findings support the suggestions that playing off students' interests is key to increasing passion in schools, as is the creation of an intellectually stimulating and challenging environment as Fredricks et al. (2010) suggest:

> Cognitively complex tasks that are both meaningful and challenging and allow youth to pose and solve real-world problems can help accomplish this goal. Providing opportunities for students to incorporate their outside interests and future plans in their schoolwork is also likely to be beneficial. Finally, teachers should give youth some choice over the types of activities they work on and some control over how they complete these activities.
>
> (Fredricks et al., 2010, p. 27)

This suggestion mirrors the Type III activities found in the Schoolwide Enrichment Model (Reis & Renzulli, 2009; see also Chapter 21 in this book). Baum et al. (1995b) and Emerick (1992) demonstrated that using students' strengths and interests through Type III activities could reverse underachievement. The use of interest- and strength-based activities in combination with mentors seemed to be quite powerful.

Rimm's Trifocal Model (2008), derived from her clinical practice, involves the collaboration of school and family in six steps:

1. Assess skills, abilities, reinforcement contingencies, and types of underachievement.
2. Communicate the results of the assessment to parents and teachers, and communicate support, rather than blame[,] while continually monitoring the student's progress through school and home communications.
3. Change the expectations of parents, teachers, peers, siblings, and the student himself that the student has the ability to achieve.
4. Locate an appropriate, achieving role model.
5. Correct any skill deficiencies—some might have developed as a result of the underachievement.
6. Modify home and school reinforcements that support underachievement.

As frustrating as underachievement is to parents and teachers, ultimately, it is the student who must be willing to change behaviors. As Whitmore (1986) noted over a quarter of a century ago, "The final choice, obviously, is the child's; he or she must want to change and believe effort will be rewarded by sufficient success and personal satisfaction" (p. 69). For some gifted students, this willingness to change comes with maturity. For others, the impetus to change occurs when the consequences of underachievement become more serious. Unfortunately, for some gifted underachievers, this willingness to change never comes. Although there is no silver bullet, it is our hope that research in this area will continue to explore ways to help gifted underachievers fully develop their talents and abilities.

REFERENCES

Albaili, M. A. (2003). Motivational goal orientations of intellectually gifted achieving and underachieving students in the United Arab Emirates. *Social Behavior and Personality, 31*, 107–120.

Baker, J. A., Bridger, R., & Evans, K. (1998). Models of underachievement among gifted preadolescents: The role of personal, family, and school factors. *Gifted Child Quarterly, 42,* 5–14.

Baslanti, U., & McCoach, D. B. (2006). Gifted underachievers and factors affecting underachievement. *Roeper Review, 28,* 210–215.

Baum, S. M., Renzulli, J. S., & Hébert, T. P. (1995b). *The prism metaphor: A new paradigm for reversing underachievement.* (CRS95310). Storrs: The National Research Center on the Gifted and Talented, University of Connecticut.

Baum, S. M., Renzulli, J. S., & Hébert, T. P. (1995a). Reversing underachievement: Creative productivity as a systematic intervention. *Gifted Child Quarterly, 39,* 224–235.

Berndt, T. J. (1999). Friends influence on students' adjustment to school. *Educational Psychologist, 34,* 15–28.

Brown, B. B., Mounts, N., Lamborn, S. D., & Steinberg, L. (1993). Parenting practices and peer group affiliation in adolescence. *Child Development, 64,* 467–482.

Butler-Por, N. (1987). *Underachievers in school: Issues and intervention.* Chichester, UK: Wiley.

Butler-Por, N. (1993). Underachieving gifted students. In K. A. Heller, F. J. Monks, & A. H. Passow (Eds.), *International handbook of research and development of giftedness and talent* (pp. 649–668). Oxford, UK: Pergamon Press.

Carr, M., Borkowski, J. G., & Maxwell, S. E. (1991). Motivational components of underachievement. *Developmental Psychology, 27,* 108–118.

Chen, X. (1997, June). *Students' peer groups in high school: The pattern and relationship to educational outcomes.* (NCES 97–055). Washington, DC: U.S. Department of Education.

Clasen, D. R., & Clasen, R. E. (1995). Underachievement of highly able students and the peer society. *Gifted and Talented International, 10*(2), 67–75.

Colangelo, N., Kerr, B., Christensen, P., & Maxey, J. (1993). A comparison of gifted underachievers and gifted high achievers. *Gifted Child Quarterly, 37,* 155–160.

Cole, N. S. (1997). *The ETS gender study: How males and females perform in educational settings.* Princeton, NJ: Educational Testing Service.

Conger, D., & Long, M. (2010). Why are men falling behind? Gender gaps in college performance and persistence. *Annals of the American Academy of Political and Social Science, 627,* 184–214.

Delisle, J., & Galbraith, J. (2002). *When gifted kids don't have all the answers: How to meet their social and emotional needs.* Minneapolis, MN: Free Spirit.

Dowdall, C. B., & Colangelo, N. (1982). Underachieving gifted students: Review and implications. *Gifted Child Quarterly, 26,* 179–184.

Duckworth, A. L. & Seligman, M. E. P. (2006). Self-discipline outdoes IQ in predicting academic performance of adolescents. *Psychological Science, 16,* 939–944.

Dweck, C. S. (2000). *Self-theories: Their role in motivation, personality, and development.* Philadelphia: Psychology Press.

Emerick, L. J. (1988). *Academic underachievement among the gifted: Students' perceptions of factors relating to the reversal of the academic underachievement pattern.* (Unpublished doctoral dissertation). University of Connecticut, Storrs.

Emerick, L. J. (1992). Academic underachievement among the gifted: Students' perceptions of factors that reverse the pattern. *Gifted Child Quarterly, 36,* 140–146.

Fehrenbach, C. R. (1993). Underachieving students: Intervention programs that work. *Roeper Review, 16,* 88–90.

Fine, M. J., & Pitts, R. (1980). Intervention with underachieving gifted children: Rationale and strategies. *Gifted Child Quarterly, 24,* 51–55.

Ford, D. Y. (1996). *Reversing underachievement among gifted Black students: Promising practices and programs.* New York: Teachers College Press.

Fredricks, J. A., Alfeld, C., & Eccles, J. (2010). Developing and fostering passion in academic and nonacademic domains. *Gifted Child Quarterly, 54,* 18–30.

Freedman, J. (2000). *Personal and school factors influencing academic success or underachievement of intellectually gifted students in middle childhood.* (Unpublished doctoral dissertation). Yale University, New Haven.

Gowan, J. (1955). The underachieving gifted child—A problem for everyone. *Exceptional Children, 21,* 247–271.

Green, K., Fine, M. J., & Tollefson, N. (1988). Family systems characteristics and underachieving gifted males. *Gifted Child Quarterly, 32,* 267–272.

Heacox, D. (1991). *Up from underachievement: How teachers, students, and parents can work together to promote student success.* Minneapolis, MN: Free Spirit.

Johnsen, S. K. (2005). *Identifying gifted students: A step-by-step guide.* Waco, TX: Prufrock Press.

Kindermann, T. A. (1993). Natural peer groups as contexts for individual development: The case of children's motivation in school. *Developmental Psychology, 29,* 970–977.

Krouse, J. H., & Krouse, H. J. (1981). Toward a multimodal theory of underachievement. *Educational Psychologist, 16*, 151–164.

Lacasse, M. A. (1999). *Personality types among gifted underachieving adolescents: A comparison with gifted achievers and non-gifted underachievers.* (Unpublished doctoral dissertation). York University, Toronto.

McCall, R. B. (1994). Academic underachievers. *Current Directions in Psychological Science, 3*, 15–19.

McCall, R. B., Evahn, C., & Kratzer, L. (1992). *High school underachievers: What do they achieve as adults?* Newbury Park, CA: Sage.

McCoach, D. B. (2002). A validity study of the School Attitude Assessment Survey (SAAS). *Measurement and Evaluation in Counseling and Development, 35*, 66–77.

McCoach, D. B. (2010). Research methods for gifted studies: Comments and future directions. In B. Thompson, & R. F. Subotnik (Eds.), *Methodologies for conducting research on giftedness* (pp. 241–252). Washington, DC: American Psychological Association.

McCoach, D. B., & Siegle, D. (2001). A comparison of high achievers' and low achievers' attitudes, perceptions, and motivations. *Academic Exchange Quarterly, 5*(2), 71–76.

McCoach, D. B., & Siegle, D. (2003a). The SAAS-R: A new instrument to identify academically able students who underachieve. *Educational and Psychological Measurement, 63*, 414–429.

McCoach, D. B., & Siegle, D. (2003b). The structure and function of academic self-concept in gifted and general education samples. *Roeper Review, 25*, 61–65.

Matthews, M. S., & McBee, M. T. (2007). School factors and the underachievement of gifted students in a talent search summer program. *Gifted Child Quarterly, 51*, 167–181.

Moon, S. M., & Hall, A. S. (1998). Family therapy with intellectually and creatively gifted children. *Journal of Marital and Family Therapy, 24*, 59–80.

Neisser, U., Boodoo, G., Bouchard, T. J., Jr., Boykin, A. W., Brody, N., Ceci, S. J. et al. (1996). Intelligence: Knowns and unknowns. *American Psychologist, 51*, 77–101.

Pendarvis, E. D., Howley, A. A., & Howley, C. B. (1990). *The abilities of gifted children.* Englewood Cliffs, NJ: Prentice Hall.

Peterson, J. S., & Colangelo, N. (1996). Gifted achievers and underachievers: A comparison of patterns found in school files. *Journal of Counseling and Development, 74*, 399–406.

Rayneri, L. J., Gerber, B. L., & Wiley, L. P. (2003). Gifted achievers and gifted underachievers: The impact of learning style preferences in the classroom. *The Journal of Secondary Gifted Education, 14*, 197–204.

Redding, R. E. (1990). Learning preferences and skill patterns among underachieving gifted adolescents. *Gifted Child Quarterly, 34*, 72–75.

Reis, S. M., Hébert, T. P., Diaz, E. P., Maxfield, L. R., & Ratley, M. E. (1995). *Case studies of talented students who achieve and underachieve in an urban high school.* (Research Monograph 95120). Storrs: The National Research Center on the Gifted and Talented, University of Connecticut.

Reis, S. M., & McCoach, D. B. (2000). The underachievement of gifted students: What do we know and where do we go? *Gifted Child Quarterly, 44*, 158–170.

Reis, S. M., & Renzulli, J. S. (2009). The Schoolwide Enrichment Model: A focus on student strengths and interests. In J. S. Renzulli, E. J. Gubbins, K. S. McMillen, R. D. Eckert, & C. A. Little (Eds.), *Systems and models for developing programs for the gifted and talented* (2nd ed., pp. 323–352). Mansfield Center, CT: Creative Learning Press.

Reis, S. M., Westberg, K. L., Kulikowich, J., Caillard, F., Hébert, T., Plucker, J. et al. (1993). *Why not let high ability students start school in January? The curriculum compacting study.* (Research Monograph 93106). Storrs: The National Research Center on the Gifted and Talented, University of Connecticut.

Richert, E. S. (1991). Patterns of underachievement among gifted students. In J. H. Borland (Series Ed.), M. Bireley, & J. Genshaft (Vol. Eds.), *Understanding the gifted adolescent* (pp. 139–162). New York: Teachers College Press.

Rimm, S. (1995). *Why bright kids get poor grades and what you can do about it.* New York: Crown.

Rimm, S. (1997a). An underachievement epidemic. *Educational Leadership, 54*(7), 18–22.

Rimm, S. (1997b). Underachievement syndrome: A national epidemic. In N. Colangelo, & G. A. Davis (Eds.), *Handbook of gifted education* (2nd ed., pp. 416–435). Boston: Allyn & Bacon.

Rimm, S. (2008). *Why bright kids get poor grades—and what you can do about it* (3rd ed.). Scottsdale, AZ: Great Potential Press.

Rimm, S., & Lowe, B. (1988). Family environments of underachieving gifted students. *Gifted Child Quarterly, 32*, 353–358.

Robinson, A., Shore, B., & Enerson, D. (2007). *Best practices in gifted education: An evidence-based guide.* Waco, TX: Prufrock Press.

Rosário, P., Costa, M., Nuñez, J. C., González Pineda, J., Solano, P., & Valle, A. (2009). Academic procrastination: Associations with personal, school, and family variable. *The Spanish Journal of Psychology, 12*, 118–127.

Ryan, A. M. (2001). The peer group as a context for the development of young adolescent motivation and achievement. *Child Development, 72*, 1135–1150.

Schunk, D. H. (1998, November). *Motivation and self-regulation among gifted learners.* Paper presented at the Annual Meeting of the National Association of Gifted Children, Louisville, KY.

Sheard, M. (2009). Hardiness commitment, gender, and age differentiate university academic performance. *British Journal of Educational Psychology, 79*, 189–204.

Siegle, D., & McCoach, D. B. (2002). Promoting a positive achievement attitude with gifted and talented students. In M. Neihart, S. M. Reis, N. M. Robinson, & S. Moon (Eds.), *The social and emotional development of gifted children: What do we know?* (pp. 237–249). Waco, TX: Prufrock Press.

Siegle, D., & McCoach, D. B. (2005). *Motivating gifted students.* Waco, TX: Prufrock Press.

Siegle, D., & McCoach, D. B. (2009, April). *Application of the Achievement–Orientation Model to teachers' of the gifted job satisfaction.* Paper presented at the Annual Convention of the American Educational Research Association, San Diego, CA.

Siegle, D., & Reis, S. M. (1998). Gender differences in teacher and student perceptions of gifted students' ability. *Gifted Child Quarterly, 42*, 39–48.

Siegle, D., Reis, S. M., & McCoach, D. B. (2006, June). *A study to increase academic achievement among gifted underachievers.* Poster presented at the 2006 Institute of Education Sciences Research Conference, Washington, DC.

Siegle, D., Rubenstein, L. D., Pollard, E., & Romey, E. (2010). Exploring the relationship of college freshman honors students' effort and ability attribution, interest, and implicit theory of intelligence with perceived ability. *Gifted Child Quarterly, 54*, 92–101.

Sternberg, R. J., & Davidson, J. E. (2005). *Conceptions of giftedness* (2nd ed.). New York: Cambridge University Press.

Supplee, P. L. (1990). *Reaching the gifted underachiever.* New York: Teachers College Press.

Thorndike, R. L. (1963). *The concepts of over and underachievement.* New York: Teachers College Press.

Weiner, I. B. (1992). *Psychological disturbance in adolescence* (2nd ed.). New York: Wiley.

Westberg, K. L., Archambault, F. X., Jr., Dobyns, S. M., & Salvin, T. (1993). *An observational study of instructional and curricular practices used with gifted and talented students in regular classrooms.* (Research Monograph 93104). Storrs: The National Research Center on the Gifted and Talented, University of Connecticut.

Whitmore, J. R. (1980). *Giftedness, conflict, and underachievement.* Boston: Allyn & Bacon.

Whitmore, J. R. (1986). Understanding a lack of motivation to excel. *Gifted Child Quarterly, 30*, 66–69.

Wolfle, J. A. (1991). Underachieving gifted males: Are we missing the boat? *Roeper Review, 13*, 181–184.

Yu, S. (1996). *Cognitive strategy use and motivation in underachieving students.* (Unpublished doctoral dissertation). University of Michigan, Ann Arbor, MI.

Zilli, M. G. (1971). Reasons why the gifted adolescent underachieves and some of the implications of guidance and counseling to this problem. *Gifted Child Quarterly, 15*, 279–292.

38

GIFTED AFRICAN AMERICANS

Frank C. Worrell

Author Note: Jesse Erwin helped with the research supporting this chapter.

It is a truism that African American students are under-represented in gifted[1] and talented education programs. Several explanations have been advanced for under-representation (Ford, 1995, 1998), but the most potent is the broader issue of the achievement gap in the American education system. Given that (a) African American students obtain lower scores, on average, on cognitive tests and tests of achievement across all academic domains than their Asian American and European American counterparts (Aud, Fox, & KewalRamani, 2010; Jencks & Phillips, 1998; Lee, 2002; Neisser et al., 1996); and (b) identification for gifted and talented education programs is often based on scores on these types of tests (Worrell, 2009b), it is inevitable that African Americans will be under-represented in programs for gifted and talented students relative to these other groups (Lohman, 2005a).

Acknowledging the role of the achievement gap also makes it misleading to calculate under-representation based only on the percentage of African Americans in a particular district or school's gifted and talented program, as this does not account for the distributions of students' achievement scores by demographic group. Of course, the reasons for the achievement gap are complex and related to differential rates of poverty and access to a quality education across ethnic and racial groups. Nonetheless, to date, there are no definitive studies on how much additional variance in under-representation, if any, is due to these other explanations that have been put forward (Worrell, 2009b).

The achievement gap notwithstanding, there are African Americans who obtain the gifted and talented label in both school-based and university-based programs. The goal of this chapter is to summarize the current knowledge base about this group of students. In keeping with the other chapters on demographic subgroups, this chapter is organized around three overarching questions. First, do African American students classified as gifted manifest different needs and strengths from the general population of students with that classification? Second, are there issues presented by African Americans that require specific accommodations in identification and service delivery models? Third, are there programs or approaches which have demonstrated evidence of efficacy in promoting the participation and success of African American students in advanced-level classes and environments?

Before proceeding further, it is important to acknowledge the difficulties inherent in answering these questions definitively. Despite a substantial literature on the under-representation of African Americans in gifted and talented programs, our evidence-based knowledge on gifted African Americans is woefully inadequate. First, the field of gifted education has no consensus definition of giftedness, and much of the data on gifted African Americans are from studies using small samples of convenience and a wide variety of definitions of giftedness. Second, since the majority of studies of gifted African Americans are not comparative with, for example, a control group, it is not possible to know if conclusions in the studies apply only to gifted African Americans, only to African Americans, or even only to gifted students. Thus, the conclusions drawn are tentative at best.

Who Are the Gifted African Americans?

In this chapter, giftedness is defined as superior performance in a given domain relative to the appropriate peer group. Nationally, African Americans make up 17 percent of the public elementary and secondary school population, but they typically constitute less than 10 percent of the students classified as gifted (Snyder & Dillow, 2010; Office of Civil Rights, U.S. Department of Education, 2006). The percentage of African Americans earning the gifted label fluctuates by state, but is consistently below the percentage in the school population.

Do Gifted African American Students Manifest Different Needs and Strengths?

This question is a contentious one and has more often been discussed in relation to underachievement rather than gifted performance. Given the current state of research findings, the best answer at this point is a qualified "maybe."

Similarities

Lohman (2005c) concluded that reading and mathematics achievement are predicted by the same general and specific cognitive abilities and to the same extent across different ethnic and racial groups. In other words, the contributions of variables like g (general intelligence), fluid intelligence, crystallized intelligence, auditory processing, and memory to actual reading and mathematics performance do not differ by demographic group. Additionally, contrary to popular belief, studies of the predictive and structural validity of cognitive test scores have revealed no bias against African Americans (Reynolds & Carson, 2005). In other words, differences among groups on cognitive measures are reflections of the achievement gaps that exist in the U.S. and are not due to the tests. Moreover, students in gifted and talented programs, including African Americans, obtain higher achievement test scores than their counterparts not in those programs, although even in gifted and talented programs, the average achievement scores of African Americans are lower than their White and Asian counterparts (Worrell, 2003).

Strengths

No research addresses the question of unique strengths of gifted African American students directly. However, there are studies suggesting that students from marginalized minority groups who have dual identities score higher on measures of academic achievement than their counterparts with non-dual identities (e.g., Oyserman, Kemmelmeier, Fryberg, Brosh, & Hart-Johnson, 2003). In this context, a dual identity refers to having a strong sense of belonging both to one's racial/ethnic group and to the larger society in which the racial/ethnic group is embedded. In a sample including African American, American Indian, and Hispanic middle school students in general education classrooms, Oyserman and her colleagues found that students with dual identities had higher grade point averages (GPAs) at the end of the semester than students who were aschematic (reported no racial/ethnic schema) or those who had an in-group-only schema. Two other studies including high-achieving African Americans also provide tentative support for this hypothesis. One was a study of students in a university-based program (Worrell, 2007); the other was a study of students in an International Baccalaureate program at an urban high school (Worrell & White, 2009). In both these studies, the researchers found that ethnic identity attitudes were negatively related to academic achievement for African American students, and attitudes indicating a willingness to engage with other groups were positively related to academic achievement. Although these studies did not test the hypothesis about dual identities directly, the African Americans had higher ethnic identity scores than European American students, suggesting that African American students with high "other group orientation scores" also had high ethnic identity scores (or potential dual identities). More research is needed in this area.

Additionally, although African American youth are more likely to live in poverty and single-parent homes, to be exposed to violence, and to experience the death of someone that they know, their rates of psychopathology, with the exception of attention deficit hyperactivity disorder (ADHD) and substance use, are parallel to or lower than those of European Americans. These findings suggest that African American students are quite resilient as a group (Worrell, 2009a).

Needs

Empirical evidence on the needs of African American students is limited, although there is a substantial amount of theorizing in this area (e.g., Ford, 1996; Graham, 2009; Worrell, 2009b). All of these authors argue that it is not possible to think about African American achievement without considering the socio-historical context of the United States, and Graham (2009) uses beliefs about ability ("Can I do it," p. 113) and beliefs about effort ("I can, but do I want to," p. 119) as a way to frame the issue.

Can I Achieve?

The societal stereotype about the low intelligence of African Americans is pervasive in the United States (Steele, 1997, 2010). This stereotype may result in doubts by both African American students and their teachers about the students' ability to achieve. This questioning of ability, coupled with the lower socio-economic status (SES) of African American students, on average, and their greater vulnerability to teacher expectation effects (Jussim & Harber, 2005) may have a negative impact on the academic self-concept and self-efficacy of this group, variables with well-established positive relationships to achievement outcomes in general and gifted populations.

The poorer performance of students from negatively stereotyped groups in contexts where the stereotype has been made salient relative to peers for whom the stereotype has not been made salient is called stereotype threat. The power of *stereotype threat* is such that researchers document substantial decreases in performance when it is invoked in laboratory settings, and there are claims that stereotype threat also affects performance in real-world settings such as classrooms (Walton & Spencer, 2009; for an alternative view, see Cullen, Waters, & Sackett, 2006).

The phenomenon of the "Big-Fish-Little-Pond" effect (BFLPE) in which students experience a drop in academic self-concept when they enter more competitive environments such as professional schools, graduate schools, or gifted and talented programs (Marsh & Hau, 2003) has been documented in all populations. However, societal stereotypes of low intelligence may make African American students more susceptible to the BFLPE when they are placed in gifted programs. In other words, African American students may interpret this normative drop in academic self-concept that happens when one's comparison group is more competitive as a confirmation of the societal stereotype; this may then result in diminished effort or an unwillingness to engage in academic pursuits at the intensity required for outstanding achievement.

Do I Want to Achieve?

Whereas stereotype threat speaks to self-doubts that African Americans may experience based on societal perceptions of their abilities, Ogbu's (2004) cultural ecological theory addresses the other issue raised by Graham (2009): choosing to achieve. Ogbu postulated that (a) historic and current discrimination against African Americans, (b) the failure of educational achievement to overcome economic and other barriers, and (c) negative societal attitudes toward African Americans result in some African Americans choosing to develop an identity in opposition to mainstream culture. This opposition is reflected in devaluing education, disengaging from schooling, and categorizing an orientation toward high achievement as acting White (Fordham & Ogbu, 1986).

Despite criticisms of the acting White hypothesis, there is growing empirical evidence in support of this claim, particularly among males. Taylor and Graham (2007) found that African American girls at all grade levels reported admiring and respecting high achievers, whereas African American boys' admiration and respect for high achievers plummeted in the seventh grade. This finding is also reflected in the huge gender achievement gap in favor of African American females (Aud et al., 2010), a gap that widens across grades K–12 and is ultimately reflected in major gender discrepancies in post-secondary education settings. Indeed, there is a growing literature on the education crisis for African American males (e.g., Garibaldi, 2007).

Ford, Grantham, & Whiting (2008) asked 166 gifted African American students (classified as gifted on the basis of either an IQ score of at least 127 or an achievement test percentile rank of at least 98) if they had heard of the phrases, "acting White" and "acting Black." If they answered yes, they were asked to explain what the phrases meant. About 80 percent of the participants reported they had heard of these two phrases and described "acting White" as completing one's homework, doing well in school, taking advanced classes, and preferring to study instead of hanging out with one's friends. "Acting Black" involved underachieving, being uneducated, and pretending not to be smart. Thus, gifted African American students may have a difficult choice:

Do they choose to be Black or to be good students; to fit in with their friends or to face accusations of betraying their ethnic heritage; or to belong to a group with whom they share an ethnic heritage or to belong to a group of high achievers that includes many individuals who are not like them and who may also not embrace them?

(Worrell, 2009b, p. 137)

What Issues Presented by African Americans Require Specific Accommodations?

Identification

All gifted and talented programs begin with the process of identification, and it is important to define the aspect of giftedness that will be served by the program prior to beginning the identification task. As noted by Johnsen in Chapter 10 in this book, identification procedures should be multifaceted and include measures of achievement, cognition, behaviors, and interests.

Achievement

The best predictor of subsequent performance in any domain is current performance in that domain. Thus, strong performance in reading or mathematics or science or drawing is important in identifying potential candidates for more advanced instruction in these subjects. Students who are performing above average relative to their peers in the classroom or on group tests should be considered for further assessment. Given that academic performance is substantially influenced by the socio-economic circumstances and the social and cultural capital of the home and school, relative strengths are as important for identifying talent as absolute strengths for students in under-represented subgroups. As Lohman (2005b, p. 38)2 put it, one should "compare each student's scores only to the scores of other students who share roughly similar learning opportunities or background characteristics." What this means is that in addition to using national norms, one should also use local (e.g., school, grade-level) and opportunity-based (e.g., similar SES, parental education, English language learners) norms, which allow for identification of students who are at the top of their specific subgroups, even if not at the highest levels of the national norm group.

Another option in assessing achievement involves using performance tasks (MacFarlane & Feng, 2010). In addition to being domain-specific, performance tasks assess fluency and complexity of responses, allow for multiple correct responses, focus on problem solving, encourage the use of metacognition, require a dynamic assessment approach on the part of the teacher or individual conducting the assessment, and are also useful in identifying African American and low-income students (VanTassel-Baska, Johnson, & Avery (2002).

Ability

Standardized cognitive measures should also be used in the identification process as these instruments' scores provide the most reliable information on both general and specific reasoning abilities (Lohman, 2005b), and also serve as indices of creativity (Park, Lubinski, & Benbow, 2007, 2008). Moreover, it is important to assess and pay attention to the cognitive score—typically, verbal, quantitative, or spatial—in relation to the domain of interest; thus, the three major areas of cognition should be assessed. As with achievement tests, cognitive tests should be interpreted in relation to national, local, and opportunity-based norms, as the scores on these measures are also affected by social and cultural capital. For example, African Americans and low-income students in Georgia were substantially under-represented in automatic referrals for gifted identification based on national norms on standardized tests (McBee, 2006).

Behaviors

Use of rating scales is also standard practice in identification. When assessing students for placement in gifted and talented programs, teachers often complete rating scales focused on characteristics of gifted students. Unfortunately, most gifted rating scales have major limitations. First, several of them have extremely limited normative samples, so the norms do not represent a national sample and often are not representative of the African American population. Second, the items are often high-inference—that is, they require respondents to infer characteristics rather than report on behaviors they have observed. Third, the items are typically grouped by sub-scale (i.e., all of the items assessing a particular construct such as motivation or intellectual capacity are contiguous), leading to response sets (i.e., responding similarly or identically to different items).

Fourth, the gifted rating scales with the most psychometrically robust scores often use IQ scores as their indicator of criterion-related validity. Although I support the use of cognitive instruments as part of the identification process, if the scores on a rating scale merely confirm what the IQ scores indicate, they provide no incremental validity in selection; and as the scales typically assess inferred characteristics of giftedness, they will identify and exclude the same students as the cognitive measures. A more useful strategy is to assess *observable* behaviors that are related to achievement and learning.

A critical concern regarding the use of rating scales when engaging in the identification of gifted students from populations that include African Americans is the person conducting the rating, typically a teacher. Although research indicates that teachers' perceptions of students are generally accurate, teachers are not immune from societal stereotypes of African Americans. In a vignette study, Elhoweris, Mutua, Alsheikh, and Holloway (2005) found that teachers were significantly less likely to refer to gifted programs African American students than European American students or students whose ethnicity was unknown, with effect sizes of .39 and .44, respectively. McBee (2006) reported similar findings based on data from the Georgia Department of Education.

Interests

Student interests have not received as much research attention as cognition and other identification variables, but are very important in an assessment of giftedness. If African American students are not interested in the topics covered in classrooms for gifted and talented students, they are less likely to engage with the material or remain in the program. Sosniak (1990) reminded us that interest plays a dual role in the development of talent. Individuals begin engaging in an activity out of personal interest and enjoyment, and at some point for those who become eminent, personal interest transforms into professional lifelong interest. Lubinski, Benbow, and Ryan (1995) showed that vocational interests assessed in intellectually gifted 13-year-olds with the Strong–Campbell Interest Inventory were predictive of interests beyond chance levels when these individuals were 28 years old.

Service Delivery Models

As noted in Section III of this text, several options are widely used for delivering services and curriculum to gifted students. One of the alternatives in the field involves the choice between enrichment and acceleration. Another choice point focuses on the location of the program. No research or theoretical literature suggests that one type of service delivery model is more beneficial than another with regard to African American students.

Location of Program

Gifted programming is typically offered in several different settings (VanTassel-Baska, 2007). The range of options varies from programs where individual teachers are expected to provide differentiated instruction in the general education classroom for students classified as gifted , through separate classrooms for identified gifted children, to pull-out programs for part of the day for those students, or even specialized schools (see Section III of this book). Delcourt, Cornell, and Goldberg (2007) compared gifted African American and European American students attending four different types of program (special school, separate class, pull-out, and within-class) to students in two comparison groups (a high-achiever group and a non-gifted group). In their data, there was no interaction between race and program type. However, on average, students in the special schools, separate classes, and pull-out programs had higher achievement than the gifted students in within-class programs, the high achievers not in a gifted program, and the non-gifted students. As a first step in examining the impact of program type on academic achievement, this project represents an important step forward. Pertinent to this discussion, the findings suggest that program type and not race is the variable that affects academic achievement.

Curriculum

As with delivery options, there is little guidance in the empirical literature about curricular options that are better for gifted African American students than for students from other groups. Several authors have proposed the use of multicultural education (Banks, 1995) and culturally relevant pedagogy (Ladson-Billings, 1995) as ways in which curriculum should be modified, interpreted, and taught for ethnic/racial minority students. Although these ideas were developed in response to student underachievement, they are useful to consider with regard to working with all students, including the gifted. Banks (1995, p. 393) proposed five dimensions of multicultural education:

a. the use of examples and content matter from a number of different cultural groups in teaching concepts;
b. explicit teaching that knowledge is built upon previous knowledge and thus influenced by context and previous experience;
c. explicit teaching of prejudice reduction;
d. the use of teaching strategies that are sensitive to students' cultural backgrounds; and
e. the systematic reorganization of the school to promote its mission in supporting diversity.

The work of Ladson-Billings (1995) on culturally relevant pedagogy overlaps substantially with the dimensions outlined by Banks (1995). She argued that culturally relevant pedagogy is particularly important when teaching African American students and other students from marginalized backgrounds. Culturally relevant pedagogy involves effective teaching of academic skills, using students' culture as one mechanism in promoting learning, and facilitating students in using their developing academic skills in critiques of "the cultural norms, values, mores, and institutions that produce and maintain societal inequities" (Ladson-Billings, 1995, p. 162).

Ladson-Billings (1995, p. 159) acknowledged that these ideas are not new or radical, and in fact, are "routine teaching strategies that are a part of good teaching." One way to think about these strategies is in terms of what have been dubbed the "new three Rs": relevance, relationship, and rigor. A basic principle of effective pedagogy has always been tying new knowledge to existing knowledge, and what better way to do so than to use students' lives and cultural experiences as the existing knowledge base on which to build? There are also scores of anecdotes about the teachers who care for students and for whom students want to work—teachers with whom students feel a connection. Teachers who weave students' cultures into lessons in meaningful and positive ways are the same teachers to whom students feel connected and for whom they want to work. Rigor is the last of the new trio and is often neglected. As noted earlier, the fundamental reason for African American under-representation in gifted and talented programs is the distribution of scores on achievement measures. The teaching of academic skills in ways that translate into outstanding performance is a necessary component of any gifted and talented program for all students in the program.

Support Systems

The types of support systems that might be useful in supporting African American students are based on the theory and empirical work described previously. As noted, culturally relevant pedagogy may be beneficial to all students, but may be particularly supportive for African Americans and other marginalized groups in the face of negative stereotypes and beliefs that high achievement and being African American are incompatible. The literature also suggests that African American males are more likely than females to have these beliefs, and developing strong academic identities in this group may require active work on the part of educators centered on cognitions of what it means to be African American, male, and a high achiever in academic domains (Whiting, 2006).

What Approaches Have Been Successful in Supporting African Americans in Advanced-level Classes and Environments?

A critical component of any approach stems from the literature suggesting that talent development in African American students is enhanced by feelings that they *belong*. Because academic talent development takes place in communities of learning (Sosniak, 1995), if students do not feel that they are a part of the community, they will be unwilling to participate. If they feel they are a part of the community, they are willing to participate, remain engaged, and ultimately return. Thus, gifted and talented programs more generally, including programs operating outside of the regular classroom, may need to develop strategies to foster a sense of belonging and inclusion in African American students. Whether one belongs in an educational setting is a message communicated by teachers and other adults. It is important to provide support to teachers so that they have high expectations for, and supportive attitudes toward, all students. In this section,

I present some data on persistence, the importance of values, and the role of feedback in supporting African American students.

Persistence

In examining the rate at which students returned to a summer program for academically talented youth, Worrell, Szarko, and Gabelko (2001) reported comparable return rates for nontraditional (primarily African American and Latino/Latina) and traditional (primarily Asian and European American) students. Further, grade point average, socio-economic status, standardized achievement scores, and final grades in the summer program classes did not reliably distinguish between returnees and non-returnees. Worrell et al. hypothesized that the comparable return rates were based on the academic, psychosocial, and financial supports provided only to the nontraditional students. These supports included (a) a pre-orientation to the program before the regular orientation; (b) books, tuition, and subway fare; (c) academic labs in small groups run by a mentor/tutor; and (d) ongoing support from a counselor specifically assigned to work with this group.

The components of the program were designed to integrate the nontraditional students into the program, creating as much of a home for them as it is for all of their traditional peers. Results from a later study also provide some support for this hypothesis. As noted previously, Worrell (2007) found a significant and substantial negative relationship between ethnic identity attitudes and *school GPA* for African American students attending a summer program for academically talented youth; however, the relationship between ethnic identity attitudes and *expected GPA in the program* was not significant nor meaningful in effect size terms, suggesting that African American students viewed the summer program differently from how they viewed their home schools.

Values

In a brief writing assignment, African American students in one group were asked to choose the value or values that were most important to them from a list of values, and to write a paragraph about why the values were important to them; African American students in the second group were asked to choose the value or values that were least important to them, and to write a paragraph about why the values might be important to someone else (Cohen, Garcia, Apfel, & Master, 2006). Students in the first group closed the achievement gap with their European American peers by 40 percent, and gains in both academic achievement and student self-perceptions were maintained two years later (Cohen, Garcia, Purdie-Vaughns, Apfel, & Brzustoski, 2009). Although it is not entirely clear why this intervention worked—replications are clearly necessary—and the students were in general education classrooms, this is one of very few studies that has used random assignment and resulted in a demonstrable increase in academic achievement. The potential impact on high-achieving African American students is exciting to contemplate.

Type of Feedback

Perhaps in response to the societal stereotypes about African Americans, African Americans are less likely to trust European Americans and their motives. Cohen, Steele, and Ross (1999) found that ratings by African American college students on instructor bias, motivation to persist on a writing task, and identification with writing skills differed on the basis of the way in which feedback was presented to them. Instructors were European American. African American students who received critical feedback in combination with an explicit invocation of high standards and the assurance that the student could meet the standards, (a) rated the instructor as less biased; (b) reported greater motivation to complete the task; and (c) reported greater identification with the academic task than peers who received only the critical feedback, or peers who received the critical feedback, specific directions for improvement, and positive comments about their general performance. European American students' outcomes did not differ according to type of feedback.

The results of this study indicate that African American students respond less favorably than European American students "when negative feedback [is] presented without additional information" (Cohen et al., 1999, p. 1313) by European Americans; and provide further support for the contention that teachers' views play a greater role in African American students' self-assessments than those of their majority peers. Additionally, the study models a way to provide academic feedback that helps to ensure African American student engagement without affecting the performance of other students.

A Few Cautions

It would be remiss not to address two common claims in the literature on gifted African Americans that have no empirical support. The first of these is the purported relationship between Black racial identity and academic achievement. Black racial identity is one of the most frequently studied constructs in African American samples. There are no established relationships between racial identity attitudes/Black racial identity attitudes and profiles and academic achievement. Thus, all claims in the literature are speculative, at best. Another frequent claim is that academic achievement is related to Black cultural learning styles. However, Black learning styles (Frisby, 1993a, 1993b) and learning styles more generally have no "practical utility" (Pashler, McDaniel, Rohrer, & Bjork, 2008, p. 117) and should not be used as the basis for interventions.

CONCLUSION

The achievement gap between African American students and many of their Asian American and European American counterparts is a long-standing and vexing problem in American education. One of its corollaries is the under-representation of African Americans in educational programs for gifted and talented youth. Although empirical literature on these issues is limited and often not based specifically on samples of the identified gifted students, the existing studies do provide suggestions with regard to identification practices, pedagogical approaches, and psychosocial supports. Important research questions still exist that must be addressed before we fully understand the performance of this group of students.

NOTES

1. Gifted in this chapter refers to those students with demonstrated achievement or intellectual ability in academic realms rather than the areas of the arts or leadership.
2. See Chapter 12 in this book for further details on Lohman's position.

REFERENCES

Aud, S., Fox, M., & KewalRamani, A. (2010). *Status and trends in the education of racial and ethnic groups.* (NCES 2010-015). National Center for Education Statistics, U.S. Department of Education.. Washington, DC: U.S. Government Printing Office.

Banks, J. (1995). Multicultural education and curriculum transformation. *The Journal of Negro Education, 64,* 390–400.
doi:10.2307/2967262

Cohen, G. L., Garcia, J., Apfel, N., & Master, A. (2006). Reducing the racial achievement gap: A social-psychological intervention. *Science, 313,* 1307–1308.
doi:10.1126/science.1128317

Cohen, G. L., Garcia, J., Purdie-Vaughns, V., Apfel, N., & Brzustoski, P. (2009). Recursive processes in self-affirmation: Intervening to close the minority achievement gap. *Science, 324,* 400–403.
doi:10.1126/science.1170769

Cohen, G. L., Steele, C. M., & Ross, L. D. (1999). The mentor's dilemma: Providing critical feedback across the racial divide. *Personality and Social Psychology Bulletin, 25,* 1302–1318.
doi:10.1177/0146167299258011

Cullen, M. J., Waters, S. D., & Sackett, P. R. (2006). Testing stereotype threat theory predictions for math-identified and non-math-identified students by gender. *Human Performance, 19,* 421–440.
doi:10.1207/s15327043hup1904_6

Delcourt, M. A. B., Cornell, D. G., & Goldberg, M. D. (2007). Cognitive and affective learning outcomes of gifted elementary school students. *Gifted Child Quarterly, 51,* 359–381.
doi:10.1177/0016986207306320

Elhoweris, H., Mutua, K., Alsheikh, N., & Holloway, P. (2005). Effect of children's ethnicity on teachers' referral and recommendation decisions in gifted and talented programs. *Remedial and Special Education, 26,* 25–31.
doi:10.1177/07419325050260010401

Ford, D. Y. (1995). Desegregating gifted education: A need unmet. *Journal of Negro Education, 64,* 52–62.
doi:10.2307/2967284

Ford, D. Y. (1996). *Reversing underachievement among gifted Black students: Promising practices and programs.* New York: Teachers College Press.

Ford, D. Y. (1998). The underrepresentation of minority students in gifted education: Problems and promises in recruitment and retention. *The Journal of Special Education, 32,* 4–14.
doi:10.1177/002246699803200102

Ford, D. Y., Grantham, T. C., & Whiting, G. W. (2008). Another look at the achievement gap: Learning from the experiences of gifted Black students. *Urban Education 43,* 216 -238. doi:10.1177/0042085907312344

Fordham, S., & Ogbu, J. U. (1986). Black students' school success: Coping with the "burden of acting White." *Urban Review, 18,* 176–206.
doi:10.1007/BF01112192

Frisby, C. L. (1993a). "Afrocentric" explanations for school failure: Symptoms of denial, frustration, and despair. *School Psychology Review, 22,* 568–577.

Frisby, C. L. (1993b). One giant step backward: Myths of Black cultural learning styles. *School Psychology Review, 22,* 535–557.

Garibaldi, A. M. (2007). The educational status of African American males in the 21st century. *Journal of Negro Education, 76,* 324–333.

Graham, S. (2009). Giftedness in adolescence: African American gifted youth and their challenges from a motivational perspective. In F. D. Horowitz, R. F. Subotnik, & D. J. Matthews (Eds.), *The development of giftedness and talent across the lifespan* (pp. 109–129). Washington, DC: American Psychological Association.
doi:10.1037/11867-007

Jencks, C., & Phillips, M. (Eds.). (1998). *The Black-White test score gap.* Washington, DC: Brookings Institution Press.

Jussim, L., & Harber, K. D. (2005). Teacher expectations and self-fulfilling prophecies: Knowns and unknowns, resolved and unresolved controversies. *Personality and Social Psychology Review, 9,* 131–155.
doi:10.1207/s15327957pspr0902_3

Ladson-Billings, G. (1995). But that's just good teaching! The case for culturally relevant pedagogy. *Theory Into Practice, 34,* 159–165.
doi:10.1080/00405849509543675

Lee, J. (2002). Racial and ethnic achievement gap trends: Reversing the progress toward equity. *Educational Researcher, 31,* 3–12.
doi:10.3102/0013189X031001003

Lohman, D. F. (2005a). An aptitude perspective on talent: Implications for identification of academically gifted minority students. *Journal for the Education of the Gifted, 28*, 333–360.

Lohman, D. F. (2005b). *Identifying academically talented minority students.* Storrs: The National Research Center on the Gifted and Talented, University of Connecticut.

Lohman, D. F. (2005c). The role of nonverbal ability tests in identifying academically gifted students: An aptitude perspective. *Gifted Child Quarterly, 49*, 111–138. doi:10.1177/001698620504900203

Lubinski, D., Benbow, C. P., & Ryan, J. (1995). Stability of vocational interests among the intellectually gifted from adolescence to adulthood: A 15-year longitudinal study. *Journal of Applied Psychology, 80*, 196–200. doi:10.1037/0021-9010.80.1.196

McBee, M. T. (2006). A descriptive analysis of referral sources for gifted identification screening by race and socio-economic status. *Journal of Secondary Gifted Education, 17*, 103–111.

MacFarlane, B., & Feng, A. X. (2010). The patterns and profiles of gifted African American children: Lessons learned. In J. L. VanTassel-Baska (Ed.), *Patterns and profiles of promising learners from poverty* (pp. 107–128). Waco, TX: Prufrock Press.

Marsh, H. W., & Hau, K. (2003). Big-fish-little-pond effect on academic self-concept: A cross-cultural (26-country) test of negative effects of academically selective schools. *American Psychologist, 58*, 364–376. doi:10.1037/0003-066X.58.5.364

Neisser, U., Boodoo, G., Bouchard, T. J., Jr., Boykin, A. W., Brody, N., Ceci, S. J. et al. (1996). Intelligence: Knowns and unknowns. *American Psychologist, 51*, 77–101. doi:10.1037/0003-066X.51.2.77

Ogbu, J. U. (2004). Collective identity and the burden of "acting White" in Black history, community, and education. *The Urban Review, 36*, 1–35. doi:10.1023/B:URRE.0000042734.83194.f6

Office of Civil RIghts, U.S. Department of Education. (2006). *Civil rights data collection.* Retrieved from http://ocrdata.ed.gov/Projections.aspx

Oyserman, D., Kemmelmeier, M., Fryberg, S., Brosh, H., & Hart-Johnson, T. (2003). Racial-ethnic self-schemas. *Social Psychology Quarterly, 66*, 333–347.

Park, G., Lubinski, D., & Benbow, C. P. (2007). Contrasting intellectual patterns for creativity in the arts and sciences: Tracking intellectually precocious youth over 25 years. *Psychological Science, 18*, 948–952. doi:10.1111/j.1467-9280.2007.02007.x

Park, G., Lubinski, D., & Benbow, C. P. (2008). Ability differences among people who have commensurate degrees matter for scientific creativity. *Psychological Science, 19*, 957–961. doi:10.1111/j.1467-9280.2008.02182.x

Pashler, H., McDaniel, M., Rohrer, D., & Bjork, R. (2008). Learning styles: Concepts and evidence. *Psychological Science in the Public Interest, 9*, 105–119.

Reynolds, C. R., & Carson, A. D. (2005). Methods for assessing cultural bias in tests. In C. L. Frisby, & C. R. Reynolds (Eds.), *Comprehensive handbook of multicultural school psychology* (pp. 795–823). Hoboken, NJ: Wiley.

Snyder, T. D. & Dillow, S. A. (2010). *Digest of education statistics 2009* (NCES 2010-013). Washington DC: National Center for Education Statistics, Institute of Education Sciences, U.S. Department of Education.

Sosniak, L. A. (1990). The tortoise, the hare, and the development of talent. In M. J. A. Howe (Ed.), *Encouraging the development of exceptional abilities and talents* (pp. 149–164). Leicester, UK: The British Psychological Society.

Sosniak, L. A. (1995). Inviting adolescents into academic communities: An alternative perspective on systemic reform. *Theory Into Practice, 34*, 35–42. doi:10.1080/00405849509543655

Steele, C. M. (1997). A threat in the air. How stereotypes shape intellectual identity and performance. *American Psychologist, 52*, 613–629. doi:10.1037/0003-066X.52.6.613

Steele, C. M. (2010). *Whistling Vivaldi and other clues to how stereotypes affect us.* New York: Norton.

VanTassel-Baska, J. (Ed.). (2007). *Serving gifted and talented learners beyond the traditional classroom: A guide to alternative programs and services.* Waco, TX: Prufrock Press.

VanTassel-Baska, J., Johnson, D., & Avery, L. D. (2002). Using performance tasks in the identification of economically disadvantaged and minority gifted learners: Findings from Project STAR. *Gifted Child Quarterly, 46*, 110–123. doi:10.1177/001698620204600204

Walton, G. M., & Spencer, S. J. (2009). Latent ability: Grades and test scores systematically underestimate the intellectual ability of negatively stereotyped students. *Psychological Science, 20*, 1132–1139. doi:10.1111/j.1467-9280.2009.02417.x

Whiting, G. W. (2006). From at risk to at promise: Developing scholar identities among Black males. *The Journal of Secondary Gifted Education, 17,* 222–229.

Worrell, F. C. (2003). Why are there so few African Americans in gifted programs? In C. C. Yeakey, & R. D. Henderson (Eds.), *Surmounting the odds: Education, opportunity, and society in the new millennium* (pp. 423–454). Greenwich, CT: Information Age.

Worrell, F. C. (2007). Ethnic identity, academic achievement, and global self-concept in four groups of academically talented adolescents. *Gifted Child Quarterly, 51,* 23-38. doi:10.1177/0016986206296655

Worrell, F. C. (2009a). Psychological health in school-age populations. In H. A. Neville, B. M. Tynes, & S. O. Utsey (Eds.), *Handbook of African American psychology* (pp. 352–362). Thousand Oaks, CA: Sage.

Worrell, F. C. (2009b). What does gifted mean? Personal and social identity perspectives on giftedness in adolescence. In F. D. Horowitz, R. F. Subotnik, & D. J. Matthews (Eds.), *The development of giftedness and talent across the lifespan* (pp. 131–152). Washington, DC: American Psychological Association. doi:10.1037/11867-008

Worrell, F. C., Szarko, J. E., & Gabelko, N. H. (2001). Multi-year persistence of nontraditional students in an academic talent development program. *The Journal of Secondary Gifted Education, 12,* 80–89.

Worrell, F. C., & White, L. H. (2009, August). *Ethnic identity and academic orientation: A complicated relationship.* Poster presented at the Annual Meeting of the American Psychological Association, Toronto, Canada.

39

ASIAN AMERICAN GIFTED STUDENTS
The Model Minority or the Misunderstood Minority?
Sarah Oh and Carolyn M. Callahan

A FAST-GROWING MINORITY POPULATION

The term "Asian American" refers to having origins in persons who came to the United States from the Far East, Southeast Asia, or the Indian Subcontinent (Office of Management and Budget, 1997). Asian groups are not limited to nationalities, but include ethnic grouping as well. Since the U. S. Census Bureau identified six Asian categories (Asian Indians, Chinese, Filipino, Japanese, Korean, and Vietnamese) in 1980, Asian Americans have been one of the fastest-growing groups in the United States. In 2010, there were more than 14.6 million Asian Americans (4.8 percent of the total population). This number represents an increase of 48 percent between 1990 and 2000, and 43.3 percent between 2000 and 2010 (U.S. Census Bureau, 2011). By 2050, the Asian American population is expected to increase to 40.6 million which will constitute 9.2 percent of the population. This tremendous growth is due in large part to continuing immigration. According to the data from the U.S. Department of Homeland Security (1991–2010), persons from Asia account for nearly 30 percent of the total number of immigrants who obtained permanent residence or naturalized citizen status in the last two decades.

A HIGH-ACHIEVING MINORITY

The success of Asian Americans, especially in education, has been well documented. As reflected in Table 39.1, attainment of Asian Americans in higher education is significantly higher than the U.S. population overall, and is greater than that of any other racial category. In 2008, 29.3 percent of Asian Americans obtained a Bachelor's degree and 19.9 percent received a graduate or professional degree (U.S. Census Bureau, 2008). Asian American students also outperformed students in other racial categories on national mathematics assessments and scored higher than or equal to their Caucasian counterparts on national assessments in reading at the elementary and secondary levels (National Center for Education Statistics [NCES], 2009a, 2009b).

Table 39.1 Educational attainment of Asian Americans

	Population (millions)*	Less than high school degree	High school degree only	Some college education	Bachelor's degree	Graduate or professional degree
Total U.S.	304	15%	28.5%	28.8%	17.5%	10.2%
Asian American	**14.8**	**14.4%**	**16.1%**	**20.2%**	**29.3%**	**19.9%**
White	203.5	10.0%	29.3%	30.1%	19.3%	11.4%
Hispanic	46.9	39.2%	26.0%	21.9%	8.9%	4.0%
African American	38.8	18.9%	31.3%	32.0%	11.7%	6.1%
American Indian/ Alaska Native	3.9	17.7%	29.4%	36.1%	11.0%	5.6%
Others	0.9	18.5%	23.1%	26.1%	19.2	13.3%
Pacific Islanders	0.7	11.5%	33.6%	37.8%	11.8%	5.3%

U.S. Census Bureau. 2008 American Community Survey.

* Note: All of the race classification in the table used numbers of the race alone and in combination with one or more other races, thus the sum of the population is greater than the total number of the U.S. population in 2008.

According to the Office for Civil Rights data (2000, 2002, 2004, 2006), Asian American students are more highly represented than any other racial category in programs for the gifted and talented and advanced academic settings nationwide (see Table 39.2) despite wide differences across states and locally in demographic profiles, definitions of giftedness, and identification policies and practices. In addition, Asian American and Pacific Islander students are also highly represented in advanced academic settings such as Advanced Placement (AP) at the secondary level. Based on the *7th Annual AP Report to the Nation* (College Board, 2011), the category of Asian American or Pacific Islander represents 5.5 percent of seniors from the class of 2010, but makes up 10.2 percent of the total AP examinees.

Explaining the High Achievement of Asian American Students

One possible explanation for the phenomena of Asian Americans' higher educational attainment and higher representation in programs for the gifted was offered by Ogbu and Simons (1998), who categorized minorities based on forms of settlement in the United States (autonomous, voluntary, or immigrant minorities; and involuntary or non-immigrant minorities). According to Ogbu and Simons, a dynamic relationship between how educational environments treat minorities and how minorities react to those educational environments causes differential academic achievement. From this cultural–ecological perspective, some Asian American students from China, India, Japan, and Korea were classified as voluntary minorities who chose to come to the United States. Consequently, they have more positive perceptions of and responses to education, with higher expectations of the future than involuntary minorities. In addition, Ogbu and Simons argued that other Asian Americans such as Cambodians, Vietnamese, and Hmong who came to the United States as refugees share certain attitudes and behaviors of voluntary minorities which contribute to school success despite non-voluntary status.

One characteristic shared by voluntary minorities is a positive dual frame of reference: one based on their situation in the United States and the other based on their situation in their place of origin. The comparison is positive as they see more opportunities in the United States. As a result, they are willing to accommodate and to accept less than equal

Table 39.2 Racial representation in gifted and talented programs

		American Indian/ Alaska Native		Asian/Pacific Islander		Hispanic		Black (non-Hispanic)		White (non-Hispanic)	
		Numbers	%	Numbers	%	Numbers	%	Numbers	%	Numbers	%
2000	Total										
	Membership	539,374	1.16	1,917,432	4.14	7,47,873	16.13	7,865,407	16.99	28,516,270	61.58
	G/T Representation	26,512	.91	207,124	7.08	279,250	9.54	240,792	8.23	2,172,356	74.24
2002	Total										
	Membership	568,710	1.21	2,074,128	4.42	8,358,243	17.80	8,057,742	17.16	27,905,339	59.42
	G/T Representation	27,837	.93	229,359	7.64	312,451	10.41	253,137	8.43	2,179,252	72.59
2004	Total										
	Membership	593,885	1.23	2,168,361	4.50	9,116,374	18.94	8,125,379	16.88	28,135,804	58.45
	G/T Representation	30,924	.97	257,790	8.05	394,805	12.33	287,828	8.99	2,231,413	69.97
2006	Total										
	Membership	600,261	1.24	2,331,028	4.81	9,896,732	20.41	8,308,762	17.13	27,360,985	56.42
	G/T Representation	31,362	.97	304,216	9.40	414,058	12.79	296,146	9.15	2,191,210	67.69

Office for Civil Rights, U.S. Department of Education. Elementary and Secondary School Survey, 2000; Civil Rights Data Collection 2002, 2004, and 2006.

⋆ Note: All of the race classification in the table used numbers of the race alone and in combination with one or more other races, thus the sum of the population is greater than the total number of the U.S. population in 2008.

treatment to improve their chances for success (Ogbu & Simons, 1998). This provides voluntary minorities with motivation to work hard to succeed. These immigrants believe discrimination is temporary and may be the result of their "foreigner status" or lack of oral English proficiency (Gibson, 1988; Ogbu, 1994). In addition, they are less conflicted about accommodating to a White society; consequently, their role models are usually those who have fully adopted the mainstream language and norms and have attained higher educational attainment and economic success. They are hard workers who have played by the rules of the system and succeeded.

Hsu (1971) and Sung (1987) identified unique characteristics associated with Asian culture to explain educational attainment. They concluded that Asian culture is highly conducive to academic achievement and that the family-centered nature of Asians is the most significant factor for Asian success. They proposed that Asian parents teach their children to work hard in school in order to uphold family honor. Suzuki (1995) added social and historical perspectives to the cultural explanation. He argued that schools reward certain cultural traits such as self-discipline, obedience, and respect for authority, thereby cementing the aforementioned cultural traits and Asian Americans' belief that education leads to self-improvement and social mobility. Further, the lack of options in traditional Asian culture for upward mobility outside of education may have resulted in Asian American parents' belief that schooling is one of the only salient avenues left for their children's upward mobility. This almost desperate faith in school was undoubtedly reinforced by the traditional veneration accorded to education in Asian societies. The schools, in turn, reaffirmed this faith by rewarding compliance, good behavior, perseverance, and docility in Asian American students.

THE "MODEL MINORITY"

The academic achievement of Asian Americans has generated frequent references to the group as a "model minority," a term coined by Petersen (1966). The use of this term has, in turn, contributed to the formation of a fixed image of a pan-ethnic category of Asian Americans. While originally used to describe the Japanese, the model minority stereotype expanded to all South Asians by the 1980s. Osajima (1988) asserted that even though the popular press began to recognize the potential negative implications of the model minority stereotype during the 1980s, it continued to reinforce the stereotype with stories of Southeast Asian refugees who overcame extreme circumstances and succeeded academically.

Critics of the model minority stereotype have argued that its emergence represented an attempt to silence the charges of racial injustices being raised by African Americans (Osajima, 1988; Sue & Kitano, 1973; Wu, 2002). Other minorities were implicitly told to model themselves after Asian Americans. Thus, as a hegemonic device, the model minority stereotype maintains the dominance of Whites in the racial hierarchy by diverting attention away from racial inequalities and by setting standards for how minorities should behave (Lee, 1996, 2009).

ISSUES HIDDEN BEHIND THE IMAGE OF MODEL MINORITY

While Asian American students as a group are heralded as a model minority, closer examination suggests they may present issues requiring specific accommodation in identification, service delivery models, counseling, and/or curriculum. First, data supporting the model minority stereotype are frequently aggregated, and aggregated data mask the tremendous differences in achievement and attainment across Asian ethnic groups (Ngo & Lee, 2007). As a result, conclusions such as those presented at the beginning of this chapter dominate discussions of Asian American students. This image of success is thought to serve as an argument to exclude Asian Americans from social and educational programs (Hurh & Kim, 1989; Lee, 2009; Nakanishi, 1995) and hides the reality of the struggle of many Asian Americans with low levels of educational attainment, with limited English proficiency, or living in poverty. When Asian Americans are viewed as a single group, the dominant success of one segment of that population may lead educators to view the whole group as successful and free of problems (Lee, 2009), providing a false sense of complacency with regard to the educational issues faced by subgroups or individuals within the larger group.

Furthermore, as Kim asserts (1997), the focus on the model minority's success has resulted in a lack of research addressing low achievement among some Asian American students; has prevented counselors, teachers, and policy makers from understanding the difficulties and problems of these students; and has, ultimately, led to official neglect of programs and services for Asian American students. Further, the model minority stereotype may have unhealthy repercussions for many high-achieving Asian American students such as increased fear of failure, chronic worry about making mistakes, and self-doubt and anxiety (Castro & Rice, 2003; Eaton & Dembo, 1997; Lee, 1996; Zusho, Pintrich, & Cortina, 2005).

Values of the Asian American culture also contribute to stereotypes of this group. For example, many Asians are implicitly taught at an early age to repress feelings for the greater good of the family or society (Kim & Omizo, 2005). They are told, for example, that it is a positive accomplishment to agree publicly with something with which they privately disagree (Kim & Omizo, 2005). Stoicism is also one of the significant hallmarks of Asian values instilled in Asian youth (Sandhu, 1997); they are encouraged from an early age to deal with their emotional distress within themselves, by themselves. Internalized pressures associated with the stereotype of the model minority leave many Asian Americans feeling that they have to live up to high expectations from parents, teachers, and classmates in order to sustain the image of the model minority student (Sue & Okazaki, 1990). This may prevent them from seeking appropriate and timely assistance for associated emotional difficulties.

In October 2009, the White House announced the "Initiative on Asian Americans and Pacific Islanders." The initiative reflects national concern about two issues in the education of Asian Americans that are hidden behind the stereotype of model minority. First, nearly one in four Asian American students has limited English proficiency and lives in a linguistically isolated household where parents have limited English proficiency. Based on the Civil Rights Data Collection in 2006, a total of 22 percent of Asian Americans and Pacific Islanders qualified for Limited English Proficiency (LEP) services and 19.9 percent of them are enrolled in the programs for LEP students (U.S. Office of Civil Rights, 2006). Second, the high school drop-out rate among Southeast Asian American students is staggering: 40 percent of Hmong, 38 percent of Laotian, and 35 percent of the Cambodian population do not complete high school (U.S. Census Bureau, 2008).

Diversity Within the Asian American Population

As the prior discussion suggests, the Asian population is not homogeneous. Asians represent over 30 countries and 100 different languages (Central Intelligence Agency, n.d.). Not only do cultural and linguistic differences exist, but there are vast differences in reasons for immigration or length of residence in the United States. So not surprisingly, the educational attainment of Asian Americans reflects diversity when disaggregated as in Table 39.3. The image of Asian Americans with high educational attainment is not applicable across different waves of immigration. Asian immigrants who came to the United States prior to 1975 had higher educational and economic backgrounds as well as different immigration experiences. Post-1975 waves of Southeast Asian refugees brought poorer and less educated immigrants (Portes & Rumbaut, 1996). Differences in educational attainment translate into economic disparities (Ngo & Lee, 2007). According to the U.S. Census Bureau (2000), Cambodian Americans, Hmong Americans, and Lao Americans earned relatively lower incomes compared to the overall U.S. population.

Acculturation or Assimilation

In addition to differences in culture, language, and length of residence across subgroups, intergenerational differences also affect the adjustment of Asian immigrants. The rise in intergenerational conflict is linked to differences in acculturation between second-generation youth and their immigrant parents (Su, Lee, & Vang, 2005; Yang, 2003). The "family first" concept of Asians plays a critical role in maintaining stability in the family. However, American-born second-generation Asians differ dramatically from their parents. Traditional values such as filial piety, expressing deference to elders, and making personal sacrifices for family members often become less meaningful to second-

Table 39.3 Educational attainment across Asian American subgroups

	Population (millions)	Less than high school degree	Only high school degree	Some college education	Bachelor's degree	Graduate or professional degree
Total U.S.	307	15%	28.5%	28.8%	17.5%	10.2%
Asian American	**15.5**	**14.4%**	**16.3%**	**20.5%**	**29.3%**	**19.9%**
Asian Indian	2.73	10%	10.5%	11.3%	31.9%	36.3%
Bangladeshi	.11	17.3%	17.2%	16.8%	27.9%	20.8%
Cambodian	.24	40.3%	24.3%	21.4%	11.0%	3.0%
Chinese	3.62	18.9%	14.6%	15.3%	25.8%	25.3%
Filipino	3.09	8.2%	15.7%	30.0%	37.5%	8.6%
Hmong	.22	39.6%	19.8%	27.2%	10.7%	2.7%
Indonesian	.08	5.9%	17.0%	32.0%	28.3%	16.8%
Japanese	1.30	7.9%	20.2%	27.0%	29.8%	15.1%
Korean	1.61	10.1%	19.6%	21.6%	32.7%	16.0%
Laotian	.21	31.6%	30.0%	24.6%	11.3%	2.6%
Pakistani	.35	14.6%	14.5%	16.0%	30.4%	24.5%
Thai	.22	16.6%	16.7%	24.2%	25.6%	17.0%
Vietnamese	1.73	26.0%	21.2%	23.4%	20.0%	9.4%

U.S. Census Bureau. 2008 American Community Survey.

generation immigrants. They may defy and reject their parents' way of living. As a consequence, painful value conflicts emerge. Children suffer conflict between the demands of fitting into American culture and the desires of their parents for them to adhere to the values of the culture of origin. Significant cultural clashes at home and at school may negatively affect performance in school and render these students more vulnerable. In several qualitative research studies, vulnerability among second-generation Hmong students was exacerbated by low expectations from teachers and tracking into lower-level courses (P. Thao, 1999; Y. Thao, 2003). According to Zhou and Bankston (1998), the highest rates of delinquency occur within the second generation who are "over-Americanized." Research on second-generation Hmong American youth also points to a rise in truancy, drop-out rates, delinquency, and intergenerational conflict (Faderman, 1998; Thao, 1999).

MAXIMIZING POTENTIAL THROUGH PARTICIPATION

The model minority status of gifted students and their over-representation in programs for the gifted have mitigated consideration of alternative approaches and assessment of evidence for the efficacy of participation and success of Asian American students in advanced-level learning environments. Presumably, the use of traditional assessments coupled with a model minority stereotype have contributed to higher rates of identification of high-achieving Asian American gifted students than other minority students. However, some Asian American students may be overlooked due to limited English proficiency or low socio-economic status.

Nearly all literature on identification of under-represented minorities for gifted programs is focused on African American or English language learner (ELL) Hispanic students (e.g., Ford & Harris, 1999; Naglieri & Ford, 2003; Lohman, Korb, & Lakin, 2008). Considering the relatively high proportion of Asian American students who are Limited English Proficient and their diverse ethnic/cultural backgrounds, recommended practices in identification of ELL minority students can be extended to those Asian American students who have been overlooked due to their limited English or different educational experiences from the dominant culture.

In earlier chapters, alternative procedures were discussed for identifying more highly able children who are second language learners or LEP and/or have had different educational experiences. Some researchers (e.g., Bracken & McCallum, 1998; Naglieri & Ford, 2003) have suggested that nonverbal ability tests can be used for screening students for participation in a program for the gifted. Others (e.g., Lohman et al., 2008) have taken the opposite stance and recommend collecting multiple sources of information from multiple time points. Dynamic assessment (Elliott, 2003; Kirschenbaum, 1998), the act of focusing the collection of data on the ability of the learner to respond to instruction/intervention (see also Chapter 16 in this book on Response to Intervention), has also been suggested as a more effective strategy for both identification and diagnostic purposes in screening and identifying students from nontraditional populations.

Teachers' perceptions of giftedness, potential cultural biases, and cultural competency should also be taken into account in the identification of minority students. Teachers are often the primary gatekeepers for gifted programs through their role in providing nominations for gifted programs or ratings of students in the candidate pool (Archambault et al., 1993; Darling-Hammond & Youngs, 2002). Minority students bring diverse linguistic and cultural backgrounds into classrooms, and teachers who misunderstand cultural differences among diverse students relative to learning, communication, and behavior style are more likely to perceive the differences as deficits (Storti, 1998). For example, Asian students are less likely to challenge authority figures through asking questions or expressing their disagreement. If a teacher is not knowledgeable about cultural differences influencing these behaviors, the teacher may judge the student as nonresponsive, reserved, or intellectually incapable. If Asian students lower their eyes as a sign of respect to the teacher when the teacher speaks, the teacher might misunderstand it as disrespectful, impolite, or rebellious.

Suggestions for potentially effective instructional modifications for gifted Asian students can be gleaned from the intersection of gifted and multicultural education as they have been studied in African American and Latino American students. These approaches to examining the role of culture in education contend that the academic demands of school cannot ignore students' community, experience, and heritage. Granada (2002) also suggests that relevant multicultural and linguistic components should be infused into curriculum design and instruction. For instance, due to a cultural emphasis on respect for authority figures, differing communication patterns and deference to others, Asian students may be reluctant to take part in discussions, especially issue-centered debates, which are common instructional strategies (Pang, 1988). Pang advises teachers to adjust by providing time for reflection about questions posed and specifying student roles and expectations in debate.

Additionally, attention to students' social and emotional needs is important to a well-designed school program for Asian gifted students. Like other immigrant minority populations, many Asian American students face acculturation stress in conjunction with pressure to meet the high expectations of parents and teachers. Although Asian Americans have a lower rate of seeking mental health counseling than other ethnic groups both within and outside of school (Kim, 2007; Kim & Omizo, 2003), this does not necessarily indicate that they are free of mental health problems. Furthermore, Asian students' high academic achievement is not necessarily an indicator of social and emotional well-being, especially if the student is reluctant to seek assistance but may be suffering from internalized pressure to live up to the model minority stereotype. Hence, recommendations for providing counseling services for Asian students start specifically with ongoing monitoring of any signs of distress, depression, or anxiety. In addition, bilingual counseling services and proactive education on counseling services for students and their parents are recommended (Kim 2007).

CONCLUSIONS

While it is problematic to generalize about Asian Americans and their characteristics, Asian students have historically been viewed as a single homogeneous group, and their struggles as immigrants have been masked by the dominance of the stereotypic "model minority" image of success. Consideration by educators of the differences within this group due to differences in cultural background and values, poverty, and/or length of residence in the United States should inform school practices and communication and collaboration with families. When immigrant students experience conflicting values, understandings, and expectations between school and home, conflict, confusion, and distress are likely by-products.

Analyzing disaggregated data on Asian American students extends our knowledge about the population as a heterogeneous group and can contribute to debunking stereotypes about Asian American students. In the education of gifted and talented students, identification and service should focus on maximizing student potential by engaging in learning that is responsive to student needs. To address gifted Asian American students' needs:

a. acknowledge and accommodate different cultural perspectives, values, and behaviors;
b. facilitate excellence in higher-order thinking skills through curricular and instructional modification;
c. provide professional development to develop cultural competency; and
d. support families in reducing generational conflict.

REFERENCES

Archambault, F. X., Jr., Westberg, K. L., Brown, B. W., Hallmark, C. L., Emmons, C. L., & Zhang, W. (1993). *Regular classroom practices with gifted students: Results of a national survey of classroom teachers.* (Research Monograph 93102). Storrs: National Research Center on the Gifted and Talented, University of Connecticut.

Bracken, B. A., & McCallum, R. S. (1998). *Universal Nonverbal Intelligence Test.* Itasca, IL: Riverside.

Castro, J. R., & Rice, K. G. (2003). Perfectionism and ethnicity: Implications for depressive symptoms and self-reported academic achievement. *Cultural Diversity & Ethnic Minority Psychology, 9,* 64–78.

Central Intelligence Agency. (n.d.). *The world factbook.* Retrieved January 21, 2011 from https://www.cia.gov/library/publications/the-world-factbook/

College Board. (2011). *The 7th Annual AP Report to the Nation.* Retrieved March 22, 2011 from http://professionals.collegeboard.com/profdownload/7th-annual-ap-report-to-the-nation-2011.pdf

Darling-Hammond, L., & Youngs, P. (2002). Defining "highly qualified teachers": What does "scientifically-based research" actually tell us? *Educational Researcher, 31,* 13–25.

Eaton, M. J., & Dembo, M. H. (1997). Differences in the motivational beliefs of Asian American and non-Asian students. *Journal of Educational Psychology, 89,* 433–440.

Elliott, J. (2003). Dynamic assessment in educational settings: Realizing potential. *Educational Review, 55,* 15–32.

Faderman, L. (1998). *I begin my life all over: The Hmong and the American immigrant experience.* Boston: Beacon.

Ford, D. Y., & Harris, J. J. (1999). *Multicultural gifted education.* (Education and Psychology of the Gifted Series). New York: Teachers College Press.

Gibson, M. A. (1988). *Accommodation without assimilation.* Ithaca, NY: Cornell University Press.

Granada, A. J. (2002). Addressing the curriculum, instruction, and assessment needs of the gifted bilingual/bicultural student. In J. A. Castellano (Ed.), *Reaching new horizons: Gifted and talented education for culturally and linguistically diverse students* (pp. 130–153). Boston: Allyn & Bacon.

Hsu, F. L. K. (1971). *The challenge of the American dream: The Chinese in the United States.* Belmont, CA: Wadsworth.

Hurh, W. M., & Kim, K. C. (1989). The success image of Asian Americans: Its validity, and its practical and theoretical implications. *Ethnic and Racial Studies, 12,* 512–538.

Kim, B. S. K., & Omizo, M. M. (2003). Asian cultural values, attitudes toward seeking professional psychological help, and willingness to see a counselor. *The Counseling Psychologist, 31,* 343–361.

Kim, B. S. K., & Omizo, M. M. (2005). Asian and European American cultural values, collective self-esteem, acculturative stress, cognitive flexibility, and general self-efficacy among Asian American college students. *Journal of Counseling Psychology, 52,* 412–419.

Kim, H. (1997). *Diversity among Asian American high school students.* Princeton, NJ: Educational Testing Service.

Kim, J. M. (2007). A push for caring imposition against passive tolerance: Reflections on the Virginia Tech massacre through a multicultural lens. *Harvard Educational Review, 77,* 354–359.

Kirschenbaum, R. J. (1998). Dynamic assessment and its use with underserved gifted and talented populations. *Gifted Child Quarterly, 42,* 140–147.

Lee, S. J. (1996). *Unraveling the model minority stereotype: Listening to Asian American youth.* New York: Teachers College Press.

Lee, S. J. (2009). *Unraveling the model minority stereotype: Listening to Asian American youth* (2nd ed.). New York: Teachers College Press.

Lohman, D. F., Korb, K. A., & Lakin, J. M. (2008). Identifying academically gifted English-language learners using nonverbal tests: A comparison of the Raven, NNAT, and CogAT. *Gifted Child Quarterly, 52,* 275–296.

Naglieri, J. A., & Ford, D. Y. (2003). Addressing underrepresentation of gifted minority children using the Naglieri Nonverbal Ability Test (NNAT). *Gifted Child Quarterly, 47,* 155–160.

Nakanishi, D. T. (1995). A quota on excellence? The Asian American admissions debate. In D. T. Nakanishi & T. Nishida (Eds.), *The Asian American educational experience* (pp. 273–284). New York: Routledge.

National Center for Education Statistics. (2009a). *The nation's report card: Mathematics 2009.* (NCES 2010-451). Washington, DC: National Center for Education Statistics, Institute of Education Sciences, U.S. Department of Education.

National Center for Education Statistics. (2009b). *The nation's report card: Reading 2009.* (NCES 2010-458). Washington, DC: National Center for Education Statistics, Institute of Education Sciences, U.S. Department of Education.

Ngo, B., & Lee, S. J. (2007). Complicating the image of model minority success: A review of southeast Asian American education. *Review of Educational Research, 77,* 415–453.

Office for Civil Rights. (2000). *Office for Civil Rights elementary and secondary school surveys 2000.* Washington, DC: Office for Civil Rights, U.S. Department of Education.

Office for Civil Rights. (2002). *2002 Office for Civil Rights elementary and secondary school survey projections and documentation.* Washington, DC: Office for Civil Rights, U.S. Department of Education.

Office for Civil Rights. (2004). *2004 Office for Civil Rights elementary and secondary school survey projections and documentation.* Washington, DC: Office for Civil Rights, U.S. Department of Education.

Office for Civil Rights. (2006). *The civil rights data collection.* Washington, DC: Office for Civil Rights, U.S. Department of Education. Office of Management and Budget. (1997). *Revisions to the standards for the classification of federal data on race and ethnicity.* Retrieved March 25, 2011 from http://www.whitehouse.gov/omb/fedreg_1997standards

Ogbu, J. U. (1994). Racial stratification and education in the United States: Why inequality persists. *Teachers College Record, 96,* 265–298.

Ogbu, J. U., & Simons, H. D. (1998). Voluntary and involuntary minorities: A cultural-ecological theory of school performance with some implications for education. *Anthropology & Education Quarterly, 29,* 155–188.

Osajima, K. (1988). *Asian Americans as the model minority: An analysis of the popular press image in the 1960s and 1980s.* Pullman: Washington State University Press.

Pang, V. O. (1988). Teaching about ethnic heritage: More than costumes and unusual food. *Learning, 16,* 56–57.

Petersen, W. (1996, January 6). Success story, Japanese-American style. *New York Times Magazine,* 20–43.

Portes, A., & Rumbaut, R. G. (1996). *Immigrant America: A portrait* (2nd ed.). Berkeley: University of California Press.

Sandhu, D. S. (1997). Psychocultural profiles of Asian and Pacific Islander Americans: Implications for counseling and psychotherapy. *Journal of Multicultural Counseling and Development, 25,* 7–22.

Storti, C. (1998). *The art of crossing cultures* (2nd ed.). Yarmouth, ME: Intercultural Press.

Su, J., Lee, R. M., & Vang, S. (2005). Intergenerational family conflict and coping among Hmong American college students. *Journal of Counseling Psychology, 52,* 482–489.

Sue, S., & Kitano, H. H. L. (1973). Stereotypes as a measure of success. *Journal of Social Issues, 29,* 83–98.

Sue, S., & Okazaki, S. (1990). Asian American educational achievements: A phenomenon in search of an explanation. *American Psychologist, 45,* 913–920.

Sung, B. L. (1987). *The adjustment experience of Chinese immigrant children in New York City.* New York: Center for Migration Studies.

Suzuki, R. H. (1995). Education and the socialization of Asian Americans: A revisionist analysis of the "model minority" thesis. In D. T. Nakanishi & T. Nishida (Eds.), *The Asian American educational experience* (pp. 113–132). New York: Routledge.

Thao, P. (1999). *Mong education at the crossroads.* New York: University Press of America.

Thao, Y. J. (2003). Empowering Mong students: Home and school factors. *The Urban Review, 35,* 25–42.

U.S. Census Bureau. (2000). 2000 American Community Survey. Retrieved January 21, 2011 from http://factfinder2.census.gov/faces/nav/jsf/pages/index.xhtml

U.S. Census Bureau. (2008). 2008 American Community Survey. Retrieved January 21, 2011 from http://factfinder2.census.gov/faces/nav/jsf/pages/index.xhtml U.S. Census Bureau. (2011). *Overview of race and Hispanic origin: 2010.* 2010 Census Briefs. Retrieved April 7, 2011 from http://www.census.gov/prod/cen2010/briefs/c2010br-02.pdf

U.S. Department of Homeland Security. (1991–2010). *Yearbook[s] of immigration statistics.* Retrieved January 2012 from http://www.dhs.gov/files/statistics/publications/yearbook.shtm

Wu, F. (2002). *Yellow: Race in America beyond Black and White.* New York: Basic Books.

Yang, K. (2003). Hmong Americans: A review of felt needs, problems, and community development. *Hmong Studies Journal, 4,* 1–23.

Zhou, M., & Bankston, C. L. (1998). *Growing up American: How Vietnamese children adapt to life in the United States.* New York: Russell Sage.

Zusho, A., Pintrich, P. R., & Cortina, K. S. (2005). Motives, goals, and adaptive patterns of performance in Asian American and Anglo American students. *Learning and Individual Differences, 15,* 141–158.

40

GIFTED LATINO STUDENTS
Overcoming Barriers and Realizing Promise
Thomas P. Hébert

INTRODUCTION

Although Mauricio Novelo's father encouraged him to pursue a career in science or mathematics, he preferred reading about the poignant love affair of Cathy and Heathcliff in Emily Bronte's *Wuthering Heights*, as well as Spanish poetry by Pablo Neruda and Antonio Machado. The young literature enthusiast applied his passion to his studies and took advantage of his high school's International Baccalaureate bilingual diploma program in which students took college-level courses in Spanish literature and English literature. As a result of his hard work and talent, the young man, a native Spanish speaker whose family had immigrated to Gainesville, Georgia from Mexico City, earned a coveted four-year scholarship to the University of Pennsylvania where he is pursuing an undergraduate degree in comparative literature (Jordan, 2009). Mauricio is just one of many gifted Latino[1] students whose intellect and passion for learning needed nurturing. Fortunately, his talents were identified and supported in one of the only public high schools in the country to offer a prestigious bilingual diploma. Unfortunately, stories like Mauricio's are rare, for many more talented Latino students in the United States face barriers and serious challenges to acquiring their education without support to overcome them.

Latinos are now the largest (41.3 million), fastest-growing, and youngest minority group in the United States (U.S. Bureau of the Census, 2000; Valverde & Scribner, 2001). According to current projections, by 2030, Latinos will comprise one quarter of all public school students in the United States (Suarez-Orozco & Paez, 2002). Latino students in U.S. classrooms represent all 22 Spanish-speaking countries and territories throughout the world. They come from countries in South America, Central America and the Caribbean and are immigrants and native-born (Bean & Tienda, 1987; Castellano, 2002, 2004). "They are a microcosm of the world" (Castellano, 2011, p. 250) and their unique experiences have influenced them in different ways both before and after immigration to the United States.

Although different Hispanic groups display diverse cultural characteristics, there are significant commonalities across the 22 cultural groups. One common characteristic is the importance of *familia*—a family commitment encompassing loyalty, a dedicated support system, a belief that a child's behavior is a reflection on the honor of the family, a hierarchy among siblings, and a duty to care for family members (Castellano, 2002; Griffith, Prezas, & Labercane, 2006; Griggs & Dunn, 1996). Hispanic families are characterized by a focus on the collective. The needs of the family have greater priority than the needs of the individual. Another deeply rooted cultural characteristic is *respeto*—the appropriate deferential behavior in interpersonal relationships, according to age, socio-economic status, gender, and authority status. Elders in a Latino family deserve respect from younger people (Comas-Diaz, 1989). Another characteristic is a strong sense of other-directedness and emphasis on cooperation in attaining goals (Castellano, 2002; Griffith et al., 2006; Griggs & Dunn, 1996).

Perrine (1989) noted that "the dynamic of families in Hispanic culture is a vital force and must be considered" (p. 15) in planning the academic experiences of Hispanic students. Perrine suggested that attention to this dynamic needs to be inclusive of parents, for parental support is a critical factor in determining whether or not children's capabilities are valued and nurtured. He indicated that several factors relating to family dynamics have the potential to diminish nurturance of giftedness and talent in school. They include the family structure, parental view of the educational process, and the family view of the general value of education and school success. The view of education held by Hispanic parents may differ from that of the school, with the child being torn between two value systems. Ruiz (1989) described this problem:

> Hispanics conceive of and define the term "education" much more broadly than do most who speak English in this society. To be *educado* goes far beyond school, or may not involve school at all; it means to be well mannered, respectful, considerate, and knowledgeable about practical things. In schools these may be recognized as admirable qualities, but not as talents. For their part, Hispanics may resist school programs that are merely cognitive in orientation—programs, in their terms that may add to one's "schooling," but not one's "education."
>
> (Ruiz, 1989, p. 62)

CHALLENGES FACING LATINO STUDENTS

The experiences of Latino students have involved difficult challenges at all levels of education in the United States (Valverde & Scribner, 2001; Wolf-Wendel, Trombly, Morphew, & Sopcich, 2004). Latino students as a group are seriously under-represented at the upper end of the achievement continuum and in gifted education programs and Advanced Placement classes (Gándara, 2007). They are at higher risk than all other ethnic groups for failure to complete high school (Harvey, 2002) and have the highest collegiate drop-out rates (The Tomás Rivera Policy Institute [TRPI] & National Hispanic Caucus of State Legislators [NHCSL], 2003). Hispanics are more likely to attend two-year community colleges where degree completion is the exception rather than the rule (Gándara & Chavez, 2003).

Numerous barriers impede the progress of Latino students in the United States. Many factors influence Hispanic students' academic achievement including: poverty, parental educational background, inadequate pre-kindergarten opportunities and early childhood literacy development, high rates of residential mobility, limited English proficiency (LEP), impersonal education environments, low teacher expectations, racism, lack of parental support, negative peer pressure, instruction not aligned with student needs, and lack of role models and mentors (Gándara, 2007; Gregory 2003; Valverde & Scribner, 2001; Zalaquett, 2005). Scholars have also identified barriers affecting Latino students in higher education: lack of strong adult supervision, misinformation about college requirements, and choice of less successful options (Harrell & Forney, 2003; Zalaquett, 2005). In addition, Latinos who demonstrate high academic ability, particularly those of Mexican and Puerto Rican ancestry, are less likely to come from economically and educationally advantaged backgrounds. The schools which these low-income students attend are less likely to provide rigorous curricula and Advanced Placement classes and they also typically have fewer qualified teachers and resources. Moreover, the aspirations of these students are often lower since neither their peers nor teachers hold high expectations for them. Gándara (2005) described their situation:

> Their academic futures may be hanging by a thin thread of hope that nothing will go terribly wrong in their extended families, or their relationship to school, to dash their dreams. And, even if they manage to make it through their entire K-12 education as outstanding students, they remain at very high risk for not realizing their academic promise beyond high school. Their academic futures could, perhaps, be characterized as "fragile."
>
> (Gándara, 2005, p. 5)

EXPLAINING LATINO HIGH ACHIEVEMENT AND GIFTEDNESS

> And my first day in it was an accelerated chemistry class. I was the first one to class. It was the first class of the day. The teacher walks in, looks at me, and walks out of the room and looks at the room number. Comes back in and asks me if I was aware that this was Chemistry 1X, rather than Chemistry 1. And I told him yes, I was aware that this was Chemistry 1X. This is where I belong. And he kind of looked at me in disbelief and just shrugged and went into his office.
>
> (Hughes, 2003, p. 233)

This interaction of a young Mexican student and his teacher on the first day of school serves as an example of the difficult challenges facing Latino students, and helps to explain why so many Hispanic students do not succeed in school. However, like the young man in the accelerated chemistry class, many Latino students do extremely well in school despite coming from adverse circumstances. The discussion that follows examines literature on high-achieving Latino students as well as research on gifted Hispanic youth. This discussion is in no way exhaustive, but represents an effort to highlight the major strands of the research literature. As Gentry, Hu, & Thomas (2008) indicated, the majority of research on ethnically diverse students has focused on under-representation in gifted education, developing alternative forms of identification, describing characteristics and experiences, and defining achievement issues. Ethnic groups identified for the majority of studies include "large sweeping groups" (p. 207) (i.e. Black, Asian, Hispanic,

Native American) and fail to distinguish among the many different subgroups that comprise the larger categories. However, in examining research on Latino groups, one must consider the nuances of the cultures that can lead to better understanding of student achievement and success.

Research by Cordeiro (1990) and Cordeiro and Carspecken (1993) involved an ethnographic investigation of 20 highly successful Hispanic high school students of Mexican ancestry, born in the United States from low socio-economic backgrounds and living with parents who had not completed high school. In order for these Hispanic achievers to succeed, they had to construct an identity at school that enabled them to divide themselves between the dominant individualistic American school culture and the minority Hispanic culture of their neighborhoods (Cordeiro, 1990). Moreover, these students shouldered the responsibility for academic success alone, without the complete understanding or support of their families or friendships with other high-achieving Hispanic students.

Cordeiro and Carspecken (1993) explained that entrance into the achieving Hispanic group involved the development of a "*success-facilitating interpretive scheme*" (p. 279) which enabled students to construct Hispanic identities distinct from what they regarded as "typically Hispanic" and "play the achiever's game" (p. 289) which included involvement in part-time jobs and extensive extracurricular activities. These researchers identified several important factors supporting the students' success: significant role models and extra-familial caregivers in the formative years, positive reinforcements (such as awards), and involvement in academically competitive Honors and magnet programs.

Several qualitative research studies conducted in the 1990s examined the experiences of high-ability Hispanic students from low socio-economic environments. Hine (1990, 1994) conducted a qualitative study to examine the perceptions of 10 gifted Puerto Rican high school students and their parents to identify family factors that contributed to their high academic achievement. Although the students came from a variety of social and economic backgrounds, they had much in common when asked what factors led to their school success. All of the participants described specific family factors which supported their academic achievement, including press for achievement, high educational and professional aspirations, a strong family support system, an optimistic outlook and lack of defeatism, extracurricular involvement and the development of a social bond with the community, strong encouragement for language development, and discomfort with cultural stereotypes and negative community expectations.

Parents of high achievers held high educational and occupational aspirations for their children and communicated to their children how they valued achievement in school by reviewing daily papers and report cards, offering praise and small rewards when their children did well, and encouraging greater effort when they believed their child was not working up to potential. All of the participants in the study were actively involved in both school and extracurricular activities with parental support for their involvement. Being involved helped to nurture a positive self-image and a commitment to school and community. The high achievers also described aspects of a strong family bond that included a sense of loyalty to family and culture, family pride and motivation, and closeness of family ties. Parents taught their children about their Spanish language and Puerto Rican heritage while the children strove to become successful in the larger culture. Both the parents and the teenagers felt it was important to understand and feel positive about their cultural heritage in order to develop a strong sense of self. Hine identified additional factors influencing academic achievement that mirror those of Cordeiro: role models beyond the family, having excellent teachers, consistently high teacher expectations, and an intrinsic drive for success.

Hébert (1996) used semi-structured interviews, observation, and archival data to identify factors that supported the high academic achievement of three gifted Latino males (two of Puerto Rican and one of Cuban descent) in an urban high school. These students were characterized by strong resilience stemming from specific sources of support including: a strong belief in self; deep religious convictions; strong family support; extra-familial support from coaches, teachers, and guidance counselors; and heavy involvement in school and extracurricular community-oriented activities. The resilience in the young men enabled them to overcome the adversity evidenced in their low socio-economic urban environment.

Within the same high school, Diaz (1998) explored the self- and environmental perceptions of six high-ability students of Puerto Rican descent who were underachieving. The most critical factor among the family, school, community, and personality issues contributing to the students' academic underachievement was the absence of early appropriate academic experiences. Low-challenge academic curricula during elementary school had a negative impact on these students' need to put forth effort, develop learning strategies, and acquire effective study habits. Although they were successful in earning high grades in elementary school, lack of academic rigor and challenge during those early years hampered the development of their academic abilities and talents for success in middle and high school.

Kloosterman (1999, 2003) investigated factors contributing to or hindering the development of bilingualism, academic achievement, and talent in 12 Latino elementary students of high ability in the same urban school district examined by Hébert and Diaz. In particular, she examined teachers' and parents' perceptions of the Latino culture and the linguistic and academic performance of the children: six boys and six girls of Peruvian, Colombian, Dominican or Puerto Rican descent, all born in the United States. The home and school environments of the children played essential roles in their cognitive and psychosocial development. Major influences encouraging the children's academic achievement, talent development, and bilingualism included: emotional support usually emanating from immediate or extended family members, family values, a strong mother, and maintenance of the Spanish language.

Kloosterman (2003) noted a lack of support for the 12 children within their school. The school predominantly represented the values, norms, and traditions of the dominant society and had limited understanding or appreciation of cultural diversity. Most teachers did not know or were not certain about the language or languages spoken by the families at home. In addition, she noted that teachers were unaware of key issues in the lives of the children such as loss of parents, economic challenges faced by the families, or visits to see extended families abroad. Teachers in this setting also lacked awareness of the students' talents, struggled with classroom curriculum differentiation, and had limited knowledge or training in gifted education.

Literature on high-achieving Latino students from low-income backgrounds includes several significant contributions from Patricia Gándara. Her ground-breaking study entitled *Over the Ivy Walls: The Educational Mobility of Low-income Chicanos* (1995) involved an examination of 50 individuals of Mexican descent who "met the most stringent criterion for academic success: a Ph.D., M.D., or J.D. degree conferred from a highly regarded American university of national stature" (p. 11). She described her study as an attempt to shed light on the "forces that push some Chicano students, born and raised in environments that typically yield academic failure, over the ivy walls of academia, and into the highest status professions" (p. xii). All participants were from the first wave of the post-war baby boom, born during the 1940s and early 1950s, and comprised the first documented cohort of Mexican Americans to complete doctoral-level education and earn places in their respective professional domains. The participants were from Arizona, California, Idaho, New Mexico, and Texas, and from families in which neither parent had completed high school. Most were sons and daughters of farm workers and other unskilled laborers. Using a structured interview protocol incorporating over 140 questions, Gándara and her research team conducted in-depth interviews with the participants in their homes or professional environments.

The parents of the 50 participants in Gándara's study stressed the development of independence, task mastery, and a high work ethic, and maintained high aspirations for their children. Parents encouraged a literacy-rich home environment with significant reading materials where intellectual discussions of politics, labor organizing, and world events were routinely discussed. Despite the limited formal education of the parents, a high premium was placed on ideas and information. Parents did not interact frequently with the schools. Instead they used their cultural capital to reinforce the mission of the schools, one that they shared from within the home. Coming from large families, the participants reported that older siblings were a great resource to them in achieving their goals, serving as role models and counselors and supporting their aspirations, even when similar opportunities had been closed to them.

Gándara found that most of the participants attended schools that were quite different from the communities in which they lived. With help from scholarships and extended family members, a large percentage of the families chose Catholic educations for their children. Many of the participants themselves, in collaboration with their siblings, chose to attend academically superior schools outside their barrios. More than two-thirds attended naturally desegregated or mostly Anglo schools in middle- or upper-class neighborhoods. Gándara (1995) noted that curriculum tracking was a significant influence in providing opportunity and shaping the aspirations of the participants. In the college-bound classes, "tracking 'cocooned' them with high-achieving peers and exposed them to information necessary for getting ahead in the system" (p. 70). Attending such schools provided them with a peer group that was savvy about opportunities, but also allowed them to gain the confidence they needed to compete later in highly selective universities.

Gándara (2002) and her colleagues (Gándara & Contreras, 2009; Gándara & Moreno, 2002) examined Latino high school students participating in a college-access intervention program aimed at supporting their goal of earning a college degree. The study found significant differences between participating and non-participating students' attitudes toward school, preparation for college, aspirations to attend college, and percentage of those going on to four-year colleges. An in-depth study of the lives of a sub-sample revealed that of the eight highest achieving students in the study, half went on to four-year colleges—their lives complicated by responsibilities, along with financial difficulties, which made the journey to acquiring a college diploma very difficult. Gándara concluded that poverty creates complex challenges for Latino students that prevent them from following through on routine academic commitments. Unanticipated events—

often related to the "daily dynamic of conducting life without a car, childcare, health care, or the money to buy books or pay for bus fare"—prevented some students from following through on school commitments (Gándara, 2005, p. 20).

She indicated that for Latino families, the challenges were sometimes related to being undocumented and being forced to carry out routine family business in roundabout ways, and to language barriers—where the students had to be available as translators or cultural brokers for other family members. Because the extended family is considered by Latinos to be "the vital network at the core of existence" (p. 20), young Latino students feel compelled to place the needs of family members ahead of their own immediate commitments. Gándara concluded that high-achieving students from low-income backgrounds were as likely to become caught up in a web of responsibilities as low-achieving students.

Gándara (2005) extended her inquiry with an analysis of Latino high achievers across two major national data sets—the Early Childhood Longitudinal Study (ECLS) and the National Educational Longitudinal Study (NELS). The ECLS data set was established by the U.S. Department of Education in 1988, with approximately 22,000 kindergarteners from across the United States participating. That same year, the U.S. Department of Education established the NELS study to follow a national sample of more than 24,000 eighth graders throughout high school and beyond to determine factors affecting high school performance and post-secondary choices. Gándara found that across the two data sets there were enduring differences between Latino and White students. High-achieving Latino students in the two samples were more likely to have parents with low levels of education, and schooling was more likely to interrupt the strong relationship between socio-economic status and achievement for Latino students than for White students. She posited that schooling has a greater effect on low-income and minority students' achievement because it "compensates for what low income homes and communities are not able to provide" (p. 16).

The extant research indicates that serious barriers exist for Latino students in American schools. In order to overcome these challenges, more needs to be done in identifying and nurturing gifts and talents in Hispanic youth. The discussion below highlights a number of exemplary approaches implemented in school districts throughout the United States to address this critical issue.

BEST PRACTICES IN GIFTED EDUCATION TO NURTURE HIGH ACHIEVEMENT IN LATINO STUDENTS

Mauricio Novelo, the young man whose story introduced this chapter, was a student in a Hall County public school in Gainesville, Georgia, a school district implementing several promising practices for identifying giftedness among Latino students and nurturing their talents. In addition to the bilingual International Baccalaureate program, the school district has implemented a secondary mentorship program. The Honors Mentor Program in Hall County high schools provides opportunities for highly motivated students who are intensely interested in a particular area of study to spend a semester pursuing in-depth learning in a professional setting. Participants are matched with professionals who serve as mentors by providing authentic career experiences. Latino males and females from all Hall County high schools have benefited from life-changing experiences working with individuals in such fields as medicine, law, and business (S. Krisel, personal communication, January 20, 2011).

Educators in this school district have recognized that teaching nontraditional gifted students involves the same teaching methods and curricula evident in high-quality programs for other gifted children, but they need to be accompanied by *scaffolding*: more assistance, time, and other supportive resources that enable students to succeed (Gándara, 2007). As a result, they designed the BRIDGES Program (i.e., Building Resources for Intellectual Development and Guided Empowerment of Students). This delivers rigorous interdisciplinary instructional units to cluster groups of identified gifted students who are joined by BRIDGES students, children who may eventually qualify for the gifted program, but are at a disadvantage because of socio-economic challenges and language barriers. Teachers have reported that BRIDGES program students have at times outperformed the identified gifted students. Hall County educators have found that this scaffolding approach enables the talents of the children to be nurtured until they are ready to be tested for the gifted education program (S. Krisel, personal communication, January 20, 2011).

Another important example of best practice has been launched by the Johns Hopkins Center for Talented Youth (CTY) at several sites throughout the United States. One example of the model in action is the CTY Prep in Los Angeles. The program offers intensive summer enrichment programs for the students identified as gifted through CTY's national testing program. Students in the CTY Prep did not meet the required 95th through 97th percentile on the program-administered test to qualify for the traditional program experience, but have shown promise and potential. Thus, the CTY Prep provides Saturday and summer enrichment programs designed by the center to help prepare children in the second to eighth grades eventually to qualify for the national Educational Talent Search program. The CTY Prep incorporates in-depth study of high-interest curricula, hands-on collaborative and discovery-oriented learning, and features university mentors guiding students through laboratory-based projects (Gándara, 2007).

Educators in El Paso, Texas have designed the Connecting Worlds/Mundos Unidos gifted and talented dual language immersion program. Supported by a Jacob K. Javits grant from the U.S. Department of Education, the goals of the program include: the identification of students typically under-identified and underserved; the development of bilingualism and biliteracy in English and Spanish; the implementation of rigorous curriculum in a 50/50 dual-language setting; parental involvement; and high-quality professional development. This dual-language immersion gifted magnet program serves students in grades 1–12 in a vertical school zone which includes an elementary, middle, and high school. The program merges second-language acquisition and the methodology of gifted education with goals of achieving high academic excellence and dual-language proficiency. Educators in the El Paso program have found that moving from one language to another in speaking, reading, and writing at an accelerated pace through cognitively rigorous curriculum requires gifted abilities in students. Students construct a solid foundation in their primary language through concept development, and then apply it to their emerging language. Such an approach increases learning and enables children to communicate and process information in two languages, skills needed for the 21st century (Green, Spivey, Ferris, Bernal & Izquierdo, 2011).

In addition to these best practices in gifted education, program designers have also considered the critical influence of rigorous curriculum for educating Hispanic youth. Rojas (2011) highlighted the power of high-quality mathematics instruction in the education of talented Latino students. Drawing from the standards of the National Council of Teachers of Mathematics (NCTM, 2000), she indicated that if mathematics classes offer diversity of assignments and products, appropriate pacing, and explicitly monitor student needs and experiences as they design a curriculum within the students' cultural context, all students will experience a non-threatening environment and a better understanding of their talents in mathematics. She called attention to research evidence indicating a positive correlation between second-language acquisition and mathematics learning, and indicated that talented Latino students arrive in U.S. schools with a high degree of mathematical knowledge and the academic language of Spanish connected to their knowledge of mathematics. In Spanish-speaking countries, the previous experiences of the students may have included gender-segregated schools and grouping according to performance level. Moreover, Latino students talented in mathematics are often afforded leadership opportunities in school as well as in their community.

Rojas (2011) highlighted several issues that educators in the United States need to recognize and address in teaching mathematics to high-ability Latinos. She maintained that in order to understand and solve mathematical word problems, talented Hispanic students need instructional support in academic English—the language required for text comprehension and success in school. She indicated that educators need to understand the mathematics knowledge and experiences that talented Latino students bring with them, assess their prior knowledge, and be familiar with the curriculum standards and teaching practices from the students' home countries. Teachers also need to be flexible with the students' use of native language in the mathematics classroom which can help them to focus on concepts and reasoning without being slowed down by their developing language skills. Gifted education teachers and administrators are encouraged to examine further the curriculum suggestions offered by Rojas (2011) in order to ensure a more equitable approach to delivering mathematical instruction to talented Hispanic students.

Embedded in all of the approaches described above is a philosophical belief in the need to identify giftedness in Hispanic students through a multiple-criteria approach. A multidimensional definition of giftedness is recognized and valued in these school districts. Multiple criteria approaches involve obtaining comprehensive information about a child's abilities by collecting and analyzing results from formal and informal procedures including: standardized measures of aptitude, achievement, and creativity in the child's native or English language; nominations by teachers, parents, community members, and peers; observations of the child in multiple contexts; evaluation of student products and performances; observations using rating scales and behavior checklists; past academic performance; and parent interviews (Aguirre & Hernandez, 2002; Castellano, 2002).

The gifted education field recognizes that multiple criteria approaches to the identification of giftedness and talent in culturally diverse populations provide for equity and excellence (Frasier, 1997). Consistent with this message is a call for more teacher training in recognizing gifted behaviors in Latino students. Teachers' limited understanding of the effects of language on classroom performance has prevented the identification of giftedness, creativity, and talent in Hispanic children (Gándara, 2007; Kloosterman, 2003; Masten & Plata, 2000; Plata & Masten, 1998). Providing for ongoing professional conversations that focus on identifying and developing talent in Hispanic children enables a school faculty to build a shared knowledge base through communication and appreciation of other cultures (Brulles, Castellano, & Laing, 2011).

CONCLUSION

Policy makers and researchers in the United States have acknowledged the significant increase of Latino students in our classrooms and have called for more school districts to provide high-quality education for Latino students and all other children in order to deliver a tremendous pool of talent ready to move the nation forward (Castellano, 2008, 2011; Gándara, 2007; Valverde, 2006; Yzaguirre, 2001). Students such as Mauricio Novelo in Gainesville, Georgia have shown us that barriers can be overcome and the promise for a better future can be realized. It is time for us to respond to the call.

NOTE

1. The terms Latino and Hispanic are used interchangeably throughout this chapter. Hispanic is the preferred term for government data collection efforts, but Latino is often preferred by members of the group. Both refer to essentially the same population, but they communicate different notions of identity. The term Hispanic is derived from the Latin word *Hispania* and describes people who trace their origins to Spain and the Spanish-speaking countries of Latin America. The term Latino is considered more inclusive, an attempt to disassociate from Spain, and represents a broader world perspective. People feel very strongly about these terms due to the inherent meaning and identification with Spanish heritage.

REFERENCES

Aguirre, N. M., & Hernandez, N. E. (2002). Portraits of success: Programs that work. In J. A. Castellano & E. I. Diaz (Eds.), *Reaching new horizons: Gifted and talented education for culturally and linguistically diverse students* (pp. 200–219). Boston: Allyn & Bacon.

Bean, F. D., & Tienda, M. (1987). *The Hispanic population of the United States*. New York: Russell Sage.

Brulles, D., Castellano, J. A., & Laing, P. C. (2011). Identifying and enfranchising gifted English language learners. In J. A. Castellano & D. A. Frazier (Eds.), *Special populations in gifted education: Understanding our most able students from diverse backgrounds* (pp. 305–313). Waco, TX: Prufrock Press.

Castellano, J. A. (2002). Renavigating the waters: The identification and assessment of culturally and linguistically diverse students for gifted and talented education. In J. A. Castellano & E. I. Diaz (Eds.), *Reaching new horizons: Gifted and talented education for culturally and linguistically diverse students*. Boston: Allyn & Bacon.

Castellano, J. A. (2004). Empowering and serving Hispanic students in gifted education. In D. Boothe & J. C. Stanley (Eds.), *In the eyes of the beholder: Critical issues for diversity in gifted education* (pp. 1–13). Waco, TX: Prufrock Press.

Castellano, J. A. (2007). The "browning" of American schools: Identifying and educating gifted Hispanic students. In J. A. Castellano (Ed.), *Special populations in gifted education: Working with diverse learners* (pp. 29–43). Boston: Allyn & Bacon.

Castellano. J. A. (2008). Critical issues and best practices in promoting equity and excellence for gifted Hispanic/Latino students. *Gifted Education Communicator, 39*(4), 24–30.

Castellano, J. A. (2011). Hispanic students and gifted education: New outlooks, perspectives, and paradigms. In J. A. Castellano & A. D. Frazier (Eds.), *Special populations in gifted education: Understanding our most able students from diverse backgrounds* (pp. 249–269). Waco, TX: Prufrock Press.

Comas-Diaz, L. (1989). Culturally relevant issues and treatment implications for Hispanics. In D. R. Koslow & E. P. Salett (Eds.), *Crossing cultures in mental health* (pp. 31–48). Washington, DC: International Counseling Center.

Cordeiro, P. A. (1990). *Growing away from the barrio: An ethnography of high achieving at risk Hispanic youths at two urban high schools*. (Unpublished doctoral dissertation). University of Houston.

Cordeiro, P. A., & Carspecken, P. F. (1993). How a minority of the minority succeed: A case study of twenty Hispanic achievers. *International Journal of Qualitative Studies in Education, 6*(4), 277–290.

Diaz, E. I. (1998). Perceived factors influencing the academic underachievement of talented students of Puerto Rican descent. *Gifted Child Quarterly, 42*, 105–122.

Frasier, M. M. (1997). Multiple criteria: The mandate and the challenge. *Roeper Review, 20*, A4–A6.

Gándara, P. (1995). *Over the ivy walls: The educational mobility of low-income Chicanos*. Albany: State University of New York Press.

Gándara, P. (2002). A study of high school puente: What we have learned about preparing Latino youth for post-secondary education. *Educational Policy, 16*(4), 474–495.

Gándara, P. (2005). *Fragile futures: Risk and vulnerability among Latino high achievers*. Princeton, NJ: Educational Testing Service.

Gándara, P. (2007). Latino achievement: Identifying models that foster success. In A. Turnbaugh Lockwood (Ed.), *An agenda for the future: Closing the achievement gap for underrepresented groups in gifted and talented education* (pp. 71–128). Storrs: The National Research Center on the Gifted and Talented, University of Connecticut.

Gándara, P., & Chavez, L. (2003). Putting the cart before the horse: Latinos and higher education. In D. López & A. Jiménez (Eds.), *Latinos and public policy in California: An agenda for opportunity* (pp. 87–120). Berkeley: California Policy Research Center and Regents, University of California.

Gándara, P., & Contreras, F. (2009). *The Latino education crisis: The consequences of failed social policies*. Cambridge, MA: Harvard University Press.

Gándara, P., & Moreno, J. (2002). The Puente Project: Issues and perspectives on preparing Latino youth for higher education. *Educational Policy, 16*, 463–473.

Gentry, M., Hu, S., & Thomas, A. T. (2008). Ethnically diverse students. In J. A. Plucker & C. M. Callahan (Eds.), *Critical issues and practices in gifted education: What the research says* (pp. 195–212). Waco, TX: Prufrock Press.

Green, F., Spivey, S., Ferris, L., Bernal, E. M., & Izquierdo, E. (2011). Our diversity, our treasure: Connecting Worlds/Mundos Unidos gifted and talented dual language immersion program. In J. A. Castellano & A. D. Frazier (Eds.), *Special populations in gifted education: Understanding our most able students from diverse backgrounds* (pp. 287–303). Waco, TX: Prufrock Press.

Gregory, S. T. (2003). Planning for the increasing number of Latino students. *Planning for Higher Education, 31*, 13–19.

Griffith, B., Prezas, R., & Labercane, G. (2006). Early experiences of young men of Latin descent. *Journal of Hispanic Higher Education, 5*(1), 22–34.

Griggs, S., & Dunn, R. (1996). *Hispanic-American students and learning style*. Champaign: Children's Research Center, University of Illinois at Urbana-Champaign.

Harrell, P. E., & Forney, W. S. (2003). Ready or not, here we come: Retaining Hispanic and first-generation students in postsecondary education. *Community College Journal of Research & Practice, 27*, 147–156.

Harvey, W. (2002). *Minorities in higher education, 2001–2002: Nineteenth annual status report*. Washington, DC: American Council on Education.

Hébert, T. P. (1996). Portraits of resilience: The urban life experience of gifted Latino young men. *Roeper Review, 19*, 142–147.

Hine, C. Y. (1990). *The home environment of gifted Puerto Rican children: Family factors which support high achievement*. (Unpublished doctoral dissertation). University of Connecticut, Storrs.

Hine, C. Y. (1994). *Helping your child succeed in school: A guide for Hispanic parents*. (Research Monograph 94202). Storrs: The National Research Center on the Gifted and Talented, University of Connecticut.

Hughes, C. A. (2003). What teacher education programs can learn from successful Mexican-descent students. *Bilingual Research Journal, 27*, 225–244.

Jordan, J. (2009, December 21). Bilingual program and love of literature pays off: West Hall student gets scholarship to Ivy League School [newspaper archives]. Retrieved February 12, 2011 from http:// www.gainesvilletimes.com/archives/27343/

Kloosterman, V. I. (1999). *Socio-cultural contexts for talent development: A qualitative study on high ability Hispanic bilingual students*. (Research Monograph 99142). Storrs: The National Research Center on the Gifted and Talented, University of Connecticut.

Kloosterman, V. I. (2003). A shameful subject: The condition of Latino students in gifted education. In V. I. Kloosterman (Ed.), *Latino students in American schools: Historical and contemporary views* (pp. 113–127). Westport, CT: Praeger.

Masten, W. G. & Plata, M. (2000). Acculturation and teacher ratings of Hispanic and Anglo-American students. *Roeper Review, 23*, 45–46.

National Council of Teachers of Mathematics. (2000). *Principles and standards for school mathematics*. Reston, VA: Author.

Plata, M., & Masten, W. G. (1998). Teacher ratings of Hispanic and Anglo students on a behavior rating scale. *Roeper Review, 21*, 139–144.

Perrine, J. (1989). Situational identification of gifted Hispanic students. In C. J. Maker & S. W. Schiever (Eds.), *Critical issues in gifted education: Defensible programs for cultural and ethnic minorities* (pp. 5–18). Austin, TX: Pro-Ed.

Rojas, E. D. (2011). Using mathematics as an equalizer for gifted Latino/adolescent learners. In J. A. Castellano &

A. D. Frazier (Eds.), *Special population in gifted education: Understanding our most able students from diverse backgrounds* (pp. 353–382). Waco, TX: Prufrock Press.

Ruiz, R. (1989). Considerations in the education of gifted Hispanic students. In C. J. Maker & S. W. Schiever (Eds.), *Critical issues in gifted education: Defensible programs for cultural and ethnic minorities* (pp. 60–65). Austin, TX: Pro-Ed.

Suarez-Orozco, M. M., & Paez, M. M. (Eds.), (2002). *Latinos: Remaking America*. Berkeley, CA: David Rockefeller Center for Latin American Studies, Harvard University, & University of California Press.

The Tomás Rivera Policy Institute and National Hispanic Caucus of State Legislators. (2003). *Closing the achievement gaps: Improving educational outcomes for Hispanic children*. Los Angeles & Washington, DC: Authors.

U. S. Bureau of the Census. (2000). *Hispanic or Latino origin in the United States*. Washington, DC: Author.

Valverde, L. A. (2006). *Improving schools for Latinos: Creating better learning environments*. Lanham, MD: Rowman & Littlefield Education.

Valverde, L. A., & Scribner, K. P. (2001). Latino students: Organizing schools for greater achievement. *NASSP Bulletin, 85*, 22–31.

Wolf-Wendel, L., Twombly, S., Morphew, C., & Sopcich, J. (2004). From the barrio to the bucolic: The student transfer experience from HSIs to Smith College. *Community College Journal of Research and Practice, 28*, 213–231.

Yzaguirre, R. (2001, April). Census shows disparity in education of Latino children. *Hispanic Magazine*, 104.

Zalaquett, C. P. (2005). Study of successful Latina/o students. *Journal of Hispanic Higher Education, 5*(1), 35–47.

41

STUDENTS FROM RURAL ENVIRONMENTS

Jonathan A. Plucker

POVERTY EXCELLENCE GAPS

Perhaps the most vexing problem in gifted education is the identification and development of talents among poor students. Although the bulk of public attention on the problem of achievement gaps has been focused on racial differences, socio-economic status (SES) represents a significant problem of its own. Adding geographic location adds to the complexity of the issue.[1]

First, considering the poverty issue, we see that more affluent students score much higher on most achievement tests than their less affluent peers, and these gaps exist at both the basic competency level and the advanced level. For example, one measure of excellence gaps is the comparison of the average scores of different groups of students at the 90th percentile of a particular score distribution, such as the National Assessment of Educational Progress (NAEP). On the NAEP mathematics and reading tests at grades 4 and 8, the gap at the 90th percentile between students eligible for free and reduced-price school meals and their non-eligible peers is more than 20 points on all four tests. Those gaps represent more than a two grade-level difference in achievement at that advanced level, a staggering difference.

But perhaps more troubling is the lack of progress in closing these particular excellence gaps over the past few years. At grade 4, NAEP mathematics and reading excellence gaps for poor students have stayed relatively constant for several years; at grade 8, the gaps have grown. These data suggest that we have made effectively no progress in closing achievement gaps for intellectually talented students from economically struggling families.

Contrary to what can be inferred in much of the general and gifted education literature, free-and-reduced-price-lunch eligibility is *not* a proxy for race. Although three-quarters of non-eligible students in 2009 were White, among those students who were eligible for free and reduced price meals, the proportions were roughly comparable: White (33 percent), Black (26 percent), Hispanic (35 percent). In other words, poverty cuts across other demographic characteristics and groups. Socio-economic status therefore represents a distinct dimension of the excellence gap, requiring a specific approach to educating and developing the talents of poor gifted students.

THE NATURE AND IMPACT OF POVERTY IN RURAL AREAS

Although many poor communities are located in urban areas, the majority of poor communities in the United States are rural in nature. And although every state may not have large urban areas, every state has rural communities. In this chapter, research on the nature of giftedness in rural environments is reviewed, with an emphasis on research-supported strategies for meeting the needs of talented students living in these communities.

Although the definition of "rural" is surprisingly vague (see, e.g., American Youth Policy Forum [AYPF], 2010; Arnold, Bisco, Farmer, Robertson, & Shapley, 2007),[2] the statement that every state has rural areas and, by extension, significant numbers of rural schools and students is not controversial. Indeed, with rare exceptions, most countries have significant populations of rural students and they face the same challenges as students in American rural areas (see e.g., Berdashkevich & Vlasov, 2010; Olgun, Gumus, & Adanacioglu, 2010), along with some of the same potential solutions (e.g., Bell & Jayne, 2010; McQuaide, 2009).

Estimates of the rural student population vary, but the trend of persistently declining enrollments over the past few decades (Jimerson, 2006) appears to have reversed, with recent data suggesting growth (Johnson & Strange, 2007). Regardless, the number of rural students is substantial:

Using the new [NCES] locale code system, in 2006, there were 9,974,462 students attending 26,390 schools in U.S. communities of under 2,500, accounting for 22% of U.S. public school enrollment. Nationally, 29% of public school students attended school in communities of fewer than 25,000 people.

(Johnson & Strange, 2007, p. iii)

Substantial, perhaps, but also somewhat invisible (Floyd, McGinnis, & Grantham, 2011). Rural areas receive little attention in education policy debates for a variety of reasons, but the lack of a persistent media presence in these communities is certainly a major factor. Much of the recent attention, led by national policy such as the No Child Left Behind Act of 2001, focused on identifying and addressing education issues in urban communities, but rural communities have rarely been the focus of prolonged discussion and debate.

In reviewing the literature on rurality, rural education, and gifted rural education, it is impossible not to notice the considerable variability in rural communities. Just as no two urban or suburban areas are identical, rural communities are very diverse, and nearly every study that includes multiple rural areas notes that any trends need to be interpreted with caution because of diversity within the sample. For example, in a comprehensive study of mobility in five states, Beesley, Moore, and Gopalani (2010) found evidence that very high student mobility tended to be associated with rural, poor districts, often near American Indian reservations, but they found tremendous variability across rural districts in mobility patterns, with some districts exhibiting very low student mobility and others extremely high mobility. Health care concerns also tend to vary considerably from community to community (Hendryx, Fedorko, & Halverson, 2010).

RURAL GIFTED STUDENTS' SPECIFIC CHALLENGES AND STRENGTHS

In one of the first comprehensive reviews of gifted rural education issues, Spicker, Southern, and Davis (1987) noted several specific problem areas that limit services for rural gifted students, all of which remain relevant today (2012). In addition, reviews by Colangelo, Assouline, and New (1999), Lawrence (2009), and Stambaugh (2010), among others, have identified additional barriers to the development of talent in rural students. Collectively, these reviews and additional empirical studies describe nine distinct problems.

First, the small size of many rural communities and the lack of scale in many rural schools often mean that few gifted students are identified within any one school or district. Given the diversity of potential talents, the odds are slim that many rural schools will have comprehensive gifted programs. Colangelo et al. (1999), in their exhaustive review of research on rural gifted education, expand on this point by noting that the small rural population often provides few peers for gifted students.

A related problem involves the often large geographic coverage of many rural districts, which creates substantial transportation issues for students (AYPF, 2010). As a result, one set of strategies often used to address gifted education concerns—school choice such as charter schools and magnet schools—is often impractical for rural students and their families due to logistical reasons such as transportation and a simple lack of options.

Second, Spicker et al. (1987) noted that the United States' poorest counties overwhelmingly tend to be rural areas. Poverty has negative effects on almost all aspects of a child's life, including education and health care (Peterson & Litaker, 2010). For example, certain types of drug abuse are more prevalent in rural areas (Havens, Young, & Havens, 2010), and student physical fitness may be low due to low self-efficacy and limited access to facilities that promote physical fitness (Shores, Moore, & Yin, 2010). Yet access to relevant health-care services, especially those services addressing mental health issues and child abuse and neglect, may be inconsistent or lacking (Choo et al., 2010; Ziller, Anderson, & Coburn, 2010). Mobility, which is often highly correlated with poverty, can be quite high in rural communities (Beesley et al., 2010), making provision of consistent education and health-care services problematic.

Third, Spicker et al. (1987) noted that the majority of identification procedures used to identify gifted and talented students included test material that was culturally unfamiliar to rural students and instruments that were not normed with rural students, providing a strong bias against the identification of talents within rural student populations. Significant developments in this area, supported in large part by funding for projects focusing on the identification of under-represented populations of students through the Jacob K. Javits Gifted and Talented Students Education Act of 1988 and reviewed below, have lessened but not eliminated assessment issues, and several studies and reviews have raised similar concerns (Colangelo et al., 1999; Fishkin & Kampsnider, 1996; Lawrence, 2009).

Fourth, rural communities can be marked by provincialism and an emphasis on self-sufficiency, often manifest as comfort with the status quo and resistance to change. At the same time, rural residents may hold to beliefs in the value of home rule, making outside influence in education difficult. Similarly, Colangelo et al. (1999) refer to the prevalence of charges of elitism leveled at attempts to implement gifted education in rural areas. A recent analysis by the AYPF (2010) noted that the nature of rural industry and agriculture is changing, forcing additional economic change on rural communities that are generally resistant to it.

Fifth, relatively low spending per pupil in rural versus suburban and urban areas has been a persistent problem. Although the transition to more equitable funding over the past 20 years has lessened this concern in some states, funding disparities remain between rural and better-funded non-rural, suburban districts.

Sixth, Spicker et al. (1987) mentioned a number of issues related to teachers and other educators, including the perception of difficult working conditions (e.g., low pay, collegial and social isolation, need for teachers to teach multiple subjects, lack of professional development) and a lack of supporting professionals such as psychologists, counselors, and other specialists, making it difficult to attract and retain highly effective teachers. These issues remain problematic (AYPF, 2010; Barley, 2009; Colangelo et al., 1999).

Seventh, the impact on gifted students of the current move toward school consolidation is difficult to predict (Plucker, Spradlin, Magaro, Chien, & Zapf, 2007; Spradlin, Carson, Hess, & Plucker, 2010). Robinson and Rud (2010) make a case that this consolidation, which generally focuses on merging small districts, may have disproportionately negative effects on rural schools and communities. However, the economies of scale that would purportedly emerge from consolidation could offer enhanced opportunities for gifted students as their numbers within rural districts increase along with the size of the district.

Eighth, Guiffrida (2008) notes that rural students matriculating at large universities may face a range of difficulties, most of them cultural in nature, that leads to lack of persistence and failure to graduate. In the same vein, bright rural students may need assistance in developing the study skills and confidence necessary to succeed in rigorous college coursework (Burney & Cross, 2006; Colangelo et al., 1999). This need for support makes sense given that public universities in many predominantly rural states have student bodies many times larger than the population of a gifted rural student's home community. Given the role of cultural identity issues as potential psychological stressors for gifted students (Worrell, 2010), this "culture clash" is not insignificant.

Finally, much has been made of the problem within rural gifted education (and rural education in general) regarding students being encouraged to leave their rural communities to further their education, careers, and well-being. Aimee and Craig Howley and their colleagues (Howley, Howley, & Pendarvis, 2003; Howley, 2009) have been especially critical of this emphasis, but it has also been discussed widely by other scholars. Although this concern is understandable, two factors appear to moderate its importance: First, bright students who seek post-secondary education opportunities generally have to leave their community to take advantage of those opportunities. Second, research on demographic trends (i.e., What percent of "leavers" eventually return to rural areas to raise families? Which characteristics of rural communities tend to attract leavers back to rural life?) is sparse and needs much greater attention. It is also difficult to imagine that a highly gifted learner, living in a small community, who desires the camaraderie of similarly talented peers is falling victim to educators' desire to feed the "national and global economic machine" (Howley, 2009, p. 552).

That said, Howley and Howley and their colleagues raise valuable points about the many positive advantages of rural communities. Going further, they often question the question, so to speak, about examining the issues related to rural gifted education. This is a fair criticism, given that all communities have their advantages and disadvantages, be they rural, exurban, suburban, or urban. Frequently cited advantages of rural education include a greater sense of community involvement, small schools and class sizes, a slower pace and greater appreciation for time, closer relationships with family and friends, and safer schools and communities (Burney & Cross, 2006; Cross & Stewart, 1995; Grace et al., 2006; Lawrence, 2009; Stambaugh, 2010). McIntire and Plucker (1996) noted that, contrary to conventional wisdom, cultural and athletic opportunities differed in kind—the local museum is not the Guggenheim—but not in terms of opportunity for exposure (e.g., for many purposes, a small community library is still a library). In light of these studies, it is not surprising that gifted rural students often express a desire to remain in rural areas despite their specific concerns about the opportunity cost of doing so (Howley, Harmon, & Leopold, 1996).

However, these positive aspects of rural areas do not necessarily translate into positive outcomes. For example, although the Early Childhood Longitudinal Study (ECLS) provides evidence that rural, preschool children have significant advantages relative to non-rural children (e.g., contact with parents, small kindergarten class sizes, safe communities), those advantages do not necessarily translate into relatively positive learning outcomes, such as early literacy (Grace et al., 2006).

PROMISING PRACTICES FOR RURAL GIFTED STUDENTS

Spicker et al. (1987) conclude their review by noting that "an effort should be made to separate the rural effects on student learning from those of ethnicity and poverty . . . [T]he true impact of rural isolation and traditional rural values has yet to be calculated" (p. 157). This remains true, despite the numerous philosophical and anecdotal analyses conducted since the 1980s, primarily because separating socio-economic factors from other variables in any research in the social sciences has proven to be highly complex (Harwell & LeBeau, 2010). However, several strategies for addressing the potential "impact of rural isolation and traditional rural values" have been proposed and implemented.

Identification

By far the most extensive—and positive—developments have occurred in the area of identification. Among the early efforts were those through the Special Populations Resource Information Network for the Gifted (Project SPRING), which largely focused on developing instruments and procedures for identifying gifted students from special populations, especially disadvantaged rural children in Illinois, Indiana, and Ohio (SPRING I) and Indiana, New Mexico, and South Carolina (SPRING II).[3] Based on the belief that traditional tools and procedures for identifying gifted students favored non-rural, economically advantaged students (in large part due to the traditional use of timed measures in artificial contexts), Spicker and his colleagues (Aamidor & Spicker, 1995; Spicker & Poling, 1993) developed a series of identification procedures that were intended to be culture-fair for rural students: contests (that provide meaningful time limits), writing samples judged less for grammar and spelling and more for creativity, Torrance Tests of Creative Thinking (with an emphasis on originality and elaboration scores), parent information about activities outside of school, teacher recommendations to help identify common characteristics of rural, gifted students (proficiency with regional and local dialects, depth of specific knowledge). Results of the SPRING I project provided evidence that the new identification procedures can lead to a greater number of rural students being identified as gifted (Spicker, 1993).

In Project Spring II, the identification procedures were significantly modified for African American and Mexican American students. For example, African American students were also tested with Raven's Progressive Matrices (Raven, 1981) (to assess pattern-recognition ability) and a storytelling festival that emphasized participation rather than competition (to assess performance ability as well as plot and character development). Identification procedures for Mexican American students were modified by adapting the instruments to account for the limited English comprehension of some students and their families, the use of the Matrix Analogies Test (later revised as the Naglieri Nonverbal Ability Test [NNAT]) to assess analogical thinking and spatial ability (Naglieri, Brulles, & Lansdowne, 2009), and the use of interviews of family and community members rather than written instruments. As was the case for SPRING I, the SPRING II identification procedures were associated with significant increases in the number of rural gifted students in participating schools (Spicker, Breard, & Reyes, 1996).

Other apparently successful efforts to increase the identification of rural gifted students take very similar approaches, with the use of multidimensional, multifaceted identification models and a mix of objective and subjective instruments that are often tailored to local values and cultural characteristics (e.g., Clark & Zimmerman, 2001; De Leon & Argus-Calvo, 1997; see several examples in Lawrence, 2009). However, one cautionary note is necessary: Recent research on the use of nonverbal ability tests—considered by many experts to be a promising area for future identification development for poor and/or rural students—suggests that using such assessments does not necessarily result in improved identification of gifted poor students; to the contrary, such assessments may be less likely to identify such students (Carman & Taylor, 2010).

Community-based Curriculum

Shamah and MacTavish (2009) suggest that integrating curriculum and instruction with local resources is an often overlooked strategy for rural education, especially within the context of narrowing curriculum and high-stakes assessment. For example, a lesson on comparative biology could be enhanced by having a class on a farm with a variety of livestock; and inviting a local banker to speak about interest rate calculations and the economic implications of changes in changing federal and state laws could enhance a lesson on that topic, and help students to understand the practical applications of the material. Incorporating community resources and local culture into the curriculum, which has also been recommended for gifted students (Stambaugh, 2010), mirrors efforts within gifted education to implement community-focused, problem-based models for enrichment (e.g., the idea of a Type III project in the Schoolwide Enrichment Model; see Renzulli & Reis, 1997); echoes calls for valuing the unique nature of rural communities (Howley, 2009); and respects rural educators' desire and need to connect with the community (Howley & Harmon, 2001). The SPRING II project developed a science curriculum that was largely community-focused, with positive results (Aamidor & Spicker, 1995; Lewis, 2000). Other traditional approaches to gifted education, such as acceleration, have also been associated with positive benefits for rural gifted students (Howley, 1989).

Regional Partnerships

Spicker et al. (1987) recommended regional or multi-district partnerships and resource sharing to address rural schools' chronic lack of resources and limited specialized expertise, although it is worth noting that this type of regional partnership has been used in rural areas at least as early as the 1970s (see Pringle, Webb, Warner, & Peterson, 1972). Colangelo et al. (1999) recommend the establishment of clearinghouses (i.e., formal collection and distribution centers) and similar networks to increase access to training and resources for rural educators concerned with giftedness; and Gentry and Ferriss (1999) describe a model for science enrichment programming coordinated through a regional vocational center. The idea of gifted education resource sharing aligns with current recommendations for rural schools to create regional partnerships (AYPF, 2010), suggesting that such arrangements are a promising and feasible intervention strategy.

Despite the difficulties caused by transportation to special schools, some states have created Magnet schools, often focused on science and mathematics, to address the needs of advanced students (Rapp, 2008). These schools are often residential in nature (Plucker, Cobb, & Quaglia, 1996), alleviating some transportation concerns but raising custodial issues for school officials. The willingness of families in rural areas to send a child to a residential high school, for example, is also not well understood at the current time.

Expanded use of Technology

The potential of technology-facilitated communication was a great source of optimism for Spicker and his colleagues (see also Aamidor & Spicker, 1995). They believed that technology would allow for greater teacher interaction and decreased collegial isolation and could facilitate social and intellectual interaction for gifted students. Other current uses, which Spicker et al. could not have imagined in the mid-1980s, include real-time delivery of instruction and professional development (AYPF, 2010; Colangelo et al., 1999; Floyd et al., 2011; Lawrence, 2009; among many others). Now that rural access to broadband internet services has increased greatly over the past decade (Sternberg & Low, 2009), access to high-quality (i.e., bandwidth-intensive) distance education has been greatly enhanced in many rural communities. Nearly all interventions for gifted rural students emphasize the critical role (and untapped potential) of advanced technology.

Comprehensive Support Models

Of course, technology is not a panacea. Policy makers' tendency to consider expanded offerings of Advanced Placement courses as equivalent to gifted education may lead to a situation in which meeting the needs of rural gifted students, at least at the high school level, is considered "mission accomplished" when AP courses are offered via distance education. Concerns about the inadequacy of simply making AP online courses a default for gifted education, led to Project Aspire (Burney & Cross, 2006). Aspire offers an intriguing model for expanding AP participation in ways that support rural gifted students appropriately: by identifying talented rural students and providing them with comprehensive support during both Advanced Placement classes *and* the courses leading up to those AP experiences. Teachers, starting as early as grade 7 and through to grade 12, received professional development in helping bright students prepare for the rigorous coursework that they would encounter later in high school, including a focus on providing instruction in critical thinking skills. School counselors also received training in the characteristics of poor, rural gifted students and subsequently provided the necessary supports to these students. Project Aspire is a unique and interesting model because it acknowledges that long-term interventions are necessary, that psychological support is just as important as academic support, that professional development is critical to sustainable success, and that the advantages of rural environments—such as smaller, more intimate learning environments—can be used to help gifted rural students achieve positive learning outcomes. In these ways, Aspire is among the first interventions that attempt to incorporate the wide-ranging recommendations and best practices in the literature (e.g., Aamidor & Spicker, 1995; Colangelo et al., 1999; Stambaugh, 2010), making it one of the most comprehensive interventions for rural gifted students to date.

CLOSING THOUGHTS

Significant advances have been made in the education of gifted rural students, especially in the areas of identification and curriculum development. In general, the existing research suggests that culturally-sensitive, creativity-focused identification practices and experiential, community-based curricular efforts provide numerous benefits to bright students living in rural areas. There also appears to be empirical evidence, albeit limited in scope, that providing comprehensive educational and counseling support to gifted rural students, especially those in high school and college, leads to greater academic success.

In addition, over the past 20 years, a hallmark of almost every successful program for gifted rural students has been intensive professional development focused on the characteristics and needs of gifted students. Of course, the positive impact of professional development is not surprising: The well-known lack of content on gifted students in most teacher preparation programs, combined with traditional rural attitudes toward giftedness, make it unlikely that many rural educators have had much exposure (or motivation to get exposure) to gifted education issues.

Despite the advances in the education of rural gifted students stretching back a couple of generations, the literature on this particular group of students is still marked by collections of presumed best practices, anecdotal evidence, and conceptual analyses. It is worth noting that the flurry of recent publications on gifted rural students focuses primarily either on conceptual analyses or reviews of literature.[4] The lack of program evaluations and empirical studies of specific interventions has delayed progress substantially. The field has a strong foundation from which to proceed, but a great deal of additional work is needed to provide educators with tools for fostering the development of gifted students living in rural communities.

Finally, educators and researchers need to keep in mind that the nature of rurality is rapidly changing. Due to broader economic, cultural, and immigration trends (and most probably, interactions among them), describing a prototypical "rural community" has become nearly impossible. For example, numerous languages are spoken in rural areas; in rural communities in Northeast Indiana, one may overhear conversations in English, German, or Spanish. The linguistic, cultural, and racial/ethnic diversity in rural communities is often noted, but rarely directly addressed in the literature on gifted students.

Addressing this rich, increasing diversity will go a long way to providing rural educators and their gifted students with the tools they need to develop student (and community) talents successfully.

NOTES

1. The author appreciates the input of Tony Phonethibsavads of Indiana University and Nathan Burroughs of Michigan State University, and is grateful for the contributions of Sam Guskin, Emeritus Professor at Indiana University, who provided access to the Project SPRING I and II archive.
2. These diverse definitions lead, somewhat predictably, to wide ranges in estimates of the number of rural schools and students (cf., AYPF, 2010; Johnson & Strange, 2007; Malhoit, 2007).
3. SPRING I focused on both rural and economically disadvantaged students. Because the project's greatest successes involved rural students, SPRING II focused specifically on that population in the participating states.
4. Like this one.

REFERENCES

Aamidor, S., & Spicker, H. H. (1995). Promise for the future: Gifted education in rural communities. *Rural Special Education Quarterly, 14*(2), 39–46.

American Youth Policy Forum. (2010). *Challenges, assets, and innovations: Considerations for secondary education in rural communities.* Washington, DC: Author.

Arnold, M. L., Biscoe, B., Farmer, T. W., Robertson, D. L., & Shapley, K. L. (2007). *How the government defines rural has implications for education policies and practices.* (REL 2007–No. 010). Washington, DC: Regional Educational Laboratory Southwest, U.S. Department of Education.

Barley, Z. A. (2009). Preparing teachers for rural appointments: Lessons from the Mid-Continent. *Rural Educator, 30*(3), 10–15.

Beesley, A., Moore, L., & Gopalani, S. (2010). *Student mobility in rural and nonrural districts in five Central Region states* (Issues & Answers Report, REL 2010–No. 089). Washington, DC: Regional Educational Laboratory Central, U.S. Department of Education.

Bell, D., & Jayne, M. (2010). The creative countryside: Policy and practice in the UK rural cultural economy. *Journal of Rural Studies, 26,* 209–218.

Berdashkevich, A. A., & Vlasov, V. V. (2010). Prospects of the development of the rural schools. *Russian Education and Society, 52*(11), 59–71.

Burney, V. H., & Cross, T. L. (2006). Impoverished students with academic promise in rural settings: 10 lessons from Project Aspire. *Gifted Child Today, 29*(2), 14–21.

Carman, C. A., & Taylor, D. K. (2010). Socioeconomic status effects on using the Naglieri Nonverbal Ability Test (NNAT) to identify the gifted/talented. *Gifted Child Quarterly, 54,* 75–84.

Choo, E. K., Spiro, D. M., Lowe, R. A., Newgard, C. D., Hall, M., & McConnell, K. (2010). Rural-urban disparities in child abuse management resources in the emergency department. *Journal of Rural Health, 26,* 361–365.

Clark, G., & Zimmerman, E. (2001). Identifying artistically talented students in four rural communities in the United States. *Gifted Child Quarterly, 45,* 104–115.

Colangelo, N., Assouline, S. G., & New, J. K. (1999). *Gifted education in rural schools: A national assessment.* Iowa City: The Connie Belin & Jacqueline N. Blank International Center for Gifted Education and Talent Development, The University of Iowa. Retrieved from ERIC database. (No. ED 430 766)

Cross, T. L., & Stewart, R. A. (1995). A phenomenological investigation of the *lebenswelt* of gifted students in rural high schools. *Journal of Secondary Gifted Education, 6,* 273–280.

De Leon, J., & Argus-Calvo, B. (1997). *A model program for identifying culturally and linguistically diverse rural gifted and talented students.* College Station: School of Education, Texas A&M University. Retrieved from ERIC database. (No. ED 406 125)

Fishkin, A.S., & Kampsnider, J. J. (1996). *WISC-III subtest scatter patterns for rural superior and high ability children.* Retrieved from ERIC database. (No. ED 394 783)

Floyd, E. F., McGinnis, J. L., & Grantham, T. C. (2011). Gifted education in rural environments. In J. A. Castellano, & A. D. Frazier (Eds.), *Special populations in gifted education: Understanding our most able students from diverse backgrounds* (pp. 27–46). Waco, TX: Prufrock Press.

Gentry, M., & Ferriss, S. (1999). A model of collaboration to develop science talent among rural students. *Roeper Review, 21,* 316–320.

Grace, C., Shores, E. F., Zaslow, M., Brown, B., Aufseeser, D., Bell, L. et al. (2006). *Rural disparities in baseline data of the Early Childhood Longitudinal Study: A chartbook.* Mississippi State: National Center for Rural Early Childhood Learning Initiatives, Early Childhood Institute, Mississippi State University.

Guiffrida, D. A. (2008). Preparing rural students for large colleges and universities. *Journal of School Counseling, 6*(14), 1–25.

Harwell, M., & LeBeau, B. (2010). Student eligibility for a free lunch as an SES measure in education research. *Educational Researcher, 39,* 120–131.

Havens, J. R., Young, A. M., & Havens, C. E. (2010). Nonmedical prescription drug use in a nationally representative sample of adolescents. *Archives of Pediatrics and Adolescent Medicine.* Retrieved January 13–15, 2011 from http://archpedi.ama-assn.org/cgi/content/short/archpediatrics.2010.217

Hendryx, M., Fedorko, E., & Halverson, J. (2010). Pollution sources and mortality rates across rural-urban areas in the United States. *Journal of Rural Health, 26,* 383–391.

Howley, A. (1989). The progress of gifted students in a rural district that emphasized acceleration strategies. *Roeper Review, 11,* 205–207.

Howley, A., Howley, C., & Pendarvis, E. (2003). Talent development for rural communities. In J. Borland (Ed.), *Rethinking gifted education* (pp. 80–104). New York: Teachers College Press.

Howley, C., & Harmon, H. L. (2001). *Small high schools that flourish: Rural context, case studies, and resources.* Charleston, WV: Appalachian Educational Laboratory. Retrieved from ERIC database. (No. ED 447997)

Howley, C., Harmon, H., & Leopold, G. (1996). Rural scholars or bright rednecks? Aspirations for a sense of place among rural youth in Appalachia. *Journal of Research in Rural Education, 12,* 150–160.

Howley, C. B. (2009). The meaning of rural difference for bright rednecks. *Journal for the Education of the Gifted, 32,* 537–564.

Jimerson, L. (2006). *Breaking the fall: Cushioning the impact of rural declining enrollment.* (Rural Trust Policy Brief Series on Rural Education). Arlington, VA: Rural School and Community Trust.

Johnson, J., & Strange, M. (2007). *Why rural matters 2007: The realities of rural education growth.* (Rural Trust Policy Brief Series on Rural Education). Arlington, VA: Rural School and Community Trust. Retrieved January 13–15, 2011 from http://files.ruraledu.org/wrm07/WRM07.pdf

Lawrence, B. K. (2009). Rural gifted education: A comprehensive literature review. *Journal for the Education of the Gifted, 32,* 461–494.

Lewis, J. D. (2000, March). *Rural gifted education: Enhancing service delivery.* Paper presented at Capitalizing in Leadership in Rural Special Education: Making a Difference for Children and Families Conference, Alexandria, VA. Retrieved from ERIC database. (No. ED 439 874)

McIntire, J., & Plucker, J. A. (1996). Availability of extracurricular and cultural opportunities for rural middle level gifted students. *Rural Special Education Quarterly, 15*(4), 28–35.

McQuaide, S. (2009). Making education equitable in rural China through distance learning. *International Review of Research in Open and Distance Learning, 10*(1), 1–21.

Malhoit, G. C. (2005). *Providing rural students with a high quality education: The rural perspective on the concept of educational adequacy.* (Rural Trust Policy Brief Series on Rural Education). Arlington, VA: Rural School and Community Trust.

Naglieri, J. A., Brulles, D., & Lansdowne, K. (2009). *Helping all gifted children learn: A teacher's guide to using the NNAT2.* San Antonio, TX: Pearson.

Olgun, A., Gumus, S., & Adanacioglu, H. (2010). Schooling and actors affecting decisions on schooling by household members in the rural areas of Turkey. *Social Indicators Research, 98,* 533–543.

Peterson, L. E., & Litaker, D. G. (2010). County-level poverty is equally associated with unmet health care needs in rural and urban settings. *Journal of Rural Health, 26,* 373–382.

Plucker, J. A., Cobb, C., & Quaglia, R. (1996, October). *Aspirations of students attending a science and mathematics residential magnet school.* Paper presented at the Annual Meeting of the National Rural Education Association, San Antonio, TX.

Plucker, J., Spradlin, T., Magaro, M., Chien, R., & Zapf, Z. (2007). Assessing the policy environment for school corporation collaboration, cooperation, and consolidation in Indiana. *Education Policy Briefs, 5*(5). Bloomington: Center for Evaluation and Education Policy, Indiana University. Available at http://ceep.indiana.edu

Pringle, R. G., Webb, J. G., Warner, D. A., & Peterson, A. V. (1972). Innovative education for gifted children in rural elementary schools. *The Elementary School Journal, 73*(2), 79–84.

Rapp, K. (2008). Special schools. In J. A. Plucker, & C. M. Callahan (Eds.), *Critical issues and practices in gifted education* (pp. 617–628). Waco, TX: Prufrock Press.

Raven, J. (1981). *Manual for Raven's Progressive Matrices and Vocabulary Scales. Research supplement No.1: The 1979 British standardisation of the Standard Progressive Matrices and Mill Hill Vocabulary Scales, together with comparative data from earlier studies in the UK, US, Canada, Germany and Ireland.* San Antonio, TX: Harcourt Assessment.

Renzulli, J. S., & Reis, S. M. (1997). *The Schoolwide Enrichment Model: A how-to guide for educational excellence* (2nd ed.). Mansfield Center, CT: Creative Learning Press.

Robinson, R., & Rud, A. G. (2010, May). *Pie suppers and cake walks: A historical perspective of a closed rural community school.* Paper presented at the Annual Meeting of the American Educational Research Association, Denver, CO.

Shamah, D., & MacTavish, K. A. (2009). Making room for place-based knowledge in rural classrooms. *Rural Educator, 30*(2), 1–4.

Shores, K. A., Moore, J. B., & Yin, Z. (2010). An examination of triple jeopardy in rural youth physical activity participation. *Journal of Rural Health, 26,* 352–360.

Spicker, H. H. (1993). *Final report of Project SPRING. Indiana site.* Bloomington: Indiana University. Retrieved from ERIC database. (No. ED 365 067)

Spicker, H. H., Breard, N. S., & Reyes, E. I. (1996). *Project SPRING II: Special populations rural information network for the gifted* (Tech. Rep. Final). Bloomington: Indiana University.

Spicker, H. H., & Poling, S. N. (1993). *Project SPRING: Identifying rural disadvantaged gifted students.* (Manual). Bloomington: Indiana University.

Spicker, H. H., Southern, W. T., & Davis, B. I. (1987). The rural gifted child. *Gifted Child Quarterly, 31,* 155–157.

Spradlin, T. E., Carson, F. R., Hess, S. E., & Plucker, J. (2010). Revisiting school district consolidation issues. *Education Policy Briefs, 8*(3). Bloomington: Center for Evaluation and Education Policy, Indiana University. Available at http://ceep.indiana.edu

Stambaugh, T. (2010). The education of promising students in rural areas: What do we know and what can we do? In J. L. VanTassel-Baska (Ed.), *Patterns and profiles of promising learners from poverty* (pp. 59–83). Waco, TX: Prufrock Press.

Sternberg, P., & Low, S. (Eds.). (2009). *Rural broadband at a glance: 2009 edition.* Economic Information Bulletin Number 47. Washington, DC: U.S. Department of Agriculture. Retrieved January 13–15, 2011 from http://www.ers.usda.gov/publications/eib47/

Worrell, F. C. (2010). Psychosocial stressors in the development of gifted learners with atypical profiles. In J. L. VanTassel-Baska (Ed.), *Patterns and profiles of promising learners from poverty* (pp. 33–58). Waco, TX: Prufrock Press.

Ziller, E. C., Anderson, N. J., & Coburn, A. F. (2010). Access to rural mental health services: Service use and out-of-pocket costs. *Journal of Rural Health, 26,* 214–224.

Section VI

Evaluation and Policy in Gifted Education

42

EVALUATING, REFLECTING, AFFIRMING, AND REDIRECTING

An Introduction to the Evaluation of Gifted Programs

Carolyn M. Callahan and Holly L. Hertberg-Davis

As we turn our attention toward evaluating gifted program processes and outcomes, it may help us to consider a metaphor. As we put together this text, we realized that the process of creating a comprehensive and defensible program for gifted students is not unlike planning a journey. What we have envisioned is that at this point in your reading, you will have read about options and determined your desired destination—that is, the appropriate outcomes for a solid and defensible program. Your destination determined, you are now prepared to make sound and carefully considered choices about who should go on this journey (definition), and how you will find these travelers (identification). You are prepared to choose and train appropriate travel guides (teachers and counselors) to lead students along their journeys. By considering all the possible points of interest along the way (the wide range of curricular options, the myriad service delivery options, etc.), you have explored the many routes that may be offered to gifted and talented students to take them to the desired destination. You very likely may have determined that not all of the students in your gifted program have to take the exact same route to get to their destinations, and accordingly planned side trips, express routes, and extended stops along the way. Now you can look at your itinerary, your roadmap, and your destination, and begin to make plans for how you will evaluate the effectiveness, efficiency, and power of the journey itself.

Developing and providing services to gifted and talented students should be based on a body of theory and research guiding best practice. The prior chapters in the book have offered background and directions for such decision making across the critical components of quality programs and services. However, as we pointed out in the very beginning of the text, there is no formula and no "right way" to provide services to gifted students. What we have continually advocated is determining best practices for the students who fit the adopted definition of giftedness and the philosophy about both gifted education and education in general held by the school.

WHY CAN WE NOT RELY ON "BEST PRACTICE" GUIDES, RESEARCH AND GOOD PLANNING?

However, even decisions based on best practices, research, and standards such as those endorsed by the National Association for Gifted Children (2010) and presented in this book can only serve as guides for planning programs, developing curriculum, and implementing programs. The decisions made after careful study and in good faith only provide the roadmap. The journey is created by many heads and hands and many interpretations of the map. Thus, we do not really have a sense of whether students have had a productive journey and arrived at the intended destination without evaluation of the program as implemented. Once programs are planned, educators are responsible for collecting systematic data about whether the individual components have been implemented as designed, and whether the implementation is yielding the expected outcomes. The potential gaps between intentions, practice, and outcomes signal a need for evaluation.

Further, what translates into best practice in one school division may not be appropriate in a different school division with a different population. What was appropriate at one point in time may not be appropriate now as the population of the school division changes, and as more has been learned about good practice in educating gifted students. Too often, educators are willing to rely on reports of "what works" garnered either from the research literature or through rumors about success from the neighboring district; consequently, they fail to determine carefully whether or not, or to what degree, a practice is indeed having the desired effect on their students.

TACKLING THE ISSUES UNDERLYING PROGRAM EVALUATION AND ASSESSMENT OF GOALS

The chapters which follow are focused on planning for program evaluation and measuring the outcomes of implementing the decisions made about how to identify gifted students, what curricula to provide to them, who will teach them, where and how to instruct them, how to provide supports such as counseling services, etc. The processes that are discussed are structured to help you focus on the goals for gifted students, the success of the program options in helping students achieve those goals, and the degree to which particular components contribute to or detract from the achievement of goals, or have unintended consequences on gifted students or other students. These chapters are intended to stimulate thinking and to guide readers in the process of formulating a plan for evaluation.

Questions to consider in applying the guidelines in the chapters on evaluation emanate from concerns about making program evaluation serve as a means to document program effects, improve program offerings, and enhance the opportunities for full development of potential.

- What are the goals of the components of the services that have been selected as appropriate for gifted students? Can I specify those in measurable terms?
- What is credible evidence that the students I work with are achieving those goals? How would I gather that evidence?
- Who would be the key stakeholders in the gifted program I conceive? What would be the questions they would ask about the program and its goals?

- Who are the best informants in providing me with the information needed to make judgments about program effectiveness and decisions about program improvement?

REFERENCES

National Association for Gifted Children. (2010). *Pre-K–Grade 12 gifted programming standards: A blueprint for quality gifted education programs.* Washington, DC: Author. Available at http://www.nagc.org/uploadedFiles/ Information_and_Resources/Gifted_Program_Standards/K-12%20programming%20standards.pdf

43

EVALUATING SERVICES OFFERED TO GIFTED AND TALENTED STUDENTS

A Planning Guide

Carolyn M. Callahan

Consider this analogy to program evaluation: the model of medical practice. When a physician prescribes interventions for a patient, those interventions range from medication to diet to exercise and physical therapy and they are drawn from the research. The physician tries to match a patient's symptoms and his or her other physical characteristics to those of subjects in that research. But the physician does not just prescribe an intervention without a follow-up plan to determine if it is having the desired effect on the patient. The patient who receives medication for high blood pressure returns to see if new readings are in the normal range. Even when the desired result is achieved, the physician questions the patient about other undesirable side effects. If the medication has not been effective or if it has produced side effects that cannot be tolerated, the physician first seeks to determine if the patient has been following the prescribed regimen of exercise and drug use. With that knowledge in hand, new medications or exercise regimes are offered.

It is also important to note the many precautions against taking medication prescribed for someone else with the same symptoms without consulting a physician. So, too, a program for gifted services should never be "borrowed" from another district. Rather, a quality program for gifted students in a school district must be developed based on the best and most current research and theory, given our best understanding of the unique educational, social, and emotional needs of the students in that school district. Additionally, we must follow through with an evaluation to determine whether the program has been implemented and is achieving its desired effects.

"IF YOU DO NOT KNOW WHERE YOU ARE GOING, HOW WILL YOU KNOW WHEN YOU HAVE ARRIVED?"

Of course the key to determining whether you have been successful in achieving the goals or objectives of services for gifted students is to specify those program goals and objectives. Goals and objectives may relate to success in implementing a particular component of the program (e.g., *Identification of gifted and talented students is carried out without bias or prejudice toward any socio-economic, ethnic, racial, or gender subgroup*). Or they may relate to student outcomes (e.g., *Students produced products that solved more advanced problems, reflected greater depth and complexity of thought, and used communication strategies that would not have been possible without the implementation of these services*).

The outcomes measured can be process outcomes which reflect whether or not the activities of the program are being carried out as designed (e.g., *Identification and selection committees are provided with staff development that prepares them for the work of the committee*). Or the outcomes measured may be product outcomes (e.g., *Teachers have acquired the knowledge and skills necessary to implement the Multiple Menu Model successfully*; or *Students in the accelerated mathematics program demonstrate achievement of mathematics at least three grade levels beyond their age peers*).

But good evaluations of services for gifted students do not focus only on process or outcomes. It is critical that an evaluation also seeks to determine the "why" underlying results. If students do not achieve the stated objectives, why is that the case? Is there a mismatch between students identified as gifted and the curriculum provided to these students? Do teachers lack the background, the training, and/or the resources necessary for carrying out the planned curriculum? Equally important, if we have evidence that students have achieved the stated goals, we need to determine which factors contributed to that achievement so that we continue practices that lead to success.

Unfortunately, it is far easier to toss around the term "goals" than it is actually to articulate them in ways that lead to clear measurement. It is critical at the stage of developing programs to specify goals in language that leads to clear agreement on meaning, and will lead to clear agreement on the kinds of evidence that will be accepted as indications of whether goals have been achieved. If done at the onset of planning, evaluation becomes much more manageable. But if goal specification is left to the evaluation stage of planning, it is no less important. Each goal must be subjected to the questions: *How will we know if the goal has been achieved? What evidence will we accept?* For example, if one goal of the program is an unbiased and fair identification process, what are the indicators that we have achieved that goal?

The combined aims of ascertaining the outcomes of services for gifted students and determining why we did or did not achieve those goals lead to the first step in program evaluation: developing a clear description of all the components of the program and the intended outcomes (goals) of all the components of all the services offered to students.

STEPS IN EVALUATING SERVICES FOR GIFTED STUDENTS

Step 1: Describing the Program

Once again we are using the term "program" as an umbrella term for all services offered to gifted and talented students. So if a school district offers early entrance to kindergarten, a full-time classroom for some gifted students, part-time resource classes for others, and a counseling program that cuts across the three service delivery options, the evaluation should be designed to gather data about all four of these services and the evaluation plan should include a description of the components of each.

The term "component" is used as a construct to describe some set of *resources*, activities, and outcomes of a functional activity in a program. For example, identification (determining which students will be considered gifted and talented and which services each of these students will receive) is a component of all services for gifted students (Callahan & Caldwell, 1995). *Resources* are used to carry out the identification function (policies including the definition of giftedness, staff time to collect and organize student data, tests, teacher time to complete rating scales, guidelines for decision making, staff time to meet and make decisions, appeals guidelines, etc.).

There are also *activities* associated with that component (e.g., testing, collecting teacher ratings on forms for assessing student behaviors, compiling student data into a format for review, meetings of selection and placement committees, time for appeals hearings, notification of parents, etc.). And the use of the specified *resources* to carry out the *activities* of a given component should lead to the expected *outcomes* or goals (e.g., creation of a fair and defensible identification process, accurate identification of students who are in need of special services, appropriate matches between identified students and the services offered to them, etc.).

The major components of most gifted programs include:

- identification, selection and placement;
- curriculum development;
- program/service delivery;
- instruction of gifted students;
- communication (within the program and to other outside groups);
- program administration and management;
- staff selection; and
- staff professional development.

Program evaluation should also be an integral component of all gifted programs, but is too often neglected.

Obviously, some resources are used in multiple components (e.g., teacher time), and the outcomes of one function may relate to the successful implementation of another. For example, an outcome of the staff development component might be teachers who have the skill and the will to teach the curriculum necessary for successful implementation of the service delivery component, which then leads, it is hoped, to the expected student outcomes.

The specification of the resources, activities, and goals of each of these components may seem to be a tedious chore; however, a clear description will not only serve as a framework for planning an evaluation, but also as:

1) a roadmap for program implementation; 2) a quick check on whether all resources are available to carry out the component, and whether all necessary activities have been planned; and 3) a check on internal consistency across components of a program or service (Callahan & Caldwell, 1995). Figure 43.1 provides an example of a graphic illustrating one way to summarize the resources, activities, and goals of one program component. Note that the lists are not aligned across the chart. Many of the listed resources may be used for one activity and many activities contribute to one of the goals. Also note that each of the stated goals needs to be elaborated into measurable indicators of success.

RESOURCES	ACTIVITIES	GOALS
Students	Pre-assess student to ascertain readiness levels	Students are engaged in learning
Teachers	Create and deliver a staff development program	Students exhibit increased achievement including proficiency in key regular curriculum concepts
Print resources and materials	Carry out classroom instructional planning based on student data	Students display more positive attitudes toward school and learning
Technology resources	Develop learning activities based on balance between acceleration and enrichment	Students exhibit more positive social behavior and exhibit emotional health
Differentiated assessment tools		Student instruction that is based on needs identified during the screening, identification, and placement process
Curriculum developed as a product from the curriculum development component		Students exhibit growth in ability to engage in advanced abstract thinking, and knowledge and understanding of interdisciplinary subject matter focusing on major concepts and issues Daily lessons are based on opportunity for student exploration of ideas of interest

Fig. 43.1 Program component: Instruction.

After the program has been fully described, it is very easy to see the wide range of possibilities and important areas to be evaluated in each component. For example, in the illustration, it is apparent that questions can be asked about the availability and adequacy of resources; questions about the degree to which pre-assessment is utilized by teachers to drive curriculum and instruction would provide useful information on the possible reasons why goals are or are not achieved; and questions about student change become evident.

Step 2: Identifying Key Stakeholders

In creating guidelines for best practice in program evaluation, The Joint Committee on Standards for Educational Evaluation included an explicit directive to include in the planning process for program evaluations the perspectives of the full range of persons and groups who have a vested interest in program activities and outcomes and/or are affected by the evaluation and the outcomes of program activities (Yarbrough, Shulha,

Hopson, & Caruthers, 2011). When Tomlinson, Bland, Moon, and Callahan (1994) identified key elements of a strong gifted program evaluation (one whose results were broadly disseminated, included recommendations for action, and outlined mechanisms for translating findings into positive program change), they found the identification of key decision makers and inviting their input into the planning process to be of critical importance to success.

The key decision makers are not only the administrators and school board in a school district, but also parents who determine whether the needs of their children are being addressed in the program, teachers who are being asked to implement a particular curriculum, other staff (e.g., counselors or media specialists) who may have additional responsibilities because of program activities, and the students themselves. When planning for program evaluation, consider all those who should have a voice in what is considered in the evaluation. Involvement of these stakeholders serves to ensure that those in decision-making positions will have the information they need and want about program effectiveness and efficiency.[1] Involve stakeholders in both formal ways (e.g., creating a program evaluation steering committee; surveying key persons in each group about the areas of concern they have) and in informal ways (e.g., informal conversations with the staff about the way the process is proceeding). The input from the formal and informal collection of data from key stakeholders is valuable in identifying areas for evaluation that may not have been evident from the program description, but is even more valuable in Step 3 of the process.

Step 3: Focusing on Key Evaluation Concerns and Generating Evaluation Questions

The purpose of developing a program description and identifying key stakeholders is to determine where the focus of an evaluation should lie. Looking at the specific resources, activities, and goals of each component will provide many areas of concern and evaluation questions that can be addressed in a program evaluation. Not all of the concerns and questions can be addressed in one evaluation, so the next step in the process is focusing the evaluation on the most important areas of concern and evaluation questions.

The focusing process should consider at least these four major questions. The first question to ask is: Which areas of the program and which program outcomes are of most concern to key stakeholders? The data collected in Step 2 will guide in answering this question. The second question is: Are there resources or activities of the program critical to program success? This is answered by examining the relationships between the components. For example, in Figure 43.1, staff development is crucial for teacher instructional competence—teaching in ways that will lead to the goals of student achievement. This suggests that the outcomes of the staff development component should be a target of the program evaluation. The third question is: Are there activities or outcomes that must be successful for other components to be successful? Again, examining the relationships between program components suggests that the curriculum development products are critical for the instructional component's success. Finally, we must ask: Are there components which past experience or logic suggest could be problematic or especially prone to snags in implementation that may inhibit the ultimate success of the program? As the prior chapters in this book have suggested, teacher training to implement the curriculum is critical for any service delivery model or curricular modification that is used to guide instruction for gifted students. This brief illustration suggests that staff development and training would be target areas for evaluation in the program described in Figure 43.1.

One misinterpretation of the evaluation process is posing the evaluation question: Should this gifted program exist? Rather, the fundamental questions should be: Is this program providing the best educational opportunities for gifted students given the constraints of the context? Which elements are working as planned and which elements can be improved? In generating the specific evaluation questions, the process must result in clearly defined concepts or the next step in the process is frustrating and often unsuccessful.

Step 4: Determining the Best Source(s) of Information and Data to Answer the Evaluation Questions

Like any data collection process, the most critical step is choosing the ways to measure the variables we are interested in assessing. This choice means being sure that we choose valid instruments—instruments that are truly assessing what we think they measure. To be sure we have valid measures, we have to be certain we have carefully defined those variables. For example, it is not sufficient to say we want to assess creativity or critical thinking. The ways in which we define those terms will guide measurement. The next chapter addresses issues that surround measurement in gifted programs.

It is also important to be sure we gather the data directly from the best source of data to answer any given evaluation question. And we are more confident about the conclusions we draw if we are able to triangulate our data—confirm our conclusions from multiple sources using multiple instruments. So if we collect data from tests or performance assessments on student achievement (the most direct and objective evidence of student outcomes), and also verify that teachers and parents have observed changes in student achievement or performance, we can have greater confidence in the conclusions we draw.

Finally, the data collection process should include both quantitative and qualitative data as appropriate to the questions being asked (NAGC, 2010; Tomlinson et al., 1994). Some outcomes can be measured by tests or surveys, but others (e.g., the quality of curriculum or the classroom activities) are best evaluated by comparing them to standards using qualitative professional judgments.

Step 5: Analyzing and Reporting the Results of Data Collection

A full discussion of creating the plan for data collection, data analysis, and reporting is beyond the scope of a general textbook (for a more in-depth look at planning and implementing an evaluation of a gifted program, see Callahan and Caldwell, 1995), but the simple guide is to ensure that the process includes sufficient sophistication to allow for questions to be answered fully. Of course, ideally, we would hope to create experimental designs for assessing outcomes of gifted programs that unequivocally justify our conclusions about the effects of instruction, but as the next chapter will elaborate, a true experimental design is seldom feasible in gifted program evaluation. Hence triangulation of data becomes more essential.

Reporting the results of any evaluation data is a very delicate and pivotal part of the evaluation process (Callahan & Caldwell, 1995; NAGC, 2010; Renzulli, 1975; Tomlinson et al., 1994). Three key points to remember: focus on *who* you deliver results to, *when* you deliver these results, and *how* you present these results. All of these elements are certainly interrelated, but each is important enough to be considered independently.

First, the *who*: Findings should be reported to those individuals who will have a key role in any decision making—whether in making adjustments in funding (e.g., school board members), program delivery services (central office administrators), curriculum (central office administrators and program teachers), or simply in whether or not a child should be part of the services offered (parents). However, not all constituents need to see all findings in a long, and potentially overwhelming, written report. While most evaluations do and should produce such a document, consideration should be given to separating parts of the report into targeted presentations or mini-reports that allow the decision makers to access the findings they need easily. Tailoring the reports to the needs of the stakeholder group also entails clear presentation of findings and recommendations in terms that can be understood by the members of the group. While avoiding condescending language, avoid use of jargon and confusing technical interpretation of data (Renzulli, 1975; Tomlinson & Callahan, 1993).

The second consideration, the *when*, relates again to decisions, but this time the focus is on ensuring that the findings are available in time to be incorporated into the assessment of needed changes. Changes recommended for budgets or staffing assignments that come after the school district's budget has been developed and submitted have little chance of being considered—not just in this budget cycle, but also in the next, as data is likely to be considered "too old" by the time the next budget cycle comes around. Recommendations for changes in the identification process should occur in time for careful planning for the subsequent round of review.

Finally, *how* results are presented will affect the likelihood of impact. Consider your own reactions to receiving any feedback relative to teaching or other aspects of your personal or professional life. The reality is that those who are either in administrative or teaching roles have heavily invested in the services that are offered, so great care must be taken to ensure that the content of the report does not generate a level of defensiveness that mitigates acceptance of findings and recommendations. One strategy is to make clear recommendations that respect prior commitments to the program while suggesting improvements. Protection of the identity of individuals in the reporting process is fundamental. A program evaluation is not a personnel evaluation, so individual teacher, counselor, administrator, and student identities should be protected. (Of course, some personnel, including people like the administrator for gifted programs/services or the superintendent of schools, will be recognizable by role.) But the identity of other individuals should be masked by aggregating data or taking care to use non-identifiable examples or quotations in the report.

CONCLUSION

There is little glamour in program evaluation, but there is great potential pay-off if the process of program evaluation is used to improve understanding of the ways in which various components of a program contribute to, or detract from, providing excellent educational opportunities. In the evaluation of gifted programs, the data from program evaluations also serves to provide documentation of the quality and importance of any special services offered to the targeted students.

NOTE

1. Some ask how students are key stakeholders and decision makers. They are perhaps the most critical decision makers as their decision to participate actively in the learning process or not is key to their learning.

REFERENCES

Callahan, C. M., & Caldwell, M. S. (1995). *A practitioner's guide to evaluating programs for the gifted.* Washington, DC: National Association for Gifted Children.

National Association for Gifted Children. (2010). *Pre-K–Grade 12 gifted programming standards: A blueprint for quality gifted education programs.* Retrieved January 28, 2012 from http://www.nagc.org/index.aspx?id=546

Renzulli, J. S. (1975). *A guidebook for evaluating programs for the gifted and talented.* Ventura, CA: National/State Leadership Training Institute on the Gifted/Talented.

Tomlinson, C. A., Bland, L. C., Moon, T. R., & Callahan, C. M. (1994). Studies of evaluation utilization in gifted education. *Evaluation Practice, 15,* 153–168.

Tomlinson, C. A., & Callahan, C. M. (1993, Fall). A planning guide for evaluating programs for gifted learners. *Quest, 4*(2), 1–4.

Tomlinson, C. A., & Callahan, C. M. (1994). Planning effective evaluations for programs for the gifted. *Roeper Review, 17,* 46–51.

Yarbrough, D. B., Shulha, L. M., Hopson, R. K., & Caruthers, F. A. (2011). *The program evaluation standards: A guide for evaluators and evaluation users* (3rd ed.). Thousand Oaks, CA: Sage.

44

ASSESSING RESOURCES, ACTIVITIES, AND OUTCOMES OF PROGRAMS FOR THE GIFTED AND TALENTED

Tonya R. Moon

The collection of good data is essential for good decision making. Therefore, the selection or construction of instruments to measure the quality of resources, program activities, and program outcomes as well as the outcomes of gifted curriculum and instruction is a critical step in completing the cycle of program planning and implementation. In addition to collecting student outcome data, program administrators need to gather information about every component of a gifted program to determine whether it is functioning as intended and whether it has achieved the outcomes expected. (See Chapter 42 by Callahan in this book for an overview of specifying components and outcomes of a program.)

TYPES OF DATA FOR EVALUATING GIFTED PROGRAMS: FORMATIVE AND SUMMATIVE DATA

There are a variety of ways of capturing data about the quality of program activities and the impacts of a gifted program on the gifted students it serves. The nature of the evaluation questions asked and the types of data collected to address these questions can be divided into two categories: (1) formative evaluation questions; and (2) summative evaluation questions. Formative evaluation questions typically focus on examining the degree to which resources are adequate, collecting data on whether activities are being implemented as described and intended, or monitoring progress toward achievement of goals. Formative evaluation may include questions such as:

- Is the gifted program operating as described in program documents?
- Are funds being appropriately spent?
- Are qualified teachers hired and retained?
- Are resources available to implement the curriculum and instruction as described?

- Is the curriculum defensible as appropriate for gifted and talented learners?
- Are students receiving appropriate counseling services?

The purpose of formative data collection is to assess the current status of a gifted program and its activities, to measure progress toward meeting program goals, and to suggest areas of needed improvement. These types of data help identify a gifted program's strengths as well as areas that may need attention so that the program can most effectively and efficiently meet its goals.

Summative evaluation questions address the gifted program's effectiveness and success in achieving its mission and goals. Sample summative evaluation questions might include:

- Is the gifted program effective in increasing student creativity?
- Does staff development result in teacher change in knowledge and in classroom instructional practice?
- Which components of the gifted program are most effective in developing students' critical and creative thinking skills?
- Are the achieved outcomes worth the cost of implementing the program (cost-benefit analysis)?
- Did students benefit from participating in the program? In what ways?

Data for addressing summative evaluation questions are collected longitudinally and may address the outcomes of all components of a gifted program and its services, including the outcomes of providing student and teacher services (i.e., professional development).

DATA AND DATA COLLECTION STRATEGIES: QUANTITATIVE AND QUALITATIVE

Regardless of the evaluation questions asked, the first key step in the collection of data to answer those questions is deciding which type of data and data collection strategies will best answer the questions and are within the scope of one's resources and skills. Data and data collection strategies fall into two categories: quantitative and qualitative.

Quantitative Data Collection

Quantitative data and strategies for gathering quantitative data are typically used to answer questions such as:

- What percentage of fourth grade gifted students demonstrated growth in the area of mathematics?
- How many students participated in each of the various types of service delivery options provided?
- What are the demographic characteristics of students served by the gifted program?
- How do parents rate various aspects of the gifted program?
- What are the qualifications of teachers teaching in the gifted program?

Instruments used to collect quantitative data can include surveys, questionnaires, tests administered to students, rating scales of student products, etc. Other quantitative data collection and analysis might include examining enrollment data for Advanced Placement courses, analyzing college acceptance ratios, or collecting ratings of curriculum development products from experts in gifted education. Quantitative data can be used to answer either formative or summative evaluation questions. It is important to note here that adequate answers to a given evaluation question might require collection of both quantitative and qualitative data.

Surveys/Questionnaires

Surveys and questionnaires can contain multiple-choice questions, rating scales and/or checklists which yield quantitative data. They might also contain open-ended items that would be considered more qualitative in nature. The more quantitative items on surveys and questionnaires are appropriate and useful under four conditions—when:

1. the goal is to gather information from many different stakeholders (e.g., students, principals, teachers, parents) and these stakeholders have data or important perceptions to offer about various aspects of the program;
2. the type of information required is specific and familiar to the respondents;
3. *a priori* questions focused on specific aspects of the gifted program can be generated based on areas of concern that have been identified by key stakeholders; and
4. the range of responses that is likely to occur in response to proposed questions is fairly well-known.

Surveys/questionnaires can be useful in gathering factual information (e.g., demographics; hours of professional development attended) as well as opinion and attitudinal data about specific components of a gifted program (e.g., questions focused on parental perceptions of communication about their children's progress).

Student Assessments

Data on student outcomes provide valuable information useful for a variety of purposes, including making curricular decisions, making decisions regarding service delivery options, and providing cost-benefit information regarding services and student outcomes. Common student assessments include classroom tests, ratings of student projects, and performance assessments, including portfolios. Other types of student assessments include end-of-course assessments, state assessments, Advanced Placement examinations, the SAT Reasoning Test, and ACT examinations.

Questions regarding validity and ceiling effects have led to considerations of alternative assessments. Callahan (2005, 2009) and Renzulli and Callahan (2008) have provided numerous examples of student outcome measures ranging from alternative objective assessments to checklists and student rating scales measuring cognitive, affective, and psychomotor outcomes. Because the use of performance-based assessments has received considerable attention as a valid strategy for measuring student outcomes in gifted programs, an introduction to the use of these assessments is provided later in this chapter.

Qualitative Data Collection

Qualitative methods are best used to seek deeper understanding about stakeholders' (e.g., students, teachers, and parents) experiences, opinions, or concerns. Questions that might be addressed using qualitative data include:

- What is the quality of the curriculum offered to gifted and talented students?
- What are the differences in the instruction offered in the special classes for gifted students and the general education classroom?
- Is there a congruent philosophy of gifted education across the various stakeholders in the school district?

The primary tools for collecting qualitative data include individual interviews, focus group interviews, and observations. Documents such as official minutes of meetings, curriculum frameworks, letters, newspaper accounts, or reports, as well as any published data about the gifted program may also provide qualitative data.

Individual Interviews/Focus Group Interviews

Interviews provide the opportunity for in-depth follow-up to delve deeply into the perspectives of key stakeholders, something that is not an option for surveys/questionnaires. Focus group interviews depend on group dynamics and, because they are social in nature, the group interaction can serve as a test of the strength and pervasiveness of perceptions of program outcomes. They can provide insights into a program that would not emerge without the interaction of the group.

Documents/Electronic Files

Existing records can provide valuable information about a program and include student records (e.g., transcripts), mission and goal statements, annual reports, official documents filed with state agencies, plans, budgets, curricula, media reports, formal presentations (e.g., presentations made to Boards of Education), podcasts, and webinars. These types of files can be useful in describing a gifted program and the types of services it provides and in identifying which program goals have been met or not met. These types of data are also useful in conducting a cost-benefit analysis.

Table 44.1 provides an overview of the various types of data collection methods including advantages and disadvantages of each.

ACCESS TO DATA FOR DECISION MAKING: ESTABLISHING A WAREHOUSE

As the discussion so far suggests, an integral component of any gifted program should be continuous and reflective use of data for program documentation and improvement. If the collection of data for decision making is left until needed for an imminent decision, there may not be an opportunity to collect the most useful data. Schools are now much more attuned to the importance of systematically and longitudinally collecting data, so the opportunity to include data relative to identified gifted students receiving services in the schools is likely to be available. Systematic, longitudinal collection of data on questions of interest to policy makers should occur through anticipation of questions. One

Table 44.1 A brief summary of data collection strategies

Data & Data Collection Strategy	Description & Use	Advantages	Challenges
Documents & Document Review	• Internal program records or external sources • Hard copy/electronic copy • Examples: reports, newsletters, meeting minutes, curriculum frameworks, student products, etc. • Can be used as a basis to determine if program implementation reflects program mission/plan • Useful in identifying public perceptions, in identifying areas of potential concern, in generating evaluation questions and/or in developing other tools for data collection (e.g., interview protocols; surveys)	• Offers historical view of program • Easily obtained (e.g., archived minutes, reports, newsletter articles)	• May be disorganized, out of date • May be incomplete or inaccurate • May be time-consuming to review and analyze
Surveys/Questionnaires Completed by Stakeholders	Paper and pencil or web-based instrument used to gather information regarding stakeholder perceptions, beliefs, attitudes, and experiences	• Allows data gathering from a large number of individuals and across groups of stakeholders • Data can be collected anonymously and at times that are convenient for stakeholder group	• Potentially low response rates from stakeholders • Respondents' reading levels can impact responses • Web-based surveys/questionnaires may not be accessible to all stakeholders
Surveys/Questionnaire Completed by Evaluator through Phone or Face-to-face Interview Strategy	Individualized questioning using a standard set of questions with options read to respondents to gather information regarding stakeholder perceptions, beliefs, attitudes, and experiences	• Reading level not an issue	Sampling • Question format or responses may lead to biases in responses • Cannot probe responses Cost • Time required to conduct interviews • Gaining access to stakeholders • Question format or responses may lead to biases • Persons administering instrument must be trained in the use of the survey/questionnaire

Data & Data Collection Strategy	Description & Use	Advantages	Challenges
Individual Interviews	Data are gathered by directly asking individual stakeholders (e.g., parents, students, teachers, administrators).	• Allows for the clarification of stakeholder responses by using follow-up questions and allows further probing on issues that emerge during the interview, or questions that have emerged from other interviews	Cost • Time required to conduct interviews • Gaining access to stakeholders • Evaluator can bias interviewee
Observation	Data are gathered by observing how people (e.g., students, teachers) react to, are affected by, the gifted program's implementation.	• Provides first-hand view of what occurs; might reveal unexpected findings • Provides knowledge of the context in which the gifted program operates	• Time-consuming • Difficult to observe the complexity of settings (many things going on at the same time) • Presence of observer can affect events
Focus Group Interviews	Data are gathered by asking small groups of stakeholders (generally 6–8 individuals) to respond to specific questions regarding the program's implementation or effectiveness.	• Generally more interesting to stakeholders than individual interviews • Degree of spontaneity of answers tends to be greater because questions are directed at the group rather than individuals	• Cost associated with collection • Moderator can introduce bias by failing to ask certain questions or delve more deeply into specific areas • Difficulty in scheduling • Some persons may dominate and/or influence the responses of others
Student Outcome Data	Ranges from standardized test data (e.g., benchmark tests, state summative tests) to alternative assessments (e.g., grades, performance assessments, products)	• May be regularly collected at the district level • Difficult to find valid published instruments	• Provides a measure of achievement of program goals • Does not provide contextual information

way to centralize data for more effective and efficient decision making is through the establishment of a data warehouse for quantitative data.

What Is a Data Warehouse?

A data warehouse is a computerized system for storing numerical data in a structured way that can be used for querying, analysis, and reporting (Kimball & Ross, 2002). While there are many sophisticated forms of data warehouses, readily available spreadsheet software programs (e.g., Microsoft Excel) can easily be used for storing gifted program data. The data warehouse provides a centralized location for student outcome data, allowing for disaggregating at the school level, grade level, or by sub-populations (e.g., race, gender, economic status, language status), or for tracking longitudinal data (e.g., types of courses taken, activities involvement) on students as they progress through a district's K–12 gifted program. Collection of such data in one data base makes it possible to examine, for example, program effects across time, relationships between type of services offered and student outcomes, or the relationship between the amount of professional development provided to teachers about identification and the rates of identification of underserved groups for placement in a gifted program.

USING PERFORMANCE-BASED ASSESSMENT TO EVALUATE STUDENT OUTCOMES

Performance-based assessments (PBA) are nontraditional assessments that require students to construct a response, create a product, or engage in some type of demonstration. In general, PBAs focus on real-world applicability, using higher-order thinking skills such as application, evaluation, and synthesis. Several types of assessment fall under the broader PBA umbrella: performance assessments, product assessments, and portfolios.

Performance Assessment

This type of assessment is designed to assess a student's ability to apply knowledge and skills to real-life challenges. Students are required to produce ideas, integrate knowledge, and apply skills in ways that parallel genuine problem solving. Performance assessments can be used appropriately to ascertain students' mastery of skills at the end of a series of lessons, at the end of a unit, or a course of study. "Excellent Experiment or Sloppy Science?" in Figure 44.1 is an example of a performance assessment that assesses application of knowledge about the scientific method and experimental design that highlights these attributes. The assessment situates the student in the role of both a reviewer and an editor like those of actual professionals (e.g., journal editors and scientists). Students are asked to analyze, synthesize, evaluate, and apply their understanding about experimental design in much the same way that editors and reviewers are asked to do in the production of peer-reviewed research journals.

In evaluating students' responses, the accompanying Experiment Review Form and rubric are used to document the student's understanding of the various aspects of the scientific method. The rubric allows for the holistic evaluation of the understanding of the scientific method and the student's ability to communicate, as demonstrated by the letter written from the student to the author of the research article.

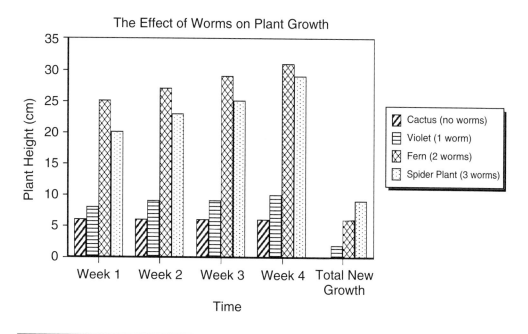

Fig. 44.1 Performance assessment.

Developed by The National Research Center on the Gifted and Talented at the Curry School of Education, University of Virginia.

Product Assessment

In product assessment, another type of PBA, students respond to a prompt or a series of prompts by constructing a tangible product that demonstrates their understanding of the identified concepts and skills. The range of product assessments is reflective of the type of tasks given to students. These types of assessment range from highly structured tasks or prompts similar to those that result from the Core Curriculum Parallel in the Parallel Curriculum Model (Tomlinson et al., 2002) to semi-structured or unstructured tasks which often occur in Type III enrichment activities in the Schoolwide Enrichment Model (Renzulli & Reis, 1985). Figure 44.2 provides a rubric that could be used for evaluating students' efforts in completing semi-structured or unstructured tasks related to a unit on poetry. Specific dimensions of the student product are systematically reviewed using the graduated descriptors in the rubric. See Figure 44.2 for an example of a rubric to rate students' poems. Product assessments may or may not reflect real-life challenges.

As with any type of assessment that involves individuals making decisions regarding levels of student performance, product assessment necessitates the use of a carefully developed scoring mechanism. Most often, product assessments are accompanied by a rubric for evaluating students' responses. Wiggins (1996) suggested four dimensions along which the products of gifted students should be evaluated:

- high *quality* (e.g., tops in its class, novel, ethical) and effectiveness (e.g., problem solved, persuasive) of responses;
- process—the degree to which the student demonstrates purposefulness (e.g., persistent, adaptive, self-regulated, self-reflective);

Set criteria Please focus on these set criteria Poet should check applicable boxes and/or circle specifics. ↓	*Rework*	**NEAR COMPLETION**	**Publishable**	Rating
❏ **Sound:** *(Music in the words)* i.e., rhythm, speed of lines, rhymes, alliteration, repetition, consonance, assonance	The words and lines do not follow the principles of rhythm or rhyme. The *sound* of the poem does not enhance the *meaning* of the poem.	The words and lines follow the principles of rhythm or rhyme. The sound of the poem supports the meaning of the poem.	The words and lines follow the principles of rhythm or rhyme and enhance the meaning of the poem: *I never saw a moor, I never saw the sea; Yet I know how the heather looks And what a wave must be.* - Emily Dickinson	
❏ **Form:** *(The poem's skeleton)* i.e., visual organization or structure: sonnet, haiku, ballad, epic, concrete, blank verse	Poem does not show a clear structure OR the structure is confusing OR the poem is not true to the selected form.	Poem deviates from structure but this does not detract from the overall effect of the poem.	Structure is clear and consistent within the selected form.	
❏ **Imagery:** *(Words that hint at the magic of the world)* i.e., metaphor, simile, symbols, pictures for the senses	The imagery is confused, clichéd or ineffective.	The imagery is effective in places, ineffective in others.	The imagery is effective, and successfully extends the meaning of the poem. *My bull is white like the silver fish in the river white like the simmering crane bird on the river bank white like fresh milk!* - Dinka Tribe	
❏ **Tone:** *(Flavor of the words, revealing how the world tastes to the poet)* i.e., ironic, objective, romantic, witty, despairing	The grouping and choice of words create a choppy or inconsistent tone.	The grouping and choice of words create a tone that is inconsistent in a few spots, but clear overall.	The grouping and choice of words create a consistent, distinct tone. *Shall I compare thee to a summer's day? Thou art more lovely and more temperate.* - Shakespeare	
❏ **Voice:** *(Synthesis of poet & world)* i.e., control of point of view, control of language in creating an individual persona	The poet's voice is indistinct and lacking control of language and/or point of view.	The poet shows a distinct voice, but this voice does not seem unique to the poet. The control of language and point of view is ordinary and expected.	The poet has such a command of point of view and language that his or her voice is personal and distinct. ***Be an outcast*** *(Uncool)* *Or line the crowded River beds With other impetuous Fools.* - Alice Walker	
Artist's criteria **Please also focus on my criteria** Poet fills in: i.e., appropriate title, invented words ↓				

Fig. 44.2 Poetry rubric for use with product assessments.

Developed by The National Research Center on the Gifted and Talented at the Curry School of Education, University of Virginia.

- *form* which is the degree to which the product is well designed (e.g., form follows function) and crafted with authenticity (e.g., precise, organized, thorough); and
- content including accuracy (e.g., valid, rigorous, justified), aptness (e.g., focused), and sophistication (e.g., insightful, powerful, expertise, depth).

Portfolios

Portfolios are collections of students' work that demonstrate either (a) students' growth, or (b) students' best work (a.k.a., showcase). As such, portfolios are not assessments at all, but rather a collection of previously completed assessments. *Best Work Portfolios* might include products from PBAs that can either be selected by the student, by the teacher or by both, and should include student reflection on the pieces, as well as the teacher's comments. When using portfolios to evaluate gifted program outcomes, the purpose of the portfolio determines the content of the portfolio, the processes by which the portfolio is assembled, and the processes by which the portfolio is ultimately evaluated. Clearly, evaluation of student success in achieving program goals will guide the selection of items to be included in the portfolio and the process of evaluating the portfolio.

SUMMARY

The evaluation of the outcomes of the various components of a gifted program completes the circle of program development, implementation, and assessment. Good decision making at all stages is based on having valid and reliable data. Careful choice of instruments to measure the process of program implementation and the effects of the services offered to gifted students will provide data to make each iteration of implementation even more successful.

REFERENCES

Callahan, C. M. (2005). Making the grade or achieving the goal? Evaluating learner and program outcomes in gifted education. In F. A. Karnes & S. M. Bean (Eds.), *Methods and materials for teaching the gifted* (2nd ed., pp. 211–246). Waco, TX: Prufrock Press

Callahan, C. M. (2009). Making the grade or achieving the goal? Evaluating learner and program outcomes in gifted education. In F. A. Karnes & S. M. Bean (Eds.), *Methods and materials for teaching the gifted* (3rd ed., pp. 221–258). Waco, TX: Prufrock Press.

Kimball, R., & Ross, M. (2002). *The data warehouse toolkit: The complete guide to dimensional modeling* (2nd ed.). New York: Wiley.

Renzulli, J. S, & Callahan, C. M. (2008). Product assessment. In J. L. VanTassel-Baska (Ed.), *Alternative assessment with gifted and talented students* (pp. 259–283). Waco, TX: Prufrock Press.

Renzulli, J. S., & Reis, S. M. (1985). *The Schoolwide Enrichment Model: A comprehensive plan for educational excellence.* Mansfield Center, CT: Creative Learning Press.

Tomlinson, C. A., Kaplan, S. N., Renzulli, J. S., Purcell, J. H., Leppien, J. H., & Burns, D. E. (2002). *The parallel curriculum. A design to develop high potential and challenge high-ability learners.* Thousand Oaks, CA: Corwin Press.

Wiggins, G. (1996). Anchoring assessment with exemplars: Why students and teachers need models. *Gifted Child Quarterly, 40,* 66–69.

45

POLITICAL ISSUES IN GIFTED EDUCATION

James J. Gallagher

SOCIAL POLICY AND ITS ROLE IN EDUCATIONAL POLICY MAKING

Understanding the political issues and the debate surrounding the education of gifted students is based on the recognition that education policy (including rules, regulations, financial allocations, etc.) reflects social policy. Therefore, defining and examining the way that social policy influences education policy is the first step in understanding the politics of education: *"Social policy creates the rules and standards by which scarce resources are allocated to meet almost unlimited social needs."* (Gallagher, 2002, p.1).

Focusing on the "scarce" resources component of this definition directs our attention to the very real fact that not all desirable actions can be taken before our resources run out. Hence, society prioritizes needs so that the most important of these are dealt with first and the most critical needs are addressed before resources are expended. In establishing policy that governs decisions in the realm of educating gifted students, social policy should answer the following questions:

- *Who receives the resources?* Which children will be identified as gifted students and become eligible for the differentiated services?
- *Who delivers the resources?* There is a need to identify the qualifications of the persons who will be the education intervention specialists and how they will be evaluated.
- *What are the resources that are to be delivered to the gifted student?* Are we to provided advanced mathematics or art or music experiences? What is the goal of intervention?
- *What are the conditions under which resources are delivered? How are they delivered?* Will resources be delivered in a special school or an advanced class or a Charter school? Could they be delivered at the student's home through the internet?

Taken together, the answers to these four questions provide a portrait of the goals, the policies, and the implementation mechanisms used to carry them out.

ATTEMPTS TO SET PRIORITIES FOR GIFTED EDUCATION

The political arguments for priorities within social and educational policy for programs for gifted students and, hence, lead to the allocation of resources for educational programs are simple and straightforward.

- The United States is engaged in economic, social, and political competition across the globe with other nations, all seeking creativity and innovation to drive their future prosperity.
- The United States needs the full and efficient performance of its most able students to compete efficiently on a worldwide basis.
- Therefore, educational resources and planning efforts should be allocated to ensure that outcome.

These propositions are not new. As Thomas Jefferson noted, "We seek talents and virtues which nature has sown as liberally among the poor as rich and which are lost to their country by the want of means for their cultivation" (Elementary School Act, 1817; see Jefferson, [1905]), and Arnold Toynbee (1964) commented:

To give a fair chance to potential creativity is a matter of life and death for any society. This is all important because the outstanding creative ability of a fairly small percentage of the population is mankind's ultimate capital asset.

(Toynbee, 1964, p. 4)

Further, the propositions have been supported by generations of scholarship that can be summarized as follows:

- Bright productive students will become bright and productive adults in the arts, sciences, politics, etc. (Tannenbaum, 2003).
- It is not true that such positive outcomes will occur automatically. There are many bright students who are underachievers and many more whose talents are hidden by unfavorable environments and circumstances (Ford, 2003).
- Opportunities and resources must be provided for these bright students to move forward, even as we also support "excellence for all," as an education policy (Renzulli, 2003).

Even as politicians and educators nod in assent to all of the above propositions, we have not seen policies initiated that would act to fulfill the promise. Any significant modification to the education of children with special gifts and talents (SGT) will require political changes to existing rules, regulations, and standards (Ambrose, VanTassel-Baska, Coleman, & Cross, 2010; Gallagher, 1975). Why have such policies not been initiated, but rather only talked about? It is not for want of attention to the issues.

Advocacy and Commissions

One of the time-honored approaches to policy change has been the assembly of a distinguished panel of experts who seek to identify what needs to be done to address a particular problem or challenge. This strategy has been used at intervals of every 10 to 15 years in efforts to create a social policy that would prioritize the education of our brightest students. The first of these, the Marland Report to the U.S. Congress on *Education of the Gifted and Talented* (Marland, 1972), provided the definition of gifted students that became the standard used for decades in establishing state and local definitions of giftedness. The report called for action in creating programs for gifted and talented students. Notably, given the important components of social policy listed above, the recommendations for personnel preparation and research were largely ignored—making it difficult for creation of social policy around the questions of which resources were to be delivered and how they were to be delivered.

The second report, *A Nation at Risk* (Gardner, 1983), used highly inflammatory language to get the attention of the American public. The report portrayed American education as failing and warned of the United States' potential loss of world leadership in science and business.

> If an unfriendly foreign power had attempted to impose on America the mediocre educational performance that exists today, we might have viewed it as an act of war … We have, in effect, been committing an act of unthinking unilateral educational disarmament.
>
> (Gardner, 1983, p.1)

Despite such stirring language, a follow-up report 10 years later found that very few of the recommendations of the report had been implemented. This third report, *National Excellence: A Case for Developing America's Talent* (U.S. Department of Education 1993), covered much of the same ground as the earlier reports (redefining gifted and talented, calling for challenge and intellectual stimulation of our brightest students, and making recommendations for advanced curriculum efforts and acceleration), but social policy has been little affected by this report.

Contrast the inaction following these reports to the major report, *Rising Above the Gathering Storm* (Committee on Prospering in the Global Economy of the 21st Century, 2007), sponsored by the National Academies of Science and produced by a distinguished panel of Nobel Prize winners, university presidents, and chief executive officers of major corporations. The emphasis of this report was on U.S. shortcomings in mathematics and science and made a series of legislative suggestions, such as preparation and four-year support of 10,000 teachers in mathematics and science. This report was quickly turned into legislation (America COMPETES Act of 2007) and became a part of the American Recovery and Reinvestment Act of 2009). Currently, the STEM (science, technology, engineering, and mathematics) programs that benefit from this legislation are funded at 3 billion dollars scattered over three departments (Education, Health and Human Services, and Energy) (Congressional Research Service [CRS],2008).

We need to ask ourselves why so little response has been made to the panels that directed attention to the gifted and talented population, all predicting national disaster in one way or another if America ignores the education of its "best and brightest." There would seem to be two major ingredients to effective action that were lacking: the will to act and the mechanism to implement needed action. Both of these seemed absent at the time of the reports focusing on gifted students. Perhaps the muted response lies in the nation's peace with the status quo at those times—a powerful and implacable enemy of change. A powerful impetus is required to abandon the rewards of stability, and there is always the fear that change might result in "out of control" effects that would be undesirable (Fullan, 2001). Or conflicts in underlying values in the American educational system may have mitigated attention to these reports.

The Will for Change

Equity Versus Excellence

The two predominant values reflected in American education are equity and excellence. On one hand, U.S. society values fair and equal treatment of all students and rejects any favoritism in the allocation of resources. One value honored in education policy is the principle of vertical equity, or the need to provide "unequal treatment of unequals in order to make them more equal." Such programs as Head Start (Zigler & Styfco, 2004) and the Individuals with Disabilities Education Act (IDEA/IDEIA, 2004) are examples of this principle in action.

On the other hand, U.S. society also wishes to support *excellence*, which is recognized as important for the broader society. All of the reports noted earlier advocated for excellence. The conflict between these two values often lies in the reality that *excellence* becomes a long-term goal while *equity*, because of its immediate crisis character, is more often a short-term goal. In democratic societies, short-term goals gain priority, and the scarce resources tend to run out before long-range goals such as climate change or mass transportation or the education of gifted students can command any significant or meaningful portion of the limited resources.

A clear example of what can happen when the "will to change" is suddenly energized occurred when there was great fear that the U.S. educational system was being eclipsed by the Soviet Union (exemplified by the Sputnik launching which received far-reaching attention in 1957). That fear resulted in the allocation of millions of dollars in multi-year efforts to reform curriculum in the sciences. The focus of all of these efforts was on high conceptual understanding of the content across science and mathematics together with practice in scientific processes and procedures, resulting in numerous curricular products including the Chemical Bond Approach, the Biological Sciences Curriculum Study, the Physical Science Study Committee materials and the School Mathematics Study Group (SMSG) (Goodlad, 1964). No similar catalytic event has mobilized educational policy that would draw attention to and rally support around the education of gifted students.

The Mechanisms for Change Implementation

Even if American society were to place a high priority on support for excellence in education for gifted students, the implementation of actions to create change would suffer because of the current structure of the educational system. That is, the current overall support systems and educational infrastructure at the national, state, and local levels are not sufficiently developed to mobilize resources effectively to utilize them in the best way in serving gifted students. Since the American public education system has grown from the bottom, or local community, up to state and federal levels, the necessary infrastructure has to be provided through special efforts. Historically, one area that has

Table 45.1 Federal special education infrastructure

Category of Support	Critical Components
Research Support	Competition for funds over multi-year periods
Personnel Preparation	Funds to provide support to institutions of higher education for graduate fellowships and qualified faculty in special fields
Demonstration Centers	Financial support for programs which illustrate best practices and provide short-term training in area of specialty
Technical Assistance	Assistance on demand to teachers and administrators provided by centers developed to provide counsel on issues of current interest
Communication	Funds for centers that would expedite the distribution (and assistance in distribution) of information derived from evidence-based best practices and identification and advice on implementation
Technology Development	Funds to support the development and testing of new ways to use technology to help children with special needs to learn
State Grants	Funds to aid states in bearing extra costs of special education
Long-range Planning	A federally funded unit designed to anticipate future needs and resources as well as set goals and objectives for a program

accomplished that process is the area of education of students with disabilities (special education). Table 45.1 illustrates the elements of the federal educational infrastructure created to support programs for children with disabilities. The public support for programs for children with special needs has allowed for major investments in research, personnel preparation, technical assistance, and evaluation which have come together to create a synergy that supports educational efforts for students with disabilities. In contrast, while there is scattered evidence of some of these components in various communities around the United States, there has been no national agenda to bring them together in a coherent plan as spurred by the Education for All Handicapped Children Act of 1975, now known as the Individuals with Disabilities [Improvement] Education Act (IDEA/IDEIA) of 2004.

Levels of Educational Policy

In the American system of government, there are three distinct levels of policy: local, state, and federal. Each of these three levels has unique goals and significant players and they can be judged separately or together in terms of their accomplishments. Table 45.2 identifies the active players and major emphases for each of these levels for the field of educating children with special gifts and talents (gifted).

Local

At the local level, the school boards, superintendents of schools, teachers, and parents often play an important role in calling for and designing special programming. At this local level, the emphasis is often on differentiated curriculum, special courses or programs such as Advanced Placement and International Baccalaureate classes and special learning settings such as resource rooms or special classes.

Since special programming options often add to the budget expense line for the school districts (due to limited funding from the state and no federal support for gifted programming), vigorous debates as to the worth of special programming often take place at

Table 45.2 Levels of educational policy for gifted education

	Active Players	Examples of Major Emphasis	Organizations
Local	• School Boards • Superintendents • Teachers • Parent Advocates	• Differentiated Curriculum • Special Classes • Acceleration	• Parent Groups (PTA) • Gifted Advocacy Groups
State	• Legislatures • Governors • State Departments of Public Instruction	• Personnel Preparation • Legislation • Special Residential Schools • Technical Assistance • Program Evaluation • Magnet Schools	• Residential School Boards • State Associations of Educators/ Parents • Governors Schools' Boards
Federal	• Congress • Courts • U.S. Department of Education • National Professional Organizations	• Research and Development • Leadership Training • Legislative Initiatives • Court Decisions • Standards	• National Association for Gifted Children (NAGC) • The Association for the Gifted (TAG) • Supporting Emotional Needs of the Gifted (SENG) • National Research Center on the Gifted and Talented

this level. Clearly, at this level, the concerns of individual parents and parent groups play a significant role in influencing social policy, and subsequently, education policy that will support identifiable programs for children with special gifts and talents. Further, even when monies for programs for the gifted and talented are allocated, other values as reflected in social and educational policy clearly come into play when the limited budget resources must be directed at limited numbers of gifted students. Which grade levels will be served in which areas of talent (academic, leadership, the arts?) and through which service delivery mechanism?

State

At the state level, different components of the infrastructure of Table 45.1 can be addressed and the state legislature may become involved in establishing programs and in funding existing programs. The State Department of Public Instruction/State Department of Education, led by the governor, can play a significant role in developing policy, rules and regulations for guiding identification of gifted students, providing program guidelines, setting standards for personnel preparation, and creating requirements for certification of teachers of the gifted who will play a special role in educating students with special gifts and talents.

In 13 states there are also residential school programs for advanced students at the secondary level often focusing upon science and mathematics (e.g., The North Carolina School of Science and Mathematics or The Illinois Mathematics and Science Academy) (Kolloff, 2003). These programs established by the state legislature invite applications from secondary school students to take a rigorous program devoted to preparing them for university work ahead. In addition, a number of states have established special summer programs, often called Governor's Schools, to provide an enriched experience for students who qualify for the high standards set out for such schools.

An example of a state initiative can be seen in North Carolina where legislation requires local education agencies to develop three-year AIG (Academically or Intellectually Gifted) local plans with specific components to be approved by local school boards, and subsequently sent to the State Board of Education and the Department of Public Instruction for review and comment. There are no options for local school districts to opt out of this program and the result has been that gifted students are planned for in every school district in the state.

Federal

Finally, at the federal level, the emphasis has historically been on funding research, model programs, and leadership training through the Jacob K. Javits Gifted and Talented Students Education Act of 1988 and the STEM programs previously noted. In addition, the federal funds from the Javits Act fund a National Research Center on the Gifted and Talented (NRC/GT), currently a collaboration of the University of Connecticut and the University of Virginia, although many other universities including Yale, the University of Georgia, Stanford University, and New York University have also been involved. The NRC/GT both synthesizes research on major topics in the field and conducts independent research on educational issues—particularly those surrounding identification and programming for students historically underserved by gifted programs.

Yet, the federal-level activities for students with special gifts and talents pale in significance when compared to federal efforts in educating children with disabilities. Despite advocacy efforts of major professional organizations like the National Association for Gifted Children (NAGC), The Association for the Gifted (TAG), a division of the Council for Exceptional Children (CEC), and Social and Emotional Needs of the Gifted (SENG), only a few million dollars are allocated each year for federal support of education programs and research in the field of gifted education, while over 11 billion dollars are invested yearly for children with disabilities. The reasons for such disparities will be dealt with later in this chapter. In the recent stimulus plan (2009) approved by the U.S. government, more than 12 billion dollars was allocated to special education funding for implementation of IDEA/IDEIA (http://www.propublica.org/special/the-stimulus-plan-a-detailed-list-of-spending#stim_education, retrieved July 8, 2011). No funds were allocated for gifted education and the existing Javits program was reduced to $0 in the budget negotiations in spring, 2011 (http://www.policyinsider.org/2011/05/department-of-education-release-final-funding-tables-idea-cut-javits-eliminated.html, retrieved July 8, 2011).

It is important to realize that all of these special programming options for identified gifted students—from Advanced Placement courses to special curriculum development to personnel preparation for teachers of the gifted and talented—do not occur by happenstance or coincidence. Each innovation has required sustained effort from professionals and parent advocates to establish their right to exist. It has been evident in the evolution of the field that policies, representing the collective will of the public, are not easy to initiate or change.

Personnel Preparation

Another player in the field of special education has been the college and university community. The significant role that higher education has played, or rather has not played, in the education of children with special gifts and talents is illustrative of the differences between special education and gifted and talented education and the influence of politics. If there are to be teachers specially certified in teaching gifted and talented students, then that preparation is most likely to be in a university setting. Also, if significant and long-range research is to be done on this topic, a university department or center or institute would be the likely venue for such activity.

If we accept these axioms, then the extremely limited role played by institutions of higher education becomes a serious detriment to progress in this special field. Those not familiar with the operation of universities would be surprised that they were not more active in such special instruction for gifted students, since colleges and universities themselves are committed to educate the best and brightest of the next generation. The problem is not intention, but economics. Lack of strong rules and regulations governing who can or should teach gifted and talented students, and lack of financial support (at the local, state, and federal levels) provided to teacher training programs for teachers of gifted students mean that a university unit or part of an education department devoted to preparing teachers of the gifted and talented would be relatively small. A university would likely be losing money hiring a full-time professor and the additional staff and graduate assistants necessary to do this task.

Some 40 years ago, professors wanting to prepare teachers for children with disabilities were faced with the exact same problem. A major effort to prepare teachers for children with disabilities would be operating at a loss because of the expense of organizing such a unit. Since that time, personnel preparation programs for children with disabilities have flourished while similar programs for teachers of the gifted and talented have languished. What was the difference? Policy—the policy that was established through legislation (the Education for all Handicapped Children Act of 1975) passed the U.S. Congress. That legislation provided handsome subsidies for universities that would agree to establish special units and hire qualified professors, and would also pay for graduate student stipends and the salaries of some of the staff. This policy, adopted in 1977, has resulted in a remarkable expansion of special education departments in universities across the United States with more than 85 million dollars invested in personnel development programs each year for the last several years (Government Accountability Office, 2010). But students with special gifts and talents were not included in the legislation; therefore, no subsidies were available to prepare teachers and leadership personnel in that field.

Similarly, research funds were set aside in the legislation for children with disabilities, resulting in even more activity in the university special education programs. Again, no such funds were available for conducting research on students with gifts and talents. As a consequence, this special field has depended upon a small group of dedicated professionals whose own personal interest kept them at a difficult task.

Professional Initiatives

Not all of the initiatives to develop programs for the gifted have come about through the support of government agencies. Dedicated professional efforts have established programs such as the Study of Mathematically Precocious Youth (SMPY) led by Julian Stanley at Johns Hopkins University (Stanley, 2005) through support from the Spencer Foundation. Although the program focused originally on the identification of talent, it soon moved into special advanced programming which combined acceleration with advanced curriculum. This program was extended with the Talent Identification Project (Duke University), the Center for Talent Development (Northwestern University), and the Rocky Mountain Talent Search (University of Denver).

RECOMMENDATION: AN INFRASTRUCTURE FOR EDUCATION

For education of the gifted to be established as a readily available option for all gifted students, educational programming for gifted students needs a support system or infrastructure similar to the one already in existence for children with disabilities. As a matter of fact, all students in education need such a support system. The components of such a system would look something like this.

Research and Evaluation

A major investment in research and evaluation could pay off in greater understanding of the needs of talented students and in understanding the learning environment which works best for them. Further, investment in developing the tools for effective evaluation of programs could save money now being spent on dubious interventions, creating more effective and efficient programming and curricular options (Callahan, 2004).

Evolving basic research on brain functioning can eventually give insight into the cortical root of giftedness, but we need educational research in the classroom to help our teachers and other specialists improve their performance. History has documented the axiom that if funds for research or development are included as part of larger block grants or folded into larger funding initiatives without clear demarcation of funding priorities (as exists in categorical funding initiatives), then funding gradually declines (Finegold, Wherry, & Schardin, 2004). And in the case of gifted education, funding disappeared in the block grant initiatives of the Reagan years (1980s). Diversion of funds would likely follow the social policy theory and be diverted to other priorities of a crisis nature.

Differentiated Curricula

One of the most pressing needs in the education of gifted and talented students is the production of valid, differentiated curricula across the disciplines. There is wide general agreement that gifted students have already mastered much of the general curriculum in the content areas in which they have been identified before it is even taught (Reis, Westberg, Kulikowich, & Purcell, 1998) and are in need of well-organized experiences that will add to their knowledge and motivation to learn. The few examples that do exist (e.g., Center for Gifted Education, 1998; and Tomlinson et al., 2009) serve as models for the much-needed expansion of these efforts. Like all efforts of this nature, the production of curriculum requires systematic, multi-year efforts by teams of specialists and therefore is quite expensive. The field must convince funding agencies such as foundations of the value of underwriting such efforts, but that too will require a realignment of the social values that drive decision making at those organizations.

Personnel Preparation

Well-trained personnel are key to effective education practice. They do not spring magically out of the mist, but rather from a well-organized university program. As noted earlier, subsidies that underwrite such programs over a multi-year basis can provide assurances to the universities that supporting such programs will not lead to financial difficulties. The program for preparing personnel to teach children with disabilities provides a fine model to follow.

Technical Assistance and Demonstration Centers

A priority service not currently available is technical assistance—help provided on a needs basis. To make the team concept real in educating our brightest students requires the opportunity for teachers to learn from short-term workshops and individual consultations from regional centers that could be established by state departments of education. Such centers, established competitively, could demonstrate the newest techniques on topics such as problem-based learning or a new mathematics curriculum. It would allow state departments of education to take a genuinely helping role instead of being the police force monitoring standards.

Technology Utilization

Grants to support translation of the latest communication developments to programs for gifted education can provide alternatives to schools and school districts which do not have such support, and may not have readily available funds to offer services to small numbers of students identified as gifted in particular areas of talent.

State Aid—Long-range Planning

If each state had a dedicated unit for state-level planning, then many of the other components of quality initiatives mentioned above would be more likely to receive needed attention.

CONCLUSION

Some form of the above recommendations for establishing an infrastructure will be necessary to have a real system of support for administrators, counselors, and teachers who are responsible for delivery of quality programs to gifted and talented students. If instituted, the system would mirror similar support systems for health and military efforts (e.g., the U.S. Army and Marines normally have only 100,000 actual fighting troops; the remainder of the military play supporting roles to those front-line soldiers). Our front-line administrators, counselors, and classroom teachers do not have that kind of support.

Until we can recognize that support efforts are fundamental to an efficient educational system, we will be captives of the status quo, stumbling through local crises, patching what can be patched, but never getting ahead of the game. Gifted education can be the pilot program by which we demonstrate what support services, linked together, can do for the larger education enterprise.

Politically we need to find "angels" who will drive and support such a program, at the state or federal level—key leaders who recognize what is at stake in our failure to adapt to the needs and forces in the 21st century. It is the role of individuals and collective groups such as our professional associations to find these persons and convince them to provide leadership in our political systems to design the policies that would serve the next generation of gifted and talented students.

REFERENCES

Ambrose, D., VanTassel-Baska, J., Coleman, L., & Cross, T. (2010). *Journal for the Education of the Gifted, 33* 453–476.

America COMPETES Act of 2007, Pub. L. No. 110-69, 121 Stat. 572–718 (2007).

American Recovery and Reinvestment Act of 2009, Pub. L. No. 111–5 (2009).

Callahan, C. M. (2004). Introduction to program evaluation in gifted education. In C. M. Callahan (Ed.), *Program evaluation in gifted education* (pp. xxiii–xxxi). Thousand Oaks, CA: Corwin Press.

Center for Gifted Education. (1998). *Persuasion: A language arts unit for high ability learners: Grades 5–7.* Williamsburg, VA: The College of William & Mary.

Colangelo, N., Assouline, S., & Gross, M. U. M. (2004*). A nation deceived: How schools hold back America's brightest students.* Iowa City: The Connie Belin & Jacqueline N. Blank International Center for Gifted Education and Talent Development,The University of Iowa.

Committee on Prospering in the Global Economy of the 21st Century. (2007). *Rising above the gathering storm: Energizing and employing America for a brighter economic future.* Washington, DC: National Academy of Sciences.

Congressional Research Service. (2008). Congressional Research Services Report.Washington DC Dec. 19, 2008. The Federal Budget. Current and Upcoming Issues.

Education for all Handicapped Children Act of 1975, Pub. L. 94–142, 89 Stat. 773 (1975).

Finegold, K., Whery, L., & Schardin, S. (2004). *Block grants: Historical overview and lessons learned.* Urban Institute Research of Record, Report No. A-63. Retrieved November 26, 2010 from http://www.urban.org/publications/310991.html

Ford, D. (2003). Equity and excellence: Culturally diverse students in gifted education. In N. Colangelo & G. Davis (Eds.), *Handbook of gifted Education* (3rd ed., pp. 506–520). Boston: Allyn & Bacon.

Fullan, M. (2001). *The new meaning of educational change.* (3rd ed.) New York: Teachers College Press.

Gallagher, J. (1975). How the government breaks its promises. *New York University Quarterly, 6*(4), 22–27.

Gallagher, J. (2002). *Society's role in educating gifted students: The role of public policy.* (Research Monograph 02162). Storrs: National Research Center on the Gifted and Talented, University of Connecticut.

Gallagher, J. J. (2006). *Driving change in special education.* Baltimore; Paul H. Brookes.

Gardner, J. (1983). *A nation at risk: The imperative for educational reform.* Washington, DC. U.S. Government Printing Office.

Goodlad, J. (1964). *School curricular reform in the United States.* New York: The Fund for the Advancement of Education.

Government Accountability Office. (2010, January). *Federal education funding: Overview of K–12 and early childhood education programs.* Retrieved June 2011 from http://www.gao.gov/new.items/d1051.pdf

Individuals with Disabilities Education Act of 1997. Pub. L. No. 105-17, §101, 111, Stat. 37 (1997).

Individuals with Disabilities Education Improvement Act of 2004, H.R.1350, 108th Cong. (2003–2004).

Jacob K. Javits Gifted and Talented Students Education Act of 1988, Pub. L. No. 100-297, §1001, 102, Stat. 237 (1988).

Jefferson, T. (1905). *The Works, Vol. 3 (Notes on Virginia I, Correspondence 1780–1782)* (Federal ed.). New York & London, UK: G.P. Putnam's Sons.

Kolloff, P. (2003). State supported residential high schools. In N. Colangelo & G. Davis (Eds.), *Handbook of gifted education* (3rd ed., pp. 238–246). Boston: Allyn & Bacon.

Marland, S. P., Jr. (1972). *Education of the gifted and talented: Vol. 1, Report to the Congress of the United States by the U.S. Commissioner of Education.* (Government Documents, Y4.L 11/2: G36). Washington, DC: U.S. Department of Education.

Reis, S. M., Westberg, K. L., Kulikowich, J. M., & Purcell, J. H. (1998). Curriculum compacting and achievement test scores: What does the research say? *Gifted Child Quarterly, 42*, 123–129.

Renzulli, J. S. (2003). Conceptions of giftedness and its relationship to the development of social capital. In N. Colangelo & G. Davis (Eds.), *Handbook of gifted education* (3rd ed., pp. 75–87). Boston: Allyn & Bacon.

Renzulli, J. S., & Reis, S. N. (1985). *The Schoolwide Enrichment Model: A comprehensive plan for educational excellence.* Mansfield Center, CT: Creative Learning Press.

Stanley, J. (1997). In the beginning: The study of mathematically precocious youth. In C. Benbow & D. Lubinski (Eds.), *Intellectual talent: Psychometric and social issues*. Baltimore: Johns Hopkins University Press.

Tannenbaum, A. (2003). Nature and nurture of giftedness. In N. Colangelo & G. Davis (Eds.), *Handbook of gifted education* (3rd ed., pp. 45–59). Boston: Allyn & Bacon.

Tomlinson, C. A., Kaplan, S. N., Renzulli, J. S., Purcell, J. H., Leppien, J. H., Burns, D. E. et al. (2009). *The parallel curriculum: A design to develop learning potential and challenge advanced learning* (2nd ed.). Thousand Oaks, CA: Corwin Press.

Toynbee, A. (1964). Is America neglecting her creative talents? In C. W. Taylor (Ed.), *Widening horizons and creativity* (pp. 3–9). New York: Wiley.

U.S. Department of Education. (1993). *National excellence: A case for developing America's talents*. Washington, DC: Author.

Zigler, E., & Styfco, S. (2004). *The Head Start debates*. Baltimore: Paul H. Brookes.

RECOMMENDED READINGS BY TOPIC

DEFINING GIFTEDNESS

Gagné, F. (2009). Building gifts into talents: Detailed overview of the DMGT 2.0. In B. MacFarlane, & T. Stambaugh (Eds.), *Leading change in gifted education: The* festschrift *of Dr. Joyce VanTassel-Baska* (pp. 61–80). Waco, TX: Prufrock Press.

Gardner, H. (2000). The Giftedness Matrix: A developmental perspective. In R. Friedman, & B. Shore (Eds.), *Talents unfolding: Cognition and development* (pp. 77–88). Washington, DC: American Psychological Association.

Lubinski, D. (2009). Exceptional cognitive ability: The phenotype. *Behavioral Genetics, 39*, 350–358.

Moon, S. M. (2006). Developing a definition of giftedness. In J. H. Purcell, & R. D. Eckert (Eds.), *Designing services and programs for high-ability learners: A guidebook for gifted education* (pp. 23–31). Thousand Oaks, CA: Corwin Press.

Renzulli, J. S. (1978). What makes giftedness? Reexamining a definition. *Phi Delta Kappan, 60*, 180–184, 261.

Robinson, N. M. (2005). In defense of a psychometric approach to the definition of academic giftedness: A conservative view from a die-hard liberal (pp. 280–294). In R. J. Sternberg, & J. E. Davidson (Eds.), *Conceptions of giftedness* (2nd ed.). New York: Cambridge University Press.

Sternberg, R. J. (2000). Patterns of giftedness: A triarchic analysis. *Roeper Review, 22*, 231–235.

IDENTIFICATION

Callahan, C. M. (2005). Identifying gifted students from underrepresented populations. *Theory Into Practice, 44*, 98–104.

Johnsen, S. K. (Ed.). (2004). *Identifying gifted students: A practical guide.* Waco, TX: Prufrock Press.

Lohman, D. F. (2009). The contextual assessment of talent. In B. MacFarlane, & T. Stambaugh (Eds.), *Leading change in gifted education: The* festschrift *of Dr. Joyce VanTassel-Baska* (pp. 229–242). Waco, TX: Prufrock Press.

Moon, T. R., Brighton, C. M., Callahan, C. M., & Robinson, A. E. (2005). Reliable and valid performance assessments for the middle school classroom. *Journal for Secondary Gifted Education, 16*, 119–133.

National Association for Gifted Children. (n.d.). *The role of assessment in the identification of gifted children.* (Position statement). Retrieved January 23, 2009 from http://www.nagc.org/uploadedFiles/assessment%20pos%20paper%20final.pdf

National Association for Gifted Children. (n.d.). *Using tests to identify gifted students.* (Position statement). Retrieved March 9, 2009 from http://www.nagc.org/uploadedFiles/PDF/Position_Statement_PDFs/pp_use_of_tests.pdf VanTassel-Baska, J., Johnson, D., & Avery, L. D. (2008). Using performance tasks in the identification of economically disadvantaged and minority gifted learners: Findings from Project STAR. *Gifted Child Quarterly, 46*, 110–123.

PROGRAM PLANNING, DESIGN, AND IMPLEMENTATION

National Association for Gifted Children. (2010). *NAGC Pre-K–Grade 12 gifted programming standards: A blueprint for quality gifted education programs.* Washington, DC: Author. Retrieved from http://www.nagc.org/uploadedFiles/Information_and_Resources/Gifted_Program_Standards/K-12%20booklet%20for%20convention%20(final).pdf

Plucker, J. A., & Callahan, C. M. (2008). *Critical issues and practices in gifted education: What the research says.* Waco, TX: Prufrock Press.

Purcell, J. H., & Eckert, R. D. (2006). *Designing services and programs for high-ability learners: A guidebook for gifted education.* Thousand Oaks, CA: Corwin Press.

Renzulli, J. S. (1977). *The Enrichment Triad Model: A guide for developing defensible programs for the gifted and talented.* Mansfield Center, CT: Creative Learning Press.

Renzulli, J. S., Gubbins, E. J., McMillen, K. S., Eckert, R. D., & Little, C. A. (Eds.). (2009). *Systems & models for developing programs for the gifted & talented* (2nd ed.). Mansfield Center, CT: Creative Learning Press.

SERVICE DELIVERY OPTIONS

Assouline, S. G., & Lupkowski-Shoplik, A. (2011). *Developing math talent: A comprehensive guide to math education for gifted students in elementary and middle school* (2nd ed.). Waco, TX: Prufrock Press.

Colangelo, N., Assouline, S., & Gross, M. U. M. (2004). *A nation deceived: How schools hold back America's brightest students* (Vol. 1). Iowa City: The Connie Belin & Jacqueline N. Blank International Center for Gifted Education and Talent Development, The University of Iowa.

Institute for Research and Policy on Acceleration, National Association for Gifted Children, & Council of State Directors of Programs for the Gifted (2009, November). *Guidelines for developing an academic acceleration policy.* Iowa City, IA: Authors.

Landrum, M. S. (2001). An evaluation of the Catalyst Program: Consultation and collaboration in gifted education. *Gifted Child Quarterly, 45,* 139–51.

CURRICULUM AND INSTRUCTION

Hockett, J. A. (2009). Curriculum for highly able learners that conforms to general education and gifted education quality indicators. *Journal for the Education of the Gifted, 32*(3), pp. 394–440.

Kaplan, S. (2008). The layered curriculum. In F. Karnes, & S. Bean (Eds.), *Methods and materials for teaching the gifted.* Waco, TX: Prufrock Press.

Kaplan, S. (2009). The grid: A model to construct differentiated curriculum for the gifted. In J. Renzulli, J. Gubbins, K. McMullen, R. Eckert, & C. Little (Eds.), *Systems & models for developing programs for the gifted & talented.* Mansfield Center, CT: Creative Learning Press.

Renzulli, J. S., Leppien, J. L., & Hays, T. S. (2000). *The Multiple Menu Model: A practical guide for developing differentiated curriculum.* Mansfield Center, CT: Creative Learning Press.

Tomlinson, C. A., Kaplan, S. N., Renzulli, J. S., Purcell, J. H., Leppien, J. H., Burns, D. E. et al. (2009). *The Parallel Curriculum: A design to develop learner potential and challenge advanced learners* (2nd ed.). Thousand Oaks, CA: Corwin.

VanTassel-Baska, J., & Stambaugh, T. (2006). *Comprehensive curriculum for the gifted.* Boston: Pearson.

SPECIAL POPULATIONS

Gifted African Americans

Cohen, G. L., Garcia, J., Purdie-Vaughns, V., Apfel, N., & Brzustoski, P. (2009). Recursive processes in self-affirmation: Intervening to close the minority achievement gap. *Science, 324,* 400–403. doi:10.1126/science.1170769

Frasier, M. M., Garcia, J. H., & Passow, A. H. (1995). *A review of assessment issues in gifted education and their implications for identifying gifted minority students.* Storrs: National Research Center on the Gifted and Talented, University of Connecticut.

Graham, S. (2009). Giftedness in adolescence: African American gifted youth and their challenges from a motivational perspective. In F. D. Horowitz, R. F. Subotnik, & D. J. Matthews (Eds.), *The development of giftedness and talent across the lifespan* (pp. 109–129). Washington, DC: American Psychological Association. doi:10.1037/11867-007

MacFarlane, B., & Feng, A. X. (2010). The patterns and profiles of gifted African American children: Lessons learned. In J. L. VanTassel-Baska (Ed.), *Patterns and profiles of promising learners from poverty* (pp. 107–128). Waco, TX: Prufrock Press.

Gifted females

Reis, S. M. (2005). Feminist perspectives on talent development: A research based conception of giftedness in women. In R. J. Sternberg, & J. E. Davidson (Eds.), *Conceptions of giftedness* (2nd ed., pp. 217–245). Boston: Cambridge University Press.

Gifted Latinos

Castellano, J. A. (2002). Renavigating the waters: The identification and assessment of culturally and linguistically diverse students for gifted and talented education. In J. A. Castellano, & E. I. Diaz (Eds.), *Reaching new horizons: Gifted and talented education for culturally and linguistically diverse students.* Boston: Allyn & Bacon.

Diaz, E. I. (1998). Perceived factors influencing the academic underachievement of talented students of Puerto Rican descent. *Gifted Child Quarterly, 42,* 105–122.

Gándara, P. (2004). *Latino achievement: Identifying models that foster success.* (Research Monograph 04194). Storrs: National Research Center on the Gifted and Talented, University of Connecticut.

Hébert, T. P. (1996). Portraits of resilience: The urban life experience of gifted Latino young men. *Roeper Review, 19,* 142–147.

Gifted males

Hébert, T. P. (2006). Gifted university males in a Greek fraternity: Creating a culture of achievement. *Gifted Child Quarterly, 50,* 26–41.

Hébert, T. P., & Kelly, K. R. (2006). Identity and career development in gifted students.

In F. A. Dixon, & S. M. Moon (Eds.), *The handbook of secondary gifted education* (pp. 35–63). Waco, TX: Prufrock Press.

Gifted students from rural environments

Burney, V. H., & Cross, T. L. (2006). Impoverished students with academic promise in rural settings: 10 lessons from Project Aspire. *Gifted Child Today, 29*(2), 14–21.

Howley, C., Harmon, H., & Leopold, G. (1996). Rural scholars or bright rednecks? Aspirations for a sense of place among rural youth in Appalachia. *Journal of Research in Rural Education, 12,* 150–160.

Lawrence, B. K. (2009). Rural gifted education: A comprehensive literature review. *Journal for the Education of the Gifted, 32,* 461–494.

Twice exceptional: emotional and behavioral disabilities

Mueller, C. E. (2009). Protective factors as barriers to depression in gifted and nongifted adolescents. *Gifted Child Quarterly, 53,* 3–14.

Rizzo, M. G., & Morrison, W. F. (2003). Uncovering stereotypes and identifying characteristics of gifted students with emotional/behavioral disabilities. *Roeper Review, 25,* 73–77.

Twice exceptional: learning disabilities

Attwood, T. (2008). *The complete guide to asperger's syndrome.* Philadelphia: Jessica Kingsley Publishers.

Gilger, J. W., & Hynd, G. W. (2008). Neurodevelopmental variation as a framework for thinking about the twice exceptional. *Roeper Review, 30,* 214–228.

doi:10.1080/02783190802363893 Newman, T. M., & Sternberg, R. J. (Eds.). (2004). *Students with both gifts and learning disabilities: Identification, assessment, and outcomes.* New York: Springer.

Underachievement

Baum, S. M., Renzulli, J. S., & Hébert, T. P. (1995). Reversing underachievement: Creative productivity as a systematic intervention. *Gifted Child Quarterly, 39,* 224–235

McCoach, D. B., & Siegle, D. (2008). Underachievers. In J. Plucker, & C. Callahan (Eds.), *Critical issues and practices in gifted education: What the research says* (pp. 707–719). Waco, TX: Prufrock Press.

Reis, S. M., & McCoach, D. B. (2000). The underachievement of gifted students: What do we know and where do we go? *Gifted Child Quarterly, 44,* 158–170.

PROGRAM EVALUATION

Callahan, C. M. (2009). Making the grade or achieving the goal? Evaluating learner and program outcomes in gifted education. In F. A. Karnes, & S. M. Bean (Eds.), *Methods and materials for teaching the gifted* (3rd ed., pp. 221–258). Waco, TX: Prufrock Press.

Callahan, C. M., & Caldwell, M. S. (1995). *A practitioner's guide to evaluating programs for the gifted.* Washington, DC: National Association for Gifted Children.

Renzulli, J. S., & Callahan, C. M. (2008). Product assessment. In J. L. VanTassel-Baska (Ed.), *Alternative assessment with gifted and talented students* (pp. 259–283). Waco, TX: Prufrock Press.

VanTassel-Baska, J., & Feng, X. (2004). *Designing and utilizing evaluation for gifted program improvement.* Waco, TX: Prufrock Press.

POLICY AND ADVOCACY

Baker, B. D., & Friedman-Nimz, R. (2004). State policies and equal opportunity: The example of gifted education. *Educational Evaluation and Policy Analysis, 26,* 39–64.

Clarenbach, J. (2010). Advocating for a difference. *Gifted Education Communicator, 41*(1), 19–22.

Council of State Directors of Programs for the Gifted, & National Association for Gifted Children. (2009). *State of the states in gifted education 2008–2009: National policy and practice data.* Washington, DC: Author.

Gallagher, J. J. (2002). *Society's role in educating gifted students: The role of public policy.* (Research Monograph 02162). Storrs: National Research Center on the Gifted and Talented, University of Connecticut.

VanTassel-Baska, J. (2006). State policies in gifted education. In J. H. Purcell, & R. D. Eckert (Eds.), *Designing services and programs for high-ability learners: A guidebook for gifted education* (pp. 249–261). Thousand Oaks, CA: Corwin Press.

Zirkel, P. A. (2003). *The law on gifted education.* (Research Monograph 03178). Storrs: National Research Center on the Gifted and Talented, University of Connecticut.

INDEX